STRUCTURE
AND PROCESS
IN INTERNATIONAL
POLITICS

Structure and Process in International Politics

RAYMOND F. HOPKINS
Swarthmore College

RICHARD W. MANSBACH
Rutgers University

HARPER & ROW, PUBLISHERS
NEW YORK, EVANSTON, SAN FRANCISCO, LONDON

CONTENTS

PREFACE

A November 1972 issue of *The New York Times* featured such stories as "Kissinger and Tho Expected To Meet Late in the Week," "Egypt Is Reported To Get Advanced Soviet Missile," "U.S. Is Said To Deliver 20 Bombers to Cambodia," "Wave of Bengalis Fleeing Pakistan," and "Pressures On Canada." Every day similar headlines catch the flavor of exciting and dangerous conflicts in a world without central authority. They highlight the bewildering character of sudden events that exhibit little apparent pattern. Sometimes our adrenalin flows, and our worst fears seem near to realization. Yet most of us recognize the impact of only few international events on the present or future. While the responsibility for human survival is concentrated in the hands of a few leaders, these leaders, regardless of their motives, rarely have the skill or knowledge that would permit them to exercise their power intelligently and humanely.

The study of international politics is a joint enterprise in which students and scholars seek to understand the genesis and implications of events as they unfold in the international arena and to provide insights for bureaucratic technicians and statesmen. The fact that there is precious little peace or human dignity in the world attests less to man's corrupt nature than to his woeful ignorance.

Men know little about the international events that shape their most central values, including life itself; they understand still less. Not long ago the study of international relations was a new discipline in the United States; graduate departments were first established at several universities in the 1930s. Yet international relations has failed to mature as a separate intellectual field, and many of these departments have been abandoned. There is no science of international relations nor, in the narrower sphere of international politics, is there a single body of information or theory that could constitute a core subject matter.

It is important to understand these limitations on both the subject matter of this book and its organization. The problems of analyzing the complex phenomena labeled "international politics" militate against any *standard* interpretation and against all existing methodological or theoretical prejudices. Such prejudices encourage misleading simplification and inadequate theories and fail to provide reliable knowledge. Our purpose is to order the existing knowledge about international politics without surveying the interests of all relevant writers and thinkers. We shall emphasize conceptual tools rather than grand theories or ready solutions, seeking to illuminate the milieu within which international events occur, the kinds of distinctions that separate actors and elements in their behavior, and that murky sector of international politics in which international business, professional, religious, and cultural groups are important in shaping global outcomes. In addition, we shall discuss strategic thinking, diplomatic bargaining, and those ecological factors of social, economic, and technological change that inexorably alter international behavior.

How do men act? How may they secure peace and dignity? Neither the utopian optimism of Edward Bellamy's *Looking Backward* nor the cynical despair of Nevil Shute's *On the Beach* contributes much of value to help answer these questions. To project only one's hopes or fears is to court irrelevance or to encourage disaster. The task of simple survival is bound up with the ability to think accurately about the unknown and sometimes even the unknowable. Above all, we want to make clear the fallibility of men who are responsible for the defense and preservation of human life, men whose sense of history and grasp of the factors that shape future events may be at best fragmentary and often illusory. We are interested not so much in criticizing past compendia of information as in highlighting some concepts, distinctions, arguments, and fragmentary data that have shaped our own mental "maps" of the world and that we believe can improve the art of thinking about international politics. We hope that this book will serve to clarify questions about what international politics is, how it can be studied, and what relevance such study has to both immediate policy decisions and long-term global transformations.

This book represents the merging of two antithetical heritages. The authors' collaboration began when we were colleagues during our first year as college instructors. Finding that we differed about what is important in international politics and how it should be studied, we began an exchange of ideas that grew into a joint seminar at Swarthmore College and continues to this day. Both of us, one historically and the other behaviorally trained, have found our styles, interests, and concerns converging. We do not agree on everything in this book, but this difference of opinion seems to us an advantage. The coherence of our analytical posture rests on a common view of the role and uses of history, the value of method, and the importance of analytical judgments both in studying international politics and in promoting adaptive and healthy policy making.

The ideas about international politics we present were influenced by teachers, colleagues, and friends who educated, inspired, and assisted us. Among those who have influenced this volume markedly and to whom we are indebted and grateful are: Hayward Alker, Garry Brewer, Ronald Brunner, Alan Bullock, Karl W. Deutsch, Robert Keohane, Wilfrid Knapp, Laurence Lafore, Harold Lasswell, Roy Licklider, Joseph Nye, James Rosenau, Bruce Russett, J. David Singer, and Kenneth Waltz. In particular we would like to thank Thomas O'Donnell, whose research assistance and helpful contributions rendered great service.

In addition we wish to thank for their encouragement and assistance Walter H. Lippincott, Editor-in-Chief, Humanities, and Claire Rubin, Rebecca Sacks, Sally Cerny, and Dorie Autilio, of Harper & Row, and Estelle Whelan, who worked with us at various stages of its preparation. Finally, we must pay tribute to our wives Carol and Rhoda, who contributed immeasurably to this book.

RAYMOND F. HOPKINS
RICHARD W. MANSBACH

STRUCTURE
AND PROCESS
IN INTERNATIONAL
POLITICS

Part I
A FRAMEWORK FOR ANALYSIS

The value of any investigation depends upon the questions asked and the means by which they are answered. Before we can pose questions intelligently, however, we must define precisely the universe with which we are concerned. At the outset of our study of international politics, then, we must define the *set* of human behavior with which we are concerned and the *units* whose activity will be the focus of our attention. Chapter 1 provides these definitions.

Once we have clarified the scope of our subject matter, we must decide how to frame our questions most profitably and efficiently. The accumulation of knowledge depends upon asking questions that are both important and answerable; otherwise we are likely to find ourselves at intellectual dead ends, unable to find much substance to support opinions about what *ought* to be done. In Chapter 2 we identify the major tools of our analysis, as well as different ways to seek answers in this complex field of study. Then we turn to the basic problems of theory in international politics, reviewing several alternative theoretical frameworks that have been developed in recent years.

Theory must be anchored in fact. To evaluate the relevance of central theoretical concepts, we must focus upon concrete events. In Chapter 3, we examine several explanations for the outbreak of World War I. Considerable information on these events is available. The war served as a watershed between the politics of the past and the politics of the present. Among its direct consequences was the emergence of a kind of international politics with many characteristics that we can still observe today. We shall test the utility of various theories and approaches to this very instructive example, so that the reader can gain a keener appreciation of the need for theory in international politics—and of the shortcomings of earlier efforts to explain international phenomena.

International politics consists of purposive units in interaction with one another. These units formulate objectives for themselves and seek to realize them in cooperation or competition with other units. In Chapter 4 we shall turn to such core concepts as goals, objectives, and influence; we shall also examine the relationship, or link, between units' aims and the means that they employ to achieve them. These complex but ambiguous concepts are central to any approach to international politics.

Chapter 1
INTERNATIONAL POLITICS: THE ACTOR AND THE DISCIPLINE

Mr. President, we and you ought not to pull on the ends of the rope in which you have tied the knot of war, because the more the two of us pull, the tighter the knot will be tied. And a moment may come when the knot may be tied so tight that even he who tied it will not have the strength to untie it, and then it will be necessary to cut that knot, and what that would mean is not for me to explain to you, because you yourself understand perfectly of what terrible forces our countries dispose—Nikita S. Khrushchev [4]

In the autumn of 1962 the United States and the Soviet Union confronted each other in an interaction that brought the world to the brink of war. The crisis was initiated by a Russian attempt to alter its military capability by secretly setting up strategic missile bases on the island of Cuba. The subsequent interaction involved threats and promises by both sides as each tried to modify the other's behavior, maximize its own gain, yet avoid a thermonuclear explosion. The stakes were high, and the protagonists bargained in an atmosphere fraught with risk. This episode exhibits the main characteristics of politics in an arena lacking authoritative institutions.

POLITICS

Politics is the process by which men pursue goals and promote values in strategic interaction with one another. Such pursuit involves independent decision making and the exercise of influence (see Chapter 4). Definitions of politics are frequently restricted to situations of conflict or struggle, but conflict, though a common element in human interaction, is by no means the only mode of politics. Values are attained through cooperation too, and efforts to achieve such cooperation are fundamental forms of political behavior. Politics, then, involves interplay of cooperative and competitive behavior, and that interplay is regulated through the use of threats, promises, rewards, and punishments. Alliances, trade, economic and political unions, and cease-fire agreements are all expressions of political behavior involving both cooperation and conflict. In domestic politics an election campaign involves conflict among candidates, but the rules governing both campaign and election are expressions of cooperation. In international politics the rules are less firmly established, apply to a narrower range of behavior, and are less commonly followed—but they exist all the same.

Many mutually beneficial daily activities depend upon a minimum of cooperation even between adversaries. Certain international customs have attained the status of "rules" through time because they have been found necessary for the conduct of international intercourse. The observance of diplomatic rights and privileges and respect for the status of embassies are examples of such rules of conduct established, maintained, and sanctioned over time, despite changing relations among specific international actors.

Even in intense international conflict at least tacit rules operate. For example, mutual recognition of what could happen were an international crisis to be mishandled has stimulated the creation of certain conventions governing behavior during such periods. Soviet and American leaders have used allies to attain objectives when direct confrontation seemed too dangerous. The 1962 Cuban missile crisis demonstrated the risks of direct confrontation.

THE ACTOR IN INTERNATIONAL POLITICS

In international politics an actor is a relatively *autonomous* unit that exercises *influence* on the behavior of other autonomous actors. Sometimes these actors are men acting on their own behalf, but more frequently they are men acting as spokesmen or surrogates for larger social units like states. Their activities help to regulate the flow and distribution of values among the units that they represent.[1] We use the term "international" solely as a convention; it suggests that the actors possess sovereignty, that is, legal independence. Only states can possess this attribute, but the complexity of international politics defies the arbitrary definition of international actors as states alone. Turning from legal characteristics to behavioral characteristics, we find certain units that appear to behave independently and to have an impact on international life yet do not possess sovereignty and do not fall within the legal definition of states. The Arab terrorist group al-Fatah, the Viet Cong in Indochina, and even the Mafia play larger roles in international politics than is customarily recognized. Organizations like the United Nations, the European Economic Community, International Business Machines Corporation (IBM), the Roman Catholic Church, and the International Red Cross, though possessing neither sovereignty nor usually territory, are nevertheless actors in international politics.

On the other hand, some units that have nominal sovereignty or are recognized as sovereign do not fulfill the behavioral criteria for international actors. The Ukraine and Belorussia are members of the U.N. General Assembly with votes equal to those of the United States and the Soviet Union, but their behavior has hardly been internationally significant since the Bolshevik Revolution in 1917. The United States continues to recognize the "sovereignty" of Latvia, Lithuania, and Estonia, which have embassies in Washington, but these states have not acted as independent entities for many years.

The defining characteristic of an international actor is thus not the legal quality of sovereignty but rather the behavioral attribute of *autonomy*. Autonomy in this context means the ability to behave in ways that have consequences in international politics and cannot be predicted entirely by reference to other actors or authorities. In practice, no actor in the contemporary international system is entirely autonomous because of the high level of interdependence among units in the system. Some actors, however, have relative autonomy, whereas others make few independent decisions. In the contemporary system nation-states behave

---

[1] Harold D. Lasswell and Abraham Kaplan suggest two categories of "values," that is, things valued by people, that incorporate many of those to be discussed here. Their first category, "welfare values," includes well-being, wealth, skill, and enlightenment. Their second category, "deference values," includes power, respect, rectitude, and affection [5].

autonomously more consistently than do other types of actors, who may manifest autonomy only under certain conditions or on specific occasions. Most individuals and groups in the United States, for example, are subject to the constraints of superior associations like the federal government. The citizen's participation in international politics is generally limited to fulfilling specified obligations like serving in the armed forces and paying taxes, which are deemed necessary to the pursuit of national objectives.

We must avoid attributing physical reality to actors; in the sense used here they are essentially artificial constructions. The only real actors are men; when we speak of a group as an "actor" we must remember that it is really men who make decisions in the name of one group or another. As we shall see, men may behave differently as representatives of the group than simply as individuals because they are subject to different influences. For example, most individuals are unwilling to murder their neighbors, no matter how disagreeable, yet are willing to serve in the armed forces of their countries and kill men of other countries. Many social groups forbid the killing of others within their units, but may sanction the murder of outsiders.

Nation-states have not always been and need not always be the dominant international actors. Before they evolved, individuals like Marco Polo, as well as cities, banks, trading companies, and religious movements, played significant, often dominant, parts in world politics. Furthermore, even today actors other than nation-states have a degree of prominence that they may have not enjoyed for some time. We can differentiate among international actors according to the tasks that they perform for their constituencies, the scope of their constituencies, and whether they are governmental or not.

Tasks Performed by Actors

All political actors perform certain tasks for their constituents. One possible ex-

planation for the emergence of new actors and the disappearance of old ones may lie in the changing ability of units to perform the tasks demanded of them. When an existing state is conquered and occupied by outsiders, as has occurred in Poland several times, the disappearance of an autonomous political unit may reflect its failure to provide its citizens with protection from other international units. Similarly, the emergence of autonomous units, like that of the United States in 1776 and Biafra in 1967–1969, is the result partly of demands for more effective performance of certain tasks like physical protection. Such demands must be either suppressed or fulfilled by the existing political unit, or they may lead to the emergence of a new unit. One of the fundamental questions that a social scientist must ask is What are the conditions under which one or the other outcome is likely to occur?

At least four kinds of tasks are performed by political systems: *Physical protection* means the protection of men and their values from coercion and deprivation either by other members within the group or by individuals or collectivities outside the group. *Economic development and regulation* includes activities intended to overcome the constraints imposed by scarcity or unequal distribution of material resources on the individual or collective capacity for self-development. *Residual public-interest tasks* are those activities intended to overcome constraints other than economic—for example, disease and ignorance—that hamper individual or collective capacity for self-development. *Provision of group status,* or "referent identification," through such symbols as ethnicity, nation, class, and kinship, binds the individual to others, provides a sense of psychological and emotional security and well-being, and distinguishes individuals from those who are not members of their group.

All decisions and activities of international actors are related to the performance of one or more of these kinds of tasks. The categories themselves are, however, only analytic; most activities belong to more than one category. Often different categories of tasks are perceived as interdependent, as when the physical protection and security of group members is considered to depend upon the efficient use and husbanding of economic resources, maintenance of in-group respect and morale, or reaffirmation of selected moral precepts and principles. Actors may assume or discard tasks and extend or restrict them over time. For example, many welfare policies have been undertaken only recently by individual nation-states and, even more recently, by interstate groups, thus enlarging the scope of activities in the residual public-interest category. Technological change encourages demands for new services, and it is already possible to foresee that demands for pollution control and population limitation on a world scale will lead to the creation of new, internationally significant political structures should existing political actors remain unable to cope with these growing problems.

The performance of these tasks becomes relevant internationally, however, only when it has an impact on other international actors. A nation may pursue economic development on behalf of its community without international consequences. But when it becomes necessary for the actor to compete or cooperate with other units to satisfy the values of his own community, the task becomes international.

The performance of any political task involves several functions: formulation and articulation of demands for services, authoritative decisions on whether or not and how the services will be provided, execution of the decisions, and, finally, channeling information on performance to decision makers. For example, the major trading nations of the West are members of an interstate organization known as the General Agreement on Tariffs and Trade (GATT). This organization provides an institutional framework within which members can negotiate reciprocal trade agreements and attempt to lower barriers to international trade. In GATT demands are brought forward by individual states, but decisions are reached and rules set by the states acting together as a group. As the organization has no executive machinery, its decisions must be carried out by the individual state governments, which must also monitor the effects of the decisions. More than one actor or type of actor—in this instance the individual states and the interstate organization—can thus be significantly involved in the performance of a single task.

The Scope of the Constituency

Beside classification according to tasks, actors can be usefully distinguished by the scope of their constituencies: individuals, small groups, even governments. The United Nations is composed of government representatives from different states; an international corporation like IBM consists of shareholders, executives, and employees from different states. We can identify at least five possible types of actors by their composition: *interstate governmental organizations,* consisting of governmental representatives from more than one state; *interstate nongovernmental organizations,* consisting of nongovernmental representatives from more than one state; *intrastate governmental organizations,* consisting of government personnel from one state; *intrastate nongovernmental organizations,* consisting of nongovernmental groups or individuals within a single state; *individuals,* who perform tasks (or parts of tasks) for themselves or for diffuse communities of individuals or groups. Individuals of the last type may appear in the previous four groups; it is only when they behave independently of these groups, as Hitler seemed to do, that we consider them internationally significant in themselves.

Table 1.1 offers several examples of significant international actors according to both task and constituency criteria. Many of these examples could be placed in more than one cell, for they are multi-

Table 1.1.
Task and Constituency Criteria of Selected Actors

Constituency	*Task*			
	Physical Protection	*Economic*	*Residual Public Interest*	*Group Status*
Interstate Governmental	North Atlantic Treaty Organization (NATO) Warsaw Pact	General Agreement on Tariffs and Trade (GATT) Council of Mutual Economic Assistance (Comecon)	World Health Organization (WHO) International Labor Organization (ILO)	Afro-Asian solidarity bloc
Interstate Nongovernmental	al-Fatah	Shell Oil Company International Business Machines Corporation (IBM)	International Red Cross Caritas	Roman Catholic Church
Intrastate Governmental	U.S. Government Biafra	Agency for International Development (AID)	TASS, the Soviet news agency	Serbia (predecessor of modern Yugoslavia) Bangla Desh
Intrastate Nongovernmental	Ibo tribe Turkish Cypriots	Boeing Corporation	Ford Foundation	American Jewish community
Individual	Gustaf von Rosen	Jean Monnet	Albert Schweitzer Andrew Carnegie	Pope John XXIII

task actors. For example, the North Atlantic Treaty Organization (NATO) is an interstate governmental organization whose fundamental task is to protect the member states, but it also promotes economic interests and group status. The Ibo in "Biafra" illustrate that a group with the same membership can shift either its primary task or, as in this instance, its status as a unit. With the breakdown of civil order in Nigeria the Ibo gathered in a single territory, formed a government, and became, at least temporarily, an autonomous state.

ACTORS IN CONTEXT: THE NIGERIAN CIVIL WAR

The civil war in Nigeria (1967–1969) demonstrates which kinds of actors participate significantly in international interaction. After two coups d'état by the Nigerian army and a period of communal violence, in which large numbers of Ibo and eastern Nigerians who had settled in the north were killed, the former Eastern Region of Nigeria declared its independence under the name Biafra. Following this declaration in May 1967 the Nigerian federal government in Lagos decided to end by police action what it called an "illegal secession." A bloody war ensued, and perhaps 1 million Nigerians either were killed or died of starvation.

What actors, beside the principals, took part in this confrontation? Perhaps the most all-encompassing interstate actor, the United Nations, took little action. It did, however, offer its diplomatic services, provide observer teams, and mobilize aid for refugees, particularly in the last stages of the conflict. Its main role in the conflict was thus limited to performing certain public-interest tasks for the adversaries. The International Red Cross, a nongovernmental group, took a more active role, entering into negotiations with both Biafra and the federal government on several occasions, in order to resolve difficulties in supplying food to noncom-

batant civilians in the war-torn eastern part of Nigeria. Because regulating food imports, an economic task, was considered an important determinant of the outcome of the struggle, each side attempted to prevent its adversary from controlling Red Cross relief efforts.

Several other transnational agencies acted relatively autonomously in the conflict. Joint Church Aid, a consortium of religious and other humanitarian organizations, was formed to work directly with Biafra to bring food supplies. The organization chartered airplanes and sponsored clandestine night flights from the Portuguese island of São Tomé in the Gulf of Nigeria to airfields in Biafra. As many residents in the eastern region of Nigeria are Roman Catholic, the Roman Catholic Church provided both food and medical care to Biafrans and exerted diplomatic pressure for a peaceful resolution of the conflict. Beside control of territory and people, access to the area's rich oil reserves was also at stake. International oil companies controlled by Dutch and British interests were thus major participants in the conflict; both Biafra and Nigeria threatened the companies with sanctions if they withheld revenues from either state. After a period of noncommital caution the petroleum interests sided with the federal government and used their influence in the United Kingdom to encourage provision of arms and military equipment to the Lagos government. The Organization of African Unity (OAU), a regional interstate body, attempted unsuccessfully to mediate the conflict on a number of occasions. It issued resolutions calling on both parties to work out a peaceful settlement in order to restore the territorial integrity of what had been Nigeria. It thus seemed to favor the federal government's efforts to reunite the country.

Single states both in Africa and outside became involved in the war. The federal government received arms, money, and advisers from the Soviet Union, the United Kingdom, and, to a lesser extent, the United Arab Republic. Whereas the British supplied primarily light arms, transportation, and radio-communications facilities, the Russians sent heavy weapons. Biafra, on the other hand, was recognized by and thus received moral support from four African states: Gabon, the Ivory Coast, Tanzania, and Zambia. It also received arms and other assistance from France, Portugal, and South Africa. This assistance, though widely recognized, was never explicitly acknowledged by the donors. The People's Republic of China also lent Biafra somewhat ambiguous diplomatic support.

Individuals rarely play important roles as actors in international politics, except through the impact of their personalities on roles within structured organizations. But the Nigerian civil war does provide an example of relatively autonomous individual action unassociated with any internationally recognized social, economic, or political organization. Count Carl Gustaf von Rosen, a middle-aged Swedish nobleman, provided and helped to fly for the Biafran government seventeen light airplanes and two old converted fighter-bombers. Von Rosen's activity may have seemed anachronistic in an age of large bureaucratic organizations and carefully guarded spheres of authority, but his assistance proved important to Biafra, and his behavior exemplifies the way in which an individual may function as an actor in international politics. Another individual who, it could be argued, played a relatively autonomous role in the war, particularly as a goal setter, was Colonel Odumegwu Ojukwu, the leader of the Biafrans. His aspirations prolonged the struggle by inspiring his followers to fight on long after they had apparently lost the war. Before Ojukwu sought asylum in the Ivory Coast he declared, "While I live, Biafra lives"—an indication of his prominent inspirational part in the Biafran events.

The Biafra example illustrates how international politics can involve actors other than nation-states and demonstrates that the traditional model of a global system of national actors alone is descriptively inadequate. Legal sovereignty is insufficient evidence of autonomy. Furthermore, different actors have different supportive or adversarial roles and perform different tasks, even in a single series of events. International politics is simply too complex to be explained solely in terms of states that are geographically defined and readily comparable.

INTERNATIONAL POLITICS AS A SUBJECT OF STUDY

International politics encompasses military, diplomatic, social, economic, cultural, psychological, legal, technical, and other interactions, provided that those who are engaged in them influence or are influenced by the behavior of other actors. It is probably not necessary to identify the boundaries of this expanding discipline too closely, however, for such boundaries shift as more data become available and new approaches are developed [7, 2, 6]. Whereas formerly the study of international politics was based almost exclusively on international law and diplomatic history, the recent increases in available data and methods have reflected borrowing from other fields of study. For example, before President John F. Kennedy journeyed to Vienna in 1961 to meet Soviet Premier Nikita S. Khrushchev, the U.S. Central Intelligence Agency engaged twenty physicians, psychologists, and psychiatrists to assess the health, personality, and negotiating style of the Russian leader.

The difficulty in fixing the precise boundaries for international politics becomes apparent when we try to distinguish it from domestic, or national, politics. One rather clear distinction is that in a domestic political system, one actor, usually a government, possesses a virtual monopoly of the means of violent coercion. For reasons rooted in tradition, culture, and this monopoly of the means of coercion, groups and individuals subject to government have developed habits of compliance and nonviolent means of resolving disputes. Intrastate conflict does occur, and in fact it may be widespread; but, except for relations between government and subject, the modes of exerting influence on other actors within the state are usually nonviolent.

In contrast to domestic politics, politics in the international arena is subject to weak authority and characterized by high conflict. There is no supreme authority that can enforce decisions. The International Court of Justice has since its inception decided few questions, and most of those have involved relatively minor quarrels. Indeed, in a recent review of the Court's activities it was noted: "Without a single case or request for an advisory opinion on its docket and with its reputation tarnished by some recent questionable decisions, the Court appears to have entered upon a period of enforced neglect" [3].

Standards of fairness and codes of conduct in international politics differ markedly from those in national politics, so much so that international law is sometimes called "the law of the jungle." Thus, enforcement of the 1972 Soviet-American strategic arms limitation agreement cannot be obtained by recourse to law but only by their mutual ability to observe and destroy each other. In low-conflict situations some operating procedures for regulating international intercourse are commonly established. But when there is active pursuit of conflicting objectives accommodation is difficult and often results only from hard bargaining and tacit maneuvers, including threats and promises. When disputes arise actors often rely on their own resources and private sanctions, and each behaves as he deems proper as long as he is able. The international system is thus in a condition resembling anarchy, which the seventeenth-century English philosopher Thomas Hobbes described as one of "continual fear, and danger of violent death."

The salient features of the international political system can sometimes be found in other arenas. Price wars[2] and gangland shootouts have been examined for parallels to international politics; bargaining strategies in labor relations and in marital relations have been used to develop theories about bargaining among international actors. A variety of psychological and "gaming" experiments have been carried out in contexts that appear to duplicate the weak-authority situation of the international political system. Although the emphasis in this book is on the activities specifically of international politics, relevant theory can be derived from any situation lacking strong institutionalized authority and containing the potential for conflict. Furthermore, domestic political phenomena often have consequences for the international system— and the reverse; we shall discuss the "links" between behavior within an autonomous unit and the behavior of this unit as an actor within the international arena.

As Biafra illustrates, the distinction between the domestic and international political realms is particularly difficult to discern in instances of civil war and internal disturbance; international law does not provide machinery for an authoritative declaration on this question [1].

The question whether or not an actor is significant internationally requires an empirical answer. At what point does a group with a set of goals different from that of the formal authority under which it resides acquire autonomy? The legal concept of "state recognition" is of little value in answering this question. Presumably, the answer is "when the group is capable of conducting relations with other actors unimpeded by some master." The American colonies rose against British rule in 1776, concluded a treaty with France, and thus behaved as autonomous actors before their independence was rec-

[2] See, for example, Ralph Cassady, Jr., "Taxicab Rate War: Counterpart of International Conflict," *Journal of Conflict Resolution,* 1 (1957): pp. 364–368.

ognized by most nations. Similarly, although the American Civil War (1861–1865) was ostensibly a matter of domestic American politics, the rebellious Confederacy negotiated with and influenced the behavior of other autonomous actors, including the British government, despite the opposition of the U.S. government. We must conclude therefore that it was an autonomous and internationally relevant actor, if only for a short time.

As we have suggested in this chapter, international politics involves actors who are autonomous only to degrees. It is precisely because no government or state, regardless of its legal sovereignty, exercises total control over the individuals and groups for which it is responsible that subnational and multinational actors can enter independently into relations with other autonomous actors.

References

1. Brierly, J. L., *The Law of Nations,* 6th ed. (New York: Oxford University Press, 1963), p. 137.
2. Dunn, Frederick S., "The Scope of International Relations," in David S. McLellan, William C. Olson, and Fred A. Sondermann, eds., *The Theory and Practice of International Relations,* (Englewood Cliffs, N.J.: Prentice-Hall, 1960), pp. 16–19.
3. "Issues Before the 25th General Assembly," *International Conciliation,* 579 (September 1970), p. 205.
4. Kennedy, Robert F., *Thirteen Days* (New York: Norton, 1969), pp. 89–90.
5. Lasswell, Harold D., and Abraham Kaplan, *Power and Society* (New Haven: Yale University Press, 1950), pp. 55–56.
6. Marchant, P. D., "Theory and Practice in the Study of International Relations," *International Relations,* 1 (April 1955), pp. 95–102.
7. Platig, E. Raymond, "International Relations as a Field of Inquiry," in James N. Rosenau, ed., *International Politics and Foreign Policy,* rev. ed. (New York: Free Press, 1969), pp. 13–19.

Suggested Reading

Lasswell, Harold D., and Abraham Kaplan, *Power and Society: A Framework for Political Inquiry* (New Haven: Yale University Press, 1950), pp. 55–73.

McClelland, Charles A., "International Relations: Wisdom or Science?" in James N. Rosenau, ed., *International Politics and Foreign Policy* (New York: Free Press, 1969), pp. 3–5.

Platig, E. Raymond, "International Relations as a Field of Inquiry," in James N. Rosenau, ed., *International Politics and Foreign Policy*, rev. ed. (New York: Free Press, 1969), pp. 13–19.

Riggs, Fred W., "International Relations as a Prismatic System," in Klaus Knorr and Sidney Verba, eds., *The International System: Theoretical Essays* (Princeton: Princeton University Press, 1961), pp. 144–148.

Singer, J. David, "Introduction," in J. David Singer, ed., *Human Behavior and International Politics* (New York: Free Press, 1968), pp. 1–20.

Young, Oran R., "The Actors in World Politics," in James N. Rosenau, Vincent Davis, and Maurice A. East, eds., *The Analysis of International Politics* (New York: Free Press, 1972), pp. 125–144.

Chapter 2
PROBLEMS OF ANALYSIS IN INTERNATIONAL POLITICS

In describing or analyzing international politics, we must constantly make difficult choices among many possible approaches. One approach, common in the writing of historians and journalists, assumes that international politics is a struggle determined by power. This interpretation goes back to Thucydides and Tacitus. In general, it is based on the assumption that "the striving for power is an aboriginal human impulse . . . which blindly snatches at everything around it until it comes up against some external barriers" [22]. This view often engenders analyses laden with moral prescriptions in defense of the status quo since any but minimal change is regarded as a threat.

A totally different approach is that of macrosystems analysis; Walter Isard and others have attempted to combine mathematical and related techniques—including game theory, graph theory, formal models, and general systems theory—with insights about human behavior and adaptability suggested by philosophers and psychologists [17].

The one approach is concrete, the other abstract. The one cites specific, possibly atypical instances to support generalizations, whereas the other deals with aggregate phenomena in order to eliminate "accidental" deviations. The former rests on the conviction that, in a complex field, judgment and insight gained through knowledge of history and philosophy are the first requirements of the analyst; the latter seeks patterns of recurrent behavior and demands that theory be subject to objective verification. The approach of historians and journalists who rely upon "power" theories is derived from "philosophy, history, and law, and [that] is characterized above all by explicit reliance upon the exercise of judgment and by the assumption that if we confine ourselves to strict standards of verification and proof there is very little of significance that can be said about international relations" [7].

The two approaches have common features. Both simplify empirical material and attempt to generalize, though in quite different ways. Implicit or explicit in both are certain views of human behavior and what policies are the most desirable or adaptive for the survival of the values that their proponents cherish.

In this book we shall try to draw upon the insights of both the historical and the quantitative approaches. We thus emphasize historical uniqueness as well as the scientific posture of contemporary political science, insisting on "the hypothetical character of all empirical knowledge. The test for communicable knowledge depends on replicability even if only in principle. . . . Even intuition requires the techniques of science to prepare the base on which new intuitions develop" [19].

Knowledge from both traditions should be *cumulative;* later scholars should be able to reproduce the procedures of earlier ones and arrive at similar conclusions. The degree to which analyses of international politics can or ought to be free of moral considerations is a subject to which we shall return in Part IV of this book. At present it is enough to remind ourselves that an analyst's preferences are implicit in his choice of questions for study.

CONCEPT FORMATION AND THEORY BUILDING

In investigating politics we must make many subjective choices. Any set of general concepts used to analyze and describe reality is artificially constructed. Let us review briefly the process of concept formation and theory building. This intellectual enterprise, sometimes heavily disguised and often poorly managed, underlies nearly every attempt to discuss international politics, whether by the most poorly informed citizen with a simple view of causality or by one trained to be sensitive to its complexity. Both men simplify, selecting concepts and symbols to organize their perceptions and building models to explain and predict actions in international politics. It is impossible to

escape the need to simplify and conceptualize in order to understand, yet, because science demands precision and accuracy, we must seek concepts that have the same meaning for everyone. We must try to find those concepts and models that encompass the widest possible range of historical events, help to clarify with the least distortion, yet yield generalizations that are not too universal in their application to have little practical value.

Concepts

Concepts are used to organize ideas, perceptions, and symbols. A concept is an abstract construction that mentally combines all the characteristics of a class of phenomena to which we want to give meaning. The concept "nation-state" refers to a large number of individuals grouped together in a specific complex pattern of behavior. Defining concepts that permit us to organize our ideas and perceptions in a way that makes reality more understandable is the first step in building theory. Such definitions are neither "true" nor "false"; they are simply declarative. A concept is more useful when it helps to organize *more* rather than *less* information; does not overlap awkwardly with other concepts; and aids in explaining phenomena in the simplest and most straightforward fashion.

In Chapter 1 we introduced three important concepts—system, autonomy, and actor. We refer to the international political "system" (see definition page 16) because the term reminds us that international politics consists of patterned interactions that are to some degree interdependent and among which we search for relationships. We use the concept "autonomy" because it enables us to distinguish those actors who directly affect events in the international political system from those who depend upon other actors. The term "actor" refers to both individuals and groups that are sources of energy or influence in international politics; it does not exclude, as would a term like "state" or "nation," those participants like international corporations that are not "sovereign" and are therefore discussed only infrequently in conventional works on international affairs. These three concepts are useful, first, because their specific connotations remind the reader of the range of ideas and events included in our discussion and, second, because they call attention to information in a particular historical context that might otherwise escape notice. In a study of bloc voting in the U.N., for instance, assuming varying autonomy among member states encourages studies of informal communications and consultations.

Some concepts are very complex. For instance "power" is both ambiguous in definition and difficult to measure empirically. We use instead the concepts of "influence," which refers to the active aspect of power, and of "resources," which connotes the passive, or supply, aspects of power. Although there is occasionally some value in using a term that has broad and ambiguous connotations, the fact that such a term can have several different meanings in the course of a single discussion is likely to engender confusion and misunderstanding, rather than clarifying or enriching interpretation. For example, at the Yalta Conference of February 1945 the Western allies and the Soviet Union agreed that the liberated states of eastern Europe should be governed in accordance with the principles of "democracy." This concept, however, had a different meaning for Franklin D. Roosevelt and Winston Churchill, the Western leaders, than for the Soviet leader, Joseph Stalin. Soviet statesmen, reasoning from Marxist premises, viewed démocracy as the achievement of economic and social equality rather than simply of political equality. The ambiguity of the concept contributed to a series of postwar misunderstandings about the fate of eastern Europe.

Theory

Once we have developed a basic set of concepts and accepted a number of con-

ventional and more specific terms, we can turn to the essential analytical task of international politics: the building of *theory*. A theory is basically a proposition that purports to explain a particular outcome or relationship. It permits the observer to make sense of apparently disparate pieces of information. A theory generally consists of "logically interconnected sets of propositions from which empirical uniformities can be derived" [23].

In attempting to develop theory the analyst uses *working hypotheses,* which reflect his ideas about the way in which an inquiry should proceed to achieve optimum results. Usually he begins with a set of *assumptions,* or untested ideas, about the problem. In the process of testing them he may develop a *model,* an artificial representation of the reality being investigated; the model is based on several assumptions and propositions linked in logical fashion. After sufficient investigation the analyst may be prepared to combine several testable propositions in a theory that he believes will *explain* a particular phenomenon. A theory "will appear as the device for interpreting, criticizing, and unifying established laws, modifying them to fit data unanticipated in their formulation, and guiding the enterprise of discovering new and more powerful generalizations" [18]. But theory must be *tested* against reality in order that its assertions of relationships may be confirmed or disproved. Once a theory has been well established, it is considered a *law.*

In confronting the difficult questions of international politics, the analyst seeks, first, to develop theories that can explain *relationships* among important variables (factors subject to change). Good theory is built on concepts that accurately describe the phenomena with which the analyst is grappling. A concept, such as gross national product, may not accurately represent an actor's capability in a theory explaining the outbreak of war. For the sake of clarity, however, some simplification is often necessary. Detailed descriptions, as in a historical account, may make it more difficult to see the overall picture clearly. Second, the analyst seeks to explain outcomes by identifying the *causal* nexus that links variables. Third, he also seeks to predict future trends and outcomes with some reliability. A single theory rarely satisfies all three goals equally. It may yield reliable predictions but inaccurate explanations. Or it may explain phenomena but be unreliable in predicting future events.

Statesmen sometimes find it necessary to consider a number of different theories about the causal connection between, for example, the change in men's attitudes and the frequency with which war occurs. They then try to build larger theoretical structures that will explain and predict the outcomes of alternative policies that they may be able to pursue. For example, if a statesman wished to increase world order, he might examine various theoretical explanations of disorder in order to allot the state's resources most efficiently to attain its goal. After examining the possible alternatives, the statesman would be able to derive policy preferences from his theoretical model. In this way, theory has important practical consequences.

Theory building involves the connection of several discrete theoretical propositions to yield more inclusive explanations of the conditioning factors at work in the contemporary environment. Good theory must be empirically testable so that analysts can replicate earlier investigations and corroborate or disprove the theory in different situations and at different times.[1]

An example of poor theory building is the following argument:

For want of a smith the horse was not shod,

For want of a horse the messenger was not sent,
For want of a messenger the news was not carried,
For want of the news, the battle was lost.

Each statement explains why a particular unavailable resource led to an unfortunate outcome. The unavailability of each item —the smith, the horse, the messenger, and the news—supposedly ensured defeat in battle. Each hypothesis is fairly specific, can be checked against data, and is related logically to the next hypothesis. These four brief explanations might thus be used to trace the failure at each point. It is a poor theory, however, because, even if all the assertions are valid, we still do not have an adequate explanation of why the battle was lost. At best we have only the direction in which to seek the reasons why news, rather than courage, firepower, superior numbers, and so forth, was decisive. At worst we must concentrate on explaining the absence of the first link, the blacksmith. Either way, we do not know which resources were really crucial for victory, nor do we know if such resources are necessary for victory in all battles or only in this one. In each statement of the theory, we have a specified condition contrary to fact: we do not *know* whether or not, had the smith been present to shoe the horse, the outcome would have been different; we know only that he was absent. If a very similar battle were staged, differing only in that both sides had enough blacksmiths, we might gain a better idea of the importance of such skills in determining battles. Without such an unlikely control, however, this kind of theory remains speculative, for it cannot be tested against alternative explanations. The general may say, "If only I had known, it would have turned out differently," but he did not "know," and he can therefore never be sure whether or not the outcome would really have been different. In theory building we should avoid inferences about situations contrary to fact.

We use a variety of specific propositions in order to build a more complex

---

[1] For an example of the importance of replicability in political science, see the analyses of the causes of Hitler's rise to power in Seymour M. Lipset, *Political Man* (New York: Doubleday Anchor, 1963), pp. 127–152; and K. O'Lessker, "Who Voted for Hitler?" *American Journal of Sociology*, 74 (July 1968): pp. 63–69. Both authors have based their conclusion on the same set of data. O'Lessker can thus criticize Lipset's theory, and the student can systematically compare and criticize the results of each.

and complete theory, or model. From this higher level of theory we should then be able to compute the future values of the variables in which we are interested. We must recognize, however, that in any model incorporating a number of hypotheses, the important variables will themselves be merely mental constructs or concepts. For example, when we try to explain why war occurs, we must first understand clearly what constitutes war. Is it hostility and slaughter, or is it merely the absence of general peace?

Universal theories of international politics not only tend to simplify reality; they also therefore frequently distort or yield erroneous predictions of real events. We prefer to use small or partial theories of international politics, rather than grand theory, in this book. Middle-range theory attempts to explain or predict events only in a particular context or among a particular subset of variables. This approach is still more useful than any general theory of international politics because the study of this complex area of human behavior has not yet achieved the regularities, predictabilities, and formal models of, for example, the study of economic behavior. The fundamental characteristics of the contemporary international system and of its predecessors are the absence of centralized or dominant patterns of control and the predominance of purposive behavior by individual constituents over common purposive behavior. A general model of such a system provides for little explanation or prediction.[2]

SYSTEMS AND SYSTEMS ANALYSIS

A *system* is an abstract concept comprising a set of units complexly interrelated through interaction. The structures and processes within a system may vary over time, and the state of the system at any point in time is the result of the inter-

action of its constituent units. This simple notion of system is fundamental to our arguments and analyses in this book. In this chapter we shall briefly explore two related analytical approaches, general systems analysis and structural-functional analysis; they have much in common with our own approach but are distinct from it. We shall also explain our own, more limited use of the concept of system as a framework for analysis.

Characteristics of Systems

Several basic features of *any* system can be described:

Interdependence. In every system there are by definition two or more interdependent units. The behavior of each unit depends partly on the behavior of others in the system. In international politics we speak of a "global system" that embraces many autonomous units among which there is a discernible pattern of interaction. Within the system there are also subsystems—specialized groups of units—whose interrelations are particular to them, often exhibiting higher levels of interdependence than those in the larger system. For example, within the global system we can identify a North Atlantic subsystem, a communist subsystem, and so on. For certain purposes these subsystems may be considered actors within the larger system [5, 4, 32, 39].

Effects of Changes. Any action by any unit in the system will have some impact on at least one other actor in the system. If France reduces the number of North Atlantic Treaty Organization (NATO) troops committed to the defense of Germany, the number of German troops assigned this responsibility may be increased. No actor other than Germany may be affected, or at least none may seem to be affected, by France's action. The system can be said to have adjusted to the initial change in one of its variables and to have achieved a new equilibrium. The initial action has had consequences for at least one other actor,

[2] Models like Quincy Wright's "field theory" and Morton Kaplan's systems analysis have yielded few useful insights despite considerable efforts by many social scientists [38, 20, 28].

Germany, which has in turn responded in such a way as to restore the status quo in the NATO alliance. If, on the other hand, Germany does not respond, the lower troop levels may have a range of consequences for all NATO members and for the opposing Warsaw Treaty Organization. The attitudes of both the members of NATO and those of the Warsaw Pact may be altered, along with their expectations and relative capabilities. Then a change in a single variable will have led to a sequence of changes in other variables, which may prove destabilizing to the entire system. Even if the system remains particularly stable, each change may lead to further changes in a slow process of system development and decay.

Purposeful Responses. Responses to changes in the behavior of one unit will be neither random nor mechanical; rather, they will be predictable, for an alteration either in the environment or in the behavior of one actor will be evaluated according to the goals and objectives of all actors affected. Their responses will be purposeful, directed toward adjustments necessary to attaining their own goals. We may therefore extend our conception of international politics: It is a system of *patterned behavior* among autonomous actors characterized by interdependence and interrelated activities in the pursuit of goals that may or may not be compatible. Cooperation may be possible when conflicting goals and objectives are changed or the means for attaining them are modified.[3]

Feedback. The effects of an action are signaled to the initiator in a form of information known as *feedback*. Feedback can be of two types, positive and negative. Positive, or amplifying, feedback communicates the consequences of the initial action in such a fashion that the original behavior is reinforced, regardless of whether or not it has furthered the

actor's goals. There is increased probability of further action of the same type. Positive feedback within a system can be pathological, causing escalating cycles of action and counteraction that are disruptive; this mechanism is often at work in panics, inflations, arms races, and other crises.

Negative feedback is a self-correcting flow of information to the initiator of an action. If the initial action has produced undesirable consequences, negative feedback will enable the actor to alter the direction of his behavior.

In human, as opposed to mechanical, systems another kind of feedback may occur: "second order" feedback, which involves the use of past experience or memory, combined with new information, to reorder an actor's goals. Purely mechanical systems, like the automatic pilot of an airplane, are incapable of learning and goal change, but human, purposive systems have this capacity.[4]

A Familiar Analogy and Its Limitations

An analogy may help to clarify our idea of system. The thermostat attached to a furnace is a simple operating system found in many homes. Let us examine its salient features. A thermometer registers the temperature within a closed area. When the temperature outside the house drops and there is some exchange between the internal and the external environments, the inside temperature is likely to fall below the "goal" set on the thermostat. This decrease in temperature is registered by the thermostat, and when the difference between the "goal" temperature and the actual temperature in the house drops below a specified limit, usually one or two degrees, the furnace is turned on

[3] J. W. Burton calls international politics a "purposeful system." See Burton, *Systems, States, Diplomacy and Rules* (New York: Cambridge University Press, 1968), pp. 6–10.

[4] Karl Deutsch has distinguished first-order and second-order feedback this way: "A first-order purpose in a feedback net would be the seeking of *immediate satisfaction*. . . . By a second-order purpose would be meant that internal and external state of the net that would seem to offer . . . the largest probability . . . for the net's continued ability to seek first-order purposes" [10, 33].

by the thermostat. The furnace, in turn, generates heat until the thermometer "reports" to the thermostat that the temperature in the house has reached or exceeded the target. Then the furnace is shut off until the temperature again drops below the desired level. The thermostat can maintain the temperature in the house at a fairly constant level, provided that adequate resources—fuel for the furnace and electricity for the thermostat —are available. Furthermore, the thermostat, like any system, is capable of operating only within certain limits. If the temperature rises or drops too quickly or too far, the heating system may be unable to cope with the change. The greater the capacity of the furnace and the more sophisticated the thermostat, the more capable the system will be of adapting to sudden or extreme changes.[5]

We can see feedback operating in this system. A change in temperature is detected and measured against a goal, and the thermostat triggers the appropriate response to return the room temperature to the desired level. All systems, whether thermostats or nation-states, that contain purposive, or goal-seeking, agents have certain common characteristics. But the thermostat lacks some qualities of the international system.

Lack of a Single Goal. The international system is not unidimensional. The members of the system are interested in pursuing more than single goals like comfortable temperature in a house; rather, they have multiple goals that they pursue simultaneously. To extend the analogy in the appropriate direction, we would have to′add several other goals to the thermostat system: perhaps maintaining desired levels of humidity, dust, and odor. Presumably we would have to add new devices to regulate them.

Decentralization. Whereas the thermostat system that we have described is cen-

tralized, the international system is highly decentralized. To maintain the analogy, we would have to think of a house with many rooms, each with its own thermostat varying in its setting for heat, humidity, odor, and so forth and each controlled by people with different preferences. In the simple heating system the major problem is to adjust temperature to the level desired by a single person. As long as adequate resources are available and the environment stays within certain limits, the system will operate in a straightforward fashion. On the other hand, if we think of a house with many devices trying to achieve many goals simultaneously for many occupants with different preferences, we shall recognize very quickly that their preferences cannot be satisfied simultaneously (provided that there is interchange in humidity, heat, odor, and so forth among the rooms), regardless of the resources available. We cannot predict what the average humidity or temperature throughout this house might be, but we can be sure that conflict resolution would have to occur before stable settings would be possible. Indeed, unless each room could be sealed off, it would be impossible to satisfy the preferences of all the occupants simultaneously.[6]

In international politics autonomous actors attempt simultaneously to maximize their varying purposes, preferences, and goals but can do so only at the expense of others' purposes, preferences, and goals. Furthermore, the system is interdependent to such a degree that corrective feedback in one sphere may affect other values, just as changes in heat affect relative humidity in a purely mechanical way. When one country attempts to improve its relations with another the result may be new enemies for the initiator. An old Arab proverb declares that

---

[5] In the same way, the more sophisticated and flexible the regulatory mechanisms in an international system, the more capable of coping with severe disruptions that system will be.

[6] For a discussion of levels of centralization and decentralization in politics as a function of the economies of supply and demand, see Manfred Kochen and Karl Deutsch, "Towards a Rational Theory of Decentralization: Some Implications of a Mathematical Approach," *American Political Science Review*, 63 (September 1969): pp. 734–749.

"a friend of my enemy is my enemy." To the extent that this proverb is accepted by Arab leaders, we can imagine that the consequences of friendliness by one Arab state toward Israel would be to increase animosity within the Arab world. International politics, then, is a mansion with many rooms and many occupants in which interdependent and multidimensional goals are pursued.

Fallibility of Feedback. Another important distinction between the thermostat analogy and the international system is in the feedback itself. If operating correctly the thermostat inevitably leads to corrective feedback. But, whereas the thermostat is virtually automatic, feedback in the international system depends on human perceptions and decisions. Because of inadequate information or irrational behavior, self-correcting feedback is not always available in international politics. Frequently actors misunderstand the extent to which they control particular situations or the actual conditioning factors at work. Perhaps another pedestrian analogy can clarify the increased probability of error in human systems. Imagine a couple settling down together with a new dual-control electric blanket in which the controls have accidentally been crossed. The wife, preferring warmth, turns up her control; the husband, finding himself too warm, turns down his control. As the wife becomes colder, she turns her control still higher. The husband, increasingly warm, turns his still lower, thus making his wife still colder. At some point the limitations of the blanket will be reached, and the couple will spend a thoroughly miserable night unless they discover the positive, or escalating, rather than self-correcting feedback situation in which they have placed themselves.

Occasionally international actors do not recognize the extent of their interdependence. To what degree are the American defense budget and arms level determined by policies made in Moscow and the reverse? When two actors incorrectly assess each other's behavior as

willful and their own as necessary—as is typical in military decisions—positive feedback occurs. Two states, however, cannot exchange control over budgetary or military decisions as readily and as safely as a couple in bed can exchange their blanket controls. It may therefore be very difficult for actors to identify the causes of such positive feedback.

Summary. The international system is decentralized, multipurpose, and conflict-ridden; it has no equilibrium point and cannot satisfy the goals of all its constituents at the same time. These characteristics have remained fairly unchanged in international systems for many centuries. But some characteristics of the international system—its underlying structure, the resources that may be committed to it, and the degree of interdependence among the units within it —have changed not only through the centuries but also in the last few decades.[7]

Further Connotations of "System"

Some theorists have tried to go beyond the simpler notion of system in order to derive additional information about international politics. Some have assumed the existence of certain "isomorphisms," or parallel relationships, between different types of systems. They have examined biological, ecological, mechanical, and astronomical systems with a view toward developing a common language to describe similar functions performed by various structures. These theorists have sought a set of integrated general concepts, hypotheses, and propositions that could be used to understand or explain events in a wide range of subject matter and to provide a universal framework for analysis; the concepts for organizing and analyzing phenomena in one system could then be used in another. This approach, known as "general systems theory," after generating initial interest among students of international politics, has now been

[7] These changes are described and discussed in Chapters 5 and 12.

recognized as operating on a level of abstraction so remote from policy considerations that it has only limited promise.

Other theorists, drawing upon work in anthropology and sociology [31, 29, 30, 21, 24],[8] have combined the idea of system with assumptions about pervasive relationships between *structure* and *function*. The tasks performed in systems are called "functions." Although it is useful to recognize that, at different times within one system or simultaneously within several systems, a similar function may be carried out, we must be careful lest we assume that systems *must* carry out particular functions. We must avoid the teleological assumption that systems are imbued with purpose, that they have been *designed* or *intended* to perform certain functions. It is unlikely that political systems are ever purposely created (except by a very loose concept of design); rather, they are produced out of the interactions of a variety of forces. They serve no particular set of functions but rather comprise a set of goal-seeking or purposive actors. The activities characteristic of a system are purposive, but the system itself has no function or purpose; it does have consequences, however. We can therefore conclude that an actor's behavior has not served his objectives, but it makes little sense to claim that his behavior has undermined some systemic requisite like "peace" or "survival." To assume that an international system must perform certain functions and to condemn behavior that undermines such performance is to build an optimistic and altogether unwarranted bias into our understanding of international politics.[9]

In this book we shall rely on a simpler

footnotes:

[8] In the 1950s this approach was introduced into political science, where it has been applied particularly in comparative political studies [2].

[9] Amitai Etzioni has outlined two models for studying change. The first, which assumes that a given system performs from the beginning all the functions that will characterize it at maturity, he has labeled "preformism." The second, "epigenesis," posits that a system can add or lose functions over time, depending upon the interaction of its components [12]. From our discussion it should be clear that we incline toward the epigenesis model.

concept of system, one that implies interdependence of units and a *boundary* between the system and its environment. By "boundary" we mean simply the point at which the system ends—that is, the line at which there is an empirically discernible and sharp reduction in interdependence. Clearly, determining such boundaries is difficult and is related to the purposes of the observer.

ANALYTIC PERSPECTIVES

Levels of Analysis

A major problem in the analysis of international politics is choosing among levels of analysis. It is possible to account for any event from three different perspectives. The observer could study international behavior of a given state as a unit responding to the larger context of the international system, as a unit whose own attributes explain its actions, or as a unit whose constituents, such as its key decision makers or interest groups, determine its behavior. The first approach is considered to be at a higher level than that of the behavior itself; the second is at the same level; the third is at a lower level (a *reductionist* approach). One of the most obvious differences between foreign-policy studies and studies of the international system is that the former concentrate on individual states' behavior and the variables that explain the critical actions of each actor, whereas the latter focus on actors from the perspective of the system as a whole [35].

Identifying the *level* of explanation helps to clarify the construction of theory and to diminish the likelihood of unjustifiable inferences. But such identification itself can be a difficult task. To explain any given event, we begin by specifying the *unit of analysis*. We can identify a number of levels or layers of behavioral systems: individual, family, neighborhood or village, city, province, nation, international region, and world. We must clarify the system level at which the unit to be analyzed resides. Congressional action on foreign aid, for example, might be considered as an action of the United States or as a collection of individual votes; the investigator should be clear which is the case. Stipulating the unit of analysis, however, is only the first step in determining the level of analysis of an investigation.

A second distinction is the *unit of explanation,* the unit whose behavior is observed and recorded. Such information as a person uses to investigate and explain any particular unit of analysis need not come from the same system level; it could be different. For instance, we well might try to account for a U.S. foreign aid decision by data on the personalities of key decision makers, on the size of the budget or past aid decisions, or on the actions of recipient nations. While units can be finely distinguished as to systemic layer, we can illustrate the point about levels of analysis by the matrix in Figure 2.1 below. It refers to only three system levels: individual, nation, and world.

Essentially, three types of levels of analysis can be seen: (1) those where the explanation is at a lower level; (2) those where the explanation is at the same level; and (3) those where the explanation is at a higher level. If we specify our unit of analysis as U.S. congressional action on foreign aid, then the early socialization experiences of individual congressmen would be reductionist—the childhood experiences of men are on a lower level than the political action of a state in which they operate. If the unit of analysis is the voting of individual congressmen, then these facts would be at the same level—both voting and the childhood experiences are individual attributes. If we tried to explain either individual votes or the group decision (as the unit of analysis) by information about activity in the world outside the United States, such as a decline in "cold war" tensions, this would be a type 3, or inductionist, analysis.

When seeking to explain the behavior of an actor *solely* in terms of the international system in which he is found, we assume that the actor's internal characteristics do not affect outcomes. Although this is seldom true, it may be a useful assumption that forces us to look at the aggregate pattern of interaction among collective actors. However, misleading or meaningless assumptions like "States behave in accordance with national interest" and "Human nature has not changed through the centuries" often are justified because they permit the analyst to look only at "the big picture."[10] On the other hand, aggregation of data at this level may permit us to recognize regular patterns of activity and to discover gross trends.

A lower level of analysis, focused on conditioning factors within a single actor, permits us to discern differences among actors, sometimes even to exaggerate them. Although such an approach may hamper generalization or discovery of global patterns, it does permit us to explain specific outcomes more fully. This level of analysis is often used to explain particular decisions; it thus introduces the important phenomenon of *perception* by individuals into the study of international politics. As J. David Singer has suggested, "if the nation or state is seen as a group of individuals operating within an institutional framework, then it makes perfect sense to focus on the phenomenal field of those individuals who participate in the policy-making process" [35, p. 88].

[10] Such assumptions are often found in analyses by "realists." See, for example, Hans Morgenthau, *Politics Among Nations,* 4th ed. (New York: Knopf, 1967). A penetrating analysis of "national interest" can be found in James N. Rosenau, *The Scientific Study of Foreign Policy* (New York: Free Press, 1971), pp. 239–249.

	Unit of Analysis		
		Individual	Nation	World
Unit of Explanation — Individual	2	1	1
Nation	3	2	1
World	3	3	2

Figure 2.1.

The outbreak of the war between India and Pakistan in December 1971 can be viewed from three perspectives. First, we can see it in its global context. It has been suggested that the attention focused by the major powers on events in Vietnam and the Middle East led to a neutral policy toward the Indian subcontinent, whereas transfers of arms by external suppliers increased the level of armament available for conflict. Long-standing tensions in this area were considered sufficiently unimportant by other major system actors to be left unresolved.

Second, at the level of the two acting units a major source of tension was the plight of Bengali refugees from East Pakistan. Their presence in India was a major burden on Indian resources. India's economy was jeopardized by a prolonged crisis between East Pakistani insurgent forces and West Pakistani troops.

Third, we could seek an explanation of the crisis by looking at key elements within each state, particularly the motivations of leaders and the attitudes of major groups like the Bengali populations found in both those countries. For instance, the decision of Pakistani President Yahya Khan to apply force in suppressing Bengali nationalist politicians and intellectuals was, in retrospect, one of the critical steps on the road to war. That decision might be explained in terms of individual or military pressures brought to bear on specific leaders.

Although we can move between different levels in analyzing an event, it is not always necessary to view it from all perspectives. When we investigate an event at a higher level, we examine the whole system and its structure by induction and seek the *emergent properties* of a particular configuration of attributes or variables. Although no one of those variables alone may have produced the outcome observed, collectively they form a whole with traits such as a high probability of violence that may not be attributes of any single actor in the system. A war would then be viewed as the product not of sinful men or autocratic states but rather of the system as a whole. A relevant question is Do the properties of a system of actors in which none can ensure his safety increase individual actors' hostility and willingness to behave aggressively?

Often such questions are supplemented by examining information about specific attributes of actors. Do increased logistical capabilities increase aggressiveness? The United States, for example, with its large capability, undertook military actions in distant areas during the 1960s, actions that a country like China was incapable of taking. Perhaps the possession of a large air force and navy permits subsequently their use. Correlations of a state's economic or social attributes with its actions, a same-level perspective, are commonly used in analyzing and predicting the policies of states. Such covariation of variables suggests that one may follow from the other—a major form of *consequences*.

Finally, when we seek explanations through examination of the elements of which an actor is composed, we engage in reductionism, reducing the actor to the parts of which he is formed. Reductionism permits the analyst to reconstruct an event still more completely, specifying mediating mechanisms that may serve as intervening variables for factors at other levels or as independent variables. Use of this approach, however, involves the risk of overemphasizing what is specific to a particular outcome at the expense of recognizing what is general in a class of similar outcomes.

As Table 2.1 shows, these three approaches involve different types of explanation and analysis.

There are many other questions involved in considerations of levels of analy-

Table 2.1.
Levels of Analysis

Level of Explanation	Class of Explanation
higher	emergent property/induction
same	consequence/correlation
lower	mechanism/reduction

sis. One is the problem of *adequacy*. What constitutes an adequate analysis of a particular aspect of international politics? Must it specify relevant underlying mechanisms and emergent properties, as well as immediate causes? Usually not. An explanation at any one level will probably suffice.

A second question is Which level of analysis is most appropriate? After the Japanese bombing of Pearl Harbor in 1941 practically any American president would have reacted as President Roosevelt did. We would not have to examine his psychological makeup, his personal background, his idiosyncracies, or his popularity with the public to predict the initial American response. In some instances we can thus ignore reductionist perspectives in predicting outcomes; higher levels of analysis will *clearly* be more appropriate. When this is not so, we consider it advisable to review all levels of analysis.

A third question is Which techniques of observation should be used? Data are facts observed or inferred from observation, and we are constantly uncovering new ways to observe and record facts or to employ facts in novel ways in explaining something. For example, it has been suggested that the changing mores of a community may be reflected in the record of books borrowed from the local library.[11] In international politics informal conversations during meetings of the United Nations have been examined for clues to delegates' behavior and their places in the international hierarchy [1]; analysis of the contents in newspapers and speeches has been used to discern values and trends within national states [11, 3]. These techniques, along with less imaginative but fairly exhaustive collections of economic, social, and "event" data, have enriched the fund of available evidence.

In determining what evidence to gather, international analysts sometimes decide

between a "macro" and a "micro" approach. This distinction freezes the level of analysis with respect to the unit of analysis. A "macro" approach involves analysis of the dynamics of aggregate interactions and emergent patterns like conflict, trade, and communications. Microanalysis is focused on the components of the pattern. It can thus be similar to what we have termed "reductionism." "Micro" studies often take the form of in-depth investigations of particular examples, whereas "macro" studies extract the outstanding features of many examples for comparison, which often requires quantification of data [15]. A macro approach can thus resemble "induction."

The question of macro- versus microanalysis is clearly related to the level of analysis, but it is a less clear distinction in international politics than in economics, where the study of a firm is micro and the total economy of a country is macro. The basic issue for us is whether to explore a single instance in depth (the life of a political leader or a nation's decision to go to war) or to extract and compare salient features from many instances (the decisions of all states to go to war). The analyst's choice of emphasizing a macro or micro approach generally depends on the problem he confronts and the data that are available.

A fourth question relevant to the level of analysis is the nature of the information in the unit of explanation. If the analyst decides to compare events, he faces the choice of whether to make his comparison over time or through space or both.[12] Historians often compare similar political phenomena over time—for instance, American foreign policy from 1800 to 1972—by means of time-series data. A single actor is isolated and his behavior is traced in order to detect changes or recurring patterns. Alternatively, the analyst can use cross-sectional

---

[11] Some of these and other novel approaches to empirical measurement are discussed in Eugene J. Webb *et al., Unobtrusive Measures* (Chicago: Rand McNally, 1966).

[12] For an excellent essay on distinctions between space and time see Johan Galtung, "The Social Sciences: An Essay on Polarization and Integration," in Klaus Knorr and James N. Rosenau, eds., *Contending Approaches to International Politics* (Princeton: Princeton University Press, 1969), pp. 243–285.

data to compare the behavior of several actors at the same point in time, as in the foreign policies of the great powers in 1970. An aggregate analysis, whether based on time-series or cross-sectional data, involves a great deal of abstraction, even quantification and statistical inference, if recurring patterns are to be revealed. Cross-sectional analysis based on measurements at one point in time and time-series analysis relying on changes in variables over time have been used to explore questions about both systems and their constituent parts.

Macro-Micro Analysis

We shall consider macroanalysis to refer to studies where the unit of explanation is outside the nation-state, and microanalysis, to studies where the unit of explanation is within the nation-state. The processes in such settings are the findings of "micro" studies, which confirm those of macroanalysis, and the relationships among variables in the two will not necessarily be the same. One common fallacy is to assume that propositions about the behavior of components also apply to the whole: the *fallacy of composition*. Hans Morgenthau, for instance, has argued that individual men seek power unceasingly, a view that has also been held by Hobbes and other political philosophers. He has concluded fallaciously that all statesmen charged with acting for their country define its interests in terms of power and can be assumed to be ready to expand their power until checked by countervailing power [27]. Similarly, even though all the people in a state are "peace loving," it does not necessarily follow that the state itself is "peace loving." Another common example of the fallacy of composition is an assumption that the objectives of an alliance or coalition equal the sum of the objectives of its members.

We could use both micro- and macroanalysis to investigate whether or not foreign aid produces political support for the donor. In a "macro" approach we might look at the per capita aid received by national states and the support that they provide the donors on key votes at the United Nations [14]. Did states that received large amounts of American assistance tend to support American positions on the admission of mainland China? Have recipients of substantial assistance from Great Britain backed the British position on Rhodesia? Such an investigation could use either time-series or cross-sectional data or both. Data on relative aid and voting patterns would indicate whether or not evidence of "buying" support could be found. Other factors might have to be included in the analysis for a satisfactory assessment of the influence of foreign aid.

In a microanalysis we might also tackle this question. We might interview bureaucrats in recipient states involved in negotiating aid agreements to discover their attitudes to donor states. Another strategy would be to simulate conditions of aid transfer in a laboratory to see whether individual subjects accorded support or respect to their benefactors.[13] The subjects of "micro" and "macro" analyses are linked; each affects but does not determine the other. The "macro" approach focuses on a market situation—a probabilities table of costs and benefits, threats and opportunities associated with various strategies—confronted by the individual international actor. Microanalysis examines the organization, resources, and goals of an actor and the possibility of pursuing separate goals that form part of the structure and pattern of the "macro" process of international politics.

The opposite kind of generalization can produce the *ecological fallacy*. If we discover that wealthy states spend proportionately more of their resources on defense, we cannot conclude that wealthy individuals do the same. Nor can we assume that during periods of great violence in international affairs more individuals are prone to violence.

[13] For more information on simulation experiments, see William D. Coplin, ed., *Simulation in the Study of Politics* (Chicago: Markham, 1968).

We may thus find different relationships among variables at different levels. Frequently stronger relationships will be detected by means of aggregate studies than by means of disaggregate studies because in the latter the processes are usually defined by a more complex model and are more subject to "noise" from outside factors. For instance, it has been postulated that trade promotes friendship. By examining trade among large aggregates like nation-states and tracing changes in trade patterns and changes in friendship over a long period, we could make an initial test of this postulate. The same relationship between friendship and trade among individuals might be found, but it is likely that, as "friendship" among individuals is more complex and more sensitive than is "friendship" among states, the relevance of trade in the two instances would also be different. In most studies stronger relationships have emerged among aggregate units than among disaggregate units [6].

THE BALANCE OF POWER: AN ILLUSTRATION

"Balance of power" is a model widely used in international politics. Thanks to both its familiarity and its ambiguity, it serves as a useful illustration of some problems in analyzing international politics. Both the concept of "balance" and that of "power" have been used with several different meanings and in relation to both "micro" and "macro" analyses. We shall describe first the historical period in which balance-of-power theories flourished most fully and then distinguish several meanings ascribed to the idea.[14]

[14] The following discussion is drawn largely from Edward Vose Gulick, *Europe's Classical Balance of Power* (Ithaca: Cornell University Press, 1955); Inis L. Claude, Jr., *Power and International Relations* (New York: Random House, 1962), chaps. 2–3; Ernst B. Haas, "The Balance of Power: Prescription, Concept, or Propaganda?" *World Politics,* vol. 5, no. 4 (July 1953): pp. 442–477; A. F. K. Organski, *World Politics* (New York: Knopf, 1958), chaps. 11, 12, 14; Morton A. Kaplan, *System*

History of the Concept

The concept of the balance of power can be traced back to ancient Greek and Indian thought [34, 9, 25]. Although aspects of politics among the Greek city-states, the Italian city-states, the Indian principalities, and the European feudal kingdoms have been described as "balance of power" systems, the clearest and best-documented historical period for such a system is eighteenth- and nineteenth-century Europe.

The period after the Treaty of Westphalia in 1648 witnessed the rise of an international system in which violence was minimized in the pursuit of specific political ends. A small group of major states emerged, and no one of them possessed the capability to dominate the others. Although they competed for markets, trade, control of border regions, and hegemony over weaker peripheral states, their behavior was characterized by common respect for one another's existence, needs, and potential importance as future allies. The number of essential states in the system alternated between five and six, as states like Turkey declined in power and others, notably Prussia, rose. Although several states did expand, such devices as compensation and realignment prevented large-scale aggression and the partition of major states. Violence was used sparingly; minor wars were conducted to achieve minor readjustments, and major wars were undertaken only to prevent a single power from achieving preponderance.

This system, which survived imperfectly into the nineteenth century, had been conditioned by several factors. At the end of the religious wars in Europe ideology became quiescent and nationalism was still dormant. Unencumbered by ideological or popular constraints diplomats enjoyed considerable flexibility. Alliances were fluid and largely pragmatic.

and Process in International Politics (New York: Wiley, 1957), pp. 22–36; and Martin Wight, "The Balance of Power," in Herbert Butterfield and Martin Wight, eds., *Diplomatic Investigations* (Cambridge, Mass.: Harvard University Press, 1968), pp. 149–175.

The business of international politics remained largely in the hands of aristocrats, kings, and a corps of cosmopolitan diplomats, who spoke the same language—usually French—had the same manners and experience, and understood one another's viewpoints. Despite their different national origins, they tended to form an international society in which rulers had more in common with their counterparts in other lands than with commoners in their own country. The ruling classes stood for conservatism and moderation, and royal families were often related through dynastic marriages.

Furthermore, in view of the excesses of the previous epoch, soldiering was not held in high esteem. Sources of government revenue were limited, and large standing armies were virtually impossible to finance. The nobility was not taxed, and neither the middle class nor the peasantry was expected to interrupt its productive labors to fight. Mercenaries were therefore recruited from the dregs of society—often someone else's society—and they showed marked willingness to avoid battle.

Technology during this period was fairly stable, and adversaries could readily estimate the military and economic strength of their opponents. This stability facilitated the task of statesmen who sought to maintain wide distribution of capabilities among major actors. The caution of statesmen and the inability of any state to achieve decisive military capability made sustained war unnecessary and unacceptable to rulers. With the exception of Napoleon's reign at the beginning of the nineteenth century, the territorial integrity of major actors was not threatened. Edward Gibbon wrote in 1782: "In war the European forces are exercised by temperate and undecisive contests. The Balance of Power will continue to fluctuate, and the prosperity of our own or the neighboring kingdoms may be alternately exalted or depressed; but these partial events cannot essentially injure our general state of happiness" [26].

The French Revolution and the Na-poleonic conquest interrupted this "felicitous" pattern of international politics. One result was that, after Napoleon's defeat in 1815, the Congress of Vienna was convened under the guidance of the Austrian statesman Prince Klemens von Metternich. This congress was the first of a series of international conferences that would be held to deal with disruptions in the system. This pattern of conference diplomacy was known as the Concert of Europe. The Concert attempted to institutionalize the pre-Napoleonic pattern of international politics and to cope with threats to the stability or security of the major actors. The basic assumptions—the propriety of international consultations to avoid major disruptions, limited objectives, and shifting defensive coalitions—continued throughout the nineteenth century and up to 1914. This system, in which a limited number of major actors, none powerful enough to dominate the others, shared similar ideologies and goals, exemplifies a historical balance of international power, with preservation of order and minimum security, rather than peace, as a goal. As Edward V. Gulick has observed, "peace was no more essential to equilibrist theory than the barnacle to the boat" [16].

Uses of the Concept

Observers have interpreted the workings of the balance-of-power system in many ways. Let us examine a few of these interpretations, in order to illustrate the conceptual confusion that exists.

Distribution. Some writers use the concept of balance of power to refer to the distribution of power resources. Contemporary statesmen who argue that the balance of power is becoming less favorable to the United States use the term in this sense. They are suggesting merely that the distribution of resources in the international system is shifting so that the United States controls a proportionally smaller share than before. Other writers imply that the balance of power means a relatively even distribution of resources among the participants. They argue that under these conditions no one state or even small coalition can endanger the autonomy of the others and that the system will be characterized by a competitive pattern of politics. The concept of even distribution has been applied both to a simple balance involving only two actors and to a multiple balance involving several actors. On the other hand, it has also been employed to signify an unequal distribution of resources in which a pacific actor can deter an aggressive one seeking to alter the distribution.

National Policy. The balance-of-power metaphor has also been used to describe a certain kind of policy, usually of forming defensive alliances in order to prevent any coalition from winning a dominant position. It has been suggested that the role of at least one major nation (actor) must be that of "balancer." This actor must consciously behave in order to prevent any other state from expanding too far by throwing its weight on the side of the defensive coalition to ensure the defeat of an aggressor. Great Britain was often the "balancer" in the eighteenth and nineteenth centuries, intervening to check the expansion of France under Louis XIV and again under Napoleon, opposing Spain's efforts to regain its Latin American colonies, and participating in the Crimean War to halt Russian expansion. At the end of the eighteenth century Edmund Burke wrote that the various nations had special roles to play in maintaining an even distribution of power: "France . . . is the natural guardian of the independence and balance of Germany. Great Britain . . . has a serious interest in preserving (a balance between France and Germany). . . . It is always the interest of Great Britain that the power of France should be kept within the bounds of moderation" [8].

Such a highly rational and determinist explanation of Great Britain's foreign policy is unsatisfactory. This policy was actually the product of the perceptions of British statesmen and of their subjective

assessments of British interests rather than a set of "objective" and unchanging interests. British behavior in this period was neither so consistent nor so straightforward as the "balancer" explanation implies. Furthermore, *why* the statesmen chose to pursue this role is not revealed in balance-of-power discussions, yet one of the most important requirements of good theory is that it explain why. A valid assessment of British policy during this era requires an investigation of other variables beside the distribution of resources in Europe. British colonial expansion in Africa, for instance, was partly the product of a curious *misperception* of the strategic importance of control of the source of the Nile River [13].

Burke's explanation of the balance of power implies that differences in the internal composition of actors have little impact on foreign-policy outputs. Another gross simplification is the assumption that all men reason in the same manner and arrive at conclusions on the basis of objective criteria of "national interest" determined largely by influences external to the state, like the strength or weakness of neighbors and opportunities for conquest. Many analysts in the eighteenth and nineteenth centuries limited themselves to identifying the "permanent" and "transient" interests of states, or raison d'état. Frederick the Great of Prussia observed that "one must blindly follow the interest of the State." Friedrich Meinecke wrote: "The policy of the great monarchies has always been the same. Their fundamental principle has constantly been to grasp at everything in order to increase their territory continually" [22].

Maintaining a given distribution of resources may not be the actual policy of a nation-state but may be favored by individuals who have internalized some of the commitments or assumptions of the kind of analysis that we are discussing. When Dean Rusk was secretary of state he implied at a news conference that unless the United States pursued a policy of containing communism in Southeast Asia, China would succeed in overturning

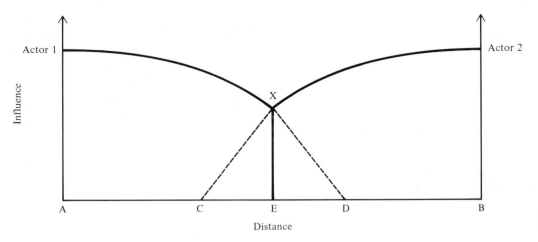

Figure 2.2. A Simple Equilibrium Model

the "balance of power" in that region [37]. This view reflects a set of assumptions about the forces maintaining such a "balance" and the consequences of withdrawing military force from the region. It also suggests that a change in the distribution of resources might injure either one actor or the system as a whole. One basis for favoring balance-of-power policies is the belief that all states have a natural tendency to expand to their limits. Leaders who act on this assumption may generate self-fulfilling prophecies, for their policies may actually encourage the already expected aggressive behavior by others. Statesmen who interpret events and promote policies of balance can be the means through which the larger pattern of balance of power is perpetuated. Certainly, the shared assumptions and expectations of key European leaders in the eighteenth and nineteenth centuries were crucial to the operation of the balance-of-power system.

Equilibrium. The third interpretation of balance of power is more abstract than are the first two. It involves a model at the aggregate level that purports to explain or predict the actions of states on the basis of systemic characteristics. Equilibrium is viewed as a relationship among the main variables of the system, like distribution of resources or attitudes

and the policies of states, so intimate that a change in one variable will inevitably lead to a change in another variable. Equilibrium is maintained only if the variables do not change too quickly or too much. This approach assumes that as long as there is a fairly equal distribution of resources among five or more actors, their policies will remain moderate, and efforts by one to achieve preponderance will be thwarted by countervailing influence.

The locus of equilibrium is the boundaries at which the diminishing domains of influence of actors meet. Influence declines through geographic, cultural, and organizational distance from the center of resource production.[15] Figure 2.2 illustrates this idea. Actors can exercise influence over a domain until they encounter an equal countervailing force. At point X the influence of the two actors is equal; AE represents the domain of the first actor's influence, BE the domain of the second actor's influence, and CD a contestable domain.

If a general equilibrium exists among all actors, when the influence of one actor increases or decreases, the equilibrium

[15] Kenneth E. Boulding suggests a gradient of diminishing influence based on geographical distance in *Conflict and Defense* (New York: Harper & Row, 1962). Geographical distance, however, is increasingly less important in limiting the extension of influence.

points will shift—unless countervailing or compensating changes occur among other actors. This model does not provide for analysis of the motives of actors; rather, it assumes that resources ensure control over a domain until they are matched by other forces.

In this interpretation of the balance-of-power model, shifting coalitions are considered to occur because states seek to maintain and can maintain a relative equilibrium. The prediction is that when there are several major actors with relatively equal resources, they will act to preserve the relative distribution. In this view states *automatically* adjust to an increase in the weight of one state either by increasing their own resource bases, by forming alliances, or by resisting the expanding state. The growth of one state, though yielding some increment in the domain of its influence, will be effectively counterbalanced by the weight of others, which may increase their own resources or shift larger portions of them to check the growth of the threatening state. Historian Arnold Toynbee has argued that the balance of power operates

to keep the average calibre of states low in terms of every criterion for the measurement of political power . . . a state which threatens to increase its calibre above the prevailing average becomes subject, almost automatically, to pressure from all the other states that are members of the same political constellation. [36]

The equilibrium model poses several problems. First, it assumes that systemic characteristics determine the strategy of actors and that the operation of the balance of power is therefore virtually automatic. In fact, historically the pattern of adjustments has not been automatic and has depended upon the ability of statesmen to perceive and interpret changes properly. Second, in the model "power" is defined as resources bringing influence. It is then suggested that a resource change can affect the balance of power only when it influences power. In specific instances it is difficult to know whether changes in resources actually increase or decrease a

single actor's influence. Finally, the model does not take into account the goals, objectives, and motivations of states, on the assumption that every state will use its influence to expand until it meets resistance. There are, however, many instances in which states have not behaved in this way and have chosen to expend only limited portions of their resources to attain influence in international politics.

Prescription. The notion of balance of power as defined in any one of these interpretations can serve as a prescription: an assumption that the "balance" *should be* preserved, usually in the interests of peace or stability. Such recommendations are often made by those who favor the status quo. Revolutionary or revisionist states, on the other hand, tend to reject "balance." In prescriptive use the metaphor provides neither a description of reality nor a theory of the behavior of states; it is, in fact, a shibboleth of conservatives. Since the Arab-Israeli war of June 1967 Israel has found the distribution of territory and military resources favorable to its security and has appealed to the United States to help "maintain the Middle East balance of power." The Arab states, on the other hand, deprived of large tracts of territory and in a position of marked military inferiority, have sought to enlist the help of the Soviet Union to "upset the balance of power."

Summary
Because "balance of power" can have several meanings, often at the same time, it can be a confusing, even a misleading concept. It may refer to the objectives of actors or to the policies recommended by some statesmen. Alternatively, it can mean a general theory that plural competition within some minimum consensus will lead to system "rules" causing every change to produce a countervailing change or adjustment. Although in some periods of history this model may have been approximated, the automatic character attributed to it is erroneous, and the underlying assumption of determinism is

unwarranted. Those who view the current balance of power favorably often make a leap from what "is" to what "ought to be" (or the reverse); the "balance" is assumed to be worth preserving.

We may conclude that the concept of balance of power is confusing because it lacks the qualities of a concept that we outlined earlier. Indeed, it is uncertain whether it is a concept, a model, a metaphor, or a theory. Consequently, it has no meaning that scholars and statesmen agree on and is virtually useless as a guide to policy making. Furthermore, it begs the question of level of analysis. Presumably, most versions of it involve macroanalysis of the anarchic international system with reductionist predictions about the behavior of individual states. In several notions of the balance of power we recognize the ecological fallacy and the fallacy of composition; analysts of the balance of power tend to make inferences about one level of analysis from the properties of another level. But we cannot conclude that Great Britain will always act as "balancer" in an international system characterized by shifting alliances, nor can we assume that when all states seek to maintain an existing distribution of capabilities, the distribution will be maintained.

THE TASK OF THE ANALYST

Confusing, ambiguous, and value-laden concepts and theories like that of the balance of power must be discarded whenever possible. Only in this way can we hope to clarify the workings of international politics.

The basic task of our analysis is the search for conditioning factors, that is, the forces that cause a particular event or pattern to emerge in international politics. To gain insights into conditioning factors, we must begin with detailed studies, selecting and differentiating among levels of analysis, using both macro- and microanalysis, but avoiding the fallacies of inference across levels. Furthermore, we must seek to build theories that are test-

able, which means theories at low and medium levels of generality.

There are, of course, other tasks for the analyst. Harold Lasswell has outlined five objectives for social scientists: clarification of goals, documentation of trends, discovery of conditioning factors, projection of future alternatives, and prescriptions for policy. We outline our choices for analytical investigation in Parts I, II, and III of this book. Ethical or normative considerations will be treated formally in Part IV. This separation does not, however, imply that we are striving to be "objective" or "scientific" in the sense of keeping our discussion of international politics value-free. The goal of developing an understanding of international politics that is both more scientific and more relevant to policy shapes our discussion throughout.

References

1. Alger, Chadwick, "Interaction in a Committee of the United Nations General Assembly," in J. David Singer, ed., *Quantitative International Politics* (New York: Free Press, 1968), pp. 51–84.
2. Almond, Gabriel A., and G. Bingham Powell, Jr., *Comparative Politics: A Developmental Approach* (Boston: Little, Brown, 1966).
3. Angell, Robert, Vera S. Dunham, and J. David Singer, "Social Values and Foreign Policy Attitudes of Soviet and American Elites," *Journal of Conflict Resolution,* 8 (December 1964).
4. Bowman, Larry W., "The Subordinate State System of Southern Africa," *International Studies Quarterly,* 12 (September 1968), pp. 231–261.
5. Brecher, Michael, "The Subordinate State System of Southern Asia," *World Politics,* 15 (January 1963), pp. 213–235.
6. Brunner, Ronald D., and Klaus Liepelt, *Data Analysis, Process Analysis, and System Change,* Institute of Public Policy Studies Discussion Paper No. 20 (Ann Arbor: University of Michigan, 1971).
7. Bull, Hedley, "International Theory: The Case for a Classical Approach," in Klaus Knorr and James N. Rosenau,

eds., *Contending Approaches to International Politics* (Princeton: Princeton University Press, 1969), p. 20.

8. Burke, Edmund, "Thoughts on French Affairs," in Paul Seabury, ed., *Balance of Power* (San Francisco: Chandler, 1965), p. 101.

9. Butterfield, Herbert, "The Balance of Power," in Herbert Butterfield and Martin Wight, eds., *Diplomatic Investigations* (Cambridge, Mass: Harvard University Press, 1968), pp. 132–148.

10. Deutsch, Karl W., *The Nerves of Government* (New York: Free Press, 1963), pp. 92, 93.

11. Deutsch, Karl W., *et al., France, Germany and the Western Alliance* (New York: Scribner, 1967).

12. Etzioni, Amitai, "The Epigenesis of Political Communities at the International Level," *American Journal of Sociology,* 68 (1963), pp. 407–421.

13. Gallagher, J., R. Robinson, and A. Denny, *Africa and the Victorians* (New York: Macmillan, 1961).

14. Gibert, Stephen P., "Soviet-American Military Aid Competition in the Third World," *Orbis,* 13 (Winter 1970), pp. 1117–1137.

15. Golden, John, "System, Process and Decision-Making: A Developing Method," in Morton A. Kaplan, ed., *New Approaches to International Politics* (New York: St. Martin's, 1968), pp. 55–70.

16. Gulick, Edward Vose, *Europe's Classical Balance of Power* (Ithaca: Cornell University Press, 1955), p. 35.

17. Isard, Walter, *General Theory: Social, Political, Economic and Regional* (Cambridge, Mass.: MIT Press, 1969).

18. Kaplan, Abraham, *The Conflict of Inquiry* (San Francisco: Chandler, 1964), p. 295.

19. Kaplan, Morton A., "The New Great Debate: Traditionalism vs. Science in International Relations," in Klaus Knorr and James N. Rosenau, eds., *Contending Approaches to International Politics* (Princeton: Princeton University Press, 1969), p. 43.

20. Kaplan, Morton A., *System and Process in International Politics* (New York: Wiley, 1957).

21. Levy, Marion, Jr., *The Structure of Society* (Princeton: Princeton University Press, 1952).

22. Meinecke, Friedrich, *Machiavellism* (New Haven: Yale University Press, 1957), p. 4.

23. Merton, Robert K., *On Theoretical Sociology* (New York: Free Press, 1967), p. 39.

24. Merton, Robert K., *Social Theory and Social Structure,* rev. ed. (New York: Free Press, 1957).

25. Modelski, George, "Kautilya: Foreign Policy and the International System in the Ancient Hindu World," *American Political Science Review,* 58 (September 1964), pp. 549–561.

26. Montross, Lynn, *War through the Ages,* 3rd ed. (New York: Harper & Row, 1960), p. 315.

27. Morgenthau, Hans J., *Politics Among Nations,* 4th ed. (New York: Knopf, 1967).

28. Palmer, Norman D., ed., *A Design for International Relations Research: Scope, Theory, Methods, and Relevance,* American Academy of Political and Social Science Monograph 10 (Philadelphia: 1970).

29. Parsons, Talcott, *The Social System* (New York: Free Press, 1951).

30. Parsons, Talcott, and Edward Shils, eds., *Toward a General Theory of Action* (Cambridge, Mass.: Harvard University Press, 1951).

31. Radcliffe-Brown, A. R., *Structure and Function in Primitive Society* (New York: Free Press, 1957).

32. Robinson, Thomas W., "Systems Theory and the Communist System," *International Studies Quarterly,* 13 (December 1969), pp. 398–420.

33. Rosenau, James N., *The Adaptation of National Societies: A Theory of Political System Behavior and Transformation* (New York: McCaleb-Seiler, 1970).

34. Seabury, Paul, ed., *Balance of Power* (San Francisco: Chandler, 1965).

35. Singer, J. David, "The Level-of-Analysis Problem in International Relations," in Klaus Knorr and Sidney Verba, eds., *The International System* (Princeton: Princeton University Press, 1961), pp. 77–92.

36. Toynbee, Arnold, *A Study of History,* vol. 3 (New York: Oxford, 1934), pp. 301–302.

37. U.S. Department of State, *Bulletin,* 57 (October 30, 1967), pp. 555–564.

38. Wright, Quincy, *The Study of International Relations* (New York: Appleton, 1955).

39. Young, Oran R., "Political Discontinuities in the International System," *World Politics,* 20 (April 1968), pp. 369–392.

Suggested Reading

Deutsch, Karl W., *The Nerves of Government* (New York: Free Press, 1963).

Kaplan, Morton A., ed., *New Approaches to International Relations* (New York: St. Martin's, 1968).

Knorr, Klaus, and James N. Rosenau, eds., *Contending Approaches to International Politics* (Princeton: Princeton University Press, 1969).

Knorr, Klaus, and Sidney Verba, eds., *The International System* (Princeton: Princeton University Press, 1961).

Morgenthau, Hans J., *Politics Among Nations,* 4th ed. (New York: Knopf, 1967).

Rosenau, James N., Vincent Davis, and Maurice A. East, eds., *The Analysis of International Politics* (New York: Free Press, 1972).

Singer, J. David, ed., *Quantitative International Politics* (New York: Free Press, 1968).

Waltz, Kenneth N., *Man, the State and War* (New York: Columbia University Press, 1959).

Chapter 3
THEORY AND EXPLANATION: THE OUTBREAK OF WORLD WAR I

The aim of causal inquiry . . . is to reveal the structure of the course of history, to disentangle the skein of great underlying cause and particular events—Raymond Aron [3]

Why did World War I occur? If a statesman or student were to ask this question of a political scientist, he would expect an answer revealing underlying causes— not an answer like "because the Germans invaded Belgium and France." By examining the sequence of events leading to World War I and several alternative theories about its outbreak, we can perhaps better understand the role of theory in the study of international politics; what tests may help us to decide whether to accept, reject, or modify a theory; the difficult and uncertain choices about "correctness" in constructing theory; and how theory can aid in avoiding future wars.

THE ROAD TO WAR

In 1914 the major states of Europe declared war on one another and fought for four bitter years in hostilities that none of the participants had fully anticipated or desired. One of every 28 Frenchmen, one of every 32 Germans, one of every 57 Englishmen, and one of every 107 Russians were killed [32, p. 488n.]. It seemed clear that the European state system that had emerged in the eighteenth and nineteenth centuries had to be reconstructed in substantially altered form if future mass destruction was to be avoided. The patterns of domestic and international politics had been shattered, and the illusion of permanent European stability had been destroyed. The peacemakers intended to build a better system, but World War II was grim testimony to their failure.

Europe Before 1870

The consolidation of Germany was completed in 1870 as a result of Prussia's decisive military victory over France at Sedan. This victory marked the culmination of a policy that Chancellor Otto von Bismarck had initiated almost two decades earlier. After the Franco-Prussian War, then, an uneasy status quo was preserved in Europe for almost half a century; during that time the European powers channeled their energies into industrial development and colonial expansion, particularly in Africa. By 1895 nine-tenths of Africa had been appropriated by the European states. The availability of colonizable territory diverted attention and reduced interstate tensions in Europe. After 1890, however, little unclaimed territory remained, and imperialist rivalries became a source of conflict.

Until his dismissal in 1890 Bismarck, through a cautious policy of compromise, readjustment, and delicate bargaining, had supported the European "distribution of power" established after the Franco-Prussian War. Germany's central geographical position and large army, combined with the chancellor's consummate diplomatic skills, had allowed Germany to exercise a moderating influence on the other European powers; only France had remained hostile because of Germany's seizure of Alsace-Lorraine in 1870. Of the "lost" province the French leader Léon Gambetta said in 1880, "Think of it always, speak of it never" [2]. A second major problem haunting the German chancellor during this period was the Balkans, where the hegemony of Turkey, the "sick man of Europe," was receding and Slavic nationalism was exacerbating a rivalry between Austria-Hungary and Russia that threatened to upset the delicate peace [23].

Bismarck's objectives were to keep Russia and Austria-Hungary from coming to blows, to isolate France from potential European allies, and to prevent Germany from becoming embroiled in imperialist competition. His scheme depended upon an intricate series of alliances that could be altered and shifted in times of crisis. Through the adroit exercise of threats and cajolery, Bismarck entered into alliances or understandings at various times with all the major powers except France. In the Balkans, however, intractable disputes over areas like Bosnia and Bulgaria made the status quo there impossible to maintain; Austria-Hungary

and Russia thus sought to prevent each other from gaining control of this vital area. Until he left office the chancellor maintained important diplomatic connections with both St. Petersburg and Vienna, advising his colleagues in the Dual Monarchy to "keep friends with Russia." After Bismarck was dismissed in 1890, however, Kaiser Wilhelm II allowed the Russo-German Reinsurance Treaty to lapse, setting Russia free to join with France. European alliances thus hardened, and it became increasingly difficult for states to change allies.

As long as Bismarck had remained chancellor, Germany had pursued limited and well-defined objectives. After his dismissal the objectives became less limited and explicit. His successors' intention of obtaining for Germany a "place in the sun" seemed ominous to the country's neighbors. Bismarck's cautious foreign policy was replaced by one calling for colonial expansion and naval armament, and the emperor spoke of Germany as having "become a world empire." Such "saber rattling" persuaded France, Great Britain, and Russia to overcome their outstanding difficulties and achieve something of a diplomatic revolution.

Bismarck's skill had enabled him consistently to achieve results favorable to Germany without sacrificing, as he remarked, "the healthy bones of a single Pomeranian grenadier." After 1890 his less astute successors began to pursue objectives for which no appropriate resources were available. The German government began to misuse its resources.

Bismarck's successors were ill suited to "Concert diplomacy." The mercurial and arrogant kaiser, described by Tsar Alexander III as "un garçon mal élevé," created frequently serious diplomatic embarrassment for the German government. In 1909, for example, an interview with a British journalist in which the Kaiser insulted Great Britain resulted in the resignation of Chancellor Prince Bernhard von Bülow.

Attempts to achieve military parity with Great Britain in the one area in which Germany remained inferior—on the seas—were characteristic of German behavior after Bismarck's dismissal. German entry on a naval arms race with the British was based on the "risk theory" of Admiral Alfred von Tirpitz. Recognizing that the German navy could never challenge Britain's worldwide naval strength, Tirpitz argued that the German battle fleet, if concentrated in home waters, could inhibit British behavior just because the British fleet was dispersed around the world.

For Germany the most dangerous naval enemy at the present time is England. It is also the enemy against which we most urgently require a certain measure of naval force as a *political power factor*. . . . Our fleet must be so constructed that it can unfold its greatest military potential between Heligoland and the Thames. [29, p. 27]

Tirpitz's idea that increasing naval resources would provide a "power factor" represents the type of misunderstanding of the nature of influence that often leads to ill-conceived policy recommendations.

Great Britain, an island nation dependent upon the seas for trade and control of the British Empire, perceived the German challenge to its naval supremacy as a threat to the empire and even to the island homeland. The British responded by increasing their own naval appropriations, outstripping German naval construction, and thus neutralizing German efforts in this area. British policy was, as Winston Churchill declared, to maintain a lead of "sixty percent in dreadnoughts over Germany as long as she adhered to her present program" and to lay down "two keels to one for every additional ship laid down by her" [6]. Tirpitz himself later lamented the folly of German policy: "We threw ourselves into the arms of others, then suddenly fell on them, we never missed an opportunity to demonstrate to others how splendidly we were doing. We never put ourselves into the position of others. We blew fanfares which never corresponded to our real position." [29, p. 28]

France was similarly preoccupied by German behavior. After the lapse of the Russo-German alliance, it succeeded in putting an end to its isolation by coming to a political understanding with the Russian government. In return the tsarist regime received needed foreign loans. This agreement destroyed one of the main props of Bismarck's system, the isolation of France. The conversion of the political understanding into a full-blown Franco-Russian alliance was completed in 1899.

Gradually an anti-German coalition began to take shape. After their confrontation at Fashoda in Africa in 1898 the British and French governments succeeded in settling their colonial differences: British supremacy in Egypt and French primacy in Morocco were mutually recognized. The German naval program also heightened French fears of German intentions in the Mediterranean, and open German antagonism toward Britain during the Boer War further convinced the British government that Germany had hostile intentions. Following the conclusion of the Anglo-French Entente in 1904 the military staffs of the two governments reached a series of secret understandings, in accordance with which the British undertook to provide naval security in the Atlantic Ocean and the English Channel and the French accepted similar responsibility for the Mediterranean. Although the Anglo-French Entente was never officially converted into a mutual-defense alliance, it began to serve the same purpose. The anti-German coalition was completed in 1907 with the conclusion of an Anglo-Russian Entente, which settled outstanding political issues between Great Britain and Russia in Persia, Tibet, and Mongolia.

The second major European coalition centered around the Austro-German alliance. This alliance, formally initiated in 1879 by Bismarck, later came to include Italy, although Italy abandoned its partners at the outbreak of war. As this coalition began to emerge, it became increasingly clear that the Austro-Hungarian

monarchy was Germany's only dependable ally. Austria-Hungary was in fact a
multinational federation of two independent states, Austria and Hungary, each
retaining considerable constitutional autonomy. In 1914 the federation had a
population of more than 50 million, one
of the largest armies in Europe, an effective bureaucracy, and rich agricultural
and industrial resources. Its weakness lay
in its bewildering patchwork of national
groups: Germans, Magyars, Serbs, Croats,
Slovenes, Rumanians, Czechs, Italians,
Poles, Ruthenes, Jews, and others bound
together only by common allegiance to
the Habsburg dynasty and Emperor Franz
Joseph. The failure of the regime to protect these various national groups, particularly the Serbs, Croats, and Slovenes,
from domination by the landed and
wealthier Hungarians threatened to destroy the unity of the empire.

The effect of the two large networks
of alliance was to magnify local differences into large-scale confrontations and
to erode the diplomatic flexibility that
had been a hallmark of the Bismarckian
period. After 1905, as the alliances were
hardened on the forge of successive crises
over Bosnia (1908), Morocco (1905 and
1911), and the Balkans in general (1912–
1913), there emerged what Bismarck
called a "damned system of alliances."

Germany's behavior appeared to Great
Britain, France, and Russia as threatening use of military force. Furthermore,
the more heavily Germany armed, the
more its insecurity grew. Far from ensuring its protection and recognition as a
world power, arming merely increased the
suspicions of Germany's neighbors so that
they reacted in ways that could only increase the German security dilemma. After
1890, ironically, the leaders of Europe's
greatest military power, with an enormous
and growing array of economic, political,
and military resources at their disposal,
found themselves increasingly apprehen-
sive about a possible British naval attack
or an onslaught of Slavic "barbarians"
from the east. Although Germany spent
more than £185 million on naval prepa-

rations from 1905 to 1914, the sum was
easily topped by Great Britain, and the
increase in the number of men in uniform
in France and Russia kept pace with German expansion in the same period [4].
This European arms race thus proved
futile, increasing insecurity and draining
resources.

The Coming of War

The "fearful concatenation of events"
that plunged Europe into war was centered in the Balkans. After a revolution
in 1903 tiny Serbia had ceased to be
loyal to Austria-Hungary and had become a focal point for Slavic nationalism.
With the tacit support of the Serbian government and Russian approval, nationalist terrorism spread within the southern
provinces of Austria. The idea of a union
of South Slavs appealed not only to the
Serbs residing in the Austro-Hungarian
Empire but also to the Croats and Slovenes. In 1908 the Serbian-speaking
province of Bosnia, which had been occupied by the Austrians some years before, was formally annexed by the Dual
Monarchy. In the Balkan Wars of 1912–
1913 Serbia was thwarted in its attempt
to gain access to the sea. As a consequence of these events, Serbian hostility
toward Austria-Hungary increased. The
latter determined to put an end to the
agitation that seemed to originate in Serbia and to threaten the empire's continued
existence. Persuaded by Foreign Minister
Count Leopold von Berchtold and Chief
of Staff General Conrad von Hotzendorf,
the Austro-Hungarian government began
to contemplate a military solution to its
domestic woes.

Russian calculations were shaped by a
disastrous defeat at the hands of the Japanese in 1905 and subsequent domestic
agitation against the tsarist regime. The
tsarist government decided that successes
in the Balkans were necessary to restore
its prestige and authority. As Turkey
grew weaker, Russian leaders sought control of the Dardenelles and the entrance
to the Black Sea, as well as influence over

areas that had formerly been subject to Turkish control. The Russian government declared itself the champion of Pan-Slavism and Greek Orthodoxy in the Balkans and the "protector" of the South Slavs.

Austria-Hungary sought German support to meet the Russian challenge, and Berlin conceded to the Austrians a "free hand" in the Balkans, which Bismarck had consistently refrained from doing. The kaiser and his advisers became convinced that Germany had to support Austrian ambitions in the Balkans to prevent the collapse of the Dual Monarchy and the subsequent isolation of Germany in Europe. Ironically, it was weakness that gave the Dual Monarchy such leverage over its German ally, and the German government increasingly permitted its weaker and more desperate partner to dominate the alliance.

For some time before the summer of 1914 German officials had been planning for an outbreak of hostilities. Taking the Austro-Prussian War of 1866 and the Franco-Prussian War as models, the German general staff had predicted that the forthcoming war would be won by speed and mobility, rather than by attrition, and had constructed an intricate system of roads and railways to facilitate movement of men and supplies. Perceiving both France and Russia as potential enemies, the general staff, under Count Alfred von Schlieffen, had in 1905 adopted a plan to nullify the numerical superiority of Germany's enemies, evade French fortifications on the German frontier, and maximize Germany's geographical and technological advantages. The Schlieffen plan called for a rapid, overwhelming flanking attack on France through Belgium toward the channel ports, "thus throwing the French armies against their own fortresses and the Swiss frontier" [15, p. 192]. In effect, German strategy telescoped immediate mobilization and war into a single action. Only the rapid conquest of France would permit the German armies to take advantage of the highly developed transportation network and turn their full

fury on Russia before the tsar's slowly mobilizing troops were prepared. The success of the Schlieffen plan would depend upon the rapid collapse of France, in repetition of 1870, and on British neutrality or inability to aid France in time. But the secret military arrangements that had been concluded between the British and French general staffs made it morally, if not legally, necessary for Great Britain to intervene if Germany invaded France. Furthermore, the traditional British objective of preventing any major continental power from occupying the channel ports in Holland or Belgium made British entry into a conflict highly likely.

The military plans of the adversaries had an air of unreality about them. With little understanding of the implications of technological developments in the latter half of the nineteenth century—barbed wire, machine guns, and large-scale industrialization—both sides thought in terms of achieving rapid victory in one "decisive" battle. Their model was the German victory at Sedan. All the actors believed that attack was the only means to victory and gave little thought to defense. We are led to conclude that German belief in the value of offensive operations resulted from recognition that Germany *could not* fight a war of attrition. "Such wars," wrote Schlieffen, "are impossible at a time when the existence of a nation is founded upon the uninterrupted progress of commerce and industry" [15, p. 187].

Bismarck had predicted that "some damned foolish thing in the Balkans" would spark war [32, p. 91], and on June 28, 1914, his prophecy was fulfilled. Archduke Francis Ferdinand, the heir to the Habsburg throne, was assassinated by a Serbian nationalist while on a state visit to Sarajevo, the capital of Bosnia. Previous crises in Morocco, the Balkans, and elsewhere had served to test and harden the European alliance system. Military plans and war technology, instead of being only means by which to achieve political objectives, had become major determinants of political decisions. Military planning required that once war seemed imminent, military considerations had to outweigh political ones. As this planning put a premium on swift and decisive action, mobilization of armies had to be initiated at once. The mobilization of one side was perceived as a deadly threat by neighbors who had not mobilized. Mobilization of the armed forces in 1914 involved a security dilemma similar to that posed by the use of nuclear weapons in the contemporary world. It could be perceived as highly provocative and essentially irreversible. The result was to deprive political leaders of their freedom to make decisions. In fact, the German chief of staff in 1914 bluntly informed the kaiser that "the strategic plans of the general staff had deprived the government of its freedom of action" [15, p. 181]. The same was true of the Russians. General Dobrolski declared: "The whole plan of mobilization is worked out ahead to its final conclusion and in all its detail. . . . Once the moment is chosen, everything is settled. There is no going back; it determines mechanically the beginning of war" [7, p. 343].

With the murder of the archduke as an excuse, the Austrian government decided that the time was ripe to crush Serbia in a rapid, limited war and to bring an end to Slavic nationalist agitation. Encouraged by Germany it sent to Serbia an ambiguous ultimatum calculated to be unacceptable. Despite a conciliatory Serbian response, it was clear that Austria-Hungary intended to invade Serbia; Russia was thus faced with a difficult problem, for its previous commitments and strategic calculations had inclined it to support Serbia. But a partial mobilization of Russian troops, stationed on the Austro-Hungarian frontier, would have left Russia exposed to Germany and would have made impossible any Russian assistance to France in the event of a large-scale war. Furthermore, Russia's lack of necessary administrative and transportation facilities probably rendered partial mobilization impossible anyway. This was because Russian troops mobilized in areas near their homes and were then dis-

patched to areas not necessarily nearest their point of mobilization. Russia thus had to choose either total mobilization or no mobilization at all. Guided by his military advisers, the tsar declared general mobilization, anticipating that Germany would intervene in the Balkan crisis. The abandonment of civilian control of policy was recognized by Foreign Minister Sergei Sazonov, who turned to the Russian chief of staff and declared: "Now you can smash the telephone. Give your orders, General, and then—disappear for the rest of the day" [7, p. 343].

In response to Russian mobilization Germany mobilized and declared war on Russia. Fearful that France would *not* declare war, thus failing to provide an excuse for setting the Schlieffen plan in motion, the German government demanded to know the French attitude toward a Russo-German conflict. France replied by mobilizing, and Germany declared war on France. With the German invasion of neutral Belgium, Great Britain entered the war. Although no one wanted large-scale war, Europe had entered a long and bloody season, and British Foreign Minister Sir Edward Grey remarked, "The lamps are going out all over Europe; we shall not see them lit again in our lifetime" [11].

One peculiarity of the European situation was that the achievement of the objectives for which alliances had been created was in conflict with the general objective of preventing a major war. The former objectives were rooted in balance-of-power and alliance thinking. Whether or not they were related to the main goals and values of the nations holding them was not considered by leaders in 1914. At the moment of choice between objectives all the participants except Italy chose to go to war to preserve the alliance system and the status quo.

THE ADEQUACY OF EXPLANATORY THEORIES: WORLD WAR I

In making decisions and fashioning policies all statesmen rely on theory of some kind, whether it be naïve or sophisticated, right or wrong. Good theory should explain more than single events. Although it is clearly useful and satisfying to be able to explain particular events, it is more useful to be able to explain *classes* of events. During World War I and the years since, many scholars and statesmen have sought to explain why the war occurred. Some of their theories seem adequate, but few, if any, have generated broader hypotheses about the outbreak of war in general. These theories are thus "noncumulative." A summary examination of a few of the more general theories applied to explain World War I will permit us to understand more clearly the advantages and disadvantages of case-generated theory.

Anachronistic Leadership

Although hundreds of diplomats and military leaders were involved in the network of decisions that culminated in the outbreak of war, certain individuals at the apex of influence within each state played critical roles in determining the outcome. According to one general explanation of what took place in 1914, had a few of these fifteen or so key leaders staunchly resisted the outbreak of hostilities, World War I might have been prevented.

The tsar of Russia and the Austro-Hungarian emperor, in particular, were rather weak men, hereditary rulers not selected for merit, superior judgment, will, or intelligence. Tsar Nicholas was indecisive, a poor judge of men, and incapable of political leadership.[1] He was less interested in ruling Russia than in enjoying the deference and license attached to the throne.[2] At the outbreak of

war, he sensed, though he did not comprehend, the magnitude of his role responsibilities; he finally loosed his generals with approval for full mobilization and retired for a walk in his garden.

The aging Emperor Franz Joseph was no longer in touch with the divisive groups in his kingdom. He lacked both the energy and the will to maintain central control, and he personally was largely responsible for the outbreak of war through his tacit approval of the initiatives of his government and military leaders. Kaiser Wilhelm, though better equipped to comprehend the exigencies of world politics, was shortsighted in his appraisal of the pressures on Germany and tended to abdicate control as the war approached.[3]

Aside from the personal weaknesses of these leaders, their attitudes and motives —fostered by dynastic interests, their education, and the outmoded government structures that they were supposed to guide—also contributed to their failure. They presided over hierarchies that had absorbed only imperfectly modern bureaucratic practices and skills. The goals, attitudes, and administrative practices of these rulers and their advisers reflected the customs and habits of the previous century rather than the realities of an age of growing industrialization.

As a result, many leaders could not perceive the greater risks and smaller gains associated with strategies of threat and force in international affairs, particularly as these strategies had worked well in the nineteenth century. Misjudgments of the probable performances of their own military organizations and the likely responses of others were grounded in unawareness of the forces at work in both domestic and international affairs.

The shared life style of nobility, reinforced by intermarriage and social intercourse, had welded an elite consensus characterized by self-importance and an

[1] One of his intimate advisers was the "mad monk" Grigorio Rasputin, whose influence over Russian state affairs grew to such alarming proportions that a group of court officials assassinated him.

[2] "The regime was ruled from the top by a sovereign who had but one idea of government —to preserve intact the absolute monarchy bequeathed to him by his father—and who, lacking the intellect, energy, or training for his job, fell back on personal favorites, whim, simple mulishness, and other devices of the empty-headed aristocrat." [32, p. 78]

[3] "As the final crisis boiled, his commentary on diplomatic telegrams grew more and more agitated: 'Aha! The common cheat.' 'Rot!' 'He lies!' 'Mr. Grey is a false dog!' 'Twaddle!' " [32, p. 95]

interest in ensuring mutual survival. Personal and royal aspirations overrode national, and even international, considerations for many of these leaders. The tsar, for example, wanted to defend the state interests and prerogatives that he had inherited. Kaiser Wilhelm was driven by personal pride and egotism. Although he privately wished to avoid war, as is revealed in his exchange with the Russian tsar in the famous "Willie-Nicki" letters, his contempt for other states and races dominated his feelings. He spoke of the British, for example, as that "nation of shopkeepers," which he hoped would "at least lose India" [25, 24].

Personal or class aspirations and ambitions are likely to have higher claims than do national priorities when the basis for leadership is a dynasty with anachronistic outlooks and interests. In the nineteenth century, dominated by skillful political leaders like Metternich and Bismarck, the influence of the aristocracy was muted or balanced in judicious fashion. But the central roles played by anachronistic leaders in 1914 have been blamed for the outbreak of war.

This explanation would be plausible if it could be argued that other leaders would have behaved differently. But English and French leaders, chosen by more democratic methods and presumably more responsive to popular preferences for peace, also vacillated and failed to grasp opportunities to avert conflict (though they were less inclined to be panicked by events). Grey, the British foreign minister, refused to clarify the British commitment to France and Belgium, and his silence encouraged German illusions that the English would remain neutral. Furthermore, the views and perceptions of the aristocratic leaders in eastern and central Europe were echoed by members of the comparable classes, with similar backgrounds and education, who served as the economic and political leaders of France and Great Britain.

Another problem is the assumption that a few leaders *could* control events, for it is possible that the aggregate of antagonistic forces present would have dominated events *even* if leaders had resisted more consistently and forthrightly the pressure toward war.

The Aggressive State

In the Treaty of Versailles German guilt for starting World War I was declared explicitly. Certainly German invasion of "neutral" Belgium and efforts to gain a quick, decisive triumph over France are evidence that Germany was an aggressor. But this swift mobilization and attack across its western frontier was precipitated *not* by a deliberate attempt to conquer territory but rather by the exigencies of military strategy under the Schlieffen Plan. "Schlieffen first created the Franco-Russian alliance; and then ensured that Great Britain would enter the war as well. The Germans complained that the war could not be 'localized' in 1914; Schlieffen's strategy prevented it" [31, p. 529].

Blaming Germany because its war strategy required a quick surprise attack is superficial. It makes more sense to ask how Germany became committed to such a plan and developed a set of potential enemies, for these factors determine the extent to which its initiation of hostilities was purposeful.

Two theories of German aggressiveness have been proposed. One declares that Germans, or at least German leaders, sought aggrandizement. Following the unification of Germany in the mid-nineteenth century, Germany had pursued a policy of consolidating and expanding the Reich. The Franco-Prussian War had ended with annexation of Alsace-Lorraine; the Congress of Berlin (1884–1885) had led to international recognition of German claims in Africa; and Kaiser Wilhelm had continued to press for increasing German strength and influence in international affairs after Bismarck's dismissal in 1890. A second view is that Germany saw itself as the target of other powerful states, which created anxiety and insecurity. As a result, German policy would have been defensive, aimed at countering the perceived hostility of France and Great Britain [1].

Several factors led Germany to behave aggressively, whether from offensive or defensive motivations. Its annexation of Alsace-Lorraine ensured permanent French animosity. Its efforts to bind Austria-Hungary and Italy in a strong alliance after letting the Reinsurance Treaty with Russia lapse hardened diplomatic relations in central Europe without increasing German security. The decision to compete with the English in naval strength by building dreadnaughts stimulated an arms race as illustrated in Table 3.1, promoted antagonism, and yielded no gain in comparative naval strength.

Furthermore, in a conference with Austrian Ambassador Szögyény in early July 1914 the kaiser promised German support for whatever the Dual Monarchy did, a virtual "blank check." From 1890 until 1914 Germany moved steadily away from acting as a cordial partner in imperial Europe to acting as a powerful divisive force that had to be reckoned with. The resulting international tensions created an atmosphere in which the Schlieffen plan seemed reasonable and necessary for German defense. They also prompted other states to consider Germany an aggressor.

As a result of propaganda there was for a long time widespread acceptance of the theory that World War I was the work of the German imperial court and general staff; as a consequence Germany, once defeated, was made to pay for its aggression and was reorganized on a "democratic" basis. This theory is now generally discredited, however. Both the proximate and more distant causes of Germany's attack on Belgium and France were basically not self-generated; they arose from the context of international hopes and fears. The Germans were not aggressive by preference, nor did they aim at changing the relative power among the major states, though such an outcome would have been welcomed. It was the Russian general mobilization that triggered the Germans' activation of their master plan for war. German aggression, to the extent that it existed, was not internally generated but was produced by German perceptions of the hostility of other states and was encouraged by misinterpretations of the intentions of other states. This perceived hostility, coupled with fears of relative decline, account for the war risks taken by Germany.

In recalling the events leading up to war Chancellor Theobald von Bethmann-Hollweg remarked:

Yes, My God, in a certain sense it was a preventive war. But when war was hanging above us, when it had to come in two years even more dangerously and more inescapably, and when the generals said, now it is still possible without defeat, but not in two years time. Yes, the generals! [8]

Table 3.1.
Defense Estimates of the Great Powers, 1870-1914 (in millions of pounds)

	1870	1880	1890	1900	1910	1914
Germany	11	20	29	41	64	111
Austria-Hungary	8	13	13	14	17	36
France	22	31	37	42	52	57
Great Britain	23	25	31	116	68	77
Italy	8	10	15	15	24	28
Russia	22	30	29	41	63	88

Source: A. J. P. Taylor, *The Struggle for Mastery in Europe, 1848-1918* (New York: Oxford University Press, 1954), p. xxviii. Reprinted by permission of the Clarendon Press, Oxford.

Weak States

A third explanation for World War I is the internal weaknesses of Austria-Hungary and Russia [23]. In both empires the old hierarchies were being challenged by forces of nationalism and reform.

In the Dual Monarchy the Serbian population, in particular, was restive as the decline of the Ottoman Empire permitted growing Pan-Slavism and demands for political union of the South Slavs. In Russia the reforms following the revolutionary uprising of 1905 had been minimal, and discontent was again on the rise. The legislative prerogatives of the Duma, never great and granted only under popular pressure in 1905, were increasingly circumscribed once again, and the impact of industrialization was creating new discontents and organizations that were slowly undermining the remaining store of credit of the old order.

The system of diplomacy that Bismarck had dominated in the late nineteenth century required states to act according to a standard set of principles that would promote peaceful solutions to conflicts over areas outside a major state's home territory. This system, however, was poorly prepared to deal with domestic or internal political crises. Nevertheless, such internal weaknesses could generate behavior, otherwise not "rational" or likely, that had international repercussions. As domestic pressures increased, Austria-Hungary sought to solve its internal problems by successful military ventures. Russia similarly resolved to go to war, rather than to admit weakness that might stimulate further domestic agitation against the regime.

This third theory holds that regimes with internal problems may be more prone to external aggression than are less troubled ones. War or the threat of war is used to divert unrest and to promote unity. When the popularity and legitimacy of a regime are low it becomes accustomed to using coercion to secure compliance. Indeed, the use of such instruments in international politics is constrained neither by popular will nor by inhibitions

about appropriateness. Weak states, it is argued, are both more prone to violence and more likely to see international conflict as either an extension of their own internal struggles or as a means of reducing domestic problems.[4]

This theory is also unsatisfactory for several reasons. Weak states are frequently *unassertive* in international affairs. Vulnerability can inhibit even imprudent leaders, and internal problems may absorb the attention and resources of the regime. For example, the Soviet Union was quite pacific during its period of internal consolidation in the 1920s and 1930s; Japan expanded militarily only after its transformation to a modern economy had been completed; and China since the Korean War has avoided actions that might match its frequently strident rhetoric. In contrast, there are many instances of weak states tempting others to enter domestic conflicts, thus internationalizing the conflicts, as in the breakup of the Ottoman Empire and the more recent Congo crisis. Although the theory may thus be applicable in some instances, it cannot serve as a general explanation, at least in this form. Furthermore, it can be easily reversed: One historian has declared that because "the statesmen of 1914 enjoyed Freedom from Fear, so far as revolution went, this made it easier for them to contemplate war as an instrument of policy" [31, p. xxxiv].

The Nature of Imperialism

John Hobson, Nikolai Lenin, and others, in trying to explain expansion of European influence around the globe, found economic factors at the basis of the war. In his essay "Imperialism, the Last Stage of Capitalism," written during the war,

[4] Rudolph D. Rummel has, however, found no apparent relationship between instances of domestic turmoil and acts of international conflict. His finding is important because of the widely held view that internal conflict tends to spill over into the global arena. See Rummel, "Dimension of Conflict Behavior Within and Between Nations," *General Systems Yearbook*, 8 (1963): pp. 1–50.

Lenin argued that as the contradictions within capitalist society increased, "bank capital" and "industrial capital" would merge and that these societies were seeking to solve their problems by creating overseas dependencies that could serve as outlets for surplus capital and markets for goods. The theory, explaining events unforeseen by Karl Marx, held that it would be possible (temporarily) to improve the lot of workers in industrial states like Great Britain or France by substituting exploitation of workers in overseas colonies and territories.

But this solution would be short-lived, for class antagonisms could be dampened only at the price of inevitable clashes among capitalist states competing to exploit overseas territory. Furthermore, a new revolutionary class would result from expanding the international proletariat, as Asians and Africans were forced from folk and feudal societies into capitalist labor markets. The general argument ran that Europe needed markets, cheap raw materials, and territories to which to export surplus population and capital. First the Americas (for a period), then Asia, and finally Africa had been incorporated into an imperial system of international capitalist exploitation.

Lenin insisted that as unclaimed territory disappeared and population migration from Europe slowed, pressures on the continent would certainly increase until imperialist competition erupted in international warfare: "When the whole world had been divided up, there was inevitably ushered in a period of colonial monopoly; and, consequently, a period of particularly intense struggle for the division and redivision of the world." World War I, according to Marxist-Leninist theories of imperialism, was thus the predictable outcome of capitalist societies' struggle to overcome their internal contradictions by internationalizing their economic dilemmas. War was inevitable once the later-developed capitalist states like Germany and the United States sought to expand abroad, only to find that early imperialists like Great Britain had *already*

divided up the world. It had only been a matter of time until German merchants from Hannover, British traders from Liverpool and London, and French businessmen from Marseilles had found their interests at odds and had used their political influence to goad their respective governments into protecting their interests, thus threatening the economic interests of other states. War had then ensued. The assassination of Archduke Ferdinand and the campaign against Serbian nationalism in Austria-Hungary were mere side events; the forces that lead states to commit their armies, it is argued, flow from the felt need to protect monopoly markets [36].

The imperialist theory of the causes of World War I has a simplifying appeal. By focusing on aggregate phenomena, it excuses us from explaining the complex web of individual calculations that led to Russian mobilization or the German decision to implement the Schlieffen plan. It is sufficient to recognize the antagonisms generated by international monopoly capital and the impossibility that it will fail to expand and exploit. This explanation is somewhat remote from reality, however. First, the war was precipitated by competition for control over a border area, not a market area. Although tensions from colonies may have contributed to tensions in Europe, major colonial crises had been settled peacefully in 1890 (Fashoda), 1905, and 1911 (Morocco), as overseas interests were accommodated among the powers. As John Strachey has declared, "The war arose, immediately, out of the rivalries of two of the landlocked, contiguous, and semi-feudal, as opposed to the oceanic, capitalist and highly developed empires, namely Russia and Austria-Hungary" [30].

Second, socialist forces in Germany and elsewhere rallied to their respective national causes, rather than denouncing the war as imperialist [28]. Finally, although some firms benefited, notably steel and munitions manufacturers, most capitalists suffered during the war, except for those in the United States, where "imperialist" economic competition with Europe was just beginning.[5]

System Overload

A final theory of the outbreak of war in 1914 may be called the "system overload" theory. The argument is that political elites in the key states of the international system, while pursuing personal and national goals, rely upon sets of learned propositions about the meaning of different cues and signals from other states and the probable consequences of various kinds of actions. These cues form patterns of *potential* actions and adjustments that constitute system rules. These rules are the guidelines that tell leaders what is important, what is expected, and what is likely in various situations. This kind of "working knowledge" is institutionalized as the product of previous experience but usually lags behind the actual range of problems that exist. The behavior to which such guidelines are supposed to apply may have changed because of technological advances, ideological shifts, or the failure of elites to invoke appropriate adjustment mechanisms. Most human systems have means of adapting to changing circumstances or to single failures without serious consequences. But occasionally the stress of change and failure of individuals in the established pattern may so overload the feedback mechanisms that the system cannot adjust rapidly enough and procedures for resolving conflict may be blocked.

A system-overload explanation can incorporate portions of the other four explanations that we have described. The interaction of two or more variables is necessary for a sufficient systemic explanation. The theory of imperialist causes of World War I is itself essentially a systemic theory. It suggests that, though there is a limit to possible expansion and exploitation, the system operates as if there were none, so that after the limit is reached the capitalist state system tries to resolve the conflict through war. The overload theory is more general, and evidence to corroborate or disprove it is easier to obtain. A group at Stanford University has examined the communication flows among the principal state leaders of the five major actors from late June 1914 until the outbreak of war in August. It was found that systematically perceived hostility had increased, leveling off in July as expectations of settlement improved but then rising drastically after the Austro-Hungarian ultimatum to Serbia. These changes were documented by means of content analysis of important written messages sent among the powers; the results are shown in Figure 3.1. The alternatives available to each state, as perceived by its leaders, declined during the period, whereas their perceptions of the options for other states reflect at least a relative increase. A feeling of resignation was widespread among the principal leaders, who believed that their hands were tied and that it was up to *others* to reduce tension or provide a path to peaceful settlement [16, 26, 17].

According to system-overload theory, the flow of communications increased, rumors and misperceptions abounded; leaders felt pressed to act quickly. Traditional diplomatic channels proved inadequate to cope with a crisis of this size and urgency, though they were still the primary agencies for handling it. The leaders who might have created ad hoc procedures or brought about a pause in the escalation of tension felt helpless to move against the weight of events. Delays in reading communiqués, interpreting their significance, and responding to new information were exaggerated by the overload of messages in the system, which conspired to make a manageable situation unmanageable.[6]

The overload of a system does not re-

---

[5] One related version of the imperialist explanation was put forward by a U.S. Senate committee, chaired by Senator Nye, in the early 1930s. This group reported on the role of several large munitions firms like Krupp and Vickers in the rapid armament before World War I. The conclusion was that a small group of profit-minded industrialists was largely responsible for the war.

[6] See the discussion on crisis in Chapter 20.

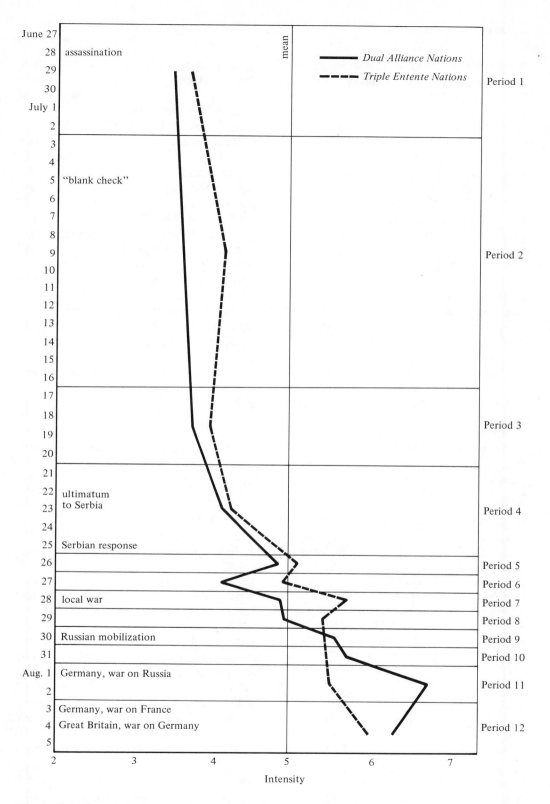

Figure 3.1. Perceived Hostility by Decision Makers of Major Powers, 1914

Source: Ole R. Holsti and Robert C. North, "The History of Human Conflict," in Elton B. McNeil, Editor, *The Nature of Human Conflict* © 1965. Reprinted by permission of Prentice-Hall, Inc., Englewood Cliffs, New Jersey.

sult from the failure of one actor to behave prudently or according to rules, nor is it a consequence of a single state's violation of international norms of conduct. Rather, some unique juxtaposition of events and personalities must overwhelm the routine functioning of the system. Occasionally, major events and crises occur because of unique combinations of circumstances. The Russian revolution of 1917 may have been such an event. That is, if one factor such as Lenin or Trotsky had been absent, the revolution might not have succeeded [12]. At other times so many factors may be pressing toward a certain outcome that altering but one circumstance can only modify its timing or magnitude. World War I is probably an example of this latter situation.

Some historians have suggested that the existing complex of circumstances— that is, the juxtaposition of social forces and attitudes among collective human organizations—would almost certainly have led to war. If the structure of the system made war inevitable, examining the private motives of key leaders is a futile exercise in the search for adequate theory. As Raymond Aron has declared:

Many historians consider research on the immediate causes of the war of 1914 devoid of interest because, in their view, it would have happened in any case. Scientifically, one cannot choose between immediate and long-range causes; either or both may attract the attention of the historian. But if he is convinced that the latter made an event *inevitable,* then study of the former loses all importance. *If* the European situation in 1914 was such that any incident could have touched off the spark, then the cause lay almost entirely in the situation and the incident was no more than an occasion for action. [3]

Perhaps fairly rapid peaceful changes in the European state structure were highly unlikely, regardless of national leaders or state problems. Then we might say that the war was "overdetermined." In this case, the presence or absence of any single factor would not have altered the outcome.[7] Systemic causation usually "overdetermines" in that the structure of the system itself is chiefly responsible for ensuring the outcome.

The major problem with such a systemic explanation is that it may explain too much and hence too little. As W. F. Ilchman and N. T. Uphoff have counseled, "the more encompassing an explanation is, the less testable, the less verifiable, and the less certain it is as a causal explanation, and thus the weaker it is as a basis for prediction and choice" [19]. System-overload theory may tell us only that the character of the European system encouraged people to see war as a rational policy and that hostilities were likely to spiral. If instability was acute within the European structure, random events would then have been sufficient to spark the cycle of expanding tension and conflict.

A "SATISFACTORY" EXPLANATION

Four Tests of Theory

There are no agreed-upon standards for determining when a theory adequately explains some event. To provide satisfactory explanation a theory should meet several tests, which help us to determine the extent to which the theory explains or predicts accurately and thus serves as a reliable guide to shaping policy. The first test was suggested in the Middle Ages by the Scholastic William of Occam. He argued that between two explanations that account for events equally well we should choose the simpler. This principle, called "Occam's razor," favored the validity of Johannes Kepler's formulas for planetary movement over the more complicated ones previously accepted. *Parsimony* in the number of variables or the specification of relationships can never be the only test for a theory, but it has been useful in clarifying and simplifying our theoretical heritage.

[7] Note that Alfred O. Hirschman's use of this term [12] is rather different.

A second test is the extent to which the theory is applicable. If it can be applied at more than one level of analysis and in several cultural settings it is more *powerful*. If it applies to only one specific kind of situation, it will not be helpful in predicting future outcomes. Theories are useful when similar patterns have been frequently observed, for they help to identify conditioning events so that some confidence can be placed in the prediction of similar consequences from similar events. The more general the theory, the more valuable it can be, but it may also have little value if it cannot satisfy the other tests. For instance, the theory that major events are "Acts of God" is all-encompassing but virtually useless, except as a bromide for ignorance, for it is non-empirical and defies disproof (our fourth test).

A third test is to determine whether or not the explanatory factors identified by the theory are *manipulatable*. If a theory specifies *only* causes over which little control can be exercised, it will be of no assistance in regulating human affairs. Explaining an event as the result of witchcraft, for instance, seems useful only to those who firmly believe in the efficacy and dependability of exorcism and ritual. Similarly, blaming the cold war on immutable communism provides few clues to how to end the conflict. If World War I was the inevitable product of the European system, no alternative outcome was possible, and we can gain no insight into how similar calamities can be avoided in the future. Identifying manipulatable factors that affect an outcome is necessary for satisfactory explanations because it permits responsibility for events to be affixed.[8]

Often the badly organized bureaucracy, incompetent leaders, inadequate proce-

dures for international conflict resolution, and similar factors are responsible only for fairly immediate causes. Yet the assassination of the archduke or the Austrian invasion of Serbia does not account for the outbreak of World War I; on the other hand gross underlying factors, like the structure of capitalist international economies, are so remote as to provide few policy guides short of a call for revolution. It may be that forces beyond human control *were* the critical determinants of World War I. A theory that allows for this possibility is not to be disparaged, for it may prevent investigators from wasting valuable time attempting to find non-existent controllable causes.

A fourth test is *empirical*. Yet when the subject is grand historical events, it is usually impossible to repeat sequences several times to satisfy the requirements of a controlled experiment. It should still, however, be possible to frame a theory in such a way that observations can *disprove* it. It may be that the opportunities even for such observations have passed; inference about what might have been based on existing data is tenuous. Nevertheless, the incompleteness of the historical record is insufficient justification for ignoring whether or not a theory can be disproved. For World War I enough documents exist so that theories about how patterns of communications were related to increasing tension, anxiety, and perceptions of narrowing choice have been subjected to reasonably critical tests and have generally been confirmed. Even careful sifting of data to corroborate or disprove a theory cannot guarantee certainty. The best that we can hope for is to discover whether or not the theory can predict correctly some relationship or fact that can then be more fully investigated. Nevertheless, such attempts to "operationalize" a theory and to compare its predictions with known or discoverable data are an important check on its value.

Whether or not an explanation is satisfactory is, finally, subjective. Why do we suggest that there is a need for theory that explains more than just specific outcomes?

---

[8] This focus on establishing moral responsibility was incorporated into international legal traditions by the Nuremburg trials after World War II. The decision that men cannot legitimately claim to have been obeying orders as part of a larger impersonal political system established the principle that they can be held responsible for acts of terror and genocide.

Because statesmen behave according to their theories. If a theory enables a person to predict with some confidence that certain behavior will produce intended results, then it is satisfactory. If his theories are not applicable to other situations, his behavior may be misguided. Statesmen between 1919 and 1939 sought to prevent a recurrence of large-scale war, but their prescriptions for peace, based on theories derived from the 1914 experience, may have encouraged the very calamity that they had hoped to avoid.

1919 and After: The Consequences of Acting on Poor Theory

At Versailles after the conclusion of World War I national leaders sought to provide a peace settlement that would prevent a similar holocaust from recurring. The war and its consequences had suggested to all that there had been weaknesses in the international system, which had been exacerbated by the stresses leading up to 1914. The major powers differed, however, in their assessments of the causes of the war and, as a result, in their prescriptions for peace. The peace settlement incorporated in the Treaty of Versailles was a compromise that embodied the different approaches of the victors.

At the time of the armistice in November 1918 the allies had not yet succeeded in entering Germany. Some German units remained intact and still able to fight. Germany was surely on the road to defeat, but the armistice did not involve "unconditional surrender." The military leaders of Germany, rather than awaiting inevitable defeat, sponsored a "revolution from above" by means of which Germany became a democratic country governed by a civilian regime; this regime was forced to negotiate the peace. After that the myth that Germany had *not* been defeated but had been "betrayed" was carefully nurtured. The harsh peace terms dictated at Versailles were viewed by many Germans as "unjust," and Germany remained a revisionist power. Partly as a consequence of the experience of 1919

and after, the allies, at the conclusion of World War II, demanded the unconditional surrender of Germany and Japan.

Other major actors were also dissatisfied with the results of the peace conference. Italy, for example, thought that it had not received a "fair" share of the spoils and that Anglo-French promises remained unfulfilled. The nations of eastern Europe, spawned in the breakup of the Austro-Hungarian Empire, were embittered by the allies' failure to satisfy their territorial and economic demands, and the newly created Soviet regime in Russia was treated by the Western allies as a virtual pariah. Even the Japanese were thwarted in their effort to have included in the treaty a clause that would recognize the concept of "racial equality." The Versailles Treaty represents an amalgam of the different "images of the situation" held by the victor nations, and World War I thus became only the first act in what Winston Churchill called "another Thirty Years' War."

President Woodrow Wilson came to the peace conference convinced that the war had begun as a consequence of the internal conditions of several of the old European states and as a result of the "power politics" of the nineteenth century. The people, he argued, wanted peace, but the existence of monarchical and absolutist institutions in Germany, Russia, and Austria-Hungary prevented their sentiments from having any effect. He believed that monarchs, in connivance with certain industrialists (the so-called merchants of death), had initiated wars for private gain and prestige. Only an international system made up of democratic nations in which all groups could exercise self-determination, concluded Wilson, could avoid the scourge of war. The world would be made "safe for democracy" *by* democracies.

Wilson sought the establishment of democratic governments in eastern and central Europe and in Germany. He opposed a punitive peace, arguing that the people of Germany should not be made to pay for the crimes of their leaders. He called for "peace without victory." Speaking before the U.S. Senate on January 22, 1917, he declared:

Victory would mean peace forced upon the loser, a victor's terms imposed upon the vanquished. It would be accepted in humiliation, under duress, at an intolerable sacrifice, and would leave a sting, a resentment, a bitter memory upon which terms of peace would rest, not permanently, but only as upon quicksand. Only a peace between equals can last.

The Germans agreed to an armistice on the expectation that the peace would be based upon Wilson's Fourteen Points, one of which called for peace by "open covenants . . . openly arrived at." This demand was in conflict with the "secret treaties" that Great Britain and France had concluded with Italy and other states in the course of the war. The British objected to some of the Fourteen Points, like freedom of the seas and free trade, because they sought to retain their naval and maritime dominance. The Fourteen Points also included a demand for the establishment of autonomous democratic states corresponding to ethnic divisions. Czechoslovakia, Hungary, Austria, Poland, and Yugoslavia thus emerged, but unfortunately the interpenetration of ethnic groups in eastern and central Europe made it virtually impossible to found national states coterminous with them. The new states all incorporated unstable ethnic minorities. In Czechoslovakia the Sudeten Germans, Slovaks, and Ruthenes were dominated by a Czech minority. In Yugoslavia, Serbs, Croats, Slovenes, Albanians, and Macedonians vied with one another for control. The "minorities question" also remained a burning issue in Rumania, Hungary, and elsewhere. Furthermore, most of the new states proved economically unviable and politically vulnerable. With the exception of Czechoslovakia, the eastern and central European countries succumbed to dictatorships like that of Admiral Míklós Horthy in Hungary in the 1920s and 1930s. Finally, economic weakness made it possible for the Nazis to obtain control over large sectors of their economies in the 1930s.

The last of the Fourteen Points called for the establishment of a League of Nations, which Wilson conceived as the main guarantor of peace in Europe and as a substitute for the balance-of-power system. He envisioned the League as an organization of equal democratic states that would act in concert if aggression were to occur.[9] The French and British agreed to establishment of the League—but a League very different from that which Wilson had envisioned.

Wilsonian idealism was challenged almost immediately. In the first British election campaign after Germany's defeat Prime Minister David Lloyd George declared, "I will make the Germans pay . . . as much as they can" [31, p. 195].

In the United States President Wilson sought a mandate for his policies and received instead a virtual vote of "no confidence" in the election of a Republican Congress. Under the leadership of Senator Henry Cabot Lodge the Republican Party, which Wilson called this "little group of willful men reflecting no opinion but their own," ultimately rejected the Versailles Treaty and prevented American participation in the League of Nations.

The French, led by Georges Clemenceau, saw German aggression as the main cause of war and an unrepentant Germany as the main threat to future peace. Their prescription for maintaining peace was therefore simple: to suppress Germany. They argued that peace could be guaranteed by disarming Germany and surrounding it by states allied with France. Poland, Czechoslovakia, and other eastern states would become France's sentries in the east, as well as serving as a *cordon sanitaire* against the advance of bolshevism. The French viewed the League as an alliance of victorious powers to maintain peace against Germany by armed might. When the League failed to take this form, the French preferred to act unilaterally, as when they

[9] For a discussion of collective security, see Chapter 10.

occupied the Ruhr in 1923 after German failure to pay reparations. Clemenceau had little regard for the abstract idealism of Wilson, and he remarked that the American president with his Fourteen Points was worse than God Almighty— for God had only ten commandments [34, p. 879].

The British statesmen, on the other hand, considered the war a consequence of the great powers' failure to uphold conference diplomacy. Because of the absence of this single coping mechanism, of a type that had figured so prominently in the nineteenth century, they believed system overload had occurred. They thus concluded that major war could be avoided if the Concert of Europe could be revived as a forum for settling differences and misunderstandings amicably. They considered the League such a forum. It was also to serve as a substitute for the inflexible alliance systems that had grown up before World War I; the British viewed this system as having been an important cause of the conflict.

The British thus did not blame Germany alone for the outbreak of war; they considered the independence of Serbia or Belgium not worth the cost of the conflict. They sought to temper French policy and argued for an Anglo-American guarantee of French security. Provided that the German fleet was dismembered and German colonies in Africa turned over to Great Britain, Germany should not be forced to bear the onus for the war but should instead be drawn as an equal into a reformed European state system, much as France had regained its status after the defeat of Napoleon.

The British did not accept the French view of an inherent expansionist tendency in the German nation. From this assumption, it followed that, by improving communications and understanding between states through mechanisms such as the League, future catastrophes could be avoided. The prominent Fabian Leonard Woolf elegantly articulated the dominant British view when he declared that a con-

ference would prevent the outbreak of war:

it prevents excitement by being so intolerably dull. . . . Even a Serbian or a German would lose interest in a question of Serbian and German nationality if he saw it discussed by diplomatists at a Conference, and not one person in a thousand would ever have thought of Sarajevo again if a conference had met in July, 1914. . . . It is darkness, doubt, and ignorance which breed fear and fear which breeds war. [35]

The results of the peace conference that assembled in Paris in January 1919 thus reflected an unwieldy compromise among the victors. Pressured by domestic groups demanding revenge against Germany, the statesmen of Versailles were peculiarly unprepared to legislate peace. "They were," one observer declared, "the merest novices in international affairs" [34, p. 876]. Of Wilson, John Maynard Keynes, the noted economist and a member of the British delegation, remarked, "There can seldom have been a statesman of the first rank more incompetent than the President in the agilities of the council chamber." Wilson's advisers he described simply as "dummies" [22]. The resulting Versailles Treaty was universally condemned as a failure. "This is not Peace," declared French Marshal Ferdinand Foch bitterly. "It is an Armistice for twenty years" [5].

Although the American proposal for a League of Nations was accepted, the Versailles Treaty can be said to represent more fully British and particularly French demands. Germany was forced to recognize its liability for the conflict in the "war guilt" clause. In addition, it was agreed in principle that the Germans should pay large-scale reparations to France and Britain, even while they were being deprived of the means to pay. Germany was forced to cede territories accounting for four-fifths of its production of iron ore, half its pig iron, one-fourth of its coal, three-fifths of its zinc, and a third of its lead. Its loss of arable land was greater in percentage terms than was its loss of population, which increased its difficulties even in feeding itself.[10] Indeed, even the industrial Saar Valley was to be occupied by France for fifteen years. Shorn of much of its ability to produce, Germany could finance its reparations payments to Britain and France only by means of loans from the United States. France and Britain, in turn, repaid American wartime loans with German reparations. This circular system continued until the Great Depression, when American loans to Germany dried up and Germany ceased paying reparations to the Western allies.

French security was to be enhanced by placing allied troops in "neutral" territory along the left bank of the Rhine. The German army was reduced to a token force of 100,000 men. The provinces of Alsace and Lorraine were returned to France, and Germany was forbidden to unite with Austria. In the east large tracts of German territory were turned over to Poland, but in a plebiscite Silesia chose to remain German. Finally, the German port of Danzig (Gdansk) was made a "free city"; it was this city that offered the ostensible justification for the Nazi attack on Poland in 1939, which opened World War II.

The peace was a vindictive one, and the bitterness that it caused ensured that Germany would accept its new status only as long as it was forced to. Although Wilson had failed to gain an even remotely satisfying outcome at Versailles, he nevertheless clung to the "sincere delusion," as Keynes called it, that the League of Nations could guarantee the peace. But, when the U.S. Senate refused to ratify either the Treaty of Versailles or the proposed Three-Power Pact with France and Great Britain, the United States withdrew into isolation.

Without the assistance of either Britain or the United States, French determina-

tion to maintain superiority over Germany was doomed to ultimate frustration. British attempts to revive the Concert of Europe could not be successful as long as German politics continued to be dominated by highly nationalistic and revisionist sentiment. German opposition to the Versailles Treaty increased, rather than decreased, as time went by; the Weimar Republic, successor to the German Empire, was buffeted successively by inflation and depression. At the same time the German population increased more rapidly than did the French population. Time was in Germany's favor. By 1933 domestic changes leading to Adolf Hitler's assumption of power had created a revolutionary state in the midst of Europe. Under such conditions the Concert could not have been successfully revived. Finally, the Americans, who had never become members of the League, turned away from Wilson and contributed to the ultimate failure of the international organization. The conflicting policies of the former wartime allies prevented any of them from realizing postwar objectives. Arguing for complete revision of the Treaty of Versailles, Keynes sagely observed in 1920, "The difference between revising the treaty at once and progressively modifying it under the force of circumstances is the difference between building a firm foundation and underpinning day by day a tottering structure" [21].

World War I and its consequences were events for which no statesmen were prepared. The leaders of the period could not meet the challenge of the swiftly changing environment, for the impoverished and inadequate theories of international politics upon which they depended were of little use.

VALUES AND THEORY

Many statesmen who have sought to explain the outbreak of World War I have failed to distinguish between explanations

---

[10] At the time Keynes pointed out the disastrous consequences of such a settlement in *Economic Consequences of the Peace* (New York: Harcourt Brace Jovanovich, 1920).

of *why* the war occurred and what they thought *ought to occur* in the future. In effect, they have failed to distinguish between their explanations and their aspirations. Confusing empirical and normative theory can serve only to complicate the task of finding explanations. "The point," Stanley Hoffmann has said, "is to keep our prejudices from becoming obstacles to the search for truth, but this does not mean the values we believe in should not serve as our guide" [13].

Normative and Empirical Theory

Partly because the prescriptions for avoiding future wars that arose after World War I were bad mixtures of theory, normative and empirical, they proved inadequate. Normative theory, once a principal concern of nearly every scholar of politics, has been increasingly relegated to a lesser status. Philosophically oriented social scientists are fewer, and their works are read less frequently by those engaged in empirical research.

Normative theory is concerned with ends and goals, how things *should* be. It is an attempt to define the "good" and to relate it to more specific events. Normative considerations play a critical role in every policy—indeed, in every conscious choice. Some principle of what is right or of what ought to be done, justified by some value considered good in itself, is always present. Most often, however, the value of certain objectives is taken for granted in reasoning about choices. As Hoffmann has noted, "Research oriented to action requires both an analysis of reality and a definite choice of values. Unfortunately, these values are not always made as explicit as they should be" [14].

The practice of medicine provides a comparison helpful for clarifying the complexity of normative views. Doctors have assumed for some time that life is better than death and that health is preferable to suffering and pain. Although they have occasionally found contradictions in these principles, these contradictions have not seriously inhibited their work in prescribing for and administering to patients. The goals of political scientists, however, tend much more frequently to be incompatible: peace versus sovereign independence or stability versus justice. Consequently basing the "should" in a policy prescription on some larger notion of good is precarious. Furthermore, no appeal to empirical theory can resolve finally a dispute among preferences.[11] Nevertheless, "It is in the areas of policymaking that the interaction between normative and empirical theory is most critical" [10].

Empirical theory purports to describe existing facts and relationships, regardless of their desirability. It consists of statements about *why* things are the way that they are: statements with "is" rather than "should." For many years empirical assertions were based on common sense or historical instances. More recently, especially since the growth of social science in the twentieth century, the use of statistics and "scientific" method has brought increased rigor and precision to empirical theory. Students of international politics have available large amounts of information to aid them in testing various empirical theories. The creation of large data banks, the expanded availability of census and survey information, and the capability of modern computers have greatly increased possibilities for manipulating data in order to test theories. The ranks of political philosophers and political historians have been joined by political sociologists and political psychologists. For the latter two groups the use of evidence in justifying theory has led to heightened attention to the types of evidence available and how they relate to empirical theory. Theories are framed in ways that permit the use of new kinds of evidence to substantiate or disprove them. Norma-

[11] F. S. C. Northrop has sought to show how empirical theory can clarify normative theories by exposing assumptions that are demonstrably false, but there is still no way to "prove" a normative theory by means of empirical evidence. See Northrop, *The Logic of the Sciences and the Humanities* (New York: Macmillan, 1947).

tive theory, though it may contain empirical assertions, primarily requires the relating of sets of statements logically in order to make consistent and coherent assertions about utility and preference [20].

Relationship of Theory and Values

The recent decline in attention to normative theory partly reflects the diffusion of shared views about certain political ends, as illustrated by the U.N. Universal Declaration of Human Rights and the rhetoric of nearly all major political leaders. Democracy, economic opportunity, equality, and justice are almost universally praised; privilege, class status, and corruption are almost universally condemned. Nevertheless, the meanings attached to these terms vary in different states. Many of the differences arise from contradictory empirical theories. Some of the major differences between Western democratic beliefs and values and those in socialist states rest on different theories about the relationship among control of the means of production, political power, and the links that establish popular control over government.

In international politics propositions related to policy may combine both kinds of theory. For instance, it has been argued that to guarantee peace more effectively, the United States should be a member of the United Nations and that to stop aggression in Southeast Asia, American troops had to be sent to Vietnam. Propositions of this kind reflect theories combining "is" and "ought" that often remain unexamined. Normative assertions enter the theoretical construction independently, for, as David Hume demonstrated convincingly several centuries ago, we cannot derive an "ought" statement from statements of fact. The belief about United Nations membership, for instance, most likely reflects empirical theories that the organization can reduce the probability of war and that American membership strengthens this ability—combined with the normative theory that the increased

probability of peace is more valuable to the United States than are the costs involved. By breaking down the clichés of politicians' rhetoric into component theories in this way, we can reveal value *assumptions* (that cannot be falsified) and examine the empirical components in the light of available evidence. Such an analytic procedure may enable political scientists to play roles comparable to those enjoyed by economists as advisers on international economic affairs.

THE FUTURE ROLE OF VALUES AND THEORY

The "Realist" school of international political theorists, whose influence reached its apogee in the mid-1950s, held that international morality is largely unenforceable. Its adherents, among them Hans Morgenthau, Dean Acheson, and Reinhold Niebuhr, argued that the ethical actor bases his behavior on considerations of power and on the will to overcome threats to peace.[12] They argued that we cannot deduce a moral policy from some universal moral principle but that in an imperfect world wise men at times must act "immorally" to preserve and strengthen national and international values. Those who have denied or suppressed freedom, like Hitler and Stalin, have to be opposed even if opposition behavior is immoral according to absolute principles or private standards. These arguments are also the foundation of the contemporary "contextualist" approach to ethics.[13] The principal weakness of the Realists' argument is its heavy deductive flavor. History and personal value commitments have shaped a set of basic axioms about politics from which the Realists have concluded that a

[12] Their ideas on ethics and morality in international politics may be found in Hans Morgenthau, *Politics Among Nations,* 8th ed., (New York: Knopf, 1967); Dean Acheson, *Power and Diplomacy* (Cambridge: Harvard University Press, 1958); and Reinhold Niebuhr, *Moral Man and Immoral Society* (New York: Scribner, 1941).

[13] This position is discussed by Abraham Kaplan in *American Ethics and Public Policy* (New York: Oxford University Press, 1963).

foreign policy should be based on power considerations. In addition, "necessity of state" can serve as a rationalization for almost any form of international behavior.

Several arguments bear upon the role of morality in international politics. One is the view that international morality or immorality emerges in the context of mixed motive interactions among states. Thus, morality is determined by the mix of cooperation or conflict existing in a given situation. Analyses of games and game situations have underlined the importance of trust, reciprocity, and commitment in bargaining when there is weak or no central authority.[14] The emerging code of behavior depends upon reciprocal mores; the behavior of each actor affects the "morality" of the others [18]. Absolute moral standards always involve conflict and ambiguity when applied in real contexts. Choices in international politics involve risking trust in other actors for mutual gain or refusing to act cooperatively in order to minimize loss [27].

A second development that has helped to reshape the study of international politics has been renewed interest in mechanisms for peaceful resolution based on the systemic study of behavior rather than institutions alone. In contrast to earlier scholars, who looked to formal intergovernmental groups like the United Nations for conflict resolution and possibly eventual world government, a younger group of scholars is attempting to study institutionalized *practices*—negotiation techniques, organizational behavior of the government units responsible for foreign policy, and strategies for accommodation and peaceful settlement in crisis and noncrisis situations. The moral or ethical imperatives that inform the practices and institutions and the impact that they have on international outcomes are also beginning to be investigated.

These trends suggest renewed concern about values and their connections with

policy decisions.[15] The values held by national populations are being studied, for they shape the goals and objectives of international actors. The point at which empirical theories are linked to normative statements to generate policy decisions has also received increased attention.[16]

The rapid expansion of data archives and methods of content analysis have facilitated systematic inquiry into values by means of both inductive and deductive analysis. Maintaining a desirable balance between these two approaches is essential.[17] Any satisfactory theory will build upon both, carefully bringing value choices to bear upon the range of theories investigated, the data collected or used, and the empirical relationships posited to link general and more specific normative statements.

Two additional research considerations may advance the cause of sounder theory and better policy. The first has to do with the basic dilemma of testing empirical theory. Much vital data is simply unavailable. Data on perceptions, ideals, and assumptions about reality held by major members of the international political elite are seldom gathered or used because of methodological difficulties.[18] Occasion-

[14] See Chapter 17.

[15] Herman Kahn and Anthony J. Weiner, in *The Year 2000* (New York: Macmillan, 1967), predict that value considerations will attract greater attention in industrialized states through the end of this century.
[16] For example, Ole R. Holsti, in "The Belief System and National Images: A Case Study" (*Journal of Conflict Resolution,* vol. 6, no. 3 (1962): pp. 244–252), has investigated how Secretary of State John Foster Dulles's values and beliefs affected his interpretation of events and his explanations to Congress of Soviet behavior and U.S. foreign policy.
[17] A somewhat intemperate exchange about reliance on inductive versus deductive approaches to theory construction vividly underlines the dangers of overemphasis on either. See Oran R. Young, "Professor Russett: Industrious Tailor to a Naked Emperor," in *World Politics,* 21 (April 1969): pp. 486–511; and the reply by Bruce M. Russett, "The Young Science of International Politics," in *World Politics,* 22 (October 1969): pp. 87–94.
[18] For an exception, see George Modelski, "The World's Foreign Ministers: A Political Elite," *Journal of Conflict Resolution,* 14 (June 1970): pp. 135–175.

ally bits and pieces appear in autobiographical form. But, in order better to understand the vertical and horizontal links that structure elite behavior and relate it to system capacity, new and more sophisticated data are needed. Aside from direct interviews—often difficult if not impossible to hold—other less direct methods might be tried, including some of those used by the psychologists who reported on Nikita Khrushchev's personality to President John F. Kennedy in 1961 [33, 9].

A second advance could be made through systemic study of erroneous decisions or predictions. The U.S. State Department, for instance, has no procedures for examining what has caused its mistakes and what are the major sources of its bias and misjudgment. As a result, little "learning" takes place, and the number of bad predictions and the amount of poor theory upon which policy is eventually based are unlikely to decline.[19] Such study and evaluation of mistaken government theories and views, detailing how they have been arrived at and eventually discovered, could improve the feedback and correction process so vital if political organizations are to adapt to a changing world environment. Furthermore, the infusion of values into the policy process might be more carefully scrutinized and described.

Attention to the role of values in explanation and policy promotion is important to clarify how they are related not only analytically but also practically. The improvement and expansion of our knowledge about international actors will provide increasing opportunities to construct and test theories about international politics. Procedures like those outlined here could also help to clarify the

role that preferences play in guiding statesmen and other international elites in their various efforts.

---

[19] An instance of unsuccessful prediction by a scholar frequently asked to advise the American Government appears in Ithiel de Sola Pool's essay "The International System in the Next Half Century," *Daedalus*, vol. 96, no. 3 (Summer 1967). He predicted, "Major fighting in Viet-Nam will peter out about 1967; and . . . Lyndon Johnson will have been re-elected in 1968" (p. 932).

References

1. Albertini, Luigi, *The Origins of the War of 1914,* 3 vols. (New York: Oxford University Press, 1953).
2. Albrecht-Carrié, René, *A Diplomatic History of Europe Since the Congress of Vienna* (New York: Harper & Row, 1958), p. 167.
3. Aron, Raymond, "Evidence and Influence in History," in Daniel Lerner, ed., *Evidence and Inference* (New York: Free Press, 1959), p. 31.
4. Barnes, Harry E., *The Genesis of the World War* (New York: Fertig, 1970), pp. 55–59.
5. Churchill, Winston, *The Gathering Storm* (Boston: Houghton Mifflin, 1948), p. 7.
6. Churchill, Winston, *The World Crisis, 1911–1918* (London: Macmillan, 1943), pp. 79–80.
7. Cowles, Virginia, *The Kaiser* (New York: Harper & Row, 1964).
8. Geiss, Imanuael, "The Outbreak of the First World War and German War Aims," in Walter Laqueur and George L. Mosse, eds., *1914: The Coming of the First World War* (New York: Harper & Row, 1966), p. 78.
9. Greenstein, Fred I., *Personality and Politics* (Chicago: Markham, 1969).
10. Greer, Scott, *The Logic of Social Inquiry* (Chicago: Aldine, 1969), p. 185.
11. Grey, Edward, *Twenty-five Years,* vol. 2 (New York: Stokes, 1925), p. 20.
12. Hirschman, Alfred O., "The Search for Paradigms as a Hindrance to Understanding," *World Politics,* 22 (April 1970), pp. 329–343.
13. Hoffmann, Stanley, *The State of War* (New York: Praeger, 1965), p. 19.
14. Hoffmann, Stanley, "Theory and International Relations," in James N. Rosenau, ed., *International Politics and Foreign Policy,* rev. ed. (New York: Free Press, 1969), p. 34.
15. Holborn, Hajo, "Moltke and Schlieffen: The Prussian-German School," in Edward Meade Earle, ed., *Makers of*

Modern Strategy (New York: Atheneum, 1967).

16. Holsti, Ole R., "The 1914 Case," *American Political Science Review,* 59 (June 1965), pp. 365–378.

17. Holsti, Ole R., Robert C. North, and Richard A. Brody, "Perception and Action in the 1914 Case," in J. David Singer, ed., *Quantitative International Politics* (New York: Free Press, 1968), pp. 123–158.

18. Hopkins, Raymond F., "Game Theory and Generalizations in Ethics," *Review of Politics,* 27 (October 1965), pp. 491–500.

19. Ilchman, W. F., and N. T. Uphoff, *The Political Economy of Change* (Berkeley: University of California Press, 1969), p. 261.

20. Kaplan, Abraham, *The Conduct of Inquiry* (San Francisco: Chandler, 1964), especially chap. 10.

21. Keynes, John Maynard, "The Economic Consequences of the Peace," in Theodore P. Greene, ed., *Wilson at Versailles* (Boston: Heath, 1957), p. 27.

22. Keynes, John Maynard, "Wilson," in Theodore P. Greene, ed., *Wilson at Versailles* (Boston: Heath, 1957), pp. 30, 31.

23. Lafore, Laurence, *The Long Fuse* (Philadelphia: Lippincott, 1965).

24. Montgelas, Max, and Walter Schücking, eds., *Outbreak of the World War: German Documents Collected by Karl Kautsky* (New York: Oxford, 1924), especially pp. 350 ff.

25. North, Robert *et al., Content Analysis* (Evanston, Ill.: Northwestern University Press, 1963), p. 175.

26. North, Robert C., Richard A. Brody, and Ole R. Holsti, "Some Empirical Data on the Conflict Spiral," *Peace Research Society Papers,* 1 (1964), pp. 1–14.

27. Rapoport, Anatol, and A. M. Chammah, *Prisoner's Dilemma: A Study in Conflict and Cooperation* (Ann Arbor: University of Michigan Press, 1965).

28. Schorske, Carl E., *German Social Democracy 1905–1917* (Cambridge, Mass.: Harvard University Press, 1955).

29. Steinberg, Jonathan, "The Copenhagen Complex," in Walter Laqueur and George L. Mosse, eds., *1914: The Coming of the First World War* (New York: Harper & Row, 1966), p. 27, italics added.

30. Strachey, John, *The End of Empire* (New York: Praeger, 1964), p. 103.

31. Taylor, A. J. P., *The Struggle for Mastery in Europe 1848–1918* (Oxford: Clarendon, 1954).

32. Tuchman, Barbara, *The Guns of August* (New York: Macmillan, 1962).

33. Wedge, Bryant, "Khrushchev at a Distance: A Study of Public Personality," *Trans-Action,* 5 (October 1968), pp. 24–28.

34. Wells, H. G., *The Outline of History,* rev. ed. (Garden City, N.Y.: Doubleday, 1961).

35. Woolf, Leonard, *International Government* (New York: Brentano's, 1916), pp. 134–135.

36. Wright, Harrison M., ed., *The New Imperialism* (Boston: Heath, 1961).

Suggested Reading

Forward, Nigel, *The Field of Nations: New Approaches to International Relations* (Boston: Little, Brown, 1971).

Greer, Scott, *The Logic of Social Inquiry* (Chicago: Aldine, 1969).

Holsti, Ole, R., "The 1914 Case," *American Political Science Review,* 59 (June 1965), pp. 365–378.

Holsti, Ole R., Robert C. North, and Richard A. Brody, "Perception and Action in the 1914 Case," in J. David Singer, ed., *Quantitative International Politics* (New York: Free Press, 1968), pp. 123–158.

Kaplan, Abraham, *The Conduct of Inquiry* (San Francisco: Chandler, 1964).

Lerner, Daniel, ed., *Evidence and Inference* (New York: Free Press, 1959).

Mueller, John E., *Approaches to Measurement in International Relations* (New York: Appleton, 1969).

Northrop, F. S. C., *The Logic of the Sciences and the Humanities* (New York: Macmillan, 1947).

Palmer, Norman D., ed., *A Design for International Relations Research: Scope, Theory, Methods, and Relevance,* American Academy of Political and Social Science Monograph 10 (Philadelphia: 1970).

Chapter 4
THE NATURE OF OBJECTIVES AND THE PROBLEM OF INFLUENCE

The study of politics is the study of influence and the influential—Harold D. Lasswell [6]

In international politics most actors obtain what they want by influencing others. In the previous chapters we have dealt with concepts and analytical approaches that permit us to examine static situations. We turn now to concepts that permit us to explore the dynamics of influence.

Every action in international politics involves a *situation* as defined by the actors, the *objectives* and *goals* of actors, and the *means* by which actors influence one another. The relationships among these factors are complex and so close that any alteration in one usually leads to alterations in the others. For instance, the objectives that an actor sets for himself may determine the means by which they can be achieved; or the available means may determine the choice of objectives.

To understand these interrelations, it is necessary to examine the components separately.

THE SITUATION

The situation is the actor's "image" of his external and internal environments—an image in the sense that the actor perceives these environments through sensory agents. An actor can have no conception of or response to an event until he receives information about that event. In Japan before the visit of Admiral M. C. Perry in 1853 the decision makers were virtually unaware of many of the great events unfolding in the rest of the world; for them these events had not taken place.

Many events that do occur are not perceived—less because observers to receive information are not functioning than because of poor "scanning," that is dedicated, careful, and complete reception. The *psychological environment* results from scanning; it is the environment of which leaders are conscious and from which they can therefore draw inferences in making policy decisions. The *operational environment* includes phenomena that actually affect the outcome of policy, whether or not they are perceived by decision makers. For various reasons the United States remained unaware of clues that might have enabled it to predict the Japanese attack on Pearl Harbor in 1941. This information, though not part of the psychological environment of American leaders, was surely part of their operational environment [15]. In a sense the psychological environment determines the outcome of the decision process, whereas the operational environment affects the outcome of policy.

Information

Leaders' interpretations and evaluations of information are affected by their own memories and by selective perceptions and advice of others inside and outside the country. Generally actors learn of an event from various sources after a time lag. Often it is ambassadors and newspaper reporters who relay information to leaders. This raw information is then processed and refined.

An actor thus defines the situation on the basis of the information received and other "cues" (from memories and theories), whether or not they accord with "objective reality." Because the event is filtered through various channels, the image that emerges will only partly correspond to it; the image can never *exactly* represent reality.

The degree of correspondence between the image and the actual event is determined by three main factors. The first is the quality of the actor's receptor devices, his ability to identify and record faithfully what has happened. This factor is critical because, as data enter a decision-making system, some of them are selected for the attention of leaders, but most of them are ignored and processed no further.

A second factor is the functioning of communications channels. How quickly and accurately is information relayed to decision makers? During the Cuban missile crisis of 1962 American intelligence agents in Havana and elsewhere had sub-

stantial information on the movement of Russian ships to Cuba and the unloading of missiles at Cuban ports. There was, however, much delay in communicating to key officials some of the information that would have assisted them in piecing together the fragmentary data that they *were* receiving because the sources were felt to be unreliable and the information contradicted expected Soviet actions.

Finally, the image evolves within a framework of continuing memory processes. American decision makers initially refused to take seriously reports that the Soviet Union was stealthily introducing offensive weapons into Cuba. Previous experience had convinced them that the Soviet Union would not dare take such a step. They were certain that the Russians were striving for a détente with the United States and would not endanger growing Soviet-American understanding. It was also widely assumed that Soviet leaders understood that the United States would not tolerate Russian offensive weapons in the Western Hemisphere [16].

Interpretation

Once information has been received, it must be interpreted. The sources of information and its interpretation can be exceedingly complex; an image usually emerges only after an intricate set of interactions between suppliers of information and interpreters of it. The reliability and accuracy of the information are important, but equally important are the factors that affect a decision maker's interpretation of that information. His health and his memory, as well as the advice of his friends and the policy of his government, are some of these factors.

Whether or not key United States leaders perceive that "aggression," for example, has occurred in some distant conflict depends upon the sources of this information and their own interpretation of it. The plea of a "friendly" government,[1] the

[1] The definition of a government as "friendly" is itself the outcome of previous information and interpretation that have been stored in memory.

communications of ambassadors and prominent citizens, the memory of comparable past situations, and a host of other factors can shape leaders' perceptions. Information about and interpretation of the same event often differ in different countries and at different times because of reliance on different sources. The Western conclusion that the Chinese invaded India in 1962, for example, has been called into question by recent information on Indian diplomatic and military activities before the outbreak of hostilities. Whether or not aggression has actually occurred is often less important than that significant decision makers in countries like the United States and the Soviet Union *think* that it has.

The probability of undesirable conflict increases as the images of major international actors become less congruent. Often the conflicting views of international leaders have equal claims to "reality." Differences arise not because certain leaders are insane or irrational but because they have different sources of information and interpretation, different value systems, and different images of reality.

VALUES, GOALS, AND OBJECTIVES

All actors in international politics pursue goals that determine, or at least affect, their behavior. These goals reflect the actors' underlying value patterns and are thus closely related to the tasks performed by an actor.[2]

Values

The values sought by individuals and groups include wealth, prestige, health or well-being, influence, enlightenment, and affection. It is difficult to determine an individual's preferences among his various values, but we can identify basic values that must be attained before any individual will devote much time or attention to attaining others.

[2] See Chapter 1, pp. 5–6.

Collective actors, however, have much more complex priority structures than do individuals, and it is impossible in the abstract to identify basic values. The values and priorities of a collective actor are not necessarily the same as those of its individual constituents. Indeed, values like national prestige can inhere only in the state. Furthermore, a collective actor may pursue certain values at the expense of others that seem to the individual more basic. The German playwright Berthold Brecht attacked the value priorities of capitalist society, because he considered them at odds with his individual values; social principles like "justice" often seem irrelevant when simple individual survival has not been ensured.

International actors may pursue values like status and prestige energetically while ignoring economic well-being, security, or autonomy. In the nineteenth century imperial China insisted that foreign "barbarians" perform the "kowtow" when meeting the emperor but refused to modernize China's economy and army to prevent foreign depredations. The value priorities of France under Louis XVI and Marie Antoinette did not reflect those of most Frenchmen at the time. Although an actor's priorities are partly determined by the social milieu in which they are conceived and by the perceived needs of individual constituents, we cannot assume a priori that the value structure of a collective actor even approximates the sum of the values of its constituents.

Goals

Although the basic values of a particular group may remain fairly constant over time, their implications for behavior will vary. Goals may be viewed as "relevant utopias," that is, as constructs of the future in which an actor envisages his values maximized, given the constraints and limitations of the present as he understands them. Goals are not extremely specific; rather they represent ranges of satisfactory futures. Actors are often inconsistent in their goals, which may be

Term	Referent
Values	desired objects
Goals	preferred future situations
Objectives	concrete steps toward goals
Policies	specific activities to further objectives

Figure 4.1. Motivational Hierarchy of an Actor

contradictory or even counterproductive yet firmly adhered to. Compromise among goals is thus sometimes required in policy making; but it has often happened that an actor has pursued conflicting goals simultaneously, and has failed to achieve any of them. Elimination of conflict, on the other hand, might have resulted in attainment of some of them. Third-world states frequently face "trade-offs" between economic independence and rapid growth. Indonesia sought both goals in the early 1960s and attained neither.

Goals represent desirable and possible future states of affairs. An important goal of Marxist-Leninists is the classless society, and American liberals consider the end of poverty in the United States a "relevant utopia." As the conditioning factors of the present situation change with time and as value priorities shift in response to changes in culture or levels of satisfaction, goals will also shift. Actors must then adjust and adapt their concrete objectives if they are to achieve their new goals. Full attainment of goals is rare, because of their tendency to change before it can occur; predicting behavior and analyzing the pursuit of goals in international politics is thus a hazardous undertaking.

Objectives

One way to simplify the problem is to identify even more concrete targets, which we call "objectives." Objectives are related to goals, and it is possible to distinguish among classes and types of objectives. If a nation values its territorial integrity and takes as a goal security from external threats, then one of its objectives is to modify the behavior of adversaries. The achievement of such an objective is presumably a major step toward the goal that expresses an underlying value. The most specific attribute of an actor's motivational hierarchy is policy. Building additional military capacity and deploying troops in certain ways are policies that might be designed to achieve the objective of modifying enemy behavior. A policy is what an actor does or refrains from doing in order to secure an objective; it involves specific exercises of influence. An objective, on the other hand, may always be stated as an *intention* to move from a present state of affairs to another state of affairs. Figure 4.1 depicts the hierarchical relationship of these four levels in the motivational hierarchy.

An objective is an actor's mental construct based on images of the present state of affairs, a predicted future state of affairs, and a preferred future state of affairs [14]. The image of a present situation consists of an *analytical* component (including the facts that the actor believes characterize the situation and the facts that explain or interpret those facts) and an *evaluative* component (judgments about whether or not the facts and their implications are desirable and important).

For each present situation an actor also has a series of alternative projected future situations in mind. Evaluation of these alternatives determines which seem most congruent with the actor's values and most significant; evaluation thus shapes the goals that the actor pursues. The need to envision as many alternative future situations as possible was recognized by President John F. Kennedy when he commented about the Cuban missile crisis, "If we had had to act on Wednesday in the first twenty-four hours, I don't think probably we would have chosen as prudently as we finally did" [13]. An actor's objectives are to see that preferred future situations occur and to avert undesirable ones.

Salience. The concept of *salience* requires some elaboration. When actors receive information that allows them to define a situation, they consciously or unconsciously accord it a certain amount of attention and a certain degree of importance. The importance of a situation is largely determined by the actor's interpretation and evaluation of the information available. If the actor concludes that the event will have significant consequences for his goals and the values that they reflect, he will accord greater attention and importance to the event. The salience of an objective helps determine the types and amounts of resources that an actor will devote to attaining the objective, provided that there is a fair chance of doing so.

Although it is difficult to measure the salience of objectives, it is reasonable to infer it from the attention that an actor pays to them. The student makes such inferences every day when he reads a newspaper, in which news is presented, organized, and analyzed according to its perceived relevance and significance. It becomes clear that an actor not only has different objectives but has also assigned priorities to them. The social scientist might be more successful in inferring the salience of objectives if he had access to telephone and written communications among high-level decision makers. As it is, we can measure salience best by examining "what important people talk and write about." Even with such limited information we can safely conclude that in the 1960s President Lyndon B. Johnson considered it more important to alter the behavior of North Vietnam than of François Duvalier, then dictator of Haiti.

The same objectives may have different salience for different actors. Whereas halting the expansion of communist influence in Vietnam may be an objective of both the United States and Great Britain, it is more salient for the former. This difference helps to explain why different actors with similar objectives devote different levels of resources to their attainment. Furthermore, as individual decision makers can deal with only limited ranges of information at once and have

only limited time to consider problems, it is likely that many less salient objectives will be virtually ignored.[3] One study of foreign trade in the United States has suggested that the "low saliency of foreign-trade matters and the competition of other matters for time means that at every level there is only a limited amount of actual communication and a great deal of speculative imagination of what each relevant group must be thinking and feeling" [2].

Objectives involve implicit or explicit comparisons and contrasts. For example, at the height of the cold war the United States sought to "halt communist aggression" in many parts of the world. This objective was based on the assumption that aggression was demonstrable from available facts. It was reasoned that if such aggression were to succeed, it would lead to setbacks for the United States and tempt adversaries to embark on further aggression. The United States viewed this state of affairs (the present situation) as important and undesirable and perceived that unless it and other countries intervened to halt and prevent the "spread" of communism, the "free world" would suffer further defeats (the predicted situation). As this predicted future situation was considered undesirable, the United States formulated an objective designed to secure a more desirable future state of affairs. The objective was to convince other actors that "aggression would not pay," and specific policies were initiated to further this objective.

The components basic to defining an objective are summarized in Figure 4.2. As one scholar has commented: "Sound political analysis is nothing less than correct orientation in the continuum which embraces the past, present, and future. Unless the salient features of the all-

[3] A similar analysis of salience is implicit in Karl W. Deutsch and J. David Singer, "Multipolar Power Systems and International Stability," *World Politics*, 16 (1964), pp. 390–406. In complex, highly bureaucratic states it is possible for a specialized set of decision makers to pursue objectives of their own relatively uncontrolled by high-ranking officials whose attention may be focused elsewhere.

Components	Present Situation	Future Situation
Analysis: Description	few facts—many facts	few facts—many facts
Causal interpretation	unexplained—explained	unlikely—likely
Evaluation: Effect	undesired—desired	undesired—desired
Salience	unimportant—important	unimportant—important

Figure 4.2. Situational Images Basic to Objectives

inclusive whole are discerned, details will be incorrectly located" [7]. Explanations of present situations reflect analysis of the causal or conditioning factors that produced them. After analyzing a present situation an actor projects future situations. The more completely an actor thinks that he understands a present situation, the more certainty he will attach to his estimates of future situations. If a government interprets certain events as hostile aggression, it may believe that unless it intervenes, the future situation is likely to be dangerous and undesirable. If the government evaluates this aggression and its future consequences as important, it will be tempted to act in order to bring about a preferable future situation. An actor's *ideology,* including most particularly his explanatory beliefs, will profoundly affect his view of the future situation. The more sweeping and unquestioned the ideology, the more likely the actor is to be certain of his predictions.

Types of Objectives. We can distinguish objectives by the *ways* in which an actor evaluates present situations and projects the future. Four possible alternative images of future situations are illustrated in Figure 4.3. We assume that facts and salience are constant for all four. The significant variables in the future situations are the probability and desirability that an actor assigns to them. As desirability is determined by goals, we can isolate at least four types of objectives on this basis. These types of objectives imply different kinds of policy initiatives.

In column A the actor's analysis of the future situation as likely and evaluation of it as desirable lead to adoption of *preservation* of the conditions that seem to ensure the future situation as an objective. Often the solution is to preserve the status quo, however, if the present situation is undesirable but changing, the actor will look upon the changes benignly. Few policies and resources will be committed

	Future Situations			
	A	B	C	D
Evaluation	desired	desired	undesired	undesired
Analysis	likely	unlikely	likely	unlikely
Objectives	preservation	securance	prevention	avoidance
Resources and initiative required by policy	low	high	high	low

Figure 4.3. Objectives Derived from Analysis and Evaluation of Future Situations

to the objective, as witnessed by U.S. policy in Latin America before Fidel Castro came to power.

When the actor deems the goal desirable but unlikely his objective is to further it, to intervene to alter the probabilities; the actor will see little chance of success otherwise. *Securance* is perceived as dependent upon the actor's own behavior. For example, President Johnson's administration considered participation of Asian allies in the Vietnam War highly desirable but unlikely without strong encouragement from the United States. Military and supply units from South Korea and the Philippines were sent to Vietnam as indications of those countries' support for American policy—but only at the cost of millions of dollars in aid to those nations explicitly for this support.

When the future situation is deemed undesirable but likely, the actor tries to reduce the probability of its occurrence through *prevention*. Designing policies of prevention probably occupies the greatest amount of decision makers' time, particularly among actors that are relatively satisfied with the existing situation and foresee its continuation. Preventing a major military confrontation in the Middle East has long been an objective of the United States and most other great powers. There is general agreement that such a confrontation would be undesirable, yet the three major clashes there since 1948 make clear that future military involvement by the great powers is quite possible. The United States, the Soviet Union, and other states have thus on a number of occasions adopted policies reflecting the important objective of preventing direct military confrontation. In 1956 the Dwight D. Eisenhower administration opposed Great Britain and France when they invaded Egypt and, with the Soviets, supported United Nations efforts to keep the conflict from spreading. Intermittent high-level talks between representatives of the United States and the Soviet Union, particularly since the Six-Day War of 1967, are further evidence of policies designed to achieve prevention. Policies limiting the scope of warfare in Vietnam have had a similar objective.

The greater the dissimilarity between the preferred and predicted future situations, the greater the influence that an actor will believe must be exercised in order to realize the preferred situation. The actor always *tries to* increase the probability of a preferred situation but expends effort unevenly.

When the future situation is undesirable but seems unlikely, the actor will feel no need to intervene. The United States surely prefers to *avoid* a situation in which the leading states of western Europe would be allied with the Soviet Union against the United States. As this event seems unlikely, however, American foreign-policy personnel spend little time designing policies to avoid it. Few policies have to be designed for avoidance of the unlikely; an actor has mainly to avoid "irrational" policies. History, of course, is replete with policies that have achieved the opposite of what was intended. In 1960, for example, the United States wished to avoid a major land war in Asia and to prevent a communist victory in South Vietnam. The policy makers had to choose between competing objectives, and presumably they weighed the relative salience of the two. A future situation in which a communist government would control South Vietnam was considered more detrimental to American interests than one that would involve American military forces. In retrospect many policy makers would revise their evaluations of the salience of these two images, placing higher priority on a policy designed to avoid the Vietnam War.

As this example illustrates, several types of objectives are usually involved in a single sequence of action, and, as we shall see, this intertwining of objectives makes simple analysis difficult. In Korea in 1950–1951, for example, the United States sought simultaneously to alter the behavior of North Korea (in order to further Korean unification) and to avoid Chinese intervention in the Korean conflict. The two objectives were extremely difficult to reconcile, as General Douglas MacArthur discovered when Chinese armies crossed the Yalu River in November 1950, catching MacArthur and his staff unprepared, and drove American and other United Nations troops southward in one of the worst defeats ever suffered by American forces.

Dimensions of Objectives. Having briefly examined four types of objectives, we turn now to the *dimensions* of objectives, which permit us to distinguish among objectives of the same type. The most significant of these dimensions are *domain* and *scope* [8, 3].

The domain is the set of actors whose behavior is to be affected. Clearly, the larger the domain of the objective, the greater will be the influence necessary to achieve it, all else being equal. Presumably it would be less difficult for the United States to affect the behavior of North Korea or Cuba than that of the Soviet Union or China because fewer resources are required for the former, less populous countries.

The scope is the range of behavior with which the objective is concerned; preventing a Soviet invasion of Berlin has a narrower scope than preventing a Soviet invasion of Europe. As the scope of an objective varies, changes in the level of resources invested and influence exerted are required.

We can generally identify the domain and scope of an objective by the way in which it is formulated. For example, the statement "The United States wants the Soviet Union to stop supplying arms to Egypt" expresses a securance objective; the domain is the Soviet Union, and the scope is supplying arms to Egypt. If the statement were changed to "The United States wants the Soviet Union and France to stop supplying arms to Egypt," the domain would have been enlarged. In "The United States wants the Soviet Union to stop supplying arms and giving moral support to Egypt" the scope of the objective has been enlarged.

INFLUENCE IN INTERNATIONAL POLITICS

A central, yet most baffling, set of concepts in political science is that of "power" and "influence." In general, we shall use the term "influence," in order to avoid some of the misleading connotations that "power" evokes—for example, the popular notion that power equals force or that the possession of resources like wealth and nuclear weapons invariably indicates possession of power. "Power," unlike "influence," cannot be used as a verb. The verbal form of "influence," on the other hand, implies causality: When one is influenced to behave in a certain way, he is *caused* to behave in that way.[4]

When one actor modifies the behavior of another actor he influences him. In this sense influence "is a property of the social relation; it is not an attribute of the actor" [4]. Influence involves at least two actors—one influencing, the other influenced—and constitutes a *relationship* between them, rather than a quality inherent in either of them. In the United States widely accepted norms dictate that the secretary of state has influence over an undersecretary and that the president has influence over both. But under certain actual conditions the president may have influence over both, over only one, or over neither. When we describe someone as "influential," we are really suggesting that he is able to influence others, but the degree and type of influence vary with the nature of the relationship. The president may have great influence over the secretary's foreign policy but none at all on his choice of a vacation spot.

This distinction leads us to the "paradox of power." We might infer that an actor has great influence by examining his resources alone; yet under certain circumstances the actor with lavish resources may have very little influence.

[4] See Chapter 5, pp. 101–105. We do, however, use the term "power" in this book to denote actors able to exercise broad and continual influence.

The United States, an apparently "power-ful" actor, was unable to influence North Korea to free the captured American sur-veillance ship *Pueblo* in 1968. Conversely, North Korea, with far fewer resources than the United States, was able to render ineffective American attempts to exercise influence in this instance. The "paradox of power" results from considering influ-ence as inherent in a single actor, rather than as a relationship between two or more actors. The opinion of many Ameri-cans, expressed by Richard M. Nixon in early 1968, that the United States should not be "pushed around by a third-rate power" like North Korea is based on mis-understanding of just this aspect of the nature of influence and power.

When an actor's use of resources is adequate for his objectives, then his chances of attaining desired outcomes are greater. An apparently powerful actor like the United States may set itself ex-tremely difficult, complex, large-scale ob-jectives that cannot be fully achieved. On the other hand, an apparently weak actor like Switzerland may set very modest objectives and achieve them fully. Switzer-land does not necessarily have more in-fluence than does the United States; it may simply marshal its resources more effectively to achieve desired outcomes. As Walter Lippmann has noted, "a for-eign policy consists in bringing into bal-ance, with a comfortable surplus of power in reserve, the nation's commitments and the nation's power. The constant pre-occupation of the true statesman is to achieve and maintain this balance" [9].

Types of Influence

There are two major types of influence, *legitimate* and *reward-coercion*, which re-flect the nature of the influence relation-ship.

Legitimate Influence. Legitimate influ-ence causes one actor to alter his be-havior because he perceives other actors' preferences as *rightfully* binding. Such in-fluence is generally based on the formal position of the influential actor, his spe-cial knowledge or competence, or his general reputation or "charisma."

When a nation attempts to become democratic "like the United States," the United States is exercising legitimate in-fluence even if it is unaware of this influ-ence. In this example the reputation of the actor is enough to encourage others to pattern their behavior on the actor's own. Much of what is called "prestige" in international politics is really legitimate influence of this type. Sometimes, how-ever, reputation can have a reverse effect. Cuba's reputation in the 1960s had a reactionary effect on conservative Latin American regimes.

Deference to an actor because of his expertise or knowledge also reflects legiti-mate influence. A doctor has such influ-ence over a patient, as do generals over politicians in matters of military strategy. For such legitimate influence to exist, the special knowledge must be related to the activity under consideration. The World Bank, for example, does not have such influence over the military affairs of a recipient nation.

Finally, legitimate influence can be the product of an actor's formal position in a hierarchy that others perceived as giv-ing him authority to make certain de-mands on them. For example, a citizen who supports the foreign policy of the president of the United States because he thinks that the office of president should be supported, regardless of its in-cumbent's political affiliation, personality, or policy, is subject to this type of legiti-mate influence. A large portion of the American populace responds in this fash-ion to foreign policy questions. Such ac-ceptance of the authority of the influenc-ing actor, rather than calculations as to the actor's specific behavior or objectives, is the basis for influence.

Reward-Coercion Influence. Reward-co-ercion influence is the manipulation of positive and negative incentives to achieve objectives. Promised rewards include redistribution of values in favor of the in-fluenced actor if his behavior accords with the wishes of the influencer. The reward itself must be distinguished from the promise of the reward. Very often the promised reward is contingent upon the desired behavior. Making promises is akin to contracting debts, which must be paid if the reputation of the actor is to be maintained.

Promised rewards may include reduction or cessation of negative incentives (withholding of sanctions). It is therefore often difficult to differentiate promising of rewards from coercion; only the recipient can make the distinction. It is debatable whether the end of American bombing of North Vietnam in 1968 was perceived by the North Vietnamese as a reward for the beginning of negotiations in Paris or as a threat that bombing would be resumed if the negotiations were unsuccessful or not conducted in good faith by Hanoi. In fact, the cessation of bombing was probably perceived as a combination of both.

Coercive influence occurs when an actor modifies his behavior to avoid or put an end to punishment and other negative incentives. Again we must distinguish between the threat of coercion and its actual application. Influence is often exercised *not* through actual pain or harm that is caused—for example, economic sanctions—but through fear that the harm will continue or increase. It is thus a threat, or implied threat, that is effective. Finally, coercion may have different consequences from those of rewards, particularly when it leads to greater depletion of base resources, as in warfare, which is likely to have higher total costs for human beings and their environment than reward-based coercion.

The exercise of any type of influence by an actor will either attract or repel other actors. Attempts at coercion are likely to stimulate resistance among other actors, especially when there is mutual, or reciprocal, influence. If an actor anticipates a future situation that will require him to exert influence over a second actor

again, he will exert influence in the present with attention to whether or not his methods will enhance or inhibit future attempts. British Prime Minister Neville Chamberlain's decision to appease (reward) Adolf Hitler at Munich in 1938 apparently encouraged Hitler to pursue an aggressive foreign policy and to doubt Chamberlain's resolve to oppose his expansionist designs. The result of Chamberlain's use of reward influence at Munich was thus to make it *more* difficult for Great Britain to influence Nazi Germany in 1939. This incident illustrates the complexity of causal relations among purposive actors in the international arena. The choice of types of influence not only facilitates or retards achievement of specific objectives but also helps to structure later interactions among international units. The outbreak of World War I was, in many respects, determined by earlier crises and their "peaceful" resolutions. Leaders expected crises to be resolved peacefully and were therefore willing to run high risks.

Dimensions of Influence

Influence, like objectives, has domain and scope, but it also has a third dimension, *weight*, which, as we shall see in Chapter 5, is important in determining causal sequences. Influence varies along these dimensions in accordance with the specific objective to be achieved, as well as with the resources to be invested.

The domain is the set of actors whose behavior is significantly affected by the application of influence. The domain of the pope's influence is restricted primarily to Roman Catholics and rarely includes Protestants or members of other religious faiths.

The scope of influence includes the set of all particular classes and functional types of behavior subject to it. The scope of the pope's influence is generally confined to matters of religion and doctrine. In voting matters his scope is probably much smaller. On the other hand, much of a child's behavior is subject to parental influence, but, as the child grows, the scope of parental authority diminishes. Conversely, the scope of the influence of the Universal Postal Union over Roman Catholics and children is limited indeed.

The weight of influence is the degree to which the target actor is influenced. For example, the Canadian economy is influenced to a greater extent by the United States than by Mexico; that is, American influence has greater weight than does Mexican influence. The weight of American second-strike nuclear capability in deterring a surprise attack on the United States may be extremely high. Its weight in preventing subversion in Southeast Asia is very low, however. This point reminds us that the weight of influence depends upon objectives and resources and is specific to situations.

The weight of influence cannot be inferred from whether or not a specific outcome is realized at a particular time; what is important is the increase in *probability* of a particular outcome after resources are invested.

The Use of Resources to Achieve Objectives

Although influence is a relational concept, it is still desirable to try to measure it. Many analysts have sought to do so. Often such measurement takes the form of "capability analysis," which involves equating influence with a capacity based upon an inventory of the actor's resources. Influence is thus inferred from resources, specifically the actor's control over those relevant to rewards and deprivations: wealth, weapons, moral force, and so on. Such resources are the clearest and most objective indicators available, and it is assumed that they can and will be transformed into influence.

Capability analysis delineates various classes of resources but frequently lapses into mere cataloguing.[5] Sometimes a dis-

tinction is made between material and nonmaterial resources. An analysis limited to material resources, which are easy to quantify and useful in making projections, does furnish a rather informative resource profile of an actor. Dealing with nonmaterial resources like morale and skill is more difficult, and many capability analyses unfortunately either ignore them or define them vaguely. The tendency to equate influence with physical resources is common among political leaders. At the close of World War II Joseph Stalin was reputed to have asked about the pope "How many divisions does he have?" His assumption that the pope, lacking an army, was without influence was, of course, incorrect. The pope's religious prestige may not have influenced Stalin, but it has influenced many others whose actions countered Stalin's desires. The tendency to equate physical resources and influence is misleading; it can be dangerous when major policies are based on it, as American efforts in Vietnam were in the 1960s.

Once resources have been catalogued, it is still necessary to discover whether or not they will be allocated to producing influence, mobilized and employed skillfully, and proven effective in producing desired outcomes. We can distinguish among current influence, probable future influence, and maximum potential influence [11]. The latter two may lead to confusion, however. Maximum potential influence is easier to infer since it does not require considering competing objectives, but it is seldom achieved, especially in relation to a single objective. Even during World War II no nation invested *all* its resources in current or future military production, and many resources were not devoted to winning the war. Instead, resources were sometimes squandered and wasted or invested in objectives unrelated to the war effort. Nevertheless, there is a tendency among leaders to examine the potential, rather than the probable, performance of other actors.

Generally several factors militate against the exertion of maximum poten-

---

[5] See, for example, Stephen B. Jones, "The Power Inventory and National Strategy," *World Politics*, 6 (1954), pp. 421–454. See also Chapter 6 in this book.

tial influence in attaining a given objective. Some of them limit the use of resources. First, the actor must determine what types of resources are available and whether or not they are appropriate to a given objective. Resources are not always easily convertible from the achievement of one type of objective to that of another. The so-called guns or butter dilemma in economics illustrates the point. Guns may be useful in ensuring the coercive influence necessary to win a war but not in satisfying the economic wants of a population, and the reverse. International prestige is not easily converted into resources necessary for military victory, and guns and bombs may be only marginally helpful in dissuading people of the virtue of their cause. In the Vietnam War Viet Cong guerrilla activity has been supported by the peasants' perceptions of reality, and American bombing of peasant villages and roads to alter those perceptions has probably been counterproductive.

A second factor affecting the use of resources is the actor's capability of mobilizing them toward a specific objective: the "resource liquidity" factor. Speed and efficiency in mobilizing vary with the communications and transportation infrastructure available and with the skills and foresight of those who coordinate mobilization. Geography partly determines the speed and efficiency of mobilization, as do the personnel available and the levels of their skills. Before World War I, for example, imperial Germany had constructed an elaborate railroad network that made rapid transport of men and supplies from west to east possible. Partly as a result of this network German leaders were confident that they could defeat France before tsarist Russia could mobilize its resources to attack Germany.

The efficiency with which an actor amasses and mobilizes his resources may determine whether or not an objective can be attained at all. A policy of using excessive resources is inappropriate. The objective may be attained but at the price of wasting scarce resources. In addition

to inefficiency due to waste, miscalculated investments may prove inefficient. Before 1914 the government of imperial Germany blustered and postured in such a way as to increase British hostility and production of new weapons, although Germany's objective was to reduce British pressures against it. The more weapons that the Germans produced, the greater German insecurity became because of the increasing fear and hostility of other countries, notably Great Britain. Germany's policies were thus ineffective, even counterproductive. Similarly, Stalin's aggressive use of the Red Army after World War II for political control of eastern Europe, while effective for that objective, sowed suspicion of Soviet intentions in the West. This led to American commitment to the defense of western Europe against anticipated Soviet incursions, presumably an unwanted objective.

Another set of factors affecting attainment of maximum potential influence depends upon the objectives. First, the greater the opposition among other actors toward a given objective, the more difficult it will be to attain it. Second, an actor generally pursues several objectives simultaneously, and they may conflict with one another. The greater the number of objectives that an actor pursues, the greater the probable number of compromises in the use of resources necessary to achieve any one of them.

In a third set of factors the *will* of an actor significantly affects the influence that can be exerted toward achieving an objective. That an actor has wealth, coercive capability, and other resources does not guarantee that he is willing to use them. Chamberlain was so horrified by the memory of the terrible war of 1914–1918, in which most of a generation of Britons had died, that he rejected the possibility of war with Hitler's Germany and therefore failed to use Great Britain's military resources to influence Nazi behavior at the 1938 Munich conference. His attitude was revealed in a radio broadcast: "How horrible, fantastic, incredible it is that we should be digging trenches and trying on gas-masks here because of a quarrel in a far-away country between people of whom we know nothing" [10]. Only when an actor uses his resources can he influence world events.[6]

Resources are limited, and it is possible that an actor may not wish to convert them into influence. Will is not itself a resource but an expression of an actor's priorities in allocating scarce resources to the attainment of different objectives. An actor's willingness to attempt influence is based on two primary considerations. The first is the salience of the objective: The more important the objective is, the more willing the actor will be to expend resources to achieve it. The second is the perceived probability that a desired future situation will be realized without deliberate investment of resources. If the probability seems high, the actor will be less likely to try to exert influence to increase it. Willingness to expend resources to achieve influence is thus directly related to the importance of the objective and inversely related to the probability of the objective's being realized without intervention (see Figure 4.4).

For example, to the United States it may be important that Mexico maintain an open border, but the likelihood that Mexico will do so without pressure is high. We expect that the United States will not exert influence on this point, for that would be a waste of scarce resources. If Mexico's policy were to change drastically, however, American priorities would presumably change as well. On the other hand, the United States considered it extremely important that Soviet missiles be removed from Cuba in 1962, but the probability of their withdrawal without American influence was very low. The United States therefore exerted a great deal of influence to achieve its objective.

Willingness to use scarce resources in

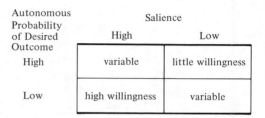

Figure 4.4. Willingness to Attempt Influence

order to exert influence thus varies from situation to situation. It is lowest when the salience of the objective is low and the probability of the preferred outcome high; it is highest when the objective is important and the probability of its realization low. When both importance and probability are high or when both are low, then there are varying degrees of medium willingness to invest resources in acquiring influence.

Complexity of International Outcomes

It is perhaps easier to infer influence from the *results* of an actor's attempt to influence another than from the resources that are used: to ask the degree to which actor B has behaved differently because of actor A's influence. The major difficulty with this approach is the complexity of international politics itself, which makes it difficult to identify specific causal sequences. The assumption that A's efforts caused B to behave in certain ways is risky, for B's behavior may have been brought about by factors unrelated or only partly related to A's attempt.

The complexity of causal sequences is perhaps best illustrated by the problem of *unanticipated effects*. Actors, like the heroes of Horace Walpole's *The Three Princes of Serendip,* make "discoveries, by accidents and sagacity, of things they were not in quest of." Such effects result from purposive behavior that is only partially congruent with the immediate objective, usually because decision makers are unaware of factors in their operational environment.

Unanticipated effects may further or

---

[6] There is one special instance in which an actor has influence *before* using his resources: when another actor perceives that the first is willing and able to use them, even before a promise or threat is made.

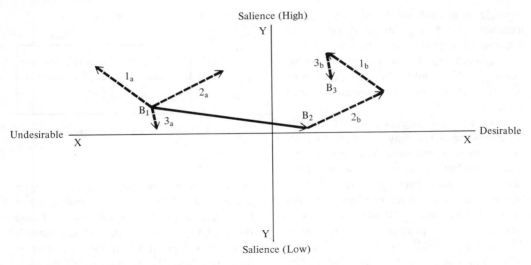

Figure 4.5. Mapping an Attempt at Influence

inhibit the achievement of an objective. They may occur within the initiator, as when British public opinion turned against the government of Anthony Eden after the invasion of Suez in 1956. They may also occur within the target actor, as American involvement in Vietnam may have caused neutral Vietnamese to join the Viet Cong out of aversion to foreign, particularly non-Asian, interference in their affairs. Finally, unanticipated effects may involve third parties, as when mainland China intervened in the Korean War. The intervention was unintentionally precipitated by the advance of the United Nations army forces to the Yalu River, the border between Korea and Manchuria. Unanticipated effects of this kind usually limit the success of the attempt at influence and may complicate the process of measuring influence. The strength of the stimulus (the attempt at influence) that we are trying to measure is further distorted by effects that may enlarge or restrict the apparent response (or outcome).

The net positive or negative effect of an attempt at influence often depends upon unanticipated effects. (In our definition of influence, we have avoided specifying that the results of an attempt to exercise it must be sought or predicted.) Indeed, the occurrence of negative unanticipated effects on a large scale may

move an actor's objective further away. Figure 4.5 may help the reader to visualize the results of an attempt at influence. It represents actor A's view of what happens to actor B in the course of A's attempt at influence. The X axis represents a continuum from undesirable to desirable behavior; the Y axis represents the continuum of salience to actor A of actor B's behavior. Point B_1 is actor B's initial position in relation to these two dimensions. Point B_2 represents the ideal result of A's influence, and point B_3 represents the final behavior of B, reflecting unanticipated effects.[7] In this illustration the action has had an enhancing effect.

In addition to the problems raised by

[7] The arrows represent the directions of an attempt at influence and its unanticipated effects. The solid arrow shows the general direction of the attempt, and its length indicates the strength of the attempt. The broken arrows represent unanticipated effects modifying those of the initial attempt. The net effect may be determined through "vector addition." The arrows labeled with b on the right side of the Y axis are the same in direction and length as those on the left; their relative positions have been shifted for purposes of measurement. A's attempt to move B from B_1 to B_2, because of unanticipated effects, has ensured that B actually will end up at point B_3. As B_3 is farther along in the desired direction, we conclude that the contingent effects *enhanced* the results of the original attempt at influence. The net influence is the distance between B_1 and B_3. Quantifiable length and direction (*slope*) permit us to diagram the magnitude of attempt at influence.

unanticipated effects, there are several other difficulties in inferring dimensions of influence from results. First, there is the special instance of an actor's adjustment to what he expects will take place. An actor may perceive the existence of another actor's resources and objectives and conclude, correctly or incorrectly, that he will be the object of a future attempt at influence. He is thus "caused" to modify his own behavior in certain ways. The actor may refrain from actions that are otherwise appealing or may initiate certain courses of behavior in anticipation that he will shortly be influenced to do so. For example, India might develop nuclear weapons in anticipation of China's attempt to use "nuclear blackmail" on New Delhi. Conversely, India might offer concessions to China in anticipation of such a blackmail attempt. Israel rarely introduces resolutions on its conflict with the Arabs into the United Nations because it perceives that most members of that organization will oppose them and that it cannot achieve a favorable outcome. Anticipated results thus narrow the policy options of Israel. Some issues are never raised because certain groups or a "mobilization of bias" would prevent a favorable outcome for those raising the issues. Certain capabilities in the international system thus remain permanently unused [1]. Sometimes a future attempt at influence is *erroneously* perceived by an actor, and it thus forecloses certain "options." In 1950 the United States tried to limit defense expenditures because it anticipated that American public opinion would not accept the necessary tax increase. Domestic considerations thus militated against demanding public sacrifices for defense, outweighing the weak expectations that military force would be needed as a means of coercive influence in Korea [12].

Another measurement problem is raised by the "chameleon effect," which involves mistaken perception of an influence relationship. When the object of the attempt at influence already intends to behave as desired by the influencer, it is a mistake to assume that influence accounts for the resulting behavior. For example, since 1961 the United States has favored British entry into the European Common Market. It would be incorrect to infer that the eventual membership of Great Britain was due to U.S. influence; indeed, American efforts may have delayed it by creating suspicion in France, rather than by encouraging it through diplomatic talks with Britain.

Finally, some actors will always follow the lead of certain other actors, and their doing so on any given occasion does not reflect additional influence by the latter. This effect may be called the "satellite effect." Bulgaria generally follows the lead of the Soviet Union in foreign policy, and for purposes of measuring influence it is irrelevant whether it happens ten times or a hundred times. Such behavior may, in fact, indicate that Bulgaria is not even an autonomous international actor.

Costs of Influence and the Consequences of Interaction

In exerting influence an actor manipulates the costs to a second actor of behaving in different ways. A threat actually creates a set of disadvantages that the second actor must consider in determining what course of action to take. Rewards make it less expensive to perform the desired action and more expensive not to perform it. The costs of flouting legitimate influence are generally psychological, that is, registered in a decline of approval for decision makers. Just as it may be painful to disobey a friend or a parent, rejecting appeals from actors with legitimacy, such as the United Nations, can lead to at least minor losses. Exertion of influence always involves costs for the initiator. The initiator, in determining whether or not to exert influence, considers the costs versus the probable returns. When the costs are higher or opportunities forgone greater, a rational actor will not exert the influence [5].

Every day we discuss a problem with a friend, obey the policeman at the corner, purchase something from a clerk in a store. In all these interactions we are trying to realize desired future states of affairs at minimum cost. Some of our interactions with others have no further consequences. When someone calls us on the telephone but has the wrong number, we tell him so and hang up; our behavior will probably have no further significance for us or the person who called. But, when the Soviet premier calls the American president on the "hot line" during an acute international crisis, the nature of the president's response will have important consequences for millions of people.

An actor who threatens force instead of offering positive inducements may find his short-term success offset by increasing long-term difficulties in gaining cooperation on other matters. Most international interactions affect other interactions and help to structure the participants' images of one another. The president's response to the call on the "hot line" will help to shape the premier's perception of the United States and its leaders. If the president is unfriendly and threatening, the premier's image of American leaders will emphasize these qualities, and it will prove difficult to create an atmosphere of mutual trust and cooperation.

Some strategic interactions, like a game of checkers, also have no further consequences for the players. A win or a loss in one particular match and the manner in which it was played have little or no effect on the next game. We might call a checker game a "single interaction without further consequences." But for a poker player with limited cash, winning or losing affects the number of hands that he can play and the amounts that he can bet. Furthermore, the ways in which the poker hands are played by each player influence the ways in which others will play future hands. The rash player may not be able to stay in the game long. The player who cheats may never be permitted to play with the same partners again. Each poker hand therefore is a "single interaction with further consequences."

Situations in international politics may also be viewed by participants as either single or repetitive interactions, but seldom if ever will they be interactions with no further consequences. For instance, the United States could threaten to invade Canada unless the latter agreed to extradite American draft dodgers. Such a threat might achieve the desired objective, but American-Canadian relations would be permanently embittered. The long-term costs of such behavior would be prohibitively high to the United States. On the other hand, offering Canada a reciprocal agreement on citizens' rights that might oblige Canada to return draft dodgers might achieve the desired objective without impairing Canadian cooperation on other matters. If the United States saw no need for further cooperation with Canada, either means to achieve the objective might be acceptable. But, in general, using resources like military force to gain acceptance of a legal procedure is not very efficient.

Much of international politics is characterized by repetitive interaction. The single interaction without further consequences is an "end of the world" game and participants tend to behave as if they are playing Monopoly and have only five minutes left. A businessman who cheats his customers can prosper over time only if he does not expect to see the same customers again and if they do not report his behavior to the authorities. Running "fly by night" businesses may occasionally be reasonable for some entrepreneurs but hardly ever for reputable statesmen. States cannot quietly fold their tents in the night and reappear in new locations with new identities. Reputation is thus a significant part of an actor's resources; if the actor violates an international treaty, he cannot expect to be trusted in the future. In the international system actors have continuing relations with one another, and their behavior in each instance helps to structure the ways in which they will be expected to behave in other interactions. Each interaction is part of a learning process that creates the conditions under which further interactions take place.

Matching Influence to Objectives

One of the major problems for international actors is to determine the relationship between potential influence and objectives. This task is critical if they are to avoid damaging miscalculations or the consequences of poor performance. Certain questions about an actor's international behavior thus become relevant: Are sufficient and appropriate resources available to achieve objectives? Is an actor willing and able to use them in ways that will create influence?

The quality of system feedback mechanisms is reflected in the answers to these questions. When there is an imbalance between influence and objectives, a corrective feedback mechanism should lead either to a change in influence or a change in objectives in order to restore equilibrium. A political system thus adjusts its policies, realigning them to government priorities. The French withdrawals from Indochina in 1954 and from Algeria in 1962 were examples of such self-correction. In both instances French decision makers recognized their inability or unwillingness to exert the influence necessary to realize their objectives. They therefore altered their objectives in order to end the imbalance between influence and objectives. In World War II the massive shift of American industry to war production is a case of a shift in resources to match objectives.

In relating influence to objectives it is crucial that an actor use resources appropriate to attaining that objective. For particular objectives only influence based on certain types of resources may be appropriate. For example, the president's legitimate influence is appropriate to the objective of changing the secretary of state's behavior in foreign-policy matters. But influence based on legitimacy is limited. It is usually less effective in influencing other countries. Foreign countries are more subject to influence through re-

wards and coercion than to legitimate influence by an international "authority."

Type of influence is not the only consideration in determining the appropriateness of a specific attempt. The character of the resource is also important. For example, the United States' possession of nuclear weapons probably helps to deter the Soviet Union from initiating an attack on this country but has little effect on the behavior of guerrilla bands seeking to capture governments in Southeast Asia. Nuclear weapons can be converted into influence only in the former instance. Nevertheless, it is likely that coercive and reward influence will be appropriate in both instances. The objective in each instance implies a certain scope of influence that would be necessary to achieve it. The scopes of the types of influence and the objectives must correspond if an effective influence relationship is to exist.

As we have seen, every objective has a particular scope and domain; each attempt at influence also has a scope and a domain. If both the scope and domain of the particular type of influence correspond with the scope and domain of the objective, there is potential for an effective influence relationship. Conversely, to the extent that either dimension does not correspond, the act of influence is inappropriate to the objective. If we imagine the domain and scope of types of influence and objectives to be represented by two circles, as in Figure 4.6, then the extent of their overlap represents the potential for an influence relationship.

An actor's failure to achieve objectives is often the result of a poor match between objectives and influence. Successful matching is based on the actor's assumptions about which policies will lead to which outcomes. The actor may also consider what feasible objectives will further his goals without jeopardizing or conflicting with other goals. Several types of mismatch occur frequently in international politics. An actor may fail to understand the conditioning factors in the environment and may thus perceive incorrectly the potential influence, thus choosing in-

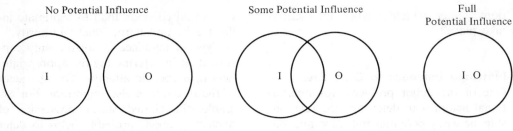

No Potential Influence   Some Potential Influence   Full
Potential Influence

Figure 4.6. The Relationship of Scope and Domain of Influence and Objective

appropriate types of influence to achieve objectives. Second, an actor may misunderstand the relationship between objectives and goals and may then select objectives that are counterproductive to his goals. Third, an actor may perceive changes in the links between objectives and goals arising from emergent properties of the international environment. For these reasons, as Robert Burns warned,

The best laid plans of mice and men
Gang aft agley.

We shall now examine how the outbreak of World War I reflected mismatching.

OBJECTIVES AND INFLUENCE IN THE OUTBREAK OF WORLD WAR I

In Chapter 3 we examined alternative theories about the conditions that allowed World War I to occur. Additional insight into the behavior of the parties to the war may be gained through an examination of the interaction of the goals, objectives, and available resources for influencing particular other actors.

We shall present some of the objectives and policies derived from broader goals that precipitated World War I.

Austria-Hungary
1. Objective: to secure an end to Serbian-supported domestic nationalist agitation.
   Policy: to inhibit Serbian independence by means of military threats and action.
2. Objective: to prevent Russia from assisting Serbia and expanding the domain of the conflict.
   Policy: to gain German support for action in the Balkans and to deter the Russians from interfering by means of the

threat of German military action against them.

Russia
1. Objective: to prevent a successful Austrian attack on Serbia that would reduce Russian influence in the Balkans.
   Policy: to promise military support for Serbia against Austria-Hungary.
2. Objective: to prevent a German attack on either Russia or France.
   Policy: to mobilize Russian armies.

Germany
1. Objective: to maintain a strong alliance with Austria-Hungary.
   Policy: to give Austria-Hungary unqualified support for its policies in the Balkans.
2. Objective: to prevent a successful Russian attack on Austria-Hungary.
   Policy: to mobilize before the Russians did.
3. Objective: to secure the defeat of France before the completion of Russian mobilization.
   Policy: to follow the Schlieffen plan, which called for a quick assault on France through Belgium.
4. Objective: to avoid behaving in such a way that British neutrality would end.
   Policy: None

France
1. Objective: to prevent a successful German attack on Russia or France.
   Policy: to achieve massive armament and mobilization in support of Russia.
2. Objective: to secure a British commitment to come to the defense of France.
   Policy: to further Anglo-French joint military planning for defense and to permit the Germans to strike first.

Great Britain
1. Objective: to prevent occupation of the

Low Countries or a successful attack on France.
Policy: to uphold commitments to Belgian neutrality.
2. Objective: to avoid full-scale commitment to defend France.
Policy: to avoid making a public commitment to France.

Table 4.1 categorizes these relevant characteristics of objectives of the major participants at the beginning of World War I as apparently they were perceived by decision makers in their respective countries.

The major actors were willing to exert influence to achieve most of their objectives. As many of their objectives were in conflict, however, the chances of confrontation were increased. Although the avoidance of a massive and costly war was an implicit objective of all the states involved, they assumed that the adjustment mechanisms of the state system, which had worked well in the past, would operate to prevent catastrophe. They therefore expended little effort in trying to avert a general conflagration.

There was not only conflict among the objectives of different actors; there were also contradictions within these sets of objectives. For example, Austria-Hungary's objectives to end Serbian agitation and to prevent Russia from assisting Serbia were contradictory. As Russian action was contingent upon Austrian behavior toward Serbia, Austria-Hungary could not effectively deal with the Serbs without bringing Russia into the conflict. Austrian leaders did not wish to broaden the conflict, but, in attacking Serbia, they could not avoid doing so. They simply assumed that the war would end quickly and that Russia would back down or settle short of war.

Similarly, Germany's objectives of securing the rapid defeat of France and of keeping the British neutral were contradictory. Germany's plan of attack against France necessitated an invasion of Belgium, but British entry into the war was contingent upon just such an action by Germany. This fact was not apparent to

German decision makers because of British vacillation during the critical days before the war.

The British objective of deterring Germany from occupying the Low Countries and from attacking France conflicted with the objective of avoiding commitment to the defense of France. The British government remained publicly silent about its intentions, thus encouraging Germany to discount the possibility of British intervention if the Schlieffen plan were instituted.

The behavior of the participants thus reveals that commitment of resources in attempts to influence outcomes was clearly inappropriate to the objectives that were pursued. Austria-Hungary's attempt to secure an end to domestic Slavic agitation took the form of an ultimatum and declaration of war against Serbia, which had the unanticipated effect of bringing about Russian mobilization. The domain of the attempt at influence was Serbia, yet it is not clear that the Serbian government controlled the behavior of nationalist elements on its soil or elsewhere, which was the essential domain of the objective. The domain of influence was thus inappropriate. A parallel occurred after the 1967 Arab-Israeli War, when Israel, in reprisals against terrorists based in Lebanon and Jordan, launched military attacks against those two countries. But the governments of Lebanon and Jordan were unable to control the terrorist groups on their territories.

The outbreak of World War I demonstrates that when actors, especially nation-states, pursue several objectives at the same time, they must try to detect incompatibilities. Objectives may conflict, and uses of influence to achieve one objective may necessitate forgoing others. Furthermore, although in isolation attempts at influence may appear appropriate to specific objectives, they may evoke consequences that render them ultimately inappropriate.

This discussion of our approach to objectives and influence has, we hope, alerted the reader to the complex interrelations of events and the consequent

Table 4.1.
Characteristics of Major Participants' Objectives at the Beginning of World War I

Actor	Type of Objective	Present Image	Future Image	Salience	Willingness	Probability	Domain	Scope
Austria-Hungary	securance	undesired	desired	high	high	low	Serbian and Slav nationalists	Slav nationalism and terrorism
	prevention	desired	undesired	high	high	low	Russia	military support of Serbia
Russia	prevention	desired	undesired	high	high	low	Austria-Hungary	action against Serbia
	prevention	desired	undesired	high	high	medium	Germany	action against Russia or France
Germany	securance	undesired	desired	high	high	medium	Serbian and Slav nationalists	Slav nationalism and terrorism
	prevention	desired	undesired	high	high	low	Russia	action against Austria-Hungary
	securance	undesired	desired	high	high	low	France	defeat of French armies
	avoidance	desired	undesired	high	low	high	Great Britain	British neutrality
France	prevention	desired	undesired	high	high	medium	Germany	action against Russia or France
	securance	undesired	desired	high	high	medium	Great Britain	British commitment to France
Great Britain	prevention	desired	undesired	high	high	low	Germany	action against Belgium or France
	avoidance	desired	undesired	high	variable	high	France	British commitment

difficulty of handling them within an analytical framework. It has also suggested
some of the chief points of analysis: the
importance of unanticipated effects, of
matching influence types to objectives,
and of autonomous probability and salience in determining an actor's willingness to commit resources. Finally, we must
emphasize that good theory, particularly
policy-oriented theory, has to account for
the policies and objectives of all relevant
actors.

References

1. Bachrach, P., and M. Baratz, "Two
   Faces of Power," *American Political
   Science Review,* 56 (December 1962),
   pp. 947–52.
2. Bauer, Raymond A., Ithiel de Sola
   Pool, and Lewis A. Dexter, *American
   Business and Public Policy* (New York:
   Atherton, 1963), p. 479.
3. Deutsch, Karl W., *The Analysis of International Relations* (Englewood Cliffs,
   N.J.: Prentice-Hall, 1968), pp. 28–35.
4. Emerson, Rupert, "Power-Dependence
   Relations," *American Sociological Review,* 271 (February 1962), p. 32.
5. Harsanyi, John C., "Measurement of
   Social Power, Opportunity Costs, and
   the Theory of Two-Person Bargaining
   Games," *Behavioral Science,* 7 (January 1962), pp. 67–80.
6. Lasswell, Harold D., *Who Gets What,
   When, and How* (New York: Meridian,
   1958), p. 13.
7. Lasswell, Harold D., *World Politics
   and Personal Insecurity* (New York:
   McGraw-Hill, 1935), p. 4.
8. Lasswell, Harold D., and Abraham
   Kaplan, *Power and Society* (New Haven: Yale University Press, 1950), pp.
   73–74.
9. Lippmann, Walter, *U.S. Foreign Policy:
   Shield of the Republic* (Boston: Little,
   Brown, 1943), pp. 9–10.
10. Loewenheim, Francis L., ed., *Peace or
    Appeasement?* (Boston: Houghton Mif-
    flin, 1965), p. 55.
11. Modelski, George, *A Theory of Foreign
    Policy* (New York: Praeger, 1962), pp.
    45–57.
12. Schilling, W. R., "The Politics of Na-
    tional Defense: Fiscal 1950," in W. R.
    Schilling, P. Y. Hammond, and G. H.
    Snyder, eds., *Strategy, Politics and De-
    fense Budgets* (New York: Columbia
    University Press, 1962), pp. 1–266.
13. Schlesinger, Arthur M., Jr., *A Thou-
    sand Days* (Boston: Houghton Mifflin,
    1965), p. 803.
14. Singer, J. David, "Inter-Nation Influ-
    ence: A Formal Model," *American Po-
    litical Science Review,* 57 (1963), pp.
    420–430.
15. Sprout, Harold, and Margaret Sprout,
    "Environmental Factors in the Study of
    International Politics," *Journal of Con-
    flict Resolution,* 1 (1957), pp. 309–328.
16. Wohlstetter, Roberta, "Cuba and Pearl
    Harbor: Hindsight and Foresight," *For-
    eign Affairs,* 43 (July 1965), pp. 691–
    707.

Suggested Reading

Claude, Inis L., Jr., *Power and International
Relations* (New York: Random House,
1962).

Dahl, Robert A., "The Concept of Power,"
Behavioral Science, 2 (July 1957), pp.
201–215.

Farrar, L. L., "The Limits of Choice: July
1914 Reconsidered," *Journal of Conflict
Resolution,* 1 (1972), pp. 1–23.

Harsanyi, John C., "Measurement of Social
Power, Opportunity Costs, and the Theory
of Two-Person Bargaining Games," *Behavioral Science,* 7 (January 1962), pp.
67–80.

Holsti, K. J., "The Concept of Power in the
Study of International Relations," *Background,* 7 (February 1964), pp. 179–
194.

Knorr, Klaus, *The War Potential of Nations* (Princeton: Princeton University
Press, 1956).

Lasswell, Harold G., and Abraham Kaplan,
Power and Society (New Haven: Yale
University Press, 1950).

McClelland, Charles A., *Theory and the International System* (New York: Macmillan, 1966), chap. 3.

March, James G., "An Introduction to the
Theory and Measurement of Influence,"
American Political Science Review, 49
(June 1955), pp. 431–451.

Singer, J. David, "Inter-Nation Influence:
A Formal Model," *American Political
Science Review,* 57 (June 1963), pp.
420–430.

Part II
THE INTERNATIONAL SYSTEM: PARTS AND WHOLES

As all human systems consist of series of interrelated, interdependent, and somewhat self-adjusting parts, it is necessary to have both an overview of the international system and some knowledge of its various parts to understand outcomes in international politics. In this section we shall examine the parts, the individual and collective actors whose behavior constitutes the empirical reality that we are studying. In our examination of macroanalysis, we found that the whole can be greater than the sum of its parts, in the sense that the uncoordinated but interrelated policies of several actors can lead to characteristics of the system inherent not in the parts but in their composition and to events not only unplanned but also, on occasion, universally undesired.

These same unplanned and occasionally undesired outcomes are also possible *within* nation-states, other group actors, and even individuals, for, although they are all of the international system, they are also themselves systems composed of various parts. We must therefore look at both the whole and the parts from a broad perspective.

We shall begin by examining the structure of the whole—the international system. In Chapter 5 we present an analysis of structure and its importance in understanding the processes of international politics. In Chapter 6 we review selected historical structures and their consequences and describe contemporary trends that seem to be shaping the current and emerging political structure.

We shall then investigate the various parts of the international system and explore their roles in international politics. In Chapters 7 through 9 we examine national actors and the individuals who constitute the major decision-making elites in these collectivities, exploring in some depth the relation of "micro" processes to "macro" outcomes, as well as the significance of various clusters of variables in determining these outcomes. In Chapters 10 and 11 we focus on collective actors other than nation-states. Several of them will seem immediately familiar to the reader, whereas others will appear less orthodox. As so many contemporary analyses focus almost exclusively on interactions among states, we expect these chapters to be especially helpful in bringing new and important questions about the roles of nonnational actors to the reader's attention and providing him with a more accurate and complete understanding of current trends in international politics.

Chapter 5
INTERNATIONAL STRUCTURE

Unevenness, structure, and distribution are fundamental physical properties of everything—all matter, all energy, all processes—in the universe we know, and even in any universe we can imagine —Karl W. Deutsch [3]

THE CONCEPT OF STRUCTURE

When we speak of the *structure* of the international system we mean the framework within which international politics occurs. An understanding of this structure in any period gives us valuable insights into the conduct of international politics. For instance, American policy in the Middle East is often justified as an attempt to maintain the balance of power between Israel and the Arab states. This explanation implies a certain structure of the international system in the Middle East, and we might outline such a structure briefly, though not completely. First, we might examine the distribution of military resources between the two sides, carefully noting the number of army divisions of each, the relative strengths of their air forces, the numbers of tanks, their technological efficiency, and so forth. We might then infer that a certain "parity" of military resources is necessary to prevent either side from initiating warfare.

We might go farther and examine the strengths of the various economies in the area, their health problems, or any other pertinent resource information. From these measurements we might construct a picture of the international system now prevailing in the Middle East. But the picture would still be incomplete, for we cannot evaluate the importance of resource distribution if we have no indication of the intentions and attitudes of the actors in this system. Surely it would be rash to suggest that another set of actors, located elsewhere than in the Middle East, would be subject to the same constraints in international politics just because they might have the same distribution of resources.

It thus would become necessary to examine the attitudes of the actors in the Middle East. What are the intentions of each toward the other? What are their expectations about future interactions? If Israel and the Arab states expected amicable relations in the future, the framework of the international politics of the area would be far different from that based on the hostile expectations prevailing after 1948, regardless of resources. We might argue, however, that distribution of resources shapes attitudes. Israel is a "have" state; the Arab states are "have nots." Would we not normally find hostile expectations coupled with such a distribution of resources? We would therefore have to examine the interdependence of resources and attitudes. Once we had done so, we would have a fairly complex picture of the international system of the Middle East, and this picture would suggest constraints and possibilities for the future of international politics in the area. Such a picture of the structure of the international system of the Middle East would incorporate what policy makers mean by the "realities of the situation." By "structure," therefore, we mean the distribution of resources and attitudes among the actors of an international system and the interdependencies among them.

The concept of structure can be better understood if we think of it as a building and examine its various characteristics. We may know that the building contains a certain number of square feet of floor space, but this piece of information is of little use to us unless we know how the space is distributed, for differences in distribution reflect quite different uses. Knowledge of the distribution of floor space does not tell us exactly what the building is used for, but it certainly suggests a possible *class* of possible uses; the engineering of the building, how it was built, may also tell us something about its ability to withstand stress from heavy objects, fire, or earthquakes.

Information about the structure of the international system tells us something about the activities that are possible within it and what the likely consequences of various changes in it are. The adaptability of the structure is critical to the stability of patterns of international interaction within a particular system. War and peace, the success or failure of international organizations, and the rise and decline of a "superstate" are not *caused*

by the phenomenon of structure, but their likelihood, magnitude, and importance are limited by the characteristics of structure.

We are not interested here in the distribution of *all* resources and attitudes. In international politics structure specifically includes those distributions related to strategic interaction among the units of the international system. We therefore exclude investigation of individual and collective actors' resources and attitudes that seem to have only marginal significance for international outcomes. The distribution of restaurants in the world, for example, would not normally be included in an analysis of international structure. Attitudes toward witchcraft are similarly excluded. But attitudes toward national or international identities of a population, friendliness or hostility toward other peoples, and views about the morality of weapons systems are significant.[1]

Having decided which structural variables are important, we must then seek to discover the *interdependence* among them. Interdependence encompasses the effects that a change in the resources or attitudes of one actor will have on the resources and attitudes of other actors. Although the number of conceivable interdependent relationships is enormous, for most purposes only a small specified set need ever be investigated.

As we examine international structure, we should keep several questions in mind. What are the most salient characteristics of a particular international structure? How can we tell? How permanent or ephemeral are these characteristics? How does a particular structure affect the opportunities for and limitations on activity within a particular political system? Finally, what are the likely consequences of particular structural features for an international system?

The two principal tasks in examining

---

[1] In both Japan and India important portions of the population are adamantly opposed to their countries' development or use of nuclear weapons. The potential international importance of these views should be obvious.

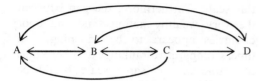

Figure 5.1. The "Sovereign Equals" Model

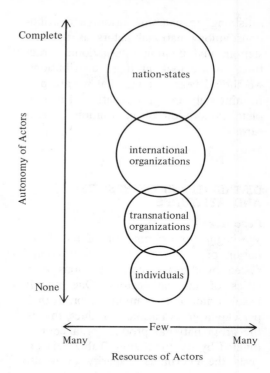

Figure 5.2. Autonomy and Resources of Actors

international structure are, first, identifying and measuring the distribution of relevant attributes and, second, specifying the degree of interdependence among variables. Research in international politics has not yet adequately accomplished either of these tasks, but in recent years several scholars have made significant advances in describing the distribution of important variables [20, 18]. Efforts at discovering the nature of interdependencies have been less successful because reliable data on their extent are difficult to acquire.

A crude picture of the structure of international politics, contrasted with the more formal "state centered" view of international politics, can be sketched, however. In the more formal model politics is considered as involving "sovereign equals." Figure 5.1 shows international political activities (represented by arrows) functioning only among sovereign states A, B, C, and D.[2] This model is composed of interactions, primarily legal, diplomatic, and commercial, among such states. The result is a unidimensional view of world politics. Disputes are jurisdictional, rather than substantial; the states debate which can decide particular issues or control certain individuals or activities. Although this model has some empirical basis, especially in reference to the eighteenth century, it has probably never been a satisfactory depiction of international politics.

Contemporary international structure is becoming increasingly complex. The structure of "power" or the potential for influence in international affairs resembles an interlocking cone of actors. Fig-

ure 5.2 illustrates the current distribution diagrammatically. In some areas like economics large international corporations may have more autonomy—and certainly more resources—than do some of the smaller states like Lesotho. The relative impacts on international politics of the disappearance of General Motors and Lesotho demonstrate the greater influence potential of the former. The circles on Figure 5.2 overlap, indicating the interdependent claims on the same resources of different types of actors. The larger the circle, the greater the resources controlled by that type of actor.

We have acquired considerable information about distribution of certain resources among nation-states. Comparable information for other collectivities like churches, businesses, international organizations, and so forth seldom exists.[3] Given these limitations, it is useful, if not

---

[2] This view is similar to that outlined by Hans Morgenthau in *Politics Among Nations*, 4th ed. (New York: Knopf, 1967) and by many international legal theorists.

[3] In 1969 the Inter-University Consortium for Political Research in Ann Arbor, Michigan, began an international data archive that may eventually fill these lacunae.

satisfying, to examine resource distributions among national actors as the first step in investigating international structure. As we look at these distributions, we should bear in mind that we are performing only an approximation of a complete exploration of international structure.

DISTRIBUTIONS OF RESOURCES AND ATTITUDES

Resources

We begin our examination of the distribution of resources in the international system by observing certain obvious properties of national actors. One readily usable criterion for ranking actors is their per capita gross national product, that is, the gross national product of a country divided by its population. Table 5.1 suggests the enormous disparity in wealth among even the top twenty countries on

Table 5.1
Gross National Product Per Capita, 1965

1.	United States	$3,575
2.	Kuwait	3,390
3.	Sweden	2,550
4.	Canada	2,470
5.	Iceland	2,470
6.	Switzerland	2,330
7.	Denmark	2,120
8.	Australia	2,000
9.	New Zealand	1,980
10.	Luxembourg	1,980
11.	France	1,920
12.	West Germany	1,900
13.	Norway	1,890
14.	United Kingdom	1,820
15.	Belgium	1,805
16.	Finland	1,750
17.	Czechoslovakia	1,560
18.	Netherlands	1,555
19.	Ireland	1,420
20.	U.S.S.R.	1,355

Source: Michael Hudson, Charles Taylor, *et al., World Handbook of Political and Social Indicators,* 2nd ed. (New Haven: Yale University Press, 1972). The figures have been rounded off to the nearest billion.

this scale. Furthermore, the gap between the very wealthy nations and the poor countries appears to be widening with time. Comparative rankings of other kinds of actors on the same scale would be most intriguing. For example, the total product divided by numbers of employees of international businesses like International Business Machines (IBM), Fiat, and Unilever could yield a similar crude approximation of the comparative productivity of corporations.

The populations of national actors furnish another readily usable scale of international structure. In Table 5.2 the populations of the 21 most populous states in 1961 and their projected populations for 1975 are listed.[4] One of the most striking revelations about population is its uneven distribution. In 1961, 21 nations out of more than 130 accounted for more than 75 percent of the world's population, and this distribution seems likely to remain fairly stable. The apparent stability of international population distribution for the immediate future is belied by important qualitative shifts in population and technological equipment among only these 21 states. Although such shifts may not be drastic, they can alter the relative influence bases among states in significant ways. China, for example, with the largest population in the world, can best achieve rapid gains in resources not by a gain in population but through technological growth and social organization.

Neither of the two indicators described can alone provide an adequate measure of an actor's resources. Other resources like average levels of skills, education, and technology are also important in international politics. A better summary picture can be obtained by examining a wide assortment of these resources. As an illustration we have chosen ten different measures; using a statistical tool called

[4] A projection is *not* the same as a prediction. Projection is a procedure by which past rates of change are computed on the assumption that they will continue into the future. Although projection tells what will happen if rates of change remain the same, it does not predict that they will remain the same.

Table 5.2.

Total Population, 1961 and 1975

	1961			Projection 1975	
Rank	Country	Population (in millions)		Country	Population (in millions)
1	China	694		China	916
2	India	442		India	600
3	U.S.S.R.	218		U.S.S.R.	280
4	United States	184		United States	233
5	Indonesia	96		Indonesia	131
6	Pakistan	95		Pakistan	126
7	Japan	94		Brazil	120
8	Brazil	73		Japan	106
9	West Germany	54		Nigeria*	70
10	United Kingdom	53		West Germany	64
11	Nigeria*	50		United Kingdom	58
12	Italy	49		Mexico	55
13	France	46		Italy	53
14	Mexico	36		France	52
15	Spain	31		Philippines	45
16	Poland	30		Turkey	43
17	Philippines	29		Thailand	41
18	Turkey	29		South Korea	38
19	Thailand	27		Egypt	38
20	Egypt	27		Poland	37
21	South Korea	25		Spain	35

*The figures for Nigeria are crudely reestimated from the 1964 Nigerian census.
Source: Bruce M. Russett *et al., World Handbook of Political and Social Indicators* (New Haven: Yale University Press, 1964).

"factor analysis," we have created two "umbrella" variables based on distinct groupings among these measures; the variables, or factors, within each grouping were found to be strongly interrelated and less related to variables in the other group. These two groupings indicate the "socioeconomic development" and "size" of each actor; these dimensions are also found in various studies cited by Bruce M. Russett and conducted by five different colleagues [18, pp. 41–46].

Socioeconomic Development

1. Number of people per physician.
2. Number of radios per 1,000 people.
3. Per capita gross national product.
4. Number of students in higher education per 100,000 people.
5. Literate percentage of population fifteen years or older.

6. Percentage of population living in cities of more than 20,000.
7. Percentage of labor force in agriculture.

Size

8. Total population.
9. Total gross national product.
10. Total land area.

In ranking nations according to these two groups of variables, we come out with two rather different lists of the "top twelve" nations (see Table 5.3). Taking "size" to indicate the availability of natural resources and "economic development" to indicate ability to use such resources efficiently, we would expect actors who appear on both lists to be among the most powerful nations in the world. The United States appears on both lists, but the Soviet Union, though third in size, ranks below twelfth in economic develop-

Table 5.3.

*Twelve Highest Ranking States on Socioeconomic Development and Size**

Socioeconomic Development	Size
United States	United States
United Kingdom	China
Canada	U.S.S.R.
Belgium	India
West Germany	Brazil
New Zealand	Indonesia
Netherlands	Pakistan
Sweden	Canada
Switzerland	Japan
Israel	United Kingdom
Denmark	France
Australia	West Germany

*These rankings are based on factor analysis of data on 133 countries from Bruce M. Russett *et al., World Handbook of Political and Social Indicators* (New Haven: Yale University Press, 1964). Varimax notation was used, and factors with eigenvalues greater than 1.0 are reported. For a discussion of factor analysis see Rudolph J. Rummel, *Applied Factor Analysis* (Evanston: Northwestern University Press, 1970).

ment, whereas China ranks seventieth. Despite their size and potential resources, these states will have difficulty matching the material influence base of the United States in the near future.

The importance of the variables included in economic development may not be immediately apparent. But better education, for instance, is associated not only with a wider range of technical and organizational skills but also with more accurate views of the relation of man to nature, the values and limits of science, and the ability to organize cognitions, to think independently, and to act when order and tradition yield confusing or unusable cues for action. The Six-Day War between Israel and the Arab states in June 1967 dramatically illustrates this point. The Egyptian army was larger and better equipped with tanks, missiles, artillery, and light weapons than was the Israeli army. Although the initial air superiority gained by the Israelis contributed heavily to their victory, it was frequently clear that the Egyptian soldiers were simply unprepared for modern war. In a culture with little experience of sophisticated technology and few habits of sustained abstract and independent thought, many Arab soldiers sought hierarchical leadership, rather than taking initiative, and, when unable to find it, abandoned their modern weapons and fled, frequently following those immediately above them in status or rank. Personal courage was no substitute for higher education and technological sophistication.

Sheer military power is, perhaps, the oldest and crudest resource available to actors in international politics. Niccolò Machiavelli declared in *The Prince,* "The chief foundations of all states, whether new, old, or mixed, are good laws and good arms" [9]. Military power is, however, difficult to measure and consequently its distribution is difficult to describe. Nevertheless, influence based on the use of armed forces is a resource jealously guarded by governments. Table 5.4 shows several indexes of military capacity among major world states, as well as selected smaller ones. It includes total military expenditures, the percentages of gross national products that they represent, the total numbers of men in uniform, and the percentages of the total populations that they represent. These figures provide crude indicators of the absolute military strength of nations, as well as of the relative salience of coercion for these states. The United States and the Soviet Union have by far the greatest military resources; Israel, Jordan, Korea, and Vietnam also assign very high priorities to military security. The total worldwide burden of military expenditures increased from $155 billion in 1964 to about $186 billion in 1969. It is estimated that an average of $52 per capita were spent in 1969, ranging from a high of $189 per person in North Atlantic Treaty Organization countries to a low of $10 per person in developing states (see Table 5.5).

As training, morale, intelligence, and strategy all affect coercive capability, we cannot offer a single summary index of this quality. Economists can construct useful cost-of-living indexes only because they can generally agree on what factors go into the index for Americans, Russians, and Argentinians; how they should be measured; where relevant information can be found; and so on. Such agreement is lacking on the components of coercive capability, and our comparisons must therefore be crude. If we could be certain of the distribution of coercive resources, war might become less attractive, for the weaker would know that they would lose, and the stronger would have nothing to fear.

We can, however, point out certain important disparities in comparisons of military resources. It is clear, for instance, that a soldier in one country is not necessarily equivalent to a soldier in another country. Americans have often been proud of the resourcefulness, skill, ingenuity, and courage of the typical "G.I.," whom they intuitively judge to be superior to any other soldier in the world. Nevertheless, the "cost effectiveness" of American soldiers today is one of the lowest in the world. The costs of recruiting, maintaining, and equipping each American soldier are very high in comparison with similar costs for a single North Vietnamese or Chinese soldier. Even though the enemy losses in Vietnam were very high compared with American losses, American soldiers were much more "expensive." It has been estimated that it cost the United States $300,000 to kill a single Viet Cong soldier.

Another problem in evaluating military resources arises from differences among various types of weapons and their relative effectiveness in different situations. How can we compare the relative effectiveness, for example, of naval vessels, infantry, tanks, and planes? They are qualitatively different resources, effective under different conditions. Nuclear weapons may be useful for eliminating cities but seem to provide no advantage in battling guerrilla movements or civil insurrections. Similarly, counterinsurgency forces and surface naval vessels are of limited use in deterring nuclear attack. The problem of the appropriateness of resources to an actor's objectives has been discussed at some length. We remind the reader of this basic point because misunderstanding of it has been the source of frequent and tragic errors by statesmen in assessing and making policy.

In the short range coercion can be a very important source of influence, but its long-range consequences and even its short-range tactical limitations must be examined carefully. In the nineteenth century military capacity was not only more evenly distributed among major actors; it was also more readily comparable. The skills, equipment, and weapons available to different states were similar. The number of men under arms and their training were, along with battlefield strategy, the critical determinants in military conflict. Technological change has, however, greatly complicated the military equation. For example, the maximum destructive radius of a single explosion increased geometrically from the middle of the nineteenth to the middle of the twentieth century. After the introduction of nuclear weapons, destructive capacity increased even more rapidly (see Figure 5.3). So far this destructive capability has remained in the hands of a few states, but more are likely to acquire it, as the projections in Table 5.6 make clear. Even so, nuclear weapons have greatly increased inequalities in destructive capacity.[5]

Along with this dramatic rise in destructive capabilities there have been parallel increases in the speed with which such weapons can be delivered. In discussing the development of nuclear weapons and their delivery systems one observer has declared that they differ from older weapons

not in the number of people they can eventually kill but in the speed with which it

[5] It is important, however, to distinguish between what one country *can* do and what it is *likely* to do in order to coerce another. This point and other considerations affecting the impact of nuclear capacity on international influence are discussed in Chapters 17 and 18.

Table 5.4.

Military Expenditures and Related Data, 1967

Country	Military Expenditures (in millions of dollars)	Gross National Product (in millions) of dollars)	Relative Burden	
			Military Expenditures (as % of GNP)	GNP (in dollars per capita)
United States	75,484	793,500	9.5	3,985
France	5,856	115,900	5.1	2,323
West Germany	5,349	121,000	4.4	2,097
Portugal	333	4,600	7.2	487
United Kingdom	6,436	110,900	5.8	2,014
East Germany	890	28,800	3.1	1,780
Poland	1,680	33,900	5.0	1,061
U.S.S.R.	52,000	384,000	(8-9)	1,630
Albania	69	700	9.9	356
Sweden	945	23,900	4.0	3,037
Switzerland	374	16,000	2.3	2,645
Brazil	940	29,743	3.2	347
Cuba	380	5,400	7.0	622
Mainland China	7,000	85,000	8.2	108
Taiwan	415	3,602	11.5	263
North Korea	600	3,000	20.0	236
South Korea	184	4,612	4.0	155
Thailand	133	5,078	2.6	149
North Vietnam	500	2,000	25.0	100
South Vietnam	419	2,980	14.1	177
India	1,486	43,650	3.4	85
Pakistan	492	13,725	3.6	113
Iraq	268	2,240	12.0	265
Israel	428	4,005	10.7	1,501
Jordan	77	575	13.4	286
Saudi Arabia	341	2,000	17.1	444
Syria	125	1,130	11.1	203
United Arab Republic	666	5,693	11.7	184
South Africa	370	13,080	2.8	698
Tanzania	12	858	1.4	73

Source: U.S. Arms Control and Disarmament Agency, *World Military Expenditures, 1969* (Washington, D.C.: Government Printing Office, 1970), pp. 11-13.

can be done, in the centralization of decision, in the divorce of the war from political processes, and in computerized programs that threaten to take war out of human hands once it begins. [22]

Figure 5.4 gives the rate (in miles per hour) at which armed men and equipment can be transported, and Figure 5.5 suggests a crude indicator of the growth in the driving force behind these tech-nological changes represented by the growth in the scientific community and the exchanges of information within it. Although the publications of individual scientists vary widely, the number of journals published provides a good indicator of the numbers of scientists working and their general productivity. Derek J. Price found a tenfold increase in the scientific community every fifty years since 1800;

Other Public Expenditures		Armed Forces		
Foreign Aid Received (in millions of dollars)	Foreign Aid Given (in millions of dollars)	Armed Forces (in thousands)	Population (in thousands)	Forces (per thousand population)
-	4,130	3,400	199,118	17
-	873	520	49,890	10
-	634	460	57,699	8
-	58	149	9,440	16
-	542	429	55,068	8
-	116	127	16,001	8
-	116	270	31,944	8
-	340	3,220	235,543	14
NA	-	38	1,965	19
-	50	65	7,869	8
-	13	12	6,050	2
283	-	225	85,655	5
1	-	200	8,033	25
-	49	2,700	789,000	4
92	-	600	13,700	44
NA	-	368	12,700	29
270	-	612	29,784	21
68	-	126	34,008	4
NA	-	447	20,100	22
450	-	465	16,973	27
1,447	-	1,200	514,200	2
533	-	360	121,760	3
14	-	84	8,440	10
85	-	80	2,669	30
50	-	50	2,013	25
−12	-	54	4,500	12
20	-	64	5,570	11
51	-	200	30,907	6
NA	-	27	18,733	1
37	-	4	12,173	*

*Less than one half-unit.

90 percent of all the scientists who have ever lived are alive today [12, 19]. Attempting to predict changes in military technology is thus a hazardous enterprise, for military technology has outstripped the development of social and political institutions designed to channel and regulate the purposes to which such technology can be applied.

Finally, the distribution of natural resources is an important attribute of international structure. The distribution of crude-oil reserves, for instance, has important consequences for international politics. Until large-scale tankers were developed western Europe depended upon shipment of crude petroleum through the Suez canal, which was known as "the lifeline of the British Empire." The British responded vigorously to any threat to

Table 5.5.
Summary Trends in Military Expenditures, 1964-1969

	1964	1965	1966	1967	1968 estimated	1969 estimated
Total			*(in billions of 1967 dollars)*			
World	155	154	166	181	185	186
Developed	137	136	148	161	162	161
Developing	18	18	18	20	23	25
NATO	81	79	89	100	102	100
Warsaw Pact	53	54	56	57	58	58
Other	21	21	21	24	25	28
Per Capita			*(in 1967 dollars)*			
World	48	47	49	53	53	52
Developed	148	144	156	168	168	165
Developing	8	8	8	8	9	10
NATO	162	155	173	193	195	189
Warsaw Pact	162	163	168	170	171	170
Other	9	9	8	9	9	10

Source: U.S. Arms Control and Disarmament Agency, *World Military Expenditures, 1969* (Washington, D.C.: U.S. Government Printing Office, 1970).

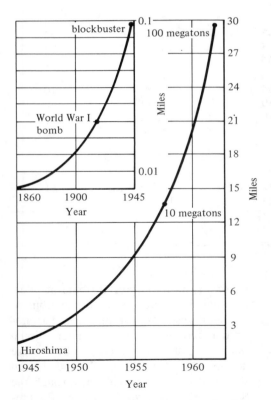

Figure 5.3. Maximum Destructive Radius of Weapons, 1860–1960

Source: Reprinted with permission of The Macmillan Company from *Trends in World Politics* by Bruce M. Russett. Copyright © Bruce M. Russett, 1965.

close it, as in their 1956 invasion of Egypt. Japan and Germany, currently the two most rapidly growing industrial states in the world, have virtually no petroleum reserves. In addition, the Soviet Union and the United States have to import vast quantities of petroleum to supplement their own production. The importance of the Middle East, particularly the oil-rich countries adjoining the Persian Gulf, is therefore obvious. As oil is basic to many industries, future exhaustion of supplies would have momentous political and economic consequences unless substitute fuels were available. As with other raw materials oil provides an incentive for strong states to interfere in the affairs of weaker states; rivalry for control of petroleum deposits constitutes a possible source of conflict among states with rapidly expanding economies. Indeed, one cause of Japan's aggressiveness before World War II was its need for petroleum and iron, critical resources in which it was deficient. As Table 5.7 illustrates, the demand for energy is likely to rise steeply in the foreseeable future. Unless alternative sources of energy are developed, areas with fuel resources will surely become even more important in international politics.

Table 5.6.

*A Primitive Model of Nuclear-Weapons Growth and Proliferation, 1945-1979**

Rank	1945	1949	1952	1955	1958	1961	1964	1967	1970	1973	1976	1979
1. United States	2	32	128	512	2,048	8,192	10,000+					
2. U.S.S.R.	-	2	16	64	256	1,024	4,096	10,000+				
3. Britain (2 in 1951)	-	-	4	24	98	396	1,584	6,336	10,000+			
4. France (2 in 1957)	-	-	-	-	4	24	98	396	1,584	6,336	10,000+	
5. China	-	-	-	-	-	-	2	16	64	256	1,024	4,096
6. Country 1	-	-	-	-	-	-	-	-	2	16	64	256
7. Country 2	-	-	-	-	-	-	-	-	2	16	64	256
8. Country 3	-	-	-	-	-	-	-	-	2	16	64	256
9. Country 4	-	-	-	-	-	-	-	-	-	2	16	64
10. Country 5	-	-	-	-	-	-	-	-	-	-	2	16

*Assuming annual doubling of output for-first three years and doubling every eighteen months thereafter until approach to saturation level of more than 10,000 warheads. The actual development of nuclear weapons may have been faster in some years and slower in others. It seems plausible, however, that the growth of nuclear stocks in each country starts slowly, then accelerates, and finally slows down near some saturation level. Countries 6-10 might be India, Japan, Israel, Germany, Italy, Brazil or Argentina.

Source: Karl W. Deutsch, *The Analysis of International Relations* © 1968. Reprinted by permission of Prentice-Hall, Inc., Englewood Cliffs, New Jersey.

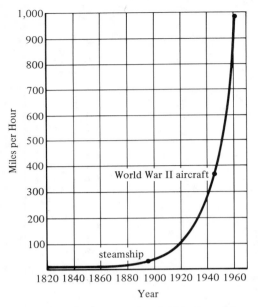

Figure 5.4. Maximum Attainable Speed for Travel over Intercontinental Distances, 1820–1960

Source: Reprinted by permission of the Macmillan Company from *Trends In World Politics* by Bruce M. Russett. Copyright © Bruce M. Russett, 1965.

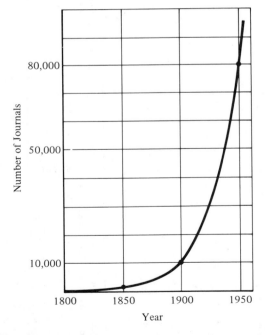

Figure 5.5. Number of Technical Journals, 1800–1950

Source: Derek J. deSolla Price, *Science Since Babylon,* (New Haven: Yale University Press, 1961), p. 97.

The distribution of resources in the international system thus suggests that destructive capacity is increasing and that the rates of change in distribution and amounts of important resources are accelerating. Furthermore, resources consumed in the processes of change and modernization are often in scarce supply and may furnish sources of current and future political conflict.

Examination of the distribution of resources suggests that the international system is not equalitarian. There are a few rich and powerful national actors and a large number of poorer, weak, and usually small states. Figure 5.6 illustrates this disparity with an approximation to actual data. The percentages of all states are represented on the horizontal axis and those of the world's resources on the vertical axis. If resources were evenly distributed among all the states of the world, the result would be a diagonal line as in the figure. The "real" distribution of resources is represented by the curve below the diagonal, showing that a few nations possess most of the world's resources.[6] So-called "developed" states control more than 75 percent of the world's wealth but account for less than one-third of the world's population. The gap between the rich countries and the poor ones (see Figure 5.7) is already enormous, and it is growing, a fact with significant implications for the future of the international political system.

If it is true that great inequality promotes instability and violence, a theory held by Aristotle and others, then the inequalities in the international system may be viewed as increasing the probability of violence and anarchy already enhanced by the absence of any supranational authority. Until mechanisms for translating extreme poverty into political action are developed, however, this feature will be less important than is another aspect of the international system: quarrels among

[6] The curved line is known as a "Lorenz curve," and the area between the curve and the line of equality (the diagonal) is a measure of the inequality of distribution. The smaller this area, the more equitable the distribution is. This measure is called the "Gini index of inequality."

Table 5.7.

*Projected Energy Consumption
(in millions of metric tons
of coal equivalents)*

Nation	Projection 1975	1985
United States	2,463.13	3,135.91
U.S.S.R.	1,284.16	1,735.52
China	811.73	1,285.73
West Germany	342.91	435.81
United Kingdom	329.31	376.55
Japan	287.27	399.87
Canada	247.25	344.47
France	212.21	279.99
Italy	163.84	235.50
Poland	147.16	183.94
India	130.33	176.87
Australia	125.42	179.89
East Germany	118.23	143.49
Czechoslovakia	111.31	142.25
South Africa	79.36	104.30
Netherlands	76.85	107.49
Rumania	64.45	90.19
Belgium	61.80	78.86
Mexico	61.11	80.51
Sweden	52.33	69.81

Source: Based on data from Michael Hudson, Charles Taylor, *et al., World Handbook of Political and Social Indicators,* 2nd ed. (New Haven: Yale University Press, 1972).

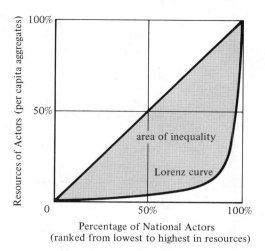

Figure 5.6. Distribution of World's Resources Among States (A rough approximation)

the great powers themselves. We may adopt a crude analogy for the international system *in this one respect,* considering it comparable to the early stages of European feudalism, when a few noblemen fought over peripheral fiefdoms while the peasants remained aloof. Not until the rise of nationalism and demands for universal equality did the expectations of common people alter the distribution of resources. The revolt of the "third world" is not likely to occur until the locus of its aspirations shifts to the global arena and its preferences coincide with the values currently shared by the wealthy North American and European states (including the Soviet Union).

Attitudes

A second major component of international structure is the distribution of atti-

tudes. Although resources *permit* international actors to take action, attitudes shape *how, when,* and *where* they act. The uses to which resources may be put are many, and it is therefore difficult to infer attitudes from resources alone with any degree of accuracy. For instance, we cannot predict that poor states will be more prone to war or that those with weapons will be aggressive. When the Soviet Union began installing antiballistic missiles in the latter half of the 1960s, it was not possible to deduce its intentions. The action was equally plausible as evidence of desire to avoid destruction or of an intended attack. The beliefs, expectations, and identifications of international actors have long been regarded as important determinants of international outcomes. Historians are apt to draw distinctions between "status quo" and "revisionist" states, suggesting that differences in these attitudes have been the sources of international conflict. At different times and in different places relevant attitude holders differ. The more "democratic" a political system, the higher will be the proportion of individuals within the system whose views and attitudes are relevant to international structure.

Investigation of the distribution of attitudes in the international system is an even more formidable task than examina-

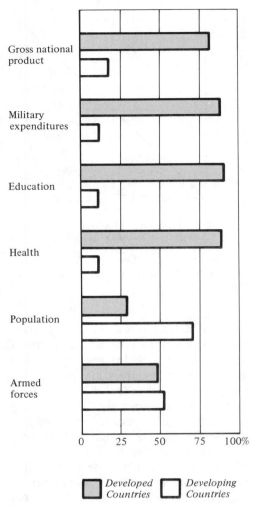

Figure 5.7. Share of Total World Resources, 1967

Source: U.S. Arms Control and Disarmament Agency, *World Military Expenditures, 1969* (Washington, D.C.: Government Printing Office, 1970), p. 4.

tion of resource distribution. Nevertheless, because attitudes shape behavior, representing subjective motivations for and constraints on the behavior of international actors, they cannot be ignored, even though systematic and reliable data are difficult to acquire.

Sometimes it is unnecessary to examine attitudes in order to explain or predict their political force. For example, a knowledge of the base resources and geographical locations of Mongolia and Chad indicates that they will have little if

any direct interdependence or interaction. These states have little in common. An analysis of relevant attitudes in Mongolia and Chad would thus add little more to our understanding of their behavior. Their few coincidental international interests can be inferred from their relative resource positions in the world [21, 18].

If we were to disregard attitudes, however, we might arrive at a similar conclusion about the relationship between Canada and Australia. These two countries are geographically far apart, have reached about the same level of economic development, and have little trade with each other. Nevertheless, the comparatively high rates of mail, migration, and travel between the two and the fact that they were allies in World Wars I and II belie such a conclusion. Information about their shared identifications, common cultural background, and similar beliefs and expectations about politics and economics is necessary to understand their cooperative and parallel behavior in international politics.

Knowledge of the distribution of attitudes also permits the observer to distinguish what is *possible* in international politics from what is *probable*. An analysis of shipping and manpower resources alone suggests that it is impossible for India to launch a major invasion of Brazil. Brazilian leaders therefore probably do not pay careful attention to the policy statements and budgetary allocations of the Indian government. On the other hand, it is possible for the United States to attack Canada, for the latter is contiguous and vulnerable. Nevertheless, the United States is undoubtedly considered a greater military threat in Moscow than in Ottawa, because the Russian and Canadian governments have different assessments not of what the United States *could* do but of what it is *likely* to do. Americans and Canadians share common identities and expectations of mutual cooperation; their beliefs and values are similar. The United States and the Soviet Union, on the other hand, have negative attitudes toward each other; each suspects that the other poses a threat to its security. *The major cleavages in the world are anchored more in attitudes than in geography.*

Identities. The first major type of attitude to be examined is the shared identifications of peoples, the extent to which they are psychologically close, for these factors may either reinforce or undermine the structural restraints of geographical distance. Individuals within actors identify themselves in myriad ways, including definitions of basic beliefs, nationality, and ownership. An understanding of *identity* is not only important in explaining possible political coalitions among major actors but may also help to reveal weak alliance relationships that analysis of resources and formal commitments might obscure. An illustration of the importance of attitudes and identifications involves Italian behavior during World War II. Although Italy was formally a member of the Axis, Italian enthusiasm and discipline were much lower than were those of Germany and Japan. In addition, large numbers of Italian-Americans had created strong links between the United States and Italy. In some respects the Italians were psychologically closer to Americans than to Germans, and this fact had important consequences for their behavior in World War II when German troops were used to reinforce their loyalty to the Axis.

The underlying propensities for action, particularly joint action, are usually determined by such common identifications, rather than by formal treaties. For instance, the United States and Pakistan are both members of the Southeast Asia Treaty Organization (SEATO), a military alliance whose principal aim is the containment of communism in Asia. Nevertheless, the arms that Pakistan has received through this agreement have been used against only one external foe, India, and one former domestic group, the Bengali population in East Pakistan. Both these enemies are also considered friends of the United States. Further-

more, Pakistan has not supported American military intervention in Vietnam and has established cordial relations with Communist China.

Goals. A second type of attitude to be examined is the demands and goals of various actors. We must ask what goals or outcomes actors seek and how compatible they are.[7] For poor countries in early phases of modernization national goals are often perfectly clear and widely accepted, though difficult to achieve. The goals of most African states, for instance, are to preserve their independence by avoiding entanglement with the great powers, to extract as many resources as possible from the international environment, and to improve national well-being.

The literature, art, philosophy, and behavior of the younger generation in countries already modernized—Sweden, the United States, and the Soviet Union, for example—suggest that at some point accumulation of material wealth and preservation of national security may decline in importance as goals. As people become more satisfied with their own positions on their chosen scales of values, they may emphasize less immediate values like affection, artistic fulfillment, and freedom of speech. Europeans who own cars for the first time in their lives talk about them, wash them, tinker with them, and drive them (however poorly) just for fun. Most Americans, on the other hand, have been raised with automobiles and have owned them from an early age, but take less pride in and care of them. Easy access reduces desirability, as familiarity breeds contempt.

Man's priorities among valued objects over which he seeks control change with time and circumstances. Certain professions gain esteem as others struggle to maintain status in the face of changing social values. Some years ago political scientist Harold D. Lasswell proposed a

[7] See Chapter 4 for an elaboration of how goals based on value priorities lead to specifically defined objectives and ultimately to policy decisions.

"garrison state" hypothesis somewhat analogous to the future described by George Orwell in *1984*. He forecast a reciprocal rise in insecurity among the large industrial nations. This rise would catapult military specialists to positions of state leadership; they would sense a need to maintain international tension in order to retain their positions and status [7]. Such garrison states have not yet emerged, partly because other values like economic productivity have taken precedence in the scale of social values. Furthermore, nuclear weapons have made strategic defense cheaper, and the major states' desire to avoid war has increased. The United States and Europe feel less threatened by communism today than they did in the 1950s.

Expectations. These changes, which have been important features of the evolving international structure since World War II, are discussed more fully in Chapter 6. Associated with them, however, are expectations, the third attitudinal element affecting international structure. What each actor expects of the other is conditioned by their reciprocal behavior and modified by various distorting and idiosyncratic factors like the personality of an important leader. These expectations are based upon and influence theories and identifications. If we believe that a certain type of behavior is good and expect another actor to exhibit it, we are more apt to identify with that actor. We least expect undesirable actions from those whom we know and trust. Suppose that a nuclear warhead were to explode tomorrow in Philadelphia. Americans would assign responsibility according to their knowledge of the capabilities of other countries and their expectations of those countries. Most Americans would expect the culprit to be China or the Soviet Union, rather than France or Great Britain. In June 1967, when the American naval-intelligence vessel *Liberty* was attacked and seriously damaged by Israeli aircraft (by mistake), many Americans found the facts difficult to believe until an explana-tion was offered; this response was radically different from American reactions when a similar ship, *Pueblo,* was seized by North Korea. The difference in responses can be attributed partly to American perceptions of other nations and to very different expectations about their rationality and intentions. Expectations serve not only to guide interpretation of behavior but also to help justify it.

Attitudes shape the goals and policies of states; they also incorporate expectations about the behavior of other actors and relevant internal elites. We are by now accustomed to considering international actors as playing "roles"—Western ally, nonaligned state, mediator, and so on—in the international system. Each of these labels suggests certain expectations and attitudes. Most relevant groups hold attitudes toward past or possible international systems that include clusters of expectations associated with roles that various actors may play [5]. For instance, in the balance-of-power system that prevailed in Europe through most of the eighteenth and nineteenth centuries, Great Britain was expected to function as "balancer."

To the extent that relevant groups, especially elites, share expectations about the roles of the various actors in the system, international politics will tend to conform to such expectations. Major shifts in the expectations of elites could signify an impending change in the system as a whole. In Table 5.8 some common ways in which various international actors perceive their own roles are listed. In most instances actors are perceived as playing several roles simultaneously. A map of their expectations for themselves and others would allow us to identify areas of congruence between perceptions by self and others. As Lasswell has argued, expectations of aggressive or violent behavior can induce corresponding and mutually destructive behavior [8, 17]. It is probable that the more nearly congruent the external and internal perceptions of roles, the more stable the international system.

Table 5.8.
Common Roles of National Actors

Role	Main Features	Examples
Bastion of revolution, liberator	ideological principles, anticolonial attitudes, desire for ethnic unity	Communist China Cuba North Korea
Regional leader	superior capabilities, traditional national role	Egypt Japan
Regional protector	perception of threat, geographic location, traditional policies, needs of threatened states	Australia New Zealand United States U.S.S.R.
Active independent	antibloc attitudes, economic needs and trade expansion, pivotal geographic location	France India Yugolsavia Rumania
Nonaligned	anticolonial attitudes, ideological principles	most African, Asian, and communist states
Mediator, integrator	traditional national role, cultural-ethnic composition of state, traditional non-involvement in conflicts	Lebanon Sweden
Regional-subsystem collaborator	economic needs, sense of belonging to region, common political-ideological traditions, geographic location	Belgium Brazil Kenya Sweden
Faithful ally	perception of threat, insufficient capabilities, traditional policies, ideological compatibility	Albania Bulgaria Portugal Great Britain
Isolate	perception of external threat, weak capabilities	Burma Laos

Source: This excerpt from "National Role Conceptions in the Study of Foreign Policy", by K. J. Holsti is reprinted from *International Studies Quarterly,* Volume 14, number 3 (September 1970), pp. 233-309 by permission of the Publisher, Sage Publications, Inc.

Trends in Distribution

Trends in the distribution of both resources and attitudes are important. They reflect visible change, altering structure and the patterns of action that structure permits. Some processes of change are relatively stable and predictable and have exhibited established rates of change over time. Other changes are more dramatic and unexpected. Earlier we described changes in the time necessary for delivering ideas, people, and weapons from one point to another: There have been dramatic increases in the speed with which people can communicate, travel, and commit mass murder.

In the future we may expect man's capacity to kill his brothers quickly and in quantity to increase exponentially, as it has done so far in the twentieth century. Although the costs of missile-delivery systems and nuclear devices may inhibit smaller states from developing them, we can imagine other trends related to the growth of weapons capacity that may further a more nearly even distribution—for instance, the spread of chemical and bacteriological means of killing. As these weapons require a smaller industrial base than do nuclear weapons, they may be more attractive to poorer countries.

In addition to rates of change in weapons development, the rate of discovery of new resources can be estimated and compared with the rate of exhaustion of known resources to yield some idea about relative future scarcity of resources. Another trend worth calculating is the rate of technological change, which can affect the adaptive capacity of actors in the international system. A high rate may keep satisfactions ahead of aspirations for bigger slices of the world pie.

Rates of change in the distribution of attitudes should also be examined, in order to see what trends are current in the identifications, demands, and expectations of key groups. In such an examination we would want to separate fluctuations of a temporary sort from trends that represent fundamental adjustments to new events or realities. What new alignments are emerging, and what old ones are breaking up? A recent poll suggests that the French now identify more closely with the Germans than with the Americans, whereas West Germans reserve their highest opinion of foreigners for Americans [4].[8]

More important than the size or capabilities of a state are its probable responses in varying situations. An analysis of structural trends can furnish information about these probabilities. Analyzing trends, projecting future trends, and making predictions are the basic requisites for a future-oriented society. For the moment, we can suggest that structural imbalances and discontinuities are likely to increase. The choice of solutions or adjustments that can ensure or preserve

minimum acceptable goals for many actors may be shrinking. In situations for which there are many possible satisfactory solutions men of limited vision and intelligence may perform effectively, though not necessarily efficiently. As the range of acceptable alternatives decreases, however, greater wisdom and expertise will be required to achieve them.

INTERDEPENDENCE

It is widely acknowledged that the world is "growing smaller" and that men's fates are becoming increasingly interdependent. Economics is characterized by the expansion of markets, the transformation and widespread sharing of modern technology, and sophisticated products dependent upon diverse technological and geographical resources. The rise of literacy and the spread of communications through movies, television, radio, international journals and newspapers, and international meetings of professional societies have promoted similarities in the understanding of technology, art, and urban life styles. Not only do the components of complex manufactured goods depend upon skills, resources, and labor from various sources, but the composition of the major media of modern communication is also increasingly international. Ideas, themes, and techniques for motion pictures and television programs; ethics and standards for journalists and news broadcasters; and format, point of view, and contributors for newspapers and magazines have all become increasingly standardized and shared. Such common features, initially produced by exchanges among elites in the various cultural fields, as well as by those in business and theology, have promoted similarities in life styles and attitudes throughout the world, particularly among urban and "modernized" populations.

Interdependence seems related to two major factors. By far the more important is the linkage of the fates of actors whose objectives can be secured and goals

[8] For other analyses of attitude changes in international politics, see Hayward Alker, Jr., and Donald Puchala [1], Puchala [13, 14], and Philip E. Jacob and James V. Toscano [6].

achieved only when there is some minimum of cooperation. The second factor is the spread of common culture and values arising from expanding trade and communications and the increased rapidity with which they function. In recent years a great deal of attention has been paid to the flow of goods and services, communications, and migration among various states. Although these currents are important in shaping common values and in creating interdependence, their importance has often been exaggerated: Despite yielding some useful and surprising insights, information on these currents does not in itself ensure that interdependence exists.

For instance, British reluctance to intervene forcibly to end the "illegal" independence of Rhodesia has been assumed to have resulted from Great Britain's economic dependence upon Rhodesia's ally South Africa. In 1965 the white-dominated government of Rhodesia unilaterally declared its independence of Great Britain. Many African and other countries demanded that the latter either intervene militarily or invoke effective sanctions against the Rhodesian regime. Although Great Britain and eventually the United Nations also invoked a series of economic boycotts and sanctions, they were ineffective, principally because the Union of South Africa supplied Rhodesia with critical imports and assisted the Rhodesian government in subverting the ban on its exports. As South Africa was thwarting the will of the world community, it would have been logical to enforce economic sanctions against that country as well. It was argued, however, that because South Africa was a major trading partner of Great Britain and the site of large-scale British investments, the cost to the British economy of imposing such sanctions would have outweighed the possible gain to be derived from renewed control over Rhodesia.

But the assumption of British dependence upon South Africa based only on trade statistics is unjustified. The extent of Britain's economic dependence upon

South Africa is determined by the costs involved in finding substitute markets for British goods and new investment opportunities for British capital. If the political stakes elsewhere in Africa had been high enough for Great Britain, some substitutes could have been found, and some economic loss would have been acceptable. That Great Britain and South Africa trade with each other does not *alone* determine interdependence.

This point can also be illustrated by the example of Cuba since 1960. When Fidel Castro's revolutionary regime began to oppose American objectives, the United States imposed a political and economic embargo upon Cuba. American citizens were forbidden to travel to Cuba; political, military, and economic assistance, including favored prices for Cuba's sugar crop, was terminated; and pressure was brought to bear upon other Latin American governments to pursue similar policies. As Cuba's economic infrastructure *seemed* highly dependent upon American technology and goodwill, these measures were expected to influence Cuba to adapt itself to American wishes. Instead of accommodating American objectives, however, Cuba sought and received the assistance of the Soviet Union. Cuba was not so dependent upon the United States that, given overriding political goals, it could not break the apparent dependence. The choices available to Cuba included ending its reliance on the American economy.

Finally, some countries, even though they are poor in resources, may not be heavily dependent upon other countries or unimportant in world politics. For example, Somalia's largest export before the closing of the Suez canal in 1967 was bananas, which were shipped primarily to Italy and other Mediterranean countries.[9] Somalia's international importance, however, is largely determined by the military potential of its geographical location on

[9] The closing of the canal brought economic problems that, combined with internal clan disputes, may have led to the military coup d'état in Somalia in 1969.

the east coast of Africa, bordering the Red Sea and across from southwestern Asia. The importance of this geographical resource in interdependence with other actors is determined entirely by the *judgments* of other states; a conclusion that Somalia was dependent upon Italy because of the banana trade would have been misleading.

This point brings up a second major problem in examining aggregate flows among states. Only two-way relationships are usually examined, whereas flows of resources may promote complex interdependence among three or more actors. For instance, alignments in the Middle East since the establishment of Israel in 1948 have become increasingly complex *not* because of the flow of goods and services between the Soviet Union and Egypt or between Israel and the United States (both of which *could* promote interdependence) but because of the possibility that resulting interdependencies may have implications for the more important interdependency between the United States and the Soviet Union. As a consequence of the increasing closeness of the United States with Israel and the Soviet Union with Egypt—and of the hostility between Israel and Egypt—the two superpowers have been drawn closer to large-scale conflict.

Despite the difficulties already mentioned, flows of trade and communications among national actors and other organizations remain indicators, albeit crude ones, of international interdependence. Such flows also have implications for international integration and disintegration and the establishment of dependency relationships (see Chapter 13).

We can examine interdependence from two points of view: first, whether or not actors' fates are linked and, second, the nature of the relationship in terms of potential influence or causal effect within the system.

Interlocking Fates

Two actors have interlocking fates when the consequences of their behavior are such that in order for one to achieve his goal some action by the other is required. The choice of one thus affects the situation and sometimes the policy of the other. Let us consider for a moment the analysis of all possible dyadic (paired) combinations in the international system. If we added to the approximately 130 nation-states such other important international actors as the 20 largest multinational corporations, the 10 largest international organizations, and the 10 largest charitable, religious, or cultural groups, we would have 14,365 possible dyadic relationships. Although transactions within many of these dyads would be few and in many more absent altogether, a sizable number of active dyads would remain. Furthermore, each remaining dyad might be investigated for overlapping areas of policy control, from which interdependence arises.

As we have suggested, one starting place would be to examine the flow of people (migration), goods (trade), and ideas (culture) among units, because these factors may contribute to interdependence. Such analyses are valuable in delineating clusters of actors, but, as we have noted earlier, they do not in themselves allow us to assume interdependence.[10] In Table 5.9 we have reproduced the results of research in which selected national attributes were used to define clusters of states as what Russett has called "regions of socio-cultural homogeneity." These regions are similar in economic and cultural features and likely to share wider ranges of interdependence. We can nevertheless note certain unusual features of the clustering. Israel turns up in the Western community, rather than among Afro-Asian states; the Philippines appears with Latin America, whereas Spain and Portugal appear to have more in common with Chile, Cuba, Puerto Rico, and Uruguay than with their Euro-

[10] See Bruce M. Russett [18] and Karl W. Deutsch, Richard W. Chadwick, and I. Richard Savage, *Regionalism, Trade and International Community* (forthcoming). In Chapter 8 of his book Russett infers interdependence from trade groupings; we prefer to consider these groupings as reflecting simply interrelationships.

Table 5.9.
Regions of Sociocultural Homogeneity

Afro-Asia	
Tunisia	Syria
Iraq	Jordan
Iran	Taiwan
India	Ceylon
Malaya	Indonesia
Turkey	Pakistan
Morocco	Egypt
Thailand	Algeria
South Korea	Mauritius
Burma	Lebanon

Western Community	
Denmark	Netherlands
Sweden	France
Norway	Iceland
United Kingdom	New Zealand
United States	Australia
Switzerland	Belgium
West Germany	Austria
Finland	Luxembourg
Canada	Cyprus
Ireland	Italy
Argentina	Israel
Japan	Malta
Greece	Trinidad

Latin America	
Colombia	Costa Rica
Honduras	Mexico
Nicaragua	Brazil
Ecuador	Bolivia
Guatemala	Paraguay
El Salvador	Panama
Dominican Republic	Philippines
Peru	Venezuela

Semideveloped Latins	
Uruguay	Spain
Puerto Rico	Portugal
Cuba	Chile

Eastern Europe	
Rumania	Hungary
Yugoslavia	Czechoslovakia
Bulgaria	East Germany
Poland	U.S.S.R.
Albania	

Source: Bruce M. Russett, *International Regions and the International System,* © 1967 by Rand McNally & Company, Chicago, Table 2.2, pp. 24-25.

pean neighbors. Communist China and the Union of South Africa fit into no group and are "unclassifiable."

Coefficients of Causation

We might wish to know how much change in the characteristics of a particular coun-try would be required to alter some sig-nificant variable of international politics like the basic alignments among states. What would be the impact of a change in a single variable of an actor upon that actor's position vis-à-vis other countries? Answering this question is important in attempting to simplify the major cleavages that separate actors and provide occa-sions for the most important conflicts in the international system.

Coefficients of causation would simply be measures of the causal effect that a policy of one actor has on the behavior of other actors. They represent the *amounts* of effect of one actor on others, and therefore they indicate the importance of an "interlocking fate" relationship. They also help to distinguish cause and effect from influence. Every instance of influence is also one of cause and effect, but cause and effect do not always signify the purposiveness of influence. As we suggested in Chapter 4, many attempts at influence have unanticipated effects. Such effects do not reflect the conscious exer-tion of influence, but they do reflect a causal sequence. Large-scale transforma-tions in attitudes and technological change may also result in changes in the distribu-tion of resources and attitudes, which may in turn lead to systemic adjustments not deliberately initiated to achieve some ob-jective. Many changes in the distribution of variables, like discovery of oil in the Middle East or Alaska and the invention of nuclear weapons, have had important consequences for international politics but have not been part of direct attempts at influence.

Examining coefficients of causation re-veals basic characteristics of structure and interdependence within structure. Essen-tially the analyst asks, For a given change in variable x (perhaps the military capa-bility of the United States) what would be the change in y (perhaps the inhibi-tions on any other actor against attacking American territory)? Such questions are often answerable only after the fact or by means of hypothetical testing of simplified models of the real world. But we can in-fer relationships from past experience, by means of either data analysis or subjective analyses by diplomats and historians. Such calculations require fundamental assumptions upon which policy must be based. Nearly every discussion of foreign policy involves assumptions about coefficients of causation. What are the real effects of heavy investment by American corporations in Latin America? Radical critics of U.S. foreign policy, for instance, insist that American investment promotes conservative domestic policies and a facade of anticommunism in Latin America that mask and therefore perpetuate social and economic inequalities. How accurate is this argument? If we could gauge the interdependence between amounts of American investment and these alleged outcomes, we might begin to answer this question.

A more manageable question is What effect would an increase or decrease of American investment have on Latin America? By separating the multitude of possible relationships and asking the effect of a specific change on some related attribute and what other changes would ensue, we can begin to approach one of the most fundamental questions in international politics: What is the chain of political causality when an attribute or the distribution of resources in the world is altered? If we could calculate the coefficients, we could predict with greater accuracy the outcomes of various policy alternatives or of changes occurring outside the control of statesmen.

One puzzle is Which states are most interdependent? Paradoxically, it may be that those most nearly equal in their attributes are the most interdependent and can influence one another the most. For instance, the United States is more able than is any other country to influence the Soviet Union—and the reverse.[11] This proposition suggests that the more nearly equal the actors, the more sensitive they will be to one another's behavior.[12] States

with vast resources also have the greatest potential for influence and for producing change. Changes in their resources and attitudes may also have significant, not necessarily planned, consequences for international politics. A recession or an inflation in the United States has consequences, often unanticipated, for many other international actors. If these consequences are viewed by others as unfavorable, they may be ascribed to deliberate attempts at influence. For example, countries have occasionally attributed drops in world market prices of major primary products like cocoa and copper to "Wall Street manipulators."

Another problem is to determine which actors actually instigate the most change in the international structure. Large states would be expected to do so because of their generally greater resources, but this expectation is not always borne out. If their chief objectives are the preservation of current distribution systems and defense of their values, they tend to ignore the discontinuities and inequalities that expanding communications networks and underlying mechanisms of change are generating. We may characterize the resulting policies as *supervisory*. When attitudes that result in demands for change become widespread, dissatisfaction increases. The responsibility for satisfying these demands often falls on the most influential actors, and pressure for "leadership" increases. When major actors pursue supervisory policies, the "colonels," or "young Turks" in the nation-state hierarchy may be tempted to oppose them, hoping to change existing distributions of resources and attitudes. The preservation of world order and a tolerable rate of change thus requires strong and gifted leadership; the only alternative is the exercise of greater influence by those who are weak but willing to take risks.

To summarize, any change in a variable may have some causal effect on another variable. Those changes that result from one actor's use of resources to alter the behavior of another actor are

[11] It seems also to be true that in Latin America those states that are most nearly equal in attributes influence one another the most [11].

[12] This proposition has also been documented in the study of social structures [2].

instances of what we have labeled "influence." Influence is not, however, always involved in cause and effect. Policy is usually predicated on the assumption that the coefficients of causal effect among variables are known and that the consequences of a particular activity can be predicted. Policies frequently fail, however, because policy makers hold mistaken theories about interdependencies. In the mid-1960s General William Westmoreland, General Craighton Abrams, and other American military leaders made several predictions about the effects of increasing the American military presence in South Vietnam; they argued that increased American military activity would alter North Vietnamese and Viet Cong cost-benefit calculations about the desirability of continuing efforts to overthrow the South Vietnamese government. This prediction seems to have been painfully incorrect.

As various actors seek to shape the world in ways more conducive to their own values and objectives, their expectations condition their predictions about the causal interdependencies of the international structure, whether these expectations are accurate or not. "Real" interdependencies will limit and shape the "realm of the possible," whereas expectations and demands distributed among actors will determine the course of events within this realm. As politics is the "art of the possible," structure is the "realm of the possible."

STRUCTURAL COMPLEXITY IN SITUATIONAL ANALYSIS

Having discussed complexity in the international distribution of resources and attitudes, we shall examine how causal interrelationships further complicate any attempt to analyze a particular situation. We shall use a modified arms-race model of the sort popularized by Lewis F. Richardson [15, 16].

Let us take two countries, A and B, which might be Egypt and Israel. Let us

assume that certain very simple processes affect the level of armaments and the degree of hostility in each country. The behavior of the rest of the world is represented by Z. The model includes two variables for each country: level of armaments and perceived threat; it also includes the simple response rule that when one country appears to be gaining clear superiority, arms are supplied to the other by third parties.

Figures 5.8–5.12 illustrate four simple processes in which the level of arms and the degree of perceived threat change over time. In Figure 5.8 decay and deterioration take place between initial time (t_0) and a specified subsequent time (t_1), and continue at $t_2, \ldots, t_n$. Weapons deteriorate and depreciate over time, and hostility and perceived threat lessen, assuming that no new stimulus increases them

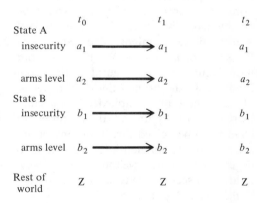

Figure 5.8. Decay in Weapons

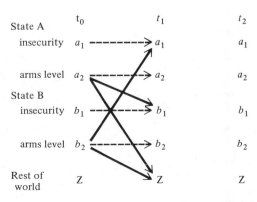

Figure 5.9. Response to Changes in Arms Levels

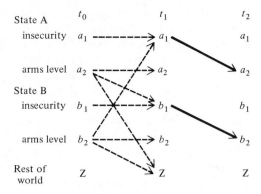

Figure 5.10. Response to Changes in National Insecurity

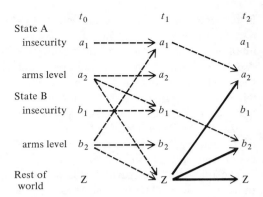

Figure 5.11. Response of the International Community (Z)

and that no new weapons are added to existing stockpiles.

Figure 5.9 suggests that the level of armaments in one country stimulates perceived threat in the other country. If A, for example, were to increase its level of arms, B's sense of insecurity would be heightened. Conversely, if A were to disarm partially, it might effectively lessen B's sense of insecurity. We have also put into Figure 5.9 the causal paths from Figure 5.8 (the broken lines) in order to illustrate how the complexity of causality increases. In Figure 5.10 responses to changes in perceived threat and insecurity are shown. Heightened insecurity leads to development of new weapons. Conversely, reduced insecurity may lead to a reduction in arms levels or deterioration of existing stocks without replacement. The final process is shown in Figure 5.11:

how the rest of the world as an aggregate might respond to changes in the arms levels of the two competing countries if it wished to maintain a balance in the levels of armaments and prevent either country from destroying the other.

When we bring these four processes together, starting at some initial point in time (t_0) and permit them to operate for three periods, or until t_3 (see Figure 5.12), we can examine the extent to which the level of armaments in country A is dependent upon previous values of other variables like that country's level of insecurity. At the end of the first period (t_1) the level of arms in state A (a_2) is a function of two causal paths leading from the level of arms of the same state at an earlier time and from its earlier insecurity. By the end of the third period we can find without difficulty sixteen

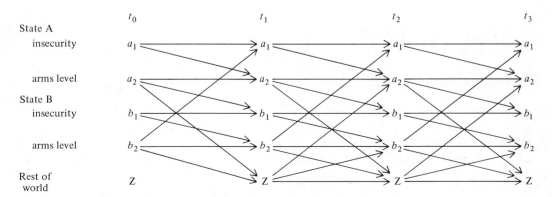

Figure 5.12. Arms Race for a Three-Period Cycle

paths of influence affecting the level of armaments in state A; they involve all the other variables in the model at certain points in time. This model is highly deterministic. Indeed the behavior of the actors is determined by paths of influence that reinforce rather than counteract one another (given the parameters, or constants of the situation, that were initially specified). Nevertheless, this example does give us some idea of the adjustment mechanisms that produce changes in structural variables. These variables are related to one another and to government policies in the two states and the rest of the world. They affect one another, even without specifying magnitude and direction, in so complex a way that, even in this simple example, it is difficult to understand or sort out the relationships. Furthermore, without specifying actual parameters, the observer cannot predict whether arms levels will increase infinitely, decrease to zero, or fluctuate between high and low points.

The purpose of this illustration is to show the complexity underlying events in the international arena, even when broadly simplified. It is not unreasonable to make simplifying assumptions if they are fairly accurate and tell us something about the properties of the underlying relationships governing behavior. Building models of international processes may lead to empirical work on causal relationships and coefficients among variables.[13]

References

1. Alker, Hayward, Jr., and Donald Puchala, "Trends in Economic Partnership: The North Atlantic Area, 1928–1963," in J. David Singer, ed., *Quantitative International Politics* (New York: Free Press, 1968), pp. 287–316.
2. Berelson, Bernard, and Gary Steiner, *Human Behavior: An Inventory of Scientific Findings* (New York: Harcourt Brace Jovanovich, 1964).
3. Deutsch, Karl W., *The Nerves of Government* (New York: Free Press, 1963), p. 21.
4. Deutsch, Karl W., *et al.*, *France, Germany and the Western Alliance* (New York: Scribner, 1967).
5. Holsti, H. J., "National Role Conceptions in the Study of Foreign Policy," *International Studies Quarterly*, 14 (September 1970), pp. 296–297.
6. Jacob, Philip E., and James V. Toscano, eds., *The Integration of Political Communities* (Philadelphia: Lippincott, 1964).
7. Lasswell, Harold D., "The Garrison State," *The American Journal of Sociology*, 46 (January 1941), pp. 455–468.
8. Lasswell, Harold D., *World Politics and Personal Insecurity*, 2nd ed. (New York: Free Press, 1965), chap. 3.
9. Machiavelli, Niccolò, *The Prince* (New York: Modern Library, 1950), chap. 12.
10. Milstein, Jeffrey S., and William Charles Wallace, "Computer Simulation of International Processes: The Vietnam War and the Pre-World War I Naval Race," *Papers of the Peace Research Society (International)*, 12 (1969), pp. 117–136.
11. Olav, Per, "International Structure and International Integration," *Journal of Peace Research*, 4 (1967), pp. 334–365.
12. Price, Derek J., *Science Since Babylon* (New Haven: Yale University Press, 1961).
13. Puchala, Donald, "European Integration: Progress and Prospects," mimeographed (New Haven: Yale University, 1965).
14. Puchala, Donald, "Integration and Disintegration in Franco-German Relations, 1954–1965," *International Organization*, 24 (Spring 1970), pp. 183–208.
15. Richardson, Lewis F., *Arms and Insecurity* (Chicago: Quadrangle, 1960).
16. Richardson, Lewis F., *Statistics of Deadly Quarrels* (Chicago: Quadrangle, 1960).
17. Rosenberg, Milton S., "Images in Relation to the Policy Process: American Public Opinion on Cold-War Issues," in Herbert C. Kelman, ed., *International Behavior* (New York: Holt, Rinehart & Winston, 1965), pp. 277–336.

[13] For one example of such work see Jeffrey S. Milstein, and William Charles Wallace [10].

18. Russett, Bruce M., *International Regions and the International System: A Study in Political Ecology* (Chicago: Rand McNally, 1967).
19. Russett, Bruce M., *Trends in World Politics* (New York: Macmillan, 1965), pp. 11–12.
20. Russett, Bruce M., *et al., World Handbook of Political and Social Indicators* (New Haven: Yale University Press, 1964).
21. Sawyer, Jack W., "Dimensions of Nations: Size, Wealth and Politics," *American Journal of Sociology,* 73 (September 1967), pp. 145–172.
22. Schelling, Thomas C., *Arms and Influence* (New Haven: Yale University Press, 1966), p. 20.

Suggested Reading

Alker, Hayward R., Jr., and Bruce M. Russett, *World Politics in the General Assembly* (New Haven: Yale University Press, 1965).

Boulding, Kenneth, *Conflict and Defense: A Theoretical Statement* (New York: Harper & Row, 1962).

Caspary, William R., "Richardson's Models of Arms Races: Description, Technique and an Alternative Model," *International Studies Quarterly,* 9 (1967), pp. 63–88.

Deutsch, Karl W., *Political Community at the International Level* (Garden City, N.Y.: Doubleday, 1954).

Deutsch, Karl W., "Toward an Inventory of Basic Trends and Patterns in Comparative and International Politics," in James N. Rosenau, ed., *International Politics and Foreign Policy,* rev. ed. (New York: Free Press, 1969), pp. 498–512.

Knorr, Klaus, *On the Uses of Military Power in the Nuclear Age* (Princeton: Princeton University Press, 1966).

Liska, George, *International Equilibrium* (Cambridge, Mass.: Harvard University Press, 1957).

Russett, Bruce M., *Trends in World Politics* (New York: Macmillan, 1965).

Singer, J. David, and Melvin Small, *The Wages of War, 1816–1965* (New York: Wiley, 1972).

Sprout, Harold, and Margaret Sprout, *The Ecological Perspective on Human Affairs* (Princeton: Princeton University Press, 1965).

See also Suggested Readings for Chapter 6.

Chapter 6
THE STRUCTURAL BASES OF SYSTEM TRANSFORMATION

Especially since the early sixties, a number of trends have manifested themselves and become interrelated in such a way that, taken together, they are substantially altering the fundamental postwar patterns of international politics—Oran R. Young [30]

Because structure largely determines the possible alternatives for behavior in international politics, fundamental transformation of the system requires a change in structure. Important shifts in the nature of international decision processes can, under certain conditions, occur with only small corresponding changes in international structure. Just as changing one card among the hands in a poker game may have no, little, or great consequences for the outcome of a particular game, so altering one structural feature may have marginal or major consequences in the calculations of international actors and in their patterned interactions. In this chapter we shall examine several types of systems for their major structural characteristics and the implications of these characteristics.

THE IMPACT OF STRUCTURE

We have already discussed the distributions, cleavages, and interdependencies that constitute international structure. So far we have concentrated on the many trees, interdependent in needs and growth, that compose the forest of international politics—but what of the forest itself? Out of the myriad possible combinations of actors, influences, and causal sequences we want to discover whether or not there are some dominant patterns and divisive issues among actors.

An examination of the impact of system structure on international politics must necessarily be focused on "macro" features. The purpose of a broad aggregate analysis is to investigate the unique concatenation of consequences attributable to international structure. The unique features of historical reality are lifted out of context, simplified, and aggregated in order to characterize the most important *emergent properties* of a system. These properties determine the effects of structure on the two dependent variables central to the concerns of the political analyst: the probability of war and the abilities of actors to fulfill their goals.

The behavior of an individual actor depends upon various influences; those unique to the actor shaping his foreign policy include the nature of the domestic political system, his value priorities and goals, available resources (including levels of technology and communications facilities), particular personalities in critical decision-making roles, and organizational procedures. Systemic, or structural, factors also help to shape an individual actor's behavior; their impact varies according to the type of international system, the degree to which the state is "engaged" in the system, and the strength of idiosyncratic and domestic political characteristics in the calculations of decision makers.[1]

Structure affects international political action in two ways: by placing constraints on what an actor can do and by providing opportunities for alternative modes of behavior. Constraints quite simply raise the cost to an actor of using resources for achieving certain objectives. Structure may also offer inducement for action. "Power vacuums," for instance, are considered to attract outside intervention.[2] After its victory over the Spanish in Cuba in 1898, the United States may have been induced by Spanish weakness also to acquire the Philippines. Weak states like Albania and Haiti, however, do manage to maintain their autonomy; inducements clearly involve more complex factors than mere distribution of resources.

Under some conditions the effect of these factors may be largely permissive. Kenneth Waltz has argued that the most salient feature of the international system is the condition of anarchy that allows wars to occur [27]. It is certainly true that the structural features of the international system have consistently made possible a higher level of organized violence among actors than normally exists within nations or integrated political communities.[3] But it is not true that the probability of violence arising from systemic factors remains constant through a succession of different historical systems. Rather, the probability of violence and the degrees to which actors fulfill their goals are partly the functions of particular features of an international structure.

EMERGENT PROPERTIES OF INTERNATIONAL STRUCTURE

The interrelated parts within a system form a whole from which emerges certain properties. The basic elements of structure outlined in Chapter 5—the distribution of resources and attitudes and the coefficients of causality relating one variable to another—provide the information necessary to specify five important systemic properties: distribution of influence, compatibility of goals, number of participant actors, interdependence, and stability.

Distribution of Influence

The resources available to each actor may be investigated in terms of their potential influence. Although influence is multidimensional and often specific to a situation, we shall assume for the purposes of this discussion that the relationship between each pair of actors can be specified in terms of one of three possibilities: independence (no direct influence), asymmetrical interdependence (one actor influences the other), and symmetrical interdependence (two actors are roughly equal in influence). As the influence domains of actors overlap, one of the latter two relationships occurs. In Figure 6.1 state A exercises influence over state B, experiences mutual influence with state C, and has no direct but perhaps some indirect influence over state D.

Influence has been distributed in many different ways throughout history, and each distribution has had implications for the degrees of order and clarity that have emerged. Figure 6.2 illustrates four ideal types of distribution on a continuum from

---

[1] The nature of domestic factors and their relative importance will be discussed in Chapters 7, 8, and 9.

[2] Balance-of-power theorists especially make this claim.

[3] Integration is discussed in Chapter 13.

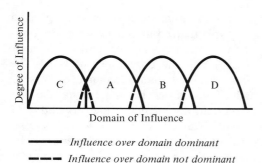

Influence over domain dominant

Influence over domain not dominant

Figure 6.1. Overlapping Domains of Influence of Several Actors

concentration to dispersion of influence. The arrows indicate direction of influence. Not all possible influence paths are shown in the figure: In the hierarchical ordering, actor A might influence actor F directly as well as indirectly, and in the absence of ordering, A and F might also be mutually influential.[4] Ordering is transitive

---

[4] If Figure 6.2 were considered to specify all possible directions of influence, then we would have to conclude that no actual influence relationship between A and F exists, though A must have *potential* influence over F when there is transitivity. See the discussions of influence concentration and status ordering by Steven Brams [4], Bruce M. Russett [20], and J. David Singer and Melvin Small [23, 24]. Specific measures of influence concentration proposed as summary devices have both advantages and disadvantages in representing specific patterns of influence.

when no actor is both dominant over one actor and yet subordinate to some other actor dominated by the former subordinate one.

In hierarchical situations—the Roman Empire, for example—in which one actor dominates the rest, the possibility of enforcing legal codes is high. Because the capacity to influence is relatively clear, hierarchical structure also lessens the probabilities of war. On the other hand, relative parity among actors, as the legal rules of the United Nations Assembly propose, tends to induce conflict because of uncertainty, or limit areas of common action. Parity encourages actors to take limited risks in pursuing goals. Most historical systems resemble the intermediate pyramidal or polyarchical distributions of influence.

Measuring distribution of influence is both important and difficult. One effort, not wholly satisfactory, has been made by J. David Singer in collaboration with Melvin Small. They have sought to measure empirically the concentration of influence resources in international politics from 1816 to 1965. In order to measure distribution, the base resources must first be enumerated and weighted. The equally weighted resources that they have used in their calculations are demographic (total

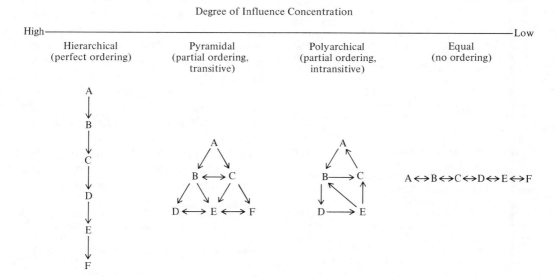

Figure 6.2. Four Ideal Types of Influence Distribution

population, urban population), industrial (energy consumption, iron and steel production), and military (total military expenditures and size of armed forces). Unfortunately, the analysis is limited to between five and eight major powers, thus eliminating considerations of the impact on concentration and overall distribution of the many states that have appeared since 1945. The measure used by Singer and Small is each major actor's average percentage share among major actors of all six variables.[5] We present their findings in Table 6.1 as an example of the ways in which influence concentration can be examined over time. Their measure of concentration ranges from 0.0 (perfect equality) to 1.0 (when one actor has 100 percent of possible influence).[6]

[5] As destructive capacity is associated with the absolute total of resources available to a state, the inclusion of all actors possessing more than a certain threshold level of resources could have yielded a more accurate picture of influence distribution, particularly in the twentieth century. Singer and Small have also emphasized the mere possession of resources, which, as we suggested in Chapter 4, provides at best a partial indicator of influence.

[6] Expanding the number of states in the calculation would not have altered the relative positions reported in Table 6.1, but both the enormous inequalities among actors and the decline in potential influence concentration that have occurred since World War II would have been more dramatically highlighted. Second, Singer and Small have used preservation of peace, measured by the frequency of war from 1816 to 1965, as the variable they wish to explain. Our view is that the actual incidence of war results from multiple and complex causes, including basic structural features and idiosyncratic and accidental factors. For conceptual purposes, the *probability* of war is more satisfying as a dependent variable than is actual incidence. Although probability and incidence are undoubtedly correlated, the effects of war and the terms by which it is ended have important effects both on structural properties and on subsequent probabilities of war that are overlooked when we use incidence of war as the measure. Finally, Singer and Small's work reminds us of the question To measure the distribution of influence, do we include all actors individually or limit their number by aggregation into alliances? For example, it sometimes seems more sensible, in measuring concentration of potential influence, to consider the Warsaw Pact nations as a single unit because their cooperation and coordination make the bloc potentially more influential than does the sum

Two alternative theories are suggested to explain the relation between distribution of resources among actors (states or blocs) and the probability of war.[7] The first, held by many "balance of power" advocates, is that the more equal the distribution, the greater is the probability of peace. The alternative view is that control of a preponderance of resources by one actor or coalition best promotes peace.

Advocates of the "peace through parity" model argue that when resources are evenly matched, inequities and the feelings of relative deprivation that encourage revisionist goals among actors are unlikely. Approximate equality makes the outcome of struggle uncertain, and risks are thus difficult to calculate. Such uncertainty, it is argued, can inhibit aggressive diplomacy [29]. This view of war assumes that structural changes apparently tending toward less equality and the potential emergence of a dominant state or coalition that could upset a "balance of power" encourage war.

The alternative theory is based on "preponderance." It is argued that clear qualitative differences in capabilities reduce the temptations and uncertainties involved in a more symmetrical distribution of resources. The hypothesis is that *weak states will not initiate war because they cannot win, whereas powerful states will not initiate war because they can exercise influence more cheaply by other means.* Furthermore, small changes in very unequal distributions are considered likely to have relatively smaller impacts on the calculations of major statesmen than they would if the distribution were nearly equal. Uncertainty and miscalculation are then less likely to cause war. Preponderance, even in the absence of global community and authoritative organizations, seems less pre-

of the resource potentials possessed by all its members. Answering this question involves another dimension of structural analysis: determining the number of actors in the system. Clearly emergent properties, though analytically distinct, are nevertheless interrelated.

[7] These models are outlined by Singer and Small [23, pp. 5–8].

Table 6.1.

Relative Capability Scores and Concentration Indexes for Major Powers, 1816-1965

Year	Nation	Percentage Share	Year	Nation	Percentage Share
1816	England	42.0	1840	England	35.5
	Russia	25.5		France	22.8
	France	16.5		Russia	19.7
	Austria-Hungary	12.0		Austria-Hungary	13.5
	Prussia	4.5		Prussia	8.7
	Concentration	.33		Concentration	.23
1890	England	29.3	1913	United States	24.8
	Germany	22.0		Germany	18.0
	Russia	17.8		Russia	16.7
	France	15.0		England	14.0
	Austria-Hungary	8.2		France	10.3
	Italy	7.7		Austria-Hungary	6.3
				Italy	5.0
				Japan	4.5
	Concentration	.20		Concentration	.20
1946	United States	52.7	1955	United States	40.5
	U.S.S.R.	26.3		U.S.S.R.	26.0
	England	15.2		China	19.2
	France	6.2		England	8.7
				France	5.8
	Concentration	.42		Concentration	.33

Year	Nation	Percentage Share
1865	England	35.3
	Russia	19.0
	France	18.7
	Prussia	9.7
	Austria-Hungary	9.3
	Italy	7.7
	Concentration	.26
1938	U.S.S.R.	25.3
	United States	23.5
	Germany	18.7
	England	10.0
	Japan	10.0
	France	8.0
	Italy	4.7
	Concentration	.22
1965	United States	36.7
	U.S.S.R.	29.2
	China	22.2
	England	6.8
	France	5.0
	Concentration	.31

Source: We wish to thank J. David Singer for permission to use these data from computer calculations. This research is to appear in J. David Singer, Stuart Bremer, and John Stuckey, "Capability Distribution and the Preservation of Peace in the Major Power Sub-System, 1816-1965," in Bruce M. Russett, ed., *Peace, War and Numbers* (Beverly Hills, Calif.: Sage, 1972).

carious and less likely to furnish inducements to risk war.[8]

The statistical analysis by Singer and Small, based upon historical incidences of war, concentration of resources, and trends in concentration for each historical period, is, by their own admission, far from conclusive. Furthermore, the second dependent variable in political analysis, the satisfaction of actors' goals, has not been considered in their assessment of distribution of influence. To the extent that the limitations, assumptions, and measurement techniques of Singer and Small are reliable, the bivariate relationships between single structural variables and warfare that they report suggest, first, that relative equality or balance is associated with less war in the nineteenth century but with more in the twentieth century. Particularly in this century, the concentration of strategic capabilities has been associated with periods of reduced deaths and duration in international war. Second, changes in distributions of capability, regardless of direction, are associated with more war. This finding accords with our view that important structural change, regardless of its ultimate effects on concentration, increases the probability of war precisely because it is destabilizing. Singer and Small's tentative findings suggest that in the twentieth century clarity of influence potential and the concentration of preponderant potential force tend to act as restraints on decisions to initiate war. As Michael Haas has argued, "Im-

plementation of rules is a function of the degree of concentration of influence within the system, because enforcement capability insures compliance with international rules" [11].

Compatibility of Goals

Attitudes—including expectations, demands, and identifications of both the leaders and the masses within international actors—help to determine the extent to which actors' goals and objectives will conflict. Degree of compatibility among goals is a second emergent property of international structure. In general actors with common cultural traits, similar value priorities, and economies at comparable stages of development tend to formulate similar goals and objectives. The distribution of influence resources has never been the sole determining factor in world structure, despite the central importance accorded to distribution of "power" by many theorists.[9] Equally important has been the distribution of goals among groups, which separates allies from enemies. The desire to increase influence per se does not necessarily generate a goal conflict. Demands for greater influence are seldom made outside the context of other conflicts. Goal conflict exists when actors seek different outcomes. It varies with the intensity with which they pursue those goals and the incompatibility of the related objectives.

In the current international system several goal conflicts divide actors. The first major cluster of issues on which actors' goals conflict involves individual freedom and desirable economic arrangements. This kind of conflict has been at the center of the cold war that took form in 1946–1947. The mission of international communism, as articulated by Soviet

---

[8] It therefore promotes system stability, the fifth emergent property to be considered. When resources are symmetrically distributed, attempts at influence may be more cautious because of uncertainty and the potential costs of their results. An increase in statesmen's efforts to avoid war may thus have led to the complex "balance of power" types of mechanisms that seem, particularly in the nineteenth century, to have reduced the consequences of war. In this instance, however, the effect of structure was to make the situation *appear* precarious, so that mechanisms for reducing uncertainty and reassuring each side that aggressive actions would be countered were encouraged. The inducements toward war in the structure were countered by delicate social mechanisms invented by nineteenth-century statesmen with many shared views.

[9] Bruce M. Russett [21, p. 4], for instance, has stated that the bipolar international system after World War II was produced by the concentration of resources in two powerful states. Kenneth Waltz [26, p. 312 *n.*] defines "structure" as "the pattern according to which power is distributed."

leaders, was the expansion of socialist, or communist, leadership to all nations. The accuracy of Soviet theories about the relationship between politics and economics and the forces behind behavior of "capitalist" states, as well as of their predictions based on communist ideology, is irrelevant to the fact that the goals of the international communist leadership were in sharp conflict with those of American and western European leaders. The perception of threat by both sides escalated as each used force and threat to oppose the other. Because of the paramount positions of the United States and the Soviet Union, especially in relation to those of other European states, China, and Japan, this conflict has remained the most important single dimension of cleavage in international politics.

Since the de facto acceptance by Western leadership of Soviet control in eastern Europe, reflected in Western passivity during the Hungarian uprising in 1956 and the Russian invasion of Czechoslovakia in 1968, the behavior of the United States and the Soviet Union has indicated an irregular decline in the comparative importance of this goal conflict. Nonaligned states have increasingly pursued independent policies without fear of actively negative responses from the two major conflicting blocs. Other submerged conflicts, both global and regional in nature, have emerged to prominence and have absorbed greater attention and commitment of resources.

A second major focus of goal conflict in the international system is economic differences; the resources of poor states—such as oil, tin, and foodstuffs—are largely extracted and enjoyed by the relatively industrialized states. As a result of existing economic arrangements, many industrialized states support highly urbanized populations by exploiting resource bases extending far beyond their own political frontiers. Under these circumstances, the poorer states are almost all pursuing the goals of economic development and industrialization so that their own societies may enjoy the fruits of modern technology

and increase their productivity. Recent studies have tended to interpret the continuing economic gap less as a consequence of the poor states' late start in industrialization than of the modes of production imposed upon them, particularly in Asia and Africa, by colonial conquest and of the economic arrangements currently imposed by foreign political and economic elites. André Frank and others have argued that the low per capita incomes of these states and the fact that they began to industrialize only in the mid-twentieth century result from exploitation by European and North American colonial powers. These writers claim that despite the political independence, which is generally of long standing in Latin America, the prevailing international economic arrangements are widening the gap between the living standards enjoyed in the mass-consumption economies of the North Atlantic area and the Soviet Union, on one hand, and the less developed economies of the "third world" [8, 2]. To achieve the objective of maintaining high levels of resource consumption and economic growth, the states to develop first created dependent economies, whose gradual "underdevelopment" made them reliable suppliers of natural resources. Imports are thus important inputs in the productive system of industrialized states. Furthermore, such resources are considered "free" goods, for which the purchaser pays only the expenses of extraction plus some "rent" to the legal owner, whether it be a domestic titleholder or a foreign government. Rents are generally based on fluctuating market conditions and international bargaining. Political arrangements, enforced by treaties and government policies designed to protect the economic interest at stake, perpetuate this situation.

Some of the consequences of permitting private, or "particularized," interests to have "free" access to seas, airways, and waterways as part of the production process have recently become apparent. Various states are beginning to question the wisdom of treating the extraction, depletion, or pollution of natural resources like petroleum, air, and water as essentially free. Strong economic interests, however, seek to maintain the largely capitalist structure of the international economy.

International economic exploitation has existed among socialist states as well. After World War II the Soviet Union entered into highly inequitable economic relationships with the countries of eastern Europe and later with China. It expropriated industrial goods and machinery from countries like Germany, Hungary, and Rumania for its own use. In addition, in eastern Europe and China it set up "joint companies" under its own control, in order to exploit the natural resources of those areas. Even after the abolition of such companies in the 1950s, the U.S.S.R. continued to control the pattern of economic development in many states through joint economic arrangements. Only recently, particularly since 1965, have certain eastern European states, notably Rumania, sought some measure of economic independence.

A third, somewhat less salient, global conflict revolves around the question of supranationalism. Many small states have sought international collaboration to deal with problems like economic development with which they cannot cope independently. Indeed, in many states, including developed ones, portions of the populations have perceived self-help as inadequate to secure goals or enforce international norms. The small states and their supporters have tried to achieve such international cooperation partly by surrendering some authority to functional bodies like the World Health Organization and to organizations like the United Nations General Assembly in which decisions are based on one-state, one-vote majoritarianism.

The third-world states seek to maximize their autonomy, to develop their own economies, and to defend their political and economic structures from intrusions especially by the great powers. But they are also prone to support supranational institutions, partly to pursue "de-

fensive" goals more effectively and partly to achieve redistribution of the world's wealth. In the late 1950s, for example, the "underdeveloped" countries sought in vain to establish a Special United Nations Fund for Economic Development (SUNFED), which would control large amounts of capital from which grants for development projects would be given on the basis of need. It was argued that the developed states should contribute SUNFED's capital at the rate of 1 percent of their respective gross national products, a percentage that exceeds the foreign-aid expenditures of most countries. The project was defeated, however, by the developed countries, primarily the United States, which exercised a "financial" veto [25].

International organizations could, if invested with authority, provide a decision-making arena in which the probabilities of goal fulfillment for poorer states would be enhanced. Supranationalism is also supported by certain groups in industrialized states that have sought to empower organizations like the United Nations to defend the status quo and prevent war. But willingness of most states themselves to relinquish the right to act unilaterally has always been very small. Although every national actor pays lip service to the goal of maintaining peace, a peace that perpetuates current economic, political, and social structures may be directly opposed to certain supranationalist aims, notably those of underdeveloped and revisionist states like China. Supranationalism is thus an issue on which actors have less consistent views than they have on the two issues described above. Proposals involving increased authority for international decision-making bodies are viewed differently in relation to different questions by the same actor. Although in many states there is some support for supranationalism on questions ranging from international narcotic controls to regional economic integration, this support fluctuates depending upon the question. General willingness to grant greater authority to supranational bodies is shared by only a thin stratum of the population in many states and by occasional leaders.

Certain states are likely to support specific proposals calling for only modest increments in the authority of an international organization, particularly a functional organization that might regulate international economic transactions or mediate conflict in regional disputes [1]. Nevertheless, self-help and bilateralism characterize the policies of most states, international businesses, and conservative institutions like the Roman Catholic Church. Supranationalism may, however, become increasingly important if interdependence in international structure or the probability of war increase.

There are other goal conflicts in international politics. The most important of them are regional in scope, however. Occasionally they become internationalized when a global conflict is superimposed on them. The internationalization of a regional conflict may result largely from the choices and perceptions of decision makers in the major powers, rather than from structural conditions. American and Soviet involvement in Southeast Asia illustrate this point. The legacy of colonialism included both "imitative" and "revolutionary" elites in the new states of Asia. Their ideals of domestic politics and economic development are in sharp conflict. Such conflict may be internationalized when these elites invoke cold-war ideology and rhetoric in attempts to defend their domestic political positions and to secure assistance from the great powers. Initial commitments by major powers and their misunderstandings may lead to heavy involvement in local contests. Once one participant in the global ideological conflict becomes involved in a regional conflict, the conflict is internationalized, and there is enormous pressure on the other side to intervene as well.[10] The conflict between Israel and the Arab states illustrates such internationalization. After 1955

the United States and the Soviet Union increasingly aligned themselves with local "pawns," which they committed themselves to defend and support with military and economic assistance.[11]

Many regional goal conflicts do not become internationalized. For example, the neighboring states of Kenya and Tanzania were in conflict over goals in the 1960s without attracting major external intervention. Kenya chose a capitalist mode of development, whereas Tanzania preferred a form of socialism adapted to its underdeveloped rural economy. This divergence was manifested in voting differences in the United Nations and the Organization of African Unity (OAU). Tanzania became one of China's closest friends in Africa, whereas Kenya forged strong ties with the United States and maintained close relations with Great Britain. Partly because their differences did not lead to territorial conflict or threaten the leadership of either state, the temptation to internationalize the regional goal conflict was minimal.

The intensity of goal conflict is reflected in the degree to which it is permitted to damage other relations. When a goal conflict between two actors is particularly bitter, it probably will affect other structural characteristics like trade flows. On the other hand, many goal conflicts remain limited and are not allowed to disrupt the relations of actors in all areas. After 1947 the ideological split between the United States and the U.S.S.R. affected all areas of their relations. Indeed, even the interest of one power in an issue was often stimulated only by the apparent interest of the adversary. After the death of Joseph Stalin in 1953, however, the Soviet-American conflict was moderated to the point at which the two nations could vie with each other over issues like domination of the Middle East while cooperating on other issues like arms control. Similarly, although the black African states have verbally attacked South Africa because of its racial policies,

[10] For a thorough discussion of intervention, see *Journal of International Affairs,* vol. 22 (1968), which is entirely devoted to this question.

[11] For a discussion of the concept of "pawn," see Bruce M. Russett [19].

Table 6.2.

The Countinuity of Issues in the General Assembly

Factor	Percentage of Variance				
	1947	*1952*	*1957*	*1961*	*1963*
Cold war	31	9	23	15	21
Self-determination*	-	24	23	32	4
Intervention in Africa	6	10	10	-	19
Supranationalism	10	12	7	12	18
Palestine and the Middle East	11	10	-	11	4
Total	59	64	62	70	66

*Included in the cold-war category in 1947 only.

Source: Bruce M. Russett, *International Regions and the International System,* © 1967 by Rand McNally & Company, Chicago, Table 4.2, p. 67.

several (Zambia and Lesotho, for example) have maintained economic relations with the South African regime for practical reasons. The ideological fervor over race in some third-world states does not extend across the broad range of international transactions especially trade.[12]

If data on the attitudes of relevant national groups were available, we might compile a list of variables related to 50 to 100 potential issue areas from which a relatively small number of common underlying dimensions, or factors, of goal conflict could be derived by statistical analysis. Such data unfortunately do not exist. Voting in the United Nations has, however, been used to analyze dimensions of conflict in international politics; in trying to obtain an accurate picture of international goal conflicts and their relative salience, however, United Nations votes have several drawbacks. First, the issues debated in the United Nations do not represent the full range of questions that stimulate international conflict. The Vietnam War, for instance, has received relatively little attention in General Assembly vot-

ing. Second, certain important actors—notably the two Germanys—are not represented in the General Assembly. Third, the choice of which votes to analyze and their relative importance is dependent upon the subjective judgment of the investigator.[13] Despite these limitations, however, United Nations voting may provide the best objective data currently available for determining goals and objectives.

Recent studies have consistently revealed underlying voting alignments in the United Nations from 1947 to 1963 that correspond to the goal conflicts already discussed. Table 6.2 represents the percentages of variance in voting accounted for by certain major issue conflicts in successive sessions of the General Assembly. Although there are flaws in this kind of analysis, as we have noted, the continuity of these issues over time supports the assumption of an underlying regularity in these issue areas, despite idiosyncratic or cyclical attention in the Assembly to specific issues in specific years.

[12] Data on trade and communications clearly reflect the ideologically imposed boundaries between eastern and western states in Europe. Although some African states have ended trade with South Africa at some cost, others have not translated their goal conflict into economic isolationism; landlocked Malawi, owing to its dependence for goods and transport, has pursued an aberrant set of goals in comparison to those of other black African states by its friendliness with South Africa [3].

[13] Representatives of states are not asked about the objectives and goals of their states, which are presumably expressed in the votes themselves—though in many instances the particular language of a proposal, rather than its substance, affects the outcome. Russett is aware of the problem of whether every vote is of equal importance and has sought to use amounts of discussion on the floor as a weighting device. See Russett, *International Regions and the International System* (Chicago: Rand McNally, 1967), pp. 59–93.

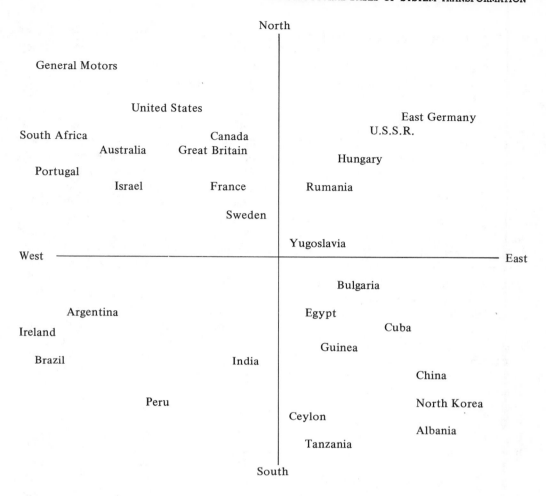

North

Goals: to maintain positions of influence (the status quo) and economic growth.
Resources: great, including industrialized economies and high GNP per capita.
South

Goals: economic growth, reduction of foreign domination.
Resources: few, because of poor, underdeveloped agricultural economies.
East

Goals: socialist economies, party rule of collectivist states.
Resources: communist or socialist ideologies, one-party rule (regimes that mobilize and control society).
West

Goals: capitalist and welfare economies, "liberal" democratic procedures.
Resources: liberal ideologies, pluralist systems with economic power.

Figure 6.3. Estimated Positions of Selected Actors on North-South and East-West Issues

Because of potential distortions in analyzing actual United Nations voting data to discover major conflicts, we prefer to map the positions of national actors in the first two goal conflicts that we have identified in this chapter. Figure 6.3 represents a set of descriptive hypotheses showing the positions at which we expect major actors in international politics would be found if a relatively complete set of data on actors' goals were available and submitted to dimensional analysis of some form (e.g. multidimensional scaling). The two major conflicts, over the cold war and economic development, can be expressed as "east-west" and "north-south" dimensions.

At the extreme western pole we find

actors claiming to support capitalism and opposed to most forms of collectivism and social planning. The opposite end of the continuum is communism and socialism. The attitudes of those at both poles have certain common emotive qualities, and are, in fact, "mirror images" of each other. Actors at each polar extreme pursue policies and objectives designed to increase the number of adherents to their ideology and opponents of that at the opposite pole.

The "north-south" continuum represents the conflict between rich and poor actors. In general, northern actors seek to perpetuate current international economic distributions and to maintain their own economic growth. Their objective is fundamentally to maintain the status quo through policies of adjustment, increases in trade, and containment of revolutionary forces. Both the United States and the Soviet Union have opposed revolutionary change in their major spheres of influence—Latin America and eastern Europe respectively. Poor states, on the other hand, tend to pursue "populist" goals and have revisionist objectives.

The distances between actors on this two-dimensional plot represent the degrees of divergence between the goals. They are not precise but reflect crude judgments of the proximity and compatibility of actors' goals. Conflict among goals does not, however, necessarily lead to physical conflict. Even though their goals for the system as a whole are opposed, two states with few resources or geographically very distant from each other will probably not become involved in physical conflict. For example, Albania and the United States have very divergent goals, yet the possibility of war between them is minimized by other structural characteristics—in particular, the marked superiority of the United States in resources and the low involvement of Albania in transactions that affect the United States.

The distances between the poles of these two continua, and of others, may change with time. The east-west ideological split, for example, has declined in

importance since 1953. During part of Dwight D. Eisenhower's presidency (1955–1956) and more consistently after the Cuban missile crisis of 1962, policies of détente and reconciliation have characterized the mutual relations of the United States and the Soviet Union. Increasing awareness of the mutual interests of the leading adversaries in the east-west conflict and the growing importance of other goals unrelated to ideological differences have lessened the salience of the conflict. Problems posed by the threat of nuclear warfare, domestic unrest, rapid population growth, increasing scarcity of certain resources, space exploration, and pollution are nonideological issues that have reduced some of the fervor of the east-west conflict. Indeed "true believers" in either the capitalist or communist "way of life" hold fewer responsible positions in the governments of major states than they did during the period of intense cold-war hostility.[14]

In contrast, awareness of disparities and inequities in the distribution of resources has increased by means of expanded world communications and diffusion of world culture; it could intensify the salience of the north-south cleavage, increasing the incompatibility of goals along this dimension. Future world structure may thus include alliances of industrialized states to protect their interests against attempts by poor states to force redistribution of resources. Ideological attacks by the People's Republic of China on the alleged collusion between the Soviet Union and the United States have, in fact, been based on an expectation that tacit coalitions among industrial states have begun to form.

Number of Participant Actors

The number of participant actors is a third property of international systems that is likely to affect the probability of

[14] For a discussion of the power of ideology to absorb the attention of people and to influence their interpretations of wide ranges of activities, see Eric Hoffer, *The True Believer* (New York: Harper & Row, 1951).

war and the success of goal fulfillment. When only two major blocs exist, polarization greatly reduces the autonomy of other actors, at least in periods of high tension. As it weakens—either through a proliferation of conflicts that cut across it or a reduction in the incompatibility of objectives—pressures uniting groups of actors into blocs may decline. A decrease in concentration of resources may also lead to fragmentation of blocs. Richard Brody found, in simulation studies of the effects of the spread of nuclear weapons to more states, that bloc cohesion declined as second and third members of each bloc acquired nuclear capability [5].

The number of independent actors is likely to increase as the distribution of resources for influence becomes more nearly equal. The increased capabilities of indigenous elites in many Asian and African states help to explain how many new actors have been able to achieve formal political independence. The enormous superiority in influence enjoyed by European nation-states at the height of colonialism in the nineteenth century eroded to the point at which the costs to Great Britain, France, and Belgium of maintaining formal hegemony over colonial areas increased rapidly. Unsuccessful French efforts to maintain domination first in Indochina and later in Algeria revealed this altered situation. Although colonies might not have been able to defeat their "mother countries," they could make the costs of political control prohibitive and thus "win" their independence. In addition, as goals become differentiated on a variety of dimensions, the number of individual actors, blocs, and alliances is also likely to increase.

There are two conflicting theories about the impact of the number of actors on the probabilities of war. The first theory maintains that when only two major states or aggregates of actors exist, the probability of major war is less. A small number of actors tends to "politicize" a wide range of foreign-policy considerations and to focus attention on the "conflict periphery" separating the adversaries. As a result, it is argued, there is a tendency toward care-

ful maintenance of the status quo and a great deal of pressure on "neutral" states or bloc members that deviate. Furthermore, a small number of actors limits the possible number of contests that can occur in international politics, concentrates attention on those possibilities, and mobilizes the energy of participants to avoid major confrontations through small-scale probing, testing of peripheries, and management of crises [28].

The opposite point of view has been propounded by Deutsch and Singer, who have argued that a larger number of actors enhances the possibilities for conflicts cutting across one another, thus shuffling friends and enemies on different issues, so that no large-scale commitment of resources to any particular bilateral conflict is likely. "Every nation's needs and supplies differ, and the more nations there are, the greater will be the number and diversity of trade-offs available to the total system" [6, p. 318]. A large number of actors not only increases the complexity of the system but also causes uncertainty about the possible source and location of conflict. Indeed, when there are more actors, there are more potential bilateral conflicts. Uncertainty about which actor poses a greater threat increases a state's insecurity and reduces the perceived threat from any single potential adversary.

Deutsch and Singer have also argued that an increase in the number of important actors will lead to a decline in the attention that each actor can pay to any one other actor. Although the distribution of attention would vary with the perceived salience of the behavior of other actors (a product of factors like their sizes and capabilities), nevertheless the amount of attention paid to any one autonomous actor would be less. They have argued further that the escalation of conflict between two actors requires that each devote a relatively high degree of attention (between 10 and 15 percent of the total attention of foreign-policy makers) to each adversary. Attentiveness leads to oversensitivity to minor moves, thus escalating the conflict with each response, as in an arms race. In a system of many important actors, one actor's attention to the behavior of any single adversary would not be likely to reach this point. Furthermore, if many actors possessed substantial capabilities, it would be possible to form various temporary coalitions and alliances, thus reducing the necessity for any single actor to increase his own armaments and participate in an arms race.

Unfortunately, this argument is based partly on an untested assumption: that some minimum percentage of an actor's attention is required before he will engage in behavior leading to armed conflict. Indeed, the opposite argument could also be made: Attention to the needs and concerns of another actor may promote harmony and even integration of political units.[15] Attention in itself does not make armed conflict more likely; it simply permits actors to be more responsive to one another's interests and actions. Whether this responsiveness leads to closer, more harmonious relations or to escalation of conflict is a function of the experience of the participants' historical interactions.

Furthermore, the idea that a large number of actors would somehow diminish the capacity of an actor to pay much attention to particular other actors seems improbable. National states with large, complex foreign offices have greater bureaucratic resources than do small states, as well as special divisions charged with attention to different parts of the world. A small state like Tanzania or Ceylon, on the other hand, has only a handful of personnel involved in political decision making. These officials tend to devote relatively large portions of their attention to important donors like the United States and the Soviet Union and important neighbors like Kenya and India respectively. The United States and the Soviet Union, with large and complex bureaucracies, may, on the other hand, focus

only small fractions of their attention on marginal actors like Tanzania and Ceylon, but the attentive capacity of even these small units—and their abilities both to perceive and to respond to the foreign policies of other states—may be greater in absolute terms than are the total capacities of many small states.

In considering the effects of the number of actors in a system, it is important to distinguish between major wars and small local conflicts. When polarization and concentration of influence reduce the number of effective actors, war is likely to spread and involve the two blocs entirely; small peripheral wars tend to be discounted or viewed as preparatory to a major contest. In a system with many autonomous actors, each with independent capabilities for influence and with individual interests and goals, the *possibilities* for war are greater, but the *probability* of major conflict seems less.[16] Although the probability of war in a more diffuse system seems higher, the wars themselves may be less threatening to the stability of the system or to the goal fulfillment of actors.

These two situations—interaction of many actors and of only two—are somewhat analogous to two situations in traffic control. At rush hour crowded conditions increase the likelihood of collisions, particularly minor "fender benders." But, when two trucks loaded with explosives approach a narrow bridge from opposite directions, there is only one possibility for a collision, the consequences of which, however, would be far greater than those of any number of minor collisions. Presumably, only a very stubborn or foolish truck driver would permit such a collision, but the structural features of the situation make the event possible.

In considering the number of actors in a system and the structural propensity for war, we need not count those units that inevitably or usually follow the lead of other actors. An alliance or bloc whose

[15] Ironically, Karl W. Deutsch is a prominent advocate of this view as well; see Deutsch, *Political Community and the North Atlantic Area: International Organization in the Light of Historical Experience* (Princeton: Princeton University Press, 1957).

[16] If many of the actors possessed nuclear weapons, however, the probability of major wars would increase sharply [18, 12].

members behave as a unit, with no independent choices, can therefore be counted as a single actor. In considering the probabilities of war in the international system of 1946–1956, we can therefore reduce the number of actors to two—the Western and Eastern blocs—because the members of those groups tended to follow the lead of the United States and the U.S.S.R. respectively.[17] Furthermore, when the behavior of states or organizations has no discernible impact on major goal conflicts or the behavior of influential actors, these bodies may also be safely excluded from macroanalysis. In macroanalysis of the probability of war, we may therefore ignore such states as Chad, Botswana, Bhutan, and Nepal without the loss of important information.[18]

The effect of the number of actors on goal satisfaction has not been mentioned. Very little research has been done on this question. In the history of international affairs, instances of increasing and decreasing political autonomy in pursuit of goals can be found; Austria-Hungary, Korea, and Pakistan split; Italy, Yugoslavia, and the United States came together. In many respects the most suitable size and diversity of an actor will depend on the interdependence involved in reaching his goals. We may agree that traffic regulation in small towns is best handled by town councils, but can we agree on how many actors can best handle atomic energy, warfare, pollution, and other problems affecting the values and goals of modern society? Efficiency and the extent of human involvement should determine the number of actors best suited to deliver political goods to the world's population. Although such rational criteria do seem to shape the number and diversity of goal-seeking actors, there is consider-

able lag in adjusting the existence and form of actors to the goals demanded by global society.

Interdependence

The fourth emergent property of structure is systemic interdependence, the degree to which the behavior of each actor is dependent upon the behavior of other actors in the system. We may imagine interdependence as a continuum along which the relationship of a single actor with the remainder of the system can be represented. At one extreme would be actors who exist in isolation; at the other extreme would be actors who are fully integrated into the system, as subnational political units are integrated into effective national states. There are three aspects of interdependence: interlocking fates, the rapidity of consequences, and the nature of the relationship between superior and subordinate.

Interlocking Fates. When actors have interlocking fates, their decisions have mutual impact, determined by two structural variables: the range and intensity of transactions between them and the potential consequences of shifts in the patterns of these transactions. Levels of trade and flows of communications provide basic information on the degree to which an actor is interconnected with the rest of the system.[19] A large number of transactions, either in absolute terms or in proportion to actors' overall economic or social activity, is not in itself an indication of strongly linked fates, however. We must also consider the impact that changes in the patterns of transactions would have. For example, the high rate of transactions between the United States and Great Britain—including travel, communications, and trade, as well as joint membership in various intergovernmental organizations—does not alone indicate the degree to which the two states are interdependent. We have to know in addition the probable costs to either state

[17] Bloc members, or "followers," may act independently of "leaders" in other ranges of activity. Distinguishing these ranges would be important for microanalysis, but they can be ignored within our present "macro" perspective.

[18] The role played by organizations like the United Nations and international corporations can be important under certain circumstances, particularly in certain issue areas. The roles of such actors are explored more fully in Chapters 10 and 11.

[19] Flows of communications can be measured by exchanges of mail, newspapers, books, films, and so forth; the measures can be weighted for the political salience of the messages.

of giving up some or all of these transactions. If they were able to cease trading
with one another and readily able to substitute other trading partners like Germany
and Japan at little cost, they would not be
economically interdependent, despite the
high level of trade between them. If, on the
other hand, finding substitute trading
partners would result in severe economic
dislocations in both countries, they could
be said to exhibit a relatively high level
of economic interdependence. If the policy
choices of one state have a major impact
on the well-being of a second state, the
latter is at least partly dependent upon
the former. If both depend upon each
other, their fates are interlocked.

When an actor's fate is interlocked with
those of other actors either within a region
or in the system as a whole, then the
actor is *engaged*. Policies of isolation like
those that the United States pursued after
the American Revolution and that China
followed during the 1960s represent deliberate attempts to withdraw from the
international system. Actors who are dependent upon others for the achievement
of goals are highly engaged in the system.[20] The impact of the system upon its
various parts is thus determined by the
interdependencies among actors.[21]

Rapidity of Consequences. A second aspect of interdependence is the rapidity
with which consequences occur. As we
noted in Chapter 5, there have been rapid
increases in the speed with which people,
goods, services, information, and weapons
can be moved about the globe. As a result the rapidity with which the consequences of one actor's policies are felt by
others has also increased. Furthermore,

as the domestic economic, social, and political affairs of each actor become more
highly integrated, any international action
that affects one element of a society may
spread its effects throughout the society
more quickly and to a greater extent than
it previously would have done. For example, owing to the high level to which
British society is integrated, an international action like the cancellation of foreign orders to construct ships in the ship-
yards of the Upper Clyde in Scotland
will *quickly* have an impact on other aspects of British society; as unemployment
grows marginally, welfare payments will
increase, national productivity will decline, the balance of payments will
worsen, and even political unrest will increase.

Superior and Subordinate. A third question related to interdependence among
actors is whether their interdependence
is asymmetrical or relatively equal. In the
first instance, one actor may be relatively
dependent upon the other; in the second,
both actors are equally dependent upon
each other. During various historical periods some actors have operated in virtual
isolation from one another; then no interdependence and no influence relationship
have existed. In the contemporary international system, however, there is potential influence among virtually all actors.
In many instances, the occurrence of few
or no transactions suggests that no influence is being exercised; the concentration
of resources represents only influence potential. That is, dependent relationships,
mutual or otherwise, do not exist. Transactions and the effects of shifts in them
are important in clarifying existing influence relationships among actors.

In analyzing dependent relationships,
we can specify the *degree* of dependence,
its *direction*, and its *form*. In analyzing
Mexican-American relations, for example,
we would want to know the extent to
which events in Mexico depend upon
American political, economic, and social
decisions. We would also want to know
whether American behavior inhibits or
assists Mexico in achieving its goals. In-

[20] Morton Kaplan meant much the same
when he wrote: "The political system is dominant over its subsystems to the extent that the
essential rules of the political system act as
parametric 'givens' for any single subsystem. A
subsystem becomes dominant to the extent that
the essential rules of the system cannot be
treated as parametric givens for that subsystem" [13, p. 16].

[21] This point is related to the nature of policy
formation by different actors as discussed in
Chapters 7–9 and the possibilities for system
growth and development as discussed in Chapter 13.

deed, it is frequently unclear whether the political and economic policies of wealthy states have positive or deleterious impacts on the abilities of "underdeveloped" states to fulfill their goals. Although the United States is a source of considerable capital for Mexico, it has also been viewed as an exploiter. Some Mexican policies, like nationalization of the petroleum industry in the 1930s, have had the objective of reducing the perceived negative consequences for national goals of economic dependence.

Dependence can take several forms, direct or indirect. Reliance upon another country for an economic market might be one form, particularly when alternative markets are not easily available. States that depend heavily upon the earnings from exports of a single major crop— Brazilian coffee, Cuban sugar, Tanzanian sisal—are particularly vulnerable to this form of dependence.[22] Dependence may also take the form of foreign control of various sectors of a nation's economy. Indeed, in France affiliates of American-based multinational corporations are prevented by *American laws* from trading with certain "hostile" states, and their sale of certain strategic products may even require the approval of the American government.[23] Other forms of dependence include reliance on foreign technicians or scientific information, the need for critical replacement parts for important weapons systems or industrial equipment, and so forth.[24] Finally, dependence may be created through overt or covert support of political or military factions within a country [22]. In general, for countries that are dependent, we expect this to intensify willingness to use force (to gain

independence) and to reduce the actor's ability to secure goals.

Stability

Stability is the fifth emergent property of international structure: It is the ability of other structural features to maintain themselves over time. A system is relatively stable when small changes in concentrations of influence capabilities or marginal alterations in actors' goals do not greatly affect the degrees of interdependence or the number of participants in a system. Stability depends upon internal properties of many of the actors, so that a system in which the goals of an important actor are subject to broad shifts, as in the Soviet Union between 1917 and 1919 and in Germany between 1933 and 1939, tends to be less stable.

Stability is also frequently linked with low probability or absence of war. From the point of view of an individual actor seeking to preserve his territorial jurisdiction and his economic and social functioning, instability seems closely linked with the probability of engagement in a major war that could threaten survival. From the systemic point of view, however, warfare may or may not be destabilizing. Unfortunately, definitions of stability often include *both* pattern maintenance and the absence of warfare, thus creating confusion in the use of the term. For example, Deutsch and Singer have remarked, "From the broader, or systemic, point of view, we shall define stability as the probability that the system retains all of its essential characteristics; that no single nation becomes dominant; that most of its members can continue to survive; and that large-scale war does not occur" [6, p. 315].[25] It is the maintenance of interna-

---

[22] Many third-world states have deliberately sought to diversify their economies and to establish alternative markets in order to avoid dependence upon the fluctuating conditions of a single market for their products.

[23] Robert Gilpin [9] has noted that the French government has been unable to purchase powerful computers needed in the production of nuclear facilities.

[24] Since the 1967 Arab-Israeli War, Israel has sought to acquire the means for constructing the Mystère jet fighter to escape dependence upon France for replacement parts or new aircraft.

[25] As, by definition, certain major wars would drastically alter international structure, such wars can be assumed to be destabilizing. What is necessary, however, is a definition that describes the boundaries within which variation can occur without violating conditions of stability. Waltz's formulations of structure and stability, though highly simplified and redundant in reference to massive warfare, come closest to the notion of stability that we propose. By "stability" Waltz means "the perpetuation of that structure without the occurrence of grossly destructive violence" [26, p. 312].

tional structure with no changes sufficient to alter the basic pattern of emergent properties—concentration of influence, nature of goal conflict, number of participants, and interdependence—that ensures stability.

Stability is most upset by rapid growth or decline in the resource capabilities of major actors. Such changes lead to reshaping of potential influence relationships among actors. It is less a question of whether or not capabilities are equally distributed than of whether or not actors *perceive* sudden changes in distribution that will enhance or reduce their relative status.

Changes in actors' goals can also affect stability. A decline in the intensity of goal conflict or a shift in goals that reduces incompatibility may lead to the creation of dominant coalitions that promote peace.[26] Such coalitions may be destabilizing initially, but if they are durable, they can enhance systemic stability. Indeed, they may lead to the institutionalization of international organizations and the transfer of authority to supranational agencies, particularly as supranationalism emerges as a more salient goal of national states. Goal shifts leading to greater incompatibility are also destabilizing. The probability of war increases, and major conflict may alter the concentration of influence, the relative statuses of participant actors, the goals of regimes, and the number of actors in the system. Such alterations were apparent after 1918 and again after 1945. The speed with which goals change is partly a function of long-term trends in the international environment and in respective national environments and of the stability enjoyed by local regimes.

As a structural property stability is essentially a *propensity*. To return to the analogy used in Chapter 5, a building may stand for many years until a strong wind knocks it over. It has not suddenly become unstable; rather, it has become gradually less stable as the relationships among its parts have changed. A stable interna-

tional structure will adapt to environmental trends in technology, population, and so forth, preserving the basic properties of the system.

Depending upon the system, war, as we have suggested, may or may not indicate instability. The small wars of the eighteenth century were viewed as stabilizing mechanisms by which the then "balance of power" could be adjusted. By contrast, the two twentieth-century world wars accelerated structural changes. After World War I actors like Austria-Hungary and the Turkish Empire disappeared, and new ones emerged. A new, hierarchical pattern of influence distribution appeared, in which states organized to prevent the recurrence of war. Finally, the internal goals and organizations of several states were drastically altered. In Russia an oligarchy with a revisionist ideology seized power. In Germany the imperial government was replaced by a tenuous constitutional democracy. Stability, then, tends to promise a less violent system, but also one in which change or expansion of goals will be more difficult.

FIVE MODELS OF INTERNATIONAL STRUCTURE

Various models of international structure have been suggested. We have chosen to discuss the emergent properties of five models that reflect the characteristics of real systems in simplified and aggregate form.

Unipolar Structure

A unipolar structure is characterized by low goal conflict among only a few leading actors, a hierarchical concentration of resources, high interdependence, and stability. Historically, unipolar systems have been nonviolent. For example, the Bismarckian period in Europe from 1871 to 1890 "was largely dominated by a single Power and a single intellect. . . . Germany was powerful enough to force peace down the throats of recalcitrant Powers, and Bismarck was not above doing so" [17].

---

[26] The American-Soviet détente may reflect the growth of such a preponderant coalition.

Ernst Haas has identified two periods of unipolarity immediately after the two great wars of the twentieth century [10, pp. 29–30]. In each of these periods the goal of building supranational institutions was prominent, and major war was improbable. Unipolarity is a consequence of the reduction of goal tension among major actors to a minimum or the emergence of one actor or coalition that is able to dominate all others.

Bipolar Structure

Bipolarity is characterized by a single dominant goal conflict, concentration of influence in two actors or blocs, and a high degree of interdependence. The dominant conflict exerts pressure on all actors to gravitate toward one or the other pole. Such structures can be either tight or loose. In tight bipolarity virtually all actors are members of the two blocs, and deviants are not tolerated. Between 1947 and 1956 a pattern of tight bipolarity existed; the leading spokesmen of both blocs, men like Stalin and John Foster Dulles, sharply criticized states that sought to remain neutral in the east-west conflict. Indeed, the bipolar mentality is illustrated by Nikita Khrushchev's description of his attempt to persuade neutralist Yugoslavia to rejoin the Soviet bloc in June 1956.

I could not quite understand Comrade Tito's attitude to the socialist camp. I said this to him, "You are a socialist state too, so why don't you join our camp?" But Comrade Tito kept saying no, he did not want to join. When I asked him, "Well, all right, you don't want to join the socialist camp, so where do you belong—surely not in the capitalist camp?" Comrade Tito said no, he did not, but he did not want to belong to the socialist camp either. He did not want to be in any camp. But how can he say that—he must belong somewhere. [31]

During this period formal alliances bound more than forty states in a series of Western defense pacts, including the Southeast Asia Treaty Organization, the North Atlantic Treaty Organization, and the Baghdad Pact. The high salience of the east-west conflict and the extraordinary concentration of resources around the poles of this single dimension were major features of the system's structure [13, pp. 43–45].

In contrast, "the loose bipolar system is characterized by the presence of two major bloc actors, a leading national actor within each bloc, non-member national actors, and universal actors, all of whom perform unique and distinctive role functions within the system" [13, p. 39]. Such a system emerged after 1956 and remained the dominant structural feature until the end of 1962.

Bipolarity tends to promote tension by fostering reciprocal suspicion of adversaries and stimulating efforts to increase military strength by means of internal efforts and defensive alliances. The structure encourages decision makers to try to balance the resources of conflicting actors and blocs. Minor structural changes are closely scrutinized by both sides, and peripheries are defended with resources exceeding the resource values of the contested areas to the dominant actors in the coalitions.

Multipolar Structure

A multipolar structure is characterized by several major goal conflicts, several major actors or coalitions, and several concentrations of influence arranged in pyramidal, polyarchical, or equalitarian form. Stability is variable, and there are wider ranges of interdependence than in other systems. Several actors may adjust their alignments in order to perpetuate an existing distribution of resources. Except when trends like rapid industrialization and increased organizational capability create major changes in the relative resource positions of one or more actors, the system is likely to be transformed only when one issue becomes dominant. In the eighteenth and nineteenth centuries multipolarity was preserved by the mechanisms of balance-of-power politics, including small wars and shifting coalitions.

Current trends, as illustrated by the goal conflicts depicted in Table 6.3, sug-

Table 6.3.
*Historical International Systems**

Period	Type of Structure	Capabilities of Concentration	Goal Conflict	Number of Participant Actors	Interdependence	Stability	Probability of War	Goal Fulfillment	Methods of Actors
			Emergent Properties					Dependent Variables	
1648-1789	multipolar	low	low	nation states formed, nonnational actors declining	minimal	high	medium	high	compensation, limited war, bilateral diplomacy, treaties
1790-1814	loose bipolar	high	high (rise of revolutionary nationalism)	decrease (during Napoleonic hegemony)	medium	low	high	low	alliances, citizen armies, propaganda, treaties
1815-1871	multipolar	medium	low	consolidation of Germany and Italy, disappearance of minor actors in west and central Europe	low to medium	medium	medium to high	high	limited war, professional armies, compensation, appeasement, deliberate policies of balance and containment of liberalism, multilateral conferences, bilateral diplomacy
1872-1890	unipolar (with France dissenting)	medium to low	low	European system expanded	medium	high	low	medium	colonial expansion, multilateral conferences, bilateral diplomacy
1891-1914	loose bipolar	low	high (Europe divided)	United States, Japan, Balkans participating more fully in system	medium	low	high	low	durable alliances, armament, limited war, propaganda
1919-1932	unipolar victors (with isolated dissenters)	medium	low to medium (rise of fascism in Italy and Japan and of communism in Russia, nationalist frustrations, peace maintained)	East European and Latin American states participating more fully in central system	medium	medium	low	medium	arms reduction, collective security, multilateral conferences, treaties

1933-1939	loose bipolar	low to medium	high (Nazism in Germany)	variable	medium to high	low	high	low	appeasement, rearmament, economic imperialism, aggression, propaganda, subversive alliances
1946-1956†	tight bipolar	high	high (east-west cleavage salient)	sharp increase in Afro-Asian states	high	high	low	medium	durable alliances, bilateral economic and military aid, multilateral technical aid, propaganda, limited war, subversion, deterrence
1956-1962	loose bipolar (France and China deviating)	medium to high	medium to high (success of nationalism in Africa and Asia, east-west conflict salient)	accelerated increase with end of colonialism	high	high to medium	medium	medium	United Nations intervention, mutual deterrence, coercive diplomacy, regional economic integration, subversion, propaganda
1962-	multipolar to complex-conglomerate	medium	medium (north-south conflict salient)	more new states	medium to high (decoupling of new actors through regional growth)	medium	medium	medium to low	arms control, limited war, mutual deterrence coercive diplomacy, regional economic integration, subversion, propaganda

*The ideas of Ernst Haas [10] and of Richard Rosecrance [11] have suggested some of the formulations and time divisions in this table.

† Haas believes that a unipolar victory group emerged at the end of World War II and lasted for perhaps two years.

gest that multipolarity is one structural feature of the contemporary international system. The existence of several conflict dimensions increases the possibility that their cutting across one another will lead to reduction in the intensity of any single conflict. Analyses of domestic politics have suggested that the existence of various issues—so that individuals who oppose each other on one issue may be allied on another—tends to moderate the lengths to which adversaries are prepared to go to win on any single issue.[27] On the other hand, because of the large number of participant actors and the lack of clarity in status ordering, limited violence is likely to characterize such a system.

The Unit-Veto Structure

The unit- or group-veto system has been suggested by Morton Kaplan as a possible future structure in which all actors will possess "weapons of such a character that any actor is capable of destroying any other actor that attacks it even though it cannot prevent its own destruction" [13, p. 50].[28] This model, unlike the multipolar one, recognizes the crucial differences between high and low levels of resource capabilities, is less hierarchical than the bipolar model, and emphasizes the countervailing or counterdestructive capacity of a number of actors that allows them to maintain the status quo as long as they are prepared to use nuclear weapons. Armed with second-strike nuclear weapons, China, Indonesia, and Japan might be able to veto one another's behavior, whereas the United States, the U.S.S.R., Europe, and even a coalition of poorer states might function as "veto groups."

Complex Conglomerate Structure

This model of international structure,

though it incorporates features of the other models, is primarily notable for its recognition of international and multinational groups and organizations beside national states as international actors. In the contemporary system, alliances are formed not only among nation-states but also between states and other types of units, as well as among other units alone. There are alignments between the United Nations and third-world states and between the United States and international corporations for certain purposes. On the issue of Angolan independence we can identify alignments involving, on the one hand, the Angolan rebels, the United Nations, many African states, the Eastern bloc, and even the World Council of Churches, and on the other, Portugal, several western European states, the United States, and some international corporations. On the issue of South African apartheid, there are alignments between the South African government, western Europe, the United States and General Motors, on the one hand, and South African blacks, many African states, the Eastern bloc, and even a minority of General Motors shareholders, on the other.

The term "conglomerate" is used here in a sense analogous to that for large corporations that supply leadership and management to a broad range of firms. Conglomerates tend to be large; smaller actors may, through possession of shares of stock, share an interest in the financial empire of the conglomerate. Conglomerates may retain controlling interests in companies in their portfolio but may share stock with banks, public institutions, private individuals, and even governments.

Although formal legal codes and practices and the weight of nationalist sentiment ensure the enduring importance of national states in international politics, the behavior of states may be increasingly part of larger and functionally diverse groupings that, though fluid in outline, nevertheless function as effective actors on certain issues.

---

[27] For a discussion of the factors that tend to reduce conflict, including the argument that diversity, rather than clustering of issues on a few dimensions, lowers the intensity of conflict, see Robert A. Dahl, *Modern Political Analysis* (Englewood Cliffs, N.J.: Prentice-Hall, 1963). Russett has described this possibility in *International Regions and the International System* (Chicago: Rand McNally, 1967), p. 229.

[28] The analysis of this system resembles

David Riesman's analysis of American politics [16].

HISTORICAL SYSTEMS AND SYSTEM TRANSFORMATION

Several of the models described here, as well as other permutations that might be specified, have historical analogues. The systems described in Table 6.3 are modifications of actual historical examples with distinctive, though not totally different, international structures. As this table suggests, stability tends to continue until mechanisms like alliance structures, balance-of-power policies, and international organizations can no longer cope with strains generated by large changes in particular actors or secular trends in the international environment. Systems then tend to enter unstable periods until they are finally transformed. Wars have often marked the breaks between one system structure and another but not always.

We have indicated how structural features may serve to induce or inhibit war, beside permitting or preventing achievement of actors' goals. But structure determines the behavior of actors only to a certain extent. Indeed, one of the important elements missing from most analyses of the impact of structure has been the mediating effects of actors' policies for adapting to or preventing such undesired outcomes as major wars. In the years before 1914, for example, the policies of actors contributed to the coming of World War I; in contrast, the Soviet Union and the United States have so far been able to cope with structural changes permitting them to acquire nuclear and thermonuclear weapons. Given structural properties that may exert pressures in certain directions, actors may still adjust to these features purposively. The fact that the Soviet Union and the United States have created mechanisms to help ensure their mutual survival despite conflicts in Europe, Asia, and Africa should not be interpreted as the result of structural properties. Rather, this behavior must be viewed, at least partly, as the deliberate policies of national leaders recognizing the dangers implicit in the international structure. These policies represent internally generated corrective responses to a threatening environment. Dean Pruitt and Richard Snyder have summarized the policies of statesmen that have been thought to contribute to system stability despite structural properties encouraging instability. These policies include strengthening military capability when potential enemies do the same, making alliances with states threatened by powerful adversaries and breaking alliances with actors who become too strong, assisting other major states when one state becomes too strong, avoiding the destruction of a major state even when it has been an aggressor, restoring defeated enemies to the community of states, and weakening a potential enemy by various strategies—even military attack [15].

System Change

There is no single point at which we can demonstrate empirically that a system has been "transformed." Indeed, as a system is partially the product of the selective focus of the observer, the variation in system properties necessary before transformation takes place is somewhat arbitrary. It makes just as much sense to conclude that in place of many international systems succeeding one another in time, there has been only a single system continuously evolving and changing. Furthermore, system transformations are rarely perceived by the actors themselves, at least until after they have occurred.

Ernst Haas has identified two models for explaining systemic change. The first involves a

kind of learning which presupposes that actors make decisions that are "rational" for them in the sense that they are designed to achieve a definable political objective. . . . Learning, therefore, is a rational process of redefining objectives and changing methods as leaders discover that persistence with the initial aims is self-defeating or overly costly. Hence international bargaining may serve as a "school" in which such lessons are learned. . . . The lessons of what could and could not be done are "fed back" into the national states. They put forward new purposes. . . . Reformulated purposes may become "functional" for system transformation. . . . [10, pp. 23–24]

According to this model, actors can consciously adapt to the contraints of structure in ways that can prevent war in a world prone to such conflict, or they can actually change the structure to lessen the probability of war. Soviet-American policies of mutual deterrence and arms control illustrate adaptation to a situation in which the probability of war may be great; the creation of supranational institutions might actually convert the existing system into a more peaceful one.[29]

In the second model, systemic change is considered beyond the deliberate control of actors:

Developments in the various social, economic, and political sectors making up the environment are conceived as proceeding more rapidly and decisively than the national learning of international feedbacks. New demands will then also be put on the system's structures. These will still encounter other new or opposing demands. The structures may not gain any net power at the expense of the member states but will be transformed just the same because the new mix of demands will result in a different task for the organization. The point which bears repetition here is the absence of any learning on the part of the national decision-makers. [10, p. 25]

Haas has concluded that the second model is closer to reality.

The Future International System
The international structure that seems to be emerging in the 1970s includes elements of all five models described. It comes closest, however, to the complex conglomerate system, with certain residual features of bipolarity at the strategic nuclear level and with a potential for limited veto features. The United States has already established a veto in connection with the safety of West Berlin, and the Soviet Union with that of eastern Europe. China and other actors may also become able to exercise limited vetoes.

Other trends include increased salience of diverse regional conflicts, which are less likely to correspond to global cleavages.[30] Consequently policy makers will face a more complex and ambiguous system requiring richer conceptual maps for the formulation of policies to secure objectives. There may also be greater difficulty in reconciling attentive publics to more complex policy analysis, particularly those publics accustomed to simpler and more stereotyped interpretations of reality. We may expect limited disengagement among major states and even greater disengagement among at least some third-world states. Pressures from large conglomerates to limit fighting in their economic interests and decline in the ideologies that generate alliances are two further apparent trends.

In addition, we expect certain current trends to continue at their same rates and in the same directions. These gradual changes in attitudes and resources may alter how actors attempt to influence one another in international politics—both their modes of action and the organizational arenas in which they act. Changes in the rules and the institutionalization of new patterns and modes of action can be examined from the points of view of system change and development (Chapter 12) and of the rise of global system dominance through processes of integration (Chapter 13).

Within twenty years, or at least by the end of the twentieth century, judgments about which actors are legitimate may become increasingly paramount, not because of threats by other actors but as they are challenged by the underlying norms of the international system. The "inherent" rights of self-defense and self-help in securing goals remain so fundamental as to offer no dimension for major conflict. But change may eventually im-

[29] See Chapters 12 and 13 for discussion of international development and integration.

[30] One author has even argued that "there is a long-term structural trend toward international fragmentation—a breakdown into subsystems" [7].

pose new structures and institutionalize new international norms that will reduce the probability of war without sacrificing the rights of all actors to fulfill their goals.[31]

References

1. Alker, Hayward R., Jr., "Supranationalism in the United Nations," *Papers of the Peace Research Society (International),* 3 (1965), pp. 197–212.
2. Arrighi, Giovanni, and John Saul, "Socialism and Economic Development in Tropical Africa," *Journal of Modern African Studies,* 6 (July 1968), pp. 141–170.
3. Bowman, Larry, "The Subordinate State System of Southern Africa," *International Studies Quarterly,* 12 (September 1968), pp. 231–261.
4. Brams, Steven, "Measuring the Concentration of Power in Political Systems," *American Political Science Review,* 62 (June 1968), pp. 461–475.
5. Brody, Richard A., "Some Systemic Effects of the Spread of Nuclear Weapons Technology: A Study Through Simulation of a Multi-Nuclear Future," *Journal of Conflict Resolution,* 7 (December 1963), pp. 663–753.
6. Deutsch, Karl W., and J. David Singer, "Multipolar Power Systems and International Stability," in James N. Rosenau, ed., *International Politics and Foreign Policy,* rev. ed. (New York: Free Press, 1969), pp. 315–324.
7. Domínquez, Jorge I., "Mice that Do Not Roar: Some Aspects of International Politics in the World's Peripheries," *International Organization,* 25 (Spring 1971), p. 178.
8. Frank, André Gunder, *Capitalism and Underdevelopment in Latin America* (New York: Monthly Review Press, 1967).
9. Gilpin, Robert, *France in the Age of the Scientific State* (Princeton: Princeton University Press, 1968).
10. Haas, Ernst B., *Collective Security and the Future International System,* Monograph Series in World Affairs, vol. 5, no. 1 (Denver: University of Denver, 1967–1968).
11. Haas, Michael, "A Functional Approach to International Organization," in James N. Rosenau, ed., *International Politics and Foreign Policy,* rev. ed. (New York: Free Press, 1969), pp. 131–141.
12. Hanreider, Wolfram F., "The International System: Bipolar or Multibloc?" *Journal of Conflict Resolution,* 9 (September 1965), pp. 299–308.
13. Kaplan, Morton, *System and Process in International Politics* (New York: Wiley, 1957).
14. Masters, Roger D., "World Politics as a Primitive Political System," in James N. Rosenau, ed., *International Politics and Foreign Policy,* rev. ed. (New York: Free Press, 1969), pp. 104–118.
15. Pruitt, Dean G., and Richard C. Snyder, eds., *Theory and Research on the Causes of War* (Englewood Cliffs, N.J.: Prentice-Hall, 1969), p. 103.
16. Riesman, David, *The Lonely Crowd: A Study of Changing American Character* (New Haven: Yale University Press, 1950).
17. Rosecrance, Richard N., *Action and Reaction in World Politics* (Boston: Little, Brown, 1963), p. 135.
18. Rosecrance, Richard N., "Bipolarity, Multipolarity and the Future," *Journal of Conflict Resolution,* 10 (September 1966), pp. 314–327.
19. Russett, Bruce M., "The Calculus of Deterrence," *Journal of Conflict Resolution,* 7 (1963), pp. 97–109.
20. Russett, Bruce M., "Probabilism and the Number of Units Affected: Measuring Influence Concentration," *American Political Science Review,* 62 (June 1968), pp. 476–480.
21. Russett, Bruce M., *Trends in World Politics* (New York: Macmillan, 1965).
22. Scott, Andrew M., *The Revolution in Statecraft: Informal Penetration* (New York: Random House, 1965).
23. Singer, J. David, and Melvin Small, "Capability Distribution and the Preservation of Peace in the Major Power Sub-System, 1816–1965" (Paper delivered at the Sixty-Sixth Annual Meeting of the American Political Science Association, Los Angeles, September 8–12, 1970).

[31] For discussion of parallels between primitive societies and the international system and between processes of development in national and international contexts, see Roger D. Masters [14].

24. Singer, J. David, and Melvin Small, "The Composition and Status Ordering of the International System, 1815–1940," *World Politics,* 17 (January 1966), pp. 236–282.

25. Stoessinger, John C., *The United Nations and the Superpowers* (New York: Random House, 1965), p. 15.

26. Waltz, Kenneth N., "International Structure, National Force, and the Balance of World Power," in James N. Rosenau, ed., *International Politics and Foreign Policy,* rev. ed. (New York: Free Press, 1969), pp. 304–314.

27. Waltz, Kenneth N., *Man, the State and War* (New York: Columbia University Press, 1959).

28. Waltz, Kenneth N., "The Stability of a Bipolar World," *Daedalus,* 93 (Summer 1964), pp. 881–909.

29. Wright, Quincy, *A Study of War,* 2nd ed. (Chicago: University of Chicago Press, 1965), p. 755.

30. Young, Oran R., "Political Discontinuities in the International System," *World Politics,* 20 (April 1968), p. 369.

31. Zilliacus, Konni, *A New Birth of Freedom? World Communism After Stalin* (London: Secker & Warburg, 1957), p. 103.

Suggested Reading

Claude, Inis L., *Power and International Relations* (New York: Random House, 1962).

Haas, Ernst B., *Collective Security and the Future International System,* Monograph Series in World Affairs, vol. 5, no. 1 (Denver: University of Denver, 1967–1968).

Kaplan, Morton A., *System and Process in International Politics* (New York: Wiley, 1957).

Liska, George, *Nations in Alliance* (Baltimore: Johns Hopkins, 1962).

Parsons, Talcott, "Order and Continuity in the International Social System," in James N. Rosenau, ed., *International Politics and Foreign Policy* (New York: Free Press, 1961), pp. 120–129.

Pruitt, Dean G., and Richard C. Snyder, eds., *Theory and Research on the Causes of War* (Englewood Cliffs, N.J.: Prentice-Hall, 1969).

Rosecrance, Richard N., *Action and Reaction in World Politics* (Boston: Little, Brown, 1963).

Russett, Bruce M., *International Regions and the International System* (Chicago: Rand McNally, 1967).

Russett, Bruce M., *et al., World Handbook of Political and Social Indicators* (New Haven: Yale University Press, 1964).

Singer, J. David, and Melvin Small, "The Composition and Status Ordering of the International System, 1815–1940," *World Politics,* 17 (January 1966), pp. 236–282.

Waltz, Kenneth N., "International Structure, National Force, and the Balance of World Power," *Journal of International Affairs,* 21 (1967), pp. 215–231.

Wright, Quincy, *The Study of International Relations* (New York: Appleton, 1955).

Young, Oran R., "Interdependence in World Politics," *International Journal,* 24 (Autumn 1969), pp. 726–750.

Chapter 7
THE FACTORS CONDITIONING FOREIGN POLICY

Politics everywhere, it would seem, are related to politics everywhere else
—James N. Rosenau [39, p. 2]

Although international structure is the framework in which events occur, the events themselves are the products of purposive behavior by individual actors. We shall now seek to identify the various factors that determine the foreign policies of actors.

THE LINKS BETWEEN DOMESTIC AND INTERNATIONAL POLITICS

During the twentieth century international and domestic politics have become increasingly interrelated. Events even in remote areas of the globe cannot be understood as isolated phenomena "but must be seen as part of a world transformation in which these particular pockets of semiautonomy are working out their distinctive yet somehow parallel destinies" [34]. American national politics have been influenced by wars in Korea and Vietnam, and, conversely, domestic decisions on taxation, economic investment, and even civil rights have had consequences abroad. Issues that originate in the domestic political arena are internationalized, and international issues become domestic political concerns. To some extent all international actors are "porous"; that is, they are subject to influences from the international system. The international system in turn is constantly subject to demands that originate in the domestic affairs of actors. Foreign policy is the point at which influences arising in the international system cross into the domestic arena and at which domestic politics is transformed into international behavior.

The traditional rather legalistic view that the international system is composed of sovereign units separated by space, in which collisions occur infrequently, is oversimplified and unrewarding. Figure 7.1 illustrates this traditional "state-centered" view of international politics. The only link between the domestic and international arenas is formal government officeholders. Such internal factors as public opinion, interest groups, and gov-

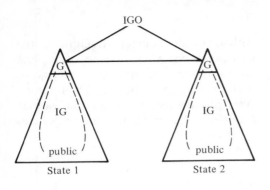

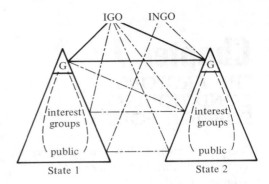

G   *government*

IGO   *intergovernmental organization*

――――   *classical interstate politics*

―――   *domestic politics*

IG   *interest groups*

Figure 7.1. Classical Restricted Model of State-Centered Politics

Source: Adapted from Robert O. Keohane and Joseph S. Nye, Jr.,"Transnational Relations and World Politics: An Introduction," *International Organization* (Summer 1971), pp. 332–334.

INGO   *international nongovernmental organization*

――――   *classic interstate links*

―――   *domestic links*

―――   *Transnational links*

IG   *intergovernmental organization*

G   *government*

Figure 7.2. Expanded Model of International and Domestic Political Links

Source: Adapted from Robert O. Keohane and Joseph S. Nye, Jr.,"Transnational Relations and World Politics: An Introduction," *International Organization* (Summer 1971), pp. 332–334.

ernment bureaucracies are purportedly focused on these officeholders, who also serve as receptors of external stimuli. In this view, interstate politics is clearly distinct from domestic politics. Transnational politics involving nonstate actors is ignored, and links appear indirect. This model is, however, increasingly inadequate to explain the full range of factors shaping the foreign policies of states and other international actors [39, pp. 1–17, 41].

Figure 7.2 presents a more complete view of international politics. The domestic pyramid of policy formation can be penetrated at several levels, and the links among actors are greatly multiplied to reflect the complex exchanges that occur. Although many domestic political issues are affected by international politics, our attention is focused here only on those outcomes that represent foreign-policy inputs in the international arena.

As links cross legal boundaries, factors conditioning policy must be sought both inside and outside the actor. American

recognition of the state of Israel in 1948 illustrates the kind of link that can exist between domestic and international politics. Israel came into existence in 1948, a presidential election year in the United States. It was necessary for both candidates to take positions on the issue of Israeli recognition, but it was particularly important that Harry S. Truman, the incumbent Democrat, adopt a favorable attitude toward the new Jewish state because he desperately needed the Jewish vote in key states like New York and the financial support that Democrats had traditionally received from the Jewish community. For President Truman Jews in Israel constituted a significant constituency because of their links with the Jewish community in the United States. He adopted a pro-Israeli position, despite the advice of members of the Departments of Defense and State who feared that such a policy would alienate the petroleum-rich Arab states. Figure 7.3 represents

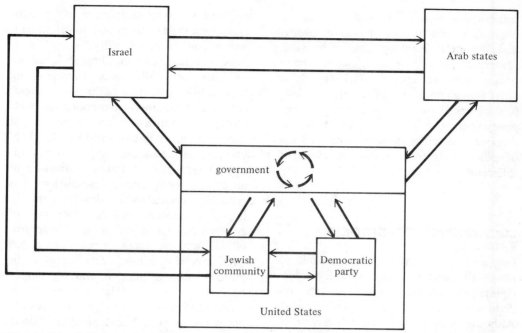

Figure 7.3. A Simple Communications Model of Israeli Recognition, 1948

schematically the links among various groups in 1948 in relation to this particular issue. Arrows designate the flow of communications among selected groups. To understand Truman's decision in detail we would have to identify and describe direct links between him and other members of government, between the government and social groups like the Jewish community and the Democratic party, and between the United States government and those of foreign countries. Furthermore, complete description would also require recognition of the direct links between the Jewish community and the Democratic party [53]. Indeed, it is possible to speak of an issue-oriented political system consisting of the American Jewish community and the state of Israel —a system that cuts across conventional national frontiers. The study of diplomatic relations among governments and intergovernmental organizations is thus no longer adequate to explain foreign policy.

In this century the art of "penetrating" a foreign state, thus reducing its autonomy, has been developed to an extent un-

precedented since the seventeenth century.[1] Propaganda, political infiltration, and foreign aid are common forms of penetration. As the Israeli example suggests, affiliations and identifications that cut across national boundaries have become important factors in foreign policy. Communist parties, *Bunds,* "international friendship societies," and "fifth columns" are other such kinds of affiliations. The connections between states and international economic enterprises are also significant. The United States limits the freedom of overseas subsidiaries of American corporations like General Motors and Ford to conduct business with other countries. These firms are, for instance, not permitted to trade freely with the countries of eastern Europe; in effect, then, they are partly instruments of American

[1] See Andrew M. Scott, *The Revolution in Statecraft: Informal Penetration* (New York: Random House, 1965); and John H. Herz, *International Politics in the Atomic Age* (New York: Columbia University Press, 1959). Herz has revised claims made earlier in "The Territorial State Revisited: Reflections on the Future of the Nation-State," in James N. Rosenau, ed., *International Politics and Foreign Policy,* rev. ed. (New York: Free Press, 1969), pp. 76–89.

penetration abroad. The systematic study of foreign policy must be based on awareness that traditional boundaries between "external" and "internal" politics have broken down at many points [12].

In this chapter we shall examine clusters of variables that affect the foreign-policy behavior of any actor and endeavor to describe the differential effects of different factors on the behavior of different types of actors.[2]

LOCATION OF CONDITIONING FACTORS

For analytical purposes it is possible to assign all variables that can influence foreign policy to five categories: external, individual, role, governmental, and societal. Although the foreign-policy behavior of all actors is influenced to some extent by all these clusters of variables, certain actors are affected more by certain types of variables than by others. Large countries with ample resources are targets for more influence attempts, but they are less likely to be influenced by external factors than are small countries with few resources. Furthermore, economically developed countries have large and complex bureaucracies to produce foreign-policy decisions, thus increasing the relative importance of governmental and role variables and limiting the scope of individual variables. By contrast, countries that are economically underdeveloped lack strong governmental and bureaucratic organizations, and consequently the personality traits of individual statesmen may more readily influence decisions. Such countries may be dominated by charismatic leaders whose behavior is not restrained by bureaucratic or role factors. Finally, when governing elites are accountable to private sectors, societal variables tend to have greater relative importance in foreign-policy decisions than they have in countries ruled by authoritarian or other undemocratic regimes. The relative impacts

[2] Our framework was developed by James N. Rosenau [40, 41].

of these variables thus seem to be associated with size, economic development, and political accountability.

As we suggested in Chapter 5, an actor's size is a dimension incorporating factors like gross national product, population, and land area. Economic development is a dimension composed of per capita gross national product, level of literacy, urbanization, and industrialization. The degree of bureaucratization of an actor's foreign-policy establishment is crudely correlated with development. In highly developed societies the type of government, the distribution of responsibilities, and the types of roles associated with official positions are likely to be more important than in underdeveloped countries in which roles are not firmly established and the foreign-policy establishments are small and undifferentiated. Accountability is the degree to which a government recognizes and responds to the demands of private citizens and groups. Democracies are open political systems in which nongovernmental influences on citizens' attitudes can play a large part in policy formation. Accountability is the degree to which certain social factors are permitted to impinge upon the foreign-policy process. Public opinion is thus a more important determinant of foreign policy in a democracy than in a dictatorship. In general, however, accountability is a less significant characteristic than is either size or development. Indeed, the distinction between open and closed societies loses much of its relevance in less developed states, most of which are relatively closed. A society tends to become more open as it develops. Using these three characteristics, James Rosenau has suggested the relative impacts of different clusters of variables on different types of actors, as shown in Figure 7.4. His formula provides a conceptual organization preliminary to theory building.

In this chapter we shall describe these five clusters in greater detail, focusing on patterns of behavior, rather than on specific actions. In suggesting the relative impacts of different variables in different

Geography and physical resources	large country				small country			
State of the economy	developed		underdeveloped		developed		underdeveloped	
State of the polity	open	closed	open	closed	open	closed	open	closed
Rankings of the variables	role societal governmental systemic individual	role individual governmental systemic societal	individual role societal systemic governmental	individual role governmental systemic societal	role systemic societal governmental individual	role systemic individual governmental societal	individual systemic role societal governmental	individual systemic role governmental societal
Illustrative examples	United States	U.S.S.R.	India	Red China	Holland	Czechoslovakia	Kenya	Tanzania

Figure 7.4. Rosenau's "Pretheory" of Foreign Policy*

Source: Reprinted with permission of The Macmillan Company from *The Scientific Study of Foreign Policy* by James N. Rosenau. Copyright © 1971 by The Free Press, a Division of The Macmillan Company.

* Five sets of variables underlying the external behavior of societies are ranked according to their relative potency in eight types of societies.

countries, we do not mean to imply that this ordering remains the same in every situation. We suggest only that over long periods of time we would expect certain variables to have a greater influence on specific actors. Even very large states like the Soviet Union and China are influenced by systemic and individual variables, and even small, "underdeveloped" states like Tanzania are affected by governmental and role variables. But the aggregate characteristics of actors make some locations appear more salient than others as sources of factors conditioning behavior.

THE INTERNATIONAL SYSTEM AS A SOURCE OF CONDITIONING FACTORS

The major variables in the international system that affect foreign policy are the relative distributions of attitudes and resources. An actor's own resources and attitudes constitute part of his internal environment, but the distribution of such factors elsewhere serves as input from the international system into the actor's decision-making process. We ask what an actor's capabilities are *relative* to those of other actors, rather than what his *absolute* capabilities are. Similarly, although

a country's geography is a societal characteristic, its strategic location in relation to other actors is a systemic property. In essence, the characteristics of the international structure are the main variables in this cluster. An actor's choices in a bipolar system are usually different from those in a multipolar system. Actors are probably subject to different sets of constraints when they are surrounded by powerful neighbors than when they are not. Alliances, alignments, and trade patterns are also significant systemic variables that impose limits on and open opportunities for policy. When they impose burdens and obligations, the actor is liable to incur costs. Systemic or external variables have greater impacts on small countries, especially those that are less developed, for they are relatively dependent upon their external environment for economic well-being and political security. Premier Pierre Werner of tiny Luxembourg has declared his country is "too small to defend itself by its own means. Luxembourg has integrated itself with a larger collectivity. Our fidelity to the Atlantic alliance and our European convictions constitute the base of our foreign policy" [22].

Students of international politics have been traditionally concerned about systemic variables, often to the exclusion of other factors. This emphasis makes foreign-policy analysis and prediction largely matters of examining the properties of the international system and deriving propositions about behavior "demanded" by the system.[3] For some purposes such simplification is helpful, *if* we are aware of the resulting limitations on explanation and prediction. Morton Kaplan has argued:

International systems are macromodels of international politics. They are not models of the foreign policy process. . . . To expect that the loose bipolar model would explain behavior within the African subsystem when it is designed to explain the overarching system of international politics would be equivalent to expecting a model of monopolistic competition to explain the economics of the garment trade in the East coast of the United States. [23]

Even when systemic factors are dominant, they must be discerned and understood—not an easy task. Aggregate patterns of international transactions and flows permit the analyst to perceive large-scale trends, but they may only partially explain the behavior of particular actors.

INDIVIDUAL IMPACT ON FOREIGN POLICY

Theorists like Thomas Carlyle have attributed nearly all change and drama in history to the wills of great men. But history is the product of both men *and* their times. We can distinguish those characteristics of an individual decision maker and his behavior—personality, experience, intellect, values, and political style —that make him unique. We can then evaluate separately the impacts of these factors on events, in order to see how much truth there is in "great men" theories when applied to particular situations. For example, former Secretary of State Dean Rusk's vigorous opposition to negotiations with the Viet Cong and North Vietnamese communists must be viewed

in the light of his previous experience as Assistant Secretary of State for Far Eastern Affairs during the Korean War. During the last stages of that war many Americans died while United Nations representatives negotiated with the enemy at Panmunjom. Rusk did not wish to see the United States suffer another such experience in Vietnam. His personal perceptions and experience exemplify what we mean by "individual variables,"[4] and a knowledge of these is necessary to understand American hesitance to negotiate with the enemy between 1965 and 1969.

As political behavior involves human behavior and as the latter is the product of environmental and psychological predisposition, the relevance of individual variables to the study of foreign policy is clear. The frequent importance of psychological data is also apparent. In the 1962 Cuban missile crisis American leaders had to make informed assumptions about the personality and belief structure of Nikita Khrushchev. How would he interpret and respond to American moves? Would he view them as a personal challenge, or would he seek to avoid a situation of inevitable conflict? Data on psychological predispositions, however, are extremely difficult to obtain and are subject to vastly different interpretations. During the missile crisis, many commentators believed that the United States should remain firm without pushing Khrushchev into a corner and forcing him to respond defensively. One analyst, however, argued that in view of the "peculiar" personalities of communist leaders, the United States should adopt an unambiguously "hard" line. Referring to an earlier study of the personalities of communist leaders, he declared:

It is tantamount to a moral imperative to the Communist leader that he must advance . . . wherever opportunity affords. . . . On the other hand, it is equally imperative that he must at no point subject to grave risk or hazard the basic achievement

---

[3] See the discussion of balance of power in Chapter 2.

[4] A very useful, concise study of the individual variable in politics has been written by Fred I. Greenstein [19].

already consolidated. . . . [I]f we wanted to be humane to him [Khrushchev], the best way of doing so was to make our threat absolutely unambiguous—to save him and his colleagues occasion for wondering whether their headlong retreat was really necessary.[5]

While individual variables can be important, they are not inevitably so. In the first place, they are difficult to separate from role variables. When an individual's behavior is identical with that of others who hold or have held similar positions, then it is likely that it results from role expectations, rather than from unique personality traits.[6] We must also distinguish individual variables from the environments in which they are formed. Individual, or idiosyncratic, traits may be products of particular social traits, but they are not the same. Finally, there is the difficult problem of determining under what circumstances individual traits are likely to have impacts on policy decisions: How would policy differ if other individuals were responsible for it?

Some situations increase the probability of individual impact on foreign policy. When the situation is fluid (as in a crisis), when few precedents exist, and when organizational interests are not threatened, individuals in strategic positions are likely to have more impact on policy. In states in which policy is largely dependent upon the attitudes of single individuals, or in "underdeveloped" societies that lack established roles or highly structured bureaucracies, individual variables have still greater impact on foreign policy.

Personality

For political scientists, the most interesting examples are those in which personality variables lead to aberrant behavior.[7] Often such behavior reflects the individual's unconscious attempt to cope with inner conflict or need—in Harold D. Lasswell's classic formulation, the displacement of private motives onto public objects. Because of its potential impact on foreign policy and other activities, this form of behavior has been the object of increasing attention [26, 3, 36, 18]. Certain emotional issues tend to evoke aberrant behavior. For example, ego-defensive behavior occurs quite frequently in agitation for or against communism, pacifism, birth control, and obscenity, as well as in sexual deviance [25]. Furthermore, as studies of prejudice have revealed, certain individuals have greater needs than do others to defend their identities. Their overt behavior, often hostile, may compensate for unconscious needs and personality defects.

When individual variables do have impact, studying a leader's life history can help us to understand his adult behavior. His relations with his parents, his education, and his socialization as a child and adolescent may have created enduring frustrations and anxieties. An analysis of President Woodrow Wilson's behavior has suggested that his independence and unwillingness to compromise with political opponents were consequences of childhood competition with his father. It has been hypothesized that he had repressed his rebellion against his father but unconsciously refused to submit to him. Consequently he "could brook no interference. *His* will must prevail. . . . He bristled at the slightest challenge to his authority" [18, p. 11].[8] Wilson's be-

[5] Letter from Bernard F. Brodie, *The New York Times,* November 13, 1962. The study to which Brodie refers was by Nathan Leites [27, 28].

[6] Individual variables are more likely than are role variables to be important in unprecedented or exceedingly complex situations. Sociologist Edward Shils has written that in novel situations "no framework of action [has been] set for the newcomer by the expectations of those already on the scene. A new political party, a newly formed religious sect will thus be more amenable to the expressive behavior of the personalities of those who make them up than an ongoing government" [47].

[7] For an examination of the components of personality, see M. Brewster Smith, "A Map for the Analysis of Personality and Politics," *Journal of Social Issues,* 24 (July 1968), pp. 15–28.

[8] A more questionable analysis of Wilson's behavior can be found in Sigmund Freud and William C. Bullitt, *Thomas Woodrow Wilson, Twenty-Eighth President of the United States: A Psychological Study* (Boston: Houghton Mifflin, 1966).

havior was unlike that of most American politicians in comparable situations.

The individual motivated by repressed hostilities may also assume a posture of moral superiority toward those with whom he is in conflict. When important members of the foreign-policy establishment adopt such attitudes, they may encourage ethnocentric international behavior [10, 13, 54]. Ethnocentrism may produce reciprocal ethnocentrism, thus contributing to a hostile international climate. Stalin's inordinate suspicion of both his colleagues and his allies during and after World War II, for instance, contributed to the cold-war climate. His successor, Khrushchev, declared: "You see to what Stalin's mania for greatness led. He had completely lost a sense of reality; he demonstrated his suspicion and haughtiness not only in relation to individuals in the U.S.S.R., but in relation to whole parties and nations [20].[9]

An individual's beliefs and the strength with which he holds them can have important effects on the way in which he deals with new information. Most people have sets of attitudes toward their environment that reflect the values they enjoy and their preferences. The stronger these predispositions are, the more contradictory evidence and information are necessary to alter the beliefs. When confronted with evidence that contradicts strong beliefs, the individual must either alter his beliefs, deny the evidence, or rationalize it so that it no longer appears contradictory [16]. A study of former Secretary of State John Foster Dulles has suggested that he consistently explained changes in Soviet behavior in terms of hostility, weakness, or treachery, which eliminated the need for him to alter his beliefs in the face of new evidence. His interpretations were colored by the be-

liefs that communism was immoral and that "atheists can hardly be expected to conform to an ideal so high [as Christian ethics]" [14, 17]. Religious beliefs frequently evoke strong attachment. In the seventeenth century, King Gustavus Adolphus of Sweden had as little use for neutrality in international politics as did Dulles in the twentieth century. To the Protestant rulers of Europe he declared: "Up for the Gospel, those of you who believe in it, or it will be the worse for you! I shall treat neutrality as equivalent to a declaration of war against me" [33].

Experience

An officeholder's previous experience helps him to interpret the problems that he faces and that shape his relations with other high officials. Former Secretary of State Dean Acheson warned that an American president "will be disappointed if he chooses [as] Secretary [of State] a man of greater political stature than himself, in the belief that the appointment will add to the power of his administration, or will placate a rival's resentment" [2]. Acheson noted that when such an appointee has held high political office before and has wielded partisan political influence, the president will have difficulty asserting his own authority. Acheson's own experience as a lawyer, his admiration for the views of Justices Louis D. Brandeis and Oliver Wendell Holmes, and his early career in the State Department during the New Deal years had shaped his commanding style of leadership and had contributed to his skepticism about ideological commitment and "instant" panaceas for difficult political problems [31, 1].

Different experiences are likely to endow officeholders with specific qualifications that may or may not be suitable for resolving the problems at hand. George C. Marshall, who served as secretary of defense in 1950–1951, had been general of the army and chief of staff. More than any other American secretary of defense since, Marshall understood the difficulties

[9] The noted Soviet writer Alexander Solzhenitsyn has described Stalin in a similar manner: "Night was Stalin's most fruitful time. His mistrustful mind unwound slowly in the morning. With his gloomy morning mind he removed people from their positions, cut back expenditures, ordered two or three ministries merged into one" [48].

confronting the military services. In addition, having previously served as secretary of state, he was in a position to judge the relations between the military services and the political objectives that they were supposed to serve.

Charles E. Wilson, on the other hand, had been president of General Motors before becoming secretary of defense in 1953. His previous experience qualified him to cut military expenditures and to design military plans that would enable the administration to maintain a balanced budget and pursue a conservative economic policy. Wilson had not had much training in military strategy, and toward the end of the Eisenhower years, professional officers were complaining that American military forces had been permitted to grow obsolete.

Robert McNamara, who assumed the post in 1961, had been president of Ford Motor Company and a pioneer in new techniques of systems analysis and program budgeting. Rejecting his predecessor's essentially passive philosophy of acting as a civilian counterbalance to the professional military officers, McNamara decided to "play an active role providing aggressive leadership—questioning, suggesting alternatives, proposing objectives, and stimulating progress. This active role represents my own philosophy of management. . . . I became convinced that there was room for and need of this kind of management philosophy in the Department of Defense" [9, 32].

Melvin Laird, who was appointed secretary of defense in 1968 by President Richard M. Nixon, had considerable political experience. As a former congressman from Wisconsin, he was appointed partly because of the need to establish good working relations with a Democratic-controlled Congress and partly because he seemed to represent the conservative wing of the Republican party, in which the president sought to consolidate his influence.

Age is also an important factor in experience. The events of the era in which an individual has been socialized are likely to be reflected in his consideration of problems. He will have different points of reference and concerns from those of an individual of a different generation.

Leadership Style

An individual's experience is likely to affect his leadership style and thus the way in which he reaches decisions. President Eisenhower, who had served much of his adult life as a high-ranking army staff officer, expected as president to coordinate the work of others and to interact with his advisers and subordinates as he had done with his military colleagues. Not only did Eisenhower solicit the advice of others and delegate authority to them, but also in an effort to achieve consensus he tried not to impose his views on them. He relied on a "committee style" of decision making, seeking to prevent interpersonal conflict and to win consensus before making decisions. Although this approach did indeed minimize conflicts among decision makers, it also tended to blur the lines of responsibility and to produce decisions at the "lowest common denominator." There was a tendency to combine elements from various points of view in an artificial way that rarely led to the decisive resolution of issues.

Eisenhower's style of leadership and the way in which he viewed the role of president were in sharp contrast to those of other American presidents. Franklin D. Roosevelt, for example, encouraged his high officials and advisers to compete with one another, making it necessary for him to serve as ultimate arbiter in the disputes that inevitably arose. Situations had to be permitted to develop, to crystallize, to clarify; the "competing forces had to vindicate themselves in the actual pull and tug of conflict; public opinion had to face the question, consider it, pronounce upon it—only then, at the long frazzled end, would the President's intuitions consolidate and precipitate a result" [46]. In this way Roosevelt sought to maximize his personal influence and to use it economically.

Health

Finally, the physical and mental health of leaders can have bearing on policy. Leaders are frequently old and unable to act as dynamically as they did when they were younger. In countries where key leaders cannot be expected to live much longer and in which the impact of individual variables is great, it is difficult to predict foreign-policy behavior far in advance.

The strain of high public office is great, and physical decay has taken its toll among leaders. Both Eisenhower and Wilson, for example, suffered serious illnesses while in office, which weakened their control over decisions. President Roosevelt was ill when he met with Stalin at Yalta in February 1945, and it has been suggested that he was therefore unable to negotiate effectively with the Soviet dictator. Prime Minister Anthony Eden was also reportedly ill at the time that he led Great Britain into the Suez crisis of 1956, and he suffered a physical breakdown shortly afterward. As pressures increase, mental illness may also become a problem. James Forrestal, the first American secretary of defense, finally suffered a breakdown and took his own life. As his biographer has suggested, "The most lasting tribute to James Forrestal would be a massive effort to reduce the incidence of physical and mental breakdown in political life" [37]. It is strange to learn that the United States requires military officers in charge of nuclear weapons to undergo extensive physical and psychological tests but provides few such safeguards for the president himself. This fact was brought home forcefully during the 1972 presidential campaign when Senator Thomas Eagleton of Missouri was forced to withdraw as Senator George McGovern's vice-presidential candidate after revealing a history of mental illness. One psychologist has declared, "When we remember that strokes, doses of tranquilizers, and many other medicinal drugs have psychological side effects, we may well be puzzled by the fact that less provision is made for detecting and helping

psychological problems in public officials than in private industrial managers" [35].[10]

In certain countries the death or incapacity of an important political leader can bring government to a halt and paralyze the decision-making process. Such a situation prevailed in the Soviet Union after the death of Stalin in 1953 and in Egypt after the death of Gamal Abdel Nasser in 1970.

ROLE VARIABLES

A role is a set of socially prescribed behaviors associated with all individuals occupying similar official positions in a political system. Such an individual assumes a set of responsibilities and undertakes to perform certain tasks. Role can be defined as the interaction of the individual officeholder's interpretation of what is expected of him, his actual behavior, and the expectations of those who are responsible for his recruitment and advancement within particular career patterns. When an individual assumes a new post his knowledge of role norms is based on the behavior of earlier occupants of the position, as well as on legal statutes, job descriptions, organizational charts, and his peer group. In addition, after exercising the responsibilities and prerogatives of his office, an individual's norms may be affected by his own personal experience.

A role is partly shaped by what relevant others expect. Individuals who seek to retain their positions or advance in their careers are likely to behave in ways that they think are expected of them. Usually a role occupant is less expected to follow his personal convictions than his obligations to the organization of which he is a member. Military officers are likely to support increased budgetary allocations for defense and the status of the military profession in society as a

[10] For an excellent study of the impact of ill health on political decisions, see Hugh L'Etang, *The Pathology of Leadership* (London: Heinemann, 1969).

whole. Those who behaved otherwise would find it difficult to advance in their profession. Similarly, an official of the Soviet Communist Party who sought to open Soviet society to other political parties would probably be dismissed. When we know the expectations and standards of those controlling role recruitment, we can predict more successfully the behavior of role occupants. Role norms limit the freedom of individuals in organizations. As a recent U.S. State Department publication notes:

The [State] Department has never succeeded in overcoming strong pressures toward conformity which have dulled its creative impulse. . . . The present highly competitive promotion system tends to stifle creativity and promote conformity. Under the present system, the key factor in determining whether an officer will be promoted is the efficiency report written by his immediate superior. The knowledge that the good opinion of his supervisor is crucial in determining whether an officer advances at a normal rate or falls behind and is eventually selected out can act as a powerful deterrent to his forthright expression of views on policy matters which may be at variance with the views of his supervisor. [51]

The obligations of a role occupant to those above him shape his perceptions of problems. A member of Congress is likely to take positions that conform to the interests of his constituents, rather than to the interests of the country as a whole [11]. Institutional loyalty also narrows the frame of reference for interpreting information and stimulates rivalries among executive departments and agencies.

A role occupant is further limited by established procedures that prescribe what he can do, with whom he can communicate, and how he can present his views. William Attwood, for example, has recalled that when he was an ambassador he had to call on the White House to see the president on important business. Most ambassadors would not have been allowed to see the president under similar circumstances because the State Depart-

ment did not have the influence to secure such appointments. But Attwood was able to gain access to the White House because he had participated in President Kennedy's presidential campaign. Generally ambassadors do not bypass the State Department; Attwood, however, had stepped outside his role [7]. Role occupants are often required to make certain decisions that as individuals they are not suited to make. Members of the U.S. Cabinet are required to make fundamental political decisions, even though some of them have little relevant experience. Finally, some positions may carry less authority than is necessary to do the job. The story of the development of the role of secretary of defense since 1947 is largely the story of the enlargement of prerogatives and powers so that the incumbent can carry out his assigned duties.

As time passes role norms become set; precedents grow, and expectations become more widely shared and more deeply anchored. It is difficult for an occupant to impose his personality on or to remold well-established roles: "A chief of state can quite honestly say: 'I must do this for my country even though it is against my principles'" [50]. On the other hand, when new positions are established or new institutions created, occupants have greater opportunities to shape roles to fit their conceptions. Stalin, as the first general secretary of the Soviet Communist Party, was able to "stamp" his personality on the Soviet Union, and leaders of countries breaking from colonial rule have been able to create new diplomatic styles for their foreign policies. But it is difficult, as Dean Rusk learned, to reshape roles for which strong expectations exist. Before becoming secretary of state he delivered a series of lectures in which he advocated that the secretary spend less time abroad servicing American alliances. Yet Rusk himself went on to log record mileage in overseas travel.

Whether or not an individual can modify role norms, then, depends upon the strength of role prescriptions, the force of his own personality and skills, and the uniqueness of the problems that confront him. McNamara's career as secretary of defense illustrates how individual factors can dominate and enlarge a role. McNamara came to office determined to "originate and stimulate new ideas and programs, not just to referee arguments" [55]. Between 1961 and 1968 he gradually expanded his role vis-à-vis Congress and the military services; reviewed the programs of the Defense Department and introduced cost-effectiveness techniques that permitted him to evaluate them relatively. As one observer concluded:

McNamara innovated both in the types of decisions that he did make and in the manner in which he made and carried them out. Both types of innovations stemmed from a conception that McNamara had of his office—a conception unlike that of any of his predecessors. . . . In making such novel decisions and in enforcing them, McNamara in effect not only asserted that a secretary of Defense can make and over-rule decisions on *military* as well as financial and administrative grounds. He also asserted that because any analytic technique can yield only so much informa-tion, it is necessary for a decision maker to make judgments and that his perspective as secretary of Defense made *his* judgments the most valuable and valid for the require-ments of *his* job. [6]

To the extent that role determines be-havior, an individual's impact on the ex-pectations of others is reduced. But an official can rationalize a policy decision by referring to the alleged demands of his role. President Nixon justified his sup-port of armed intervention in Cambodia in 1970 and Laos in 1971 by means of the requirement of his role as com-mander-in-chief that he protect American troops. The role of president of the United States affords wide latitude to in-dividual occupants in certain areas, espe-cially in foreign policy, as studies of pub-lic opinion have indicated [52]. Americans tend to accept a president's policy in for-eign affairs far more readily than in other areas. As the president has a national constituency and is responsible for sev-eral functions, he can choose to empha-size a particular one at a specific mo-ment.[11]

Other political role occupants have more limited discretionary responsibilities. They have less scope for individual initia-tive, and the role expectations of their organizations and bureaucracies reflect more parochial interests. Role prescrip-tions can be impressed upon individuals in various ways but primarily through so-cialization and recruitment. Individuals recruited for positions in the Soviet hier-archy, for example, are checked for their adherence to the party's official "line." Similarly, members of American govern-ment bureaucracies tend to recruit indi-viduals with similar beliefs and back-grounds. Role prescriptions are thus perpetuated by self-selection. Sometimes the results can be catastrophic. Before the Russian revolution of 1917 the leaders of the tsarist government were recruited only from a small aristocratic stratum of the population; the result was ineffectual leadership that in some regards aided revolutionary forces. After the revolution the new bolshevik government also re-cruited from a relatively limited group. Although the bolshevik government con-sisted almost entirely of members of the Communist Party or sympathizers, social class was relatively unimportant as a cri-terion for entry. University intellectuals, professional political organizers, workers, peasants, and even a few former tsarist officials composed the revolutionary re-gime. Although requiring ideological con-formity, the bolsheviks sought personnel throughout Russian society, particularly people who had technical skills and other expertise. On the other hand, the British have for some time recruited according to merit and achievement. The parliamen-tary form of government, the electoral system, and the existence of competitive political parties representing different so-cial groups increase the possibility that

[11] Clinton Rossiter has identified some of the presidential functions as chief of state, chief executive, commander-in-chief, chief diplomat, chief legislator, and chief of party [42].

individuals with various backgrounds, skills, and opinions will enter government. Even in Great Britain, however, there is a tendency for the political parties to nominate candidates and for the civil service to appoint individuals who have attended the "right" schools and who speak with the "appropriate" accent. There is thus a self-selection process that encourages the entry of individuals with backgrounds and views similar to those of the existing elite. Finally, in the less developed countries the absence of institutions of higher learning forces governments to recruit from among those who have been educated abroad, but the latter may have adopted values of the societies in which they were educated and may apply them to important decisions.

Those who are recruited and able to advance themselves have generally proved able to internalize role prescriptions, that is, to adopt them as personal role conceptions. The more complex and bureaucratic the foreign-policy process, the greater is the impact of institutionalized role prescriptions. As such prescriptions are generally resistant to change, highly bureaucratic countries are likely to pursue relatively conservative foreign policies.

GOVERNMENTAL VARIABLES

Governmental variables that shape policy differ from role variables as a machine differs from its parts. The types of governmental institutions, the distribution of influence among them, the means by which personnel are selected and recruited, the interests that they represent, and the degrees to which governmental institutions are open to social influences are all relevant to foreign-policy behavior. In addition, the larger the government, the more information it can handle, and the greater the attention it can pay to selected problems. On the other hand, as the size of a government increases, more people must approve each decision, which may slow down policy decisions.

Different governments make important decisions in different ways. In comparing these ways we must ask where decisions are made and what points of view are considered. Identifying the loci of decisions may thus assist us to understand the decisions themselves. For instance, when a legislature effectively represents social interests, we can expect less speed in adopting policies, more penetration by nongovernmental groups, and more continuity in foreign policy than when the legislature is either ineffective or unrepresentative. Walter Lippmann has argued that the democratic system places checks on government leaders and inhibits them from adopting foreign policies that they know to be necessary but unpopular:

The devitalization of the governing power is the malady of democratic states. . . . It can be deadly to the very survival of the state as a free society if, when the great and hard issues of war and peace, of security and solvency, of revolution and order are up for decision, the executive and judicial departments, with their civil servants and technicians, have lost their power to decide. [29]

It is important to discover whether the executive is strong or weak and whether influence is centralized or decentralized as in a confederation. In 1914 the centralized government of tsarist Russia was able to reach decisions more quickly than was the government of Austria-Hungary, in which both an Austrian and a Hungarian parliament had to approve a declaration of war. The tsarist government also had only an impotent legislature, the Duma, and was able to act more decisively than was the British government, which had to act through Parliament.

The nature of a regime may also be a factor in its foreign-policy behavior. A constitutional regime presumably operates under greater restraints than does an authoritarian one. Regimes with similar forms are more likely to ally with one another. If a regime is representative— because of contested elections, multiple political parties, and open nominating processes—it usually must take into account a wider range of views than if it represented only a limited segment of society. As a result, in representative systems the links between domestic pressures and foreign interests may be more important.

This last consideration leads to another, closely related one: the means by which government personnel and high-ranking political leaders are recruited and selected. Recruitment largely determines the character of government leaders as a whole. Are leaders appointed by other leaders, or are they selected by various social strata and groups outside the government itself? To what extent do those recruited represent different regional, age, sex, racial, language, class, and nationality groups in the population? If any one group is "overrepresented" its preferences are likely to be an important factor in government decisions. Are leaders and bureaucrats selected according to merit or according to other criteria like ideological conformity and family ties? If personnel are selected from a single social group or stratum, particularly one with a strong ideology, they will be less likely to have wide-ranging skills, less receptive to information that challenges their ideological predispositions, and more limited in their views of the community's interests in foreign policy.

Another significant variable is the extent and nature of bureaucratization. As one observer has noted, "The very bigness of governmental activities demands compartmentalization and specialization" [15]. When a nation modernizes and develops economically, its government is likely to become bureaucratically more complex as new ministries and departments, often with overlapping responsibilities, are created. "Modernization" tends to increase demands for rational problem solving and to mobilize parochial interests within the government. As modernization progresses "skilled" and differentiated interest groups emerge, broadening "the base of the ruling group as the sources of recruitment change from landownership to business, commerce, and areas of activity requiring university-trained specialists" [8].

There are both advantages and disadvantages in the involvement of large-scale bureaucracies in making foreign policy. As bureaucratic specialization increases, more information can be gathered and processed, but this increased information, unclear lines of responsibility, and proliferating "organizational" views and interests tend to promote inertia and reduce the possibility of decisive action. Such bureaucracies may become inimical to innovative and adaptive behavior. As we shall see, when distribution or redistribution of resources or authority is involved, foreign policy may be largely the product of competition among organizational interests and internally generated needs. The larger and more complex the government, the more political decisions may be a result of struggles among bureaucratic agencies. The smaller and less complex the government, the less information and expertise are available to make satisfactory choices, but speed in deciding is more likely.

The relationships between bureaucracies and executives or legislatures vary from actor to actor and from issue to issue. Sometimes legislatures or executives can control decision making and force bureaucracies only to implement policy. Kemal Ataturk at the height of his power dominated the Turkish bureaucracies. Alternatively, executives or legislatures may simply lay down general guidelines while delegating specific decisions to bureaucracies. Congressional relations with the military in the United States resemble this alternative. Occasionally bureaucracies are only monitored by other institutions, behaving as they wish until they make serious mistakes. The relationship between the British Cabinet and the corps of professional civil servants or between the French Cabinet and French bureaucracies, particularly when recurring issues are concerned, is of this type. Undoubtedly the relative independence of bureaucracies has an impact on foreign policy. For example, the more independent the foreign office, the more consistent foreign policy is likely to be. One of the determinants of European foreign policies in the eighteenth and nineteenth centuries was the relative independence of the respective foreign offices. In the Soviet Union and eastern Europe today foreign-policy decisions are generally taken by high-ranking members of the Communist Party; ministries of foreign affairs are relegated to implementation.

Continuing debate over the relative efficacy of democratic and authoritarian political systems in international affairs reflects a divergence of opinion on the degree to which social groups should be permitted voices in the making of foreign policy. Do governments that are responsible to electorates behave differently from the ways in which authoritarian regimes behave? Do multiparty or two-party systems operate differently from the ways in which single-party or nonparty systems operate? It has been argued that democracy hampers effective foreign policy by forcing leaders to respond to the whims of an ill-informed and mercurial electorate, rather than to external realities. The Greek leader Pericles, under attack by his fellow Athenians for having counseled war against Sparta, complained that it is "not like you to be so confounded with your domestic afflictions as to give up all thoughts of the common safety" [50]. John Locke, a democratic theorist, argued nonetheless that

what is to be done in reference to foreigners, depending much upon their actions and the variation of designs and interests, must be left in great part to the prudence of those who have this power committed to them, to be managed by the best of their skill for the advantage of the commonwealth. [30]

In a similar vein Lippmann and Alexis de Tocqueville have argued that democracies are unable to behave consistently in foreign affairs and that the parochial interests and opinions of private men should not be permitted to influence the conduct of foreign policy. The thrust of their criticism of "democratic" foreign policy is that open competition among groups with different values and priorities yields

ineffective compromises; the test of "good" policy is not its effectiveness in furthering objectives but its ability to attract popular endorsement.

Authoritarian governments have the advantage of being able to initiate and change policy quickly and decisively without restraint by nongovernmental groups. In 1939 it was relatively simple for the Soviet Union and Adolf Hitler's Germany, previously bitter adversaries, to sign a mutual nonaggression treaty with little domestic opposition. President Roosevelt, on the other hand, though he feared the growth of nazism from at least 1937, had to wait until the 1941 Japanese attack on Pearl Harbor before the United States could enter the war. What authoritarian regimes lose in consistency, they may gain in speed and secrecy.

The debate about the relative efficacy of democratic and authoritarian governments in foreign policy centers around the effects of accountability and publicity on policy decisions, but much of the debate has been essentially speculative. Stephen Salmore and Charles F. Hermann have, however, discovered that more "accountable" governments initiate relatively fewer foreign-policy actions than do less accountable ones, suggesting that the latter are indeed freer to behave decisively. They have also found that governments that are more accountable are relatively less hostile in their diplomatic exchanges than are unaccountable governments, though this finding may have been coincidental, a result of other factors [45].

SOCIETAL VARIABLES

Nongovernmental aspects of a society— its economic capability, political culture, and so on—also define opportunities for foreign-policy behavior. We must therefore ask specific questions about such social factors as degree of industrialization, territorial size, natural resources, social cohesion, and basic values.

The human and other resources available to an actor limit the potential influence of his foreign policy. The territorial size and geographic location of actors, though once quite important, have had declining impact on foreign policy recently. The city-states of ancient Greece, for example, were unable to unite partly because of mountainous terrain that inhibited communications and central control; nevertheless they could fight one another intermittently. The isolation of islands like Great Britain and Japan, as well as of continents like North America, have been important factors in defense policies and in those areas' aloofness from international affairs for long periods of time.

Toward the end of the nineteenth century an American naval officer, Alfred Thayer Mahan, argued that international influence is largely determined by control of the seas and that strategic geographic positions astride the great sea-lanes of international commerce gave certain states decided advantages. Some years later on the eve of World War I a British geographer, Sir Halford J. Mackinder, observing the growth of German power, began to doubt that naval superiority was sufficient to ensure Great Britain's international status. He particularly feared a combination of Russia and Germany because their geographic position would permit them to control the "world island"—Europe, Asia, and Africa—and would thus ensure them world supremacy. He summed up his view of geopolitics:

> Who rules East Europe
> commands the Heartland;
> Who rules the Heartland
> commands the World Island;
> Who rules the World Island
> commands the World. [49]

Both Mahan and Mackinder shared the common belief then that geographical position is the major determinant of international influence and status. Such beliefs have been undermined by technological advances. However salient geography may once have been in shaping goals or determining influence, it no longer plays a dominant role.

A second resource factor includes natural resources and fertile land. Those countries that are relatively self-sufficient in terms of natural resources are less likely to expand than are those that lack resources. Japan's attack on Pearl Harbor and its advance into Southeast Asia have been explained by its desire to secure sources of petroleum and iron ore to sustain its highly industrialized economy. Japanese expansion into this area and the attack on Pearl Harbor followed an American embargo of these products to Japan. On the other hand, actors who are naturally well endowed with resources may be more able to conduct vigorous and independent foreign policies.

Economic factors like the levels of industrialization, technological skills, productivity, demands for consumption, and available investment capital, as well as the presence or absence of military strength, can influence foreign-policy behavior. Whether well-endowed actors have greater incentives to use their resources in the exercise of influence is debatable.[12] Marxists have argued that excess capital creates incentives for imperialism, but other theorists have insisted that economic development actually reduces incentives to expand because leaders are relatively satisfied and perceive greater risks in international adventures than they do when they have "nothing to lose."

Under certain circumstances specific economic factors have clear impacts on foreign-policy decisions. China and the Soviet Union, both in need of wheat, have overcome ideological predispositions and have concluded trade agreements for the importation of wheat from Canada and the United States respectively. Thus, extensive crop failures in 1971–1972 seemed a major factor in persuading Soviet leaders to adopt a "soft" foreign policy in 1972. Societal factors in general merely determine what range of means may be available to an actor and the kinds of

---

[12] Recent research has suggested that available economic wealth is an excellent predictor of the outcome of war. But the measure does *not* predict the likelihood of going to war [38].

values on which decision makers are likely to rely in formulating goals.

It is difficult, however, to establish a firm causal connection between resources and foreign policy. A prevalent error in evaluating this connection is the fallacy of "post hoc, ergo propter hoc," the mistaken assumption that because a certain event occurred after certain factors were present, those factors necessarily *caused* the event. That Great Britain and France had surplus investment capital in the nineteenth century and invested this capital abroad does not mean that their possession of it *caused* the investment (though it made investment possible). The limitations and opportunities implied by certain resources are important to the degree that they are recognized by relevant leaders. Resource and capability analyses therefore have limited implications.

A second major category of societal variables includes political culture: the pattern of beliefs, identifications, and values held by the members of society. Whether they share or reject the goals adopted by their government may be a critical determinant of foreign policy. Simply stated, the more unified a society, the more likely it is to be effective in its foreign relations. History, myth, education, language, experience, and ideology are all factors affecting national pride, identity, and common goals.

In examining political culture we must first ask which groups are relevant to foreign policy. As we have already indicated, the more centralized the foreign-policy process is and the more concentrated political influence is, the less important social norms are. Nevertheless, to the degree that a government requires maintenance in the form of taxation or conscription, there must be some political support in the society at large. In each society some individuals may be "parochials," with little interest in or awareness of political events; others may be "subjects," aware of politics but not participants; finally, some citizens may be "participants," making demands upon the government or

taking part in its decisions. When parochials and subjects predominate in society, as they do in Albania and Laos, there is little social impact on foreign policy [4, 5]. The greater the number of participants in a society, the larger the number of relevant political groups will be. One comparative survey has revealed that 66 percent of American respondents believed that they can do something about an unjust law, whereas only 33 percent of Mexican respondents believed that they could have such an effect [5, p. 173].

A second question about political culture involves the degree to which it is homogeneous. Is the society relatively integrated, with little extreme opposition or division? Or does it include significant groups that are alienated from the remainder of society? Pakistan, for example, was deeply divided between the Punjabis of the west and the Bengalis of the east, whereas Denmark has been relatively homogeneous for some time. The less fragmentation within a society, the more stable its foreign policy can be. If a polity is deeply divided its government may seek to ally itself with external actors to protect itself against internal opposition; or it may simply be averse to risks in foreign affairs because of its vulnerability. It was largely to secure themselves against internal adversaries that some South Vietnamese leaders sought American assistance after 1954 and some Hungarian leaders sought Soviet assistance in 1956. A deeply divided society is also much more easily penetrated by external actors and may become a battleground, as did the Congo in 1960 and Jordan in 1970. Table 7.1 lists some of the countries in which foreign military intervention has occurred since 1960 partly as a consequence of internal divisions.

If a society is relatively homogeneous we can try to characterize its culture and predict the effects that its core values will have on foreign policy. These values can be predominantly instrumental (pragmatic) or consummatory (ideological). Only in societies in which instrumental values predominate would we expect to

Table 7.1.
Foreign Military Intervention Related to Domestic Conflict, 1960-1971

Country	Year of Intervention	Principal Intervener
Brunei	1962	Indonesia
Cambodia	1970	United States, North Vietnam
Central African Republic	1967	France
Chad	1968	France
Zaire	1960-1964	United Nations
Cyprus	1964-	United Nations
Czechoslovakia	1968	U.S.S.R.
Dominican Republic	1965	United States
Gabon	1964	France
Haiti	1968	Dominican Republic
Honduras	1969	El Salvador
Jordan	1970	Syria
Laos	1971-	South Vietnam, North Vietnam
Northern Ireland	1969-	Great Britain
South Vietnam	1961-	United States, North Vietnam
Yemen	1962-1967	Egypt

find organized social groups impinging upon the foreign-policy process with any regularity. These groups would be organized around specific common interests and would seek voices in foreign policy when foreign relations appeared to bear on those interests. In societies dominated by single ideologies most groups are manipulated by those who shape the ideologies; the only significant social groups are likely to be single political parties that define and uphold ideology. It has been asserted that foreign-policy formation in an ideologically oriented society is easier and more consistent because values and priorities are settled by the ideology itself [21, 24].

In practice most societies are fragmented to some degree. Heterogeneity in political socialization may result in conflicting values and fragmented political culture; under such circumstances common orientations toward the political process will be absent. Two important questions, then, are how much political fragmentation there is and what its consequences for foreign policy are. One type of fragmentation may reflect unequal property and income distributions, perhaps even opposition of different social classes. Sectional conflicts may also occur when inhabitants of one area develop strong group consciousness. As in the American and Nigerian civil wars, these conflicts can break into open strife. Finally, conflicts may center around issues like religion, race, language, or ethnic origins, and may explode into fighting as well. Northern Ireland has been torn by religious strife; India has been plagued by recurrent religious and linguistic quarrels since independence; and the original division of India and Pakistan was based on Muslim-Hindu hostility. Cyprus, on the other hand, has been split on the basis of nationality, between Greeks and Turks. In each instance internal conflicts have dominated foreign-policy calculations, have moved the country to adopt less coherent foreign policies, and have increased its vulnerability to external penetration.

It is commonly believed that the link between societywide variables and foreign policy lies in the tendency of actors with similar socioeconomic traits to behave in similar fashion and to cooperate in international relations, weakening or strengthening alliances according to the degree of cultural affinity [22]. One observer has suggested, "The more similar two nations are in economic development, political orientation, Catholic culture, and density, the more aligned their voting in the United Nations and the less conflictful their interactions will be" [43]. But the author of another empirical study has concluded:

Overall, *none* of the five characteristics—clustering by common institutional membership, proximity, economic interdependence, socio-cultural similarity, or similarity in UN voting behavior—in itself makes war between two countries *less* likely. . . . Clearly the conventional wisdom which asserts that political institutions always bring an end to war, or that "Good trade insures good will," is very mistaken. None of these relations is sufficient to prevent war. [44]

This statement reminds us that factors like common trade and geographical proximity *permit* conflict to occur by increasing the number of issues on which disagreements can arise.

In Chapter 8 we shall examine the factors conditioning foreign policy in more detail, exploring how their impacts vary in different situations even for a single actor. In this way we can perhaps gain greater insight into the differential effects of variables on foreign policy.

References

1. Acheson, Dean, *Present at the Creation* New York: Norton, 1969).
2. Acheson, Dean, "The President and the Secretary of State," in Don K. Price, ed., *The Secretary of State* (Englewood Cliffs, N.J.: Prentice-Hall, 1960), p. 35.
3. Adorno, T. W., *et al., The Authoritarian Personality* (New York: Harper & Row, 1950).
4. Almond, Gabriel A., and G. Bingham Powell, Jr., *Comparative Politics: A Developmental Approach* (Boston: Little, Brown, 1966), p. 53.
5. Almond, Gabriel A., and Sidney Verba, *The Civic Culture* (Boston: Little, Brown, 1965).
6. Art, Robert J., *The TFX Decision, McNamara and the Military* (Boston: Little, Brown, 1968), p. 166.
7. Attwood, William, *The Reds and the Blacks* (New York: Harper & Row, 1967).
8. Black, Cyril E., *The Dynamics of Modernization* (New York: Harper & Row, 1966), p. 79.
9. Borklund, C. W., *The Department of Defense* (New York: Praeger, 1968), p. 125.
10. Bronfenbrenner, Urie, "The Mirror Image in Soviet-American Relations: A Social Psychologist's Report," *The Journal of Social Sciences,* 17 (1961), pp. 45–56.
11. Clapp, Charles L., *The Congressman: His Work as He Sees It* (Washington, D.C.: Brookings, 1963).
12. Deutsch, Karl W., "External Influences on the Internal Behavior of States," in R. Barry Farrell, ed., *Approaches to Comparative and International Politics* (Evanston: Northwestern University Press, 1966), pp. 5–26.
13. Druckman, Daniel, "Ethnocentrism in the Inter-Nation Simulation," *Journal of Conflict Resolution,* 12 (March 1968), pp. 45–68.
14. Dulles, John Foster, *War or Peace* (New York: Macmillan, 1950), p. 20.
15. Farrell, R. Barry, "Foreign Policies of Open and Closed Political Societies," in Farrell, ed., *Approaches to Comparative and International Politics* (Evanston: Northwestern University Press, 1966), pp. 167–208.
16. Festinger, Leon, *A Theory of Cognitive Dissonance* (Stanford: Stanford University Press, 1957).
17. Finlay, David, Ole R. Holsti, and Richard Fagen, *Enemies in Politics* (Chicago: Rand McNally, 1967), pp. 25–96.
18. George, Alexander, and Juliette George, *Woodrow Wilson and Colonel House* (New York: Day, 1956).
19. Greenstein, Fred I., *Personality and Politics* (Chicago: Markham, 1969), pp. 46–57.
20. Gruliow, Leo, ed., *Current Soviet Policies—II* (New York: Praeger, 1957), p. 183.
21. Hoffmann, Stanley, "Restraints and Choices in American Foreign Policy," in Hoffmann, ed., *The State of War* (New York: Praeger, 1965), pp. 160–197.

22. Holsti, K. J., "National Role Conceptions in the Study of Foreign Policy," *International Studies Quarterly*, 14 (September 1970), pp. 267–268.

23. Kaplan, Morton A., "The Systems Approach to International Politics," in Kaplan, ed., *New Approaches to International Politics* (New York: St. Martin's, 1968), pp. 381–404.

24. Kissinger, Henry A., "Domestic Structure and Foreign Policy," in James N. Rosenau, ed., *International Politics and Foreign Policy*, rev. ed. (New York: Free Press, 1969), pp. 261–275.

25. Lane, Robert E., and David O. Sears, *Public Opinion* (Englewood Cliffs, N.J.: Prentice-Hall, 1964).

26. Lasswell, Harold D., *Psychopathology and Politics* (Chicago: University of Chicago Press, 1930).

27. Leites, Nathan, *The Operational Code of the Politburo* (New York: McGraw-Hill, 1951).

28. Leites, Nathan, *A Study of Bolshevism* (New York: Free Press, 1953).

29. Lippmann, Walter, *The Public Philosophy* (New York: Mentor, 1955), p. 29.

30. Locke, John, *The Second Treatise of Government*, Thomas P. Peardon, ed. (New York: Liberal Arts Press, 1952), chap. 12, para. 146.

31. McLellan, David S., "The Role of Political Style: A Study of Dean Acheson," Naomi Rosenbaum, ed., *Readings on the International Political System* (Englewood Cliffs, N.J.: Prentice-Hall, 1970), pp. 158–159.

32. McNamara, Robert F., *The Essence of Security* (New York: Harper & Row, 1968).

33. Montross, Lynn, *War Through the Ages*, 3rd ed. (New York: Harper & Row, 1960), p. 280.

34. Nye, Joseph S., Jr., and Robert O. Keohane, "Transnational Relations and World Politics: An Introduction," *International Organization*, 25 (Summer 1971), pp. 329–350.

35. Riggs, Fred W., "The Theory of Developing Politics," *World Politics*, 16 (October 1963), p. 171.

36. Rivera, Joseph H. de, *The Psychological Dimension of Foreign Policy* (Columbus, O.: Merrill, 1968), p. 206.

37. Rogow, Arnold, *James Forrestal* (New York: Macmillan, 1963), p. 351.

38. Rosen, Steven, "What is War Power?" (Paper delivered at the Sixty-Sixth Annual Meeting of the American Political Science Association, Los Angeles, September 8–12, 1970.)

39. Rosenau, James N., "Political Science in a Shrinking World," in Rosenau, ed., *Linkage Politics* (New York: Free Press, 1969).

40. Rosenau, James N., "Pre-Theories and Theories of Foreign Policy," in R. Barry Farrell, ed., *Approaches to Comparative and International Politics* (Evanston: Northwestern University Press, 1966), pp. 27–92.

41. Rosenau, James N., *The Scientific Study of Foreign Policy* (New York: Free Press, 1971), pp. 95–150.

42. Rossiter, Clinton, *The American Presidency*, 2nd ed. (New York: Mentor, 1960), pp. 13–40.

43. Rummel, R. J., "Some Empirical Findings on Nations and Their Behavior," *World Politics*, 21 (January 1969), p. 238.

44. Russett, Bruce M., *International Regions and the International System: A Study in Political Ecology* (Chicago: Rand McNally, 1967), pp. 198–199.

45. Salmore, Stephen A., and Charles F. Hermann, "The Effect of Size, Development, and Accountability on Foreign Policy," *Peace Research Society Papers*, 14 (1969), pp. 15–30.

46. Schlesinger, Arthur M., Jr., *The Coming of the New Deal* (Boston: Houghton Mifflin, 1958), p. 528.

47. Shils, Edward, "Authoritarianism: 'Right' and 'Left,' " in Richard Christie and Marie Jahoda, eds., *Studies in the Scope and Method of "The Authoritarian Personality"* (New York: Free Press, 1954), pp. 44–45.

48. Solzhenitsyn, Alexander, *The First Circle* (New York: Harper & Row, 1968), p. 94.

49. Sprout, Harold, and Margaret Sprout, *The Foundations of National Power* (Princeton: Van Nostrand, 1951), p. 155.

50. Stagner, Ross, *Psychological Aspects of International Conflict* (Belmont, Calif.: Brooks/Cole, 1967), p. 3.

51. U.S. Department of State, *Diplomacy for the 70's* (Washington, D.C.: Government Printing Office, 1971), pp. 3, 21–22.

52. Waltz, Kenneth N., "Electoral Punishment and Foreign Policy Crises," in James N. Rosenau, ed., *Domestic Sources of Foreign Policy* (New York: Free Press, 1967), chap. 10.
53. Westerfield, H. Bradford, *Party Politics and Foreign Policy: Pearl Harbor to Korea* (New Haven: Yale University Press, 1955), pp. 227–239.
54. White, Ralph K., "Images in the Context of International Conflict," in Herbert C. Kelman, ed., *International Behavior* (New York: Holt, 1965), pp. 238–276.
55. Zuckert, Eugene M., "The Service Secretary: Has He a Useful Role?" *Foreign Affairs,* 44 (April 1966), p. 464.

Suggested Reading

Almond, Gabriel A., and G. Bingham Powell, Jr., *Comparative Politics: A Developmental Approach* (Boston: Little, Brown, 1966).

Barber, James D., *The Presidential Character: Predicting Performance in the White House* (Englewood Cliffs, N.J.: Prentice-Hall, 1972).

Cartwright, Dr. Frederick F., *Disease and History* (New York: Crowell, 1972).

Farrell, R. Barry, ed., *Approaches to Comparative and International Politics* (Evanston: Northwestern University Press, 1966).

Greenstein, Fred I., *Personality and Politics* (Chicago: Markham, 1969).

Herz, John H., "The Territorial State Revisited: Reflections on the Future of the Nation-State," in James N. Rosenau, ed., *International Politics and Foreign Policy,* rev. ed. (New York: Free Press, 1969), pp. 76–89.

Kelman, Herbert C., ed., *International Behavior* (New York: Holt, 1965).

Rosenau, James N., ed., *Linkage Politics* (New York: Free Press, 1969).

Rosenau, James N., *The Scientific Study of Foreign Policy* (New York: Free Press, 1971).

Singer, J. David, ed., *Human Behavior and International Politics* (Chicago: Rand McNally, 1965).

Waltz, Kenneth N., *Foreign Policy and Democratic Politics* (Boston: Little, Brown, 1967).

Wilkinson, David O., *Comparative Foreign Relations: Framework and Methods* (Belmont, Calif.: Dickenson, 1969).

Chapter 8
DECISION MAKING AND THE DETERMINANTS OF INTERNATIONAL BEHAVIOR

I sit here all day trying to persuade people to do the things they ought to have sense enough to do without my persuading them—Harry S. Truman [40]

Factors internal to a particular unit, like perception, motivation, and organization, are crucial to full and accurate explanations of its behavior in international politics. Through examining an actor's internal environment we can learn something about how domestic and foreign variables interact in the process of decision making. We shall explore several models of decision making, focusing on how variables shape foreign-policy outcomes under different circumstances.

INTERNAL FACTORS AS MEDIATING VARIABLES

Some extreme explanations of foreign-policy behavior emphasize external or internal factors exclusively. In contrast, others, such as the mediated-response model, include both sets of factors. From a perspective emphasizing external factors, an actor's behavior is treated as a simple stimulus-response model. Individual characteristics of leaders and states are ignored. By closely observing reactions to selected stimuli over time, analysts hope to discover the probabilities of certain responses and to predict future behavior [30, 32].[1] They err in seeking conditioning factors only within the system itself, rather than also within the actors that constitute it. Each actor is viewed as participating in an international "marketplace" in which behavior is determined largely by "market factors." This stimulus-response approach seldom explains the behavior of actors adequately, for it assumes that responses to specific stimuli are already "set." To explain why individual actors behave as they do, some scholars, including Hans Morgenthau, have argued that the restraints and opportunities confronting an actor in the international system define "national interest" [25, 36]. Their reasoning is that an actor's primary goal is survival, which is

---

[1] Graham T. Allison calls this approach the "rational policy model" of foreign policy [2].

154

guaranteed only when the "rules" of the system are followed. It is therefore in a state's "national interest" to pursue certain policies and to abjure others. In particular, because the international system is characterized by decentralized decision making, it is in an actor's "national interest" to expand his "power."

The main signpost that helps political realism to find its way through the landscape of international politics is the concept of interest defined in terms of power.... We assume that statesmen think and act in terms of interest defined as power.... The idea of interest is indeed the essence of politics and is unaffected by the circumstances of time and place. [37]

This explanation does not stand up under scrutiny, however. If the structure of the system *requires* certain behavior to secure an actor's interests, then statesmen ought to be able to agree on an optimal course of behavior. But they are not. Upon close examination, national interest usually turns out to be the interest of a particular group in society or the subjective interpretation of a small group of political leaders. The so-called laws of prudent policy formation are not laws at all but merely policy prescriptions that different statesmen interpret differently. Furthermore, national-interest reasoning tends to ignore the extent to which individuals can alter policy. The model is attractively simple, for the analyst need not know what occurs within each actor; he need only explain and predict international behavior much as one might explain the caroms and rebounds in a pinball machine. As a highly rational model it tempts observers to define unexpected behavior as "irrational"; it thus does not account for the myriad objectives and behavior patterns actually found in the international system.

At the other extreme from the stimulus-response model, would be a model that takes no account of inputs from the international system in explaining the behavior of actors. It can be called the "autistic" model. Policy making would be considered to be completely divorced from

external stimuli and behavior to be governed entirely by internally generated forces. Policies would be pursued and evaluated by individuals for domestic reasons, regardless of their external impacts. When a state's foreign-policy decisions are based solely on ideology or on the whims of a single leader, its behavior is autistic. Failure is likely, because calculations are not based on external "reality." Adolf Hitler's invasion of the Soviet Union in 1941 and his failure to take account of his adversaries' overwhelming superiority in resources may have been an example of such autistic behavior.

In practice most actors are influenced by both systemic and subsystemic factors. To understand how an actor's behavior is shaped, we must therefore seek a model that includes both. Earlier we saw how the structure and shape of the international system present opportunities for and constraints on behavior of international actors. We suggested that the emergent properties of a system cannot be understood by reference to any of its parts alone. Nor can the foreign policies of specific actors be explained or predicted by reference only to systemic properties. Although the international system and its structure do influence the formation and execution of policy, each actor's specific policies owe much to internal influences and pressures. Because the international system is decentralized, policy decisions are made in accordance with the parochial perceptions of "local" statesmen. These perceptions are in turn conditioned by a host of internal and external variables. Focusing on the actor not only emphasizes the impact of internal factors but also implies that variations in national policies in time can stimulate changes in the international political system.

In seeking to explain the behavior of particular actors, we can divide the internal foreign-policy process into two distinct phases, which correspond approximately to an internal response and stimulus parallel to the familiar mediated-response model of psychology. In other words, an external stimulus triggers a series of responses—including perception, definition of the situation, evaluation, and assignment of responsibilities. These internal responses serve as stimuli for behavior that will be perceived by other actors as an external response [42, 18]. Figure 8.4 illustrates the way in which the behavior of other actors serves as a stimulus for internal processes which in turn culminate in external policy. This policy, the external response of one actor, is then an external stimulus for others.

The mediated-response model reminds us that foreign policy is not the result of a single decision by a single individual. On the contrary, it is the product of continual decisions, which often compete with or contradict one another. Such decisions modify and nullify previous decisions and help to structure future decisions. An actor's policy response to an international stimulus is the product of a process of deciding on principles and objectives, allocation and application of resources, and evaluation of previous decisions. Frequently these decisions are made by different individuals in different organizations. Foreign-policy outcomes are the products of complex interaction among many groups and individuals both within and outside the official government structure. They are, in effect, the emergent properties of these many discrete decisions. Furthermore, relevant groups and individuals vary with the actors and the nature of the issue.

MAJOR DECISION-MAKING FACTORS

Rationality

Foreign policy is, in the final analysis, the product of decisions by relevant individuals in a complex organizational setting. A decision is basically a choice among alternatives; ideally, individual decisions are reached through rational selection of the "best" among "all" alternatives— that is, the alternative that promises to maximize the actor's values. We might construct a model of how an individual

"ought" to decide in order to maximize his benefits. The decision-making calculus of such a model would take the following form: utility = (probability of desired outcome) × (value of outcome) + (probability of undesired outcome) × (value of undesired outcome) [48, pp. 107–112].

In international politics, however, limited information, the costs in time and manpower of acquiring more, and the frequent need for secrecy and dispatch prevent decision makers from considering all possible alternatives [35]. "Rational" decisions therefore usually entail selecting "satisfying" alternatives from among those that are apparent. The costs of extended searching usually outweigh the potential gains in additional alternatives. Time is one of the least elastic resources available to leaders [55, 63].

We suspect that decisions are never based on such rational calculations. It is virtually impossible for a decision maker to determine with much certainty the values and probabilities of different alternatives. At best he can make "educated guesses." Furthermore, the shortage of time and the press of other issues make even the desirability of such a formal, rational process doubtful.

The use of the rational-utility model to account for decisions by collective actors like states and intergovernmental organizations raises even greater difficulties. Again values and probabilities are difficult to determine and alternatives costly to discover. But these problems are even more acute for collective actors because different individuals and elites have different perspectives that can foster conflict and inconsistency in decisions. Besides, the utility model ignores the variety of pressures and influences that impinge on decision makers at all stages of the process.

Despite these difficulties, however, there is a tendency to expect such "rational" calculations to guide the behavior of others. For many years it was fashionable in the United States to interpret the behavior of the Soviet Union and its satellites as the product of central control and management according to a "master plan" for communist expansion. Indeed, many prominent Americans lamented the inability of the United States to deal effectively with the "coldly rational and calculating Russians" [33]. Soviet leaders on their part are reluctant to consider Western behavior as unplanned or the result of complex and fortuitous circumstances [28].

In seeking an alternative to the rational model of decision making, we must explore more closely the processes of the mediated-response model. Typically policy making involves several steps, during each of which individuals and groups are called upon to make decisions discretely. These steps include the perception of

events and receipt of new information, interpretation of new data, consideration of possible alternative responses, execution of policy, and appraisal of the action undertaken. Focusing on the flow of information during this process, Karl W. Deutsch has developed a crude model for charting the functional relations among the various stages of the communications process. This chart, reproduced in Figure 8.1, presents a shrewd summary of the foreign-policy process that we now wish to analyze. As references to "consciousness," "attention," and "memory" suggest, Deutsch views institutional decision making as analogous to the functioning of a human brain. The scheme includes in altered form the major variables of the mediated stimulus-response model. While

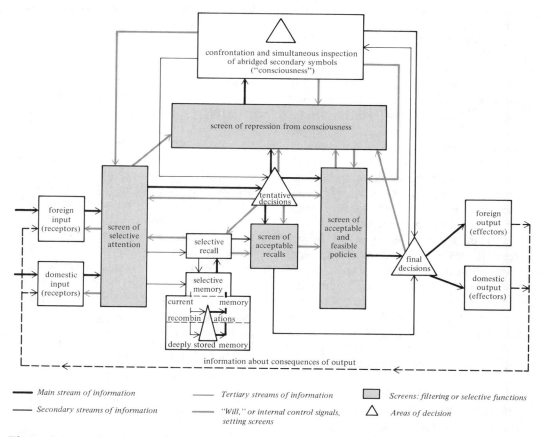

Figure 8.1. A Functional Diagram of Information Flow in Foreign-Policy Decisions
Source: Reprinted with permission of The Macmillan Company from *Nerves of Government* by Karl W. Deutsch. Copyright © 1963 by The Free Press, a Division of The Macmillan Company.

we will refer only to the most salient of the factors in the Deutsch diagram, the scheme reveals the complexity of the communications process in decision making.

Perception

The logical first phase of decision making begins when the actor becomes aware of events and demands that seem to call for response. They may arise from the international environment or from the actor's own internal environment. A Soviet diplomatic note or a demonstration by college students may serve as initial inputs into the American foreign-policy establishment. The actor's awareness is the first stage of the internal response process to which we referred earlier. The *accurate* perception of an intial input is critical if the actor is to deal effectively with problems. A red light at a street corner causes the average individual to stop; the light is a perceived stimulus. A blind person who cannot see the red light receives no stimulus, is not alerted to a changed situation, and may not stop; the red light is not part of his psychological environment. Serious consequences may ensue for the individual who is unable to perceive a stimulus. International actors evolve elaborate "eyes" for themselves: intelligence organizations, diplomats, news agencies, military personnel. These groups scan, encode, and interpret incoming information. They select information for further attention. Only a fraction of the total information input can be passed along to others in the foreign-policy community because of the limited capacity of the communications network and its channels. At this stage, as at all stages in the policy process, information is refined and filtered, and misperceptions and distortions can occur. Initial selection and screening (what Deutsch calls the "screen of selective attention") is critical because too much information may disguise what is important and may clog communications channels so that decisions cannot be made at all. As with a radio receiver, it is desirable that "static" be eliminated and that only information that has a bearing on an actor's policies and is comprehensible to him be processed.

Often there are multiple perceptions of a single event, especially an important one. For example, there were at least three separate sources of information for American leaders during the initial North Korean invasion of South Korea in June 1950 [48, p. 48].[2] How information is encoded, what is transmitted and what is not, and how information is interpreted at the primary source are important in determining subsequent events.[3] One common kind of distortion results when individuals relay only what they believe that their superiors wish to hear. Ian Fleming, himself a former intelligence agent, once wrote, "Wishful intelligence, the desire to please or reassure the recipient, was the most dangerous commodity in the whole realm of secret information [11].[4]

Interpretation and Definition of the Situation

Once information has been perceived and encoded, it is transmitted for further evaluation and interpretation. At this point the vast bureaucracies that constitute modern governments typically become involved. Once again various individual and organizational biases may lead to distortion. Incoming information is winnowed according to certain criteria of importance. Information is interpreted on the basis of frames of reference and then pieced together to make a complete picture of what is occurring and to permit evaluation in terms of the actor's values

[2] The sources included the American ambassador in South Korea, United Press International, and the Tokyo headquarters of the American Far East Military Command.

[3] An excellent fictional account of an attempt by communists in a small Southeast Asian nation to manipulate initial American perceptions of a crisis in that country is contained in William J. Lederer and Eugene Burdick, *Sarkhan* (New York: McGraw-Hill, 1965).

[4] For an excellent discussion of difficulties involved in intelligence, see Roberta Wohlstetter, *Pearl Harbor: Warning and Decision* (Stanford: Stanford University Press, 1962).

and objectives. Current information is thus combined with individual and collective memories of past events ("selective recall" in Figure 8.1). This stage is critical because discrete pieces of "raw" information seldom convey immediate and clear meanings.

The Korean invasion again illustrates the point. Shortly before it began, the American ambassador requested more military assistance in South Korea to counter a buildup of North Korean forces along the 38th parallel. The U.S. State Department judged the request unnecessary and filed it away because its definition of the situation differed from that of the ambassador. At that time the department viewed Europe as the most likely arena for Soviet aggression and consequently as the chief concern of American policy makers.[5] Second, the Soviet Union was considered incapable of fighting a major war with the United States because of its inferiority in nuclear weapons and therefore unlikely to initiate a major provocation. Third, the American ambassador was perceived as strongly sympathetic to South Korea, and his request was considered a reflection of this sympathy, rather than an accurate assessment of the North Korean threat. Finally, the South Korean armed forces were mistakenly believed to be stronger than those of North Korea and in need of no further American assistance.[6]

The distinction between the actor's psychological and operational environments is relevant here [59]. When the latter, consisting of "real" conditions that will affect the actor whether he is aware of them or not, differs sharply from the actor's perceived or psychological environment, policy failures are likely. Such was the case in the period preceding the outbreak of the Korean conflict. Similarly, the operational environment impinged on American alternatives and potential outcomes even before American decision makers became aware of the Japanese naval task force in December 1941 or of Soviet missiles in Cuba in the autumn of 1962. The psychological environment includes the information on which plans and expectations are founded. American planners in 1941 and 1962 shaped policy in terms of their psychological environments, an imperfect guide. As one team of scholars has suggested,

> With respect to policy-making and the content of policy decisions, our position is that what matters is how the policy maker imagines the milieu to be, not how it actually is. With respect to the operational results of decisions, what matters is how things are, not how the policy maker imagines them to be. [60, p. 328]

The Decision and the Situation

The number of people involved in making a decision and how incoming information is likely to be processed are largely functions of three perceptual variables: *awareness, degree of threat,* and *decision time.* Awareness is the degree to which a particular situation or type of situation is anticipated by decision makers. Some events, like the murder of the Austrian Archduke Francis Ferdinand in 1914, completely surprise political leaders; others, like the defeat of Chiang Kai-shek's Nationalist regime in China in 1949, are anticipated. The latter are likely to involve planning,[7] usually at many echelons of government bureaucracy. The existence of plans is likely to reduce innovative behavior or rapid casting about for new alternatives.

---

[5] The North Korean regime was perceived as a "puppet" government unable to act without Soviet approval.

[6] For an excellent though somewhat dated essay on how information is processed by the U.S. State Department, see Charlton Ogburn, Jr., "The Flow of Policy Making in the Department of State," in H. Field Haviland, Jr., *et al.*, eds., *The Formulation and Administration of United States Foreign Policy: Report of the Committee on Foreign Relations of the United States Senate* (Washington, D.C.: The Brookings Institution, 1960), pp. 172–177.

[7] Before Chiang's defeat, the United States government had circulated to its embassies abroad a description of what American foreign policy toward a communist-controlled China would be.

The more a situation promises to produce consequences contrary to an actor's basic values, the more threat is involved. Such a situation becomes salient for leaders and increases the likelihood that decisions will be made by top leaders rather than by low- or middle-level bureaucrats following established procedures. Very threatening situations are rare and usually require innovative responses.

Decision time is the time that decision makers think they have in which to decide before a situation has evolved significantly. For example, at the beginning of the Cuban missile crisis President John F. Kennedy and his advisers perceived that it was only a matter of weeks before Soviet missiles in Cuba would be operational. They believed that they had to make a decision before that happened. The less time perceived for decisions, the more likely it is that the decision-making group will remain small in order to facilitate the building of consensus. Furthermore, when little time is perceived, there is a less extensive search for alternatives than there would be without a perceived time limit.

Using these three variables Charles F. Hermann has described eight alternative situations, which are represented in a "situational cube" in Figure 8.2. With this typology we can identify different situations that generate different styles of response. Crises, for example, are characterized by high threat, short decision time, and surprise. The decision group is likely to be small and to include only top political and administrative leaders. At the other extreme, when threat is low, the event unsurprising, and the time available for decisions great, the response process is likely to involve lower bureaucratic echelons behaving in routine ways. For example, the arrest of an American student in Beirut for drug trafficking excites few people and is handled routinely by the American consulate there. The authorization of visas for travel in India is dealt with by low-level Indian diplomatic personnel following standard procedures.

Between these two extremes we can identify several variations. When the threat is high, the situation unanticipated, and decision time extended, we can more readily expect innovative behavior. Perception of the situation as threatening ensures that the response will not be routine and that it will be handled by high-level decision makers. The time available permits them to explore various alternative responses in search of the most appropriate one, which encourages innovation and the suggestion of new ideas. The decision to propose the Marshall plan in 1947, or Richard M. Nixon's decision in the summer of 1971 to impose restrictions on the conversion of gold into dollars, exemplifies the likely process under this set of circumstances [22]. Innovation is unlikely, however, when decision makers have extended time to deal with a surprising, but not very threatening situation. The absence of threat provides little incentive to innovate, and the extended decision time permits desultory deliberations. As the situation is unanticipated, no plans are available that might be put into operation automatically. Few substantive decisions are likely to be made in this situation, and inertia may result. If, on the other hand, the threat is low, the event surprising, and decision time short, there may be greater incentive to act. Other, more pressing problems may, however, ensure inertia again. When there are no other important problems, policy makers may recognize a rare opportunity to make consequential decisions. An anticipated situation perceived as highly threatening to core values and a short time in which to make decisions present opportunity for extensive preplanning by leaders, as in American policy in Berlin in 1948. Because of the limited time available to decision makers once the event has occurred, plans will probably be prepared in advance so that they can be put into operation almost reflexively. Finally, in a situation involving high threat, little surprise, and extended decision time, there is opportunity both before and after the event for many groups to participate in the decision. The importance of the situation provides an incentive for involvement, and there is likely to be consider-

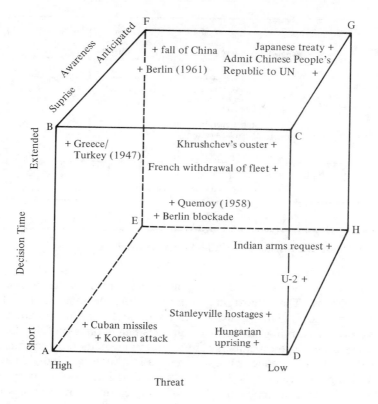

Figure 8.2. A Situational Cube*

A. *Crisis situation*
   High threat/short time/surprise
B. *Innovative situation*
   High threat/extended time/surprise
C. *Inertia situation*
   Low threat/extended time/surprise
D. *Circumstantial situation*
   Low threat/short time/surprise

E. *Reflexive situation*
   High threat/short time/anticipated
F. *Deliberative situation*
   High threat/extended time/anticipated
G. *Routinized situation*
   Low threat/extended time/anticipated
H. *Administrative situation*
   Low threat/short time/anticipated

Source: Charles F. Hermann, "International Crisis as a Situational Variable." Reprinted with permission of The Macmillan Company from *International Politics and Foreign Policy* by James N. Rosenau. Copyright © 1969 by The Free Press, a Division of The Macmillan Company.

* The representation of a three-dimensional space in a two-dimensional diagram makes it difficult to interpret the locations of the situations; their positions should not be considered exact in any case.

able controversy and competition among and within groups for the adoption of policies.[8]

Implementation of Policy

As we have suggested, the internal response of an actor to a situation eventually includes the assignment of different

[8] For a more extensive discussion of this typology, see Charles F. Hermann, "International Crisis as a Situational Variable," in James N. Rosenau, ed., *International Politics and Foreign Policy*, rev. ed. (New York: Free Press, 1969), pp. 409–421.

groups within the foreign-policy establishment to handle and process information about the situation or external stimulus. Once these individuals and groups have formulated and debated alternative responses to the challenge, they enter the second stage of the mediated-response model, that of internal stimulus. The internal stimulus involves the determination of policy and its implementation. Implementation is considered an internal stimulus because it sets in motion those activities that are perceived by other international actors as the actor's external

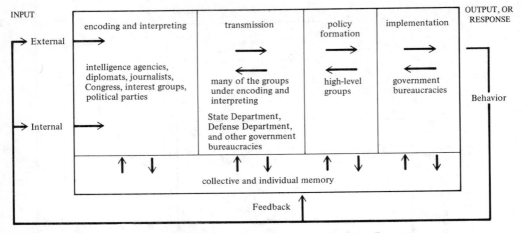

Figure 8.3. A Schematic Representation of the American Decision Process

response. The implementation stage also requires many decisions. The allocation of resources, the timing of initiatives, and the choice of means for carrying out policy involve discrete decisions by members of the civil and military bureaucracies. The implementation of policy and the reactions of other international actors are monitored by various agencies and individuals, and their appraisals constitute feedback. Ideally such feedback permits decision makers to discontinue or modify unsuccessful policy initiatives and to continue or intensify successful ones. Figure 8.3 represents schematically the process as it occurs among policy groups in the United States.

Although the figure suggests that specific groups are entrusted with each step of the process, this suggestion is deceptive. Different individuals and groups tend to become involved in different types of situations, and consequently different situations are treated in different ways, ranging through rapid action by high-level decision makers, bureaucratic conflict and cooperation, and routine processing by lower-level bureaucrats. Nevertheless, the functional specialization suggested by the figure tends to characterize the United States.

Appraisal and Memory

Past experience shapes an individual's or an organization's image of the environment and influences responses to current information. Memory not only fills in missing pieces of information as it organizes perceptions but also facilitates interpretation of those perceptions. An organization, like an individual, may be regarded as having a memory, one based on complex information retrieval systems. Behavior is "learned" from previous experience, and responses are shaped by expectations of reward and punishment derived from past behavior. Deutsch's concepts of "selective memory" and "selective recall" in Figure 8.1 suggest that, like current information, stored information is also subject to a screening and selection process. Memory affects current decisions in the form of feedback inputs as illustrated in Figures 8.1 and 8.3. The concepts of memory and feedback are based on the study of what Norbert Wiener has termed "cybernetics," the science of control and communication.

Memory is not solely a repository of facts about the past; it also contains evaluations related to the environment. Successful responses are rewarding, predisposing the actor toward similar behavior when confronted with analogous events.[9] Punishment, on the other hand, generates feedback inhibiting the repetition of the behavior and promotes a search for alternative responses to similar situations.

[9] Reinforcement is perceived largely in the form of political support by important domestic groups [44].

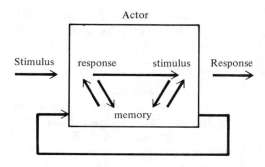

* Stimulus = *objective external action*
response = *actor's perception of and feeling toward external action*
stimulus = *actor's perception of his intentions, purposes, and behavior toward other actors*
Response = *actor's objective external action*

Figure 8.4. Expanded Mediated-Response Model with Memory and Feedback

Reward or success, on the other hand, generates hope. The fear or hope generated as responses in past situations become stimuli in current situations. It is this affective element in the memory that assists in the evaluation of new events (see Figure 8.4). In practice, the affective element is a prime determinant in the search for innovative responses.[10] For example, the failure of the Bay of Pigs invasion in 1960 has made the United States wary of engaging in similar operations. Great fear may even "short-circuit" the feedback process, that is, prevent consideration of certain courses of action owing to their lack of success in the past. The success of the Berlin airlift of 1948, on the other hand, may have contributed to American willingness to seek "technological" solutions to political dilemmas.

A faulty feedback process may lead to consistently inaccurate responses to external events. The cause may be misperception or distortion of information at any stage of the foreign-policy process. Furthermore, domestic objectives may shape an actor's foreign policy; then his foreign behavior is less likely to be effective in obtaining external objectives. Indeed, the pursuit of foreign objectives can lead to

[10] For an elaboration of learning models, see John R. Raser [46] and Herbert O. Mowrer [38].

undesirable domestic consequences. President Lyndon B. Johnson suffered political defeat because of public unwillingness to support a limited war for an extended time.

Amplifying feedback from an actor's memory can stimulate unwarranted fears, so that external events may appear increasingly dominant, as in Germany immediately before World War I. A high level of tension can further distort the perception of new information and lead to collective paranoia. In the contemporary international system the rhetoric of the People's Republic of China reflects somewhat paranoid perceptions of the international environment. Because it perceives itself as surrounded by enemies, China's behavior toward other actors has been predominantly hostile. Data collected by Charles A. McClelland and his associates show that between 1966 and 1969, 93 percent of China's behavior toward the Soviet Union was hostile, as was 91 percent of its behavior toward the United States and 67 percent of its behavior toward the rest of the world [31]. Such behavior can actually stimulate hostility on the part of other actors, thereby becoming a self-fulfilling prophecy.

STYLES OF DECISION MAKING

Once information has been perceived and evaluated, various forces for response are engaged. These forces may take several forms, depending upon the actor and the nature of the perceived situation. Such forms define the decision-making style of an actor, his predispositions toward certain kinds of organization, and the latitude allowed to decision makers. Although there are many permutations in styles of decision making, there are a few that predominate among most actors.

Incrementalism: Two Steps Forward, One Step Back

Roger Hilsman has picturesquely characterized the incremental style that dominates many aspects of foreign policy:

[I]t is an uneasy . . . compromise among competing goals. . . . A government does not decide to inaugurate the nuclear age, but only to try to build an atomic bomb before its enemy does. . . . Rather than through grand decisions on grand alternatives, policy changes seem to come through a series of slight modifications of existing policy, with new policy emerging slowly and haltingly by small and usually tentative steps, a process of trial and error in which policy zigs and zags, reverses itself, and then moves forward. [16]

As Hilsman has suggested, formation of foreign policy is in most instances incremental. Rarely are there basic changes in an actor's orientation toward his external environment—at least not precipitate or planned changes. The bulk of an actor's foreign policy involves routine procedures in the maintenance of ordinary relations with other actors and of bureaucratic competition in the pursuit of parochial goals. Large, highly modernized actors shift their foreign-policy postures largely through incremental decisions on very specific issues.

In view of their imperfect information and inability to foresee accurately the consequences of their own decisions, it is perhaps desirable that leaders proceed cautiously. Furthermore, radical shifts are inhibited by the numerous cross pressures and influences to which foreign policy is subject. Statesmen are bound by their own roles and by the push and pull of parochial interests. If policy were formulated in response only to external inputs, as claimed by certain "national interest" theorists, we might expect larger investments in planning and prediction than are usual. The factors that shape foreign policy, however, particularly in modern bureaucratic states, arise from many varied sources. A major analysis of decision making has identified thirteen sources of such influence [58]. In large bureaucratic states like the United States these forces interact, mingling formulations of objectives and analysis of means with considerations of precedent, bureaucratic harmony, and organizational interest. "Good" policy is often policy on which different groups can agree, rather than policy offering the greatest probability of positive outcomes [29, 4].

Small-Group Decisions

Some situations, like international crises, elicit less formal responses from small groups of high-level leaders. In the 1962 Cuban missile crisis, for instance, President Kennedy bypassed the ordinary mechanisms of policy formation and set up a small group of approximately fifteen trusted advisers, which came to be known as "Ex Comm." The need for secrecy, innovative behavior, and consensus restricts the size of decision-making groups in crises. Although most groups could be smaller than fifteen members, the psychological pressure of responsibility for weighty decisions leads decision makers to spread this responsibility as widely as possible (within the limits imposed by the need for secrecy and speed) and to seek advice and additional information from specialists.

Small-group decision making differs from that of large organizations in a number of ways. First, the parochial interests of the group members' bureaucratic organizations (in which the individuals may occupy high places) are somewhat subordinated to the purposes of the ad hoc group, which tends to behave cooperatively and expeditiously. Furthermore, the shortage of time in which to make decisions and the threat of the situation generate stress. Although individuals tend to perform least effectively under conditions of intense stress, there is evidence that mild pressure actually increases productivity and efficiency, heightens morale, and enhances problem-solving abilities in small groups [27, 14]. Up to some inflection point, then, stress facilitates innovative and adaptive behavior; beyond that point it impairs such behavior.[11] When there is either too little or too much in-

---

[11] This relationship between performance and stress has been found in research on World War I and during runs of Inter-Nation Simulation, an experimental game in which small groups play the role of decision makers in a mock international system [17, 53].

formational input, the group's ability to process it suffers.

Some stress seems to reduce selfish behavior and to increase group cooperation. When the pressure of time is perceived, groups are more able to reach agreement quickly; this cooperation may facilitate decisions, but it can also lead to bad ones, particularly if no one present offers divergent views [12]. Robert Kennedy has argued that if President Kennedy and his advisers had been forced to make a decision during the Cuban missile crisis twenty-four hours before they did, they would have chosen to initiate a preventive air strike against Soviet bases in Cuba, rather than to blockade the island.

The ability of individuals in small groups to deal with complex information and to combine it with stored information is another crucial determinant of the effectiveness of such groups in crises. When more individuals are able to process information efficiently, there will be greater interpersonal conflict, but this conflict will be helpful in the synthesis and integration of policy alternatives. By contrast, in organizations that penalize innovative behavior, alternatives will not be presented. Soviet bureaucrats (the *apparatchiki*) under Joseph Stalin and American State Department bureaucrats during the era of Senator Joseph McCarthy of Wisconsin tended to transmit only information that they believed that their superiors wanted. Rarely did they offer imaginative or innovative alternatives to existing policy.

In conditions of stress and limited time, the members of small groups tend to rely on their own memories of past events, rather than on the research facilities of the large bureaucracies. Their memories may, however, suggest simplified comparisons and analogies with past events. President Harry S. Truman's determination that Korea should not be "another Munich" and Robert Kennedy's concern lest his brother be viewed as "another Tojo" suggest that simple analogies may prove potent in the decisions of small groups.

In noncrisis situations small groups may develop sets of behavioral norms for their members that resemble the standard operating procedures of large bureaucracies. These norms and the threat of punishment for deviant behavior may restrict opportunities for innovation. Individuals' perceived needs to win group acceptance may cause many of the difficulties apparent in organizational behavior: routinization and primary emphasis on response to internal, rather than to external, stimuli [54]. In noncrisis situations, then, ad hoc groups may come to resemble the many special committees and commissions that are established in the United States to study particular problems but that rarely evolve imaginative or innovative proposals. Small groups usually cannot cope with the vast day-to-day business of conducting foreign policy. The bulk of foreign policy is conducted by larger organizations, acting within general guidelines and avoiding major deviations from past behavior patterns.

Bureaucratic Competition

The incremental model of foreign-policy formation presupposes the existence of a government that consists of "a conglomerate of semi-feudal, loosely allied organizations, each with a substantial life of its own" [2, p. 698]. The existence of such organizations encourages another style of decision making—bureaucratic competition. Policy is the product of interaction among a large number of relatively independent governmental and nongovernmental organizations and groups; the assumption that "rational" decisions are based on "national" needs therefore seems remote from reality. In practice much foreign policy is the outcome of highly political intragovernmental processes involving competition and bargaining among bureaus; the outcome depends as much on the "relative power" of the participants as on the "cogency and wisdom of the arguments used in support of the policy adopted" [15].

This characterization is particularly apt in relation to situations perceived as important, when time is available for decisions, and when decisions can lead to the distribution or redistribution of resources within or among public and private bureaucratic organizations. In such circumstances coalitions are likely to arise across organizational boundaries, in order to secure the interests of the participants. Representative Mendel Rivers of South Carolina, long chairman of the House Armed Services Committee, and representatives of the military services often worked together against a coalition of liberal congressmen and representatives of the State Department to ensure a high level of defense expenditures and to safeguard the military establishment from civilian interference. When such coalitions form in the United States, senators and representatives are often included on each side [65]. In addition, the process may be characterized by expanding or shifting areas of conflict in which the original "losers" may shift a policy debate from one arena into another, often larger or more public arena, in order to gain new support for their views. For example, in 1971 supporters, including the Nixon administration, of the proposal to fund and construct a supersonic transport plane in the United States, having apparently lost one battle in Congress, began to broaden the debate by soliciting the support of interested labor and management leaders. When a conflict involves a general issue like the level of military expenditures and the nature of national priorities, adversaries may also clash over more specific issues in different arenas. Opponents of high defense expenditures in the United States in the late 1960s attacked the war in Vietnam as immoral and inexpedient, investigated alleged waste and corruption in the armed services, emphasized the wisdom of a détente with the Russians and the Chinese, and sought in general to increase domestic expenditures. Finally, a decision may be aimed at protecting bureaucratic interests or may simply follow accepted practice. Compromises on the sizes of defense budgets and the allocation of funds among the services are often of this kind. It is easier

not "to rock the boat" than to establish new procedures or violate widespread expectations.

In comparing the foreign-policy behavior of different types of actors, it becomes clear that the domestic setting is a critical determinant of policy output. In the United States, for instance, influence on foreign policy is widely distributed. In fact, the authors of the Constitution set out to create a system of checks and balances that would institutionalize conflict. There may be no alternative to some fragmentation of decision making in modern states. Issues are too complex and information too plentiful to be processed and interpreted effectively by single small groups. Although nondemocratic governments can restrict the influence of private groups on foreign policy, fragmentation still occurs as a consequence of bureaucratization of the policy process. Such bureaucratization increases the effectiveness of governments in the face of expanding inputs and increasing demands [34, 8]. Executives use bureaucrats to collect, process, and interpret information, as well as to allocate resources and responsibility for performing critical tasks. Except for the highest-ranking political directors such bureaucracies are composed of appointed career officials. The pattern of recruitment and the types of individuals recruited for important posts have significant consequences for foreign-policy performance. For example, the typical Communist Party *apparatchik* recruited for administrative positions during the Stalin era was rarely personally innovative.

In any actor each relevant organization, including bureaucratic agencies like the U.S. State Department, political parties, and major private interest groups, forms a separate and distinct subsystem with its own memories, routines, and sources of current information. Through the competitive interplay of these separate subsystems, policy is produced. When innovation is required, central control and coordination may be disadvantages; inter- and intraagency conflict, on the other hand, may lead to compromise. Each structure defines the system's overall goals from a different perspective, depending upon its own role and position in the system. Ministries of defense, for instance, tend to view "national interest" as requiring increased armaments for greater security. What are basically the parochial interests of the ministries are perceived by them as the interests of the system as a whole. Similarly, the major economic elites tend to view the national interest in terms of economic prosperity and well-being, even at some cost in military security. The budgetary process is often the most important battleground for competing interests.[12] Although it has been suggested that bureaucratic competition can be avoided only through reorganization, "The choice of organization is a political choice. The 'best' organization is that which distributes power and responsibility in such a fashion as to facilitate the policies you favor [51]."

The parochial interests and perceptions of groups rarely coincide, and some bargaining is therefore necessary before consensus can be achieved on a single policy. Failure to achieve consensus may lead to "minimal decisions," even on the most important issues; such decisions can have far-reaching consequences. For example, as a result of a dispute between the U.S. Defense Department and the U.S. Atomic Energy Commission, President Truman chose in January 1950 to make only a limited commitment to developing the hydrogen bomb. He chose to continue research on the weapon and to develop a few prototype devices, in order to foreclose the fewest alternatives until sometime in the future when a consensus that would offend relatively few people might develop. Most of the major questions about the hydrogen bomb were left undecided, but the minimal decision created a momentum and had enormous consequences [50]. Shortly thereafter the

U.S.S.R. developed a similar weapon. Once the first hydrogen bombs had been developed, pressures for continuing the arms race in both the United States and Soviet Union were heightened. Each country was aware that the other now had the technological ability to build many hydrogen devices, thereby seriously changing the strategic balance. President Nixon's decision in March 1969 to embark on construction of two antiballistic-missile sites away from major cities, in order to protect existing strategic-weapons installations, was a similar decision. The fierce controversy over antiballistic missiles persuaded Nixon to decide in a way that would not foreclose future options yet would not alienate most protagonists now. He did not commit the United States to embark on large-scale construction of antiballistic missiles, but he did not abandon the project. The Soviet-American strategic arms agreement in the spring of 1972 may, however, prevent the arms race that took place in the 1950s from recurring.

Even when an actor's general goals are agreed on, the priorities among them and their interpretation vary from group to group. Some groups may perceive common or complementary interests and may ally themselves against other groups. In the United States, for example, military officers seeking promotion and influence, defense contractors seeking government contracts, and congressmen whose districts contain defense-oriented industries tend to work together.

Elites and the Foreign-Policy Process

An international actor is composed of different groups connected in complex fashion. Deutsch has identified five levels of elite opinion in most Western countries: the socioeconomic elite, the political and governmental elite, the mass media, the opinion leaders, and politically relevant strata of the general population.[13]

---

[12] For excellent discussions of the politics of defense budgets and strategic choices, see Samuel P. Huntington [19, 20] and Warner R. Schilling, Paul Hammond, and Glenn Snyder [52].

[13] A similar typology of elites is outlined in Gabriel A. Almond, *The American People and Foreign Policy* (New York: Harcourt Brace Jovanovich, 1950).

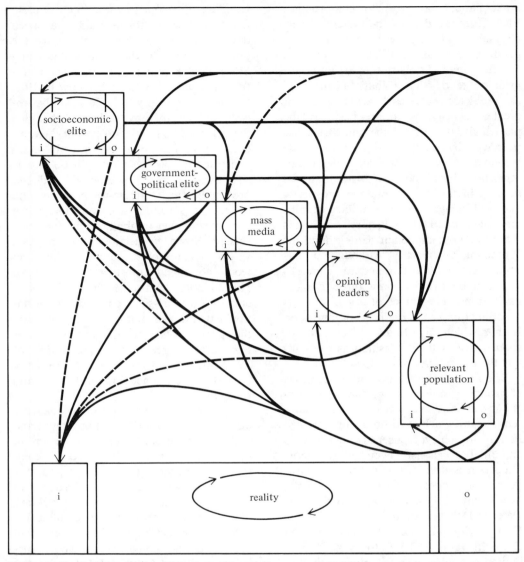

Figure 8.5. Communication Flow in a 5-Level System and Its Environment
Source: Karl W. Deutsch, *The Analysis of International Relations* © 1968. Reprinted by permission of Prentice-Hall, Inc., Englewood Cliffs, New Jersey.

Deutsch views communication among the elites as consisting of several "streams" of information flowing up and down among them much like a "cascade" (see Figure 8.5). Socioeconomic leaders have access to important government bureaucracies and significant influence in Congress. They can also influence the mass media, but their contact with local leaders and the bulk of the population is limited. By contrast, the mass media have access to the population at large and to local leaders whose perceptions and opinions they help to shape.[14] Local leaders are in direct daily contact with the general public and serve to filter and transmit information to and from it.

Each elite is relatively autonomous,

[14] The role of the mass media in policy formation has been described by Douglass Cater, Jr. [5], Bernard C. Cohen [6], and James Reston [47].

with its own sources of information and its own means of processing it. As Deutsch has suggested:

All together, every one of the five levels of our cascade is partly autonomous but also partly interdependent with the other levels. . . . Each of these interdependent levels of communication is itself composed of diverse interest groups and institutions, and there are further coalitions among groups at different levels in the communication system. [7]

The behavior of different international actors is affected by the nature of their elites, the relative complexity of their communications systems, and the perceptions and interests of the discrete groups within each elite. Except for routine decisions in accordance with established procedures, foreign-policy decision making, then, involves both vertical and horizontal communication and bargaining. Horizontal bargaining occurs within elites. For instance, defense industries compete with one another for limited numbers of contracts; congressmen compete for limited federal funds; and the military services vie with one another for funds and a greater voice in the determination of overall strategy. Vertical bargaining is even more complex: It takes place among different elites.

The relationships between high-level political leaders and relevant elites are reciprocal.[15] Leaders require the support of important elites; in democratic systems such support takes the form of electoral backing and campaign contributions, bureaucratic assistance and advice, and so on. Conversely, the elites make demands upon leaders. If such demands remain unsatisfied support may be withdrawn and electoral defeat, open opposition, even revolution, may ensue.[16]

The political elite includes government bureaucracies, political parties, and legislatures, but in authoritarian political systems bureaucratic elites are likely to be more influential than are the other two.[17] Even in democratic political systems, however, the legislatures and the political parties are usually able only to approve or reject foreign-policy initiatives; rarely can they initiate specific actions. In general such groups are more concerned about domestic than about foreign issues and lack the expertise and time to consider foreign policy in much detail. Consequently their behavior tends to reflect a general "mood," rather than specific foreign-policy positions.

The socioeconomic elite is composed of associational groups characterized by particularistic interests for which they mobilize resources to influence leaders and members of the political and governmental elite. Such groups are more significant in open political systems, though even in relatively closed systems they exist and try to influence policy. In Spain, for example, the Roman Catholic Church is a significant interest group. Interest groups may use techniques ranging through face-to-face contact, letter-writing campaigns, financial support, and publicity to bring pressure on other groups for support. Nevertheless, they are rarely able, even in democratic societies, to exert as much influence as is sometimes attributed to them. One study of American business interests has revealed that they are "restrained in exerting pressure or woefully ignorant of where pressure could be profitably exerted" [3].[18]

At the bottom of the cascade are local leaders and the general population. This large group constitutes what has often been called "public opinion." In authoritarian systems, governments are largely able to manipulate popular opinion through control of the mass media and the means of political socialization. In open political

---

[15] It should be recognized that high-level political leaders are often recruited from business and other relevant elites.

[16] The reciprocal nature of supports and demands in all political systems has been stressed by writers like David Easton [9].

[17] In authoritarian systems dominated by a single ideology, like that of the Soviet Union, the bureaucrats are likely to be members of the single political parties as well.

[18] For an opposing view, see Morton Mintz and Jerry S. Cohen, *America, Inc.* (New York: Dial, 1971).

systems the relationship between public opinion and the government is reciprocal. Leaders are influenced by the public mood and are in turn able to influence that mood through the mass media and public-relations and information campaigns. Nevertheless, as the mass media are independent and social groups and institutions relatively unfettered, many views and opinions other than official ones can influence the public. The relationship between the mass public and the government is not direct. It is mediated through local leaders and influential individuals who interpret and filter information up and down the system. There is what has been called a "two-step flow of communication. . . . Influences stemming from the mass media first reach 'opinion leaders' who, in turn, pass on what they read and hear to those of their every-day associates for whom they are influential" [23, 24, 62]. Survey research has suggested that, on the whole, the general public is ill informed about foreign policy, cannot provide specific policy direction or initiative, and is manipulatable.[19] In the 1950s and 1960s, for example, it was argued that closer relations between the United States and Communist China were impossible because American public opinion would not permit them. In fact, it appears that, had American political leaders and bureaucrats been prepared to promote such a course, the public could have been persuaded of its benefits [61].[20] The American Congress, in particular, seems able to persuade the general public, as it did in the late 1960s, when it opposed increasing American participation in the Vietnam War. Public opinion, then, may "be used as an *active* and *manipulatable* resource, as a way of increasing the prominence and credibility of initiatives and responses in international competition" [49].

[19] A contradictory example has been reported by Benjamin I. Page and Richard A. Brody [43].

[20] This conclusion has been confirmed by the positive reaction of American public opinion to the announcement of President Nixon's trip to mainland China in the summer of 1971.

The existence of competing bureaucracies and elite groups highlights a variety of problems in making foreign policy. First, this type of decision process precludes consideration of an entire foreign-policy question in a single context. When responsibilities of different agencies and groups are unclear, a kind of paralysis may develop, or weak compromises may be adopted. Public and private groups with particular interests and priorities may resort to deception in dealing with other groups; they may even sabotage the implementation of policy decisions by manipulating or filtering information in such a way as to prejudice outcomes. Organizations tend especially to forward information that will support their ideas and perpetuate their roles. Furthermore, they tend to summon specialists predisposed to their assumptions and priorities. In the 1969 dispute over whether or not the United States should develop an antiballistic-missile system, both sides called upon "their" scientists to testify in favor of their respective positions. Under such conditions experts who also have strong political views become advocates.[21]

Standard Operating Procedures

Bureaucracies devise procedures for dealing with problems effectively by routine. Such procedures are particularly useful in dealing with recurring problems and situations, for most leaders have neither the time nor the expertise to handle all of them effectively. On the many routine issues that arise low-echelon bureaucrats can act within policy guidelines approved by their political superiors. Most foreign-policy actions are, in fact, determined in this manner. It is only in the case of salient and unexpected issues that top leaders are likely to become deeply involved; under other circumstances "routinization" is the order of the day. Although general procedures are necessary

[21] For detailed discussions of experts as political advocates, see Albert Wohlstetter [67], Robert Gilpin [13], William R. Nelson [39], Eugene B. Skolnikoff [56], Harold K. Jacobson and Eric Stein [21], and C. P. Snow [57].

to deal with masses of incoming information, it may be that "What passes for planning is frequently the projection of the familiar into the future" [26].

Routine decisions can, of course, have far-reaching consequences. The U-2 affair in May 1960 illustrates this point. Early in his term of office President Dwight D. Eisenhower had authorized a series of "spy flights" over the Soviet Union to gather intelligence. Specific decisions on particular flights were taken routinely by the Central Intelligence Agency in accordance with its objectives. On the eve of the summit conference to be held among Eisenhower, Nikita Khrushchev, Harold Macmillan, and Charles de Gaulle in Paris such a flight was authorized; the plane, piloted by Francis Gary Powers, a civilian working for the Lockheed Aircraft Corporation under government contract, was shot down over the Soviet Union near Sverdlovsk. The news was released by Khrushchev, who demanded an American apology and an end to such flights. The incident proved painfully embarrassing to Eisenhower, who had apparently been unaware that the specific flight was taking place. The administration denied that the violation of Soviet air space had been intentional, but its claims were proved false by the Soviet Union, which had succeeded in capturing and questioning Powers, as well as examining the wreckage of the U-2. Khrushchev canceled the summit conference [66, 45].[22]

To the extent that standard operating procedures prevent innovation, they limit opportunities for dealing with unusual or important problems. An incident during the dramatic Soviet-American confrontation over Cuba in 1962 illustrates this point. Having decided to institute a naval quarantine of Cuba to prevent further shipments of Soviet missiles to the island, President Kennedy and his advisers left implementation to the navy. To make certain that the operation was being carried

out as the President desired, Secretary of Defense Robert McNamara visited the office of Admiral George W. Anderson, Chief of Naval Operations. McNamara inquired about the details of the blockade, explaining that the administration was trying to communicate a political message to the Soviet Union while avoiding incidents that could result in uncontrolled escalation. Anderson was affronted by what seemed to him unwarranted interference by civilians in military matters. When McNamara asked him what the navy would do if a Soviet ship refused to comply with the blockade, Anderson is reported to have waved the *Manual of Naval Regulations* at him, saying, "It's all in there." McNamara retorted: "I don't give a damn what John Paul Jones would have done. I want to know what you are going to do now." Finally, Anderson declared, "Now, Mr. Secretary, if you and your deputy will go back to your offices, the Navy will run the blockade" [1].[23] In this instance standard operating procedure overrode detailed control by decision makers; the navy could operate in only one way—by the book!

The fragmentation of the decision process makes it peculiarly difficult to coordinate the implementation of policy. Leaders may find it necessary to intervene personally in order to have a policy carried out as they want, but usually such intervention is neither possible nor desirable. Leaders seldom have the time, information, or expertise to supervise every aspect of policy directly. At best they may concentrate on those aspects of most immediate interest and importance to them, ignoring the others.[24] Dictators who have sought to supervise personally all aspects of policy implementation have generally produced poor policy or policy paralysis. Furthermore, such supervision defeats the purpose of division of labor designed to free top leaders for

---

[22] A similarly embarrassing incident for the United States involved the "routine" return of a defecting Soviet seaman by American authorities in the winter of 1970–1971.

[23] Shortly afterward Admiral Anderson was made ambassador to Portugal.

[24] President Lyndon Johnson is reported to have personally supervised the details of the bombing of North Vietnam from 1965 to 1968.

the most important tasks. The president of the United States who expects to give orders and have them carried out as he desires is bound to be disappointed. As President Truman remarked of his successor: "He'll sit here and he'll say, 'Do this! Do that!' And nothing will happen. Poor Ike—it won't be a bit like the Army" [41, p. 9]. Even President Franklin D. Roosevelt, who was noted for his ability to control and "tame" his executive departments, was frequently frustrated in the effort. At one point he exclaimed:

You should go through the experience of trying to get any changes in the thinking, policy, and action of the career diplomats and then you'd know what a real problem was. But the Treasury and the State Department put together are nothing as compared with the Na-a-vy. . . . To change anything in the Na-a-vy is like punching a feather bed. You punch it with your right and you punch it with your left until you are finally exhausted, and then you find the damn bed just as it was before you started punching. [10]

Bureaucratic organizations can only infrequently be galvanized and mobilized. Leaders can alter standard operating procedures, priorities, and organizational perspectives, but such alteration is a long-term process at best. Furthermore, one observer has suggested that a president of the United States requires at least two years of on-the-job training before he can begin to run the executive branch of government effectively [41, p. 198].

If leaders are not careful, they may find executive bureaucracies performing most policy-making functions. Kenneth Waltz has attributed what he considers the growing ineffectiveness of the British government to an increasing separation between politicians and the permanent bureaucracies that handle the day-to-day affairs of government [64]. Under such conditions an actor will be poorly prepared to cope effectively with unusual inputs for which the bureaucracies have devised no routine or standard procedures.

It is clear that the "learned" behavior of an international actor is the product of the memories and inclinations of many groups, organizations, and individuals participating in the foreign-policy process, as well as of their perceptions of incoming information. To understand the foreign-policy process, however, it is necessary not only to be familiar with the components of the process but also to view it as it varies from actor to actor. In Chapter 9 we shall examine briefly four national actors to discover the characteristics of their foreign policies and the factors that determine their international behavior.

References

1. Abel, Elie, *The Missile Crisis* (New (New York: Bantam, 1966), p. 137.
2. Allison, Graham T., "Conceptual Models and the Cuban Missile Crisis," *American Political Science Review,* 63 (September 1969), pp. 689–718.
3. Bauer, Raymond A., Ithiel de Sola Pool, and Lewis A. Dexter, *American Business and Public Policy* (New York: Atherton, 1963), p. 484.
4. Braybrooke, David, and Charles E. Lindblom, *A Strategy of Decision? Policy Evaluation as a Social Process* (New York: Free Press, 1963).
5. Cater, Douglass, Jr., *The Fourth Branch of Government* (Boston: Houghton Mifflin, 1959).
6. Cohen, Bernard C., *The Press and Foreign Policy* (Princeton: Princeton University Press, 1963).
7. Deutsch, Karl W., *The Analysis of International Relations* (Englewood Cliffs, N.J.: Prentice-Hall, 1968), p. 110.
8. Downs, Anthony, *Inside Bureaucracy* (Boston: Little, Brown, 1967).
9. Easton, David, *Analysis of Political Life* (New York: Wiley, 1965).
10. Eccles, Marriner, *Beckoning Frontiers* (New York: Knopf, 1951), p. 336.
11. Fleming, Ian, *Thunderball* (New York: New American Library, 1961), p. 109.
12. Frye, R. L., and T. M. Stritch, "Effect of Timed vs. Nontimed Discussion upon Measures of Influence and Change in Small Groups," *Journal of Social Psychology,* 63 (June 1964), pp. 139–143.
13. Gilpin, Robert, *American Scientists and*

Nuclear Weapons Policy (Princeton: Princeton University Press, 1962).

14. Hare, A. P., *Handbook of Small Group Research* (New York: Free Press, 1962), pp. 265–271.

15. Hilsman, Roger, "The Foreign Policy Consensus: An Interim Research Report," *Journal of Conflict Resolution,* 3 (December 1959), p. 365.

16. Hilsman, Roger, *To Move a Nation* (Garden City, N.Y.: Doubleday, 1967), p. 5.

17. Holsti, Ole R., "The 1914 Case," *American Political Science Review,* 59 (June 1965), pp. 365–378.

18. Holsti, Ole R., Richard A. Brody, and Robert C. North, "Measuring Affect and Action in International Reaction Models: Empirical Materials from the 1962 Cuban Crisis," *Journal of Peace Research,* 1 (1964), pp. 170–190.

19. Huntington, Samuel P., *The Common Defense* (New York: Columbia University Press, 1961).

20. Huntington, Samuel P., "Strategic Planning and the Political Process," in James N. Rosenau, ed., *International Politics and Foreign Policy* (New York: Free Press, 1961), pp. 234–240.

21. Jacobson, Harold K., and Eric Stein, *Diplomats, Scientists, and Politicians* (Ann Arbor: University of Michigan Press, 1966).

22. Jones, Joseph M., *The Fifteen Weeks* (New York: Viking, 1965).

23. Katz, Elihu, "The Two-Step Flow of Communication: An Up-to-Date Report on an Hypothesis," in J. David Singer, ed., *Human Behavior and International Politics* (Chicago: Rand McNally, 1965), p. 293.

24. Katz, Elihu, and Paul Lazarsfeld, *Personal Influence* (New York: Free Press, 1955).

25. Kennan, George F., *Realities of American Foreign Policy* (Princeton: Princeton University Press, 1954).

26. Kissinger, Henry A., "Domestic Structure and Foreign Policy," in James N. Rosenau, ed., *International Politics and Foreign Policy,* rev. ed. (New York: Free Press, 1969), p. 264.

27. Lanzetta, J. T., "Group Behavior Under Stress," *Human Relations,* 8 (1955), pp. 29–52.

28. Leites, Nathan, *A Study of Bolshevism* (New York: Free Press, 1953), pp. 67–73.

29. Lindblom, Charles E., "The Science of Muddling Through," *Public Administration Review,* 19 (Spring 1959), p. 81.

30. McClelland, Charles A., "Action Structures and Communication in Two International Crises: Quemoy and Berlin," *Background,* 7 (1964), pp. 201–215.

31. McClelland, Charles A., "World Event Interaction Survey" (Los Angeles: University of Southern California, unpublished).

32. McClelland, Charles A., and Gary Hoggard, "Conflict Patterns in the Interactions Among Nations," in James N. Rosenau, ed., *International Politics and Foreign Policy,* rev. ed. (New York: Free Press, 1969), pp. 711–724.

33. May, Ernest R., "The Nature of Foreign Policy: The Calculated Versus the Axiomatic," *Daedalus,* 91 (Fall 1962), pp. 653–667.

34. Merton, Robert K., *et al., Reader in Bureaucracy* (New York: Free Press, 1952).

35. Miller, George A., "The Magic Number, Plus or Minus Two," in *The Psychology of Communication: Seven Essays* (New York: Basic Books, 1967).

36. Morgenthau, Hans J., *Dilemmas of Politics* (Chicago: University of Chicago Press, 1958).

37. Morgenthau, Hans J., *Politics Among Nations,* 4th ed. (New York: Knopf, 1967), pp. 5, 8.

38. Mowrer, Herbert O., *Learning Theory and Behavior* (New York: Wiley, 1960).

39. Nelson, William R., ed., *The Politics of Science* (New York: Oxford, 1968), pp. 269–357.

40. Neustadt, Richard E., "The Presidency at Mid-Century," *Law and Contemporary Problems,* 21 (Autumn 1956), p. 625.

41. Neustadt, Richard E., *Presidential Power,* rev. ed. (New York: Wiley, 1968).

42. North, Robert C., "Research Pluralism and the International Elephant," in Klaus Knorr and James N. Rosenau, eds., *Contending Approaches to International Politics* (Princeton: Princeton University Press, 1969), pp. 218–242.

43. Page, Benjamin I., and Richard A. Brody, "Issue Voting and the Electoral Process: The Case of Vietnam" (Paper delivered at the 1971 Annual Meeting of the American Political Science Association).

44. Paige, Glenn D., *The Korean Decision* (New York: Free Press, 1968), p. 317.

45. Powers, Francis Gary, *Operation Overflight* (New York: Holt, Rinehart & Winston, 1970).

46. Raser, John R., "Learning and Affect in International Politics," in James N. Rosenau, ed., *International Politics and Foreign Policy*, rev. ed. (New York: Free Press, 1969), pp. 432–441.

47. Reston, James, *The Artillery of the Press* (New York: Harper & Row, 1967).

48. Rivera, Joseph H. de, *The Psychological Dimension of Foreign Policy* (Columbus, O.: Merrill, 1968).

49. Rosenberg, Milton J., "American Public Opinion on Cold-War Issues," in Herbert C. Kelman, ed., *International Behavior* (New York: Holt, Rinehart & Winston, 1965), p. 279.

50. Schilling, Warner R., "The H-Bomb Decision: How to Decide Without Actually Choosing," *Political Science Quarterly*, 76 (March 1961), pp. 24–46.

51. Schilling, Warner R., "The Politics of National Defense: Fiscal 1950," in Warner R. Schilling, Paul Hammond, and Glenn Snyder, eds., *Strategy, Politics, and Defense Budgets* (New York: Columbia University Press, 1962), p. 230.

52. Schilling, Warner R., Paul Hammond, and Glenn Snyder, eds., *Strategy, Politics, and Defense Budgets* (New York: Columbia University Press, 1962).

53. Schroder, H. M., M. J. Driver, and S. Streufert, *Human Information Processing* (New York: Holt, Rinehart & Winston, 1967), pp. 67–105.

54. Sherif, Muzafer, *et al.*, *Intergroup Conflict and Cooperation: The Robbers' Cave Experiment* (Norman: University of Oklahoma Institute of Group Relations, 1961).

55. Simon, Herbert, *Administrative Behavior: A Discussion of Decision-Making Process in Administrative Organization*, 2nd ed. (New York: Macmillan, 1961).

56. Skolnikoff, Eugene B., *Science, Technology, and American Foreign Policy* (Cambridge, Mass.: MIT Press, 1967).

57. Snow, C. P., *Science and Government* (Cambridge, Mass.: Harvard University Press, 1961).

58. Snyder, Richard C., H. W. Bruck, and Burton Sapin, eds., *Foreign Policy Decision-Making* (New York: Free Press, 1962).

59. Sprout, Harold, and Margaret Sprout, *The Ecological Perspective on Human Affairs* (Princeton: Princeton University Press, 1965).

60. Sprout, Harold, and Margaret Sprout, "Environmental Factors in the Study of International Politics," *Journal of Conflict Resolution*, 1 (1957), pp. 309–328.

61. Steele, A. T., *The American People and China* (New York: McGraw-Hill, 1966).

62. Truman, David, "The American System in Crisis," *Political Science Quarterly*, 74 (December 1959), pp. 481–497.

63. Verba, Sidney, "Assumptions of Rationality and Non-Rationality in Models of the International System," in Klaus Knorr and Sidney Verba, eds., *The International System: Theoretical Essays* (Princeton: Princeton University Press, 1961), pp. 93–117.

64. Waltz, Kenneth, *Foreign Policy and Domestic Politics* (Boston: Little, Brown, 1967).

65. Westerfield, H. Bradford, *Foreign Policy and Party Politics* (New Haven: Yale University Press, 1955).

66. Wise, David, and Thomas B. Ross, *The U-2 Affair* (New York: Random House, 1962).

67. Wohlstetter, Albert, "Scientists, Seers, and Strategy," *Foreign Affairs*, 41 (April 1963), pp. 466–478.

Suggested Reading

Allison, Graham T., *Essence of Decision: Explaining the Cuban Missile Crisis* (Boston: Little, Brown, 1971).

Bauer, Raymond A., Ithiel de Sola Pool, and Lewis A. Dexter, *American Business and Public Policy* (New York: Atherton, 1963).

Braybrooke, David, and Charles E. Lindblom, *A Strategy of Decision? Policy Evaluation as a Social Process* (New York: Free Press, 1963).

Hermann, Charles F., "International Crisis as a Situational Variable," in James N. Rosenau, ed., *International Politics and Foreign Policy,* rev. ed. (New York: Free Press, 1969), pp. 409–421.

Hilsman, Roger, *To Move a Nation* (Garden City, N.Y.: Doubleday, 1967).

Lindblom, Charles E., "The Science of Muddling Through," *Public Administration Review,* 19 (Spring 1959), pp. 79–88.

Paige, Glenn D., *The Korean Decision* (New York: Free Press, 1968).

Raser, John R., "Learning and Affect in International Politics," in James N. Rosenau, ed., *International Politics and Foreign Policy,* rev. ed. (New York: Free Press, 1969), pp. 432–441.

Rivera, Joseph H. de, *The Psychological Dimension of Foreign Policy* (Columbus, O.: Merrill, 1968).

Rosenau, James N., "The National Interest," in James N. Rosenau, ed., *The Scientific Study of Foreign Policy* (New York: Free Press, 1971), pp. 239–249.

Snyder, Richard C., H. W. Bruck, and Burton Sapin, eds., *Foreign Policy Decision-Making* (New York: Free Press, 1962).

Chapter 9
FOUR INSTANCES OF FOREIGN-POLICY BEHAVIOR

We say that the state acts when we mean that the people in it act, just as we say that the pot boils when we mean that the water in it boils. . . . To continue the figure: Water running out of a faucet is chemically the same as water in a container, but once the water is in a container, it can be made to "behave" in different ways—Kenneth N. Waltz [95, p. 80]

A comparison of the foreign-policy processes in the Soviet Union, a large, developed, but closed system; the People's Republic of China, a large, underdeveloped, and closed system; the United States, a large, developed, and open system; and Tanzania, a small, underdeveloped, and closed system, will illustrate how the determinants of foreign-policy behavior vary from actor to actor.

THE SOVIET UNION

The Soviet Union, like other actors, seeks to ensure its security, to preserve or enhance its influence abroad, and to perpetuate the regime at home. In addition, its foreign policy includes an active ideological component, which helps to shape perceptions of external events and provides an abstract theory for defining goals and interpreting events. According to Marxist theory, the state is the instrument of the ruling economic class, and its foreign policy reflects class interests abroad; diplomacy represents the means by which such class interests are implemented. This ideology implies that foreign policy is a function of a society's economic "substructure" and that international politics as such will disappear after the inevitable world revolution.[1]

Ideology plays a greater role in authoritarian polities in general. Authoritarian governments tend to have fewer sources of information than do democratic regimes and thus depend to a greater extent upon information generated from within the governments themselves. Because of the absence of other influences, a single ideology may bias the selection and interpretation of information.

When the views of the leadership are well known, the words which subordinates throw

[1] For a summary of the Marxist model of international politics, see Kenneth N. Waltz [95, chap. 5]. For discussions of the role of ideology in Soviet foreign policy, see, for example, Daniel Bell [5], Adam B. Ulam [92], Zbigniew K. Brzezinski [8], Milorad M. Drachkovitch [25, 26], and Bertram D. Wolfe [98].

back at it tend to confirm its beliefs rather than to challenge its analyses. . . . The danger in the case of the Soviet Union is accentuated by the rigid doctrinal stereotypes about the outside world which acceptance of the Communist ideology imposes. [28]

In the Soviet Union the institutionalized ideology is one of the few potent societal variables. The extent to which it affects foreign policy is the subject of considerable debate, for the impact of ideology is not uniform. The ideology itself has been revised from time to time to bring it more into line with external and domestic realities. Lenin himself rejected ideological "dogmatism" in favor of flexibility, what he called "living Marxism." One quantitative analysis has revealed that ideological considerations are more prominent in the verbal behavior of older members of the Communist Party of the Soviet Union (CPSU) whose careers have been shaped mainly by work in the party itself, than in that of younger officials whose careers have been launched in the government apparatus or technical and professional fields. The same study has suggested that greater attention is paid to ideology in foreign affairs than in domestic questions, particularly by those members of the Soviet elite who are not foreign-policy specialists. Furthermore, Marxism-Leninism appears to be more salient in Soviet analyses of long-term trends than in those of short-term trends. "We must note that the content analysis performed here definitely rejects the possibility that Soviet foreign-policy decision-makers draw all their premises from Marxism-Leninism or even that all empirical premises are doctrinally distorted in their perception" [88, p. 125]. When events preclude a doctrinaire approach to problems, Soviet leaders are not averse to sacrificing ideological considerations to expedience.[2]

It is apparent that in the Soviet Union

role, individual, and governmental variables have greater relative impacts on behavior than do societal variables, with the exception of ideology. The vast Eurasian land mass and the extensive resources of the Soviet Union permit it to conduct a foreign policy of considerable scope; they also generate particular foreign-policy concerns, notably in eastern Europe and China. Since its inception the Soviet regime has taken pains to preclude the formation of groups outside the control of the Communist Party and has succeeded in preventing the growth of private associations among the mass of peasants and workers. Nevertheless, it appears that societal variables will become more significant as the Soviet Union continues to mature economically. Already unofficial groups, comprising individuals who identify themselves as members of nonparty elites with common interests, expectations, and priorities, can be observed. Groups of specialists, or "technocrats," less imbued with an ideological outlook and with more instrumental views on problems, are emerging. "The general trend is toward increased specialist elite perceptions of their participatory role in the policy-making arena" [57].[3] (See Tables 9.1 and 9.2.)

From Revolution to Revision

After a brief and thoroughly disappointing attempt to stimulate world revolution after they assumed power in 1917, the bolsheviks came to realize that such an immediate policy would further isolate the Soviet regime internationally, stimulate "imperialist" intervention, and perpetuate economic backwardness, and that it was necessary first to consolidate revolutionary gains at home.

The issue of world revolution versus consolidation of the Soviet regime came to a head after the death of Lenin in 1924. Joseph Stalin adopted the slogan

---

[2] During World War II, for instance, Soviet leaders made few references to Marxism-Leninism, emphasizing instead patriotic and nationalist themes.

[3] For more information on this question, see Joel J. Schwartz and William R. Keech [81], William Zimmerman [101], and Brzezinski and Samuel P. Huntington [10].

Table 9.1.

Elite Perceptions of the Soviet Policy-Making Arena, 1952-1965

Policy making is the responsibility of
1.0 party participation solely
2.0 party participation primarily
3.0 joint party-specialist elite participation
4.0 specialist participation primarily
5.0 specialist participation solely*

Elites	1952	1953	1955	1957	1959	1961	1963	1965	All Years
Party	1.9	1.9	2.0	1.4	2.9	2.7	1.7	2.3	2.1
Economic	0.0	2.5	2.3	1.5	3.2	3.0	2.8	3.6	2.5
Legal	0.0	1.3	2.3	2.9	1.7	4.0	2.5	3.8	2.7
Military	(1.8)†	(1.6)†	1.6	1.3	0.0	2.2	3.3	2.7	2.1
Literary	1.8	1.0	1.8	2.9	2.4	2.0	2.5	3.1	2.3
All elites	1.8	1.6	1.9	2.1	2.5	2.6	2.7	3.2	2.4
Specialists	1.8	1.6	1.9	2.1	2.4	2.8	2.8	3.3	2.4

$F (33,106) = 3.089$, significant at .001.

*An example of position 5.0, taken from the material used in training the coders:
The formation of our military world view has taken place in a creative atmosphere. . . and is the result of the common effort of military theorists and practical military people. Thanks to this, we have developed a body of unified theory on the basis of which a broad state program has been carried out to prepare the country and armed forces for the defense of the Fatherland. (*Kommunist Vooruzhenuykh sil,* no. 10 (May 1962), p. 12)

†Data for the military are unavailable for 1952 and 1953. The mean scores for all elites have been assigned to the military for those two years and noted in parentheses.

Source: Milton C. Lodge, *Soviet Elite Attitudes Since Stalin* (Columbus, O.: Merrill, 1969), p. 12.

"socialism in one country," which meant in effect that the preservation and development of the Soviet Union were to take priority over revolutionary goals. Gradually but inexorably Stalin identified the interests of international communism with the interests of the Soviet state. In the process the Communist International, or Comintern, formed in 1919 to promote the goal of world revolution, came to serve as an arm of Soviet foreign policy.[4] While paying lip service to the cause of international revolution, the Soviet Union adopted conventional diplomatic practices to prevent foreign intervention in Soviet affairs and thus give the country time to develop militarily and economically. By the end of the 1920s Stalin dominated Soviet policy making, and under his leadership the Soviet Union embarked on an ambitious program of industrialization.

[4] For a study of Stalin's rise to power, see Isaac Deutscher, *Stalin: A Political Biography* (New York: Oxford University Press, 1949).

New bureaucracies evolved, with stakes in the existing social order and with less concern about foreign policy than their revolutionary predecessors had felt.

In the face of German and Italian fascism in the 1930s the Soviet Union sought to forge alliances in the West, but mutual suspicion of motives and mutual ideological aversion made cooperation difficult, as Anglo-French appeasement of Adolf Hitler at Munich in 1938 demonstrated. On August 23, 1939, in a sudden reversal of policy, Stalin concluded a nonaggression treaty with Hitler. Two years later, however, Hitler turned on the Soviet Union. Consequently Stalin rapidly concluded another alliance with the United States and Great Britain and urged communists throughout Europe to resist the nazis. The Soviet Union emerged from the war in control of much of eastern Europe and Germany. North Korea was also occupied for a time, and within a few years communist regimes had seized

Table 9.2.

Elite Attitudes Toward Participation in the Soviet Policy-Making Arena, 1952-1965

Policy-making *should* be the responsibility of
1.0 party participation solely
2.0 party participation primarily
3.0 joint party-specialist elite participation*
4.0 specialist participation primarily
5.0 specialist participation solely

Elites	1952	1953	1955	1957	1959	1961	1963	1965	All Years
Party	1.9	1.4	1.5	2.1	2.1	2.2	2.0	2.4	1.9
Economic	1.0	1.2	3.0	1.6	2.9	3.4	2.7	3.1	2.2
Legal	1.2	1.4	1.9	2.9	2.7	3.2	3.7	3.3	2.5
Military	(1.3)†	(1.3)†	1.4	2.8	2.3	2.4	3.2	3.4	2.3
Literary	1.4	1.3	2.9	2.7	2.8	3.0	3.1	3.6	2.6
All elites	1.3	1.3	2.1	2.5	2.6	2.7	2.9	3.2	2.4
Specialists	1.2	1.3	2.3	2.5	2.7	3.0	3.2	3.4	2.4

$F(38,177) = 7.246$, significant at .001

*An example of position 3.0 is contained in a speech by Nikita S. Khrushechev at a meeting of agronomists: You say "Comrade Khrushchev said thus and so." Am I the highest authority in agricultural science? You are President of the Ukraine Republic Academy of Sciences and I am the Secretary of the Party Central Committee. You must help me in these matters, and not I you. I might be wrong, and if I am, you, as an honest scientist, should say: "Comrade Khrushchev, you do not quite understand the matter." If you explain things to me correctly, I will thank you for it. Let us say I was wrong. But you will say, "Comrade Khrushchev said this and I supported him." What sort of scientist is this comrades? This is toadyism and timeserving. (*Pravda*, December 25, 1961)

†Data for the military are unavailable for 1952 and 1953. The mean scores for all elites have been assigned to the military for those two years and noted in parentheses.

Source: Milton C. Lodge, *Soviet Elite Attitudes Since Stalin* (Columbus, O.: Merrill, 1969), p. 14.

power in China and North Vietnam as well.[5]

The Soviet domination of eastern Europe and China was essentially contradictory to Communist ideology. In states like Yugoslavia and China, where the Communist parties had come to power mainly through their own efforts, Stalin's argument that strengthening the Soviet Union would foster international communism seemed a mask for Soviet imperialism. After Stalin's death in 1953 his successor, Nikita S. Khrushchev, sought to place the communist bloc on a new footing. He not only repudiated Stalin's leadership but also began to work through formal interstate organizations like the Council for Mutual Economic Assistance (CEMA) and the Warsaw Pact, instead of relying solely on coercion and party ties to reconcile the growing autonomy of bloc members; his objective was to sustain bloc unity. The Soviets were increasingly faced with "polycentrism," involving nearly all their "satellites" in the eastern bloc.[6]

Khrushchev's policy was relatively successful, except for the growing rift between the Soviet Union and the People's Republic of China, which became apparent after 1960.[7] Several factors contributed to this split, including personal

[5] The Soviet take-over of eastern Europe has been described and analyzed in Hugh Seton-Watson, *The East European Revolution*, 3rd ed. (New York: Praeger, 1956).

[6] There is considerable literature on the development and decay of the Soviet bloc in eastern Europe. See, for example, Brzezinski [9], Alexander Dallin [22], William E. Griffith [38], Richard Lowenthal [59], and Robert H. McNeal [61].

[7] For an outline of the main factors behind the growth of the Sino-Soviet conflict, see Griffith [37, 39], Donald S. Zagoria [100], Lowenthal [58], John Gittings [35], Harrison Salisbury [79], and Chu-Yuan Cheng [13].

rivalry between Khrushchev and Mao Tse-tung and their different international objectives and concerns. Societal variables also contributed to the growing schism, for the Soviet Union had become a modern, economically developed "have" nation that required slackened international tension and uninterrupted economic and technological growth to attain its goals. China, on the other hand, remained an underdeveloped and relatively primitive actor with revisionist goals greatly influenced by the ideology of Mao. The risk of nuclear warfare became a grim reality for Soviet leaders as they acquired a stake in the existing international order. By contrast, China was imbued with revolutionary ardor and the desire to achieve "great power" status; it therefore favored an "adventurous" foreign policy.

Stalin had considered the world divided between two hostile camps, but Khrushchev initiated a reexamination of Soviet relations with the West and with the less developed countries of the "third world." At the Twentieth Congress of the Soviet Communist Party in 1956, besides attacking Stalin's rule, he claimed that the world was divided into three, rather than two, camps, with the neutral countries forming the third bloc. He also argued that war between capitalist and communist states is not "fatally inevitable" and that confrontation should be replaced by "peaceful, competitive coexistence" in nonmilitary spheres. Beginning in 1954 the Soviet government reached agreement with the West on several outstanding issues, and a limited détente began to evolve.[8]

One of the major issues dividing the Soviet Union and Communist China is what constitutes an acceptable risk of escalating conflict with the capitalist adversaries. The Chinese argue in favor of a more militant policy and accuse the Soviet Union of "selling out" the ideals of Marxism-Leninism. Since Khrushchev's overthrow in 1964 his successors Leonid

[8] See, for example, Wolfgang Leonhard [53], Michael P. Gehlen [33], Marshall Shulman [83], Ulam [91], and Zimmerman [102].

Brezhnev and Alexei Kosygin have also pursued a conservative, low-risk foreign policy. It appears that

the multiple constraints superimposed on Soviet risk-taking . . . have been such that the resulting level and pattern of Soviet risk assumed in twenty-nine crises have been *low* and *narrow*. Soviet crisis behavior was found to be conservative rather than radical, cautious rather than reckless, deliberate rather than impulsive, and rational (not willing to lose) rather than nonrational. [88, p. 346]

The Chinese, on the other hand, unable by themselves to pursue a "forward" foreign policy, have demanded a harder line against the West. By 1966 this split in the international communist movement had become a fact; many Communist parties were divided on the issues in the dispute.

Systemic Factors

Several major characteristics of the international system seem to have substantial influence on Soviet foreign-policy behavior. The bipolarity of certain major aspects of international structure, such as the distribution of strategic weapons, has created a condition that stimulates conflict with the United States and its allies. Each bloc is perceived by the other as a threat to its own core values, and competition between the two blocs has occurred in virtually all spheres of international activity, including economic, armaments, and space developments. Each has sought to deny the other opportunities for influence among the uncommitted nations of the world and to take advantage of such opportunities itself, and both have vied in the military, political, and economic arenas for fear that a gain by the other side would lead to a loss by its own side.

The perceptions of conflict resulting partly from a decaying bipolar world configuration have led the Soviet Union to try to delay growing "polycentrism" within its own bloc. The Soviet occupation of Hungary in 1956 and the invasion of

Czechoslovakia in 1968, coupled with the so-called "Brezhnev doctrine," illustrate that the Soviet Union is prepared to act forcibly when changes in eastern Europe threaten communism in those countries or when such "reformism" threatens to spread to Soviet society as well.[9]

A third important calculation in Soviet foreign policy is China. The rapid rise of China has created a new element in the previous bipolar international configuration. The continuing hostility of a powerful neighbor has forced the Soviet Union to allocate considerable resources to the defense of its Asian frontiers. In addition, it has been forced to compete with China in the "third world" and in the international communist movement. The Chinese have accused Soviet leaders, with some truth, of seeking domestic affluence and the interests of the existing Soviet social order at the expense of revolutionary ideals.[10]

The existence of a large number of uncommitted Afro-Asian nations is one of the major deviations from the bipolar model. These areas thus appear as stakes in Soviet-American competition. Many of these nations are newly emerged from colonial status, poor, and politically unstable; they thus offer opportunities for increasing Soviet influence and heighten Soviet interest because of their possibly important role in East-West competition. They also serve as arenas in which the Soviet Union and the United States can compete by "proxy" if necessary, reducing the risk of thermonuclear confrontation. Soviet aims in these areas have ranged from converting these countries to Soviet communism, on one hand, to simple denial of their resources to the West, on the other. Unlike Stalin, Khrushchev and his successors have supported "libera-

tion" movements even when they have had "bourgeois" leaders.

The Soviet Union has also sought to increase its influence through trade and foreign aid. Originally such aid was "opportunistic," concentrated in particular "show projects." The Soviet Union offered Egypt assistance in the construction of the Aswan High Dam after the United States had withdrawn its own promise of aid, and it extended assistance to India to construct a steel mill after American refusal. Returns in the form of political support were, however, initially disappointing to the Soviet Union, and its economic aid began to decline until the Chinese became competitors in the early 1960s [36, 4, 93, 34, 14].

Individual Variables

Since the death of Stalin no single individual has been permitted to control Soviet foreign-policy decisions completely. Nevertheless, the existence of a "cult of personality" around Stalin and, to a lesser extent, around Khrushchev suggests that idiosyncratic factors have considerable impact on Soviet foreign-policy behavior. As little is known of the personal backgrounds of Soviet leaders, it is difficult to evaluate the ways in which personality factors affect their politics. But the absence of an institutionalized process of succession encourages conflict among individuals at the highest levels of government and stimulates the creation of temporary alliances and factions within the party [17, 18, 74, 75]. Different individuals tend to associate themselves with different groups in their attempts to gain power. Such alliances are generally short-lived, however, and individual leaders, shifting their institutional bases of influence with some frequency, rarely internalize the role norms of the institutions that they purport to represent. Even though there is an uneasy collective leadership at the present time, some individuals at the top are able to leave their personal imprints on policy. The impact of individual variables is reinforced by the

[9] American behavior in Santo Domingo in 1965 and in Vietnam suggests that the United States is equally affected by the fear of "losing" areas to its main adversary.
[10] The unpredictability of "the Chinese factor" in what had been fundamentally a bipolar world was prominently recognized after the sudden Chinese attempt to improve relations with the United States in the spring of 1971.

concept of "democratic centralism" that governs Soviet administration; it requires that decisions of leaders must be accepted without question, though they are expected to consult with others beforehand.

Leadership positions are won and held by virtue of individuals' abilities to manipulate support within a small group of elites. As there is no regular succession, there are fewer "forward" role links for a potential leader to consider than there are in democratic societies. Current Soviet leaders were socialized during the height of the Stalin era. As political survival under Stalin meant avoiding responsibility and initiative, the present leadership, according to one Soviet critic, represents "Stalin's Committee of Eunuchs.... A timid (though sometimes panicky) mediocrity has replaced Stalin's raging will" [19]. As postrevolutionary figures, the present Soviet leaders have been socialized into a functioning political system and are considerably more conservative than were their "heroic" predecessors. Recruitment, though based partly on performance, depends also upon careful conformity to party norms of correctness *and* upon personal ties with those in high places—patrons who maintain their own positions by promoting their clients. This conservatism and the resulting mediocrity make it unlikely that the Soviet Union will soon act as "a positive and creative force" in international politics [7].

Governmental and Role Variables

Few groups outside high party and governmental circles influence policy. No political parties other than the Communist party itself are permitted. In practice, as Figure 9.1 suggests, there are two parallel institutional hierarchies relevant to foreign policy—that of the party and that of the government. They merge at the top in the Politburo, a small party committee of high-level leaders. Both party and government have become highly bureaucratic, and their memberships overlap, particularly at higher levels. Consequently a "new class," a ruling class with many of

the traits of traditional ruling elites, has formed in what was supposed to become a "classless" society. This class has acquired a privileged position, in terms of income and prerogatives, in Soviet society, and it therefore has a vested interest in the status quo. It maintains itself through self-selection and intergenerational transfer of wealth and status [23, 24]. The "new class," however, does not consist solely of members of the party *apparat* or bureaucratic hierarchy, as it did in Stalin's day; it has come to include several specialist and technocratic elites as well. As Suzanne Keller has written, "No single strategic elite can today know all there is to be known, and none can perform all the functions involved in social leadership" [50].

In general, the ruling groups in the Soviet Union tend to be conservative and to view foreign policy largely in terms of their domestic political and economic positions. Under Khrushchev issues of war and peace came to be evaluated in terms of their effects on the fortunes of the several elites, rather than in terms of the interests of a single dictator and the small clique of individuals surrounding him. Soviet foreign-policy decisions are thus frequently based on predicted political advantages to particular factions or groups in the struggle for power, beside providing justification for the continuation or modification of existing domestic policies, practices, and distribution of resources. Despite differences among and within the elites, they are all united in their determination to perpetuate the social system and the Soviet state, the source of their privileged positions. The early goal of world revolution has been replaced by that of "building communism" at home and perpetuating the socioeconomic system that benefits the elites. One author has even declared that the Soviet leaders "would risk thermonuclear destruction rather than allow the Soviet social order to be disestablished" [1].[11]

[11] Certain groups in the United States share similar priorities.

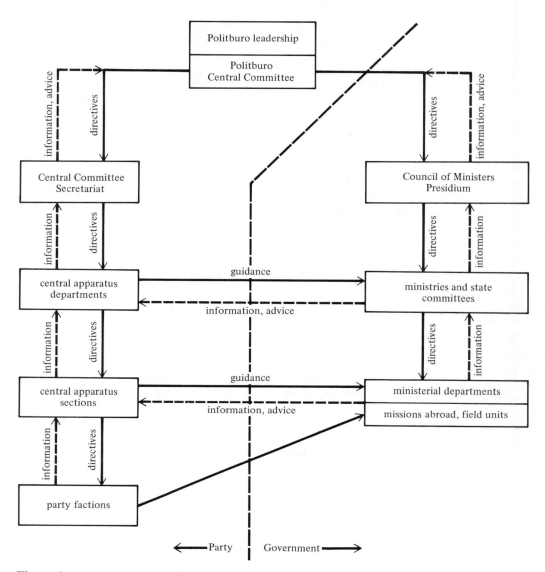

Figure 9.1. Institutionalized Relationship of Party and Government in the Soviet Union
Source: Reprinted by permission of The Macmillan Company from *Soviet Foreign Policy* by Jan F. Triska and David D. Finley. Copyright © The Macmillan Company, 1968.

The Soviet government includes both legislative and administrative organs. Constitutionally the Supreme Soviet, which is the highest legislative body, and its Presidium are vested with sovereignty. In practice the Supreme Soviet serves as a forum for the pronouncement of important policies; the Presidium acts for the Supreme Soviet when it is not in session. The primary administrative body is the Council of Ministers, which is too large for effec-

tive decision making; it is generally represented by its own Presidium. The Council of Ministers' formal powers include many of the same rights and duties as those of the American Cabinet. It administers the numerous ministries and agencies involved in foreign and domestic policy. The most important administrative agencies in the formulation and administration of Soviet foreign policy are the Ministry of Foreign Affairs, the Ministry of Defense, the Ministry of Foreign Trade, the State Committee for Foreign Economic Relations, the State Committee for Cultural Relations with Foreign Countries, and the Committee for State Security. In both theory and practice, however, these government agencies defer to and seek guidance from the Communist Party.[12]

According to the Soviet constitution the party represents "the most active and politically-conscious citizens in the ranks of the working class, working peasants and working intelligentsia" and is "the vanguard of the working people in their struggle to build communist society and is the leading core of all organizations of the working people, both public and state." Important party members are concentrated in government positions, particularly in the higher ranks, and the party tends to initiate and oversee foreign policy, leaving implementation to the organs of government. The party also neutralizes other potential interest groups by control of the media, as well as of the instruments of coercion [30].[13]

The most important party organ is the Politburo of the Central Committee, a small group that decides major questions of foreign and domestic policy. Its members are mainly full-time party officials, like the general secretary. Under Stalin the role of general secretary developed, and the Politburo as a whole lost its preeminent position.

Stalin does not "command," he merely "suggests" or "proposes." The fiction of voting is retained. But the vote never fails to uphold his "suggestions." The decision is signed by all ten members of the Politburo, with Stalin's signature among the rest. Yet everyone knows that there is only one boss. [3][14]

Under Khrushchev the Politburo was restored to its former position of authority.

The second major party organ is the Secretariat of the Central Committee, which controls the recruitment of personnel and is the source of much of the Politburo's information. In effect the Secretariat controls and administers the party hierarchy, or *apparat,* which in turn oversees all levels of the government bureaucracy. Both Stalin and Khrushchev used the position of general secretary to achieve and consolidate their own political influence. Nevertheless, under Kosygin and Brezhnev this role has changed and become more institutionalized. As the Soviet Union has become modernized and bureaucracies with stable expectations have evolved, it has become more difficult for a secretary general to use his position to become dictator.

Within the Soviet foreign policy establishment several distinct roles are discernible (see Figure 9.2). The party apparat, more than any other group in the Soviet Union, has a vested interest in maintaining the status quo. Its function is basically nonproductive, and it profits from being the articulator of official ideology. Since the ascendance of Khrushchev it has to a greater extent taken for itself the role of "building communism" in the Soviet Union. Although party leaders may differ on specific policies, they are united in seeking to perpetuate the authority of their ideology. If they can do so by neglecting the international revolution and emphasizing internal economic goals instead, they will. On the other hand, international tension allows the party to demand greater ideological conformity in the face of alleged "foreign enemies." Sustained economic and technological progress requires more than Marxism-Leninism alone can offer. It requires technical and scientific expertise that can be furnished only by other elites whose interests are often at odds with those of the apparat. To a greater extent than under Stalin, therefore, the party bureaucracy is now being staffed with

[12] See, for example, John A. Armstrong, *The Soviet Bureaucratic Elite* (New York: Praeger, 1959); and David Granick, *The Red Executive* (Garden City, N.Y.: Doubleday, 1960).

[13] For greater detail on the functions and composition of the Soviet Communist party, see Gehlen [32] and Abdurakham Avtorkhanov [2].

[14] Currently Mao Tse-tung rules the People's Republic of China with similar stature.

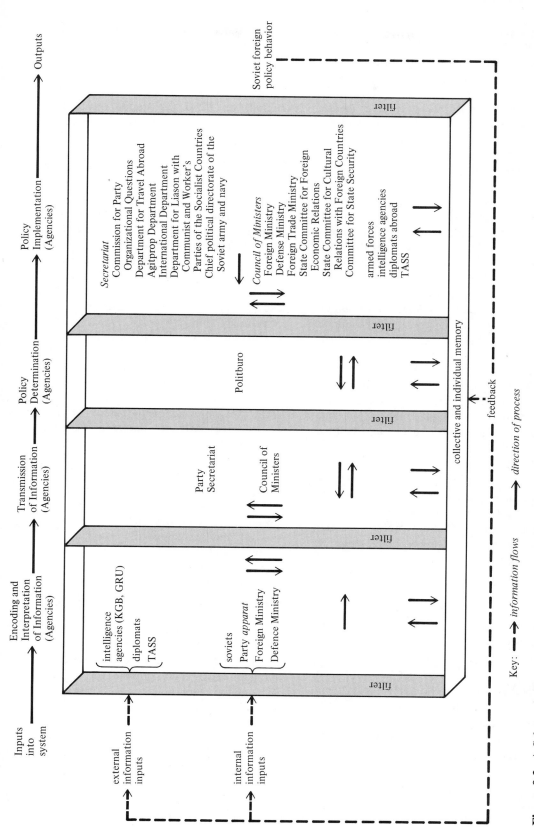

Figure 9.2. A Schematic Representation of the Soviet Foreign-Policy Process

Inputs into system

Encoding and Interpretation of Information (Agencies)

Transmission of Information (Agencies)

Policy Determination (Agencies)

Policy Implementation (Agencies)

Outputs

external information inputs

internal information inputs

intelligence agencies (KGB, GRU)
diplomats
TASS

soviets
Party *apparat*
Foreign Ministry
Defence Ministry

filter

Party Secretariat

Council of Ministers

Politburo

Secretariat
Commission for Party Organizational Questions
Department for Travel Abroad
Agitprop Department
International Department
Department for Liason with Communist and Worker's Parties of the Socialist Countries
Chief political directorate of the Soviet army and navy

Council of Ministers
Foreign Ministry
Defense Ministry
Foreign Trade Ministry
State Committee for Foreign Economic Relations
State Committee for Cultural Relations with Foreign Countries
Committee for State Security

armed forces
intelligence agencies
diplomats abroad
TASS

Soviet foreign policy behavior

collective and individual memory

feedback

Key: ——▶ *information flows*   ——▶ *direction of process*

individuals who have professional training and specific expertise.[15]

A second important elite, the military, has a greater interest in maintenance of international tension. When tension is high the armed forces receive greater shares of resources and esteem and are less subject to party controls. For these reasons the military has occasionally allied itself, on matters of foreign policy, with more conservative members of the party bureaucracy, as well as with the managers of heavy industry, who are loath to permit production of consumer goods to take priority over production of industrial and military equipment. In practice the Soviet military officer probably has a greater interest in the continuation of international tension than does his American counterpart because the opportunities available to the retired American officer for careers in business and politics are not available to the retired Soviet officer.

Other significant elites in the Soviet system include the state bureaucracies, the managers of light industry, agricultural managers and experts, and cultural and professional groups. Their roles are generally not directly associated with foreign policy, except as it serves or detracts from their particular interests. Both the intelligentsia and the managers of light industry and agriculture prefer reduction of international tensions, which generally permits them greater shares of resources and eases the pressure for ideological conformity.

In summary, the Communist Party, as an organization controlled by a small elite, still occupies the commanding heights of Soviet policy formation. To the extent that international tensions increase ideological uniformity, the party favors them. To the extent that they detract from the party's role as the "builder of communism" within the Soviet Union, it seeks to keep them within manageable limits.

[15] The problem of reconciling the party's political control with the needs of economic and technological development has been very well described by Gehlen [32].

THE PEOPLE'S REPUBLIC OF CHINA

The People's Republic of China is a large country of 800 million people, about one-quarter of the world's total population. Its gross national product is about $200 billion, or $250 per capita [86]. The country's partially developed resources and capabilities, however, do not permit it to play as important an international role as that once played by imperial China.[16] As one observer has suggested: "This discrepancy between China's traditional status, particularly as viewed through Chinese eyes, and the country's current position in the world undoubtedly stimulates contemporary leaders towards persistent, sometimes massive, national efforts in the pursuit of prestige, influence, power, and probably a certain kind of primacy" [68, 90].

Current Chinese leaders have been variously labeled "communist revolutionaries," "Chinese nationalists," "domestic modernizers," and "agrarian reformers." All these labels reflect aspects of the truth, but none adequately describes the behavior of Mao and the other Chinese communists since their victory in 1949. The People's Republic has sought to lead the underdeveloped world against the developed West and the Soviet Union. The Maoist regime has consistently opposed the last vestiges of Western colonialism and has supported "wars of liberation" and radical insurgent movements in countries like the Philippines, Malaysia, Thailand, Indonesia, and Vietnam. Chinese foreign policy has racial overtones as well; the regime identifies itself with the "underprivileged masses" of Africa and Asia against the "white" capitalists of the West. Moreover, the Chinese communists depict themselves as the rightful heirs of the revolutionary mantle allegedly discarded by the Soviet Union.

Chinese foreign policy has been largely characterized by ambivalence and inconsistency. China has supported radical and revolutionary political movements throughout the world, while at the same

[16] This statement remains true despite development of Chinese nuclear weapons.

time it has sought to normalize relations with existing governments and to gain acceptance within the international system.[17] In large measure China's international involvement has been limited to verbal and material support for liberation movements, participation in nonaligned conferences, and verbal abuse of the two principal "enemies," the United States and the Soviet Union. Actual Chinese foreign interventon has been limited to areas on the Chinese periphery like Korea (1951–1953), Quemoy and Matsu (1954–1955, 1958), Tibet (1959), the Sino-Indian frontier (1959, 1962), and the Sino-Soviet border (1968–1969).[18] In addition, China has sought to exert influence in selected areas of the "third world" [84, 40].

China's xenophobic views of the United States and Westerners in general cannot be understood without reference to its political history, a societal variable. This history has shaped values, goals, and the frame of reference for viewing the outside world [29]. In the seventeenth century China's population began to increase rapidly, but the nation failed to compensate for this explosion through modernization and industrialization as western Europe, the United States, and Japan did. Consequently by the nineteenth century the European powers and Japan were able to penetrate deeply into China and to demand numerous trade and other concessions that effectively limited Chinese sovereignty. In 1911 the feudal Chinese empire was finally overthrown by modernist forces; a period of civil war, political disintegration, and additional

foreign encroachment ensued. Internal divisions kept China weak and pliant before foreigners until the communists came to power.[19]

In the 1920s two significant political movements developed, the Kuomintang (nationalists) and the communists. Both movements received assistance from the Russian bolsheviks, and the two collaborated until 1927, when the Kuomintang, under the leadership of Chiang Kai-shek, turned upon the communists and crushed them. Despite this initial victory, the Kuomintang was unable to cope effectively either with the continued autonomy of regional warlords, runaway inflation or persistent communist opposition.[20] Furthermore, after 1931 China was occupied by the Japanese, which forced the Kuomintang and the communists again into an uneasy alliance. Once Japan had been defeated, the alliance rapidly disintegrated, and the Kuomintang's hold on the country rapidly weakened. After a period of civil war the nationalist regime collapsed in 1949 and fled to the island of Taiwan [89, 54, 85].

Chinese communist hostility toward the United States developed shortly afterward, when, at the beginning of the Korean War, the United States embraced the nationalist regime on Taiwan and refused to recognize and even actively harassed the communists [97]. These early patterns of American-Chinese interaction were filled with conflict, and they continued through the late 1960s; American support for the rival nationalist regime on Taiwan has been the main focus of Communist China's hostility.

Chinese mistrust of the Soviet Union

[17] The inauguration of "ping-pong diplomacy" in the spring of 1971 illustrates the latter point. The dualism of Chinese foreign policy resembles that of Soviet foreign policy in the 1920s and 1930s, when the young bolshevik regime sponsored and supported communist revolution abroad while seeking acceptance in the international community. Chinese inconsistency in foreign affairs is partly a product of domestic political struggles that have pitted leaders against one another.

[18] For a summary discussion of crises involving the Chinese People's Republic between 1949 and 1965, see Robert C. North [68, pp. 78–80].

[19] Chinese resentment of foreigners and their determination to oust them and to regain former national status are expressed in Chiang Kai-shek, *China's Destiny* (New York: Macmillan, 1947).

[20] After their defeat in 1927 the Chinese communists retreated to remote regions of the country, where, under Mao's leadership, they perfected the strategy of political and guerrilla warfare that finally enabled them to overthrow Chiang without Soviet assistance. For studies of the development of Maoist strategy and tactics, see Jerome Ch'en [12] and Henry G. Schwarz [82].

can be traced to early developments in the Chinese communist movement. After Mao had become undisputed leader of the Chinese Communist Party in 1935 the Soviet Union appears to have made several attempts through Moscow-oriented Chinese to replace or undermine him. During the civil war the Chinese communists received little support from the Soviet Union, and after their success Stalin sought to impose his will on the new regime. After Stalin's death, his denunciation by Khrushchev, and the subsequent eruptions in eastern Europe, Mao sought the position of doctrinal leader of the international communist movement and a status for China within the movement equal to that of the Soviet Union. In addition, the Russians refused to back Chinese attempts to seize Taiwan and the offshore islands of Quemoy and Matsu by force or to supply the Chinese with nuclear weapons. These incidents, cultural and ideological differences, and territorial competition opened a Sino-Soviet split that widened rapidly, culminating in sharp clashes along the common frontier in 1968 and 1969. Competition with the Soviet Union within the international communist movement, including North Vietnam, and in the underdeveloped regions of the world has become a hallmark of contemporary Chinese foreign policy.[21]

Despite industrial and technological advances, China's major foreign-policy objectives remain largely regional; the country lacks the capabilities to bring about the global changes embodied in Mao's revolutionary ideology. The most momentous event in recent Chinese history has been the Great Proletarian Cultural Revolution, which was inaugurated in May 1966 and officially terminated in

[21] For an excellent study of Sino-Soviet competition in Vietnam, see Zagoria, *Vietnam Triangle* (New York: Pegasus, 1967). A quantitative analysis of the deterioration of Sino-Soviet relations has been published in Ole R. Holsti, "External Conflict and Internal Cohesion: The Sino-Soviet Case," in Jan F. Triska, ed., *Communist Party-States: Comparative and International Studies* (New York: Bobbs-Merrill, 1969), pp. 337–353.

April 1969. The cultural revolution was fundamentally an attempt by Mao to transform and revitalize the growing institutional elites of the large party and state bureaucracies. Mao had been increasingly frustrated in carrying out reforms and in implementing policies. The growing institutionalization of roles, the parochial and conservative outlook of government and party officials, and the growing pragmatism of the bureaucracies led him to turn upon the institutions of party and state that he himself had created. He complained:

During the past decade, not a single comrade suggested and dared to expose analytically and systematically to the Center the defects in our plan in order to seek adjustments. I have never seen such a man. I know there are such people, but they dared not appeal to the top echelon by bypassing proper echelons. [73]

In order to produce social change, Mao elected to exacerbate social tensions in China, taking advantage of conflicts between the army and the state bureaucracy, between town and country, and between generations to strengthen his own hand. As a result, the influence of government bureaucrats and conservative members of the party was weakened.

As a consequence of this domestic turmoil China became less active in international politics after 1965, concentrating on the tasks of administrative reorganization and the restoration of political stability. Chinese leaders turned their attention inward, and, except for support of North Vietnam, Chinese foreign policy came to a virtual halt as many ambassadors were recalled from their host countries. Since then control of foreign policy has remained largely in the hands of Mao and his closest associates, notably Premier Chou En-lai. Indeed, one plausible explanation for the cultural revolution is that Mao was seeking for himself "revolutionary immortality" and was looking to restore ideological "purity" both in domestic and foreign policy, putting an end to the instrumental and pragmatic approach to questions of policy that had been adopted by the bureaucracies [55].

Since the cultural revolution China's governmental and party structures have become fluid, and few institutionalized roles currently exist. Chinese foreign policy is therefore influenced in large measure by individual variables. The charismatic figure of Mao dominates Chinese politics, and Maoism continues to serve as the ideological framework through which China views the world. Mao's views about "wars of national liberation" are derived largely from his own revolutionary experience. His personal influence was revealed in the resolution of a conflict over the course of Chinese economic development, which had an important effect on Chinese foreign policy. One faction, led by Marshal Lo Jui-ching, Chief of Staff of the People's Liberation Army (PLA), favored Chinese intervention in Vietnam and elsewhere to counter "imperialist aggression." To undertake such a policy China required a modern professional army equipped with the latest weapons, as well as a strong and stable economy. As the Soviet Union appeared to be the only possible source of outside assistance in rapidly developing the Chinese economy, this faction argued in favor of closer relations with the Soviets. A second faction, led by President Liu Shao-chi, the titular head of state, favored peaceful coexistence with both the United States and the Soviet Union, in order to permit steady economic progress. For both these groups the objective of rapid but balanced economic growth seemed to demand closer association with the Soviet Union. Mao, however, argued that "ideological incentives" can substitute for material incentives in economic development and that China should pursue a foreign policy that, though not provocative, would reduce Chinese dependence upon other actors and increase China's ability to determine its own destiny. Both opposition factions were defeated during the cultural revolution, and Mao's fierce determination to control the political destiny of his

country and impose his own foreign and domestic priorities upon China has prevailed.

Although Mao rarely participates in day-to-day policy making, he frequently intervenes to initiate new programs or redirect old ones. His major weapon for ensuring compliance is the accusation that an official has deviated from Maoist doctrine. As the first leader of the People's Republic Mao has been able to shape his own role. One of his former colleagues has noted, "Mao Tse-tung is more familiar with Chinese history than any other comrade in the Party, and ... the first emperor of any dynasty is always strong handed and brilliant."[22] Maoist ideology, however, may impose strong role constraints on his successors. The cultural revolution also broke down many existing bureaucratic patterns and destroyed those internalized norms that had fostered resistance to pressures for change from above. Consequently role variables are generally weaker in China than might have been expected from James N. Rosenau's analysis.[23]

Mao's emergence from the cultural revolution as the undisputed leader of China means that the "thought of Chairman Mao" will remain China's guiding ideology for the near future. This ideology is based principally on China's domestic experiences, and the attempt to generalize such lessons to foreign policy may be unsuccessful. In fact, Mao's "little red book" contains little of relevance to foreign policy except general approval of wars of national liberation and the assertion that "imperialists are paper tigers." After 1955 Mao shifted from a policy of seeking close relations with existing non-aligned governments to one of militant support for internal revolutions "from be-

[22] P'eng Teh-huai [73, p. 341]. There is a parallel with Soviet history: As long as Stalin was alive he was able to make "Stalinism" reflect his personal preferences. After Stalin's death, however, Khrushchev needed only a few years before he was able to alter the content of the doctrine.

[23] See Chapter 7, p. 137, Figure 7.4.

low," that is, for revolutions carried out by local communists with minimum local "bourgeois" or foreign assistance.[24] Mao has been ambivalent about peaceful coexistence with the capitalist states. He is convinced that the Soviet Union has abandoned the revolutionary struggle and has entered into a tacit coalition with American "imperialists." The tactic of supporting "revolution from below," like the similar Soviet policy in the 1920s, has had few successes despite Mao's assertion that revolutionary forces "will assuredly win still greater victories" [80, p. 414].

The succession is unclear, and Mao's death may lead to a new struggle for power or a military take-over. The Chinese leaders' collective lack of firsthand experience with the noncommunist world inhibits them from accurately perceiving or understanding demands arising elsewhere in the international system. Mao perceives China as a besieged nation; it is "encircled ring upon ring by the imperialists and the modern revisionists" [80, p. 437]. Such a belief can become a self-fulfilling prophecy; it stimulates China's adversaries and neighbors to behave aggressively and hostilely. In Mao's view, however, though China is isolated, it has the strength ultimately to triumph.

In summary, the making of China's foreign policy has resembled the autistic model that we described in Chapter 8, but one centered on a few individuals, rather than on institutionalized role and governmental variables. Chinese foreign policy is formulated in something of a vacuum, with little corrective feedback from either the internal or external environments. As a consequence wider and more erratic shifts are possible, and they may stimulate defensive hostility among other states.

[24] In at least one instance, the attempt by Indonesian communists to seize power in a coup d'état in 1965, this policy ended in unmitigated disaster. A countercoup launched by the Indonesian Army culminated in the slaughter of many communists and their sympathizers and led to the overthrow of President Ahmed Sukarno.

TANZANIA

Tanzania, a recently independent state on the east coast of Africa, exhibits many characteristics typical of the host of Afro-Asian nations that have broken from European colonialism since World War II. The country is economically underdeveloped and poor, with more than 90 percent of its population living in rural peasant communities and a per capita income of approximately $70 a year. Although Tanzania occupies a land area about the size of Germany and France combined, it is populated by only 14 million people, who are unevenly distributed through this large territory. It is an underdeveloped state, with a political system that is closed to most of the population, and its foreign policy can thus be understood primarily in terms of systemic and individual variables. Since independence (for mainland Tanganyika) in December 1961 Tanzania has pursued a policy of nonalignment in foreign affairs, coupled with hesitant attempts to achieve regional leadership. The early postindependence goal of regional integration, partly achieved through the merger with Zanzibar in 1964, has been abandoned owing to disagreements with Kenya and Uganda, Tanzania's northern neighbors.

The primary concern of the Tanzanian government, led by President Julius K. Nyerere, has since been socialist economic development. At the same time Tanzanians have been wary of becoming dependent upon any of the major powers and thus suffering infringement of their new independence. In the parliamentary debates preceding independence Joseph Nyerere, the President's younger brother, argued that his nation should avoid all diplomatic relations except through the United Nations. Although his suggestion was not accepted, it reflected the widely shared fear that African countries remain in danger of losing their independence through the penetration of the great powers. In general the nonaligned countries of Africa and Asia fear that participation in the cold war will lead to loss of sovereignty and divert important resources from economic development. Although it is impossible for Tanzania to retreat into diplomatic isolation, owing to its need for foreign assistance in economic development, President Nyerere has declared:

It is a fact of our life that if any of the big powers attacks us with military force our only hope is to wage a prolonged guerrilla warfare; and as yet very few of us would be very proficient in waging such a war. . . . The real and urgent threat to the independence of almost all the non-aligned states thus comes not from the military, but from the economic power of the big States. . . . [71]

Nonalignment is the typical response of more than fifty states like Tanzania to the impact of systemic variables.[25] In discussing the states that follow this policy, however, we must recognize that they are, in fact, a loosely knit group with a diversity of backgrounds and goals.[26] This nonalignment is basically a rejection of permanent involvement in cold-war conflicts on either side. Underdeveloped states are partly dependent for trade and aid upon the developed countries, for only in this way can they obtain the capital necessary to develop their own resources. A policy of isolationism is thus undesirable, and traditional neutrality, as practiced by Switzerland and to a lesser extent Austria and Sweden, would place underdeveloped states in a passive or defensive posture vis-à-vis the developed world. In contrast to traditional neutralism, nonalignment is an attempt to maximize trade and aid flows while maintaining political independence through active involvement with other international actors. The doctrine has not prevented nonaligned actors from taking public positions on *particular* cold-war issues. For instance, many of them have condemned United States involvement in Indochina and have taken sides in the Arab-Israeli controversy. Nevertheless, nearly all carry

on trade, and several maintain armament agreements with great powers.[27]

The concept of nonalignment, which Prime Minister Jawaharlal Nehru of India labeled "positive neutralism," has been justified as a strategy to prevent the cold war from spreading to the underdeveloped areas of the world. It first arose in an Afro-Asian movement that originated during the organization of the United Nations in 1945. In 1954 at a meeting in Colombo, Ceylon, Nehru and China's Chou En-lai agreed on five principles that were subsequently adopted at the nonaligned conference at Bandung in 1955. They were respect for one another's territorial integrity and sovereignty, mutual nonaggression, noninterference in one another's affairs, equality and mutual benefit, and peaceful coexistence. Curiously four of these five principles are directed toward relations *among* the nonaligned states, and only the last one refers to their common posture toward the major powers.[28]

As Tanzania's experience suggests, the goals of nonalignment can come into conflict, and choices must be made among them. Tanzania has sought to maintain relations with countries of both the Eastern and Western blocs while diversifying trade and aid patterns in order to deal with a broad spectrum of states and remain independent of all of them. Initially dependent upon its former colonial ruler, Great Britain, for close to 90 percent of its economic assistance, Tanzania has

[25] Fifty-four states participated in the third conference of nonaligned countries in Lusaka, Zambia, in 1970.

[26] Tanzania is generally more militant in its foreign policies than are its nonaligned fellows.

[27] Many African members of the former French community and most Latin American countries have such agreements with France and the United States respectively. Nonalignment is hardly a novel policy for poor, newly independent states. For nearly a century after its independence the United States eschewed "European quarrels." For studies of the theory and practice of nonalignment, see J. W. Burton [11], Cecil V. Crabb, Jr. [21], Laurance W. Martin [62], and Alvin Z. Rubinstein [78].

[28] In the autumn of 1962, when China attacked India, it appeared that the five principles had been abandoned. Both sides, however, made efforts to restrain their behavior while Burma, Ceylon, Indonesia, and Cambodia offered their good offices in search of a settlement. India accepted the offer, and China countered with a unilateral cease-fire and partial withdrawal.

shifted partners, so that by 1969 Great Britain accounted for only 31 percent of the total aid received, whereas the People's Republic of China and the United States provided 23 percent and 20 percent respectively. Tanzania's most important single development project is the Tan-Zam railway linking Dar es Salaam with Zambia's copper belt. Construction of this railway was undertaken by the Chinese after both Great Britain and the United States rejected pleas for assistance [67]. In the process of readjusting its diplomatic and aid alignments Tanzania has decisively asserted its independence on several occasions, scuttling agreements with West Germany in a dispute about the establishment of an East German consulate, recalling its ambassador from the United States after accusing two American diplomats of spying, and breaking off diplomatic relations with Great Britain after Rhodesia had declared unilateral independence. These actions have cost Tanzania millions of dollars in economic assistance and loans, but they have established the country's political sensitivity and determination to remain independent.

Apart from reasserting national independence by seeking new trade and aid partners, Tanzania's leaders have seen the need for active participation in international affairs in order to create conditions more favorable to themselves. This participation has been concentrated, in the United Nations and in African regional associations, on efforts to unite the underdeveloped states against the developed ones. As President Nyerere has noted, apart from opposition to colonialism and imperialism, "all that the non-aligned nations have in common is their non-alignment; that is, their existence as weak nations, trying to maintain their independence, and use it for their own benefit in a world dominated politically, economically, and militarily by a few big powers" [49]. Although the nonaligned countries are bound by certain common interests, local conflicts, boundary disputes, and problems of nascent nationalism remain

salient. The Organization of African Unity (OAU) has been active in seeking to resolve intra-African quarrels, particularly by limiting the numbers of participants in disagreements.

Most nonaligned states give the United Nations and functional international agencies extensive support. They regularly press for increases in the budgets of such organizations. As their voting strength exceeds their resources and as they are the greatest beneficiaries of the redistribution of wealth and services that such agencies undertake, this policy seems more self-serving than necessarily progressive or "international." [29] Indeed, as Nyerere's comment suggests, there is a discernible decline in supranational identities among elites in the underdeveloped areas and increased emphasis on nationalism, sovereignty, and reduced interdependence with the outside world. Many of these states are nationalizing foreign industries, erecting trade barriers, reducing imports through tariff barriers that foster infant industries, and restricting foreign travel by their own nationals. Economic unions in East, Central, and West Africa have either declined or disintegrated, and the growth of Latin American trade areas has been spotty at best, with major economic benefits going to the largest states. Furthermore, several national units have disintegrated: India and Pakistan were separated, Singapore seceded from Malaysia and Bangladesh from West Pakistan, and irredentist or separatist movements remain active in Chad, Sudan, Iran, Pakistan, and the Philippines. In states like Kenya, India, Malaysia, Ceylon, and Nigeria secessionist movements are now dormant, having already erupted in varying degrees.

Tanzania's foreign policy reflects its status as an underdeveloped and nonaligned state, as well as its regional role in East Africa. Five foreign policy objectives arise from the country's posture of dynamic nonalignment. Tanzania has

[29] For investigations of African behavior in the United Nations, see Ali Mazrui [63] and Benjamin Meyers [64].

acted as a mediator to reduce tensions among states, particularly in Africa. Its recognition of Biafra in 1968 was partly an effort to bring an end to the Nigerian civil war after it had become protracted and bloody. In addition, Tanzania has acted to mediate disputes between Kenya and Somalia and among competing black nationalist factions from white-controlled areas of southern Africa.

Tanzania's second objective has been to take the initiative in promoting peace among the major bloc actors. To this end, it has maintained diplomatic relations with both sides and has established a record of independent voting in the United Nations, thus establishing a reasonable "third party" reputation in the East-West conflict.

Even more significant is Tanzania's third objective, to set an example for other weak actors. Nyerere has endeavored to demonstrate that independence can be secured only through cooperative action among the nonaligned states against foreign interference. Tanzania immediately severed diplomatic relations with Great Britain as a result of the latter's failure to end the independence of the white-dominated government of Rhodesia. When other African states vacillated and backed away from such a step because of economic considerations, Nyerere did not hesitate to denounce the lack of will to make sacrifices necessary to guarantee and promote nonalignment.

Tanzania's fourth objective has been to promote liberation movements in southern Africa by providing material assistance and training camps, as well as by permitting Chinese communist advisers to operate in them. Tanzania has been in the forefront of OAU efforts to organize forces directed against the Union of South Africa, Rhodesia, Southwest Africa, and Portuguese-controlled Mozambique. In particular the clandestine Mozambique Liberation Front (FRELIMO), a guerrilla movement directed against the Portuguese, has operated out of Tanzania with greater success than any similar movement has had.

Finally, Tanzania has sought to galvanize world public opinion against those states that flagrantly violate accepted international norms of behavior. It has denounced American behavior in Indochina, Israel's continued occupation of Arab lands, and the Soviet invasion of Czechoslovakia, despite the fact that all three nations had provided large amounts of assistance to Tanzania.[30]

The architect of Tanzania's foreign policy has been the first president of the country, Nyerere. He exhibits the spirit of proud and sometimes defiant self-reliance that shapes Tanzanian behavior.

We shall deal with each problem as it occurs, and on its own merits. We shall neither move from particular quarrels with individual countries to a generalized hostility to members of a particular group, nor to automatic support for those who also happen to be, for their own reasons, quarrelling with the same nations. We wish to live in friendship with all states and all peoples. [72, 70, 69]

Nyerere's role in policy formation is decisive. In 1965, for instance, his government was one of the few to break diplomatic relations with Great Britain over the Rhodesian issue, and it was the only one (besides Ghana, which restored those relations after the overthrow of Kwame Nkrumah) that had strong economic ties with Great Britain to do so. Although Tanzania's East African common-market partners, Kenya and Uganda, voted with Tanzania in the OAU to sever relations, they failed to act on their decision. Tanzania did so, largely on the initiative of Nyerere. The decision was made essentially single-handedly, with little or no consultation. This episode reflects the general style of Nyerere's direction of Tanzanian foreign policy.[31]

Nyerere's political style, which includes

[30] In fact, after the Soviet invasion of Czechoslovakia, the Tanzanian minister of state for foreign affairs personally led a protest march against the Soviet embassy in Dar es Salaam.
[31] For a discussion of Nyerere's style of executive leadership, see Raymond F. Hopkins, *Political Roles in a New State* (New Haven: Yale University Press, 1971), chap. 6.

194

a disarming frankness about the costs of pursuing an independent foreign policy, and his own personal popularity enable him to command support from within the government, as well as from relevant constituencies in Tanzania. He remains relatively free to scrutinize and shape Tanzania's foreign policy. The country has had only one minister for external affairs, Oscar Kambona, a popular politician who lacked administrative acumen. After Kambona's period of service the portfolio of foreign affairs was moved to the presidential office, where Nyerere has been able to exert even stronger influence over foreign policy than he had done previously.

The diffuse and less direct impact of other variable clusters ensures domination of the foreign-policy process by individual and systemic factors. Tanzania's underdeveloped economy and primitive rural society, though providing impetus toward economic development, do not furnish the basis for foreign-policy pressure groups or an alternative ideology. Nyerere's successful disregard of economic considerations in foreign policy indicates the weakness of economic elites. As economic development is managed directly by the central government, the principal area of potential conflict is with the donor states, rather than with domestic groups. The political system, though democratic in form, incorporates few constraints on foreign policy, and Nyerere's immense personal popularity with the electorate and his paramount influence within the only legal political party, the Tanzanian African National Union (TANU), permit him to impose his personal views. The absence of clearly established foreign-policy precedents and patterns, the result of Tanzania's recent entrance into the international system, permit Nyerere himself to create such precedents.

Governmental variables also place few constraints on foreign policy, other than limiting its potential scope and domain. It is difficult in an underdeveloped country like Tanzania to create the bureaucratic instruments necessary to sustain an active foreign policy. There are severe shortages of trained and educated manpower. In 1970 the Tanzanian foreign ministry employed only 180 people, most of whom were in Dar es Salaam; the country has few trained diplomats, and most of them are required within the country [87]. The cost of maintaining overseas embassies is burdensome, and Tanzania supported only sixteen such embassies in 1970. The consequent lack of contact with other actors is compensated for by the many foreign embassies in Tanzania. The United Nations also serves as a medium through which Tanzanian diplomats can conduct relations with others. The small foreign-policy establishment—and we stretch the meaning of the term "establishment"—has developed few institutional interests, in contrast to those in countries like the United States or the Soviet Union. On the other hand, the small size of the establishment itself is a major constraint on the range and effectiveness of the diplomatic communications in which Tanzania can engage.

Role variables have so far little importance in Tanzania. The role of the president has largely been defined by Nyerere himself, the first occupant of this post. His role is, to a greater extent than in most countries, the product of his own personality and inclinations. Those roles that have developed in Tanzania revolve around a system of "closed politics"; that is, political disputes are resolved *within* the single political party, though open debate is permitted there. In other areas of government, roles are developing and will in time come to influence foreign policy to a greater extent than they do today.[32]

In general the governmental, social, and role variables relevant to policy formulation are similar in many underdeveloped states. Government bureaucracies

[32] For a discussion of roles in Tanzania, see Hopkins, "The Role of the M. P. in Tanzania," *American Political Science Review*, 64 (September 1970), 754–771.

have few trained diplomats and they are usually more skilled in protocol than in negotiating trade agreements.[33] These states often have small armies or at least small nuclei of professional officers, and when conflict has erupted they have fared poorly in battle.[34] A cynic might explain these failures by noting that many military officers are preoccupied with running their respective countries, as in Indonesia, Thailand, South Vietnam, South Korea, Burma, Pakistan, Nigeria, the Congo, Argentina, Brazil, and Bolivia, to name a few.

In addition to bureaucratic and military weakness, national identity and territorial nationalism are frequently also fragile and fragmentary. Indeed, accusations of diabolical attempts by outside powers to divide these countries can be more accurately understood as manifestations of this weak nationalism. Vitriolic attacks on foreigners and the nonalignment posture serve to reduce the tendency for competing factions to line up at the "special fund" troughs of the big-power embassies. Nonalignment thus also serves the domestic purpose of providing a defense against reinforcement of internal splits by the external East-West cleavage.[35]

[33] In many African states, at least during the 1960s, trade agreements and management contracts with international firms were drawn up by foreign advisers. Furthermore, the planning and accounting procedures expected by overseas donors like the United States, Great Britain, and West Germany are frequently impossible for national governments desiring assistance. As a result, American Agency for International Development (AID) personnel seconded to foreign governments have occasionally negotiated these agreements with American AID field personnel.

[34] The surprising ease with which the military forces of Indonesia, Egypt, the Congo, and East Africa were defeated in engagements during the 1960s attests to this weakness.

[35] The incidence of foreign support for domestic political movements or particular leaders in the third world and nonaligned states is widespread. Some efforts by the Soviet Union and China have already been mentioned. The United States, France, and Great Britain also engage in such activities, often indirectly. Aside from direct "bribes," kickbacks to politicians from private foreign businesses are a flagrant example of such tacit behavior by Western states.

Another characteristic of these states is that their political systems lack historical precedents, shared expectations for behavior, and historical accumulations of legitimacy. Their frontiers often cut across ethnic groups, and border conflicts have thus become dangerous focuses of attention. Recent examples of border conflict in underdeveloped areas include those between India and Pakistan; Somalia, Kenya, and Ethiopia; and Morocco and Algeria.

In summary, nonaligned actors like Tanzania seek greater prestige in the international system, the liberation of remaining colonized areas, maximum foreign assistance, and avoidance of direct involvement in both the cold war and local or regional conflict. Their major goals are to extract resources from the developed states, to secure greater redistribution of resources from international corporations (particularly from those controlling primary resources), and to retain a free hand in solving their internal problems without interference by the great powers. In addition, many wish to exercise the "right" to take ideological stands in the great-power controversies. The underlying rationale of all these goals is expressed in the African proverb that when two elephants fight, it is the grass that suffers [21, p. 2].

THE UNITED STATES

The United States is a large, economically developed, and accessible political system. Among international actors it ranks highest in size and development. In contrast to Tanzania, it possesses the resources and manpower to sustain an active foreign policy throughout the world and to influence other actors more than it is influenced by them. American foreign policy is characterized by high levels of interaction with other actors. American behavior is likely to have formidable impacts on other actors, so that shifts in United States policy are salient factors in shaping other states' behavior.

Since World War II the touchstone of

American foreign policy has been opposition to the creation of new communist governments and regimes. As a "status quo" power, the United States has opposed revolutionary and radical movements in Asia and Latin America, and is the leader of anticommunist alliances in Europe and Asia. It has also exercised "leadership" in Latin America and the Caribbean and has sought to maintain its hegemony in the Western Hemisphere.[36]

As a developed state the United States possesses a highly bureaucratic foreign-policy process. That is, its foreign policy is greatly influenced by government and role factors [99, 43, 45, 52, 48, 41, 42]. As the political process is relatively open, foreign-policy elites must be responsive to societal pressures. Owing to the deference of the majority of citizens to the authority and expertise of political leaders in foreign policy, public opinion can be manipulated within certain limits; only a small portion of the population is attentive to foreign-policy issues. But major socioeconomic groups do have access to the governmental arena and can exercise indirect and even direct influence on many decisions. As a result, decisions with consequences for foreign policy are often taken to satisfy internal constituencies, rather than deliberately to shape the external environment. George F. Kennan has declared that his first lesson on becoming a diplomat was on

one of the most consistent and incurable traits of American statesmanship—namely, its neurotic self-consciousness and introversion, the tendency to make statements and take actions with regard not to their effect on the international scene to which they are ostensibly addressed but rather to their effects on those echelons of American opinion, congressional opinion first and foremost, to which the respective statesmen are anxious to appeal. [51, p. 53]

Public opinion can flow into the foreign-policy process through various channels—in particular, elections, mass media,

political parties, Congress, and interest groups. For political parties or elections to function as effective channels of such opinion, foreign-policy questions must be issues with ramifications in the domestic political arena. Survey research suggests that foreign-policy attitudes in the United States are rarely translated into electoral or partisan support. Indeed, both major political parties have tended to support rather similar foreign policies under the label of "bipartisanship" [96, 47, 20].

In the presidential election of 1968 the Vietnam War was a major issue, but the candidates did not take discernibly different stands on it; the Democrats seem to have suffered simply by having been in office while the war grew. During the campaign and after his assumption of office, President Richard M. Nixon rejected attempts to end the war quickly. Referring to antiwar sentiment, the President declared, "Under no circumstances will I be affected whatever by it."[37] In practice the President *was* influenced by the antiwar climate. This fact became clearer as American troops were gradually withdrawn from Vietnam between 1969 and 1972, and "rumors" of an armistice with North Vietnam grew just before the 1972 presidential election. As Presidents Harry S. Truman and Lyndon B. Johnson had discovered before him, the American public will not support a limited war that is not an apparent success, especially one that is remote from the United States both geographically and culturally. Other than issues directly related to war and taxes, however, foreign-policy questions seldom play dramatic roles in American politics. As Rosenau has suggested, unless a foreign-policy issue involves an important investment of resources or a significant challenge to existing socioeconomic relationships, it will not be drawn into the domestic political process but will be handled by the foreign-policy establishment [77, 60]. As one analyst has observed, "The chances that a President will be unable to carry out even a controver-

[36] For critical evaluations of American foreign policy, see David Horowitz [46], J. William Fulbright [31], S. Brown [6], Theodore Draper [27], and George Liska [56].

[37] *The New York Times,* September 27, 1969, p. 14.

sial policy are slight, nor is it at all likely that he will be dissuaded from pursuing a difficult and possibly unpopular line of policy by fear that he and his party will be electorally punished" [94].[38]

Individuals have little impact on legislators or bureaucrats through letters, telegrams, or visits because they generally lack sufficient organization and resources. Except when such communications are part of a well-organized public protest, it is unlikely that government representatives will pay attention. Congressmen, for instance, are seldom amenable to the opinions of those who appear to have no direct economic interest in the foreign-policy issue under discussion. Most influence by nongovernmental groups thus revolves around economic issues, is handled by professional lobbyists, and works through stimulation of latent congressional and bureaucratic support. A study of the influence of constituency attitudes on the views and votes of congressmen has shown foreign policy to be an area of far less possible influence than domestic policy [65].

The most influential groups are those that represent particular economic or cultural interests on issues that appear to affect them directly. For instance, the fishing industry of the West Coast had a significant voice in shaping the peace treaty with Japan, because one of the subjects dealt with in the treaty was international fishing rights [16]. Bernard C. Cohen has observed that "the span of influence of specific groups seems to be limited to the area of their special policy interest; this limitation seems to hold even though an organization may take an articulate public position on the entire range of foreign policy issues" [15]. Sometimes informal coalitions develop between special interest groups and congressional committees or executive agencies responsible for selected areas of policy. Such coalitions on matters of foreign policy are, however, even less formal than are those on questions of domestic import.

In the twentieth century congressional influence on American foreign policy has been considerably less than that of the executive. One study has concluded: "Congressional participation in foreign policy decisions is principally in the recommendation and prescription stages of the decision process. . . . [T]he domain of Congressional influence, especially when it is initiative, tends to be on marginal and relatively less important matters" [76]. Congressional weakness in foreign-policy formation partly reflects lack of information and the exigencies of time, for situations frequently require such prompt action that congressional consultation becomes at best pro forma. Many congressmen also lack the expertise and time to pursue foreign-policy questions constructively.[39] In addition, only the executive branch has the ability to bring together competing interests in foreign policy, particularly as many of these interests are in fact centered in executive agencies. Although committees of the two congressional houses—Foreign Relations, Foreign Affairs, Atomic Energy, Armed Services, Appropriations, and so on—are all concerned with aspects of the foreign-policy process, none is able to take the necessary overview of policy. "Consequently," one observer has declared, "congressional bodies may become advocates of particular programs, but they lack sufficient political competence to determine an overall program" [47, p. 132]. Congress influences foreign policy mainly through budgetary appropriations, public hearings and debate, and indirect means that frequently amount to lobbying.

Governmental variables are therefore rather more significant than are societal ones. The day-to-day conduct of foreign policy is handled by a variety of government agencies, including the State De-

---

[38] Before becoming President, John F. Kennedy wrote a Pulitzer Prize-winning book, *Profiles in Courage* (New York: Harper & Row, 1956), in which he praised statesmen who had shown the courage to resist popular pressures in order to do what they thought was right.

[39] Some congressmen, however, particularly committee chairmen who have served on relevant committees for long periods of time, come to be experts in foreign policy, with greater experience in their areas of competence than even their executive counterparts have.

partment, the Central Intelligence Agency, and the Department of Defense. Foreign policy is characteristically incremental, as many different groups within the government seek to achieve consensus on the bewildering array of issues with which they are confronted.[40] The dominance of organizational variables in this process leads to generation of highly institutionalized roles that limit the behavior of individuals.

Individual variables have relatively small impact on American policy, except in crises. There is little opportunity for specific individuals to affect policy and even less opportunity for personality factors to affect outcomes. Even the president is limited in his ability to change policy radically, regardless of his intentions. For a president to take initiative successfully, the cooperation of many may be required, and this cooperation must usually be induced, rather than commanded. Richard E. Neustadt has declared, "Underneath our images of Presidents-in-boots, astride decisions, are the half-observed realities of Presidents-in-sneakers, stirrups in hand, trying to induce particular department heads, or congressmen, or senators to climb aboard" [66, 44]. The political system itself inhibits radical innovation. Each decision maker is caught in his own network of constituencies and clients demanding satisfaction. In addition, the bureaucratic policy machinery often presents the president and his advisers with "yea"-or-"nay" decisions, and they are rarely able to develop sets of alternatives for themselves. Opposition to presidential action or inaction is greater to the extent that the president appears to violate role expectations. When President Nixon decided to dispatch American troops to Cambodia in May 1970, he provoked considerable opposition, particularly in Congress, many of whose members thought that he had violated their firm expectations: A great deal of public and private concern was

aroused by the President's failure to consult with or to brief prominent members of Congress beforehand, a normal practice in such situations. Finally, the cross pressures generated by the president's multiple responsibilities may lead to his "immobilization," as he seeks to make decisions that will foreclose the fewest possible alternatives in the future.

In the exceptional instance of a severe international crisis, when there is no time for the regular bureaucratic processing of foreign policy, individual variables may have greater salience. Thus, the personalities of President Kennedy and his brother Robert were significant determinants of American behavior during the Cuban missile crisis of 1962. However, it is remarkable how little American foreign policy has actually changed since World War II, despite changes in individuals and parties with supposedly different philosophies and beliefs.

Although the presidential role offers limited scope for the impact of an individual, the recruitment patterns of the government and political parties constrain those in high office even more. For example, Vice-President Hubert H. Humphrey apparently sought privately to change President Johnson's Vietnam policy, though he supported it in public. When questioned about his position on the Vietnam issue, Humphrey, who ran unsuccessfully for the presidency in 1968, remarked that "Humphrey as captain of the team would be different from Humphrey as a member of the team."

In summary, American foreign policy is the outcome of an extremely complex process of vertical and horizontal interaction within the foreign-policy establishment and between it and the remainder of society. In such an institutionalized process, governmental and role factors are of extraordinary importance.

CONCLUSION

In this and the previous chapter, we have discussed the importance of five clusters

[40] Frequently the model of fragmented decision making is applicable to the American foreign-policy process. See Chapter 8, pp. 165–167.

of variables and their interdependence in the making of foreign policy. It is clear that the importance of these clusters varies as the international system changes and its structural properties are altered. These properties are essentially what we have called "systemic variables." As we suggested in Chapter 6, the international system is shifting from bipolarity to less rigidity. In a bipolar world, systemic variables have greater impact on the foreign policy of *all* actors than they have in a multipolar system. But, as the international structure has become more complex, resources have been more evenly distributed, and ideological dimensions have multiplied beyond the simple East-West dichotomy, the effects on policy determination of structural or systemic features have declined, and other variable clusters have become more important.

As bipolarity has decayed, a new class of international and transnational actors has emerged; we shall turn our attention to it in subsqent chapters. These actors —international organizations and multinational corporations—and their activities, which are increasingly important for political outcomes, fall into the interstices of "traditional" analyses of international relations. Furthermore, the capacity of older political organizations like nation-states to regulate the activities of these new actors is declining just when the need to regulate them is increasing. Public international law, for instance, previously regarded as the summation of national interests, cannot regulate international corporations effectively. As a result, limited jurisdiction and conflicting legal constraints create opportunities for these extranational actors that are not available to actors caught within a national territorial framework.

Although there are clearly growing bonds *among the parts* of the system, the bonds *between the parts and the system as a whole* are not so obvious. As we have suggested, the breakdown of bipolarity means that we can analyze the policy processes of large actors like the United States with little reference to the larger international system. In some instances the internal processes are *more* separable from the processes of the international political system as a whole than they were before. As we shall see in Chapter 23, the growth of "system level" demands and problems has outstripped the growth of comparable institutions and attitudes necessary to manage them.

References

1. Aspaturian, Vernon V., "Internal Politics and Foreign Policy in the Soviet System," in R. Barry Farrell, ed., *Approaches to Comparative and International Politics* (Evanston: Northwestern University Press, 1966), p. 249.
2. Avtorkhanov, Abdurakham, *The Communist Party Apparatus* (Chicago: Regnery, 1966).
3. Barmine, Alexander, *One Who Survived* (New York: Putnam, 1945), p. 213.
4. Beim, David, "The Communist Bloc and the Foreign Aid Game," *Western Political Quarterly,* 17 (December 1964), pp. 784–799.
5. Bell, Daniel, "Ten Theories in Search of Reality," *World Politics,* 10 (April 1958), pp. 327–365.
6. Brown, S., *The Faces of Power* (New York: Columbia University Press, 1968).
7. Brzezinski, Zbigniew K., "Five Years After Khrushchev—A Symposium," *Survey,* 72 (July 1969), pp. 39–72.
8. Brzezinski, Zbigniew K., *Ideology and Power in Soviet Politics* (New York: Praeger, 1962).
9. Brzezinski, Zbigniew K., *The Soviet Bloc: Unity and Conflict,* rev. ed. (New York: Praeger, 1961).
10. Brzezinski, Zbigniew K., and Samuel P. Huntington, *Political Power: USA/USSR* (New York: Viking, 1965).
11. Burton, J. W., ed., *Nonalignment* (London: Heinemann, 1966).
12. Ch'en, Jerome, *Mao and the Chinese Revolution* (New York: Oxford University Press, 1967).
13. Cheng, Chu-Yuan, *Economic Relations Between Peking and Moscow, 1949–1963* (New York: Praeger, 1964).

14. Clemens, Walter C., Jr., "Soviet Policy in the Third World in the 1970's," *Orbis*, 13 (Summer 1969), pp. 476–501.

15. Cohen, Bernard C., *The Influence of Non-Governmental Groups on Foreign Policymaking* (Boston: World Peace Foundation, 1959), p. 12.

16. Cohen, Bernard C., *The Political Process and Foreign Policy: The Making of the Japanese Peace Settlement* (Princeton: Princeton University Press, 1957).

17. Conquest, Robert, *Power and Policy in the U.S.S.R.* (New York: Macmillan, 1961).

18. Conquest, Robert, *Russia after Khrushchev* (New York: Praeger, 1965).

19. Conquest, Robert, "Stalin's Successors," *Foreign Affairs*, 48 (April 1970), p. 509.

20. Crabb, Cecil V., Jr., *Bipartisan Foreign Policy: Myth or Reality?* (New York: Harper & Row, 1957).

21. Crabb, Cecil V., Jr., *The Elephants and the Grass: A Study of Nonalignment* (New York: Praeger, 1965).

22. Dallin, Alexander, ed., *Diversity in International Communism: A Documentary Record, 1961–1963* (New York: Columbia University Press, 1963).

23. Djilas, Milovan, *The New Class* (New York: Praeger, 1957).

24. Djilas, Milovan, *The Unperfect Society: Beyond the New Class* (New York: Harcourt Brace Jovanovich, 1969).

25. Drachkovitch, Milorad M., *Marxism in the Modern World* (Stanford: Stanford University Press, 1965).

26. Drachkovitch, Milorad M., *Marxist Ideology in the Contemporary World: Its Appeals and Paradoxes* (New York: Praeger, 1966).

27. Draper, Theodore, *Abuse of Power* (New York: Viking, 1967).

28. Fainsod, Merle, *How Russia is Ruled*, rev. ed. (Cambridge, Mass.: Harvard University Press, 1963), p. 341.

29. FitzGerald, C. P., *The Chinese View of Their Place in the World* (New York: Oxford University Press, 1969).

30. Fleron, Frederic J., Jr., "Toward a Reconceptualization of Political Change in the Soviet Union—The Political Leadership System," *Comparative Politics*, 1 (January 1969), pp. 228–244.

31. Fulbright, J. William, *The Arrogance of Power* (New York: Vintage, 1966).

32. Gehlen, Michael P., *The Communist Party of the Soviet Union* (Bloomington: Indiana University Press, 1969).

33. Gehlen, Michael P., *The Politics of Coexistence* (Bloomington: Indiana University Press, 1967).

34. Gibert, Stephen P., "Soviet-American Military Aid Competition in the Third World," *Orbis*, 13 (Winter 1970), pp. 1117–1138.

35. Gittings, John, *Survey of the Sino-Soviet Dispute* (London: Oxford University Press, 1968).

36. Goldman, Marshall I., "A Balance Sheet of Soviet Foreign Aid," *Foreign Affairs*, 43 (January 1965), pp. 349–360.

37. Griffith, William E., *Albania and the Sino-Soviet Rift* (Cambridge, Mass.: MIT Press, 1963).

38. Griffith, William E., ed., *Communism in Europe: Continuity, Change, and the Sino-Soviet Dispute* (Cambridge, Mass.: MIT Press, 1964–1965).

39. Griffith, William E., *Sino-Soviet Relations, 1964–1965* (Cambridge, Mass.: MIT Press, 1967).

40. Halperin, Ernst, "Peking and the Latin American Communists," *China Quarterly*, 29 (January–March, 1967), pp. 111–154.

41. Hammond, Paul Y., "Foreign Policy and Administrative Politics," *World Politics*, 17 (July 1965), pp. 656–671.

42. Hammond, Paul Y., "The Political Order and the Burden of External Relations," *World Politics*, 19 (April 1967), pp. 443–464.

43. Hilsman, Roger, "The Foreign Policy Consensus: An Interim Research Report," *Journal of Conflict Resolution*, 3 (December 1959), pp. 361–382.

44. Hilsman, Roger, *To Move a Nation* (Garden City, N.Y.: Doubleday, 1967), p. 539.

45. Hoffmann, Stanley, "Restraints and Choices in American Foreign Policy, in Stanley Hoffmann, ed., *The State of War* (New York: Praeger, 1965), pp. 160–197.

46. Horowitz, David, *The Free World Colossus*, rev. ed. (New York: Hill & Wang, 1971).

47. Huntington, Samuel P., *The Common Defense* (New York: Columbia University Press, 1961), pp. 234–267.
48. Huntington, Samuel P., "Strategic Planning and the Political Process," *Foreign Affairs*, 38 (January 1960), pp. 285–299.
49. Hveen, H., and P. Willets, "The Practice of Non-Alignment" (Paper delivered at the Social Science Conference, University of Dar es Salaam, December 27–31), p. 3.
50. Keller, Suzanne, *Beyond the Ruling Class: Strategic Elites in Modern Society* (New York: Random House, 1963), p. 70.
51. Kennan, George F., *Memoirs 1925–1950* (Boston: Little, Brown, 1967).
52. Kissinger, Henry, "Domestic Structure and Foreign Policy," *Daedalus*, 95 (Spring 1966), pp. 503–529).
53. Leonhard, Wolfgang, *The Kremlin Since Stalin* (New York: Praeger, 1962).
54. Lewis, John W., "Leader, Commissar, and Bureaucrat: The Chinese Political System in the Last Days of the Revolution," *Journal of International Affairs*, 24 (1970), pp. 48–74.
55. Lifton, Robert, *Revolutionary Immortality: Mao Tse-Tung and the Chinese Cultural Revolution* (New York: Random House, 1968).
56. Liska, George, *Imperial America* (Baltimore: Johns Hopkins University Press, 1967).
57. Lodge, Milton C., *Soviet Elite Attitudes Since Stalin* (Columbus, O.: Merrill, 1969), pp. 11–12.
58. Lowenthal, Richard, "Russia and China: Controlled Conflict," *Foreign Affairs*, 49 (April 1971), pp. 507–518.
59. Lowenthal, Richard, *World Communism: The Disintegration of a Secular Faith* (New York: Oxford University Press, 1964).
60. Lowi, Theodore, "Making Democracy Safe for the World," in James N. Rosenau, ed., *Domestic Sources of Foreign Policy* (New York: Free Press, 1967), pp. 295–332.
61. McNeal, Robert H., ed., *International Relations Among Communists* (Englewood Cliffs, N.J.: Prentice-Hall, 1967).
62. Martin, Laurance W., ed., *Neutralism and Nonalignment* (New York: Praeger, 1962).
63. Mazrui, Ali, "The United Nations and Some African Political Attitudes," *International Organization*, 18 (Summer 1964), pp. 499–520.
64. Meyers, Benjamin, "African Voting in the United Nations General Assembly," *Journal of Modern African Studies*, 4 (October 1966), pp. 213–228.
65. Miller, Warren, and Donald Stokes, "Constituency Influence in Congress," *American Political Science Review*, 57 (March 1963), p. 56.
66. Neustadt, Richard E., *Presidential Power* (New York: Wiley, 1960).
67. Nnoli, O., "Diplomacy and the Extractions of External Resources: Tanzania's Experience" (Paper delivered at the Social Science Conference, University of Dar es Salaam, December 27–31, 1970).
68. North, Robert C., *The Foreign Relations of China* (Belmont, Calif.: Dickenson, 1969), p. 9.
69. Nyerere, Julius K., *Freedom and Socialism* (New York: Oxford University Press, 1968).
70. Nyerere, Julius K., *Freedom and Unity* (London: Oxford University Press, 1967).
71. Nyerere, Julius K., "Non-alignment in the 1970s" (Address delivered to the Preparation Meeting of Non-Aligned Countries, April 13, 1970).
72. Nyerere, Julius K., *Tanzanian Policy on Foreign Affairs* (Dar es Salaam: Ministry of Information, 1967).
73. Oksenberg, Michel C., "Policy Making Under Mao Tse-tung, 1949–1968," *Comparative Politics*, 3 (April 1971), p. 331.
74. Ploss, Sidney I., *Conflict and Decision-Making in the Soviet Union* (Princeton: Princeton University Press, 1965).
75. Ploss, Sidney I., "Soviet Politics on the Eve of the 24th Party Congress," *World Politcs*, 23 (October 1970), pp. 61–82.
76. Robinson, James A., *Congress and Foreign Policy-Making*, rev. ed. (Homewood, Ill.: Dorsey, 1967), pp. 14–15.
77. Rosenau, James N., "Foreign Policy as an Issue Area," in Rosenau, ed., *Domestic Sources of Foreign Policy*

(New York: Free Press, 1967), pp. 11–50.

78. Rubinstein, Alvin Z., *Yugoslavia and the Nonaligned World* (Princeton: Princeton University Press, 1970).

79. Salisbury, Harrison, *War Between Russia and China* (New York: Norton, 1969).

80. Schram, Stuart R., ed., *The Political Thought of Mao Tse-Tung,* 2nd ed. (New York: Praeger, 1969).

81. Schwartz, Joel J., and William R. Keech, "Group Influence and the Policy Process in the Soviet Union," *American Political Science Review,* 62 (September 1968), pp. 840–851.

82. Schwarz, Henry G., "The Nature of Leadership: The Chinese Communists, 1930–1945," *World Politics,* 22 (July 1970), pp. 541–581.

83. Shulman, Marshall, "Recent Soviet Foreign Policy: Some Patterns in Retrospect," *Journal of International Affairs,* 22 (1968), pp. 26–41.

84. Slawecki, Leon M. S., "The Two Chinas In Africa," *Foreign Affairs,* 41 (January 1963), pp. 398–409.

85. Snow, Edgar, *The Other Side of the River* (New York: Random House, 1961).

86. Snow, Edgar, "Talks with Chou En-lai," *The New Republic,* March 27, 1971, pp. 20–23.

87. *Tanzania Directory* (Dar es Salaam: Government Printer, September 1970).

88. Triska, Jan F., and David D. Finley, *Soviet Foreign Policy* (New York: Macmillan, 1968).

89. Tsou, Tang, *America's Failure in China, 1941–1950,* 2 vols. (Chicago: University of Chicago Press, 1963).

90. Tuchman, Barbara, *Stilwell and the American Experience in China* (New York: Macmillan, 1970).

91. Ulam, Adam B., *Expansion and Coexistence* (New York: Praeger, 1968).

92. Ulam, Adam B., "Soviet Ideology and Soviet Foreign Policy," *World Politics,* 11 (January 1959), pp. 153–172.

93. Valkenier, Elizabeth Kridl, "New Trends in Soviet Economic Relations with the Third World," *World Politics,* 22 (April 1970), pp. 415–432.

94. Waltz, Kenneth N., "Electoral Punishment and Foreign Policy Crises," in James N. Rosenau, ed., *Domestic Sources of Foreign Policy* (New York: Free Press, 1967), p. 283.

95. Waltz, Kenneth N., *Man, the State, and War* (New York: Columbia University Press, 1959).

96. Westerfield, H. Bradford, *Foreign Policy and Party Politics: Pearl Harbor to Korea* (New Haven: Yale University Press, 1955), p. 12.

97. Whiting, Allen S., *China Crosses the Yalu* (New York: Macmillan, 1960).

98. Wolfe, Bertram D., "Communist Ideology and Soviet Foreign Policy," *Foreign Affairs,* 41 (October 1962), pp. 152–170.

99. Yarmolinsky, Adam, "Bureaucratic Structures and Political Outcomes," *Journal of International Affairs,* 23 (1969), pp. 225–235.

100. Zagoria, Donald S., *The Sino-Soviet Conflict, 1956–1961* (New York: Atheneum, 1967).

101. Zimmerman, William, "Elite Perspectives and the Explanation of Soviet Foreign Policy," *Journal of International Affairs,* 24 (1970), pp. 84–98.

102. Zimmerman, William, *Soviet Perspectives on Internation Relations, 1956–1967* (Princeton: Princeton University Press, 1969).

Suggested Reading

I. *The Soviet Union*

Aspaturian, Vernon, V., "Internal Politics and Foreign Policy in the Soviet System," in R. Barry Farrell, ed., *Approaches to Comparative and International Politics* (Evanston: Northwestern University Press, 1966).

Dallin, Alexander, "Soviet Foreign Policy and Domestic Politics: A Framework for Analysis," *Journal of International Affairs,* 23 (1969).

Modelski, George, "Communism and Globalization of Politics," *International Studies Quarterly,* 12 (December 1968), pp. 380–393.

Rubinstein, Alvin Z., *Communist Political Systems* (Englewood Cliffs, N.J.: Prentice-Hall, 1966).

Rubinstein, Alvin Z., *The Foreign Policy of the Soviet Union* (New York: Random House, 1966).

Triska, Jan F., ed., *Communist Party-States* (New York: Bobbs-Merrill, 1969).

Triska, Jan F., and David D. Finley, *Soviet*

Foreign Policy (New York: Macmillan, 1968).

II. *The People's Republic of China*

Fairbank, John K., *China: The People's Middle Kingdom and the U.S.A.* (Cambridge, Mass.: Harvard University Press, 1967).

Hinton, Harold C., *China's Turbulent Quest* (New York: Macmillan, 1970).

Hinton, Harold C., *Communist China in World Politics* (Boston: Houghton Mifflin, 1966).

Ho, Ping-ti, and Tang Tsou, eds., *China in Crisis: China's Heritage and the Communist Political System,* 2 vols. (Chicago: University of Chicago Press, 1968).

Ho, Ping-ti, and Tang Tsou, eds., *China in Crisis: China's Policies in Asia and America's Alternatives* (Chicago: University of Chicago Press, 1970).

Schurmann, H. Franz, *Ideology and Organization in Communist China* (Berkeley: University of California Press, 1966).

Schurmann, H. Franz, and Orville Schell, eds., *Communist China: Revolutionary Reconstruction and International Confrontation, 1949 to the Present* (New York: Random House, 1967).

III. *Tanzania*

Bienen, Henry, *Tanzania: Party Transformation and Economic Development* (Princeton: Princeton University Press, 1967).

Cliffe, Lionel, ed., *One Party Democracy* (Nairobi: East African Publishing House, 1967).

Hopkins, Raymond F., *Political Roles in a New State: Tanzania's First Decade* (New Haven: Yale University Press, 1971).

Nye, Joseph S., Jr., *Pan Africanism and East African Integration* (Cambridge, Mass.: Harvard University Press, 1965).

Wallerstein, Immanuel, *Africa: The Politics of Unity* (New York: Random House, 1967).

Welch, Claude E., *Dream of Unity* (Ithaca: Cornell University Press, 1966).

IV. *The United States*

Appleton, Sheldon, *United States Foreign Policy* (Boston: Little, Brown, 1968).

Armacost, Michael H., *The Foreign Relations of the United States* (Belmont, Calif.: Dickenson, 1969).

Hoffmann, Stanley, *Gulliver's Troubles* (New York: McGraw-Hill, 1968).

Rosenau, James N., ed., *The Domestic Sources of Foreign Policy* (New York: Free Press, 1967).

Sapin, Burton M., *The Making of United States Foreign Policy* (Washington, D.C.: The Brookings Institution, 1966).

Scott, Andrew, and Raymond Dawson, eds., *Readings in the Making of American Foreign Policy* (New York: Macmillan, 1965).

Waltz, Kenneth N., *Foreign Policy and Democratic Politics* (Boston: Little, Brown, 1967).

Chapter 10
INTERSTATE GOVERNMENTAL ACTORS—REGIONAL AND GLOBAL ORGANIZATIONS

International institutions, in their political processes and in their functions, reflect and to some extent magnify or modify the dominant features of the international system—Stanley Hoffmann [23]

For centuries theorists have argued that peace could be ensured if states would join in organizations to foster cooperative ventures and thwart the designs of leaders who encourage war for parochial purposes. In the eighteenth century Immanuel Kant proposed a treaty among nations that would bring "perpetual peace" and compensate for the weaknesses of the international system [30, 52]. Discord arises, he thought, from mistaken beliefs, defective governments, and inadequate education, and he believed that these faults can be remedied by universal education and republican governments. Republican governments, according to Kant, generate no external dissension and give scope to men's basically peaceful instincts. In calling for international organization, he argued that if nations were to band together voluntarily in an international federation, war could be prevented.

But if all states were peaceful such a treaty would not be needed. On the other hand, when some states are aggressive, there is no guarantee that republican governments can prevent war except by resorting to war themselves.

Since the nineteenth century there has been a steady increase in the number of international organizations that have sought to deal with the sources of international conflict. In this period the number of both nations and intergovernmental organizations has grown (see Figure 10.1). Increasingly these organizations have been regional, rather than global, in scope. Table 10.1 shows the number of international organizations founded between 1815 and 1965 and the percentages that have been regional. In 1969 there was a total of 221 interstate governmental organizations,[1] including those that are multifunctional and unifunctional and those that encompass few and many national actors. Some, like the European Common Market and its agencies, have

[1] This figure has been compiled from Eyvind S. Tew, ed., *Yearbook of International Organizations (1968–1969)*, 12th ed. (Brussels: Union of International Associations, January 1969).

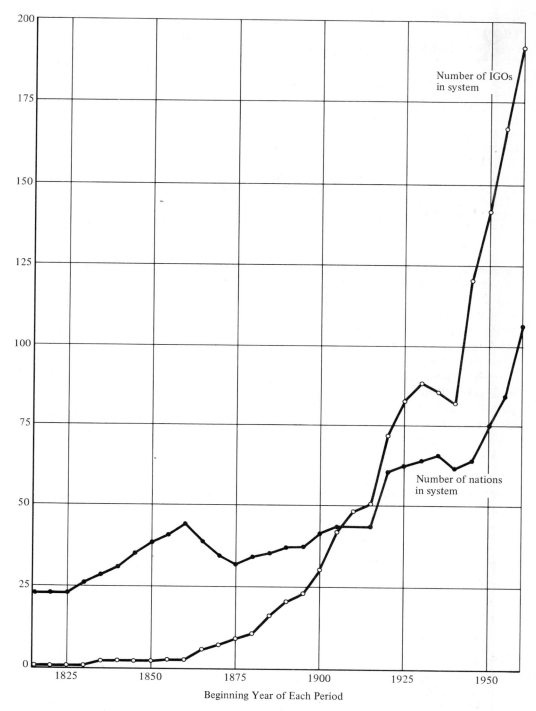

Figure 10.1. Numbers of Nations and Intergovernment Organizations in the International System in Successive Periods

Source: J. David Singer and Michael Wallace, "Intergovernmental Organization in the Global System, 1815–1964: A Quantitative Description," *International Organization,* 24 (Spring 1970), p. 277.

Table 10.1.

Intergovernmental Organizations Founded 1815-1965

	Total	*Regional*	*Regional as Percentage of Total*
1815-1914	49	14	28
1915-1944	73	27	37
1945-1955	76	45	60
1956-1965	56	41	73
Founded	254	127	50
Terminated	(65)	(27)	
Total	189	100	53

Source: From *Peace in Parts,* J. S. Nye, p. 4. Copyright © 1971 by Little, Brown and Company, Inc. Reprinted by permission.

predominantly economic functions; others, like the International Labor Organization and the World Health Organization, perform social services. Still others, like the North Atlantic Treaty Organization and the Southeast Asia Treaty Organization, are military alliances. Some organizations, like the United Nations, on which we shall concentrate in this chapter, seek to perform many such functions for their members. Table 10.2 shows the functional and geographic distribution of intergovernmental organizations, not including the United Nations (and its satellite agencies), the European Economic Community, and the European Free Trade Area. Many of these organizations have been established to deal with the perceived sources of *previous* wars. Rarely have they proved responsive to new dilemmas. Nevertheless, scholars have only recently approached the study of international or-

Table 10.2.

*Intergovernmental Organizations**

Type Function	*Africa*	*Asia*	*Afro-Asia*	*North America*	*South America*	*Americas*
Economic	6	5	1	0	5	5
Social and technical	18	4	2	0	7	11
Security	0	0	0	0	1	2
Political	3	0	1	0	0	0
Combined (general aims include all four)	2	0	0	0	1	0
Total	29	9	4	0	14	18

Total 183

*This list excludes the United Nations, the European Community, and the European Free Trade Area.
**Organizations listed in this category include members from any other three or more categories, except "Other."

ganizations with critical eyes. No longer is it assumed that such organizations can eventually produce peace, and new efforts are being made to explain more realistically what their possible roles in international politics are. The impact of global organizations like the League of Nations and the United Nations on prevention of war is unclear. In fact, it has been suggested that since 1815 there has been "almost no discernible correlation" between the existence of international governmental organizations (IGO) and the outbreak of war in ensuing periods [45]. Even though international organizations do not guarantee peace, they can at least promote understanding and cooperation through transnational contacts. "One of the best demonstrated theories," one observer has declared, "is that contacts made in small intimate groups tend to produce favorable attitudes toward one another among the members" [5]. But improved understanding among the representatives of states does not necessarily lead to improved relations among the states themselves. Furthermore, increased contacts themselves offer new opportunities for disagreement and conflict.

Cooperation in one area may encourage cooperation in others. Functionalist theorists have argued that when states collaborate in solving relatively uncontroversial problems like technical questions of health or economic development, cooperative habits are learned and may lead to cooperative ventures in politically sensitive areas. They assume that cooperative habits acquired in one functional area can be translated into collaboration in other areas and that ultimately functionally specific international organizations will take over the tasks currently performed by sovereign nation-states.[2]

The experiences of organizations like the European common market (EEC) and the United Nations, however, suggest that this kind of "pebble in the water" effect does not occur in politically sensitive sectors. Autonomy is an intrinsic goal

[2] For somewhat differing versions of this theory, see David Mitrany [34] and Ernst B. Haas [20, 22]. See also Chapter 13, pp. 283–286.

Europe	British Commonwealth	Americas, Europe	Mixed**	Communist	Arab	Other†
4	0	0	4	1	0	5
17	5	0	40	0	2	14
0	0	0	0	1	0	2
3	2	0	6	0	0	0
1	0	1	0	0	1	0
25	7	1	50	2	3	21

†Organizations listed in this category include members from any two areas not listed here and those whose composition is not clear.

of all international actors, and states do not willingly cede functions to international organizations when such organizations seem likely to impinge on their own capacity for self-determination. There is a strong positive correlation between the number of international organizations and the number of independent nation-states in the international system. For example, since the breakup of most European colonial empires and the emergence of large numbers of African and Asian states, there has been a marked rise in the number of international organizations, notably those of a regional kind.

REGIONAL ORGANIZATIONS

Regional organizations constitute only one facet of the phenomenon of regionalism. In Chapters 5 and 6 we identified regional groupings on the basis of geographical proximity, culture, trade and mutual economic dependence, communications, and joint membership in intergovernmental organizations. The structural importance of regionalism is not in the creation of formal organizations that may function as semiautonomous actors but in the constraints on overall patterns of international activity that it makes possible and probable. The activities of such organizations may, however, serve as indicators of underlying mutual interests and of economic, social, or political integration among participating states. In contrast to the more generally understood "region," regional organizations have with few exceptions (like the British Commonwealth) cores of members located in single geographical areas, the sizes of which can vary widely. The capitals of the Benelux countries are all within 200 miles of one another, whereas the distance between the two most widely separated capital cities of the members of SEATO is nearly 11,000 miles. Regional organizations for principally economic tasks tend to consist of geographically contiguous members, whereas military organizations often include members from

areas remote from one another. Regional organizations are generally the formal expressions of regional interests, ranging from ad hoc and poorly financed intergovernmental collaborations represented by conferences of nonaligned states to the professionally staffed central institutions of the EEC.

Regional organizations exhibit partial autonomy in international politics. Occasionally, as with the High Commission of the EEC, they may take the initiative in promoting common interests among states. More often they act as intermediaries, responding to various pressures and problems that confront member states. Some organizations like NATO and SEATO exist primarily to defend the interests of major actors outside a region through the formal alliance of these actors with partially subservient political elites in some states within the region.[3] Other regional organizations act to defend the interests of regional actors against the intrusions of larger and more powerful outside interests. The Organization of African Unity (OAU), for example, has sought to promote collective action among the African states in the United Nations and other arenas, in order to maximize pressure on the cold-war blocs. Regional organizations can also provide new arenas for bargaining. The Organization of American States (OAS), for instance, provides organizational legitimacy for United States pursuit of its policy of preventing foreign penetration in Latin America. It also provides the smaller Latin American states with an organizational means by which to bargain collectively with the United States, rather than bilaterally. A similar role may be played by the eastern European regional organizations, notably the Council of Mutual Economic Assistance (CEMA), in which the former Soviet satellites are able to negotiate with their Soviet mentors in a multinational, rather than a bilateral, context.

A regional organization may deal with various specific critical problems that tax

[3] Military alliances are discussed in Chapters 14 and 15.

the governments of a region. The Arab League, for example, was a useful channel for negotiations between the Arab states and the Palestine guerrilla organizations during the apogee of their influence in the Middle East in 1968–1970. Formulating and enforcing mutually beneficial economic transactions is one of the most important functions of regional organizations. The General Agreement on Tariffs and Trade (GATT) regulates trade and establishes reciprocal codes and standards for its members. GATT prevents such trade discrimination as unfair import quotas and tariffs and helps to resolve disputes over alleged infractions. Between 1964 and 1966 it served as the forum in which the United States and the members of the EEC attempted to find a formula for eliminating EEC tariffs on American exports to Europe—the so-called "Kennedy round" of bargaining. As GATT was established primarily to serve the developed states, some less developed states established through the United Nations a rival organization, the U.N. Conference on Trade and Development (UNCTAD), aimed at adjusting trade and tariff agreements to give preference to third-world commodities and products and at creating an improved international climate for the economic development of the member states. It provides another example of the north-south split that affects the politics of international organizations.

For the maintenance of international peace and stability the two most important types of regional organizations are those related to economic collaboration (the EEC, the Central American Common Market [CACM], and the East African Common Market [EAC]) and those, like the OAS and the OAU, aimed principally at resolutions of regional conflict.

Several arguments for the efficacy of regional economic organizations in maintaining regional peace have been put forward. The first is based on the assumption that economic interdependence increases the costs of war and thus creates incentives to seek peaceful solutions. A second

is that the increase in transactions among members creates a sense of common identity among member states, thus generating a "security community" in which interstate violence is "unthinkable." A third argument is that interdependence alters the perceptions of leading statesmen, so that they seek alternative goals and objectives, rather than permitting confrontations with other members; in effect, they seek "integrative solutions" by creating common objectives [34, 35].

Joseph S. Nye, Jr., has reviewed the respective roles of the EEC, CACM, and EAC in disputes over the future of the Saar region in the early 1950s, the El Salvador-Honduras "football war" of 1969, and the differing political orientations of Kenya and Tanzania; he has concluded that "there is evidence for the regionalist claims that micro-regional economic organization can help to prevent conflict by raising its price and can promote resolution of conflict through integrative solutions or the creation of a sense of community [36, p. 125].[4]

It has been argued, on the other hand, that regional organizations like the OAS promote peace primarily by limiting the scope of disputes and preventing them from merging with existing global cleavages. As we shall see, this argument reverses the original assumption of collective security held by the founders of the League of Nations—that peace throughout the world is "indivisible." Table 10.3 summarizes the weighted findings of Nye's study [36, pp. 129–172]. Although it is extremely difficult to evaluate "success," because of problems in defining conflict and intensity, as well as difficulties in resolving the dispute and isolating the compelling causes of settlement, it nevertheless appears that regional organizations have succeeded reasonably well in comparison with the United Nations. Ernst B. Haas has studied fifty-five disputes in which the United Nations has become involved; in thirty-two of them

---

[4] We shall return to these questions, as well as to the question of integration, in Chapters 12 and 13.

Table 10.3.
Performance of Regional Organizations in Conflict Resolution

	Number of Cases	Average Importance of Conflicts (max 9,800)	Average Unweighted Success				Average Weighted Score*
			Helped Isolate	Helped End Fighting	Helped Abate	Helped Settle	
OAS	11	44	91%	60%	73%	30%	858
OAU	5	222	60%	25%	40%	20%	418
Arab League	3	154	33%	0%	33%	67%	263

*Weighting was done by taking account of magnitude of organizational resources involved and degree of organizational activity.

Source: From *Peace in Parts,* J. S. Nye, p. 171. Copyright © 1971 by Little, Brown and Company, Inc. Reprinted by permission.

armed hostilities occurred. He has found that seven disputes were settled by means of United Nations resolutions, eleven partly by this means, and thirteen wholly outside the United Nations. Twenty-four disputes were not settled [21, p. 44]. About the regional organizations that he studied, Nye has concluded:

[M]acro-regional political organizations have helped to isolate conflicts among their members in 74 per cent of the relevant cases, helped contribute to the abatement of conflict in 58 per cent of the cases, helped end fighting in 44 per cent of the relevant cases, and helped to provide a lasting settlement in 32 per cent of the cases. When we weighted the cases by the intensity of hostilities and seriousness of the probable alternatives, however, we found that the successes were restricted primarily to cases of low intensity and that there were important differences between the poor performance of the Arab League and the more successful records of the OAS and OAU. Even with the latter organizations, we noted that success had been limited to interstate conflicts and in the case of the OAS to the area proximate to the United States. [36, p. 175]

In general such organizations were relatively unsuccessful in resolving important conflicts or matters of civil strife and subversive penetration. Furthermore, it is possible that when regional organizations dominated by major powers have intervened—as the OAS intervened in the

1965 war in the Dominican Republic— the results have been reduced effectiveness of the United Nations and preservation of regional hegemony by the major powers.

THE LEAGUE OF NATIONS AND ITS PREDECESSORS

Since at least the time of the Greek city-states, international organizations have been used to coordinate the international system's response to stress. "Functional" international actors, whose task is to foster cooperation in the resolution of common problems, date from the early nineteenth century, when organizations like the Central Rhine Commission (1804), the European Commission for the Control of the Danube (1856), the Universal Postal Union (1874), and the Pan-American Union (1890) were established. Most of these organizations were intended to deal with technical questions, rather than with the great issues of war and peace. Jealous of their sovereign prerogatives the European nation-states that rose after the Peace of Westphalia in 1648 relied on self-help when conflict occurred among them.

Nevertheless, as we have seen, the balance-of-power system in the eighteenth and nineteenth centuries was marked by alliances of short duration among actors seeking limited objectives. Conventional

211

diplomacy, limited war, and short-term alliances served as systemic "coping" mechanisms during this period. After the Congress of Vienna in 1815 (multilateral diplomacy known as the Concert of Europe predominated) [19]. The Concert, an informal organization of the great powers of Europe, functioned through a series of ad hoc multilateral conferences that were summoned whenever disturbances threatened the stability of the system. Four major conferences were held between 1815 and 1822 alone and others in 1856, 1871, 1878, 1884, 1906, and 1912. The conference pattern became so institutionalized that many European statesmen erroneously attributed the outbreak of World War I merely to the failure to hold another conference in 1914. Joint consultation, then, was an institutionalized "coping" mechanism of the balance-of-power system and reflected the expectations among European political leaders in the nineteenth century that the status quo could be maintained. Expectations of multilateral consultation in times of stress were widespread.

Conferences were convened in the Hague in 1899 and 1907. They differed from previous meetings in the scope of the issues discussed and the number of participants. They were also intended to remedy defects in the system itself, rather than only to "cope" with specific situations. It was proposed that meetings be convened regularly and that a more formal conference structure be established. At the first Hague conference, beside codifying certain international norms, the participants adopted a convention specifying peaceful ways to settle disputes, established the Permanent Court of Arbitration, and provided for ad hoc international commissions of inquiry.

The Hague conferences and the functional organizations of the nineteenth century were precedents for the League of Nations after World War I. During the war influential groups in France, Great Britain, and the United States had called for a permanent global organization to maintain the peace. Particularly influen-

tial were proposals put forward in 1915 by a group headed by Lord Bryce in Great Britain [13]. The concept of "a general association of nations," arising from a rejection of "power politics," received added impetus when President Woodrow Wilson and his adviser Colonel E. M. House included it in the Fourteen Points, a set of proposals for ending the war and settling future disputes.

The Covenant of the League was the work of a special committee of the Paris Peace Conference of 1919; it incorporated the diverse ideas of the victorious states.[5] The Covenant was incorporated into the Treaty of Versailles and was ratified by most of the treaty's signatories, with the notable exception of the United States.

The Covenant established three permanent organs: the Assembly, the Council, and the Secretariat. In addition, the Permanent Court of International Justice and the International Labor Organization were to be closely affiliated with the League. The Assembly functioned as a regular diplomatic conference in which each member exercised a single vote; it was empowered to deal "with any matter within the sphere of action of the League or affecting the peace of the world." Although it shared power with the Council in matters of enforcement, the Assembly exercised exclusive control over such matters as the admission of new members and the League budget.

Like the Assembly, the Council was permitted to deal with all matters affecting peace in the world. Although provision was made for permanent, as well as temporary, members of the Council, the former were to have no special prerogatives. Decisions of both Council and Assembly required unanimous votes. This provision, which gave every member a veto, reflected the ideas of sovereignty, equality, and self-determination in extreme form and made it nearly impossible for the League to reach decisions on consequential matters. Neither body was vested with special powers over the other,

[5] See Chapter 3, pp. 48–51.

and both were deemed appropriate forums for discussion of threats to peace.

Wilson's idea of collective security was never fully incorporated in the League structure and thus was never really tested. The theory of collective security was predicated on the assumption that all the members of the organization would combine to halt aggression against anyone anywhere. Members were expected to resist any aggressor, regardless of whether it was considered friend or foe. "One for all and all for one" was the underlying principle, implying that peace is indivisible and that alliances foster conflict. Each member's commitment to peace and to the stability of the international system as a whole was to take precedence over its other commitments, and aggression would be prevented because of the certain knowledge that it would be punished by the combined might of other League members. Underlying Wilson's theory was the liberal belief, similar to that of Kant, that war is caused by the behavior of "bad states" ruled by autocrats and that peace will ensue when the true sentiments of mankind are respected. The few "bad" actors will be deterred by their expectation of punishment.

There could be no toleration of "limited war" because such conflict could spread or embolden potential aggressors. This assumption was elegantly expressed by the representative of Haiti during League debate over the Italian invasion of Ethiopia: "Great or small, strong or weak, near or far, white or coloured, let us never forget that one day we may be somebody's Ethiopia" [51]. It was assumed that the collective interest of all equals the sum of the interests of individual actors and that this interest is the preservation of the status quo. In meeting aggression promptly states would be serving the collective good, even if they suffered economic or military losses as a consequence. Collective security demanded that actors be prepared to surrender their autonomy in questions of war and peace to the League of Nations as a whole. In effect, actors were to surrender control over the fundamental aspects of their foreign policy—an unrealistic assumption in an international system built on the notion of "sovereign equality" [37].

Collective security can function effectively only in an international system in which actors trust one another and can expect assistance if attacked. In the absence of such mutual trust no state is content to depend upon others for its security. Collective security can be sustained only if there is nearly universal agreement on the desirability of the status quo. The presence of revisionist actors like Germany, Italy, Japan, and the Soviet Union after World War I challenged the theory throughout the interwar period.

Other aspects of the international structure of the time did not favor collective security. Ideally the latter required a relatively wide distribution of military capability throughout the system, rather than concentration in the hands of a few actors. Nevertheless, several dissatisfied states possessed the military capability to resist the combined sanctions of others. Widespread dissatisfaction with the status quo was reflected in the absence of major actors from League sessions throughout the organization's existence. Furthermore, the aim of disarmament to render all actors vulnerable to collective sanctions was impractical until all actors could trust one another. Collective security was thus never institutionalized because of incongruence among the attitudes of the member states of the League.

Although Article 11 of the Covenant authorized the League to undertake collective action when aggression occurred or threatened, it proved ineffective because of the unanimous-vote provision, which permitted any member (including a party to the dispute) to thwart the will of the majority. The first step toward collective sanctions was to be "the severance of all trade or financial relations" with the aggressor. Obviously this response would be effective only if the target of the sanctions was vulnerable to it and if the major economic powers were to participate fully. In 1921 the Assembly further weakened the obligation to undertake collective action by deciding that each state retained the right to determine for itself when economic sanctions were appropriate.

The attempt to invoke economic sanctions against Italy when it invaded Ethiopia in 1934–1935 failed precisely because major states carried out their obligations half-heartedly. Great Britain supported sanctions but refused to stop the flow of petroleum to Italy or to close the Suez canal to Benito Mussolini's shipping. The British government was unwilling to undertake any action that would precipitate a sudden break with Italy, which it saw as a potential ally against Adolf Hitler in Europe. Of British Prime Minister Stanley Baldwin, Winston Churchill wrote, "The Prime Minister had declared that sanctions meant war; secondly, he was resolved there must be no war; and thirdly, he decided upon sanctions" [9, p. 175]. The British, in trying thus to square the circle, initiated limited economic sanctions against Italy, which did not greatly affect Mussolini's operations in Ethiopia but which did alienate the Italian government. Although Article 16 authorized the use of collective military force against aggressors if economic sanctions proved inadequate, no major state seriously considered invoking this provision against Italy [44].

In general the League avoided invoking sanctions and instead employed more moderate measures like mediation to settle disputes peacefully. In the early 1920s the League enjoyed a certain measure of success in such conflicts as the Greco-Bulgarian War of 1925. In most instances, however, it vacillated and left problems to be resolved by the major powers on their own. It played only a peripheral role in resolving the 1921 dispute among Albania, Yugoslavia, and Italy over the boundaries of Albania. Several times the League took no action at all, as when the Poles seized Vilna from Lithuania in 1920 and when the French occupied the Ruhr in 1923. Clearly, even in the 1920s

League behavior fell far short of the collective-security ideal.

When disputes involved larger states the League was virtually helpless. In 1923 the murder of an Italian diplomat in Greece led Mussolini to bombard and then to occupy the Greek island of Corfu. The League left the matter in the hands of a "conference of ambassadors" from the great powers, which decided that Greece would have to pay an indemnity to Italy. In 1931, on the occasion of the Japanese invasion of Manchuria, the League responded leisurely. The major European powers were unprepared to antagonize Japan, and the League carried out its obligations to the extent of dispatching a commission to the Far East to study the problem. The initial attempt by the Council to enforce a cease-fire was vetoed by Japan. By the time that the commission reached the scene in the spring of 1932 Japan had already established the puppet state of Manchukuo and had attacked Shanghai. The League merely censured Japanese behavior with no effect other than to provoke Japan to leave the organization. Caught in the Depression and fearful of events in Europe, the major powers refused to commit themselves to decisive action far from the focus of their primary interests [46, 50, 12].

The assumptions on which the theory of collective security was based proved invalid in the international system of the 1920s and 1930s. Of thirty-seven disputes between 1920 and 1937 only fourteen were referred to the League. Only six of the fourteen were settled in any way through the League [21, p. 34]. The increasing agitation of dissatisfied states made it impossible for the League to cope with the continual disruptions in the system. In fact, had the assumptions of the theory of collective security been valid, the League would have been unnecessary in the first place. As it was, the major actors behaved as did George Bernard Shaw's Englishman, who "never forgets that the nation which lets its duty get on the opposite side of its interest is lost."

THE ORGANIZING PRINCIPLES OF THE UNITED NATIONS

The United Nations and its associated agencies represent the most ambitious experiment in international organization in history. In an era of rapid change its survival for more than a quarter-century is remarkable. Although its record in maintaining peace is, on balance, poor, its peripheral utility in enhancing international stability has been considerable.

Unlike many of their predecessors, the founders of the United Nations recognized the intimate relations among the world's ills and acknowledged that the goal of international peace and security requires efforts to prevent instability arising from a variety of sources. The organization's purposes were defined broadly, and, though its primary task was to end large-scale conflicts, it set out to achieve this goal by modifying conditions like colonialism, poverty, inequality, and ignorance, that were considered to cause war.

The creation of the United Nations generated high hopes for the role that it would play in the postwar period, but many of the assumptions on which the United Nations was founded quickly proved unrealistic, and the organization has undergone a series of changes. The U.N. Charter has been altered to suit political reality as it is currently perceived by the dominant actors in the organization. In one sense we can view the United Nations history as a search for a legitimate role in a world still dominated by sovereign nation-states. As the international system has changed, the United Nations has also changed in order to achieve a balance between the expectations of national leaders and its ability to meet those expectations.

The Charter was the product of a series of wartime conferences among the leaders of the allied powers. American planning for the postwar organization, directed by Secretary of State Cordell Hull, started early in the war. Intensive joint planning among the allies began at Dumbarton Oaks in August 1944 and continued at the Yalta conference in February 1945.

It reached its climax at the U.N. Conference on International Organization convened by the allies in San Francisco in April 1945. Although the conference resulted in certain modifications of earlier ideas in deference to the smaller countries, the crux of the Charter had already been settled by bargaining among the United States, the Soviet Union, and Great Britain.

The framers of the Charter consciously sought to update the League Covenant and to avoid its weaknesses. The United States' decision to begin bipartisan planning long before the end of the war reflected determination to prevent repetition of Wilson's humiliation when the Senate rejected the League in 1919. Furthermore, the founding of the United Nations was separated from the general peace settlement; the idea was not to repeat the errors of the peacemakers of 1919, who had established the League and negotiated the Treaty of Versailles at one sweep. The League had thus come in many quarters to be considered an instrument for enforcing an unjust peace, rather than an institution for reconciling peace with change.

Although an effort was made to present the United Nations as a substantially new organization, many of its features were adopted from the League. Its main organs had parallels in the League structure; prewar associated agencies like the International Labor Organization were integrated into the new system. Similarly, the statute of the new International Court of Justice was "based upon the Statute of the Permanent Court of International Justice" of the League period (Article 92 of the Charter).

The United Nations has six main organs: the Security Council, the Secretariat, the International Court of Justice, the General Assembly, the Trusteeship Council, and the Economic and Social Council. In addition, several functionally specialized agencies are associated with the body. The United Nations, like the League, is a voluntary association of sovereign nation-states, and at no time did the organization's founders consider the United Nations a means of undermining sovereignty. The United Nations maintains the fiction of "sovereign equality," however unrealistic in terms of the distribution of resources and capabilities, particularly in the General Assembly, where all states from the Soviet Union to the Fiji Islands possess one vote each. In ridding itself of the requirement for unanimous voting, the General Assembly instituted a form of international majoritarianism, which constituted an advance in recognizing international realities. As one observer has noted:

The cumulative effect of these developments has been to make majority rule in some form normal practice instead of a strictly limited exception to normal practice. The process of development has reached its culmination in the provisions of the Charter of the United Nations which involve the complete abandonment of the requirement of unanimity. [28]

On "important" questions the General Assembly requires a two-thirds majority to decide. The United States consistently demanded that the question of Communist China's admission to the United Nations be considered "important."

In practice the formal majoritarianism of the General Assembly is tempered by the informal influence exercised by the great powers and the use of the veto in the Security Council, which imply that though "all states are equal, some are more equal than others." Furthermore, the United Nations remains financially dependent upon the large states, particularly the United States, and is rarely able to undertake important initiatives without their acquiescence. In 1963, for example, more than half the members paid only 3 percent of the budget; the five permanent members of the Security Council contributed more than two-thirds of the total. The United States alone contributed almost one-third of the budget in that year [47]. As the realities of international politics do not accord with majority rule, usually only recommendations of mar-

ginal significance are determined by simple majority.

As the leader of a permanent voting minority the Soviet Union has steadfastly opposed majoritarianism in the United Nations. With the admission of large numbers of African and Asian states unsympathetic to American attitudes on many issues, the United States has also become notably lukewarm to this feature. Currently the majoritarian principle is most strongly favored by small nonaligned countries.

Article 2 of the Charter leaves little doubt about the framers' views on sovereignty. "The Organization," it declares, "is based on the principle of the sovereign equality of all its Members." Paragraph 7 of the same Article forbids the United Nations to intervene "in matters which are essentially within the domestic jurisdiction of any state. . . ." In practice, this provision has been variously interpreted. Racial injustice in the Union of South Africa and in the Republic of Rhodesia have been the subject of numerous General Assembly and Security Council debates and resolutions. Furthermore, it has become increasingly difficult to maintain a distinction between those issues that are international and those that are domestic. Many of the global system's greatest challenges have originated in internal crises and civil strife, and trends suggest, as British Prime Minister Edward Heath noted at the opening of the 1970 General Assembly session, that such challenges will become increasingly important to international stability in the coming decade.

With the experience of the League still fresh in their memories, the framers of the United Nations hoped to devise an instrument that would conform more closely than had the League Council to the realities of political inequality in the international system. Throughout its existence the League had been plagued by the absence of one or more of the great powers from its sessions. In the Charter they recognized that the great powers would have to play a special role in the maintenance of stability in the postwar world. The Security Council veto was intended to ensure that no major state would find it necessary to leave the organization to protect its interests. According to Article 27 of the Charter, Security Council decisions on all substantive, as opposed to procedural, questions are to be made with the concurrence of the five permanent members: The United States, the Soviet Union, Great Britain, France, and China.[6]

The Security Council was expected to exercise paramount influence both in peaceful settlement of disputes and in applying sanctions against aggressors, and the permanent members were expected to dominate the Council. Their influence was to be strengthened by the fact that whether or not a question is considered substantive or procedural is itself defined as a substantive question subject to the veto. The Charter thus instituted a "double veto" system under which the great powers must be in agreement before the Security Council can act. A permanent member is unable to cast a veto only in matters involving peaceful settlement procedures in which it is a participant in the dispute. Furthermore, Articles 108 and 109 empower permanent members to veto any amendment to the Charter that might undermine their voting powers. Cooperation among the great powers was considered the sine qua non of an effective Security Council.

After the beginning of the cold war it became impossible to achieve consensus among the great powers in the Council. The Soviet Union, in particular, has exercised the veto to protect its interests (see Table 10.4). The number of Soviet vetoes is, however, deceptive, for many of them have been "repeats" on the same issues, brought on by members who have insisted on reintroducing issues, often for the purpose of achieving a propaganda advantage over the Soviet Union. Many vetoes have been cast against admitting new members to the United Nations and have been intended either to prevent the bal-

ance in the General Assembly from becoming more unfavorable to the Soviet Union or to force the United States to support Soviet candidates for admission. Other Soviet vetoes have been cast to protect Soviet or its allies' interests. For example, an American attempt to censure the Soviet invasion of Hungary in 1956 and a United Nations proposal to investigate the communist coup in Czechoslovakia in 1948 were vetoed. Furthermore, many Soviet vetoes have been overruled by actions of other United Nations organs or by changed circumstances.

The ratio of Soviet to American vetoes is also deceptive. Many Soviet vetoes, far from reflecting mere Soviet intransigence, have reflected the unfavorable voting distribution for the Soviet Union in the United Nations as a whole. Until the rapid growth in membership after 1955 the Soviet Union could expect to be consistently outvoted on any issue in any organ of the United Nations.[7] The United States did not have recourse to the veto until 1970 because it could command a voting majority. Matters in which the United States could be expected to cast vetoes were anticipated by its allies, and anti-Soviet voting majorities were mobilized. In 1950, for example, the American delegate threatened to veto any candidate nominated to replace Trygve Lie as secretary-general. Consequently Lie was reelected to the position [33, pp. 379–381]. In this way, the United States has exercised "anticipated influence" in the United Nations, and its veto has been an implicit, rather than an explicit, instrument. Secretary of State Hull, far from opposing the veto arrangement, declared that the United States would not remain in the Security Council "a day without retaining its veto power" [26].

On issues that have threatened direct Soviet-American confrontation the veto has merely reflected the realities of an international system in which the Soviet Union can effectively undermine United

---

[6] In 1965 the Charter was amended to increase the size of the Council from eleven to fifteen and the required majority from seven to nine.

[7] The Soviet Union has consistently been the least successful member of the Security Council in having its draft resolutions adopted [49].

Table 10.4.

United Nations Vetoes by Country and Issue, 1946-1967

Soviet Union		France		Great Britain		China	
membership questions	51	Spanish question	1	Suez question	2	membership	
Congo question	6	Indonesian question	1	Southern Rho-		question	1
Palestine question	5	Suez question	2	desia question	1		
India-Pakistan question	2						
Lebanese complaints	2						
appointment of secre-							
tary-general	2						
request for investiga-							
tion of bacterial							
warfare	2						
Korean question	2						
U.N. commission							
reports	4						
Spanish question	4						
Czechoslovak question	2						
Indonesian question	2						
RB-47 aircraft							
overflight	2						
Malaysia-Indonesia							
question	1						
Goa question	1						
Kuwait question	1						
Hungary question	1						
overflights by							
American aircraft	1						
Guatemala question	1						
Thailand question	1						
complaint of bombing							
of China	1						
Berlin question	1						
Corfu channel question	1						
Syria-Lebanon question	1						

Source: Security Council Official Records, 1946-1967 (New York: United Nations, 1946-1968).

Nations action, regardless of the voting. Had the United Nations attempted often to act despite Soviet or American displeasure, it would have run the risk of being wrecked on the shoals of great-power conflict. The veto, supported in principle by all the permanent members of the Security Council, has served to prevent the United Nations from going beyond its expected role. Without such a device it is likely that the Soviet Union would have been forced to leave the United Nations, particularly in 1945–1955, when the organization came near to functioning as an American pawn in the cold war. The United Nations would thus have embarked on the unfortunate path that the League had taken earlier.

The risks to an international organization when it exceeds its role were illustrated during the Congo crisis of 1960–1964. After gaining independence from Belgium, the Congo (now Zaire) faced a period of civil strife and political turmoil. Supported by both the Soviet Union and the United States, the United Nations initially intervened to prevent the conflict from spreading and to bring about withdrawal of Belgian troops. In the course of the conflict, however, the organization sided with the government of President Joseph Kasavubu against Soviet-supported Premier Patrice Lumumba. Furthermore, the United Nations failed to act quickly to end the secession of the mineral-rich province of Katanga led by Moise Tshombe and supported by the Belgians.

Both the Soviet Union and France subsequently refused to pay the special assessments levied by the General Assembly for the Congo operations, thus creating a constitutional crisis for the organization and threatening it with bankruptcy. In addition, the Soviet Union sponsored an attempt at revision of the Charter that would have substituted a three-man "troika," consisting of representatives from the communist bloc, the Western countries, and the neuralist countries, for the single secretary-general.

The veto thus reflects political realities and functions to protect, rather than impede, the United Nations. An international organization that exceeds the expectations of its strongest members runs grave risks. It may be perceived as illegitimate by its former supporters, and conflict may ensue. Under such conditions the organization itself will probably be the loser. In a nuclear era it is not easy to coerce a superpower, regardless of the provisions of the Charter. As one American has noted, the veto is "the safety-valve that prevents the United Nations from undertaking commitments in the political field which it presently lacks the power to fulfill" [32].[8]

The United Nations was intended as a "universal" organization of all "peace loving" states. The original membership included fifty-one states, among them the Soviet provinces of Belorussia and the Ukraine, which were admitted as part of a bargain among the great powers. The original members had been allied against the Axis during World War II, and enemy states were initially not permitted to join. In accordance with Article 4 of the Charter, states were to be admitted "by a decision of the General Assembly upon the recommendation of the Security Council."

[8] See also Chapter 12, pp. 262–263.

The rapid growth in United Nations membership as a consequence of decolonization has had a major impact on procedures and has contributed to the evolution of the organization.[9] Membership and organizational objectives have a reciprocal relationship. Members determine the issues with which the United Nations will deal, and the nature of these issues influences the pattern of membership in the organization. Admission of new members, then, involves political judgments. Even today several major international actors, including the divided countries of Vietnam, Korea, and Germany, and neutral Switzerland, remain outside the organization.[10]

Through much of the United Nations history, its most notable nonmember was the Chinese regime of Mao Tse-tung. The government of the Republic of China was not only a founding member of the organization but was also awarded the status of "great power" and a permanent seat on the Security Council. By the end of 1949, however, Chiang Kai-shek's nationalist regime had been driven by the communists from the mainland to the island refuge of Taiwan (Formosa). The question of which regime's credentials should be accepted by the United Nations as the legitimate representative of the Chinese people has remained a source of controversy for many years. Largely at American insistence Mao's regime was kept out of the United Nations. The United States claimed until 1971 that the Peking government did not "deserve" membership because it was not a "peace loving" state as required in Article 4. The United States insisted on treating the

[9] The decolonization process has been so complete that the Trusteeship Council has almost no remaining responsibilities.
[10] Switzerland and West Germany do, however, participate in many agencies of the United Nations. The relationship between membership and organizational focus is illustrated by the evolution of the European Common Market. Because western European prosperity has been the objective of the EEC, that organization has restricted its membership to the countries of continental Europe. It is feared that if the organization were to expand, its objectives would change, to the detriment of the founding members.

Chinese-membership question as a moral one, rather than as a practical question of which regime more fully represented the majority of the Chinese people. A "two China" solution was proposed by Richard M. Nixon's administration: Both regimes would be admitted. But this proposal did not resolve the difficulty of which regime would receive the permanent seat in the Council, and both Chinese governments indicated that this solution was unacceptable. The American proposal was thus turned down by the United Nations.

The entry of the Peking regime into the United Nations increases the scope and the cleavages of the organization. American policy for more than two decades had helped to prevent the United Nations from achieving the universality to which it aspires. This former policy was summed up by the late Secretary of State John Foster Dulles: "It was assumed that you would be good before you get in and not that being in would make you good" [11, p. 89]. Indeed, for much of this century, particularly during the era of the "Wilson doctrine," the United States has insisted on considering "subjective" rather than merely "objective" criteria before according recognition to new regimes.

The politicization of the membership question was inevitable in the early years of the cold war, when the organization ran the risk of becoming an American-led alliance against the Soviet Union. The most revealing example of American control during that period was the response to the North Korean invasion of South Korea in June 1950. Only a series of fortuitous circumstances permitted United Nations action at the time. A United Nations observation team was already stationed in South Korea and could provide accurate information about North Korean behavior. In addition, the United States had troops in Japan and Okinawa that could intervene swiftly. Finally, the Soviet delegate was absent from the Security Council at the time in protest against the continued refusal of the United Nations to seat the Chinese communist delegation. In the absence of the Soviet dele-

gate the Security Council recommended military intervention in Korea; it was undertaken by the United States, with some assistance from its closest allies. Military decisions were made and later negotiations with the North Koreans and Chinese communists were led by the United States, which merely reported its decisions to the United Nations.[11]

Shortly after the intervention of the Chinese communists in the Korean War, a new means of evading the veto provision was instituted. The General Assembly, led by the United States, passed the Uniting for Peace Resolution (General Assembly Resolution 377A[V]) over the objections of the Soviet bloc. Its main feature is establishment of a procedure by which the General Assembly can be summoned into session within twenty-four hours by a vote of *any* seven members of the Council or by a majority of the members of the Assembly itself. The General Assembly is empowered to make "recommendations to Members for collective measures, including in the case of a breach of the peace or act of aggression the use of armed forces when necessary" when the Security Council is unable to act. Although the resolution violates in spirit the Charter's separation of powers, it is technically legal because the Assembly can only request its members to act and cannot command them to do so.

In practice the Uniting for Peace Resolution has been invoked only five times since the Korean War, and on none of these occasions has the General Assembly tried to organize collective sanctions.[12] The procedure enabled the General Assembly, which was controlled by the

[11] Of the U.N. forces actually committed at the time of peak strength, 50.32 percent of the ground forces, 85.89 percent of the naval forces, and 93.38 percent of the air force was furnished by the United States. In view of the Republic of Korea contributions of 40.10 percent, 7.45 percent and 5.65 percent, respectively, the military contributions of the remaining members of the United Nations were obviously small. [39]

[12] Ironically it was used during the Suez canal crisis of 1956 to evade the veto of the United States' two closest allies at that time, Great Britain and France.

United States, to usurp certain prerogatives of the Security Council. The United
Nations served American interests by
legitimating American behavior in Korea;
this service was, however, a dubious
precedent for an organization that must
be considered authentically impartial [10].
By the late 1950s the United States was
no longer so strongly in favor of the
change that it had sponsored. The enlarged membership of the General Assembly meant that the United States was
no longer assured of a voting majority on
all issues and that the General Assembly
might become a weapon to be used against
American interests.[13]

CHANGE AND DEVELOPMENT
IN THE UNITED NATIONS

Until 1955 United Nations membership
increased very slowly. From the beginning the Soviet Union insisted that an ap-
plicant's wartime conduct should be an
important criterion for determining membership. The Soviet Union vetoed the
applications of Ireland and Portugal, as
well as that of Jordan, in 1946, ostensibly
because these states had not supported
the allied cause during World War II.
For its part the United States blocked the
admission of Albania and Mongolia, two
Soviet candidates. To break this deadlock
the United States unsuccessfully proposed
a "package deal" by which all five candidates would be admitted together. In the
next few years, however, the principal
protagonists reversed positions; the Soviet
Union came to sponsor a "package deal,"
and the United States demanded that each
membership application be judged on its
merits. The deadlock was finally broken
during a relaxation of the cold war in
1955. Despite an opinion by the International Court of Justice that "package
deals" are illegal, sixteen new members
were admitted in 1955 as part of such an
agreement; they included such controversial candidates as Albania, Bulgaria,

Hungary, Italy, Portugal, Rumania, and
Spain. Since 1960 membership in the
United Nations has grown rapidly owing
to liquidation of the colonial empires.
Current United Nations membership is
131 (see Table 10.5).

The increasing burdens placed on
United Nations facilities by this increase
in membership and the enlarged scope of
organizational concerns are reflected in
the annual budget, estimated at almost
$184 million for 1971. By contrast, the
United Nations budget for 1948 was a
mere $39 million. The budgetary problem
is exacerbated by the fact that many of
the newly admitted "ministates" like the
Fiji Islands, Mauritius, South Yemen, the
Maldive Islands, and Botswana are each
able to contribute only 0.04 percent, the
legal minimum, of United Nations costs.

Also as a consequence of increasing
membership, New York City, the site of
the organization's permanent headquarters, has become the scene of intensive
and virtually continuous diplomatic activity. The range and number of issues that
are discussed have made it necessary for
governments to staff large and diversified
missions and to coordinate diplomacy at
the United Nations with other foreign-
policy activities. The U.S. Department of
State has established a functional sub-
division known as the Bureau of International Organization, and since 1953 the
chief American representative to the
United Nations has been accorded Cabinet status.

The maintenance of adequate permanent staffs is an onerous burden for
many of the smaller countries, which can
spare neither the skilled diplomatic personnel nor the necessary financial resources to support them. On the other
hand, many states that do not have mutual diplomatic relations can interact at
the United Nations. Many United Nations ambassadors are also accredited to
the United States or Canada or both. One
participant has described the activities
of such a staff:

Preparations for forthcoming meetings,
preliminary negotiations, and the task of

---

[13] For more information on collective sanctions and the Korean example, see Leland M.
Goodrich [17] and Arnold Wolfers [53].

Table 10.5.
Geographical Distribution of United Nations Membership*

Year	Western Europe	Eastern Europe	Asia	Africa	Latin America	Other	Total Membership
1945	8	6	9	4	20	4	51
1946	10	6	11	4	20	4	55
1947	10	6	13	4	20	4	57
1948	10	6	14	4	20	4	58
1949	10	6	15	4	20	4	59
1950	10	6	16	4	20	4	60
1955	16	10	21	5	20	4	76
1956	16	10	22	8	20	4	80
1957	16	10	23	9	20	4	82
1958	16	10	22	10	20	4	82
1960	17	10	22	26	20	4	99
1961	17	10	24	29	20	4	104
1962	17	10	24	33	22	4	110
1963	17	10	25	35	22	4	113
1964	18	10	25	36	22	4	115
1965	18	10	26	37	22	4	117
1966	18	10	27	39	24	4	122
1967	18	10	27	40	24	4	123
1968	18	10	28	42	24	4	126
1970	18	10	29	42	24	4	127
1972	18	10	34	42	24	4	132

*In some years total membership and admission figures do not correspond because of the unification of Syria and Egypt from 1958 to 1961, the union of Tanganyika and Zanzibar in 1964, and the withdrawal of Indonesia from the United Nations from 1965 to 1966.

becoming acquainted with representatives of 99 countries take time. A considerable amount of work is done on items and issues which may never formally come before any U.N. body. Continuous working relations must be maintained with the Secretary-General and key members of his staff. . . . [38]

Consequently states like the Soviet Union and the United States, which can maintain large staffs and research facilities, serve as sources of information and advice for less well informed delegates. The missions of the great powers contribute to their influence in the United Nations and create a tendency for many small states to rely on the larger ones.

Diplomats can maintain wider ranges of personal contacts at the United Nations than elsewhere; they also find it easier to exchange information informally and to make contact with the representa-

tives of unfriendly states. Furthermore, experience in the General Assembly tends to broaden the delegates' awareness of issues and actors [1]. It appears that common membership in international organizations like the United Nations provides a more efficient means of interstate contact for most actors than do traditional diplomatic relations [2]. This observation in turn suggests that the United Nations has proved a profitable enterprise, at least as an international forum, and has facilitated diplomatic exchange. The United Nations system has become a vast information net. Information originates with member states and the Secretariat itself, and feedback is virtually continuous. Exchanges occur in the public glare of the Assembly chamber and in the more private recesses of committee rooms, corridors, bars, and lounges. The provision of novel channels of communication may be the most valuable United Nations contribution to the contemporary international system.

The sheer magnitude of the United Nations enterprise has brought in its train an enlarged corps of international civil servants who constitute the Secretariat. Its tasks range from staff work for conferences and large-scale research in many fields to publishing and mediation. In the field United Nations operatives function as technicians, policemen, doctors, and administrators. "The United Nations secretariat is a collective jack-of-all-trades, a global mother whose work is never done" [11, p. 181]. Such a development, in one sense the mark of true international organization, is very recent, dating only from the establishment of the League of Nations and the International Labor Organization. International organizations had previously employed citizens of the host countries in which they found themselves.

The decision of Sir Eric Drummond, the first secretary-general of the League, to create "a secretariat international alike in its structure, its spirit, and its personnel" was a landmark in the development of international organization. The U.N. Charter provides for an international civil service that should not receive its instructions from outside the organization. According to Article 101, the criteria for employment are to be "the highest standards of efficiency, competence, and integrity." In addition, however, the Charter makes clear that geographical distribution will also be considered a criterion for recruitment.

The Secretariat, like any bureaucracy, must meet the demands of specialization, functional distribution, and hierarchical organization. The task is complicated by the problem of coordinating a multinational and multilingual group with different standards of competence and different cultural backgrounds. Furthermore, the demands of efficiency and geographical distribution often conflict. Because of the scarcity of trained administrative and technical personnel a large percentage of the United Nations employees initially were Americans or western Europeans. To satisfy the demands of the communist and underdeveloped states, the United Nations has been forced to take cognizance of geographical origins, as well as of other qualifications, in recruiting staff. Even though many of the smaller countries can ill afford losing trained personnel, even temporarily, many of them have demanded a "fair share" of appointments as tokens of national prestige. A related problem is to retain international civil servants for an extended period of time during which they can acquire the necessary experience and skills, rather than being rotated in and out of the organization. For political reasons the Soviet Union has refused to permit its citizens to accept permanent employment at the United Nations, and many of the African and Asian states frown on long-term appointments because of their pressing domestic need for skilled personnel. In fact, because it employs Asians and Africans for two or three years, the United Nations is an important training ground for civil servants and diplomats.

An even more difficult problem for the Secretariat is that of "internationalizing" the loyalties of its employees. An excellent formulation of an "international outlook" has been stated by C. W. Jenks, the current director general of the International Labor Organization:

A lack of attachment to any one country does not constitute an international outlook. A superior indifference to the emotions and prejudices of those whose world is bounded by the frontiers of a single state does not constitute an international outlook. A blurred indistinctness of attitude toward all questions . . . does not constitute an international outlook. The international outlook required of the international civil servant is an awareness made instinctive by habit of the needs, emotions, and prejudices of the peoples of differently-circumstanced countries . . . accompanied by a capacity for weighing those frequently imponderable elements in a judicial manner before reaching any decision. . . . [29]

To some extent, particularly among United Nations technical experts, the acquisition of such an international outlook has indeed taken place [16].

The problem of ensuring impartiality among international officials is not easy to solve. Except for those who remain with the United Nations permanently, most civil servants must expect to return to their own countries. Possible escape from national loyalties is therefore hindered by anticipated career patterns. Although the problem is perhaps most acute for officials on loan from communist countries, others must also wear "two hats" simultaneously. The most egregious violation of the Charter's injunction against members' seeking to influence nationals in the Secretariat service occurred in 1952 and 1953, when the United States sought control over the Secretariat's hiring of Americans. In an atmosphere largely generated by Senator Joseph McCarthy of Wisconsin, Congress successfully intimidated Secretary-General Lie, forcing him to discharge American employees who allegedly had past affiliations with the American Communist Party and to employ only Americans who had been cleared through American security procedures [48].[14]

The problem of remaining impartial has made it difficult for international civil servants, including the secretary-general, to take novel or dramatic initiatives. In his attack on Secretary-General Dag Hammarskjöld's direction of United Nations operations in the Congo, Soviet Premier Nikita S. Khrushchev declared that "there are no neutral men." Hammarskjöld responded: "I am not neutral as regards the Charter. . . . I am not neutral as regards facts. . . . But what I do claim is that even a man who is in that sense not neutral can very well undertake and carry through neutral actions, because that is an act of integrity" [6].

Since the founding of the League of

Nations, several different conceptions of the role that the secretary-general ought to play in the resolution of international conflict have predominated. Sir Eric Drummond of the League of Nations considered his role essentially apolitical and was determined to function mainly as an administrator of the decisions of member states. "Drummond was . . . strong in the belief that a Civil Service 'had to be politically celibate.' He showed no wish to enlarge either the authority or the public image of his office" [7]. By contrast, Trygve Lie, the first United Nations secretary-general, felt obligated to "strengthen . . . the office of the Secretary-General" [33, p. 411]. As a consequence of his behavior during the Korean War Lie found himself distrusted by the Soviet Union and realized the weakness of his post. Sensing himself less a "general" and more a mere "secretary," he asked "where were his divisions?" [33, p. 42]. Until his death in 1961 Lie's successor, Hammarskjöld, had an even more vigorous interpretation of the role. "Is it possible," he asked, "for the Secretary-General to resolve controversial questions . . . without obtaining the formal decision of the organs?" [14, p. 346]. In his opinion, it was indeed. Hammarskjöld's behavior during the Congo crisis so infuriated the Soviet Union that it not only challenged him but also attacked the office itself. Although the Soviet proposal for a "troika" was defeated, Hammarskjöld's experience influenced the behavior of his successor, U Thant, who carefully avoided taking dramatic initiatives on sensitive issues. However, his successor, Kurt Waldheim, has indicated that he is prepared to behave more vigorously than did U Thant.

Even the many tasks performed daily by the Secretariat may have important political ramifications. The secretary's preparation of the annual budget, for example, is fraught with political implications. Research by the Secretariat can influence the behavior of states. The policies and guidelines of such agencies as the World Bank and the International Law Commission affect the interests of states

---

[14] The League of Nations experienced even greater difficulties, owing to the efforts of Germany and Italy to subvert the independence of their citizens in service with the Secretariat [40].

in fields like economic development and human rights, and these issues may have important political consequences. In 1948, for example, the General Assembly, on the advice of the International Law Commission, passed the Genocide Convention, which prohibits mass murder for reasons of race, religion, or national origin. Nevertheless, as late as 1973 the United States had refused to ratify the convention because various domestic groups interpreted it as an infringement of the prerogatives of the American government. Similarly, we might imagine that issues like disease prevention would create little political conflict. Nevertheless, it took nine international conferences on plague and cholera epidemics between 1850 and 1903 before an agreement was reached to enforce quarantines on affected areas, because of British reluctance to support any measure that might disrupt its commerce with India [20, pp. 14–19].

The secretary-general is by no means barred from exercising political initiative. He is empowered by Article 99 of the Charter to "bring to the attention of the Security Council any matter which in his opinion may threaten the maintenance of international peace and security." But his ability to take initiatives is circumscribed by the expectations of member states about his role. In the Congo operation Soviet expectations clearly did not coincide with the secretary-general's own conception of his role. To be effective, the secretary must be considered impartial and independent and must have access to necessary resources and information [54].

There are several possible means by which the secretary-general can exert influence in resolving international conflict. He can attempt to call to the attention of adversaries important interests that they share. U Thant attempted to do so during the Cuban missile crisis of 1962 by emphasizing the deadly risks that the Soviet Union and the United States were running. He can also try to enunciate impartially the issues in a dispute, pointing out the areas of agreement, as well as of dis-

agreement. As one observer has suggested, "The formulation of an issue may stake out the starting points and limits for concessions, fix the bench marks for evaluating gains and losses, and circumscribe areas where pressures, threats, and inducement can be used" [27]. This procedure can facilitate bargaining by clarifying the problems and articulating internationally held norms.

The secretary-general or his representative may be permitted to participate actively in bargaining, suggesting possible settlements of which the adversaries are not aware or which they themselves do not dare to suggest lest they weaken their respective bargaining positions. Through "quiet diplomacy" he can facilitate bargaining by holding private discussions with the interested parties. In this way Hammarskjöld was able to arrange for the release of American airmen held captive by the Chinese communists in 1955. In 1958 Hammarskjöld's representative, Johan Beck-Friis of Sweden, was able to mediate a border dispute between Thailand and Cambodia, and Ellsworth Bunker was successful in mediating the Dutch-Indonesian conflict over West Irian (West New Guinea) in 1962. Since 1967 Gunnar Jarring has, with limited success, attempted to mediate the Arab-Israeli dispute. A third party may have the opportunity to collect and disseminate useful information to adversaries and to provide additional direct and indirect channels of communication necessary in periods of conflict.

The United Nations may even be called upon to interpose itself between adversaries. The U.N. Emergency Force (UNEF), for example, established United Nations presence between Egyptian and Israeli forces from 1956 to 1967. Currently a United Nations force is providing similar assistance in Cyprus, preventing clashes between warring Greek and Turkish factions. Once agreements or cease-fires have been reached the United Nations may be able to furnish the means for monitoring them, as it has done in the Middle East, Kashmir, and North Borneo.

Owing to enlarged membership and to changes that have occurred in the international system since 1945, the voting pattern in the United Nations and the salience of certain issues have also changed.[15] In contrast to the situation in the early 1950s, the United States is no longer assured of controlling votes, and the cold war is no longer the only major political issue. Since about 1960 the General Assembly has become a major forum for the discussion of colonialism, racism, and economic development, and a channel through which new demands have been imposed on the international system itself. The Soviet Union has been able to take advantage of the anticolonialism of many African and Asian members. Unlike the United States, which must take into account the interests of allies like Portugal and Great Britain, which are perceived by the Africans and Asians as colonial powers, the Soviet Union has been free to support the anticolonial majority in the Assembly. Consequently it has reaped a rich propaganda harvest through its consistent anticolonial voting record and its alignment with Afro-Asian states on these issues [24, 42].

Within the United Nations framework there are several groups of states that caucus among themselves to discuss issues, exchange ideas, and formulate tactics. Although such a group does not imply voting solidarity, it "has some degree of formal organization, and is concerned with substantive issues and related procedural matters before the sessions of the General Assembly" [25]. During the 1960s there were nine identifiable caucuses in the United Nations: the Soviet bloc, the Arab League, the Afro-Asian countries, the African states, the British Commonwealth, the western European countries (including Canada, Australia, and New Zealand), the Benelux countries, the Scandinavian countries, and the Latin American states. The United States was not a member of any caucus. There

were overlaps among the groups, and several states participated in more than one caucus. Nigeria, for example, attended the meetings of the Afro-Asian group, the African group, and the Commonwealth. Of these groups the Soviet bloc most consistently voted together, and the Commonwealth countries exhibited the least voting solidarity. The Commonwealth and Afro-Asian groups have such diverse memberships with so many different interests that any attempt to enforce bloc voting upon them would inevitably lead to disintegration [43].[16]

Voting solidarity varies considerably with the issues. Western Europeans and the United States vote together more consistently on issues related to the cold war than they do on issues like colonialism and economic development. The Afro-Asian group votes together on "north-south" issues more often than on "east-west" issues [4]. Although there has been a certain consistency in the types of issues raised over time, there has also been a discernible shift in questions relating to colonial self-determination, economic development, and racial problems in South Africa, Rhodesia, and Angola [43, p. 336; 3].

To some extent influence in the United Nations reflects the distribution of resources and capabilities in the international system. This reflection is modified by the voting system of the General Assembly and by the fact that Assembly actions take the form of unenforceable resolutions. As in other areas of international politics, influence is often achieved by means of threats and promises, but legitimate influence, arising from diplomatic skill and governmental reputation, functions in the United Nations as well. Countries like Ireland, Yugoslavia, Can-

---

[15] For discussion of changing goal conflicts in the international system, see Chapter 6. pp. 112–118.

[16] By means of factor analysis of votes during the 1963 session of the General Assembly, Bruce M. Russett has identified eight groups: the Western community, Afro-Asians, Brazzaville Africans (largely consisting of former French colonies), communist nations, conservative Arab states, Spain and Portugal, the Latin American states, and Scandinavia. See also Robert O. Keohane [31].

ada, and Sweden exercise disproportionate influence there, largely because they are moderate on most issues and not deeply involved in them. On the other hand, the Union of South Africa, because of its policy of apartheid, is held in low esteem by most members of the United Nations.

THE EVOLUTION OF UNITED NATIONS PEACEKEEPING FUNCTIONS

In seeking to encourage peaceful change, the U.N. Charter actually provided two separate and distinct procedures for preventing international violence. These procedures, defined in Chapters VI and VII of the Charter, are related to peaceful settlement and peace enforcement.

The provisions for peaceful settlement assume that many wars result from misunderstandings or miscalculations. As modern warfare had become so destructive of life, property, and values, the framers of the Charter saw an acute need for a pacific equivalent to war. If conflict could be postponed and the parties to a dispute forced to discuss their differences at the conference table, it was assumed that many wars brought on by national pride, the ignorance of leaders, and heated emotions could be avoided.

Similar assumptions were at the core of the nineteenth- and twentieth-century liberal view of war; they were specifically resurrected in interpretations of the outbreak of World War I. These assumptions were particularly popular among American leaders, who viewed the international system as analogous to their own national system and looked for solutions to the problem of international conflict in the domestic experience of the United States. Provisions for delaying the outbreak of war through mediation, arbitration, and adjudication had been incorporated in the Hague Convention of 1899 for the Peaceful Settlement of International Disputes and in a series of bilateral treaties negotiated in 1913 by Secretary of State Wil-

liam Jennings Bryan, in which the signatories pledged to delay the outbreak of war for a year in order to permit arbitration. The League Covenant also provided for postponement of hostilities to permit peaceful resolution of disputes.

The methods of peaceful settlement, however, are useful only when the adversaries wish to avoid hostilities. They are not effective when the disputants are seeking fundamental alterations in the status quo and view war as less serious than failure to bring about the proposed changes. Dissatisfied actors often find violence the only way to bring their grievances to the attention of the international community. Bureaucrats tend to overlook or to obscure revisionist claims until the threshold of violence is reached.

Furthermore, it is difficult to coerce adversaries in a serious dispute into accepting outside recommendations that do not favor their interests. In certain instances, like the Indian-Pakistani quarrel over Kashmir and Jammu and the Arab-Israeli dispute, peaceful settlement procedures have temporarily reduced the level of violence, but the basic political differences between the adversaries remain unresolved, and their respective positions may even harden with time. Actors have tended to use peaceful settlement procedures to denounce adversaries, in order to reap propaganda advantages. The organs of the United Nations have frequently served as forums in which actors have indulged in the intemperate abuse of others, in order to strengthen themselves domestically or to impress allies. Such behavior merely exacerbates political differences.

Unlike enforcement of peace, peaceful settlement does not involve assignment of guilt. As it is assumed that the causes of war lie in the weaknesses of the system itself, assignment of guilt, it is argued, is unjust and can serve only to embitter the accused, as in Germany after 1919. Such judgments are sometimes accurate, but they can also lead to blatant hypocrisy.

Under Article 33 of the Charter parties to a dispute are encouraged to "seek a solution by negotiation, enquiry, mediation, conciliation, arbitration, judicial settlement, resort to regional agencies or arrangements." Article 35 permits any member to bring a dispute to the attention of the Security Council or General Assembly. The wording of the Charter suggests that the Security Council was to enjoy a preeminent role in the resolution of such disputes: It is specifically empowered by Article 34 to "investigate any dispute, or any situation which might lead to international friction or give rise to a dispute." Under this provision "disputes," as opposed to "situations," are not subject to the veto, although a decision about whether the issue constitutes one or the other can be vetoed. If actors fail to carry out the provisions of Article 33, they are instructed to refer the issue to the Security Council.

The peaceful-settlement procedure has been used with some success in various disputes among minor powers, including the achievement of Indonesian and Libyan independence in 1949 and 1951 respectively, the settlement of the Franco-Tunisian conflict of 1952–1961, and the resolution of the Cambodian-Thai border dispute of 1958–1962. It has been only marginally successful, however, when hostility has been deep-seated and a common inclination to avoid war has been absent.

The peace-enforcement procedure is outlined in Article 2, paragraph 4 of the Charter, which enjoins members to "refrain in their international relations from the threat or use of force against the territorial integrity or political independence of any state." The scope of the injunction, however, is limited to interstate relations, as opposed to colonial repression or internal subversion. Furthermore, the relation of this commitment to the "inherent" right of self-defense claimed by all states and recognized in Article 51 is ambiguous. This "right" has been used to justify military arrangements like the North Atlantic Treaty Organization and the Southeast Asia Treaty Organization. Furthermore, Article 52 specifically provides that noth-

ing in the Charter "precludes the existence of regional arrangements or agencies for dealing with such matters relating to the maintenance of international peace and security as are appropriate for regional action." Finally, Article 53 empowers regional organizations to undertake enforcement against "any enemy state" without the authorization of the Security Council. The phrase "enemy state" refers to Germany, Japan, and others that supported the Axis in World War II. The formation of the Soviet-led Warsaw Pact in 1955 was justified under this provision.

Chapter VII of the Charter provides the core of the peace-enforcement structure. Initially it was expected that the procedure would be directed mainly against small actors and would be carried out by the permanent members of the Security Council. For it to succeed as planned, the continued unity and dominance of the five great powers was required, and it therefore constituted essentially a unilateral guarantee of the security of small powers by the permanent Council members. Not only did the peace-enforcement structure not provide for handling disputes among the permanent members, but also the Charter guaranteed their immunity from its provisions through the veto. As one observer suggested, "It certainly depended for its effectiveness on recognition by the permanent members that they had a common interest in keeping the peace and that they should compromise their differences in order that they might cooperate in furthering this common interest" [18].

As initially conceived, the Security Council was to have primary responsibility for peace enforcement. Articles 39–42 empower the Council to issue orders to member states and to take whatever action, including resort to force, that it deems necessary to maintain or restore peace. Articles 43 and 45 were intended to provide the Council with "teeth"; they call upon members to negotiate agreements that will provide military contingents for the Council. Articles 46–48 set out arrangements for a military-staff committee that will coordinate and implement the decisions of the Security Council. But the cold war has rendered these provisions inoperative. No agreements were concluded under Article 43, and the military-staff committee was consigned to obscurity. As many issues pitted the United States against the Soviet Union, the Security Council found itself unable to agree on joint action.

The constitution therefore evolved, and the task of peace enforcement was taken over for a time by the General Assembly. The occasion for this shift was, as we have seen, the invasion of Korea and the passage of the Uniting for Peace Resolution in 1950 (see Table 10.6 for a summary of the evolution of United Nations peacemaking approaches). Based on the assumption of continued American dominance in the General Assembly and continued American strategic superiority over the Soviet Union, the Uniting for Peace Resolution for a while enabled the United States to circumvent the Soviet veto and to mobilize the General Assembly for Western objectives. The small countries in the General Assembly were permitted to play a more active role in

peace enforcement, and the permanent members of the Security Council (notably the Soviet Union) were no longer to be exempt from enforcement action.

By 1956 a new concept of the United Nations' role in securing peace had developed. Fostered by Secretary-General Hammarskjöld, it involved recognition that Chapter VI of the Charter is too weak to deal with serious disputes and that Chapter VII is too strong. Hammarskjöld saw the United Nations as playing a special role in those disputes that are not part of the main cold-war conflict or its periphery. He declared:

These efforts must aim at keeping newly arising conflicts outside the sphere of bloc differences. Further, in the case of conflicts on the margin of, or inside, the sphere of bloc differences, the U.N. should seek to bring such conflicts out of this sphere through solutions aiming, in the first instance, at their strict localization. [14, pp. 302–303]

Hammarskjöld considered that the United Nations' greatest opportunity for success lies in resolving disputes among the nonaligned and between colonial and anticolonial states. He hoped that, in this way, a balance between the expectations of the major actors and the capabilities of

Table 10.6
Evolution of United Nations Peacekeeping

	Early Charter (1945-1949)	Uniting for Peace (1950-1954)	Preventive Diplomacy (1956-1962)	Détente Diplomacy (1963-)
Salient U.N. organ	Security Council	General Assembly	Secretariat	Security Council
Salient members	permanent members of Security Council	Western allies and small powers	small states	permanent members of Security Council
Type of action	coercive enforcement	coercive enforcement	noncoercive interposition	coercive enforcement
Object of action	small states	major states	small states	small states
International system	emergent bipolarity	tight bipolarity	loose bipolarity	multipolarity, complex conglomerate

the United Nations would be restored. Drawing on provisions from both Chapters VI and VII of the Charter, he tried to create for the United Nations a role in preventive diplomacy, localization of limited conflict, and the isolation of the "third world" from great-power disputes and the politics of the cold war. This new role deemphasized both the use of force and the assignment of guilt. Although United Nations action of this sort still required the authorization of either the Security Council or the General Assembly, it relied heavily on the initiative and dynamism of the secretary-general himself. A further shift in the locus of peacekeeping thus took place, this time from the General Assembly to the Secretariat.

The Hammarskjöld system made use of small military contingents for interposition, observer teams, and representatives of the Secretariat. In 1956 a U.N. emergency force was sent to Egypt to supervise the withdrawal of Anglo-French forces and to maintain the uneasy ceasefire between Egypt and Israel. The United Nations also supervised the clearing of the Suez canal in 1957 and established observer teams in Lebanon and Jordan in 1958. The authorization of United Nations intervention in the Congo in 1960, after that country had been rent by civil war and Belgian occupation, represented the high-water mark of United Nations operations of this kind. Although Hammarskjöld's action precipitated a constitutional and financial crisis in the organization, U Thant continued to use Hammarskjöld's approach. He continued the Congo operation until 1963 and arranged for United Nations presence in West Irian (1962–1963), Yemen (1963–1964), North Borneo (1963), and Cyprus (1964–   ). However, he studiously avoided going beyond the mandates of the Security Council and sponsored operations that were relatively inexpensive.

As under the Uniting for Peace Resolution, the role that Hammarskjöld developed for the United Nations heavily involved the small countries of the General Assembly. United Nations forces were drawn exclusively from smaller powers like Ireland and Yugoslavia, and representatives from small countries were called upon to act as advisers for the secretary-general. United Nations forces, operating under strict guidelines, were permitted to shoot only in self-defense and to enter the territory of a state only with that state's consent [8]. In 1967, when Gamal Abdel Nasser demanded that the UNEF withdraw from the ceasefire line in Egypt, it left quickly [15, 41].

The Hammarskjöld peacekeeping system functioned effectively only to the extent that the United States and the Soviet Union voluntarily restrained themselves from seeking short-run advantages over each other in certain situations. The great powers had to have some common interest in declaring certain areas, particularly in Africa and Asia, "out of bounds" for cold-war politics. The moderate success enjoyed by Hammarskjöld and U Thant has owed much to the growing Soviet-American realization, from the mid-1950s on, that intervention in local conflicts could lead to dangerous confrontation and global crisis.

Soviet opposition to Hammarskjöld's initiatives in the Congo and the ensuing financial crisis of the United Nations led to a slackening of United Nations efforts at peacekeeping. Furthermore, the increasing pattern of Soviet-American cooperation in certain matters and the decreasing salience of cold-war issues have revived interest in the Security Council as a viable organ for maintaining the peace. In April 1966 the Security Council was able to agree that Rhodesia's unilateral declaration of independence from Great Britain and its policy of racial inequality constituted a threat to the peace. Consequently, the Council authorized Great Britain to use force if necessary to halt the shipment of petroleum and petroleum products to Rhodesia. Some months later the Council ordered an embargo on shipment of oil and arms to Rhodesia and a boycott of Rhodesian exports. This boycott has not proven successful, however, owing in part to the assistance of Rho-

Table 10.7.
Disputes Referred to the United Nations, 1945-1965

Period	Number	Disputes Referred to but Not Settled by U.N.	Disputes U.N. Settled or Helped to Settle
1945-1947	11	French withdrawal from Levant Franco government in Spain status of Trieste Kashmir Palestine South African race policies revision of 1936 Suez Canal- Sudan agreement	Azerbaijan Balkans Corfu channel Indonesia
1948-1951	6	Berlin blockade communist coup in Czechoslovakia Hyderabad Iranian oil nationalization	Korea withdrawal of Republic of China troops from Burma
1952-1955	3	North African decolonization future status of Cyprus Guatemala	none
1956-1960	10	Hungary Syrian-Turkish border Laos civil war Tibet South Tyrol U-2 flights	Suez war Lebanese-2nd Jordanian unrest Nicaraguan-Honduran border Thai-Cambodian border
1961-1965	17	civil unrest in Oman Cuba (Bay of Pigs) Cuban intervention in Dominican Republic Goa Iraq-Kuwait (U.K.) Portuguese colonies in Africa Cuban missile crisis British Guianan-Venezuelan border Dominican intervention in Haiti Malaysia-Indonesia Senegalese-Angolan border Yemen civil war Cyprus civil war Greek and Turkish hostilities Panama canal U.S. and North Vietnam (Gulf of Tonkin) U.S. intervention in Dominican Republic	Congo West Irian Bizerte Southern Rhodesia Aden-Yemen border Cambodia-South Vietnam (U.S.) Stanleyville air rescue India-Pakistan war

Source: Ernst B. Haas, *Collective Security and The Future International System,* University of Denver Monograph Series in World Affairs, vol. 5, no. 1 (Denver: 1967-1968), p. 46.

desia by South Africa and France and to continued American importation from Rhodesia of strategic materials, such as nickel and chromium.

United Nations efforts to maintain peace and to find peaceful solutions to troublesome political issues have met with varied success. Table 10.7 summarizes the disputes that were referred to the United Nations between 1945 and 1965. On the basis of his review of United Nations activity in this period, Haas has made several observations about the organization's success in dealing with different kinds of issues at different times [21, pp. 51–69]. Here are some of his more salient observations:

1. The combined action of General Assembly and Security Council brought results; the General Assembly alone was ineffective.
2. Of the various modes of resolving disputes, collective mediation and conciliation were most successful.
3. Settlement was most frequent in disputes about colonial issues.
4. Many of the disputes that were settled *did* involve major powers; disputes involving only small nonaligned actors or members of the same alliance were least susceptible to United Nations settlement.
5. For ending hostilities, the combined efforts of the Security Council and the General Assembly and the imposition of a truce were effective.
6. The United Nations was ineffective in ending hostilities involving cold-war issues.
7. United Nations success in ending hostilities declined sharply after 1945.
8. The United Nations became more successful in settling colonial disputes and less successful in resolving cold-war issues.
9. Major powers increasingly resisted United Nations intervention in hostilities in which they are involved.

Our overall conclusion about the performance of the United Nations is that it has shown ability to aid economic and social development, settle disputes, and diminish colonialism, but not to end wars. Lack of success in Vietnam, the Middle East, and Rhodesia testify to the inability of the United Nations to enforce its will or bring about peaceful settlements. It has been of some assistance in cases where force is invoked, but not when a major power was directly involved. Under Hammarskjöld, U Thant, and Waldheim, institutionalized organizational patterns have emerged, but activities of the United Nations continue to be shaped principally by cleavages in international structure and the goals of individual member states.

In Chapter 11 we shall turn from intergovernmental organizations to nongovernmental organizations, notably international corporations. The growing autonomy of such actors has been an outstanding feature of the international system since 1962.

References

1. Alger, Chadwick F., "United Nations Participation as a Learning Experience," *Public Opinion Quarterly,* 27 (Fall 1963), pp. 411–426.
2. Alger, Chadwick F., and Steven J. Brams, "Patterns of Representation in National Capitals and Intergovernmental Organizations," *World Politics,* 19 (July 1967), p. 662.
3. Alker, Hayward R., Jr., "Dimensions of Conflict in the General Assembly," *American Political Science Review,* 58 (September 1964), p. 651.
4. Alker, Hayward R., Jr., and Bruce M. Russett, *World Politics in the General Assembly* (New Haven: Yale University Press, 1965).
5. Angell, Robert C., *Peace on the March: Transnational Participation* (New York: Van Nostrand Reinhold, 1969), p. 30.
6. Bailey, Sydney D., *The Secretariat of the United Nations,* rev. ed. (New York: Praeger, 1964), p. 28.
7. Boyd, Andrew, *United Nations: Piety, Myth, and Truth* (Harmondsworth, Eng.: Penguin, 1963), p. 87.
8. Burns, A. L., and Nina Heathcote, *Peace-Keeping by U.N. Forces,* (New York: Praeger, 1963).
9. Churchill, Winston S., *The Gathering Storm* (Boston: Houghton Mifflin, 1948), p. 175.
10. Claude, Inis L., Jr., "Collective Legitimization as a Political Function of the

United Nations," *International Organization,* 20 (Summer 1966), pp. 367–379.

11. Claude, Inis L., Jr., *Swords into Plowshares,* 3rd ed. (New York: Random House, 1964).

12. Clubb, O. Edmund, *Twentieth Century China* (New York: Columbia University Press, 1964), pp. 149–184.

13. Durbin, Martin David, "Toward the Concept of Collective Security: The Bryce Group's Proposals for the Avoidance of War, 1914–1917," *International Organization,* 24 (Spring 1970), pp. 288–318.

14. Foote, Wilder, ed., *Dag Hammarskjöld: Servant of Peace* (New York: Harper & Row, 1962).

15. Frye, William R., *A United Nations Peace Force* (New York: Oceana, 1957).

16. Galtung, Ingrid E., "The Status of the Technical Assistance Expert: A Study of U.N. Experts in Latin America," *Journal of Peace Research,* 4 (1966), pp. 359–379.

17. Goodrich, Leland M., "Korea: Collective Measures Against Aggression," *International Conciliation,* 494 (October 1953).

18. Goodrich, Leland M., *The United Nations* (New York: Crowell, 1959), p. 162.

19. Gulick, Edward V., *Europe's Classical Balance of Power* (Ithaca: Cornell University Press, 1955).

20. Haas, Ernst B., *Beyond the Nation-State* (Stanford: Stanford University Press, 1964).

21. Haas, Ernst B., *Collective Security and the Future International System,* University of Denver Monograph Series in World Affairs, 5, no. 1 (Denver: 1967–1968).

22. Haas, Ernst B., *The Uniting of Europe* (Stanford: Stanford University Press, 1958).

23. Hoffmann, Stanley, "International Organization and the International System," *International Organization,* 24 (Summer 1970), pp. 389–390.

24. Hovet, Thomas, Jr., *Africa in the United Nations* (Evanston: Northwestern University Press, 1963), p. 181.

25. Hovet, Thomas, Jr., *Bloc Politics in the United Nations* (Cambridge, Mass.: Harvard University Press, 1960), p. 31.

26. Hull, Cordell, *The Memoirs of Cordell Hull,* vol. 2 (New York: Macmillan, 1948), p. 1664.

27. Iklé, Fred C., *How Nations Negotiate* (New York: Praeger, 1967), p. 218.

28. Jenks, C. W., "Some Constitutional Problems of International Organizations," *British Yearbook of International Law* (London: Oxford University Press, 1945), p. 35.

29. Jenks, C. W., "Some Problems of an International Civil Service," *Public Administration Review,* (Spring 1943), p. 95.

30. Kant, Immanuel, "Eternal Peace," in Carl J. Friedrich, ed., *The Philosophy of Kant* (New York: Modern Library, 1949), p. 448.

31. Keohane, Robert O., "Political Influence in the General Assembly," *International Conciliation,* 557 (March 1966).

32. Leonard, Larry, *International Organization* (New York: McGraw-Hill, 1951), p. 208.

33. Lie, Trygve, *In the Cause of Peace* (New York: Macmillan, 1954).

34. Mitrany, David, *A Working Peace System* (London: Royal Institute of International Affairs, 1943).

35. North, Robert C., Howard E. Koch, Jr., and Dina A. Zinnes, "The Integrative Functions of Conflict," *Journal of Conflict Resolution,* 4 (1960), pp. 355–374.

36. Nye, Joseph S., Jr., *Peace in Parts: Integration and Conflict in Regional Organization* (Boston: Little, Brown, 1971).

37. Organski, A. F. K., *World Politics* (New York: Knopf, 1958), p. 373.

38. Pederson, Richard F., "National Representation in the United Nations," *International Organization,* 15 (Spring 1961), p. 257.

39. Plano, Jack C., and Robert E. Riggs, *Forging World Order* (New York: Macmillan, 1967), p. 255.

40. Ranshofen-Wertheimer, Egon, *The International Secretariat: A Great Experiment in International Administration* (Washington, D.C.: Carnegie Endowment for International Peace, 1945), chaps. 16, 17.

41. Rossner, Gabriella, *The United Nations Emergency Force* (New York: Columbia University Press, 1963).

42. Rowe, Edward T., "The Emerging Anti-Colonial Consensus in the United Nations," *Journal of Conflict Resolution,* 8 (September 1964), pp. 209–230.

43. Russett, Bruce M., "Discovering Voting Groups in the United Nations," *American Political Science Review,* 60 (June 1966), pp. 327–339.

44. Schaefer, Ludwig F., ed., *The Ethiopian Crisis* (Boston: Heath, 1961).

45. Singer, J. David, and Michael Wallace, "Intergovernmental Organization and the Preservation of Peace, 1816–1964: Some Bivariate Relationships," *International Organization,* 24 (Summer 1970), pp. 520–547.

46. Smith, Sara R., *The Manchurian Crisis 1931–32: A Tragedy in International Relations* (New York: Columbia University Press, 1948).

47. Stoessinger, John G., *et al., Financing the United Nations System* (Washington, D.C.: The Brookings Institution, 1964), pp. 293–306.

48. Stoessinger, John G., *The United Nations and the Superpowers* (New York: Random House, 1965), pp. 37–48.

49. Todd, James E., "An Analysis of Security Council Voting Behavior," *Western Political Quarterly,* 22 (March 1969), p. 66.

50. Tuchman, Barbara W., *Stillwell and the American Experience in China, 1911–45* (New York: Macmillan, 1970).

51. Walters, F. P., *A History of the League of Nations,* vol. 2 (London: Oxford University Press, 1952), p. 653.

52. Waltz, Kenneth N., "Kant, Liberalism and War," *American Political Science Review,* 56 (June 1962), pp. 331–340.

53. Wolfers, Arnold, "Collective Security and the War in Korea," in Wolfers, *Discord and Collaboration* (Baltimore: Johns Hopkins Press, 1962), pp. 167–180.

54. Young, Oran R., *The Intermediaries* (Princeton: Princeton University Press, 1967), pp. 80–81.

Suggested Reading

Claude, Inis L., Jr., *Swords into Plowshares,* 3rd ed. (New York: Random House, 1964).

Cox, Arthur, *Prospects for Peacekeeping* (Washington, D.C.: The Brookings Institution, 1967).

Deutsch, Karl W., *et al., France, Germany and the Western Alliance* (New York: Scribner, 1967).

Haas, Ernst B., *Beyond the Nation-State* (Stanford: Stanford University Press, 1964).

International Political Communities: An Anthology (Garden City, N.Y.: Doubleday, 1966).

Larus, Joel, ed., *From Collective Security to Preventive Diplomacy* (New York: Wiley, 1965).

Nye, Joseph S., Jr., *Peace in Parts: Integration and Conflict in Regional Organization* (Boston: Little, Brown, 1971).

Plano, Jack C., and Robert E. Riggs, *Forging World Order* (New York: Macmillan, 1967).

Scheinman, Lawrence, and David Wilkinsen, eds., *International Law and Political Crisis: An Analytic Casebook* (Boston: Little, Brown, 1968).

Young, Oran R., *The Intermediaries: Third Parties in International Crises* (Princeton: Princeton University Press, 1967).

Chapter 11
NONGOVERNMENTAL ACTORS: THE INTERNATIONAL CORPORATION

Those who manage great enterprises have ceased to think in the classical pattern of producing goods for the home market and exporting the surplus overseas. Today they operate and think on a worldwide scale—George W. Ball [1]

In recent years there has been growing interest among students of international politics in explaining the role of nongovernmental institutions, organizations, and groups in the international system. There has been increasing recognition that the governments of national states and official intergovernmental organizations are *not* the only actors in international politics. To proceed as if they were is misleading and confusing. As J. David Singer has observed, "it becomes reasonable to expect that a fair amount of world political interaction will take place directly between and among international associations other than foreign ministries, or any official agencies for that matter" [31, 15]. The daily newspaper contains many references to such actors and their relatively autonomous behavior. For example, officials of the International Red Cross effectively intervened in the Nigerian civil war and several Middle East disputes; the Black Panther party has opened an "international section" in Algiers; the International Telephone and Telegraph Corporation has sought to subvert the regime of Chile's President Salvador Allende; and an organization known as Amnesty International has undertaken to obtain the release of political prisoners in many countries. Currently there are more than 2,000 transnational nongovernmental organizations of varying importance.

Unlike national governments and organizations like the United Nations, these groups tend to function in specific fields, furthering relatively narrow ranges of goals (see Table 11.1). As we suggested in Chapter 1, political systems perform several tasks—promoting physical protection, economic development and regulation, public welfare, and group status. Nongovernmental international actors tend to expend much of their effort on single tasks, often for fairly limited groups of people. International corporations and labor organizations, for instance, largely concentrate on obtaining economic benefits for shareholders and workers; the Roman Catholic Church seeks the spiritual well-being of its membership. By contrast, governments attempt with variable success to perform all four major types of tasks for geographically defined populations.

The spread of nongovernmental organizations is part of a transformation of the international system that has taken place since 1945.[1] With resources less concentrated in the hands of a few leading actors, new conflicts centering on race and poverty have become salient. Along with the increase in the number of participant national actors in the system, extranational units have emerged. Many governments, particularly those in the "third world," are unable to meet the demands and needs of their populations or to regulate extranational competitors. Arab guerrilla groups like al-Fatah have formed because many Palestinian Arabs perceive themselves as having been denied justice, respect, influence, understanding, and welfare through the three wars between Israel and its neighbors. States like Jordan and Syria can exert only limited control over Palestinian groups. Clearly, structural changes now place fewer constraints on autonomous behavior by groups that are only partially controlled by nation-states; this easing of constraints has created incentives for the formation of more such groups.

Perhaps the most dramatic evidence of increased transnational activity has been the emergence of autonomous economic institutions as part of a growth in international trade and economic flows. Charles P. Kindleberger, a noted international economist, has declared: "The nation-state is just about through as an economic unit. . . . The world is too small. It is too easy to get about. Two-hundred-thousand-ton tank and ore carriers and containerization, airbuses, and the like will not permit sovereign independence of the nation-state in economic affairs" [16, pp. 207–208]. Although some legalistic scholars persist in claiming the separation of economic and political activity, the past forty years have witnessed an alteration of expectations and attitudes among both elites and masses that has created an intimate association between economic and political systems. The set of demands and expectations evoked by the phrase "welfare state," the prevalence of government intervention in economic affairs at all levels of the community, and the growing economic gap between the "have" and "have not" states have injected political considerations into economic matters throughout the world. In addition, as Kindleberger has suggested, the politicized economic system has developed complex transnational links that do not correspond to national frontiers. The emergence of international corporations in the "interstices" between nation-states is typical of a complex conglomerate system.

International political and economic activities are not very easily isolatable as separate systems. Recurrent liquidity crises, economic integration, and trade restrictions are subjects of considerable intergovernmental political conflict and cooperation. Europeans have accused the United States of "exporting inflation," and underdeveloped countries have denounced the economic hegemony of manufacturing countries banded together in the General Agreement on Tariffs and Trade. For its part, the United States exercises considerable influence abroad through its dominance of such institutions as the Import-Export Bank and the World Bank. "We are now beginning to discover," wrote French journalist J. J. Servan-Schreiber, "what was concealed by 20 years of colonial wars, wars that dominated our thoughts and our behavior: the confrontation of civilizations will henceforth take place in the battlefield of technology, science, and management" [29, p. 275]. Most governments can no longer segregate economics from politics, either in their domestic or in their external behavior. One American policy maker has declared: "The outward surge of American corporate enterprise at its present magnitude has a powerful impact on a broad spectrum of policy issues. . . . It becomes difficult to know where business ends and foreign policy, political and economic, begins" [28].

[1] See Chapter 6.

Table 11.1.

Interstate Nongovernmental Organizations, by Function and Region

Type of Function	Africa	Asia	Afro-Asia	North America	South America	Americas
Bibliography, documentation, press	2	2	0	0	3	3
Religion	1	0	0	0	2	0
Social Sciences, humanistic studies	0	0	0	0	0	1
International relations	0	1	0	0	1	3
Politics	0	0	0	0	2	0
Law and administration	1	0	0	0	0	3
Social welfare	0	0	0	0	1	0
Professions, employers	0	0	0	0	1	3
Trade unions	4	2	2	0	1	4
Economics, finance	0	0	0	0	1	1
Commerce, industry	0	1	2	0	1	5
Agriculture	0	0	0	0	3	0
Transport, travel	0	0	0	0	3	4
Technology	0	0	1	0	0	4
Science	2	0	0	0	0	3
Health, medicine	0	0	0	0	7	8
Education, youth	1	0	0	0	4	1
Arts, broadcasting, television, cinema	0	0	0	0	0	1
Sports, recreation	2	6	0	1	3	0
Total	13	12	5	1	33	44
Total Listed	1869					

National Organizations in Consultative Status with U.N. Economic and Social Council

Total	0	2	0	6	0	0
Total Listed	15					

Source: Data are taken from Eyvind S. Tew, ed., *Yearbook of International Organizations (1968-1969)*, 12th ed. (Brussels: Union of International Associations, January 1969).

At the same time that questions of international economics are acquiring more political significance, important decisions on the international allocation and distribution of goods and services are coming to be made in the board rooms of international corporations, rather than in government ministries. Unfortunately, political scientists have been too much preoccupied with the behavior of national states and have made few systematic efforts to investigate such extranational ac-

		Region				
Europe	British Commonwealth	Americas and Europe	Mixed	Communist	Arab	Other
10	0	5	34	1	0	7
10	0	0	82	0	0	10
4	0	8	58	0	1	9
15	0	9	72	0	0	20
5	1	3	7	0	0	1
5	0	2	37	0	0	4
19	0	0	53	0	0	13
34	0	5	53	0	0	11
11	0	1	28	0	0	1
19	0	2	21	0	0	4
125	2	11	67	0	0	18
18	1	7	43	0	0	10
18	0	2	40	0	0	7
24	1	4	52	0	0	12
11	0	6	85	0	0	54
32	0	7	133	0	0	20
14	1	1	65	0	0	14
9	1	3	52	0	0	9
8	0	1	63	0	0	12
391	7	77	1045	1	1	236
0	0	0	2	0	0	5

tors as corporations. "The poverty of contemporary international theory," one critic has argued, "must be attributed to the fact that it functions as no more than the ideology of the nation-state system" [20]. Some years ago Adolf A. Berle, Jr., declared, "Corporate power in international affairs becomes a matter of major concern in the twentieth-century world" [3, p. 116]. Yet only now are students of international politics beginning to shift their attention to such actors. "Power is shifting away from the nation state to international institutions both public and private. . . . The international corporation is acting and planning in terms that are far in advance of the political concepts of the nation state" [2]. At least four approaches to the study of international corporations have so far been suggested.

First, international corporations can be viewed as extensions of national states. In this approach it is assumed that international corporations act according to a set of rules established by states and that their activities are controlled by individuals who are responsible citizens of those states, hence subject primarily to state laws and policy. We would thus focus analysis on domestic interrelations, assuming the primacy of government over corporation. This approach entails little more than an examination of national foreign-policy formation, particularly of the internal processes that lead to decisions, yet many international corporations operate against the objectives of their home governments or without reference to them. In early 1941, for example, one corporate executive argued with an American undersecretary of state that foreign policy was of no concern to his corporation.

His argument was direct and simple. His corporation, he said, was not in politics of any kind. If the United States government wished to have a quarrel with the Nazi government of Germany, that was the government's privilege; but his corporation with its foreign operations could not be involved, and did not feel bound to accommodate itself to American policy expressed in a "moral embargo." [3, p. 133]

Analyzing the international corporation from this perspective seems analogous to —and as helpful as—trying to explain E. I. du Pont's nationwide interests in the United States as extensions of the state of Delaware in which the company is incorporated.

Second, the international corporation may be considered as controlling and directing the foreign policies of national states, the reverse of the relationship assumed in the first approach. Essentially this approach is based on the Marxist interpretation of the role of the international corporation.[2] As influence is not identical with control, there is a prima facie argument against assuming that the government-corporation relationship is one of subordinate to superior. During wartime, for instance, governments are generally able to manipulate corporative behavior in order to achieve national objectives.

Third, the international corporation may be viewed as a "good citizen" of the host countries in which it operates. In this approach it is assumed that the international corporation will seek to accommodate its objectives to the domestic political and economic interests of host countries. Companies do occasionally adopt this attitude but not always. Usually there is bargaining between host countries and corporations, a means by which the latter can reshape the domestic objectives of the former.

Finally, we can analyze the international corporation as a relatively autonomous international actor, comparable in certain important aspects to national governments and international organizations. We can assume that corporations enjoy a peculiar mix of autonomy and constraint that permits them to collaborate with or oppose governments. As the number of international corporations that behave in this way is increasing, we have selected this approach as the most profitable for our analysis of corporate behavior in international politics.

THE DEVELOPMENT OF THE INTERNATIONAL CORPORATION

As early as the seventeenth century, corporations were active in the international system. The European national states granted charters to explore, trade with, and conquer vast tracts of the rest of the

[2] For a recent provocative attempt to update the work of Nikolai Lenin and John A. Hobson, see Harry Magdoff, *The Age of Imperialism* (New York: Monthly Review, 1969).

world. England, France, Portugal, and the Netherlands all chartered such companies in the early 1600s. Typical of these charters was that given to the Dutch East India Company in 1602: The company was permitted to make war and peace, seize foreign ships, establish colonies, construct fortresses, and coin money between the Cape of Good Hope and the Straits of Magellan. In return Holland was guaranteed a share in the profits. Beyond the initial charter the shareholders were guaranteed no further support in their ventures by the parent country [21]. Similar firms, like the Hudson Bay Company in North America, the Portuguese Mozambique Company, and the British and French East India Companies, played leading roles in the expansion of European influence and indeed in the expansion of the international system. It was they that first established regular contacts between Europe and China, Japan, India, Indonesia, and certain African kingdoms. At about the same time that they were vested with the right to make war and negotiate peace, Thomas Hobbes was arguing that in theory these activities are the exclusive prerogatives of the state. Nevertheless, the early conquest and administration of India by the British was undertaken almost entirely by the British East India Company on its own initiative. "Seldom in human history has a small, chance-picked body of men had so much actual cash to gain and to lose" [34].

The rise of the modern international combine began in the early years of the twentieth century in the extractive industries, particularly the oil industry. After the breakup of the Standard Oil Trust in the United States in 1909, Standard Oil of New Jersey began to expand its operations overseas, in order to discover new sources of petroleum, especially in Venezuela and the Middle East. European-based firms like Royal Dutch/Shell and other American companies followed suit, and by the late 1920s seven oil companies, known in economics literature as the "seven sisters," had achieved a virtual oligopoly over the production, refining,

and distribution of oil.[3] Not until after World War II, however, did manufacturing industries begin to invest heavily in overseas subsidiaries. American direct investments are clearly the largest part of world overseas investments (see Table 11.2), though they do not constitute an overwhelming force in international business. It has been estimated that the value of the goods produced as a consequence of American corporations' overseas investments exceeds $500 billion, equivalent to more than 25 percent of the gross national product of the entire noncommunist world.[4] When we compare the gross national products of the major national states with the annual sales of major corporations, we find that no fewer than thirteen corporations are among the fifty-one largest economic units in the world (Table 11.3) and that in 1970 General Motors had net sales valued at more than the gross national product of all but twenty-two states. As the sales of international corporations are increasing more rapidly than are gross national products, it is likely that in the future we shall find more international corporations on the "top fifty" list.

As corporations grow and diversify their products, it becomes more and more difficult for any *single* national actor to control them because their operations are so widely dispersed. It also becomes increasingly difficult to view them as mere extensions of their nations of origin. "Their identity," economist Raymond Vernon has written, "is likely to become more and more ambiguous in national terms. Commingling human and material resources of many nations, formulating problems and solutions on lines uninhibited by national boundaries, multinational enterprises may not be easy to classify in terms of national association" [38]. In-

---

[3] The "seven sisters" are Standard Oil Company of New Jersey, Royal Dutch/Shell, British Petroleum, Gulf Oil, Texaco, Standard Oil of California, and Mobil Oil.

[4] When we include the production of these corporations in their home countries, it is likely that their actual sales are greatly in excess of $500 billion [37, p. 388].

Table 11.2.

Direct Foreign Investments as Accumulated Assets by Major Countries, 1966 (book values, in millions of dollars)

	World*	United States	United Kingdom	France	Germany	Sweden	Canada	Japan
Petroleum	25,942	16,264	4,200	§	200	††	††	††
(LDC)†	(11,892)	(6,975)	(2,167)	(670)	(65)	††	††	(222)
Mining and smelting	5,923	4,135	759	††	100	††	2508§§	††
(LDC)†	(2,801)	(1,827)	(298)	(200)	(38)	(65)	(202)	(71)
Manufacturing	36,246	22,050	6,028	††	1,800	††	2,988	††
(LDC)†	(8,047)	(4,124)	(1,471)	(1,230)§§	(645)	(96)	(332)	(270)
Other	21,472	12,113	5,015**	††	400	††	††	††
(LDC)†	(7,230)	(3,915)	(2,255)	††	(97)	††	††	(33)
Total	89,583	54,462	16,002	4,000§§	2,500	793	3,238	1,000
(LDC)†	(29,970)	(16,841)	(6,184)	(2,100)	(845)	(161)	(534)	(605)

*Data for Italy, Holland, Switzerland, and Belgium are not available; total Australian investment was $300 million.
†Less developed countries.
**Including agriculture of 1.022 (864 in the less developed countries).
§Total French oil production estimated at 57.1 million tons in 1966.
††Not available.
§§Estimated.
Source: Sidney E. Rolfe and Walter Damm, eds., *The Multinational Corporation in the World Economy* (New York: Praeger, 1970), p. 8. Reprinted by permission. Published by Frederick A. Praeger for the Atlantic Institute, the Committee for Atlantic Economic Cooperation, and the Atlantic Council for the United States.

241
NONGOVERNMENTAL ACTORS: THE INTERNATIONAL CORPORATION

Table 11.3.
Gross National Products of Countries and Net Sales
of Corporations Interspersed (by rank as of 1970 in billions of dollars)

1.	United States	$927.6	27.	Standard Oil(N.J.)	16.6
2.	Soviet Union	468.0	28.	Ford Motor	15.0
3.	Japan	185.6	29.	Denmark	14.6
4.	West Germany	172.7	30.	Austria	13.2
5.	France	138.0	31.	Indonesia	12.8
6.	United Kingdom	111.8	32.	Royal Dutch/Shell	10.8
7.	Italy	87.3	33.	Norway	10.1
8.	China	86.0	34.	Venezuela	10.1
9.	Canada	75.0	35.	Iran	9.9
10.	India	50.0	36.	Finland	9.7
11.	Poland	46.1	37.	Sears Roebuck	9.3
12.	East Germany	39.7	38.	Greece	9.0
13.	Brazil	33.7	39.	General Electric	8.7
14.	Czechoslovakia	32.5	40.	Philippines	8.5
15.	Australia	31.6	41.	Turkey	8.2
16.	Mexico	31.6	42.	Korea	7.8
17.	Spain	30.7	43.	IBM	7.5
18.	Netherlands	29.8	44.	Mobil Oil	7.3
19.	Sweden	29.4	45.	Chrysler	7.0
20.	Belgium	24.1	46.	Unilever	6.9
21.	Argentina	21.0	47.	Thailand	6.8
22.	Switzerland	19.6	48.	Colombia	6.6
23.	General Motors	18.8	49.	IT&T	6.4
24.	Pakistan	17.2	50.	Chile	6.3
25.	AT&T	17.0	51.	Texaco	6.3
26.	South Africa	16.8			

Source: The Washington Monthly/January 1972, p. 29.

deed, the international corporation is an integrating factor in certain narrow economic areas, whereas nation-states cannot fulfill this function alone. The corporation is adjusting to increasing international economic interdependence more quickly than are national governments.

Not all firms with overseas branches are "international." To be international, a corporation must manifest international economic attitudes, beside having an international distribution of assets: "A company is multinational [international] when it no longer distinguishes between domestic and international business. Domestic business is subordinated to and fully integrated with a global plan of action. The head office management staff becomes multinational in outlook and responsibility" [18]. We can distinguish several types of firms with international interests. Kindleberger has identified the national firm with foreign operations, the multinational firm, and the international corporation. The first remains essentially the "citizen" of a single national state. Its foreign operations constitute only a small fraction of its total interests, and its monetary operations and corporate planning are tied to the home country. The multinational corporation, on the other hand, identifies its interests with those of the host countries. It hires local citizens in middle-management positions, accepts local investment, and generally seeks to cooperate with host countries. By contrast, the international corporation is willing to invest wherever there is a potential for return. It is prepared to speculate in currency, even against the interests of its "home" and "host" countries. Indeed, it recognizes few obligations to specific national actors and is prepared to "emigrate" in search of optimum operational conditions. "The international corporation," Kindleberger has declared, "has no country to which it owes more loyalty than any other, nor any country where it feels completely at home" [16, p. 182]. The international corporation does not hesitate to come into conflict with nation-states when its objectives diverge from theirs. As a corporation alters its structure, the attitudes and expectations of management will probably also evolve. Management of an international corporation is thus likely to be characterized by geocentric or world-oriented views. National firms are likely to be "ethnocentric," oriented to their home countries, and multinational firms will shift directions, depending upon the issue and the current comparative yields of their domestic and international operations [24].

Although we might expect management attitudes to reflect the distribution of assets and ownership, this does not necessarily occur. Indeed, an international outlook does not even seem to require that a firm be incorporated in more than one state. That firms in the United States are incorporated in particular states, particularly in "tax havens" like Delaware, does *not* guarantee that they are oriented toward those states. In fact, international corporations have increasingly sought to establish their head offices in such "tax havens" as Monaco, Switzerland, Lichtenstein, Liberia, and Panama. Currently much of the world's commercial shipping is registered in small countries like Panama and Liberia, even though its ownership is foreign.

THE INTERNATIONAL CORPORATION: OBJECTIVES AND INFLUENCE

It appears that the objectives of international corporations and national states are not comparable, first, because those of the former are usually specific and simple, whereas those of the latter are diffuse and complex. As we saw in Chapter 4, the nation-state pursues a variety of objectives simultaneously, and it is difficult to find a single measure of policy success or failure. By contrast, profits appear to offer a single readily quantifiable measure of success or failure for the international corporation. Concepts like "national interest" and "balance of power" are imprecise measures of goal fulfillment. An international corporation can readily compare its position in a given market relative to those of its competitors.

In practice, however, defining the goals and objectives of an international corporation can be as complex as is defining the goals and objectives of a nation-state. Considerations of time, risk, and even social goals must be confronted. For example, should profitability be measured over the long run or the short run? An investment may be profitable over a twenty-year span but not over a ten-year period. Compounding this problem is the element of risk present in all forecasts, both political and economic. The element of risk is far greater for an international enterprise than for a domestic one. An American corporation assumes that the flow of goods and money in the United States will remain relatively stable for the foreseeable future. It also expects that the United States will not become socialist. But the international corporation can depend upon few such certainties and must engage in political analysis very much as does a national state. Whereas a domestic corporation need not concern itself about most political questions other than marginal changes in consumer safeguards, labor regulations, and tax laws, the international enterprise must evaluate the stability of autonomous political units and try to foresee changes in the international system. Profit maximization is an objective difficult to operationalize because of subjective assessments of risk and time span.

We can identify at least four general interrelated goals of the international corporation: profits, sales growth, security, and autonomy.[5] The relative importance of each of these goals varies from situation to situation and from corporation to corporation. Except for profits, these goals are analogous to those pursued by nation-states. To achieve them, corporations must interact and bargain with one another and with nation-states.

Profits

Profits for shareholders are the sine qua non of any business operation, and no corporation can continue to exist if it fails to become profitable sooner or later. If the time horizon is extended far enough, however, almost any decision that the international corporation makes can be justified as "profitable."[6] "While few companies are likely to incur important financial obligations in the absence of profit opportunities," one economist has declared, "there have been recent instances where investments apparently have been made by large companies in underdeveloped countries as much for social as for economic reasons" [32]. International corporations are sometimes prepared to accept losses in the hope of future profits. Indeed, their behavior resembles that of the United States and the Soviet Union in the cold war; each has been prepared to incur high costs for long periods of time to prevent its adversary from making advances. Corporate investment decisions are often based less on immediate returns than on desire to keep abreast of the competition. Many international corporations thus maintain losing operations in order to stay in the market. In South America, for example, automobile manufacturers continue to compete for markets that are barely able to support a single producer. "For some reason other than profits," one observer has noted, "Ford, Chrysler, and GM stay in Brazil, expand, and hope for the *mañana* that never seems to come" [35, p. 246]. The rule of thumb seems

to be that such corporations continue to compete in the hope of a brighter future [4, p. 191 n]. The ability to support unprofitable or inefficient operations is one indication of the overall vigor of certain corporations. As one economist has suggested, "One measure of wealth is the waste one can afford" [27]. The point is, of course, that the profit motive does not adequately explain many specific decisions by international corporations.

Sales Growth

The decision makers in international corporations often perceive the absolute growth of their enterprises as inseparable from profits, even though growth in sales alone does not automatically reflect economic efficiency. Unlike profitability, which involves subjective assessments of future expectations, sales growth provides a ready measure of comparative success. It is easier to see whether or not sales of a specific enterprise have grown than to evaluate potential profitability. Furthermore, corporate bureaucrats constitute an interest group, which John Kenneth Galbraith has called the "technostructure"; its interests are not necessarily the same as those of the shareholders or owners of the corporation.[7] A growth in profits benefits the bureaucrats only if they share in ownership of the corporation. Galbraith has argued that, once an adequate level of earnings has been reached, the "technostructure" seeks to promote the autonomy and growth of the corporation as measured by increased sales. "Expansion of output means expansion of the technostructure itself," with an increase in benefits like promotion and salaries [10]. Such considerations lead to a corporate ideology that is "inherently expansive" [11].

Security and Autonomy

The goals of security and autonomy involve the maintenance and extension of

---

[5] This typology is drawn from Jonathan F. Galloway [11].

[6] Economists call this principle "the maximization of profits in infinity."

[7] This distinction is similar to that between government bureaucracies and the remainder of a nation's citizens.

the domain and scope of corporate activities relative to those of governments and actual or potential corporate competitors. The international corporation, like the nation-state, seeks to make itself invulnerable to the influence of other actors.

But, unlike its domestic counterpart, the international corporation functions in an anarchic environment. There are few institutionalized norms governing the behavior of corporations toward one another or toward governments. For the domestic corporation, contracts have the force of law. International corporations, on the other hand, conclude contracts with governments knowing that either party may violate them if conditions change sufficiently to make violation desirable. "Long term contracts or concessions running to 99 years are no barrier. . . . Facts are more compelling than sanctity of contract. When the country overcomes the initial advantages that the company brought to the bargaining table, the call for new contracts becomes irresistible" [16, p. 151]. Through expansion international corporations become less dependent upon particular governments. The impact of losses that they may suffer from expropriation of their property in one country is smaller, as the scope of their activities grows. "We have assets in seventy countries all over the world," one corporate executive has noted. "Some substantial portion of them at any one time will block the transfer of profits. But this will never be true of them all. If we can make enough profits in local currency, we can transfer enough home from some countries to make it worthwhile" [16, pp. 199–200]. We can thus view corporate activities much as we view those of national actors in a multipolar system: they shift their activities and alliances in order to avoid dependence upon other actors and to secure for themselves sufficient resources to compensate for declining relations with any one country.

In its quest for security and autonomy the international corporation tends to pursue certain specific policies. First, it generally seeks to retain full ownership of its foreign subsidiaries in order to prevent local stockholders whose objectives diverge from those of the corporation as a whole from gaining control. Rarely are investors in host countries invited to acquire ownership of subsidiaries, lest they acquire greater stakes in the subsidiaries than in the international corporation itself. The Ford Corporation's European division, for example, spent more than $500 million to buy out local investors in Europe, and the parent company currently owns more than 99 percent of outstanding shares in its overseas operations. "With such control," one observer has commented, "it could do what was necessary regardless of where the profits were made" [35, p. 261; 39, pp. 454–455]. Second, an international corporation tends to avoid investing in countries that require local partnership. Where local partnership exists, it often reflects pressure from the host government. Third, product diversification and production of all components of products are also means by which an international corporation seeks to protect itself. Finally, an international corporation can make alliances either with other corporations (cartel agreements) or with selected national actors. Not all these strategies are available to all corporations in all situations, so these corporations vary in their security and autonomy, depending upon the nature of their enterprises and the circumstances in which they find themselves.

In seeking to influence other actors, the international corporation has several strengths and weaknesses. Its foremost weakness is its lack of resources for coercion. Unlike a national actor it is rarely able to resist an attempt by a nation-state to seize its physical assets. Although the corporation may be fundamentally domestic in character, its foreign interests have often been protected by an alliance with the home country government whose interests have been considered parallel to those of the corporation. The United States government, for instance, actively encouraged American corporate expansion into Latin America during the early years of this century. As General Smedley D. Butler of the U.S. Marines remarked in 1931:

I helped make Mexico safe for American oil interests in 1914. I helped make Haiti and Cuba a decent place for the National City Bank boys to collect revenues in. I helped purify Nicaragua for the international banking house of Brown Brothers. . . . I helped make Honduras "right" for American fruit companies. Looking back on it, I might have given Al Capone a few hints. [5]

This statement suggests how businesses can provide their home states with interests in other countries and how states can promote the interests of corporations. Corporate expansion thus engenders various complex interdependencies.

Developments in the international system have made unilateral military intervention in support of business interests politically costly. Furthermore, although home countries will occasionally assist their corporations abroad today, the interests of corporations and states no longer coincide so closely. For example, from the early 1960s international corporations of American origin have accelerated their direct investments overseas, leading to steep growth in sales and profits. Simultaneously the American balance-of-payments situation has deteriorated to the point at which there has been grave concern over the weakness of the dollar. This chronic American deficit has been aggravated by the direct flows of investment overseas. In addition, rather than exporting goods made in the United States, which would aid the American balance of payments, international corporations have increasingly preferred to produce overseas, in order to reduce costs. The interests of many international corporations have thus clashed with the American government's interest in halting the outflow of dollars. As direct investment grows, there is likely to be increasing conflict between the international planning of corporations and the national planning of states [13, p. 90].

The international corporation itself often possesses resources that permit it to influence even the largest nation-states either directly or indirectly through other governments. These resources include technical expertise, capital, and flexibility in their use. Indeed, as conflict between corporations and national units becomes more common, corporations will increasingly seek to develop resources that can be used to influence nation-states. As one economist has noted:

There is nothing unusual in the observation that conflicts confronting the multinational firm must be resolved through the use of power. . . . One can see no logical reason why power should not be just as normal and proper a basis for settling conflicts in the relationships of the multinational firm as in any other type of conflict. [8, p. 114]

The bargaining strength of an international corporation depends partly upon the nature of the business in which it engages and upon the way in which it is organized. A corporation involved in the extractive industries has fewer bargaining advantages than does a manufacturer, for it remains at least partly dependent upon the national actor with jurisdiction over the natural resource. Often it cannot move its operations or assets easily. The relationship between such corporations and underdeveloped countries in particular is beginning to shift. Alternative sources of raw materials like petroleum and copper are no longer easily found. Although the producing countries still may require foreign expertise to operate extractive industries efficiently, there are frequently alternate sources of such expertise—in other international corporations or in the Soviet Union or the People's Republic of China. The problems of the extractive industries in producing countries have been illustrated by negotiations between the Organization of Petroleum Exporting Countries (OPEC), which includes representatives of the world's leading oil-producing countries—Iran, Iraq, Indonesia, Saudi Arabia, and so on—and the "seven sisters" of the international petroleum business. In 1966 the seven companies had total gross sales of almost $40 billion, far exceeding the combined gross national product of the OPEC countries. Nevertheless, during negotiations in 1970, 1971, and 1972, OPEC was able to win substantial price concessions and contractual revisions in its favor. The states that the petroleum companies serve, particularly in Europe, can ill afford to have oil supplies cut off. Furthermore, with the demise of the colonial empires and the growing determination of underdeveloped countries to modernize themselves, international corporations have faced increasingly militant opposition. As the demand for certain natural resources continues to climb, producing countries will find themselves in still more favorable bargaining positions vis-à-vis international corporations. Finally, certain international organizations, like the International Coffee Organization, have been created to protect states producing primary products by stabilizing the prices paid for commodities.

International manufacturing corporations have considerably greater flexibility than do those in extractive industries. Personnel, capital, and production facilities can be moved elsewhere if a host country becomes either too demanding or too restrictive. This flexibility functions as an implicit threat in bargaining situations. Ford of England has announced that it will relocate in West Germany because of the disruptive practices of British labor unions; this possibility had been recognized by the British government for some time. Former Prime Minister Harold Wilson warned striking Ford workers of it some years ago. Having a viable alternative, Ford is not subject to the same difficulties as is a domestic British automobile producer.

Among the problems of the developed countries are those related to the balance of payments and the instability of the international monetary system. Many of these countries have sought to resolve these difficulties at the national level, though some efforts at multinational resolution have also been made. The international corporation is in an excellent position to bypass controls and thus to have

significant impact on both the domestic and international economic systems. There are almost 200 American corporations with large-scale foreign holdings. Almost one-quarter of their sales are outside the United States. They are able to transfer assets across national boundaries and thus to influence the balance of payments significantly. In the Ford example Great Britain will lose an important export industry, and its imports will rise as Fords manufactured in Germany are sold to the British. In addition, an international corporation can evade national anti-inflation policies by borrowing abroad. It can also avoid national controls by centralizing its bookkeeping outside the host country or by pricing intracorporate transfers among countries in such a way as to avoid taxes. The international corporation rarely has to threaten a national actor overtly. Merely by making the latter aware of its alternatives, the corporation can often achieve its purposes.[8]

In recent years international corporations, particularly those owned predominantly by Americans, have found themselves in an increasingly hostile international climate. They have therefore developed an international version of public relations, seeking to create a climate favorable to their activities. Public relations is essentially the propaganda arm of the corporation, comparable to the U.S. Information Agency; the corporation seeks to put the best possible face on its activities, altering opinions in ways favorable to the corporate image. As one veteran of these operations has noted, the job of public relations is "to smooth the way for a company's foreign operations" and "to help make . . . profits" [14].

Closely related to public relations is the attempt to form coalitions with interest groups in host countries. There is, in particular, an attempt to develop ties with members of the "third culture," individuals whose nationalism is tempered

---

[8] Louis T. Wells, Jr., has argued that many of these advantages accrue only to manufacturing firms organized by geographic area, rather than by product line [39, pp. 435–457].

by a positive orientation toward foreign investment [8, pp. 111–112]. These efforts occasionally yield substantial benefits to international corporations. For example, after the 1956 Suez crisis there was considerable hostility in the Middle East toward Western-controlled petroleum companies; pipeline facilities were sabotaged and even closed. The Trans-Arabian Pipeline (Tapline), however, continued to operate throughout this period because "for years prior to the crisis, Tapline management had worked out a modus vivendi with its local hosts, which included central and local government officials, journalists, local businessmen, and other key figures in society." This result "involved years of hard work at building up a local relationship which endured some very violent and trying times" [7]. When we consider that this pipeline runs through Saudi Arabia, Syria, Jordan, and Lebanon, it is clear that management had done a superb job in cementing ties.

Finally, corporations can exert influence on national units by forming alliances with other international corporations. For the most part, overt cooperation among corporations is minimal and limited to industrywide conferences or organizations like the International Chamber of Commerce. Like national units international corporations have been wary of delegating authority to larger organizations. In some industries, however, cartel arrangements have existed. The best known of these cartels is the international petroleum cartel that flourished at the beginning of the century. As recent negotiations with OPEC suggest, the "seven sisters" still coordinate their activities and cooperate in bargaining with alliances of nation-states. In general corporate alliances exhibit far more flexibility than do intergovernmental alliances in the current system.

THE DETERMINANTS OF CORPORATE POLICY

As we have suggested, the international corporation is more than an enterprise

with multinational assets. Its managers, like international civil servants, are characterized by a set of attitudes that distinguish them from other citizens of any particular nation-state. Specifically, the corporation's interests are placed on a level with or even above those of nation-states. Although certain corporations have manifested such attitudes since before World War II, it is only since 1945 that many have adopted them.

The development of these attitudes has been largely the result of significant shifts in the structure of the international system. Before the war, governments and corporations based on their territories tended to act in harmony much of the time, thus stimulating the Marxist interpretation of governments as the "enforcement agencies" of corporate policies. The era of "gunboat diplomacy" in China and Latin America, for example, reflected the congruence of corporate and national interests in the United States. Furthermore, other industrial nations, like Nazi Germany, Japan, and the European colonial powers, eagerly supported national enterprises with overseas interests. Under these conditions there was little necessity for corporations to develop "international" attitudes. Indeed there was little incentive to behave autonomously at the international level; domestic lobbying sufficed.

The situation was not altered notably in the years immediately after the war. The United States government encouraged direct investment in war-ravaged Europe as a means of promoting recovery. As a bipolar system emerged, American corporations involved in overseas activities found their interests closely allied with those of the American government. Both government and corporate leaders perceived the cold war as a clash between social and economic systems with profound implications for the international economic system as a whole. The concentration of resources in the United States immediately after the war also tended to make corporations more dependent upon the United States, for the Soviet bloc offered little possibility for alternative allies. Capitalism and Western democracy were perceived as natural allies in the struggle against Marxism-Leninism. The extension of corporate influence abroad was regarded by relevant elites in the United States as part of the overall struggle against the Soviet Union and its allies. To this day, even though corporate and government interests have begun to diverge, this view persists in many government circles. In 1965 Secretary of the Treasury H. H. Fowler called international corporations "those mighty engines of enlightened Western capitalism" [9, p. 3]. As long as cold-war attitudes predominated and a bipolar distribution of resources and attitudes characterized the international system, there was little opportunity or incentive for corporations to behave autonomously.

By the late 1950s, however, the interests of international corporations and of the United States government had begun increasingly to diverge. The completion of postwar recovery in Europe reduced the need for a dollar outflow to stimulate European economies. Although the United States began to view with reserve dictatorships vulnerable to communist infiltration, corporations found them receptive to foreign investment. During the tenure of President John F. Kennedy the American government began to grapple with the problem of underdeveloped countries with strong socialist inclinations. Finally, as the cold war declined in intensity, the dichotomy between capitalism and communism became less salient. In addition, the American balance-of-payments deficit became increasingly salient, and direct corporate investment abroad was clearly a major contributor to this deficit. Government intervention in the affairs of small states has become increasingly unrewarding, as recent American experience in the Dominican Republic and Vietnam has suggested. Consequently, American corporations can no longer count on the support of the American government, backed by the threat of military sanctions, in the event of conflict with other states.[9] The

disappearance of the tight bipolar structure and the emergence of new political divisions cutting across the cold war have thus left many international corporations to fend for themselves in the international system. Under these conditions international corporations are behaving with autonomy in international politics.

Changes in the international system, however, have afforded corporations only the *possibility* of developing as international actors. Some corporations have retreated from this prospect and have sought instead to balance the demands of the various countries in which they operate. One high-ranking corporate executive, for example, has argued that "U.S. companies abroad should conduct their operations in complete harmony with the political, economic, and social objectives of the host country" [19]. Nevertheless, there are indications that corporate attitudes are generally becoming more supportive of an international, or "stateless," orientation. The negotiations conducted between the international petroleum corporations and the members of OPEC in 1970 suggest the nature of these new attitudes. In describing the negotiations, Standard Oil of New Jersey has stated:

Faced with this alarming spiral of escalating demands (from OPEC), international petroleum companies recognized an urgent need for stability in arrangements for the production and sale of petroleum. The U.S. companies *advised* the U.S. government of the seriousness of the situation and then joined with other international companies to negotiate a settlement.[10]

This description reflects the fact that petroleum companies bargain for themselves and "advise" governments of their activities. Clearly, international corporations must take cognizance of the possible political consequences of their behavior [22].

---

[9] The Peruvian seizure of American fishing vessels, the various expropriations of American petroleum interests, and the Chilean expropriation of American copper companies lend weight to this hypothesis.

[10] Standard Oil Company (New Jersey), "Letter to Shareholders," *1970 Annual Report*, p. 3; the emphasis is added. For more on the petroleum corporations, see J. E. Hartshorn [12] and Robert Engler [6].

Perhaps the most persuasive indication of attitude changes comes from the corporations themselves. In 1962, Frederick Donner, Chairman of the Board of General Motors, declared:

It is the emergence of the modern industrial corporation as an institution that is transcending national boundaries. These great concerns of the Free World, both here and abroad, are no longer adequately described as Dutch, German, French, Italian, British or United States corporations. We may be approaching a stage where we will not think of them primarily in terms of a single country nor will we think of their benefits as flowing especially to any one country. In interests and ambitions, in investments, in employees, in customers, they are an international resource. [4, pp. 190–191; 33, p. 123]

Another view is that corporate attitudes, though they have changed and become more international, have not changed as much as the previous quotation suggests. Raymond Vernon has argued that the "relative weight of U.S.-based considerations has declined, even if the rank-order position of such considerations has not yet changed" [37, p. 382]. Vernon has claimed that, though corporate nationalism is declining, the home country remains the object of the greatest relative affection of the corporation. Corporate executives' difficulties in understanding foreign mores and their latent racism may inhibit the development of an international outlook. "An inflexible policy against entering any joint ventures," Richard Robinson has declared, "was always a veneer covering basic distrust by United States businessmen, and possible dislike, of non-Americans" [25].

In our discussion of foreign-policy behavior in Chapter 8, we discussed nation-states in terms of size, development, and accessibility. We suggested that these three variables appear to be related to the impact of certain conditioning factors on the actor's behavior. The variable clusters are individual, societal, governmental, role, and systemic. A similar framework for analysis is appropriate when investigating international corporations.

Policy making in the international corporation appears to be no more governed by models of economic rationality involving least-cost considerations than the nation-state is governed by the rational model of decision making, popular images to the contrary. Furthermore, the general goals of the corporation provide no better guide to its actions than do the general goals of national actors. As do large developed states, the international corporation tends to "muddle through," trying to balance the demands and needs of other actors, its own bureaucracies, foreign cultures, and shareholders.

Most international corporations are economically developed, with large bureaucracies and highly institutionalized role patterns. Furthermore, most are governed by elites that are not readily accountable to shareholders. There are few routine processes of leadership change; proxy fights resemble coups d'état, rather than orderly transitions. Although the size of most corporations cannot be measured in terms of territory, population, and the like, it can be measured in terms of the assets that they control. As we suggested earlier, many corporations can be considered relatively large in terms of sales.

The complex bureaucracies that constitute most of the great international corporations permit little scope for individual decision makers to have much impact on policy. Recruitment patterns and role norms encourage the growth of "techno-structure." The role of management is well defined and has a powerful effect on corporate policy. Even when executives are recruited from different countries their behavior seems motivated largely by a relatively homogeneous conception of role. Kindleberger has noted that even a multinational staff "is likely to be committed to the aggrandizement of the corporation, and of their own incomes and stock options" [16, p. 210]. The measure of "managerial skill" used to evaluate professional competence is determined by previous practices, as well as by the expectations of other bureaucrats and shareholders. Furthermore, most international corporations are still governed by white Western executives who bring similar conceptions of efficiency and skill to the job.[11] Role and governmental variables thus have greater impacts on corporate policy than do individual or idiosyncratic variables.

The technostructure operates largely unchecked by any constituency within the corporation. Shareholders are generally satisfied as long as they receive reasonable rates of return on their investments. Even when their opinions are sought, they are generally asked to choose between "yes" and "no," and most shareholders tend to abdicate their corporate responsibility by turning over proxies to management. Lower-grade employees are usually organized in labor unions and seldom concern themselves about corporate policy belond the immediate question of contract terms; they rarely demand participation in the decision-making process.[12] Societal factors are thus relatively unimportant in the determination of corporate policy. The decision-making process of the corporation resembles that of communist states: Bargaining and competition among elites largely determines policy outcomes. International corporations have tended to structure their organizational patterns to permit greater centralization of decision making and less freedom for local subsidiaries to make their own decisions. The corporate elite can therefore behave very flexibly in its relations with other actors, constrained only by the limitations typical of highly bureaucratic structures.

Along with other international actors, international corporations have developed the means by which to conduct diplomatic relations and to collect information. Indeed, international corporations seek to recruit personnel who have had experience in the U.S. Foreign Service [3, p. 140]. The International Business Machines Corporation, for instance, maintains a permanent staff in Washington, D.C., to deal directly with the representatives of foreign governments. Corporate spying is a well-established practice. For example, the president of Burlington Industries alluded in a symposium on Japanese industry to the existence of corporate spy systems on an international scale. He offered, perhaps somewhat facetiously, to rent Burlington's intelligence operations to other companies: "Well, Burlington's spy system may be a little bit more effective than somebody else's, and we would be glad to service anybody for a fee."[13] Clearly, knowledge about the behavior of other international actors is as crucial to decision making in the international corporation as is the development of bargaining and negotiation skills.

In addition, the international corporation must deal regularly and directly with local and unofficial groups in many states (Figure 11.1). Nongovernmental groups generally deal only indirectly with similar groups in other states or with foreign governments; that is, they operate through their own governments. The international corporation, however, is able to deal directly and effectively with groups in many nation-states. It must be prepared to deal with strikes, riots, boycotts, and other forms of behavior inimical to its interests but beyond the control of host governments to regulate. The Ford Motor Company had to be prepared to deal directly with British labor unions, which would not heed the pleas of their own government to moderate their demands. The international corporation faces a multitude of cultures, traditions, and societies in its daily operations.

The growth of the international corporation and the development of its capability to act autonomously threaten the sovereignty of some nation-states. Economic processes that have heavy impacts

---

[11] For instance, a study of the fifteen largest American-based international corporations has revealed that, whereas one-fifth of their employees were foreign, only 1.6 percent of their leading corporate managers were also foreign [30].

[12] For discussion of labor's response to the international corporation, see Robert W. Cox, "Labor and Transnational Relations," *International Organization*, 25 (Summer 1971), pp. 554–584.

[13] Ely Callaway, Jr., quoted in "Free Trade v. the New Protectionism," *Time*, 97 (May 10, 1971), p. 91.

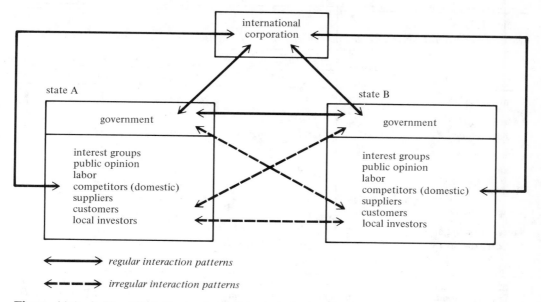

Figure 11.1. A Simplified Illustration of the Interaction Between the International Corporation and Nation States

on nation-states' abilities to reach their goals are increasingly beyond their control. For many years the threat to sovereignty was viewed by the leaders of the large industrial states as applicable only to small underdeveloped nations. The latters' intense nationalism was viewed as fundamentally defensive, part of an attempt to erect "vertical" barriers against the "horizontal" intrusions created by international economic enterprises. But more recently the largely inadequate attempts by major industrial states to cope with their own recurring liquidity crises suggest that the shoe is now on the other foot and beginning to pinch.

At best, it is difficult for national units to resist the growth of international corporations. Countries that seek to exclude direct foreign investment risk falling behind in economic growth and technological development and incurring the wrath of internal constituencies whose interests coincide with those of the corporations. On the other hand, unimpeded corporate investment may encourage evolution of instrumentalities that are only partly under the jurisdiction of the home country. Canada is a state whose sovereignty has been

partly limited through direct foreign investments (Table 11.4). Foreigners control more than one-third of the Canadian industries represented in the table and more than half the enterprises engaged in such crucial industries as resource extraction. The Canadian government has become increasingly concerned about the implicit threat to its control over vital sectors of the Canadian economy. Indeed, the presence of American investment in Canada is so pervasive that Premier Pierre Trudeau has commented: "Living next to you is in some ways like sleeping with an elephant. No matter how friendly or even tempered the beast ... one is affected by every twitch and grunt" [26]. The Canadian government cannot, however, afford to cut off foreign investment flows without a severe reduction in the Canadian standard of living. Its predicament illustrates the ways in which high interdependence acts as a structural constraint on national behavior. If national governments continue to grow weaker in relation to international corporations, "the model for the future may be the urban crisis, where strong national corporations confront weak city governments" [13, p. 90].

Table 11.4.

Nations Controlling Selected Canadian Industries (in percentages)

	End of 1959			End of 1963		
	Canada	*United States*	*Other*	*Canada*	*United States*	*Other*
Manufacturing	43	44	13	40	46	14
Petroleum and natural gas	27	67	6	26	62	12
Other mining and smelting	39	53	8	41	52	7
Railways	98	2	0	98	2	0
Other utilities	95	4	1	96	4	0
Merchandising and construction	91	6	3	88	7	5
Total	68	26	6	66	27	7

Source: Dominion Bureau of Statistics, *The Canadian Balance of International Payments 1963, 1964 and 1965 and International Investment Position*, reproduced from Sidney E. Rolfe and Walter Damm, eds., *The Multinational Corporation in the World Economy* (New York: Praeger, 1970), p. 92. Reprinted by permission. Published by Frederick A. Praeger for the Atlantic Institute, the Committee for Atlantic Economic Cooperation, and the Atlantic Council of the United States.

Nation-states have not so far created mechanisms for dealing with the growing strength of the international corporations. One possible approach would be cooperative efforts among states to control the activities of the corporations. But this approach would involve the surrender of some national sovereignty to an interstate organization, rather than to the corporations. As the influence currently available to individual states is rarely appropriate to the task of reestablishing governmental hegemony over international corporations, an obvious approach would be the merger of national states in larger political units [17]. This approach would also involve relinquishing the myth of sovereign independence.[14] "There is a stubborn life and

[14] Nongovernmental groups might be expected to develop mechanisms of their own to deal with international corporations on an international basis. Walter Reuther, the late president of the United Auto Workers (UAW), proposed in 1962 to organize automobile workers in fourteen countries, in order to bargain effectively on an international scale. But little has been done to implement this proposal. It is ironic that, instead of the growth of the international proletarian movement prophesied by Karl Marx and Lenin, it is capital that has become international, weakening the bargaining position of labor.

purpose in the system of nation states, and there is a tenacious capacity on the part of mankind indefinitely to disregard the seemingly inevitable . . . even when the apparent cost of the identity and control seems all out of proportion to its value . . ." [36].[15] If the domain and scope of the international corporation continue to expand, the sovereignty of nation-states will continue to erode.

CONCLUSION: TRENDS AND PROSPECTS

Direct investment and the expansion of the international corporation seem likely to continue at an accelerating rate, but the pattern of growth will be uneven, and the geographical distribution of investments will continue to shift. If the demand for raw materials continues to rise, the international corporation will operate in underdeveloped countries to a greater degree than it does at present. The decline in the rate of foreign investment by American-based corporations is not paralleled by

[15] For discussion of the problems of international integration, see Chapter 13.

the activities of corporations based in other countries. Japanese-based corporations in particular are moving aggressively toward obtaining larger shares of the international market.

Recently Servan-Schreiber has argued persuasively that American investment in Europe constitutes a serious threat to European independence [29]. He has called for mergers of European industries to resist this challenge, but his assumption that the "challenge" is primarily American is dubious. As we have suggested, the major corporations are becoming international, and their allegiance to the United States government cannot be assumed. Furthermore, direct investment by European-based corporations in the United States was equal to 40 percent of American direct investments in Europe in 1967 and growing at a faster rate than was the latter. The challenge is not American but international, and Servan-Schreiber's own prescription would serve only to augment the strength of the international corporation in relation to national units. As Stephen Hymer and Robert Rowthorn have argued, "the main result of the strategy of 'positive measures' to help large firms will be to change European business qualitatively towards multinationalism, rather than to raise the relative growth rates of European firms" [13, p. 83].

What, then, are the possible roles of the international corporation in the international system? Most obvious is that of contributor to the decline of national sovereignty. Also possible is that of political middleman among nation-states. As the international corporation has no strong ties with particular nation-states, it can behave as an "honest broker" among states.[16] It is even possible, though not likely, that the international corporation will facilitate the further integration of disparate communities in the world.

Although we cannot confidently predict which of these roles the international corporation will assume, there is no doubt

that it will continue to have important consequences for the international system as a whole. At the very least the corporation will encourage marked alterations in the international distribution of resources and attitudes. One major question is whether the result will be to promote international peace and stability or new forms of international conflict. In the nineteenth century, theorists like Auguste Comte considered the development of large corporations conducive to peace; Marx and Lenin, on the other hand, predicted that corporate growth and internationalization would promote imperialist wars leading to international class conflict. Similar divisions of opinion exist today. One economist has argued that "since the super-giant firms will be represented in all countries war will not be possible" [23, p. 8]. In the absence of firmly established norms and expectations for proper behavior of the international corporations, others foresee an even more anarchic international system than the present one. International corporations, they argue, will conduct trade wars for markets and supplies first in the underdeveloped areas and later throughout the world. In the absence of parallel governmental regulatory agencies international corporations will increasingly penetrate declining nation-states. [13, pp. 83–91].

---

[16] For the strongest presentation of this argument, see J. E. Hartshorn [12, especially chap. 23].

References

1. Ball, George W., "The Promise of the Multinational Corporation," *Fortune,* 75 (June 1, 1967), p. 80.
2. Barber, Arthur, "Emerging New Power: The World Corporation," *War-Peace Report,* 8 (October 1968), p. 7.
3. Berle, Adolf A., Jr., *The Twentieth Century Capitalist Revolution* (New York: Harcourt Brace Jovanovich, 1954).
4. Chamberlain, Neil W., *Enterprise and Environment* (New York: McGraw-Hill, 1968).
5. Dia Alejandro, Carlos F., "Direct Investment in Latin America," in Charles P. Kindleberger, ed., *The International Corporation* (Cambridge, Mass.: MIT Press, 1970), p. 320.

6. Engler, Robert, *The Politics of Oil* (Chicago: University of Chicago Press, 1961).

7. Farmer, Richard N., and Barry M. Richman, *International Business: An Operational Theory* (Homewood, Ill.: Irwin, 1966), p. 116.

8. Fayerweather, John, *International Business Management* (New York: McGraw-Hill, 1969).

9. Fowler, H. H., "National Interests and Multinational Business," *California Management Review* (Fall 1965).

10. Galbraith, John Kenneth, *The New Industrial State* (Boston: Houghton Mifflin, 1967), p. 171.

11. Galloway, Jonathan F., "Multinational Enterprises as Worldwide Interest Groups" (Paper delivered at the Sixty-Sixth Annual Meeting of the American Political Science Association, September 1970).

12. Hartshorn, J. E., *Politics and World Oil Economics*, rev. ed., (New York: Praeger, 1967).

13. Hymer, Stephen, and Robert Rowthorn, "Multinational Corporations and International Oligopoly: The Non-American Challenge," in Charles P. Kindleberger, ed., *The International Corporation* (Cambridge, Mass.: MIT Press, 1970).

14. Kean, Geoffrey, *The Public Relations Man Abroad* (New York: Praeger, 1968), p. 204.

15. Keohane, Robert O., and Joseph S. Nye, Jr., eds., "Transnational Relations and World Politics," *International Organization*, 25 (Summer 1971), pp. 329–349.

16. Kindleberger, Charles P., *American Business Abroad* (New Haven: Yale University Press, 1969).

17. Kindleberger, Charles P., *Power and Money* (New York: Basic Books, 1970), pp. 180–181.

18. Litvak, I. A., and C. J. Maule, "The Multinational Corporation: Some Perspectives," *Canadian Public Administration Quarterly*, 13 (Summer 1970), p. 130.

19. Model, Leo, "The Politics of Private Foreign Investment," *Foreign Affairs*, 45 (July 1967), p. 651.

20. Modelski, George, "The Promise of Geocentric Politics," *World Politics*, 22 (July 1970), p. 619.

21. Parry, J. H., *The Establishment of the European Hegemony: 1414–1715* (New York: Harper & Row, 1961), pp. 100–101.

22. Penrose, Edith, *The Large International Firm in the Developing Countries* (Cambridge, Mass.: MIT Press, 1968), p. 89.

23. Perlmutter, Howard V., "Super-Giant Firms in the Future," *Wharton Quarterly* (Winter 1968).

24. Perlmutter, Howard V., "The Tortuous Evolution of the Multinational Corporation," *Columbia Journal of World Business*, 4 (January–February 1969), p. 11.

25. Robinson, Richard D., *International Business Policy* (New York: Holt, Rinehart & Winston, 1964), p. 148.

26. Rolfe, Sydney E., and Walter Damm, eds., *The Multinational Corporation in the World Economy* (New York: Praeger, 1970), p. 30.

27. Rosenstein-Rodan, P. N., "Multinational Investment in the Framework of Latin American Integration," in *Multinational Investment in the Economic Development and Integration of Latin America* (Bogotá: Inter-American Development Bank, 1968), p. 87.

28. Samuels, Nathan, "American Business and International Investment Flows," *Department of State Bulletin* (January 12, 1970), p. 33.

29. Servan-Schreiber, J. J., *The American Challenge* (New York: Atheneum, 1968).

30. Simmons, Kenneth, "Multinational? Well, Not Quite," *Columbia Journal of World Business*, 1 (Fall 1966), p. 118.

31. Singer, J. David, "The Global System and Its Subsystems: A Developmental View," in James N. Rosenau, ed., *Linkage Politics* (New York: Free Press, 1969), p. 25.

32. Steiner, George, "Comparison of Principles and Practices of Multinational Corporate Planning," in George Steiner and Warren Cannon, eds., *Multinational Corporate Planning* (New York: Macmillan, 1966), p. 316.

33. Steiner, George, and Warren Cannon, eds., *Multinational Corporate Planning* (New York: Macmillan, 1966).

34. Strachey, John, *The End of Empire* (New York: Praeger, 1964), p. 23.

35. Sundelson, J. Wilner, "U.S. Automotive Investments Abroad," in Charles P.

Kindleberger, ed., *The International Corporation* (Cambridge, Mass.: MIT Press, 1970).

36. Vernon, Raymond, "Economic Sovereignty at Bay," *Foreign Affairs*, 47 (October 1968), pp. 120–122.

37. Vernon, Raymond, "Future of the Multinational Enterprise," in Charles P. Kindleberger, ed., *The International Corporation* (Cambridge, Mass.: MIT Press, 1970).

38. Vernon, Raymond, "The Role of U.S. Enterprises Abroad," *Daedalus*, 98 (Winter 1969), p. 129.

39. Wells, Louis T., Jr., "The Multinational Business Enterprise: What Kind of International Organization?" *International Organization*, 25 (Summer 1971).

Suggested Reading

Connery, Robert H., and Eldon L. Jones, eds., *Control or Fate in Economic Affairs* (New York: Academy of Political Science, 1971), pp. 30–33.

Cox, Robert W., ed., *International Organization: World Politics, Studies in Economic and Social Agencies* (London: Macmillan, 1969), especially part III.

Galloway, Jonathan F., "Worldwide Corporations and International Integration: The Case of INTELSAT," *International Organization*, 24 (Summer 1970), pp. 503–519.

Keohane, Robert O., and Joseph S. Nye, Jr., eds., "Transnational Relations and World Politics," *International Organization*, 25 (Summer 1971), pp. 329–349.

Kindleberger, Charles P., *American Business Abroad* (New Haven: Yale University Press, 1969).

Kindleberger, Charles P., ed., *The International Corporation* (Cambridge, Mass.: MIT Press, 1970).

Modelski, George, "The Promise of Geocentric Politics," *World Politics*, 22 (July 1970), pp. 617–635.

Penrose, Edith, *The Large International Firm in the Developing Countries* (Cambridge, Mass.: MIT Press, 1968).

Rolfe, Sidney E., and Walter Damm, eds., *The Multinational Corporation in the World Economy* (New York: Praeger, 1970).

Servan-Schreiber, J. J., *The American Challenge* (New York: Atheneum, 1968).

Chapter 12
CHANGE AND DEVELOPMENT IN THE INTERNATIONAL SYSTEM

If there is any similarity between the basic political structure of government in a new state and in our international system, then perhaps models developed in one might shed light on the other
—Fred W. Riggs [22]

Patterned relations among states and other actors depend upon procedures for regulating and coordinating behavior. Since the emergence of the modern nation-state the international system has made use of such regulating mechanisms as specialized foreign ministries, conferences, treaties, alliances, and legal conventions governing both peaceful relations and warfare. Despite considerable continuity, however, the properties of the system have changed. The rising importance of extranational actors, increased interdependence, and the cutting across vertical barriers of nationalism by horizontal ideologies like imperialism and communism have led to adjustments in the traditional pattern of decentralized politics among "sovereign equals." These changes have produced new pressures and problems that have helped establish new mechanisms, both formal and informal, for responding to the changing structure.

As the consequences of international politics have come to affect a wider range of activities and a larger portion of the world's population, these mechanisms have grown in scope and complexity. Part of this growth—notably the creation of major international organizations—has resulted from broadly felt needs generated during major wars or crises. Other changes —for example, the evolution of rapid communications and transportation networks across vast distances—have been slower and less dramatic. These changes have implications for the patterns of international politics, as relatively decentralized and anarchic conditions of the past centuries are eroded.

The stateless structure of a primitive political system may be tolerably stable, despite reliance on self-help; a similar structure in a complex system of international politics may well lead to chaos. Even in a primitive world, contact with a more "advanced" people has often meant rapid subjugation of a society lacking government institutions. It is all the more to be expected, therefore, that the present structure of the international system is essentially transitional and that considerable changes will occur in the next century [16].

POLITICAL DEVELOPMENT

To assess the probable effects of these changes, we draw upon the concept of political development. The study of political development first emerged as a major concern of social scientists after the breakup of large colonial empires and the emergence of more than fifty new states since World War II. We shall explore how ideas about political development, initially elaborated in a national context, may be applied to the international arena [21, 1, 25]. We hope, through examination of international politics in a developmental perspective, to focus on critical aspects of change and to describe how the *relative* development of the international political system may be conceived and measured.

The concept of development has a long and respectable history. Both Aristotle and Plato discussed characteristics of an ideal state and pondered conditions that might foster or sustain "developed" political systems. In one way or another nearly every major political theorist has addressed the question of how to realize a healthier political order.

Development, in the sense that we shall use it, is a *contextual,* rather than a universal, concept. A system is "developed" in relation to changing standards of performance among those who live within it. Some "primitive" societies might be considered developed because of their success in meeting the needs of their populations. Systemic development is not necessarily equivalent to modernization or administrative elaboration. Development in international politics is analogous to human growth, not in the sense that psychologists use the term meaning successful maturation to adulthood according to fairly static criteria, but in the evolutionary sense of adaptation by the human species as it has evolved from primitive forms of life.

Even in this sense development is both a normative and a "relative" concept. It implies movement from one situation to a preferable one. The preference of a more "developed" situation, however, is not based on some ultimate purpose toward which the political system moves; rather it is based on values and goals that are, it is to be hoped, widely shared. Although chroniclers of world events may agree that movement or change has occurred in a particular political situation, they may disagree about whether this change represents development or decay.[1] For example, the political system in Cuba changed markedly after Fidel Castro came to power in 1959. But was the change positive or negative? Clearly the answer depends largely upon whom we ask. Similarly, the international political system underwent profound changes between 1914 and 1918; the invention of nuclear weapons in the 1940s also brought important changes. These and other less dramatic alterations in the structure and process of international society have had consequences for development. We wish especially to evaluate those alterations that, singly or cumulatively, have significant political consequences.

The Greek philosopher Heraclitus once remarked that one cannot step in the same river twice; it flows constantly and is therefore never the same river. There is a sense in which the world too is always changing, and we never act in the same world more than once. Historian Stewart Bruchey has concluded:

To every event there belongs a temporal singularity, a contextual particularity, and it is because of this that all historical being possesses a quality of never quite the sameness. But it is equally true that the essence of a thing is not altogether its separateness. There is essential sharedness as well as essential singularity, and if this were not so, all experience [would be] a succession of differentiated particulars,

[1] For elaboration of concepts of political development, see Robert Packenham [18] and Lucian Pye [20]. For a critique of some theories of development and a discussion of development and decay, see Samuel P. Huntington [14, 13].

without meaning because nothing would be recognizable. [6, p. 10]

By comparing relatively similar historical systems and situations we can develop generalizations that will enable us to understand and possibly even to shape the flow of history. As Bruchey has claimed, "The method of comparison . . . makes it possible to conduct a causal inquiry affording a means of coping with what would otherwise be the nearly illimitable . . . ["anarchy of data"] [6, p. 13].

Political scientists, in examining the development of national political systems, judiciously select points in time and then try to assess whether the change from one time to another has been positive (development) or negative (decay). Similar analysis can be applied to the international political system. In what ways has the contemporary system changed from the 1950s, from the 1930s, from the nineteenth century? Should we evaluate these changes as development or decay? On what basis should we make such judgments?

We may begin by defining the international political system as more developed when its outputs have greater effects on the behavior of actors within it (system growth), when it is more difficult for any actor to change the patterns and procedures of the international system, and when the demands placed on the system by its various constituents are more successfully met. The international political system has grown as the number of actors, rate of transactions, and degree of interdependence have increased. Not all changes increase its capacity to fulfill these criteria, however, and we therefore cannot assume that change automatically means development. Change and development are related but distinct notions. Even when development has occurred, we cannot assume that every person has improved his lot or even that all people agree that the change has been for the better. For instance, the introduction of nuclear weapons has been hailed by some as making general war unthinkable. Such reasoning lay behind the statement by President Richard M. Nixon in 1971 that he expected no more wars. Others have viewed the expansion of destructive capability as frightening, reducing the control that outsiders can exert on those who possess such weapons and increasing the possible damage from international combat without reducing the willingness of actors to make war. If men disagree about whether a particular change is good or bad, how can we develop a set of criteria for evaluating change?

Consummatory Criteria

There is one set of criteria that we may call the "consummatory conditions of development," which, when satisfied, ensures that the physical and culturally acquired needs of men will be met. These criteria are *not* the factors that constitute system development; rather they reflect the intrinsically held values by which the developmental features of change are assessed. These consummatory criteria provide the final justifications for assessments of development and constitute the values of the global system. Various lists of values or goals can be used in examining changes in the situation of men throughout the world.[2] They may include improving the health and well-being of men, increasing their liberty, extending justice, and promoting men's sense of personal accomplishment and capacity to manage their environment.[3] In effect, this set of criteria accommodate the long-range or ultimate goals of men, which are sought by specific policies or system changes. Thus we speak of advances in medicine as improving the health and well-being of men. Medical advances themselves, however, are what we shall call instrumental changes whereas the consummatory criteria of health and well-being are concepts with which to measure the specific changes that have occurred.

[2] See Harold Lasswell and Abraham Kaplan [15] for a list of eight such values [19, 26].

[3] Cultural needs may change in time and place. The needs of a Roman citizen were greater than were those of feudal serfs in a later age but less than those of men in twentieth-century society.

Instrumental Criteria

The second type of criteria for assessing development is instrumental. Instrumental criteria of development are policies and changes that are believed to promote the fulfillment of consummatory criteria. Technological advances permitting increases in food production, per capita wealth, available energy, for example, are perceived as furthering consummatory goals. Similarly, industrialization, freedom of the press, and the increased availability of consumer goods are viewed as instrumental for attaining consummatory goals. Instrumental goals thus range from increasing the availability of material goods like food and shelter to furthering social and political beliefs like socialism or capitalism. In the latter category, for example, some political sociologists have suggested that the acquisition of a secular achievement orientation toward political activity is a mark of development. Yet these and other elements of modernity are valued not because of their intrinsic merit but because they promote scientific advancement or the selection of more talented individuals for important positions. But science and a merit system of selection are also not valued for themselves; rather it is believed that they will promote certain basic values like security and justice. In this context scientific advancement and merit selection are deemed instrumental to goals like peace. Such distinctions, however, do not take us very far. Reliance entirely on measures of achievement, for instance, in predicting the effectiveness of individuals recruited for political posts may be misleading, for occasionally recruitment by ascription can prove more effective. A head of state may be better served by someone whom he knows and trusts than by an adviser with a superior professional record. President John F. Kennedy selected Robert F. Kennedy for attorney general because he wanted in the position someone of whose loyalty and trust he had no doubt.

Instrumental criteria for evaluating whether or not change is developmental should thus focus on the effective consequences of change. Democratic control of leadership is a goal of many actors, but it is not developmental in all contexts. If it were incongruent with patterns of decision making in schools, families, and work situations, it might serve to increase instability and decrease development. To call for elections in South Vietnam, a country to which such a practice is alien, is probably ill conceived[4] because such elections would probably promote greater instability and chaos, making it still more difficult for the South Vietnamese to realize consummatory ends such as peace and happiness.

It is through positive furthering of consummatory ends that instrumental changes can be assessed. Instead of describing any particular form of developed international system, we shall emphasize interaction between the system and environmental pressures in order to establish what policies and changes lead to development. We shall thus call the international political system "developed" when it satisfies the demands made upon it by its component actors. Although some "needs" for which the international system is responsible are subject to dispute, few people would argue that preventing a nuclear Armageddon and avoiding mass death from pollution are important tasks facing international society today. There have been increasing demands for solution to these problems, yet solutions do not depend upon single actors (see Part IV).

In contemporary international politics instrumental development is indicated by increases in the stability of commercial life and reduced physical or psychological threats of foreign invasion. In current conditions such changes would appear to promote the prospects for human survival and well-being.

THREE DIMENSIONS OF DEVELOPMENT

Development has at least three principal dimensions: institutionalization, scope and

[4] For discussion of the importance of congruence, see Harry A. Eckstein [9, 10].

domain, and balance. The first two are essentially instrumental; the third incorporates both consummatory and instrumental criteria. The international system develops when an increase in one or more of these dimensions is not offset by a comparable decline in another.

Institutionalization

Institutionalization is the establishment of dependable and enduring patterns of activity; it occurs when structural relationships in the international system are complementary, reinforcing conformity to established patterns among actors. In an institutionalized system actors share expectations about the ways in which they ought to behave toward one another; behavior is thus largely predictable. Procedures for handling international transactions are so well established that violations are more costly than beneficial to actors. Institutionalization thus involves the creation and maintenance of customs and norms accepted by most actors as "right."

The role behavior of international civil servants, whether in Interpol or the United Nations, is widely accepted and emulated by others in national and international agencies whose positions require them to interact with or to at least pay attention to these civil servants. These other individuals, whose judgments constitute part of the rewards or punishments for role occupants, are "role alters" [2]. International organizations like the United Nations are institutionalized in the international political system to the extent that there is wide agreement on what can and cannot be done by spokesmen like the secretary-general. When actors behave consistently with consensual expectations of alters, institutionalization is reinforced. We can also seek to discover national "role" behavior; the actions expected of individuals in official positions define a collective "role" for a nation-state or transnational organization. K. J. Holsti has discussed how both systemic and national factors shape norms to provide "roles" for nation-states [11]. Figure 12.1 depicts the flows of attitudes and influence that define such a role for international actors. Expectations for a set of officeholders, whether leaders of a government, of a business, or of an international organization, may constitute a fairly coherent

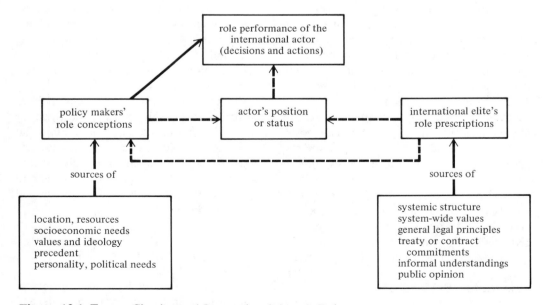

Figure 12.1 Factors Shaping and International Actor's Role
Source: Adapted from K. J. Holsti, "National Role Conceptions in the Study of Foreign Policy," *International Studies Quarterly,* 14 (September 1970), p. 245.

set of role norms for the collective actor. Holsti has said:

Typical national role conceptions would be *regional defender,* with the function of protecting other states in a defined area, or *mediator,* with the continuing function of assisting in international conflict resolution. National role conceptions are, in short, an important aspect of the total intellectual setting in which day-to-day decisions on foreign policy are made. [11, p. 246]

Constraints on the range of actions that a member of the international elite can undertake are imposed through definition of roles and careful recruitment and socialization of individuals into these roles. Such practices ensure some continuity and prohibit radical departures from behavior practiced by previous incumbents. The previous roles and experiences of an individual also shape his disposition to act and serve as barriers against deviation in high positions; they thus constitute the "backward links" of role occupants. "Forward links" also constrain individuals by encouraging anticipation of the requirements of future situations and conformity to expectations associated with desired future roles, usually to be attained through promotion.

In nearly all organizations there are established criteria of "success" that control patterns of recruitment and advancement. It is important to understand how Presidents Kennedy and Nixon, Prime Minister Edward Heath, President Charles de Gaulle, and Party Secretary Leonid Brezhnev have been limited in their authority to sponsor activities. As their positions are at the pinnacle of the international hierarchy, the individuals who occupy them are chosen partly because of their acceptability to various validating agencies and critically placed observers. An individual may find himself faced during his career with various demands to which he wishes to respond in one manner, but to which he feels that he must respond in another because his behavior will affect his subsequent recruitment for more coveted positions. Elected political leaders usually weigh heavily the calcu-

lated impacts of decisions on the probabilities of their reelection.[5] Anticipatory responses relevant to potential roles thus link a succession of roles that an individual occupies during his career. These role linkages tend to tie individuals to standard, or "conventional," procedures. Comparable career patterns within national bureaucracies and international corporations also tie individual leaders to their past experiences and to roles that they anticipate filling.

There is another way in which forward and backward role linkages tend to stabilize the international political system. Individuals occupying elite positions find their roles linked to *other* roles. Each shares some portion of another's *clientele,* that is, the groups within competing subsystems that observe role performances and demand satisfactions from them. The President of the United States, for example, has backward linkages with the principal groups that promoted his election, including key urban and rural leaders and important members of the labor and business community. The presidential role is also linked externally to major foreign leaders in the international system; their behavior is important in his efforts to fulfill his role obligations.

The individual has to anticipate his obligations both to subnational and to international observers who provide the sanctions for his behavior. As a result, his judgments are limited and shaped by his information about their expectations, demands, and identifications. He may choose to ignore the expectations of others, but he can also shorten his tenure in office by this means. Forward and backward role linkages thus constrain an individual's actions by fostering anticipatory responses and "selecting" certain kinds of prior socialization. The linkages among particular roles in the international political system constrain these roles, lim-

---

[5] Such considerations may have been among the most important factors inhibiting Prime Minister Harold Wilson from acting forcibly in 1965, when Rhodesia defied Great Britain and declared its independence.

iting the degrees to which initiative and novel behavior will occur.

In Chapter 7 we described how role variables affect behavior. There we considered roles principally as defined from *within* a particular international actor. We shall now emphasize the extent to which the normative expectations of external elites shape the actor's role behavior. These effects are more readily visible among individual leaders of relatively dependent actors like the states of eastern Europe. Walter Ulbricht, leader of the Communist Party in East Germany for more than twenty years, consistently responded to the expectations and demands of leaders in the Soviet Union. Figure 12.1 illustrates how perceptions of other actors can influence role expectations and behavior.

The dynamics of this process are revealed in analysis of the emergence of norms for critical individual roles. Let us consider the United Nations Congo operation in 1960 and the behavior of Secretary-General Dag Hammarskjöld. When disorder and political disunity erupted in the Republic of the Congo (Zaire) shortly after it received its independence, the Congolese government requested United Nations assistance. Because there were no precedents for this, expectations of the United Nations' response were neither widely shared nor deeply anchored in the opinions of the international elite. Initially, support for United Nations intervention, particularly among major powers that feared a cold-war battleground in mid-Africa, was strong and resulted in a massive commitment of troops and technical personnel. Once the United Nations had assumed responsibility for maintaining public order and had begun to assist in the training of Zairian nationals for important posts in the technical infrastructure of the country, however, it also found itself deeply involved in Zaire's domestic politics.

Partly through initiatives of the Secretary-General, the United Nations was forced into domestic controversies. It did not assist Prime Minister Patrice Lu-

mumba in his quarrel with President Joseph Kasavubu. The Soviet Union, which had hoped to gain influence in the country through friendly relations with the "progressive" Lumumba, therefore withdrew political and financial support from the United Nations' Congo operation. The United Nations also intervened to help suppress a secession led by Moise Tshombe in the copper-rich Katanga region in then southeastern Congo. This move earned it the enmity of France and Belgium, which had financial interests in this region and regarded Tshombe as a moderate with whom Europeans could deal. France, like the Soviet Union, subsequently refused to support the United Nations operations. By 1963 the organization was facing a severe financial crisis and was forced to withdraw its military and many of its technical personnel from the Congo. Because Hammarskjöld had not acted in a manner that it had predicted or approved, the Soviet Union proposed a change in the institutional structure of the United Nations, in order to divide the secretary-general's responsibilities among a three-man team, or "troika."[6] Hammarskjöld's death in an airplane crash near the Zambian border; the caution of his successor, U Thant; and the opposition of "third world" states to paralysis of the United Nations' highest post caused abandonment of these efforts to weaken the organization of the United Nations executive.

Expectations about the limited scope of United Nations autonomy and initiative in managing conflicts have become more widely shared since the Congo episode, thus increasing the institutionalization of a set of narrower operating procedures for the United Nations and its secretary-general. To some extent, the "lessons" of the Congo have increased the range of shared expectations among international

[6] "Troika" is the Russian term for a team of three horses harnessed together to pull a sled or carriage. The Soviet proposal called for three men, one each from the West, the East, and the "third world," to make decisions jointly; unless all agreed to an action, the troika would not be able to move.

elites for a limited role for the United Nations and its personnel and have fostered a deeper anchoring of these expectations.

Steady rates of change in the forces shaping role expectations; the increased weight of external or systemic forces shaping policy formation; greater consensus about and congruence among actors' roles; and stronger, more entrenched attitudes and beliefs among international elites can all promote institutionalization. Not all changes in or persistence among these variables will do so, however.[7]

Institutionalization is instrumental in furthering intrinsic ends for several reasons. Stable and dependable roles ensure trade and exchange of physical necessities and make demands for abstinence from violence more credible. They are more a necessary than a sufficient condition of development, however. Random or idiosyncratic factors like a drunken or berserk missile commander are less likely to have large and disturbing effects on the system. Institutionalization does not guarantee that a system *will* cope better with people's needs—only that it *can*.

Scope and Domain

The scope and domain of a political system describe the kinds of activities and the number of individuals or territories over which it has influence. The lives of a Kentucky farmer or of a Madras factory worker tend to be only marginally affected by events in the international political system, short of war or a major catastrophe. Such people therefore probably devote little attention to international affairs.

When Christ was living, several international political systems existed in nearly total isolation from one another. The Roman Empire maintained nominal control over the interstate relations of its

various colonies and tutelary states along the shores of the Mediterranean sea and extending into Europe. In India a delicate balance of power was maintained among a shifting coalition of states. Farther east Chinese scholarship, commerce, and culture had spread beyond the central Mandarin kingdom to function as a framework for international politics among its neighbors and its occasionally unruly subordinate units. Other isolated systems existed among various Indian nations on the American continents. Each of these international systems was clearly smaller in domain than is our contemporary global system. Each operated independently of the others and encompassed only limited territory and numbers of people.

The scope of human affairs also varied among these systems. The Roman Empire was more centralized; it controlled a broader range of behavior than did the other systems at that time and, in many respects, more than the contemporary international political system does.

Our present global system had its origins in the European state system of the seventeenth century after the conclusion of the worst of Europe's religious wars. This system increased its domain by reaching out to embrace the rest of the world. At the same time its increased domain undermined the control over individuals among local political systems in Africa, America, and Asia. At the beginning of the nineteenth century the major events of European politics, like the Napoleonic wars and the Congress of Vienna, touched the lives of millions of people in Asia and Africa barely, if at all, and only indirectly affected the former or soon-to-be liberated colonies of the Americas. A hundred years later large-scale warfare broke out again on the European continent. The interdependence of the developing global system soon involved, directly or indirectly, all the major nations and many of the peripheral regions of the world. Twenty-five years later World War II made it virtually impossible for any human being of the "civilized" world to escape the effects of

[7] For instance, if incongruent role expectations were held with greater conviction, role occupants would experience increased stress and institutionalization would decline. Various possibilities, which need not be elaborated here, are discussed in Raymond F. Hopkins, *Political Roles in a New State* (New Haven: Yale University Press, 1971), chap. 2.

war. National budgets and wide ranges of human activity were affected by the millions killed and by perhaps a billion who had changed their occupations in some way.[8] In the Soviet Union alone over 20 million were killed.

Scope and domain raise an important analytical question. Does increasing interdependence within the system necessarily mean that it has greater scope and domain, or is it necessary only for the system's subsystems—nation-states, international enterprises, and so on—to have increased their scopes and domains?[9] This question can be answered only when the distinction between the system and its components is operationally sound, but that distinction is difficult to make. When the lives and well-being of individuals around the globe have become increasingly dependent upon decision makers outside their immediate political communities, then the scope and domain of the international political system can be said to have increased. The international political system no longer encompasses only the elite layers of member societies and groups; at least in connection with major issues, it has an impact on the daily routines and individual rewards of the masses.

Decision making in the contemporary global system remains largely decentralized. Policies are made and resources are most often committed as if actors were playing poker, rather than in an orchestra concert. When systemic outcomes affect a greater range of activity and a wider domain of people, then the system has grown, regardless of whether these systemic outcomes are determined discretely by autonomous subsystemic actors or by a central body of decision makers.[10]

Decentralization occurs in geographical areas with high levels of internal transactions among actors—as in the subsystems of Asia, Africa, and so forth [3, 5, 28, 4]—and in functional systems that cross state boundaries. The following list, adapted from the work of Huntington, suggests some of the functional components in the international political system:

1. Political culture, that is, values, attitudes, orientations, myths, and beliefs relevant to politics.
2. Formal organizations: bodies like governments and intergovernmental organizations that make authoritive decisions through their respective executive, legislative, and other components.
3. Social and economic groups, both formal and informal, that make demands on such political structures as international corporations and the Roman Catholic Church.
4. Leadership: those individuals in political institutions and groups who exercise personal influence.
5. Policies: conscious allocation of resources to affect the distribution of benefits and penalties within international society.

Changes in the scope and domain of the system might be investigated through changes in these components. The relationship between the growth of transnational groups and institutional evolution could be studied, as could the effects on international relations of policy and leadership changes: for example, the effects of the detente between communist and noncommunist states in the 1970s or of the fall of "third world" leaders like Nkrumah and Sukarno. The starting assumption would be that although components are always changing, the rate, breadth, and direction of such change vary [13].

Balance

Balance is the ratio between the loads or demands placed upon the system and its

[8] For a discussion of the impacts of World War II on the fabric of American society, read Andrew Hacker, *The End of the American Era* (New York: Atheneum, 1970). Hacker has argued that the impacts of inflation, army life, and social displacement on millions of American working-class youth have altered the dominant values of American society.

[9] Oran R. Young [27] has raised a similar question in comparing the relation to the global system of regional subsystems in Europe and Asia; interests and efforts at influence in the global system may either reinforce or conflict with one another.

[10] This conclusion also raises several normative questions, which we shall discuss in Part IV. That a system has greater effects does not mean that it has better effects.

capacity to handle them. Theorists of national political development have discussed the concept of balance as the critical ratio between two specific complex processes: mobilization (or participation) and institutional strength or capacity [8, 14].[11] On one hand, changes in the objectives of individuals and groups, brought about either by shifts in tastes or values or by the failure of systems previously relied upon to satisfy these objectives, can lead to changes in the strength and content of constituents' demands on the international system. On the other, the capacity of the system can change as individual and collective actors become more highly mobilized and organized in collectivities, more affected by "world culture" and modern technology, and more affluent. The ability of bureaucratic standard operating procedures and of ad hoc arrangements to respond to demands is an important element in institutional capacity, which, essentially, is the potential influence of the system itself. In this dimension the instrumental and consummatory criteria of development are merged through the concept of system loads, which represent the valued ends of actors.

Loads and Capacity. At times loads on a system decrease, as when weak states grow stronger and more self-reliant. Then their demands for resources and attention and their tendency to defy international conventions decrease. As the states of the "third world" achieve their goals of economic development and political autonomy, their demands for special economic and political arrangements, expressed through the United Nations and other organs, may decline. As nationalism increases and the ratio of trade to the total national economy declines, such a state may turn inward, seeking to develop economically through its own efforts and to become less dependent upon the aid and trade policies of wealthy states.

[11] Huntington has concentrated on the balance between participation and institutionalization (in a broader sense than the one adopted here).

A decline in aspirations, in organizations, or in international routines on which demands can be focused will also lower demands themselves. Such change can be engineered by national leaders. Such a general decline may be reflected in an upsurge of reliance on policies of self-help. For example, the Kellogg-Briand Pact of 1928 reflected widely held expectations that the international system could respond to threats to peace in routine ways. World War II shook confidence in such legalistic undertakings, however. After the war demands for institutional peacekeeping arrangements encouraged establishment of the United Nations. By the 1970s these demands on the United Nations had declined, as major problems like arms control, the Vietnam War, and the Middle East conflicts were managed through ad hoc talks among the principals.

The capacity of the international political system also varies with time (see Figure 12.2). Capacity depends upon the resources available for implementing international decisions by actors in common situations or by collective bodies like the United Nations. In 1938 the system lacked the capacity to respond effectively to the ultimatums of Adolf Hitler. This weakness was reflected in the limited resources allocated to restraining Germany and in the timidity of key national leaders. Germany, under Hitler's leadership, greatly increased the loads upon the system, outstripping its capacity to maintain peace.

Technological Change and Capacity. It is easy perhaps to visualize how technological changes have led to increased loads on the international system. Increased and more rapid travel have heightened the possibility that mass epidemics may sweep the globe. There has been a greater demand by local public-health officials for more, and more widely enforceable, regulations relevant to the health and immunization of international travelers. Since 1947 the budget of the World Health Organization (WHO) has grown at an average of nearly 9 percent a year, lending it major influence in questions of

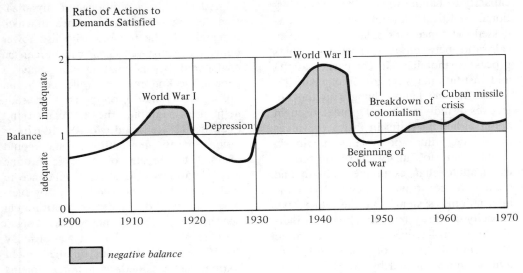

Figure 12.2. Approximate System Capability over Time, 1900–1970

international health care. The rapidity with which wars can erupt and run their courses has produced a need for more, and more regular, channels of communication among potential enemies and, indeed, even for duplicate and emergency channels of communication. Such networks expand the capacity of the international system to transmit messages among critical decision makers rapidly and accurately.

Coping Mechanisms. When the ratio of load to capacity increases, coping mechanisms, the means by which individuals and organizations try to adjust load to capacity, are taxed. Procedures like negotiations, United Nations debate, and war are examples of such mechanisms. Before World War I informal diplomacy supported by an ideological homogeneity among royalty and the diplomats and by reliance on an established code of diplomatic conduct were the principal coping mechanisms of the system. After the war the League of Nations was established as a formal coping mechanism for dealing with international conflicts. The League became institutionalized, with a set of operating procedures, rules for conduct, and modes of debate, all of which proved inadequate when Japan invaded Man-

churia, Italy attacked Ethiopia, and Germany marched into the Sudetenland. The subsequent German invasion of Poland and the Japanese attack on Pearl Harbor were never seriously debated by the League. Although expectations about the League's limitations were widely shared in the 1930s, a few desperate statesmen like Haile Selassie of Ethiopia tried unsuccessfully to make the organization live up to the ideal of collective security.

When loads on the system are increased by shifts in demands or by technological change that creates interdependencies beyond what coping mechanisms can handle, there is imbalance between system performance and environmental pressures. In periods during which demands exceed capacity the system is likely to be characterized by acute international crises. Political decay takes place, and the system is less able to respond to variations in demands without changing any of the relatively fixed aspects of the system, that is, any of its parameters; such change may involve the demise of a significant national actor, an accepted code of conduct, or an international structure like the League of Nations. Recognition of such changes, especially those calling for responsive adjustments, is, however, extremely difficult in any system that is at least partially institutionalized.

There are many forces promoting inertia or maintenance of the status quo. The expectations of political elites determine the types of responses to which they are most prone. Individuals establish the procedures, organizations, and patterns of behavior that constitute the international political system. It is their efforts to gain conflicting objectives and to obey internal bureaucratic rules, as well as their likely responses to various contingencies, that constitute the systemic repertoire of coping mechanisms. In effect these mechanisms are discrete sets of actions by which the international system is likely to respond to disturbing events or situations. These mechanisms usually reflect the shared goals for preservation of some elements of the existing order, but they can also reflect actors' objectives to change the international system in order to satisfy the demands of their populations.

Institutionalization is related to balance. Coping mechanisms that become standardized and deeply rooted in the expectations of principal members of the system are difficult to change even when they are no longer adequate to the problems that confront actors. Individuals and groups seek to deal with problems arising either from basic needs or from more complex learned motivations. The pattern of behavior that is successful in solving one problem may then be adopted for general use on apparently similar future problems. Positive feedback increases the likelihood that such behavior will be resorted to repeatedly. The institutionalization of this pattern of behavior means that it becomes embedded in individuals' personalities and memories or in organizational codes, perhaps retarding the search for new coping mechanisms. The earlier successful behavior pattern will be "selectively recalled" (see Figure 8.1). If the pattern is inappropriate to subsequent situations, the difficulty of maintaining the balance between loads and capacity may increase. In this sense, the system can become "overinstitutionalized"—unable to respond to rapid changes in its environment.

A spiral of demands and loads may result. A well-known quip among critics of the military is that generals always plan to fight the last war. France prepared for World War II by constructing the Maginot Line, a massive concrete fortification to halt an invasion of the type experienced in 1914. Although it would perhaps have been superior to the trenches actually used in World War I, the Maginot Line was simply outflanked by the Germans in 1940. Political leaders also tend to alter their expectations and to devise operating procedures in order to solve problems that generated the *last* disaster. The League of Nations was designed to stop World War I. Its organization and charter reflected a number of misconceptions and animosities that had arisen during that war. Similarly, the United Nations was designed to forestall the rise of another Hitler and of another revanchist imperialist state. But the limited war in Korea and the protracted guerrilla conflicts in Southeast Asia have exposed the weaknesses of this coping mechanism in resolving current controversies. Indeed, the Vietnam War and the 1968 Soviet invasion of Czechoslovakia suggest that the United Nations arrangements are largely irrelevant to "liberation" movements against which the great powers intervene.

When relatively uncontroversial and widely shared needs, like those related to health or regulation of international mail, are involved, agencies for coping have not only been established but have also adapted and survived. The Universal Postal Union (UPU) and the World Health Organization have been successful in solving the particular international problems for which they were designed. Both these organizations are institutionalized, but the changes in demands have been so great that the organizations have had to grow to maintain the balance between load and capacity.[12]

[12] WHO has, however, largely avoided dealing with controversial health problems like birth control.

LEGITIMACY: BAROMETER AND RESOURCE

Legitimacy is a critical resource of a developed system. When people accept a political structure as "right and proper," they endow its leaders and their roles with the authority to make decisions that will be complied with by members.

In international politics there is no single coherent political structure or government. The system's legitimacy therefore depends upon the acceptance of the actions of important leaders by politically relevant strata around the globe. Although these leaders may act legitimately according to the norms of their organizations (nation-states or corporations), their behavior may not be legitimate in the international system. For instance, it may be legitimate for the president of the United States, in his role as commander in chief, to send troops to the Dominican Republic but illegitimate in the eyes of most of the international community, including some of the United States' allies and neighbors. It may similarly be appropriate for executives of an international corporation to invest solely on the basis of profit maximization, but the legitimacy of their international operations may be undermined by such a criterion, especially among leaders in socialist states. Stockholders may applaud them, but many international political leaders, especially those in poor states, may not.

The consistent failure of the international system to solve perceived problems or to satisfy perceived needs may result in withdrawal of legitimacy from the "authorities." Although we more frequently think of actions that overstep legal or moral bounds as illegitimate, legitimacy may also be undermined by simple failure to perform expected or demanded behavior. There is thus a connection between legitimacy and balance; if the rate of change and the capacity to cope with it are in imbalance, legitimacy will decline. The moral rejection of "power politics" after World War I, exemplified in the ideas of Woodrow Wilson, illustrates such withdrawal of legitimacy from political practices that have failed to meet the demands placed upon them. Legitimacy, though a resource of the system, is actually dependent upon the attitudes of those individuals who are influential in the components of the system.

Peter Merkl has noted how German trust in international institutions has varied as apparent threats from the Soviet Union and allied support for German goals have been altered by events:

The dramatic impact of the construction of the Berlin Wall in 1961, and perhaps also the impression of headless confusion of the Western reaction to it, hit the West German population quite unprepared, giving them a sudden sense of insecurity, of being helpless, and of their lives being directly threatened. It produced a regression to residual, older attitudes of dependence on leaders and powerful protectors, even old-fashioned German nationalism. . . . The acute fear of war and desire for peace rose sharply in reaction to the upset of the status quo. [17]

The trusting or fearful attitudes of a nation's public toward various foreign states and alliances are an important variable in the interpretation of events and of the responses to them.

There are various tests of legitimacy within the international system. Karl W. Deutsch has suggested that whether or not individuals and organizational actors exhibit guilt over violating international norms or laws is one such test. When guilt feelings are intense, individuals modify their behavior; they may also refuse in advance to violate norms that engender such feelings. The strength of such norms exemplifies "legitimate influence." During the Cuban missile crisis, for example, President Kennedy and his advisers were sufficiently concerned about the propriety of their actions to ask the State Department to draw up legal arguments justifying the decisions that had already been made. Although Kennedy may have felt no guilt over his decisions, his actions, and the inhibitions about a sneak bombing raid expressed by his brother, indicate sensitivity to norms of conduct.

Another test of legitimacy is whether or not compliance with an international decision occurs without the threat or use of coercion. As no single actor or group of actors is generally accorded by all others the right to make all decisions, coercion is frequently necessary if decisions are to be carried out. But, the more legitimate an action, the less likely it is that coercion or threats will be necessary.

A third test is whether or not people trust the decision maker to do what they think it should. When general distrust of some international unit develops, stories, cartoons, and crude popular jokes will reflect this distrust and disrespect.[13]

The legitimacy of the international system is a barometer indicating whether the immediate future will be stormy or tranquil. When the legitimacy of individuals who exercise the most influence in the international system is called into serious question, the system may not be responding adequately to the demands placed upon it. A crisis may be imminent. An increase in legitimacy may spur the growth of capacity to match or exceed demands, so that future challenges can be met more easily. Legitimacy not only reflects satisfaction with the roles and structure of the international political system, but also provides a resource that can be helpful in expanding capacity.

Changes in legitimacy are likely to occur before other, more drastic, changes. When there is widespread trust that international authorities will do the right thing, their behavior will be viewed as appropriate or legitimate. Legitimacy plays a role similar to that of "confidence" in economic life. Loss of confidence in international economic decisions can lead to dramatic moves and countermoves by

actors attempting to defend themselves against expected harmful and illegitimate decisions by other, relatively autonomous economic actors. In international finance speculation against a national currency is often encouraged by loss of confidence in that country's economy. Changes in confidence usually precede changes in support for one or more major currencies. Similarly, in international politics a decline in legitimacy may precede an escalation of conflict as important leaders and attentive publics lose confidence that the leaders of other units will continue to act in "right" ways.

After 1946, when American leaders no longer trusted Soviet leaders to behave properly in international affairs, they raised doubts about the legitimacy of Soviet leadership in the authority structure of the international community. A distinction between the basically good Russian people and the bad Soviet leadership was frequently invoked; this kind of distinction is common when states are in severe conflict over goals. Americans changed their expectations of what Soviet leaders would do. To them it seemed less probable that these leaders would perform as American leaders considered appropriate to ensure world peace. With increasing mutual suspicion among the superpowers, the legitimacy of the entire system declined. Americans and Russians turned to self-reliance, building massive national systems of defense and initiating the most dramatic and prolonged arms race in history.

Legitimacy in the international system differs from legitimacy accorded to "rulers" within national political systems in that it is much more diffuse; the trust accorded to decision-making bodies outside those identified with one's own interests tends to be highly circumscribed. International legitimacy is also related to institutionalization, for it too is derived from the structure of attitudes bearing on international politics. We have already noted that the international system is more institutionalized when there is broad consensus on what various actors are ex-

[13] In eastern Europe, especially Czechoslovakia, jokes indicate disrespect for the Soviet Union—and expectations that Russian agents will do what they should not. Here is an example that was current in 1969:
PRAGUE CITIZEN: "Help! Help! A Swiss soldier has just stolen my Russian watch."
POLICEMAN: "Excuse me, you must mean a Russian soldier has just stolen your Swiss watch."
CITIZEN: "You said that, I didn't."

pected to do.[14] Consensus on expectations engenders a set of norms that are clear and likely to be deeply rooted. These norms in turn shape the behavior of system members. Legitimacy exists when there is structural agreement, or "fit," between what people *expect* authorities to do and what they think such authorities *should* do. Just as we expect antisocial behavior from a gangster, we expect illegitimate behavior from individuals or organizations that we distrust. Indeed, it sometimes happens that once we have learned to expect improper behavior from another actor, all his behavior is automatically assumed to be improper and against the best interests of the world community [12].[15]

Legitimacy is also related in somewhat complex ways to the balance between loads and capacity. When it is high the decisions of influential actors are likely to evoke compliance. When legitimacy is accorded to individuals or organizations that control material resources, their capacity to exercise influence is expanded. Increased legitimacy for international authorities thus characterizes increased development, for greater capacity is available to balance loads. Legitimacy is important in ensuring that decisions by recognized international authorities will be accepted without coercion. It thus enhances the effectiveness of existing coping mechanisms.

WAR AND SYSTEM DEVELOPMENT

Conflict, even the use of force, does not necessarily indicate the absence of devel-

---

[14] The institutionalization process continues as attitudes change; legitimacy is not an end in itself.

[15] In response to reporters' questions about Soviet troop reductions in 1956, Secretary of State John Foster Dulles stated that the move would not reduce world tensions. Asked if he would prefer that the Soviet Union keep these men in the armed forces, he replied, "Well it's a fair conclusion that I would rather have them standing around doing guard duty than making atomic bombs" [12, p. 249]. Dulles was interpreting new information to fit his model of Soviet intentions, rather than changing the model.

opment. Conflict can even become institutionalized and ritualized and deeply embedded in a pattern of systemic action. Jousting among knights in the Middle Ages and codes of warfare that have protected elites are examples of such institutionalized patterns. Thus, the chivalry of knights in the Middle Ages, as dramatized in the *Song of Roland,* forbade striking an unarmed or unprepared foe and included elaborate norms for conflict. A system's capacity to solve problems may be quite underdeveloped, even though the system itself is highly institutionalized, as when a large portion of its members' demands for status, wealth, and well-being can be fulfilled only through system-level controls or international collaboration. If leaders whose actions guide the system are individually unable to satisfy such demands, then the institutionalized system itself is not adequately developed. When coping mechanisms prove inadequate, the system is no longer self-regulating; legitimacy is likely to decline rapidly, resources are likely to contract, and institutionalization of the system is also likely to decay. The system becomes more volatile, more subject to rapid change; systemic transformation is then more probable.

The most critical institution in international politics is war. For centuries men in separate communities have turned to warfare to resolve their conflicts. As one observer has suggested, "When two groups make mutually exclusive claims to the same values, war is an instrument of decision to choose between the groups, to decide what share of the contested values will go to each of the contenders" [23]. War has thus been a major coping mechanism. Because both sides share some mutual interests during war, however, various norms and routines have been adopted to prevent killing that does not affect the outcome. The list of such measures is extensive, including the wearing of uniforms to encourage morale and to promote ready identification of friend and foe; codes of chivalry; hierarchical chains of command and military discipline; elaborate strategies and guides to appropriate tactics, attitudes, and legal obligations of combatants both to their allies and to their enemies.

The legacy of the institutionalization of war continues to manifest itself in the great respect and deference accorded to those who serve in the armed forces of most states.[16]

War is accepted by the majority of people throughout the world as an appropriate means for resolving international disputes when other methods seem to have failed—it is thus legitimate, at least in the abstract. Even India, despite its success in following Mahatma Gandhi's philosophy of nonviolence, employed large-scale armed force three times in the 1960s—against the Portuguese, the Chinese, and the Pakistanis—after only minor domestic soul-searching. In 1971 India again had few reservations about going to war against Pakistan. Although men may disagree about what conditions constitute a "just" war or what the specific conditions actually are, few question the legitimacy of war itself as a last resort for allocating values in international politics. The attraction of pacifism has waxed and waned, but its adherents, such as the Quakers, Gandhi, or the Russian author Leo Tolstoy, have never constituted more than a fraction of the population of any major national or extranational participant in international politics.

Frequently, however, war is considered counterproductive for both sides. The outbreak of war, in fact, usually signals failure of the existing coping mechanisms to respond to pressures in the international system. War is in one sense the ultimate coping mechanism, adopted by actors in pursuit of their own particular objectives and applying their own norms, observations, and prescriptions. War attests to

the breakdown of the system, not because it retards institutionalization or further unbalances the ratio of demands to capacity—although it may do both—but because it represents the withdrawal of resources and legitimacy from the international system. Increased reliance on self-help is the result, leading to a decline in system dominance and an increase in the importance of subsystems.

Two trends in the legitimacy of international authority have emerged in recent years. First, there has been an increase in the number of people, particularly among American and other youth since the beginning of the Vietnam War, who do not accept war as a legitimate mode for resolving international disputes. American military desertion rates in Vietnam are far higher than for any previous conflict. In 1944 72.9 men per 1,000 in uniform deserted. In 1970 the rate was 142.2 men per 1,000.

Since 1967 more than 350,000 American servicemen have deserted; more than 61,000 were granted "conscientious objector" status in 1971, in comparison with only 17,000 in 1960.[17] The second trend is an increase in the number of individuals who attend and respond to the behavior of the international elite. The scope of the international system is expanding downward into its various subsystems. Such increased participation means that new strata can affect the system. Some people in each nation follow international affairs carefully, watching the behavior of leaders in Germany, trends in Soviet politics, and United Nations actions with at least as much proprietary concern as a governor of New Jersey or California might feel about the actions of a New York congressman or senator. The whole range of technological and cultural changes that seem to have expanded the scope of the international system may explain why more people are interested in international politics.

If these trends prove to be of long

[16] The occupational prestige of the military varies among countries and in time. During a war it usually rises noticeably. Harold D. Lasswell has suggested a "garrison state" hypothesis: that specialists in warfare may exacerbate cold-war rivalries in order to maintain political ascendance. Some theories about military intervention in Latin America incorporate declining prestige as a precipitating factor.

[17] See "70,000 to 100,000 Young Men Could Face Prosecution," *The New York Times*, December 28, 1971.

term, rather than simply cyclical fluctuations in public moods, then the relevant audience for legitimating authoritative behavior in the international system may be expanding while some of the most prominent and carefully studied coping mechanisms in international politics, including warfare, may be losing their legitimacy.

FUTURE POSSIBILITIES

Should the use of war and other coercive practices decline, what new coping mechanisms can take their place? Various forms of world government have been proposed,[18] but none has been based on projections of systemic change and development. Changes in scope, institutionalization, and balance result from the complex interaction of large-scale processes, including fairly universal ones like the spread of culture and relatively limited ones like the trends in multinational business and "third world" states. Without reliable forecasts about these processes and interactions, proposals for systemic reform seem pointless. To outline a scheme for world government without greater understanding of the social processes of change seems to us noble foolishness. Previously such proposals have been largely ignored by policy makers—and for good reasons.

We hope that the developmental perspective outlined in this chapter will provide a framework for analyzing change, so that evolutionary processes can be studied and evaluated more effectively *before* policy recommendations are made. Changing the present system to make the world a more sane and secure place to live is obviously necessary, but what kinds of change are needed? Whether one or another change will more effectively further development is a difficult question, but we hope to begin to answer it by examining particular processes and their dynamics and by exploring alternatives

[18] See Grenville Clark and Louis B. Sohn [7], Andrei D. Sakharov [24], and various publications of the United World Federalists.

for the future (see Part IV). Large and rapid changes in the structure of the international political system are unlikely, but within the context of the present system, with all its structural propensities for conflict, there are possibilities for change toward a more developed system.

References

1. Alger, Chadwick F., "Comparisons of Intranational and International Politics," *American Political Science Review,* 57 (June 1963), pp. 406–419.
2. Biddle, Bruce J., and Edwin J. Thomas, eds., *Role Theory* (New York: Wiley, 1966).
3. Binder, Leonard, "The Middle East Subordinate International System," *World Politics,* 10 (April 1958), pp. 408–429.
4. Bowman, Larry W., "The Subordinate State System of Southern Africa," *International Studies Quarterly,* 12 (September 1968), pp. 231–261.
5. Brecher, Michael, "International Relations and Asian Studies: The Subordinate State System of Asia," *World Politics,* 15 (January 1963), pp. 213–235.
6. Bruchey, Stewart, *The Roots of American Economic Growth, 1607–1861: An Essay in Social Causation* (New York: Harper & Row, 1965).
7. Clark, Grenville, and Louis B. Sohn, *World Peace Through World Law,* 2nd ed. (Cambridge, Mass.: Harvard University Press, 1962).
8. Deutsch, Karl W., "Social Mobilization and Political Development," *American Political Science Review,* 55 (September 1961), pp. 493–514.
9. Eckstein, Harry A., "Authority Relations and Governmental Performance: A Theoretical Framework," *Comparative Political Studies,* 2 (October 1969), pp. 269–235.
10. Eckstein, Harry A., *A Theory of Stable Democracy,* Center for International Studies, No. 10 (Princeton: 1961).
11. Holsti, K. J., "National Role Conceptions in the Study of Foreign Policy," *International Studies Quarterly,* 14 (September 1970), pp. 233–309.
12. Holsti, Ole, "The Belief System and National Images: A Case Study," *Jour-*

nal of Conflict Resolution, 6 (September 1962), pp. 244–252.

13. Huntington, Samuel P., "The Change to Change: Modernization, Development and Politics," *Comparative Politics,* 3 (April 1971), pp. 283–322.

14. Huntington, Samuel P., *Political Order in Changing Societies* (New Haven: Yale University Press, 1968).

15. Lasswell, Harold D., and Abraham Kaplan, *Power in Society* (New Haven: Yale University Press, 1950), p. 87.

16. Masters, Roger D., "World Politics as a Primitive Political System," in James N. Rosenau, ed., *International Politics and Foreign Policy* (New York: Free Press, 1969), p. 116.

17. Merkl, Peter, "Politico-Cultural Constraints on West German Foreign Policy: Sense of Trust, Identity, and Agency," *Comparative Political Studies,* 3 (January 1971), p. 446.

18. Packenham, Robert, "Approaches to the Study of Political Development," *World Politics,* 17 (October 1964), pp. 108–120.

19. Pennock, J. Roland, "Political Development, Political Systems, and Political Goods," *World Politics,* 18 (April 1966), pp. 415–434.

20. Pye, Lucian, *Aspects of Political Development* (Boston: Little, Brown, 1966).

21. Riggs, Fred W., "International Relations as a Prismatic System," *World Politics,* 14 (October 1961), pp. 144–181.

22. Riggs, Fred W., "The Nation-State and Other Actors," in James N. Rosenau, ed., *International Politics and Foreign Policy* (New York: Free Press, 1969), p. 92.

23. Rosen, Steven, "A Model of War and Alliance," in Julian R. Friedman, Christopher Bladen, and Steven Rosen, eds., *Alliance in International Politics* (Boston: Allyn & Bacon, 1970), pp. 217–218.

24. Sakharov, Andrei D., *Progress, Coexistence and Intellectual Freedom* (New York: Norton, 1968).

25. Singer, J. David, "The Global System and its Subsystems: A Developmental View," in James N. Rosenau, ed., *Linkage Politics* (New York: Free Press, 1969), pp. 21–43.

26. Singer, J. David, "Political Development of the Global System since 1815: Some Problems of Measurement" (Paper delivered at the Annual Meeting of the American Political Science Association, Washington, D.C., September 1968).

27. Young, Oran R., "Political Discontinuities in the International System," *World Politics,* 20 (April 1968), pp. 369–392.

28. Zartman, W. I., "Africa as a Subordinate State System in International Relations," *International Organization,* 21 (Summer 1967), pp. 545–564.

Suggested Reading

Alger, Chadwick F., "Comparisons of Intranational and International Politics," *American Political Science Review,* 57 (June 1963), pp. 406–419.

Aron, Raymond, *Peace and War* (New York: Praeger, 1968).

Deutsch, Karl W., *The Nerves of Government* (New York: Free Press, 1963).

Lasswell, Harold D., *World Politics and Personal Insecurity* (New York: Free Press, 1965).

Modelski, George, "The Foreign Ministers as a World Elite," *Peace Research Society Papers (International),* 14 (1970), pp. 31–46.

Riggs, Fred W., "International Relations as a Prismatic System," *World Politics,* 14 (October 1961), pp. 144–181.

Rosenau, James N., ed., *Linkage Politics* (New York: Free Press, 1969).

Part III
THE DYNAMICS OF THE INTERNATIONAL SYSTEM

Up to this point we have examined selected approaches to the study of international politics and the operation of the various units that compose the international system. In this part we shall turn to the processes by which international systems are transformed and shall try to identify and describe some of the means by which autonomous actors seek and attain objectives.

Systemic transformation can bring men closer to realization of their major values or can endanger the attainment of such ends. In Chapter 12 we examined selected criteria of development and decay in international systems, relating changes in structure and process to the attainment of central values. In the process of change new international actors appear, and old ones disappear. Larger units are created to serve common and complementary interests; as values change and interests shift, existing units may appear anachronistic to members, which weakens support for them. In Chapter 13 we shall focus on processes of integration and disintegration and examine selected theories about these processes. We shall then turn, in Chapter 14, to theories of coalitions and alliances and the functions of such organizations in international politics. Historically alliances have been a means by which actors can pool their resources to achieve desired international outcomes while maintaining their autonomy. The North Atlantic Treaty Organization will be analyzed in Chapter 15, as an illustration of the tensions and contradictions inherent in such organizations.

Throughout history violence has been the ultimate arbiter of international disputes. War has been an accepted international strategy. Theorists who favor "domestic" solutions to international problems through such devices as a world state, international organization, or international law, have tended to regard war as characteristic of international anarchy and decentralized authority. In Chapter 16 we shall take a brief look at the historical role of violence in international relations, emphasizing interpretations by selected philosophers and statesmen of past epochs.

War, as a means of achieving desired outcomes in a competitive framework, is an extension of political bargaining and a mode of regulating international behavior. In Chapers 17 and 18 we shall discuss the game and simulation approaches to understanding conflict and bargaining that have recently been developed by mathematicians and economists. In Chapter 19 we shall analyze the roles of communication and violence in attaining particular political ends and in satisfying the demands of international actors. In the light of this analysis, we shall then examine the strategic choices that actors make. Finally, in the last two chapters of this section, we shall turn to the special problem of acute international crises and examine the ways in which desired outcomes have been obtained without resorting to war.

In an era in which technological development has rendered war a less acceptable and potentially more dangerous practice, an even higher premium is placed on managing conflict and planning in order to avoid large-scale hostilities that might lead to the destruction of the very values that men pursue.

Chapter 13
THE DYNAMICS OF INTEGRATION

One major normative utility of the study of regional integration is its contribution as a conceptual, empirical and methodological link between work on the future of the international system and the future of nation states whose interrelationships make up the system—Ernst B. Haas [*11, p. 645*]

Let us imagine a world in which the great powers of the contemporary system have been joined by a few regional groupings —Europe, the Middle East, South America, and possibly one or two partially integrated Asian units—each with massive destructive capabilities and increasingly self-centered attitudes toward world order. Contrast this with a multileveled, complex, and fragmented set of actors in overlapping economic, social, or cultural conglomerates. The regionally integrated world would be able to contain within each region a high percentage of the world's economic and social conflicts and transactions. The other would be characterized by ad hoc transnational bodies for regulating particular spheres of activity or subdivided by the emergence of partially autonomous subnational actors in such areas as Quebec and Tamil (or Dravidian-speaking) India and by clandestine counterregimes in states as divergent as Ethiopia and South Africa. Which version of world order would be more conducive to human safety and survival? In the various configuration of forces at work in contemporary politics, which situation is more likely to occur? An analysis of regional and global integration processes may help to answer such questions.

The study of integration illuminates the dynamic forces leading international actors into institutionalized joint decision-making endeavors. From a global perspective integration and development are complementary concepts. Integration is a process of change in which the dominance of larger political systems increases or new, more comprehensive units are deliberately created. The eventual result of integration is a political community in which previously autonomous actors, whether individuals or national states, are bound together. Global integration would result from development of the international system; regional or subsystem integration might detract from or promote global integration, depending upon the goals and interdependencies among the emerging regional conglomerates.

Integration occurs under two circumstances. When the decision procedures and institutions of a more comprehensive community must handle a growing portion of decisions, "integrative growth" has occurred. Such growth is a product of changes in the nature and interdependence of social and economic processes—and thus in the decision-making arena to which problems are "normally" referred. A separate but not necessarily independent aspect of integration is the combination of separate units into a more comprehensive community, which serves as the basis for decision-making authority. We shall call this process "integrative transfer" (or "shift"). Both integrative growth and transfer are accompanied by public reevaluation of the importance of decisions made in the larger system, but integrative transfer also requires shifts of loyalties and identifications to a larger group and promotes expectations that tasks will be handled at a *new* decision center.

All men have multiple, and frequently overlapping, loyalties. Historically, substate loyalties manifested in separatist and nationalist movements, as in the Irish break from British rule, have been common. Suprastate loyalties have also existed, as when the Serbs sought to forge a common unit among the South Slavs in the Balkans. As the deepest loyalties of men shift to smaller or larger communities, integrative change occurs.

Probably no political community is ever fully integrated in the sense that no members wish to withdraw or to merge with other groups. Nevertheless, we can posit such a political community as an ideal. Men would be bound together in a decision system of mutually reinforcing habits of compliance with rules and decisions made by legitimate, popular decision makers. International integration poses some basic question about politics. What is the most important political community today? Which is the most involved in day-to-day decisions? Which is the most powerful? And which commands the deepest loyalties?

Throughout history loyalties have been anchored in many groups: family, tribe, village, city-state, kingdom, empire, nation, religion, secular faiths like socialism or communism, regional communities, and even world community. We can trace the various units that have formed the dominant political communities at different times. Aristotle extolled the virtues of the Greek *polis*, a small, well-integrated unit. Such city-states, separated by geographic barriers that fostered different values and identities, were not, however, politically or militarily viable against external threats.

The Roman Empire embraced the entire Mediterranean community. Despite highly developed communications, it wielded only marginal control of outlying areas. Its leaders pursued a colonial policy, exacting tribute and compliance as conditions for security of local inhabitants from the Roman legions.

Medieval political thought in Europe centered on Christendom and the rights and duties of kings. It was shaped by precedents from the "dark ages" after the destruction of Rome and insights of biblical exegesis. The emphasis was on man's spiritual unity and obedience to temporal leadership. Niccolò Machiavelli considered the focus of men's loyalties to be on the political actions of princes who might unify ever larger areas by force, fraud, skill, and boldness. Thomas Hobbes and Jean Bodin, who wrote when nation-states were first emerging, did not stress national identity. Rather, they emphasized the need for a strong impersonal state to end lawlessness and to protect the "natural rights" of men in a somewhat artificial community.

By the nineteenth century the national state had fully emerged as a focus of commitment and loyalty; this focus is reflected in the writings of men like Georg Wilhelm Friedrich Hegel. Yet even in that period political thinkers like Karl Marx and Immanuel Kant were examining the possibilities and needs for more inclusive political units. Today political scientists like Karl W. Deutsch and Ernst B. Haas, skeptical of the survival prospects of the nation-state, have sought to discover the mechanisms of integration, the paths by which influence and authority pass from small parochial units to larger, more inclusive ones.

Integration is an important concern of theorists of international politics for two reasons. First, many international and supranational organizations already exist or have been proposed. Among the most important just since World War II are the European Economic Community (EEC), the North Atlantic Treaty Organization (NATO), the European Free Trade Association (EFTA), the Organization of African Unity (OAU), the Organization of American States (OAS), the Council for Mutual Economic Assistance (CEMA), the Warsaw Pact, the Arab League, the abortive Mali and Malaysian Federations, and the East African Common Market (EACM). The experiences of these organizations have revealed basic factors that, with varying force, affect integration.

The second reason for studying integration is related to one of the major historical tasks that national states have performed: the defense of their citizens. Modern technology has made this task all but impossible. As Deutsch has argued:

All the nation-state can do now is to risk or spend the lives of its soldiers and its cities as gambling stakes on the gaming tables of power, strategy or ideology, in games which none of the players control or fully understand. The nation state is thus in danger of becoming for its people a cognitive trap in times of peace and a death trap in the event of war. [5, p. 218]

THE PHENOMENON OF INTEGRATION

There has been considerable debate about what integration is. Some consider it a *process* in which several units merge into one unit or at least certain functions of several units are combined under a single coordinated direction. Others consider it a *condition* defined by certain properties of a political community. The debate has done little to clarify this problem, but it has been helpful in revealing logical flaws in various theories about integration. For example, communications theorists have proposed that people in an integrated society communicate frequently with one another and that increases in communications might thus be a measure of integration. But increasing frequency of communications among states does not in itself indicate integration. For example, before World War I a large-scale increase in international communications occurred. Furthermore, measurement of communications has been used for various purposes: to indicate a desired end, to indicate a cause of that end, and to indicate a process leading to that end [22].

We shall use the term "integration" for a process of change and the term "political community" or "integrated society" for the result of integration. This result encompasses such features as low probability of violence in disputes, organizations for achieving and distributing mutual benefits, and high levels of interdependence and transactions. The exact thresholds at which these conditions obtain are not easily agreed upon; the choice rests partly on one's specific purpose in studying integration. To avoid some problems that others have encountered, we shall focus on integration as movement to lower probabilities of violence and increased interdependence and scope for the larger system.

Philippe Schmitter has argued that organizations tend to maintain an "equilibrium" among forces of integration so that little change may occur between two specific points in time. Such "plateaus of integration" may characterize the process of change over long periods. Partly integrated units may fail to reach full integration, at least through continuous historical process. States may also regress from a "zone of indifference," an area in which their functional activities are accepted, as one or another group seeks to withdraw some of the authority previously invested in common institutions of decision making. Figure 13.1 focuses on

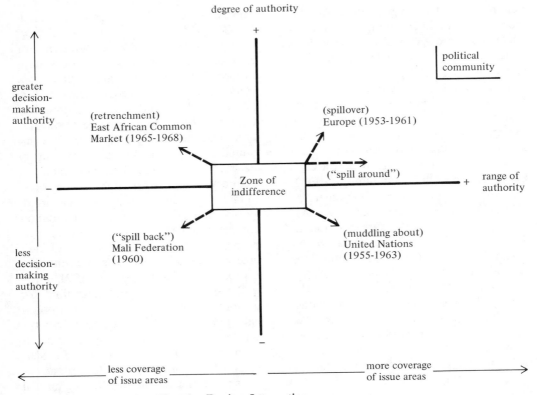

Figure 13.1. Alternative Changes During Integration
Source: Adapted from Philippe C. Schmitter, "A Revised Theory of Regional Integration," *International Organization,* 24 (Autumn 1970), p. 845.

changes in the number of steps in the decision process and in the scope of issues controlled by central authority. Collective outcomes are "system dominant" when decisions arrived at through mutual bargaining and adjustment, or through interstate or intergovernmental organizations, are generally accepted as authoritative. Changes in integration over time are represented by the arrows from the "zone of indifference." Movement toward greater authority occurs when joint decisions by actors embrace more steps in the decision process (see Chapter 1, pp. 5–8). For instance, joint agencies might first begin to identify problems or to formulate solutions; eventually they might implement and enforce those solutions. If these steps in the decision process had previously been reserved to authorities identified with single actors, their transfer to agencies or spokesmen at a higher level would

signify an increase in the degree of authority. Movement from left to right in Figure 13.1 represents an increase in the scope of authority, that is, the number of issues on which it is effective. At the global level, for instance, the United States refrained from signing the U.N. Declaration of Human Rights because it has feared providing a basis for United Nations assertion of authority over new issues, including civil rights inside the United States. The High Commission of the EEC has suggested new areas in which to coordinate national policies. This effort has increased the number of issues that it encompasses, a step toward broader scope, or "spill around."

"Spill back" is a decline in integration. It occurred dramatically in the Mali Federation in West Africa in 1960, when the political union between Senegal and the Sudan broke up after only a few months in existence. Both countries withdrew decision-making authority from the common structure and established harsh new restrictions on trade and communications between them, which included cutting the railroad link between Dakar and Bamako. Sudan kept the name Mali [7].

THEORIES OF INTEGRATION

Major theories of integration include federalism, communications theory, and neofunctionalism.[1] All stress the existence of mutual interests among units moving toward higher levels of integration. Such interests are affected by various forces, especially slowly changing "preconditions," "background features," and "integrative potential." The theories disagree on the relative importance of these structural factors and, more important, on which specific mechanisms generate direct pressure to integrate. Short-term, "accidental" factors, like the influence of specific statesmen and the occurrence of particular events, may help to determine an outcome when competing long-term forces are in balance and may thus affect a whole range of subsequent events related to integration. Communications and neofunctionalist theorists have focused primarily on preconditions and process mechanisms, federalists on critical political decisions.

Alliances are based on mutual interests, usually defense against common threats, and can represent a step on the path to creation of more comprehensive political communities. In 1775, for example, a defensive alliance was formed among the American colonies. In 1789 the process of integration, bolstered by the success of the cooperative war effort, resulted in a federal union. The United States remained a political community despite forces of disintegration that erupted in the Civil War.

What are the chances that NATO, the

[1] These three general theoretical categories have been suggested to us by Haas [11, pp. 624–629].

EEC, or the eastern European bloc might similarly be transformed from a loose military or economic alliance into a more unified community? Would such a group of states follow a path similar to that of the American colonies? Forecasting specific outcomes is particularly difficult because it requires separation of long-term and short-term trends and determination of their relative effects on particular outcomes. What we shall try to do here is to distinguish these theories, drawing upon historical events to illustrate their major points. Emphasis on the common features of theories involves some distortion, but this penalty seems minor in view of the admitted infancy of contemporary integration theory [11, pp. 607–646].

Federalism

Federalism includes theories of integration focusing on important political decisions, usually formal, that can create or destroy unified political organizations. Federalists are often concerned about formulating constitutions and distributing rights and duties among various agencies, executive bodies, courts, and geographical divisions within constitutional domains. Attention to these factors reflects the view that congruence between existing conditions and formal location of authority is more conducive to the federation's success. Every political union thus involves acts of will by the legitimate spokesmen of the merging communities. It is their ratification and their continued occupancy of authority positions that ensure the future of the nascent political community. They consider an integrated society the product of "a stroke of the pen and a stroke of genius."

Stanley Hoffmann, for one, has criticized theorists of European integration who emphasize transactional and functional trends for ignoring what he calls "high politics," the political forces that involve individual personalities and patriotism. He has argued that political leaders do not necessarily follow cost-benefit calculations and do not necessarily move toward common interests through sharing of productivity and resources. He points out that while they may seek economic and social integration, they may resist political integration. Indeed, the threat to autonomy inherent in negotiation over economic benefits may strengthen the determination of leaders to resist integration. French policy under Charles de Gaulle in the mid-1960s—aimed at exclusion of Great Britain from the Common Market and prevention of further integration within the market itself—as well as reluctance among many Britons to join the economic community, seems to justify Hoffmann's skepticism about the determinacy of economic forces [13].

Federalists also emphasize the sequence of historical events and the interaction of spokesmen for various interests during the formative phases of federation. The sequence of bargaining and the ad hoc compromises reached during this process are considered important determinants of the success or failure of federation. This approach thus tends to stress political, rather than economic, factors. The kind of integration that evolves over a long period and remains unrecognized in legal arrangements or the establishment of central political organizations often falls outside the focus of federalist theory.[2]

Communications Theory

A second major approach to study of the integration process is derived from general communications theory. Some political scientists believe that high levels of communications and transactions among actors are a critical indicator of, and probably a causal factor in, the formation of an integrated society. A rise in the level of communications would be marked by more exchange through mass media—shared radio and television programs, newspapers, and movies—and by increases in interpersonal communications measured by mail flows and telephone calls. Widespread and frequent communications accelerate the exchange of information and expand the pool of memories and mutual perceptions shared by elites and ordinary citizens.

Communications theorists are interested in all types of transactions but pay particular attention to trade flows. Increasing trade, they argue, creates interdependence and preferences for an "in-group." Partners that willingly accept one another's products may come to perceive one another as trustworthy and dependable suppliers of economic needs. Furthermore, such transactions increase interdependence, at least in the short run, for shifting from one supplier and market to another would involve some cost.[3]

Increasing flows of information and economic goods and services tend to promote the unilateral and joint adoption of administrative measures to smooth exchanges. To the extent that such exchanges are perceived as "rewarding," they are likely to promote increased respect for and reliance on other units. It has been suggested that in this process the number of errors in mutual pursuit of interrelated objectives and policies declines. Mutual understanding of interests and means of attaining them permits more realistic prediction of the consequences for others of one's actions, and greater sensitivity to and awareness of one another's values. High levels of communications should thus lessen the lag in perception of problems; clearer perceptions may permit actors to anticipate and forestall possible difficulties in cooperative relationships.

The relationship between the United States and Great Britain may serve as an example. Bruce M. Russett has analyzed a mass of transaction data for trends in relations between these two actors and has concluded that changing relative world status has been reflected in the relative attention that each has paid to the other [24]. The broad range of transactions,

[2] For examples of federalist theories, see Carl J. Friedrich [9], Thomas N. Frank [8], and William H. Riker [23].

[3] See Deutsch [6], for a general discussion of the operation of such factors in historical instances of integration.

supported by elements of shared culture and language, has created a high degree of mutual responsiveness to needs and problems. Richard E. Neustadt has described how such responsiveness has been taken for granted on both sides of the Atlantic and has suggested the crises that may occur when even minor miscalculations or misperceptions occur [20].[4] When one actor is responsive to the problems and needs of the other, mutual trust, compatible values among elites, and feelings of identification—all rather slowly changing structural features—are likely to be strengthened. The end result of the integration process is what Deutsch has called a "security community." Such a community usually enjoys peaceful resolution of disputes, but it need not have a high level of interdependence or central political organizations to enforce joint decisions. There are two types of security community. One is an amalgamation resulting from unification movements, as in nineteenth-century Italy and Germany. The other form is a pluralistic community, exemplified by the current Nordic community or that between the United States and Canada. The distinction is based on whether or not constituent units retain their legal independence and separate governments. In either type expectations of mutual violence among member actors are low, and the level of transactions among them is high. Formal political institutions are not necessary to support the social and economic solidarity of pluralistic communities; instead the emphasis is on peaceful resolution of disputes among member units [6].

Communications theorists believe that a rising volume of transactions enhances the structural propensity for integration

by encouraging learning. Learning based on shared information and common enterprises generates the knowledge and values required for mutually responsive behavior. We should note, however, that as in the case of the federalists, communications theorists also tend to ignore the impact of "high politics."

Functionalism and Neofunctionalism

Toward the end of World War II David Mitrany put forward certain proposals for a future world order and the process by which a more secure peace might be established [19].[5] His basic concept of functionalism is not complex. It is the assumption that the supplies must match demands for fulfillment of such basic human needs as food, shelter, and security. Increased specialization and broader exchanges of goods and people have increased the consequences of such problems as economic depression and epidemics. As a result, small groups have become less able to handle them. At each stage in history, actors' facilities have been increasingly taxed by their efforts to obtain adequate goods and services. As a result, according to the theory, international bodies have been created to resolve "international" problems.

Such specialized organs of the United Nations as the Food and Agricultural Organization (FAO) have been viewed as "stones cast into a pond." After the initial impact each is likely to generate widening "ripples" as its regulatory capacity increases. The need and demand for performance of certain international functions —in matters like health, food distribution, and agricultural production—have created demands for establishment or expansion of international agencies. As we noted in Chapter 11, a similar process occurs in the international corporation. As its transactions increasingly fall outside the jurisdiction of a particular national state, the need for "international" regulation be-

---

[4] Neustadt concluded his book on a somewhat solemn note, arguing that minor failures in responsiveness among states that are generally quite familiar with and attentive to one another, as are the United States and Great Britain, can lead to serious crises in their relations; relations among states with very few communications and little social or economic interaction seem extremely unlikely to be based on accurate images of one another's needs and of likely responses to one another's policies.

[5] For more recent treatments of functionalism, see Inis L. Claude, Jr. [3] and James P. Sewell [26].

comes increasingly acute. The establishment of the Universal Postal Union to ensure the orderly flow of messages, of the International Red Cross, and of the International Court of Justice can be explained as reflecting recognition of sets of needs best served by international regulatory or service agencies.

Functionalists believe that some regulatory agencies in specific functional and "nonpolitical" arenas will, once established, grow beyond the bounds of explicit political expectations among those who created them. At some point they will emerge as powerful institutionalized agencies serving as bases for more integrated formal political organizations. Functional integration, it has been argued, will create a system that may ensure international, if not domestic, peace.

Functionalists foresee an integration process that will go no farther than the minimum necessary to achieve cooperative solutions to common problems. Although in the long run the autonomy of nation-states may be undermined if states could not individually cope with problems in their remaining spheres of jurisdiction, this result seems at least several generations away. The essence of the functionalist approach is that it avoids a frontal attack on national sovereignty, but the converse is also true; integration is considered a process that does not necessarily undermine the nation-state until the latter has already ceased to be an important political entity. In this sense functionalism represents a "minimalist" approach. As Sewell has declared: "Is peace the aim? Its foundations must be laid by piecemeal international efforts in commonly recognized transnational problem areas which are readily acceptable to the procedures shaped and accepted by modern man" [26, p. 3].

The decades since the end of World War II have *not* produced continuous institutional and organizational growth of international organizations. Because of certain inadequacies in pure functionalist theory, its adherents have not predicted accurately. First, organizations like the economic and social agencies of the United Nations represent interstate alliances based on limited common interests; they are not generally indispensable. As they deal with relatively uncontroversial problems, there is little reason why incremental growth should enable them to cope with major political problems without the formal consent of national political elites. Second, as all but the most basic needs are culturally shaped, most can be satisfied only within the framework of the nation-state. It seems likely that functional organizations reach various plateaus of growth. Unless important structural changes occur, so that the learned attitudes, expectations, and demands of ordinary citizens and elites are altered to give high priority to universal standards of health, welfare, and well-being, expansion can remain within relatively narrow confines without leading to further integration.

A more persuasive version of the functionalist approach is neofunctionalism [12, 16]. It combines elements of both communications and pure functionalist theory, emphasizing the dynamics of international agencies. It posits that units established by agreements among nation-states, notably in connection with common markets or economic agreements, though attending to the mutual interests of member states, may also create pressures for broadening or strengthening their own authority. Neofunctionalist theory does not depend upon environmental changes to create needs for expanded international organization; rather it relies on existing organizational activity to generate pressures for expansion.

The European Common Market is the organization most closely studied by neofunctionalists, though the East African and South American common markets have also been examined. The common authorities created by economic unions—such as the European High Commission, for one—face the task of balancing both mutual and antagonistic interests. The High Commission or the United Nations secretary-general is frequently charged with finding formulas on which a required minimum number of members can agree. As integration proceeds, this minimum may be reduced. In the European Common Market, for example, steps to reduce the requirement for foreign ministers' agreement on particular issues from unanimity to two-thirds have been taken, though President de Gaulle blocked them in 1965.

Economic decisions affect wage levels, tax structures, and a variety of domestic political interests. Indeed, the adoption of a common set of agricultural policies in the European Common Market will lead to a new distribution of rewards and costs within and among the member states. Neofunctionalists are particularly interested in the consequences of "package" arrangements that will have profound economic impacts on many spheres within the member actors. Such packages can create new focuses of attention for lobbies and pressure groups within nation-states. These groups may seek to establish direct bargaining relations with central or supranational authorities and to develop alliances with similar groups in other countries to secure mutual interests. In this way domestic interest groups may become increasingly internationalized and may be encouraged to deal with supranational authorities directly, rather than indirectly through their national governments. Haas has called this phenomenon "spillover." Initial decisions on a limited economic issue have consequences for related areas; "spillover" occurs when areas with which the central agency has initially dealt expand *and* the authority of its decisions increases. If the agency's activities simply spread into new areas without this increase in authority, what Schmitter has called "spill around" occurs. New areas of interest are brought into the common decision-making framework without increasing the authority of the common institutions.

The "spillover" effect enlarges the scope of the bargaining process at the international level. Traditional diplomacy, particularly bilateral diplomacy, is superseded by more complex and structured bargaining in which national governments confront coalitions of labor unions, business interests, or political parties, as well as supranational agencies like the High Commission. To the extent that central agencies can take initiatives, their role may extend beyond mere implementation of joint decisions by member states. Occasionally the High Commission has played a decisive role in resolving deadlocks within the EEC; it was, for example, able to use its independent and "neutral" position to propose a package solution to the agricultural problem that member states found difficult to reject, even though it meant some losses for each of them [16]. European experience, at least until 1964–1965, encouraged neofunctional analysts to believe that "spillover" from the establishment of economic unions would lead to continual "upgrading of the common interest" and increasing growth in the authority of communitywide supranational agencies. The subsequent deadlocks and failure to move toward political unification within the EEC, arising initially from Gaullist intransigence and subsequently from a more complex set of disagreements, have posed serious challenges to the idea that bargaining and "spillover" inevitably lead to higher levels of integration.

Revised neofunctionalist approaches have focused on the possibilities for decreased integration and leveling off of the integration process around a "zone of indifference." Further efforts have been made to incorporate some of the ideas of communications theorists into a more exhaustive model of integration.

Theories of integration all include long-range, middle-range and short-range, or crisis, factors. The federalists emphasize political personalities and specific political formulas that emerge at the formative stages of a political community, when treaties, charters, or constitutions are being drafted. Communications and functionalist theories stress social and economic factors that create common interests and bring them to the attention of political elites. Sketching some of the major factors that appear to be involved in integration will provide us with a broad paradigm for analyzing the integration process and a better basis for comparing the three theories of integration.

STRUCTURAL FACTORS IN INTEGRATION

Long-term factors, or "preconditions," determine the potential for integration among any set of international actors. Let us imagine a list of all important nation-states, transnational groups, and intergovernmental organizations. If we were to draw sets of names from this list at random, we would have different numbers and types of actors in each set. The potential for integration in each of these sets might be evaluated through application of several hypotheses about the effects of structural factors. The two major structural factors in this connection are attitudes of those residing within the selected actors and the distribution of physical resources among actors.

Attitudes

Attitudes provide important information on two features that affect propensities to integrate. First, complementarity among elite values is important. If elites have undergone similar family or career socialization or have joined in such cooperative endeavors as negotiations and intergovernmental organizations, they may share similar outlooks on related problems and may even have developed personal camaraderie. Even more important is whether or not their ideologies are compatible. Men who work through problems in similar ways or who have similar commitments to political goals will find it easier to translate the mutual interests of the organizations that they represent into joint policies. Soviet ideology and American faith in civic man permit little complementarity of values. One of the factors in the failure of the federation that East

African leaders announced for June 1963 was the growing awareness of different value commitments among Kenyan and Tanzanian politicians. Tanzania subsequently inaugurated a "socialist" state, nationalizing all important industries, whereas Kenya has pursued "capitalist" development, encouraging private foreign investment.

A second attitudinal factor is identifications among populations. The extent to which entire populations share common religion, language, and customs is an important determinant of the inclusiveness of their "we" feelings. When such feelings exist trust is more easily generated, and there may be greater willingness to participate in jointly beneficial undertakings and common organizations. Positive identifications can make leaders' efforts at amalgamation with others more popular and thus enhance individual leaders' political careers. Thus, popular identification within both halves of divided Germany may ultimately facilitate the reunification of that country.

Resources

The distribution of resources has several possible effects on integration. The first is associated with relationships among units. The total number of units to be integrated can be critical. Three units may find it difficult to integrate, for within the larger community a coalition of two against the third might occur; if such a coalition seemed likely to be permanent, the third member might hesitate to place its fate in the hands of the other two. A larger number of actors may resist formation of alliances because of disparity among goals but may thus further integration by reducing the probability that any single unit will be exploited. Knowing only the number of actors is therefore not sufficient to determine whether integration will be inhibited or promoted.

A second dimension in relationships among units is relative size. Great differences in per capita income inhibit a wide range of transactions. Joseph S. Nye, Jr., has pointed out what seems to be a clear relationship between the degree of trade integration within economic unions and the parity of members' economic development [21]. Relative equality among units may also be important in generating commitments. Wide disparities in the resources and potential influence of units may promote a hierarchical or elitist structure among them, causing in weaker units contempt and fear of stronger ones.[6] States at low levels of development may find it difficult to negotiate integrative agreements regardless of equality. The East African Common Market, for example, is the product of disintegration of an economic union that existed in 1963. The unequal benefits received by Kenya, as a result of the concentration of industry around Nairobi, offset the "spread effects" that all three East African states gained from economic union. Sensitivity to Kenya's relative economic advantage was particularly acute in Tanzania, which saw high opportunity costs in maintaining the union, that is, costs incurred by forgoing special deals or protection for its economy.[7]

Equality may not always be important. Deutsch has argued that "core areas" may be a more significant precondition for integration. He has found that a marked increase in political and administrative capability of some units, coupled with high potential for overall economic growth, has been a critical initial feature in several instances of successful integration [6]. Equality may be more important at some stages than at others. For economic unions equality appears to be salient when members are at low levels of economic development and again at high levels. In making adjustments for relative advantages to units of joining a partially integrated community, there may be room for bargaining and integrated policy mixes from which all appear to gain some bene-

fit. Gains and losses in status are more difficult to assign in such a situation. During periods of modernization, however, problems of national consolidation may inhibit such bargaining, unless the core area can offer quite special advantages.

Another factor in the relations among units is physical distance. Although communications and travel time have become less important barriers to integration, distance remains significant in separating people and creating costs in the distribution and exchange of resources.

Economic development is still another important structural feature. The level of economic development indicated by gross national product per capita appears to affect possible levels of trade among states and to help to determine the complementarity of their economic systems. Two features that accompany economic development also figure prominently in shaping integration potential First, states at low levels of development tend to have many domestic problems, both economic and social. When large segments of the population are agrarian, the national infrastructure not fully developed, and communications poor, political penetration of the state and the establishment of a modern economy may pose massive problems. Consequently, the attention and sacrifices required for integration in a larger community may be beyond the capacity of political leaders. More developed units, on the other hand, can bear such costs of integration more easily, and they have complex domestic structures capable of redistributing these costs in ways that can reduce domestic opposition. Interested organizations and groups can bring pressure for integrationist policies on the government. Haas has found that economic leaders exerted pressure on European governments to form the European Coal and Steel Community and continued to exert pressure during the formative stages of the EEC. By contrast, the abortive federations in Malaysia and Mali were largely fashioned by elites and lacked the support of interlocking interests among groups cutting across national boundaries.

---

[6] On the question of inegalitarian versus elite unions see Amitai Etzioni, *Political Unification: A Comparative Study of Leaders and Forces* (New York: Holt, Rinehart and Winston, 1965), pp. 296 ff.

[7] Such opportunity costs would be extremely difficult to calculate with precision.

These long-term and slowly changing factors help to determine the integration potential among any proposed set of actors. It should be immediately clear that a group consisting of Mexico, New Zealand, and China would have less such potential than would one consisting of France, Holland, and Belgium. It is less obvious whether France, Holland, and Belgium now have more or less potential for integration than did the six member states of the EEC after 1957. Is political integration more probable in a European community of six states or in a larger community including Great Britain? Integration theorists have not yet tested propositions specific enough to permit answers to these questions.

PROCESS (MIDDLE-TERM) FACTORS IN INTEGRATION

Among those units or states that have integration potential, a series of process mechanisms that affect integration can be identified. Their "middle-term" effects are usually more visible than are those of long-term structural factors and are often associated with policy decisions. Whereas structural factors represent environmental constraints that can determine whether purposeful attempts at integration will succeed, various process mechanisms are the main locus of the dynamics of integration.

There are at least four principal process mechanisms: economic and political inducements, social and economic transactions, functional links, and learning and socialization.

Process factors may affect structural factors positively or negatively. Multiplication of transactions and functional links among states may create a "crisis" if the resulting pressure for change exceeds the supportive capacity of structural conditions or runs counter to underlying propensities, thus threatening political leadership. Leaders may then reject opportunities for integration or abandon membership in common organizations. On the other hand,

by promoting identification among populations, greater equality in their levels of development, and common economic opportunities, these process factors may buttress structural factors and increase the potential for integration. Process mechanisms may also affect one another. For example, learning induced by the results of process mechanisms can influence the subsequent operation of other process mechanisms.

Economic and Political Inducements

The benefits that each actor expects from collaboration in integrated enterprises can profoundly affect his behavior. Decision makers' perceptions that economic collaboration offers benefits may spur further integration. By contrast, perceived possibilities of loss may offset actual gains, particularly if steps toward integration seem to threaten the economic or political bases of important individuals or groups. Political theorists like Alfred Cobden have argued that free trade will promote the interests of all participants, disregarding the special benefits that individual states might derive from national encapsulation (exclusionary self-help policies). Economic factors may be important inducements to integration, but political calculations can also be salient, particularly those related to domestic politics. For example, transnational alliances among certain political groups may strengthen opposition to existing political elites.

Judgments about possible benefits may be affected by the actual conditions that produce benefits or costs, the accuracy of perceptions of these conditions, and the relative distribution of perceived benefits or costs. Underlying structural factors determine the extent to which gains from a common market are concentrated in more advanced areas of the community, limit the range of goods and services that can be traded among members, and define possible benefits and costs. The conditions that shape economic inducements tend to be evaluated in terms of their marginal impacts on member units: How much growth, added value, or increase in skills is one country likely to enjoy as a result of wider markets for its products and cheaper imports? Marginal analysis is also applicable to calculating effects on political support for incumbent elites. Election laws and political attitudes toward party and ideology are structural determinants that shape the marginal impacts of integration on politics. A "10 percent shift" in voting would be evaluated differently by elites if it represented a rise in opposition strength from 10 to 20 percent, rather than from 41 to 51 percent.

Selective perception of the marginal effects of integration distorts reality. Individuals with different frames of reference select those elements of reality that seem important and organize them according to their own theoretical understanding. Decision makers may fail to recognize certain effects as inducements; indeed, some consequences of a move toward integration are always unforeseen and *cannot* act as inducements.

"Fairness" in short-term relative gain is another element determining the impact of inducements. If one partner in a group appears to enjoy most of the early advantages from integration, others may feel deprived and disinclined to proceed with arrangements, especially when comparative standards are used to calculate utility. On the other hand, if a country were to compare its current position with its probable position after integration, aside from whether or not it will be better off than will others, then only the absolute level of probable benefits would be important. The question of "equity," however, almost always arises when states bargain over integration. Although not a controlling factor, "inequity" can lead elites to perceive only small positive gains as negative inducements.

Economic and Social Transactions

Transactions can be divided between two major categories: economic and sociocultural. They are *not*, however, independent. Business transactions lead individuals from various units to interact socially. The growth of transnational society, drawn particularly from international corporations, has been accompanied by increases in international travel and communications.

In a community undergoing at least economic integration, we would expect not only that the volume of economic transactions would rise but also that an increasing percentage of each member's trade would be with other members of the community. When the level of economic transactions within a group is higher than that of transactions with actors outside the group, then the group is linked in mutually beneficial ways. In an integrated national state the internal market absorbs a very large proportion of the total production of the society. For example, "interstate commerce" in the United States is extremely large; foreign commerce represents only about 7 percent of gross national product.

Studies of the European Common Market have brought together the greatest amounts of systematic data on economic transactions. France and Germany constitute the core of the EEC. Table 13.1 shows the growth of trade between these two countries between 1938 and 1965. Donald Puchala has shown that during the formative period of the EEC, as well as after its official establishment, reciprocal acceptance among members of one another's products was both higher than had been expected, and growing. We can derive an index of reciprocal acceptance (RA), which measures the difference between what a state actually exports to another state and what might be expected on the basis of the relative size of the states and their total international trade:

Hence, if a unit contributes 20 percent of the total transactions in a system, we expect, under the null model, that this unit will contribute 20 percent of the transactions for every other unit in the system. Actual flows may deviate from this expected 20 percent, and these deviations, positive or negative, large or small, become the basis for computing the relative acceptance

Table 13.1

Trends in Franco-German Economic Transactions
(trade flow as index; in millions of dollars)

Year	Total Trade	French Exports to West Germany	German Exports to France	Percentage of French Exports to Germany	Percentage of German Exports to France
1938	148.3	56.4	91.9	6.7	4.4
1954	699.0	351.8	347.2	8.8	6.8
1957	1,213.6	545.8	667.8	11.3	7.9
1965	3,940.5	1,990.8	1,940.5	21.5	13.1

Source: Donald J. Puchala, "International Transactions and Regional Integration," in Leon N. Lindberg and Stuart A. Scheingold, eds., *Regional Integration: Theory and Research* (Cambridge, Mass.: Harvard University Press, 1970), pp. 144-145. Copyright 1970, 1971, by the President and Fellows of Harvard College. Reprinted by permission of the publisher.

measure. If two units share many more transactions than expected on the basis of their total transactions, RA scores will be positive and high. If they share many fewer transactions than expected, scores will be negative and low. Since the computing formula for the RA index calls for dividing the difference between actual and expected transactions by expected transactions (RA = actual − expected ÷ expected), relative acceptance scores may take values ranging from −1.0 (no transactions at all) to 0.0 (transactions as expected) to infinity (a great many more transactions than expected). [22, p. 738]

From examination of RA scores for European Common Market states, as shown in Table 13.2, we can see that relative acceptances of national exports by the European "Six" have not only been positive but have also increased since 1938 for all states except Italy. As the third section of the table makes clear, international economic transactions among the six European states remained high during a period in which trade with other areas was declining. In particular, relative acceptance between the "Six" and the Scandinavian countries, which was fairly high before the creation of the European Community, has dropped noticeably.

This community, established in Europe after 1957, represents an impressive undertaking. The budget for Common Market organs in 1965 was $783 million compared to less than $500 million for the entire United Nations system in 1964.[8] This budget, however, represented less than 1 percent of the total government expenditures of the six member states. Economic integration in Europe, as measured by economic transactions and budgetary expenditures, after impressive expansion during the 1950s, seems to have leveled off at a moderately high plateau. The functional economic agencies of the EEC, though commanding substantial resources, remain puny in comparison with those of the national governments.

Social communication and cultural exchange among states, reflected in figures on international travel, mail flows, and exposure to foreign films and television programs, offer another set of indicators of integration. Table 13.3 shows a marked growth in mail communications among the Common Market states from 1937 to 1961. This measure is particularly impressive in comparison with that for mail flows between the European Six and others.

One of the major questions that vexed the Common Market in the 1960s was the possible entry of Great Britain. France in particular erected barriers; we should not

[8] These figures are taken from Leon N. Lindberg and Stuart A. Scheingold, *Europe's Would-Be Polity: Patterns of Change in the European Community* (Englewood Cliffs, N.J.: Prentice-Hall, 1970), p. 75.

Table 13.2.

Emergence of the European "Six" as a Transaction Network

	1938	1954	1963
Relative Acceptance of Exports from the "Six" to Country			
France	.2	.3	.7
Germany	.5	.9	.9
Belgium-Luxembourg	1.0	1.4	1.2
Netherlands	1.0	1.0	1.7
Italy	.7	.4	.3
Relative Acceptance of Exports from Country to "Six"			
France	.4	.4	.6
Germany	.5	.9	.8
Belgium-Luxembourg	1.0	1.4	1.0
Netherlands	.7	1.1	.9
Italy	.5	.3	.5
Region-to-Periphery and Periphery-to-Region Relative Acceptance of Exports			
"Six" to "Six"	.6	.8	.8
"Six" to Scandinavia	.7	.7	.1
Scandinavia to "Six"	.2	.2	.1
"Six" to Anglo-American area	−.5	−.5	−.6
Anglo-American area to "Six"	−.5	−.4	−.5
"Six" to world beyond Atlantic area	.1	−.1	−.1
World beyond Atlantic area to "Six"	.0	−.1	−.1

Source: Donald J. Puchala, "International Transactions and Regional Integration," in Leon N. Lindberg and Stuart A. Scheingold, eds., *Regional Integration: Theory and Research* (Cambridge, Mass.: Harvard University Press, 1970), pp. 148-149. Copyright 1970, 1971, by the President and Fellows of Harvard College. Reprinted by permission of the publisher.

Table 13.3.

Relative Acceptance of Mail in the "Six" EEC Countries

	1937	1955	1961
"Six" to "Six"	.3	.6	.9
"Six" to Scandinavia	.2	.0	.0
Scandinavia to "Six"	.0	.0	−.1
"Six" to United Kingdom	−.4	−.5	−.5
United Kingdom to "Six"	−.4	−.5	−.5
"Six" to World beyond Atlantic area	.1	−.1	−.1
World beyond Atlantic area to "Six"	.1	.0	.1

Source: Donald J. Puchala, "International Transactions and Regional Integration," in Leon N. Lindberg and Stuart A. Scheingold, eds., *Regional Integration: Theory and Research* (Cambridge, Mass.: Harvard University Press, 1970), p. 149. Copyright 1970, 1971, by the President and Fellows of Harvard College. Reprinted by permission of the publisher.

therefore be surprised that, although the percentages of French exports, letters, tourists, and exchange students to Great Britain have declined steadily since 1925, those to Germany have grown dramatically (see Table 13.4).

More frequent transactions appear to be part of a broader nexus of phenomena that appear during the integration process and continue after its successful completion. But they should not be viewed by themselves as causes of integration or as

Table 13.4.

French Transactions with Great Britain and Germany (as percentage of total foreign transactions)

	To Great Britain	To Germany
	Exports	
1938	12.4	6.7
1954	6.0	8.8
1957	5.7	11.3
1965	4.9	21.5
	First-Class Mail	
1937	12.5	4.6
1961	8.5	11.7
	International Tourists	
1929	14.2	7.4
1961	5.1	9.1
	International Student Exchange	
1925	9.9	1.8
1952	6.3	5.8
1957	7.2	27.4
1960	3.4	25.2

Source: Adapted from Donald J. Puchala, "International Transactions and Regional Integration," in Leon N. Lindberg and Stuart A. Scheingold, eds., *Regional Integration: Theory and Research* (Cambridge, Mass.: Harvard University Press, 1970), pp. 144-146. Copyright 1970, 1971, by the President and Fellows of Harvard College. Reprinted by permission of the publisher.

evidence of movement toward greater integration. The underlying causal factors reflected by rates of transaction may be part of a general pattern of change. Increased exposure, through travel and other transactions, to foreign situations may also promote more "international" attitudes. As attention is focused on a wider arena of activity, appreciation of foreign culture may increase. In one study, Raymond A. Bauer, Ithiel de Sola Pool, and Lewis A. Dexter found that American businessmen with considerable foreign experience hold more liberal views on tariff and trade policy than do other businessmen and generally favor greater international economic intercourse [2].

Transactions may, therefore, serve as an indicator of the short- to middle-term prospects for integration among states. As Hayward R. Alker and Puchala have suggested, "Because intense, enduring, and rewarding transactions are characteristic of international or supranational communities, we may use measures for the extent of economic transactions—in particular, trade—as one among many indicators of the existence of the international community" [1]. Although the causal significance of these indicators has been seriously questioned by Haas, Leon Lindberg, and others, their role in integration has generally been acknowledged by both communications and neofunctionalist theorists.

Functional Linkage

Haas and Lindberg have shown how one apparently discrete step toward interstate cooperation can generate support for increased decision-making authority at the community level. This change can in turn facilitate subsequent expansion of the scope of community authority. As a result, transnational linkages may form along functional lines. For example, when the production of a particular industrial good requires the coordination of firms, workers, and marketing facilities in several countries, demands for common systems of calculating taxes may arise. Similarly, a common agricultural pricing system may result in pressures for governments to agree on further common policies in the agricultural sector.

Joint enterprises among states may thus generate further indirect links, previously unforeseen, which can result in decisions to enhance the scope and degree of community authority. This kind of functional link is what the neofunctionalists call "spillover." One possible process mechanism begins when a high level of transactions enhances functional interdependence; such interdependence may require system-wide coordination. Intergovernmental organizations may then be established to administer common trade, tariff, and tax policies and to arbitrate related disagreements. The activities of such agencies may generate further functional interdependence as they increase the scope and importance of links among what were previously domestic processes. As domestic decisions in one country become important for the businessmen of another, pressures to bring such decisions under the control of the wider community may arise. Common regulation of food and health standards, coordination of shipping, and joint currency regulation are a few examples of existing functional links, particularly in Europe.

Learning and Socialization

The final process mechanism for integration involves learning and socialization processes among elites and ordinary citizens. Perceived benefits, multiplication of transactions, and increased interdependence can provide a schedule of rewards and punishments analogous to the simple psychological model of learning. In the formation of the European community, for instance, political and economic elites seem to have "learned" about integration. Tentative steps to establish functional agencies, like the Coal and Steel Community and Euratom, were successful and encouraged other, more comprehensive steps toward integration. Perceptions of

probable benefits from integration appear to have been reflected in more positive and supportive attitudes within a broader community. Table 13.5 shows the relatively high and increasing support for European unification among mass publics in 1957–1962. Greater political support made leaders willing to transfer national autonomy to community-level organs. Social learning for both elites and masses began with their perception of rewarding experiences as linked to the community, greater trust was thus "learned," and it led finally to demands for increasing decision-making authority at the community level.

Although support for the Common Market has grown in most member countries, it has declined in Great Britain. It has been suggested that one reason is a sense of rejection among British leaders and the British public, arising from the failure of their initial efforts to join the EEC. Negative reinforcement may have "taught" the population negative attitudes toward the EEC. British admission may reverse these attitudes, albeit slowly.

There is a lag in the effects of experience on attitudes. Positive experiences promote identifications and complementarity of elite values; they thus have gradual impacts on structural features. The pace of European integration seems to have slowed during the 1960s, and integration has remained largely within the zone of indifference [25]. Yet the community "learning" experiences appear to have resulted in stronger support for integration among the young than among members of other age groups. This situation confirms Ronald Inglehart's argument that the young generation in Europe is more "European-minded" than are present elites and may provide new impetus for integration when its members begin to assume higher positions in national political and economic structures. These differences in attitudes are reported in Table 13.6.

There is still uncertainty about the actual impacts of international transactions and mutual inducements on nascent transnational identifications. Some theo-

Table 13.5.
European Integration

Question: Are you in general for or against making efforts toward uniting Western Europe?

Date	Sept. 1952	Oct. 1954	Feb. 1955	Dec. 1955	Apr. 1956	Nov. 1956	May 1957	June 1962
France								
N =	1345	847	900	805	800	1227	1200	1307
For	60%	63%	49%	45%	53%	67%	55%	70%
Against	16	9	15	12	14	7	9	8
DK	24	28	36	43	33	26	36	22
Total	100%	100%	100%	100%	100%	100%	100%	100%
Italy								
N =	1505	808			911		1269	
For	57%	63%	NA	NA	66%	NA	59%	NA
Against	14	9			7		7	
DK	29	28			27		34	
Total	100%	100%			100%		100%	
West Germany								
N =	1591	836				1159	1299	
For	70%	82%	NA	NA	NA	82%	75%	NA
Against	10	4				5	7	
DK	20	14				13	17	
Total	100%	100%				100%	99%	
Great Britain								
N =	1503	832						
For	58%	78%	NA	NA	NA	NA	NA	NA
Against	15	4						
DK	27	18						
Total	100%	100%						

Source: Richard L. Merritt and Donald J. Puchala, eds., *Western European Perspectives on International Affairs: Public Opinion Studies and Evaluations* (New York: Praeger, 1968), p. 283. Reprinted by permission of the publisher.

rists suggest that the reinforcements that they provide are the major elements in the kind of social and cultural learning that advances integration. Social learning and purposive behavior may be equivalent formulations that describe the patterned sequences of change over time, as elites and mass publics change their attitudes and behavior in response to what they have learned about the value of international intercourse and cooperation. Patterns of identification that have previously

Table 13.6.

Percentages Favoring Three Proposals for Supranational Integration, by Country and Age Group, 1970

Age Group	Germany	Netherlands	France	Belgium	Italy	Great Britain
"United States of Europe"						
21-34	75	69	71	67	66	33
35-49	75	61	66	67	63	30
50-64	64	65	71	61	57	30
65+	57	60	60	42	42	24
British Entry into Common Market						
21-34	75	80	69	60	58	23
35-49	73	78	64	71	54	20
50-64	65	80	65	59	49	17
65+	59	73	66	57	36	14
Supranational European Government Responsible for Foreign Affairs, Defense, and Economy						
21-34	66	54	53	52	57	28
35-49	60	49	51	60	53	22
50-64	53	51	51	51	49	21
65+	42	45	40	37	33	14

Source: Ronald Inglehart, "Public Opinion and Regional Integration," in Leon N. Lindberg and Stuart A. Scheingold, eds., *Regional Integration: Theory and Research* (Cambridge, Mass.: Harvard University Press, 1970), p. 183. Copyright 1970, 1971, by the President and Fellows of Harvard College. Reprinted by permission of the publisher.

sustained nation-states continue to anchor populations in communities. The learning experiences during integration will eventually determine whether these deep loyalties are being shifted from the ship of the nation to some other vessel.

"ACCIDENTAL" FACTORS IN INTEGRATION

The final set of factors involved in the integration process tend to be short-term and fairly concrete. They are often associated with specific steps in integration and are frequently flavored by tension and drama. The impacts of such factors tend to be greatest during the final events preceding unification and to diminish fairly rapidly afterward, though their consequences may linger for a considerable period.

Five short-term factors have been identified in discussions of integration. They are external (catalytic) factors, ideological appeals, bargaining solutions, responsiveness, and specific leaders. In certain contexts some of these factors may have middle-range effects. For instance, common defense responses to perceived external threats, which helped to produce NATO, grew out of a cold-war context that has proved most durable. There is nothing sacrosanct in the assignment of factors to the three categories that we have chosen.

External (Catalytic) Factors

A commonly perceived outside threat to the values of several actors may lead to demands for an alliance and integration measures. Although such threats are frequently military, they need not be exclusively so. NATO, the Warsaw Pact, SEATO, and other alliances, initially based on common military interests, have spilled over, at least marginally, into other functional activities.[9] Other groups, like the Conference on Nonaligned Nations

[9] For example, NATO has promoted cooperation in scientific, technical, and cultural affairs by sponsoring symposiums and awarding fellowships.

and the Organization of African Unity, were created to defend social and economic, as well as military, interests. Agencies and organizations within the United Nations, especially under the leadership of Latin American states and individuals (like Brazilian economist Raoul Prebish), have taken steps to defend the economic interests of the "third world."

Ideological Appeals

Sometimes leaders and organized groups deliberately use potent "ideological" symbols to promote or attack specific steps in an integration process A certain excitement and promise inhere in the formation of a new community; they can be exaggerated through the formulation of a grand scheme or the vision of a particular leader or group and can be described with potent historical imagery.

In Africa symbols of independence and unity were once used to evoke the powerful image of a "United States of Africa." This image, promoted zealously by Kwame Nkrumah, captured the imagination of African elites [17]. But its power far outstripped structural supports, and middle-range process mechanisms had only minimal positive impact. By 1966, when Nkrumah was toppled from power in Ghana, pressure for political integration of Africa had largely abated [15, 27].[10]

Bargaining Solutions

A third specific factor is the deliberate steps in bargaining for a coalition agreement. The quality and style of bargaining and the size and diversity of the

[10] Before independence the African colonies had been protected from international intercourse and closely tied to their metropolitan centers. Their communications and the organization of their trade were heavily distorted, to the degree that in 1960 a long-distance telephone call between Accra in Ghana and Lome in Togo, less than 100 miles apart, had to be routed through London and Paris. Language and technological barriers limited the possibilities for increased transactions. Since independence some positive steps toward increasing intra-African trade have been taken, but they have not been large, nor has their impact spread to many other social and political processes.

agreements "package" may depend upon particular features of the bargaining process. In Europe, for instance, the High Commission has played an important role in the bargaining process, designing packages that have resolved difficult conflicts of interest among member states through complex agreements involving mutual concessions in timing, side payments, and escape clauses. Effective bargaining and innovative "packages" are conducive to specific agreements that can generate support for both their initial ratification and subsequent implementation. Federalists, in particular, are concerned that agreements be enforceable and acceptable. They must therefore reflect underlying interests and the realities of resource distribution among the parties to them. Although the integration of the thirteen American colonies was furthered by a common interest in fighting the English enemy and by the ideological appeal of such slogans as "United we stand, divided we fall," the actual organizational structure that emerged was the result of an intricate bargaining process. Negotiations first produced an inadequate package of agreements, the Articles of Confederation, but eventually the leaders wrote a document that has proved both flexible and realistic.[11]

Responsiveness

Responsiveness to the sensitivities of other actors is important in promoting trust and complementarity of values among elites. Empathy across national boundaries can be important in sustaining other forms of integration. Occasional domestic pressures in one state may necessitate actions that may be perceived as hostile or detrimental by other states. Mutual responsiveness tends to dampen, rather than to intensify this impact. For instance, currency imbalances among countries frequently gen-

[11] The American Constitution remains a landmark for federalist analysis of integration. Its virtues have been debated since *The Federalist*. For application of communications theory to the foundation of the United States, see Richard L. Merritt, *The Growth of American Community* (New Haven: Yale University Press, 1966).

erate antagonism, as speculators endanger the smooth functioning of a state's economy. During the last decade a number of "financial crises" involving the devaluation of the franc and the pound, the revaluation of the mark, and the floating of the dollar have created considerable short-term alarm. But adjustments have been made after long consultations and consideration of possible consequences for relevant actors. These unilateral steps have been accepted by elites in other states. The sensitivity necessary for mutual responsiveness, as we have suggested, is rooted in a broad range of transactions, particularly social communications, that promote assimilation and common feelings. Efforts to calculate how the "other fellow" will think or feel about certain actions are also occasionally undertaken in the foreign offices of nation-states alert to the value of responsiveness in realizing mutual goals.[12] Social learning, supported by increases in rewarding communications and economic transactions, can be an important mechanism for enlarging capacity for responsiveness among actors. Richard Meier has argued: "A large continuous flow of information makes it possible to mobilize the requisite experience and data . . . to bring the anticipated crisis to the attention of decision-makers sooner than would otherwise occur. Large flows of information . . . make it possible to reduce the chances of blundering into international conflicts" [18].

Leaders

Finally, leaders can have important effects, at least in the short run, on the success or failure of integration efforts. Fred I. Greenstein has shown how the location of an individual in a particular critical position, not strongly determined by role norms, may have significant historical impact [10]. Occasionally powerful political

---

[12] Neustadt has pointed out that U.S. State Department officials charged with European affairs were highly sensitive to the potential impact of the crisis over cancellation of the Skybolt missile in 1962 on Prime Minister Harold Macmillan and the British government [20].

leaders like Roy Welensky of Rhodesia and Tunku Abdul Rahman of Malaysia are able to use their personal popularity to help create a federation. But long- and middle-range factors have not sustained the amalgamations inaugurated by these leaders. Similarly, the presence of moderate pro-European leaders like Alcide de Gasperi of Italy, Robert Schumann of France, Konrad Adenauer of Germany, and Ernest Bevin of Great Britain stimulated the movement toward European unification in the late 1940s and early 1950s.

Conversely, a strong leader like de Gaulle can block integration. Inglehart has argued that de Gaulle's personal vision, his disregard for unpopularity, and his actual authority as president and as the man who had rescued France from civil war permitted him to play a unique role in the European integration process. Although economic pressures and popular opinion favored further integration, they were effectively neutralized by de Gaulle. Through a sequence of "crises" in the 1960s he was able to impose a French veto on a number of proposed steps toward integration, but his popularity and authority were largely derived from the fact that he was perceived as "indispensable," the one man who could ensure both political and economic stability for France [14, p. 780]. Once French domestic crises had subsided, Inglehart has argued, de Gaulle's stand on European integration became an important factor in the subsequent decline of his popularity and electoral support. Those who had supported both de Gaulle and integration drifted from his camp. After his ineffective performance during the students' and workers' uprisings in May–June 1968, he no longer seemed indispensable. Georges Pompidou, his successor, moved discreetly toward a more "European" position. In his election campaign he persuaded leading European-oriented politicians to his side and subsequently appointed several of them to key positions in his cabinet [14, pp. 781–782]. The underlying process mechanisms favoring further European integration and a "European" orientation are likely from here on to influence the positions taken by leading politicians in France and throughout Europe, at least by men less driven by inner visions than de Gaulle was.

INTEGRATION AS AN EMERGENT PROPERTY

Figure 13.2 illustrates these three types of factors and their impacts on the integration process over time. The vertical axis represents the impact and the horizontal axis represents time. Integration is essentially the emergent property of the interaction among these factors. In general, we suspect that short-term factors have great immediate impact but only marginal impacts over time. Long-term factors, though changing at a slow and fairly constant rate, may pass a threshold beyond which they have increasingly powerful effects in moving a nascent community toward greater concentration of central authority. In the ideal instance of integration, illustrated by the straight line in Figure 13.2, initial factors (like a perceived common enemy) or leading personalities (like Konrad Adenauer and Jean Monnet) might promote integration. Through these efforts a large formal step toward integration may occur while underlying structural features change only minimally. The average weight of short- and long-term factors thus falls along the straight line. If all factors maintain a constant and positive impact on integration over time, the ensuing sequence of middle- and then long-term factors will create an ever-firmer institutional base for the emerging community. In reality, however, such a straight-line progression is extremely unlikely. "Spill back," or prolonged plateaus of relative stagnation, may therefore occur in the movement toward a larger political community. Furthermore, the assumption of constant rates of change in these factors is also unrealistic. An accurate illustration of the impacts of various forces along the two axes in Figure 13.2 would probably include a ragged pattern.

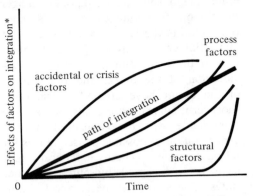

Figure 13.2. Curvilinear and Phase Effects of Factors Affecting Integration

* Definition of this dependent variable remains ambiguous and depends partly upon the specific purpose of the research. For our purposes, a low probability of violence (ensured by mechanisms for joint decision making) will suffice.

INTERNAL OUTCOMES AND THE EUROPEAN COMMON MARKET

As integration proceeds, four types of outcome seem to occur.[13] The first is that social and economic changes among integrating units create pressures for politicization; they involve actions by legitimate spokesmen of individual actors to formalize the sets of transactions and interdependencies that have arisen. A second type of outcome is the narrowing of limits on viable alternatives for a member of the nascent community. "Politicized" arrangements and changing structure tend increasingly to tie the policy alternatives of an actor to decisions taken by other members. A third outcome may be greater recognition of the differences between external units and the community itself. One of the important objections to Great Britain's entry into the Common Market was that it has special ties with the United States and the Commonwealth that would be incompatible with the obligations of a full-fledged "European" state. As integration proceeds, actors within the community tend to behave as a group toward external units. A fourth outcome may be increased differentiation in the bargain-

[13] These outcomes have been discussed by Nye [21] in his summary of the views of various writers.

ing process, resulting in more complex arrangements. Increased differentiation means that problems will be considered separately and resolved according to their own merits rather than necessitating "package" solutions that indicate a lack of trust. Such adjustments are particularly noticeable in the economic sphere, with agreements affecting labor migration, arbitrage, and relative market equilibrium (before transportation costs).

These four outcomes primarily reflect the adjustment of the domestic processes of member units to integration. All seem to have occurred during the integration of the EEC. Although it may have reached a plateau in its movement toward an integrated society, the EEC nevertheless exhibits the complexity of a partially integrated community in which process mechanisms, including functional links among economic and political activities, are widespread. Figure 13.3 illustrates the decision-making process of the European community and the units that play parts in the process. Such supranational organs as the European Parliament, Court of Justice Commission, various legislative and executive bodies, and the still-critical Council of Ministers, make the European Economic Community the most important example of integration in the twentieth century. Integration in the community has occurred through both growth and transfer. Supported by rising intra-EEC patterns of trade, functional agencies were created. These led to the limited transfer of authority, most dramatically after the Treaty of Rome (1957). During the 1960s there was little further transfer, as the move from requiring unanimity in decision making was deferred. Nevertheless, a study of decisions reached by the community from 1950 to 1970—encompassing military, political, social, and economic issues— shows that a trend toward greater community authority persisted (see Table 13.7).

Figure 13.4 illustrates the process and sequence among various factors during integration. It is important to observe that these processes can affect one another over time. Recalling the complexity of structure in social systems (see Chapter 5), we note that until the third or fourth cycle every variable has at least one lag and at least one interdependent relationship with another variable, though many of these relationships may be weak and unimportant.

The complexity of the integration problem has both challenged and hampered scholars in their efforts to clarify the phenomenon.

CONCLUSION AND FORECASTS

The process of integration remains a fascinating and central topic in international politics. The factors that determine the paths by which groups of actors move toward integration constitute possibly the most long-term force in international politics.

There is a relationship between system transformation resulting from integration and reduced probability of violence in international politics, as Figure 13.5 illustrates. At the first stage, before integration begins, relatively independent actors interact. Shifts in process and "crisis" factors like the unique leadership of Adolf Hitler in Germany can exert strong influence on outcomes in international politics. Probabilities of violence can vary widely, depending upon fluctuations in the compatibility of actors' goals. Once an integration process is underway, whether or not it has reached a plateau, a partial loss of autonomy by actors will occur. Process and crisis factors continue to be important. But, if integration proceeds or at least remains at some intermediate level, factors favoring integration will reinforce one another. As a result, factors inimical to integration, like de Gaulle's intransigence, may cause only small backward fluctuations during a long period of relatively steady transition. On the other hand, though structural factors may reduce or limit the probability of violence, integration may not yet be ensured. The underlying structural conditions for an in-

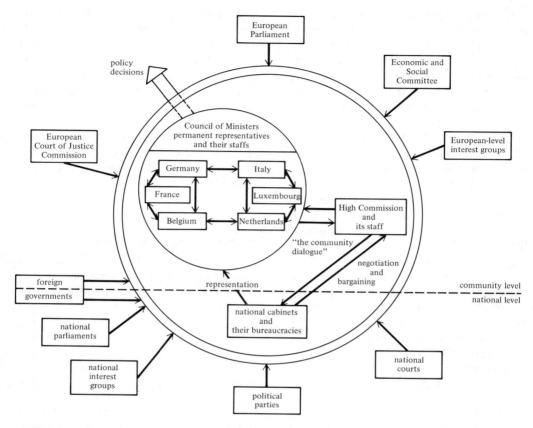

Figure 13.3. Actors in the Community Legislative Process
Source: Leon N. Lindbery and Stuart A. Scheingold, *Europe's Would-Be Polity: Patterns of Change in the European Community,* © 1970. Reprinted by permission of Prentice-Hall, Inc., Englewood Cliffs, New Jersey.

Table 13.7.

Changes in Decision-Making Locus for all Ranges of Issues, 1950-1970

	Locus of Decision	*1950*	*1957*	*1968*	*1970*
Within states	all national	22	15	5	5
	only very beginning community	0	7	9	5
Within the community	both but national predominating	0	0	6	8
	both but community predominating	0	0	2	4
	all community	0	0	0	0

Source: Leon N. Lindberg and Stuart A. Scheingold, *Europe's Would-Be Polity,* © 1970. Reprinted by permission of Prentice-Hall, Englewood Cliffs, New Jersey.

tegrated society may be reversed by failures in bargaining and process mechanisms. During the transition period, then, the will of individual leaders remains critical in determining the extent to which in-

tegration will proceed and even its eventual success or failure.

Once integration has passed certain critical thresholds, structure and process factors may continue to institutionalize

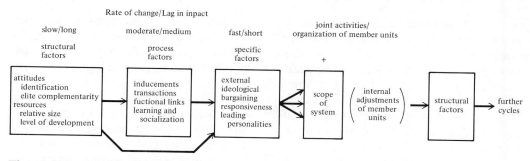

Figure 13.4. Factors in Integration Processes over Time
Source: Suggested by a similar formulation by Joseph S. Nye, Jr., "Comparing Common Markets: A Revised Neofunctionalist Model," *International Organization,* 24 (Autumn 1970), p. 813).

Conditions	Stages		
	First	Second	Third
degree of autonomy	autonomous actors ready for assimilation	partial loss of autonomy (transformation process; see Figure 13.4)	nearly complete loss of autonomy
structural factors	permissive	unstable	prohibition of violence
effects of process and crisis factors	strong effects on unstable probabilities of violence	effects on bargaining and phasing of change	weal effects on community formations; probability of violence increased only by changes in structure
probability of violence	high to low	medium to low	low

Figure 13.5. Stages in Integration

integration. The autonomy of individual actors may decline precipitously, and the future community will be only modestly affected by process and crisis factors—and even then after considerable lag. Disintegration of an integrated community can be expected to occur only through changes in structural factors. Disaffection, as in subnationalist and separatist movements, might still occur after successful international integration. Nevertheless, except in extreme instances, the probabilities of violence within the community should remain low.

At the beginning of this chapter we suggested two possible future world systems. The first is characterized by integration in several regions, reducing the number of actors and ensuring more equitable distribution of influence. Despite some trends in Europe, a future international system of this sort seems less likely than one of the second kind: a complex, multileveled, but fragmented set of actors with overlapping and conflicting goals. This alternative seems more likely for several reasons. First, in the less developed parts of the world formation of national identities remains a major goal. As social mobilization continues during coming decades, internal turmoil and fragmentation are likely. The disintegration of political unions like the Malaysian Federation, the Central and East African unions, the Mali Federation and the West Indian Federation are not merely post-independence aberrations. Linguistic differences in India remain deep and capable of fueling full-fledged separatist movements. The defeat of Biafra by federalist forces in Nigeria does not ensure that separatist movements will not occur again in Africa. New states will therefore erect interstate barriers in order to promote domestic unity and attempt to enhance their own autonomy at the expense of international integration. They are likely to continue demands for recognition of "sovereignty," territorial integrity, and economic autonomy (see Chapter 9).

Among the more developed states the emergence of "postindustrial" societies and the technological ability to produce nuclear weapons strongly suggest that a unit-veto type of international structure is possible, at least on some issues. Although a critical breakthrough in arms reduction and limitation could alter this picture *somewhat*, technological trends limit the potential effects of any such agreement among the major states because they retain the capacity to act on their own.

The trend in less developed areas thus tends toward less integration, increased sovereignty, and conscious efforts to inhibit interdependence. Among the developed states accumulation of technological and welfare resources may accompany increasing social and economic interdependence and may enhance awareness of this interdependence among mass societies. Long-term structural factors affecting assimilation and identification are probably *not* changing rapidly enough to encourage or even to permit formal political amalgamation under the aegis of regional, let alone global, political organizations. But a reservoir of support for increased integration may be created.

Such a complex, less "integrated" world would conform to the predictions of Haas and, to a lesser degree, to those of Deutsch. Although it would permit, and perhaps encourage, a great deal of local violence, it might "bar global conflict because of its very fragmentation."[14]

[14] Haas has considered such a development comparatively positive from the point of view of world peace and global integration. See also Deutsch's discussion [4].

Under these circumstances we may expect systemic development without integration; the result may resemble the system of feuding principalities in fifteenth-century Italy, which, although geographically close, were unable to identify with one another or to accept a common authority. The global processes of change make it unlikely that actors' capabilities for violence will be reduced. How long the rights of individual states to initiate war unilaterally will remain depends upon whether or not a more limited set of prerogatives and rights for nations will evolve from redirecting the will of both elites and masses and from the institutionalization of new sets of authoritative expectations among leaders.

References

1. Alker, Hayward R., Jr., and Donald Puchala, "Trends in Economic Partnership," in J. David Singer, ed., *Quantitative International Politics* (New York: Free Press, 1968), p. 288.
2. Bauer, Raymond A., Ithiel de Sola Pool, and Lewis A. Dexter, *American Business and Public Policy* (New York: Atherton, 1963).
3. Claude, Inis L., Jr., *Swords into Plowshares,* 3rd ed. (New York: Random House, 1964), chap. 17.
4. Deutsch, Karl W., "The Future of World Politics," *Political Quarterly,* 37 (January–March 1966), pp. 9–32.
5. Deutsch, Karl W., "Nation and World," in Ithiel de Sola Pool, ed., *Contemporary Political Science: Toward Political Theory* (New York: McGraw-Hill, 1967).
6. Deutsch, Karl W., *et al., Political Community and the North Atlantic Area: International Organization in the Light of Historical Experience* (Princeton: Princeton University Press, 1957).
7. Foltz, William J., *From French West Africa to the Mali Federation* (New Haven: Yale University Press, 1965).
8. Frank, Thomas N., ed., *Why Federations Fail* (New York: New York University Press, 1968).
9. Friedrich, Carl J., *Trends of Federalism in Theory and Practice* (New York: Praeger, 1968).

10. Greenstein, Fred I., "The Impact of Personality on Politics: An Attempt to Clear Away the Underbrush," *American Political Science Review,* 61 (September 1967), pp. 629–641.

11. Haas, Ernst B., "The Study of Regional Integration: Reflections on the Joy and Anguish of Pretheorizing," *International Organization,* 24 (Autumn 1970), pp. 607–646.

12. Haas, Ernst B., *The Uniting of Europe: Political, Social and Economic Forces, 1950–1957* (Stanford: Stanford University Press, 1958).

13. Hoffmann, Stanley, "Obstinate or Obsolete? The Fate of the Nation State and the Case of Western Europe," in Joseph S. Nye, Jr., *International Regionalism: Readings* (Boston: Little, Brown, 1968), pp. 177–230.

14. Inglehart, Ronald, "Public Opinion and Regional Integration," *International Organization,* 24 (Autumn 1970), pp. 764–795.

15. Legum, Colin, *Africa: Pan-Africanism* (New York: Praeger, 1962).

16. Lindberg, Leon, *The Political Dynamics of European Economic Integration* (Stanford: Stanford University Press, 1963).

17. Mazrui, Ali A., "On the Concept 'We are all African,'" *American Political Science Review,* 57 (March 1963), pp. 88–97.

18. Meier, Richard, "Information, Resources and Economic Growth," in J. J. Spengler, ed., *National Resources and Economic Growth* (Washington, D.C.: Resources for the Future, n.d.), p. 113.

19. Mitrany, David, *A Working Peace System* (London: Royal Institute of International Affairs, 1943).

20. Neustadt, Richard E., *Alliance Politics* (New York: Columbia University Press, 1970).

21. Nye, Joseph S., Jr., "Comparing Common Markets: A Revised Neofunctionalist Model," *International Organization,* 24 (Autumn 1970), p. 815.

22. Puchala, Donald J., "International Transactions and Regional Integration," *International Organization,* 24 (Autumn 1970), pp. 732–763.

23. Riker, William H., *Federalism: Origin,* *Operation, Maintenance* (Boston: Little, Brown, 1964).

24. Russett, Bruce M., *Community and Contention: Britain and America in the Twentieth Century* (Cambridge, Mass.: MIT Press, 1963).

25. Schmitter, Philippe C., "A Revised Theory of Regional Integration," *International Organization,* 24 (Autumn 1970), pp. 836–868.

26. Sewell, James P., *Functionalism and World Politics* (Princeton: Princeton University Press, 1966).

27. Wallerstein, Immanuel, *The Politics of Unity* (New York: Random House, 1967).

Suggested Reading

Cooper, Richard N., *The Economics of Interdependence: Economic Policy in the Atlantic Community* (New York: McGraw-Hill, 1968).

Deutsch, Karl W., *et al., Political Community and the North Atlantic Area: International Organization in the Light of Historical Experience* (Princeton: Princeton University Press, 1957).

Etzioni, Amitai, *Political Unification: A Comparative Study of Leaders and Forces* (New York: Holt, Rinehart and Winston, 1965).

Haas, Ernst B., *Beyond the Nation-State: Functionalism and International Organization* (Stanford: Stanford University Press, 1964).

Jacob, Philip E., and James V. Toscano, eds., *The Integration of Political Communities* (Philadelphia: Lippincott, 1964).

Kitzinger, Uwe W., *The Politics and Economics of European Integration: Britain, Europe, and the United States* (New York: Praeger, 1963).

Lindberg, Leon N., and Stuart A. Scheingold, *Europe's Would-Be Polity: Patterns of Change in the European Community* (Englewood Cliffs, N.J.: Prentice-Hall, 1970).

Lindberg, Leon N., and Stuart A. Scheingold, "Regional Integration: Theory and Research," *International Organization,* 24 (Autumn 1970).

Nye, Joseph S., Jr., ed., *International Regionalism: Readings* (Boston: Little, Brown, 1968).

Chapter 14
ALLIANCES AND COALITIONS IN INTERNATIONAL POLITICS

Alliance is as original an event in politics as is conflict.... It is impossible to speak of international relations without referring to alliances.... For the same reason, it has always been difficult to say much that is peculiar to alliances on the plane of general analysis—George Liska [24, p. 3]

Cooperative activities among actors are as central to international politics as is conflict. Alliances and coalitions are formed for a variety of reasons, among many kinds of formal and informal groups, from ad hoc and purely defensive associations to functional organizations and the United Nations. The dynamics of coalition behavior are similar to those of the formative stages of integrated communities. Increased interdependence in the global system has made collective behavior more important—and more frequent—than it has been in previous historical periods. The burgeoning number and types of collective ventures throw doubt on interpretations by balance-of-power theorists who have argued that coalitions result simply from perceptions of external threats by countries banded together to prevent domination by a single adversary or group of adversaries. Many contemporary alliances and coalitions seem to amount to more than such transient arrangements.

Actors are rarely able to realize international objectives without the cooperation of others. Furthermore, unilateral behavior is generally "convention-breaking" and likely to be regarded as "intervention or neoimperialism" [34]. By contrast, collective behavior often gains acceptance, even legitimacy, whereas similar behavior would be condemned if undertaken unilaterally.

The politics of cooperation raises several questions. When and why do actors engage in such behavior? What types of coalition occur? Why do some actors find collective behavior more congenial? Why do some collective endeavors persist and others end quickly? What principles determine the number of actors involved in a collective venture? How do coalitions of equals differ from coalitions in which some actors are dominant? Why are some collective arrangements formal whereas others remain loose and informal? Answering these questions is our task in this chapter.

FROM SERENDIPITY TO MALICE AFORETHOUGHT

Actors with similar or compatible objectives often undertake collective behavior with little prior planning. For instance, in the U.N. General Assembly, where each member has a single vote, semipermanent coalitions and even subcoalitions vote together on particular types of issues. The size of the General Assembly, the variety of issues before it, and the "one man, one vote" rule have engendered these alignments. African and Asian nations, for example, tend to vote together on issues involving colonialism and economic development but to divide on cold-war questions. The General Assembly has become "a meeting ground where alignments without alliances could be nurtured" [36]. (See Chapter 10, pp. 225–226.) Despite formal cooperation in some voting "groups," they have not crystallized into blocs; their "interrelationships are symptoms of a fluid political process characterized by ad hoc coalitions, independent decision-making by states, and the absence of any effective system to coordinate voting among large numbers of countries" [21]. Since 1957 majorities in the General Assembly have been more ad hoc, and coordination has been correspondingly difficult [1].

Countries that engage in ad hoc cooperation may in time undertake more formal collaboration as they discover shared interests. For example, the experiences of several leading nonaligned nations in the United Nations have paved the way for more formal periodic conferences to coordinate policy.

Alliances involve greater planned cooperation than do alignments. Actors bargain with one another, coordinate strategies, and seek agreement on objectives. Often alliances are formalized through treaties specifying the intended collective behavior and the obligations of the participants. But many less formal agreements are also concluded among national representatives. The president of the United States, for example, can commit

his government by "executive agreements" with representatives of other states. Such agreements do not require ratification by the Senate and have the force of treaties in American courts.[1]

Treaties often specify conditions in which they will function. In the sense that each party undertakes to behave in certain ways as long as the others do the same, treaties are similar to contracts in domestic law. But in contrast to contracts, there is seldom an authority that can adjudicate disputes over the terms of the treaty or enforce its commitments. Several principles of international law have been evolved to deal with this problem. The principle of *pacta sunt servanda* obligates actors to honor their international agreements. In addition, when no termination date has been specified, the principle of *rebus sic statibus*—that a treaty is valid only while the conditions under which it was signed persist—applies. Attempting to enforce agreements that no longer reflect mutual interests can generate conflict.[2] The principle was explicitly recognized by the authors of the Covenant of the League of Nations, who included it as Article 19.

---

[1] In its decision in Missouri v. Holland in 1920 the U.S. Supreme Court ruled that acts of Congress in pursuance of international treaties take precedence over rights reserved to states in the Constitution. "No doubt the great body of private relations usually fall within the control of the State," the Court declared, "but a treaty may override its power" [17]. Fearing that international treaties and executive agreements might erode constitutional guarantees, Senator William Bricker of Ohio in 1953 sponsored a constitutional amendment that would have subjected all "enabling legislation" to constitutional review and all executive agreements to congressional approval. The measure, however, failed to obtain the necessary two-thirds vote in the Senate.

[2] The legal theorist Hugo Grotius considered resort to war to enforce treaties "just." He believed it a "rule of the law of nature to abide by pacts." For him, treaties of alliance were evidence that international law exists. "We see that even the most powerful peoples and sovereigns seek alliances, which are quite devoid of significance according to the point of view of those who confine law within the boundaries of states" [15].

STRANGE BEDFELLOWS: TYPES OF ACTORS IN ALLIANCES

Today coalition behavior is increasingly typical not only of national governments but of all types of international actors as well. The Communist International (Comintern), for example, was a formal alliance of communist parties throughout the world. Nor is it unusual for governments to align or ally themselves with nongovernmental or "transnational" groups or organizations. Let us consider for a moment the Middle East situation during the summer of 1970. When, in July, the United States proposed a ninety-day cease-fire between the Arabs and the Israelis, the major antagonists found themselves in difficulties with their extra-national allies. Egypt, in accepting the cease-fire proposal, not only angered Arab states like Algeria and Iraq but also inflamed Palestinian commando organizations and refugee groups in Jordan, Syria, and Lebanon, which looked to President Gamal Abdel Nasser for leadership and support. The commando organizations sought to undermine the cease-fire by continuing hostilities against Israel and conducting a terrorist campaign that included the highjacking and destruction of several Western commercial airplanes. Israel sought to use its connections with the American Jewish community to apply pressure on Richard M. Nixon's administration to increase military assistance. Jewish-American groups functioned as allies through which the Israeli government might influence American decision makers. Loose coalitions of both long and short standing and not limited only to states thus participated in the bargaining.

Similarly, international corporations engage in joint development schemes with governments or join together in cartels and consortiums to protect their common interests. One such alliance provoked an international crisis in 1953: the agreement between the Iranian government and the Anglo-Iranian Oil Company for joint development of Iran's petroleum resources. In 1951 the government nationalized the oil industry and attempted to turn it into a government operation. Pressure exerted by the company and fear of increasing Soviet influence in the Iranian oil fields induced the United States and Great Britain to support a clandestine operation to overthrow the government of Premier Mohammed Mossadegh. Subsequently a new international consortium concluded a twenty-five-year agreement with Iran for development of the oil fields [45].

The kidnapping and murder of foreign diplomats by Latin American revolutionary groups illustrates one way in which nongovernmental actors have sought to force unwilling governments to ally with them temporarily. On several occasions in 1969 and 1970 foreign diplomats were seized in efforts to force their governments to press the host countries to release imprisoned guerrillas or to accede to other demands. In one instance the Guatemalan government refused to capitulate to rebel demands, and a German ambassador was murdered.

Studies of alliance behavior that focus only on formal agreements among governmental actors fail to account for the broad scope of alliance behavior. The collaboration of the People's Republic of China, North Vietnam, and the Viet Cong between 1954 and 1972 and the alliance among governments in exile, United Nations allies, and resistance movements in Europe during World War II are good examples of other important kinds of alliance behavior.

THE MOTIVES FOR FORMING ALLIANCES

Those who assume that all international actors seek to maximize autonomy, always consider alliance behavior "extraordinary." "Tradition," one observer has suggested, "has . . . given a status of normality to alignment, because of its prevalence, whereas it is nonalignment which is the 'norm' of foreign policy, the independent equilibrium position as it were, from which nations are moved by pressures and circumstances" [5]. Largely on the basis of this single assumption many theorists have sought to explain alliances as reluctant efforts of actors to combine in the smallest groups necessary to enable them to achieve objectives. An actor who can achieve all his objectives alone has no motive to enter into an alliance in which he must surrender some of his autonomy to his alliance partners. The party to an alliance has obligations and responsibilities to his allies, and his freedom to maneuver is thus circumscribed.

An actor may have several motives for entering into an alliance. He may be seeking an objective for which his own resources are insufficient. For example, the United States accepted the cooperation of the British in the nineteenth century because it was incapable of enforcing the Monroe Doctrine alone; only the British possessed the naval strength necessary to prevent other European nations from interfering in the affairs of the Western Hemisphere; Britain also shared the American interest in preventing European penetration in the area.

An actor may seek an alliance to lessen the costs of attaining an objective. Although such an alliance may not be *necessary,* it is advantageous to the actor. For example, the United States has sought to spread the costs of deterring Soviet expansion among its European allies, even though American resources are sufficient to the task. The North Atlantic Treaty Organization reduces American costs in manpower and hard currency—beside strengthening the credibility of the American commitment to deterrence. By pooling resources and using them efficiently actors can sometimes reduce costs for all. Economic groups like the European Economic Community, in which partners build on one another's strengths, are examples. Or the government of a "third world" state may contract with an international corporation to build an industry because it is less expensive to import capital than to raise it and less expensive to bring in trained personnel than to train

it abroad. Finally, an actor may join with others to reduce his share of responsibility. By fighting the Korean War under United Nations auspices, the United States sought to avoid the onus of unilateral intervention. In all these instances the actor also reduces his freedom to maneuver and increases his dependence upon others.

It is usually difficult to predict precisely what resources will be necessary to achieve an objective. Candidates know precisely how many votes they need to win nominations or elections. But, as our discussion of influence revealed, it is extremely difficult to measure with any certainty what resources will be required to achieve an objective. In international politics, although information on tangible resources of allies and even of adversaries may be available, equally reliable information on intangible factors like morale and stability rarely is. There is a tendency to "play it safe" by overestimating an adversary's tangible resources and underestimating one's own. An alliance may therefore appear desirable to ensure a winning margin or to distribute the costs of achieving a common objective. It was because of uncertainty about winning, for example, that Winston Churchill argued vainly in 1939 that Great Britain should conclude a military alliance with the Soviet Union against Germany despite British aversion to bolshevist ideology [7].

An alliance may enable an actor to gain an objective more quickly than he otherwise would. When Franklin D. Roosevelt met Joseph Stalin at Yalta in February 1945, he was confident that the United States could defeat Japan unaided, but he insisted that the Soviet Union enter the war in Asia to bring about a speedier and less expensive victory. "To President Roosevelt at Yalta," Averell Harriman testified in 1951, "the lives of American fighting men were at stake. He had been advised by the Joint Chiefs of Staff that the defeat of Japan would take many months after VE-Day . . ." [19].

Finally, an actor may seek an alliance in order to establish a pattern of cooperation that can prove useful in the future.

Part of the initial thinking behind President John F. Kennedy's proposal for the Alliance for Progress in 1961 was the assumption that endorsing orderly economic and political change in Latin America, rather than defending the status quo, would win and maintain for the United States the good will of emerging leaders in the area. Similarly, the admission of Mongolia to the Council of Mutual Economic Assistance in 1962 reflected Soviet expectations that this country would become increasingly important as the Sino-Soviet rift widened [27].

An actor's reasons for seeking a particular alliance influence the commitment, compromises, and energy that he brings to the effort. An alliance based on necessity, rather than on convenience, will evoke greater commitment from an actor; because the actor perceives no alternative to a coalition if he is to achieve his objectives, he is prepared to surrender more autonomy than he otherwise would.

INTERESTS AND OBJECTIVES: THE BASES FOR ALLIANCE

The number of common or complementary interests and objectives in an alliance influences the specificity of the agreement, its duration, and the commitment of resources that partners are prepared to make. According to the Greek historian Thucydides, the strongest alliances involve partners that can "be persuaded of each other's honesty. . . . [But] the only sure basis of an alliance is for each party to be equally afraid of the other" [42]. Real "union," Thucydides believed, requires a broad range of common objectives, and limited cooperation requires reciprocity and sanctions against parties that renege.

Actors' interests in seeking alliances vary widely. An alliance may satisfy the needs of specific leaders, domestic groups, even domestic economic interests [16, pp. 48–68]. The propensity of actors to join particular combinations seems to depend partly upon historical experience: States that have long attained objectives by their own efforts, as have Switzerland and Sweden, are less prone to collaborate with others [16, p. 54; 41].[3]

Actors tend to prefer as alliance partners those other actors with whom they share cultural and ideological values and economic interests.[4] Common, or at least not incompatible, ideological commitments generally provide impetus for alliance behavior, though they rarely provide a sufficient basis for a durable alliance. Distribution of capabilities also seems to affect the choices of alliance partners, but there is little agreement among scholars on precisely how. Do weak powers join with stronger ones, or do they seek allies with similar capabilities?[5]

One of the most striking developments since World War II has been the increased emphasis on broad mutual interests among allies. Technology has been a major force behind formation of alliances involving more than traditional military, economic, and political interests. Sociocultural interests, ideology, common race and religion, and human-welfare goals like preservation of ecological balance and population control are becoming significant variables in alliance behavior.

The Anglo-American coalition exemplifies the extent to which some associations are based on broad common interests and the ways in which cooperation can "escalate." The coalition can be dated from 1895, when a boundary dispute involving Venezuela nearly brought the United States and Great Britain into open conflict until the British agreed to arbitration. War was avoided partly because a security community between the United

[3] This hypothesis has been reinforced by one study of postwar Swedish and Norwegian behavior. Norway joined NATO and Sweden remained neutral partly because of their different experiences during World War II [3].

[4] The preconditions for alliances appear to be similar to those for integration; see Chapter 13, pp. 286–298.

[5] For discussion of this question, see George Liska [24, pp. 13–14], Charles P. Schleicher [38], and Kenneth Waltz [44].

States and Great Britain had been evolving since the 1820s. The British, one historian has argued, "sacrificed their prestige to the belief that war with the United States was unthinkable" [2]. Despite several disputes between the two nations in the 1920s, particularly one concerning the relative size of their navies, the experience of fighting together in World Wars I and II have cemented the Anglo-American community. The conviction of Churchill (whose mother was American) that his country and the United States share enduring interests was expressed in a letter to President Roosevelt in 1940:

[I]t seems to me that the vast majority of American citizens have recorded their conviction that the safety of the United States, as well as the future of our two Democracies and the kind of civilization for which they stand, is bound up with the survival and independence of the British Commonwealth of Nations. [8, 10]

Shared experience, culture and language, and close economic and personal ties have all contributed to this "special relationship." In addition to pragmatic objectives, "nonutilitarian" factors thus help to shape cooperation. Bruce M. Russett has suggested that many United States senators have extensive personal and economic ties with the British and that they are therefore likely to be sympathetic to British needs [37].

The extent to which actors will be able to recognize mutual interests appears to depend partly upon the relative distribution of capabilities among them. "In an alliance of states very unequal in size and strength," Henry A. Kissinger has written, "differences are almost certain to arise" [22, p. 226; 46; 35]. It has also been argued that democratic states are less reliable allies because of frequent changes in government and determination of policies in accordance with domestic sentiment. Nevertheless, history does not reveal patterns that permit a conclusion on this point [18]. As defense policies result partly from bargaining within complex domestic bureaucratic structures, it is probably true that alliances are unstable

to the extent that allies fail to understand one another's bureaucratic politics. Such domestic bargaining leads to definition of interests and objectives, and insensitive allies may be unresponsive [22, pp. 225–226; 29].

Types of interests and objectives—whether they are common or complementary—affect the durability of an alliance. A common interest is one in which two or more actors have the same objective. For instance, the allies had a common objective in defeating Germany during World War II. A complementary interest, on the other hand, is one in which actors have different ends but discover that mutual assistance will enable each to achieve his own. The alliance between the Soviet Union and Egypt after 1967 was based on complementary objectives. The Soviet Union seeks primarily to increase its influence in the Middle East and the eastern Mediterranean and to undermine Western influence in these areas; Egypt seeks to recover Arab lands from Israel, which conquered them in June 1967.

Alliances based on complementary interests tend to be of shorter duration than do alliances based on common interests. The former very likely occur because joint resources will enable each actor to achieve his separate objectives, but the links among allies are tenuous: Once either party has attained its objective, it will have little incentive to continue the alliance. Moreover, the opportunity for misunderstandings is great within such alliances. Their potential fragility is illustrated by President Anwar el-Sadat's sudden expulsion of his Russian allies from Egypt in July 1972. Sadat's decision was based on his belief that the Soviet Union's global interests prevented Soviet leaders from appreciating Egypt's regional objectives.

Strains may develop within alliances that have lasted for considerable periods because changing conditions alter members' objectives. On the other hand, if the alliance is not founded purely on expediency, its sheer survival may enhance its solidarity: Habits of cooperation and mutual responsiveness may develop, and institutional links may come to be valued, regardless of whether or not they any longer serve the original purposes of the alliance.

As we have suggested, coordination and decision making within an alliance vary from informal, or tacit, collaboration to institutionalized and centralized processes. When an alliance arises mainly from immediate expedience, a formal, centralized structure may contribute to its overall efficiency; "because of its control over resources, it can readily respond to external threats or opportunities" [26]. But pluralistic alliances may permit members to oppose one another on specific issues without destroying the alliance itself. The very rigidity of certain alliances may be a source of internal tension, and the need to suppress deviation may increase internal stresses [35, p. 178; 11; 6].

The greater the number and the wider the range of common objectives, the less likely it is that alliance commitments will be set forth in official documents. The formalization of an alliance is generally a means of defining the scope and domain of partners' obligations. When there is a wide range of common interests, such explicit definitions may exclude areas of cooperation and even reduce them. Furthermore, formalization may be redundant. The United States and Great Britain have cooperated for many years on a broad range of issues without formalizing their bilateral obligations; both nations are members of NATO, but this alliance mainly binds them with other states.

On the other hand, the greater the number of alliance partners, the greater is the need to formalize the alliance, for greater numbers generate difficulties in coordination and control, which require formal structure and procedures to ensure the effectiveness of the alliance. The more inclusive the alliance is, the more difficult it becomes for one actor to be responsive to the needs of each of the others, for his attention must be spread more thinly. In such an alliance it is expedient for a single actor, particularly a smaller one, to limit his contribution because it will appear to make little difference in the strength of the alliance as a whole. "In short," Mancur Olson, Jr., has declared, "the larger the group, the less it will further its common interests" [30]. The inclusion of many actors increases the probability that divergent interests will also be present. Recent French efforts to establish a European community that would exclude the United States and Canada can be viewed as an attempt to increase cohesion among Europeans, which, the French argue, is diluted by the active presence of a superpower with global responsibilities and interests.

The difficulties experienced by global organizations illustrate this point. United Nations sanctions against white-controlled Rhodesia have been largely ineffective because of the diverse interests and merely voluntary commitment of the members of the organization. Similarly, efforts by the League of Nations to invoke sanctions against Italy on the occasion of Benito Mussolini's invasion of Ethiopia in the 1930s floundered in indecision because of the member states' divergent interests. Great Britain and France in particular vacillated because they perceived that their security against Germany would be impaired by antagonizing the Italians. For a large alliance to be effective, then, the obligations of the members usually have to be specified and agreed upon at the outset and formalized through a treaty.

The fewer the common interests shared by allies, the greater is the need for a formal alliance. When allies are bound by few common interests, specifying obligations and terms is necessary to facilitate cooperation. Arms-control agreements between the United States and the Soviet Union, like Phase I of the SALT talks concluded when President Nixon visited Moscow in the spring of 1972, must be extremely detailed. The wartime alliance of the United States, the Soviet Union, and Great Britain, which was based on only one common objective, required constant reinterpretation of obligations and many high-level conferences to work out detailed plans and common language. As the interests of the three allies diverged at many points, mutual suspicion was endemic.

Although shared objectives and common characteristics usually further cooperation, they may also lead to conflict. Actors with similar attributes often seek similar objectives, but if the potential benefits cannot be easily divided, conflict may arise. Geographical contiguity, trade relations, and the like may *permit* discord that would be absent if actors were isolated from one another. The more salient the initial collective goals, the more bitter the resulting conflict may be if disagreement occurs and perceptions of "betrayal" ensue. That both the Soviet Union and the People's Republic of China are governed by Marxist-Leninist elites has not prevented a bitter schism between the two. In fact, it may have promoted their rivalry for the role of leader of international communism.

The number and range of common interests and objectives will influence the durability of an alliance significantly. *The greater they are, the longer the alliance will persist.* As common objectives reflect common goals, which can seldom be fully achieved, it is likely that related collective behavior will last for relatively long periods. Groups like the European Common Market, whose long-range objectives represent shared goals, tend to endure. Alliances based on a few common objectives tend to dissolve when the objectives have been achieved. The wartime alliance against Adolf Hitler broke up shortly after Germany had been defeated; its single objective had been realized.

When broad common objectives and long-range goals are shared, commitment is more credible and more easily communicated. The American commitment to NATO is substantially more credible than is its commitment to the Southeast Asian Treaty Organization. Visible and extensive American interests in Europe and the sharing of values and goals among NATO partners make the American commitment to European defense more convincing.

These elements are lacking in Southeast Asia, and SEATO has therefore enjoyed little success as a deterrent since it was founded in 1954. Only when goals and objectives are sufficiently compatible to permit staff and logistical coordination will the strength of the alliance exceed the total strength of its individual members.

An alliance based on common interest in preserving the status quo will tend to last longer than will an alliance based on revisionist objectives. As long as the status quo is maintained, the former alliance is fulfilling its task. Furthermore, the preservation of the status quo is not an objective that can be realized once and for all. At no point can the participants claim that their joint endeavor has been conclusively accomplished. After the defeat of Napoleon Bonaparte in 1815, for example, the major actors interested in preserving the European status quo continued a loose alliance known as the Concert of Europe until World War I altered the nineteenth-century international system.

By contrast, a revisionist alliance tends to disintegrate more rapidly after either achieving alteration of the status quo or finding its objective unattainable. Preservation of the status quo is a broad goal encompassing many specific objectives. By contrast, revisionist alliances tend to involve a few short-term objectives. Italy, for example, withdrew from the Axis in 1943, when it began to become apparent that the alliance with Germany could not help it to realize its objectives. Even a victorious revisionist alliance may disintegrate under the strains of dividing the "spoils."

George Liska has argued that "Alliances are against, and only derivatively for, someone or something" [24, p. 12].[6] However, an alliance based only on the perception of a common external threat promises to be relatively short-lived, for it lacks the sense of community resulting from broad common goals, objectives,

---

[6] K. J. Holsti has argued that "common perceptions of threat are probably the most frequent sources of alliance strategies" [20].

and values. As the threat that originally gave birth to the alliance begins to diminish, the cohesion of the alliance begins to decline. In periods of intense threat allies may be prepared to follow the lead of a single actor and to subordinate their divergent objectives to the common good [14, 40], but this cohesion tends to fade as international tension lessens. Cohesion also suffers when only some members of an alliance are threatened. Finally, if one ally is able to eliminate its own danger, even at the expense of its partners, the cohesion of the coalition will be severely damaged.

Unlike alliances formed in opposition to other actors, those formed against "nature" tend to last. Environmental challenges like overpopulation, food shortages, pollution, and epidemics are not easily overcome; they do not disappear; they therefore encourage long-term cooperation. Functional organizations like the World Health Organization and Interpol have existed for a long time and now tend to be taken for granted.

THE DYNAMICS OF ALLIANCE BEHAVIOR

Although the objectives of alliance members vary, alliances themselves may be classified according to the types of benefits that they produce. These benefits significantly affect the dynamics of alliances, in particular their sizes and the distribution of their rewards and costs. Furthermore, the effects of symmetry or asymmetry within an alliance differ according to the benefits produced.

Two basic types of benefits can be defined as collective and private. Collective benefits cannot be denied to any potential consumer, whether or not it is a member of the alliance. Their enjoyment by one actor does not reduce their availability to others. Collective benefits are sometimes called "nondistributive" because they cannot be parceled out among members of the alliance. The ability of NATO to deter Soviet aggression in western Europe,

for example, is a benefit that may be enjoyed by any nation in western Europe, regardless of whether or not it is a member of the alliance. It is unnecessary for Spain or Ireland to join NATO to be protected from Soviet invasion. Labor unions exemplify alliances that produce collective benefits: Any worker, whether or not he belongs to the union, receives the benefits of a union-negotiated contract. Unless all workers are forced to join the union and pay dues, the benefits from union efforts will be available to nonmembers as well.

Private benefits, on the other hand, are available only to members of the coalition; they are usually (but not always) distributive. Victorious military coalitions often secure private benefits; after a war the victors may demand from the losers reparations, territory, and resources that they can share among themselves to the exclusion of outsiders. Such spoils of war are distributive.

In an alliance that produces only collective benefits, the costs are distributive, even though the benefits are not. *No matter how much or how little an alliance member contributes, its returns will be the same.* As membership in the alliance is not a prerequisite for receiving these benefits, there is little advantage in belonging. The only privilege that a member receives is that of paying for something that it might have received anyway—which is why labor unions insist on compulsory membership of all workers in an industry and governments penalize tax evaders. In both cases, the opportunity to receive the group benefits while not having to pay for them creates an incentive to be a "freeloader." Actors will be reluctant to join an alliance that produces only collective benefits because they may incur costs greater than any additional "private" benefits that can be obtained. Those who are already members will seek to reduce their shares of the cost either by withdrawing or by encouraging others to join. It is thus in the collective interest of United Nations members that everyone pay assessments (thus reducing the costs to each), but it is also in the interest of *each* state to pay as little as possible.

An alliance that produces only collective benefits must deal with certain inherent stresses. On one hand, its members will seek to expand to include 100 percent of all potential members, as long as the increase in size reduces only costs and not benefits. On the other, there is little incentive to join or remain in such an alliance, which may cause disintegration (or make it impossible to organize the alliance in the first place). A paradox is thus apparent. Even though many collective benefits may be perceived as desirable by everyone, it may be difficult to motivate individual actors to participate actively in their attainment; the interests of the group and of the individuals that compose it thus diverge. For example, farmers have occasionally sought to unite to drive up the price of agricultural products by restricting supply. Such collective ventures are, however, usually unsuccessful because individual farmers desert the coalition to sell their products as prices begin to rise.

Alliances that produce only private benefits behave very differently from those that produce only collective benefits. Potential members seek to obtain shares of the benefits; the members, on the other hand, try to restrict membership to the smallest number necessary to achieve the desired objectives and consequently the private benefits. The members of such a "minimum winning coalition" will each receive the largest possible share of the payoffs; the addition of new members only reduces the portion available to each. William H. Riker has elaborated the idea that members of an alliance will seek to keep it as small as possible consonant with success and that nonmembers will seek to join in order to gain a share in the benefits [33].[7]

[7] Riker's argument revolves around the "size principle," which is, briefly, that coalitions tend toward minimum "winning" size. The size principle is based less on empirical observation than on the deductive logic of N-person game theory (game theory involving more than two players) and provides an example of the uses of mathematical reasoning in social science.

The Soviet entry into the war against Japan in the summer of 1945 illustrates conflicting tendencies in an alliance that promises private benefits. Until the United States was certain that Japan was on the verge of defeat, it sought to bring the Soviet Union into the anti-Japanese coalition. Pursuant to a nonaggression treaty with Japan, the Soviet Union had previously remained neutral in the war in the Pacific. But American policy shifted once the United States believed that it had accumulated the minimum winning resources necessary to win over Japan with-

According to this principle, actors enter into alliances in order to "win" with as few partners as possible so as to maximize their shares of the benefits. As for NATO, Riker has argued that the United States can perform by itself the function of a minimal winning coalition against the Soviet Union but seeks to maintain the alliance for other reasons; the United States will therefore either bankrupt itself by granting "side payments" to unnecessary allies or will retreat into isolation [20, pp. 231, 242]. This argument has several shortcomings, however. First, the "size principle" is based on assumptions that *only* private benefits are involved in an alliance and that members are in a zero-sum contest to distribute them. A zero-sum contest is one in which the gain of one actor equals the losses of others. But, neither of these assumptions applies to all alliances. For example, the benefits to be derived from "status quo" alliances like NATO are collective and can be distributed noncompetitively. If American and Soviet alliance policies were analyzed in terms of the collective benefits that they produce, these nations' behavior would seem more logical than Riker believes. Furthermore, it is extremely difficult to measure capabilities accurately enough to define a minimum winning coalition. Finally, as we have suggested, alliances are formed for reasons other than the simple accumulation of capabilities. "Nonutilitarian" motives based on ideology or values may figure heavily. For an explanation of Riker's and other similar coalition theories, see Jerome M. Chertkoff, "Socio-psychological Theories and Research on Coalition Formation," in Sven Groennings, E. W. Kelley, and Michael Leiserson, eds., *The Study of Coalition Behavior: Theoretical Perspectives from Four Continents* (New York: Holt, Rinehart and Winston, 1970). For cogent criticism of Riker's thesis, see Russett, "Components of an Operational Theory of International Alliance Formation," *Journal of Conflict Resolution*, 12 (September 1968), pp. 285–301; and Steven Rosen, "A Model of War and Alliance," in Julian R. Friedman, Christopher Bladen, and Steven Rosen, eds., *Alliance in International Politics* (Boston: Allyn & Bacon, 1970), pp. 215–237.

out the help of the Soviet Union. It has been suggested that the American decision to drop atomic bombs on Hiroshima and Nagasaki was influenced by a desire to end the war before the Soviet Union could enter and demand a share in the occupation of Japan. The Soviet Union eagerly entered the conflict shortly after the bomb had been dropped and did in fact share in the fruits of victory. In accordance with the Yalta protocol, it obtained the Kuril Islands, Sakhalin, and special privileges in the Chinese cities of Dairen and Port Arthur.

The cohesiveness of an alliance appears, then, to be associated with the types of benefits that the alliance produces. We would expect alliances that produce only collective benefits to be less cohesive and less effective than those that also produce private benefits would be. This hypothesis is corroborated by the results of a simulation experiment in which groups of actors were differentiated according to whether their alliance provided collective benefits alone or both collective and private benefits. The results of the simulation suggest that actors are more prepared to contribute to enterprises that promise private, as well as collective, benefits [4]. In fact, the inclusion of private benefits in the form of side payments may further the achievement of collective ones.[8]

Another important factor determining the cohesiveness of an alliance is the distribution of capabilities within it. Although most alliances consist of actors who are formally equal and independent, these actors rarely possess equivalent capabilities. An *asymmetrical alliance* is one in which one or a minority of members have the capabilities to alter significantly the costs and benefits for all members. The participation of superpowers in the Warsaw Pact and NATO make them asymmetrical. In a *symmetrical alliance,* on the other hand, no single member possesses the capabilities to affect signifi-

cantly the costs or benefits for other members. A labor union is a symmetrical alliance.

It has generally been assumed that the influence and benefits of alliance members reflect their relative capabilities within the alliance [43; 28; 24, p. 88], but in certain circumstances weaker partners in an asymmetrical coalition exert influence out of proportion to their capabilities. For one reason, the stronger partner may be at a disadvantage in bargaining because it is more strongly motivated to maintain the alliance [23]. In addition, a weaker ally in danger of defeat may be able to commit its stronger partner. Austria-Hungary, for example, appears to have found itself in this position vis-à-vis Germany in 1914. Weaker allies generally have greater bargaining leverage when the international system is highly polarized, for then large actors have difficulty finding substitute partners. These observations lead us to several general hypotheses about the impact of symmetry or asymmetry on an alliance.

First, *in a symmetrical alliance producing collective benefits, costs will be distributed evenly among members.* Let us consider again the labor union. The costs of its operation are beyond what any one member can pay, and the withdrawal of his dues does not much affect the resources available to the group. There is thus no material incentive for the individual union member to pay more than his "fair share" or indeed to pay anything at all once the union has been established. Nor is there any reason to permit him to pay less. His participation is neither more nor less necessary to the survival of the union than is that of any other member. Under these conditions costs will be evenly distributed. Functional agencies like the Universal Postal Union come closest to these features in the international system.

Second, *when an asymmetrical alliance produces collective benefits, it may be to the advantage of one member to pay more than its "fair share" of the costs.* The value of the collective benefit is dif-

[8] For an elaborate presentation of the theory of private and collective benefits, see Olson [30].

ferent for each member of the alliance. If no member values it highly, the alliance will probably disintegrate. If, however, one member considers the collective benefit vital, as the United States considers the defense of western Europe, it may contribute a disproportionate share of the costs. This member may end by paying virtually all the costs and distributing private benefits in order to keep the alliance intact. Small members may tend to pay less as they recognize that the larger member considers the alliance vital and has the resources to pay for it alone [31].

The problem of costs in an alliance like NATO is complicated by the question of risk. Although NATO lowers the probability of war in Europe, countries like Belgium and Germany, because of their locations, run high risks of enormous damage if war does occur. A "limited" war in Europe constitutes a lower risk for the United States. Therefore, although the United States commits more resources to the alliance, it does not incur as high a risk as do its European allies. Neutral countries like Switzerland, Sweden, and Ireland, which are not members of NATO, are "freeloaders." Their risks are minimal, their costs nonexistent, yet they benefit from deterrence of Soviet aggression.

Unequal distribution of costs, then, is characteristic of NATO, and American allies have collected "side payments" in return for their cooperation. Similarly, in Vietnam the United States has been forced to underwrite the contributions of allies like Thailand and South Korea. If one member values an alliance highly, it is unreasonable to expect other members to be "grateful." American frustration at the alleged "ingratitude" of SEATO and NATO allies that have refused to contribute their "fair share" is illogical, for the United States values these alliances more highly than do the allies and incurs lower risks from membership than they do.

Third, *in symmetrical alliances producing private benefits, members that join early are likely to receive greater shares of the benefits.* The most profitable situation for a potential member of an alliance that produces private benefits is to be necessary to creation of a "minimum winning coalition." In a universe of five equally potent actors the one whose behavior makes possible a coalition of three will be in a position to extract maximum concessions from his partners. In a symmetrical alliance, however, it is often difficult or impossible to identify which member has put the alliance "over the top." National presidential nominating conventions illustrate the problem. In no convention has a candidate lost after having gained more than 40 percent of the votes on a single ballot (or 59 percent when there is a two-thirds requirement) [13]. Once the coalition has achieved a certain size below the optimum, there is a rush ("the bandwagon effect") to join what appears to be a winning coalition in order to share in the payoffs. The members who have joined a coalition in this final rush have little or no bargaining strength in the alliance, for, if they had not joined, others would have. "Latecomers," even those that actually put the alliance "over the top," are often regarded as less important than are members that have been "steadfast and true" from the first.

Fourth, *in an asymmetrical alliance that produces private benefits, the member that clinches a minimum winning coalition often gains a larger share of the benefits than do earlier members.* It is usually easy to identify which potential member will enable an asymmetrical alliance to "win." Often this member will appear *absolutely* necessary to create a winning coalition, as did the United States during World War I. Under these circumstances this potential member is in an enviable bargaining position, for without its participation the others will receive no benefits. They may therefore be prepared to promise a disproportionate share of these benefits to persuade this actor to join. In 1915, when it appeared that the support of Italy would determine the outcome of the war, France and Great

Britain made clear that they were prepared to concede to Italy a large share of the postwar spoils if it would join the anti-German coalition—even though Italy was militarily weaker than either of them and had deserted its German ally before the onset of war. The Italian contribution appeared sufficient to tip the scales in favor of the Western alliance.

In practice, most international alliances, particularly those of a military nature, are asymmetrical and produce both private and collective benefits. Their stability and cohesiveness are thus significantly affected by the numbers of members that can alter the benefits or costs to other members. The emergence of more than one major actor in the Soviet bloc as a result of the consolidation of Mao Tsetung's regime in China thus increased intraalliance conflict [25].

Fifth, *the greater the number of actors who can significantly alter the distribution of costs or benefits, the less efficient the alliance will be in achieving its objectives.* The actors will bargain among themselves over the precise methods of achieving objectives. Such bargaining usually involves compromises, takes time, and may not even result in solutions. The alliance may then find its objectives more difficult to achieve than if there had been only one dominant member.

The old balance-of-power system and the alliance structure that supported it were based largely on the distribution of private benefits. Diplomatic activity in the late nineteenth century was largely focused on division of overseas territory and markets, which served as private benefits for alliance members. States acted in concert to secure such benefits and to maintain the status quo in Europe. They shifted alliances when greater potential payoffs offered themselves. Only rarely were alliances formed solely for collective benefits. When Napoleonic France threatened to undermine the European state system many of the remaining European rulers combined forces to restore the former status quo, a collective benefit for them. Alliances promising mainly collective benefits have become common since World War II, however. They range from military organizations like NATO, SEATO, and the Warsaw Pact to regional political groups like the Arab League, the Organization of African Unity, and the Organization of American States.

ALLIANCES AND THE PROBABILITY OF WAR

There is little consensus among scholars on whether alliances increase or decrease the probability of international conflict. Balance-of-power theorists generally argue that alliances serve a positive function by preventing or at least limiting war. This argument takes several forms. It has been claimed that alliances prevent imbalances of power. "In short," according to Julian R. Friedman, "the principal functions of alliance or alliance process in the international order are, first, to sustain continuity . . . and, second, to uphold balance of power (by facilitating alert responses to developing imbalances)" [12]. But even balance-of-power theorists insist that, in order to function in this way, alliances must be temporary and flexible. As Quincy Wright has observed:

Analysis of the relationships between the variable factors in the balance of power seems to warrant the following conclusions. . . . First, stability will increase and the probability of war will decrease as the number of states in the system increases. . . . So also the grouping of states in permanent alliances . . . would tend to reduce the number of independent entities in the system and so would decrease stability. As a consequence, on the assumptions of the balance of power, policies of rigid neutrality and of permanent alliance both make for instability. With all power concentrated in two alliances, stability is reduced to a minimum and war can be expected. . . . [47]

In opposition to balance-of-power theorists, many scholars and statesmen have argued that alliances, whether temporary or permanent, actually foster the conditions in which wars occur. After World War I, it may be recalled, Woodrow Wilson denounced alliances and balance-of-power politics as the causes of the conflict. Clearly, alliances are incompatible with collective security because the latter requires *every* state to oppose any would-be aggressor. As Inis L. Claude, Jr., has argued:

Collective security implies a general alliance, a universal alliance, which is disentangling in the sense that it eliminates the pattern of *competitive* alignments. . . . It calls for an alliance system which *unites* the nations in defense of the order of the community, instead of one which *divides* them into antagonistic groups. . . . [9]

Nevertheless, although particularist alliances may be incompatible with collective security, their abolition would not be a sufficient condition for establishment of an effective collective-security system.

Another major criticism of alliances is that they encourage formation of opposing alliances. Then no actor is able to increase his security; the alliances actually divide actors and increase international tension. Such, in fact, are the grounds on which many leaders of the "third world" have condemned existing alliances.

Few systematic studies have been undertaken to determine the impacts of alliances on the probabilities of war. J. David Singer and Melvin Small have, however, examined all alliances formed between 1815 and 1939 (118 were identified) in a statistical analysis correlating the outbreak of war with the existence of alliances [39]. The tentative conclusion is that formation of alliances and the outbreak of war have been positively correlated in the twentieth century but not in the nineteenth century. This conclusion suggests that the temporary coalitions of the last century were less conducive to war than are the more durable coalitions of this century. But other variables probably intrude, so that possibly the relationship between alliance and war is actually a product of such factors as changes in capabilities, and in types of regimes.

Many of these hypotheses about alliance behavior have still to be firmly proved. The relationship between war and alliances remains far from clear. And, as many of the hypotheses are quite abstract, a decision maker may find in them "very little that is useful for him" [32]. Greater insight into the working of alliances may therefore be gained by turning to an actual example.

References
1. Alker, Haywood R., Jr., and Bruce M. Russett, *World Politics in the General Assembly* (New Haven: Yale University Press, 1965).
2. Brebner, John Bartlett, *The North Atlantic Triangle* (New Haven: Yale University Press, 1945), p. 251.
3. Burgess, Philip M., *Elite Images and Foreign Policy Outcomes* (Columbus: Ohio State University Press, 1967).
4. Burgess, Philip M., and James A. Robinson, "The Alliance and the Theory of Collective Action: A Simulation of Coalition Processes," *Midwest Journal of Political Science,* 13 (May 1969), pp. 194–218.
5. Burton, J. W., *International Relations: A General Theory* (New York: Cambridge University Press, 1965), p. 170.
6. Cartwright, Dorwin, and Alvin Zander, *Group Dynamics: Research and Theory* (New York: Harper & Row, 1960), p. 87.
7. Churchill, Winston S., *The Gathering Storm* (Boston: Houghton Mifflin, 1948), p. 373.
8. Churchill, Winston S., *Their Finest Hour* (Boston: Houghton Mifflin, 1949), p. 558.
9. Claude, Inis L., Jr., *Power and International Relations* (New York: Random House, 1962), pp. 144–145.
10. Dawson, Raymond, and Richard Rosecrance, "Theory and Reality in the Anglo-American Alliance," *World Politics,* 19 (1966), pp. 21–53.
11. Fedder, Edwin H., "The Concept of Alliance," *International Studies Quarterly,* 12 (March 1968), p. 83.
12. Friedman, Julian R., "Alliance in International Politics," in Julian R. Friedman, Christopher Bladen, and Steven

Rosen, eds., *Alliance in International Politics* (Boston: Allyn & Bacon, 1970), p. 20.

13. Gamson, William, "Coalition Formation at Presidential Nomination Conventions," *American Journal of Sociology,* 58 (September 1962), pp. 157–171.

14. Gordon, Morton, and Daniel Lerner, "The Setting for European Arms Control: Political and Strategic Choices of European Elites," *Journal of Conflict Resolution,* 9 (December 1965), pp. 419–433.

15. Grotius, Hugo, *Prolegomena to the Law of War and Peace,* trans. by Francis W. Kelsey (New York: Bobbs-Merrill, 1957), p. 16.

16. Guetzkow, Harold, "Isolation and Collaboration: A Partial Theory of Inter-Nation Relations," *Journal of Conflict Resolution,* 1 (March 1957), pp. 48–68.

17. Gunther, Gerald, and Noel T. Dowling, *Cases and Materials on Constitutional Law* (New York: Foundation Press, 1970), p. 398.

18. Haas, Ernst, and Allen S. Whiting, *Dynamics of International Politics* (New York: McGraw-Hill, 1956), p. 182.

19. Harriman, W. Averell, "Statement Regarding Our Wartime Relations With the USSR, Particularly Concerning the Yalta Agreement," in Richard F. Fenno, Jr., ed., *The Yalta Conference* (Boston: Heath, 1955), p. 65.

20. Holsti, K. J., *International Politics* (Englewood Cliffs, N.J.: Prentice-Hall, 1967), p. 11.

21. Keohane, Robert O., "Political Influence in the General Assembly," *International Conciliation,* 557 (March 1966), p. 13.

22. Kissinger, Henry A., *The Troubled Partnership* (New York: McGraw-Hill, 1965).

23. Lall, Arthur, *Modern International Negotiation* (New York: Columbia University Press, 1966), p. 182.

24. Liska, George, *Nations in Alliance,* 2nd ed. (Baltimore: Johns Hopkins University Press, 1968).

25. Mansbach, Richard W., "Bilateralism and Multilateralism in the Soviet Bloc," *International Organization,* 24 (Spring 1970), pp. 371–380.

26. Masters, Roger D., "A Multi-Bloc Model of the International System," *American Political Science Review,* 55 (December 1961), p. 795.

27. Mitchell, R. Judson, "A Theoretical Approach to the Study of Communist International Organizations," in Jan F. Triska, ed., *Communist Party-States* (Indianapolis: Bobbs-Merrill, 1969), p. 94.

28. Morgenthau, Hans J., "Alliances in Theory and Practice," in Arnold Wolfers, ed., *Alliance Policy in the Cold War* (Baltimore: Johns Hopkins University Press, 1959), p. 190.

29. Neustadt, Richard E., *Alliance Politics* (New York: Columbia University Press, 1970), p. 140.

30. Olson, Mancur, Jr., *The Logic of Collective Action* (Cambridge, Mass.: Harvard University Press, 1965), p. 36.

31. Olson, Mancur, Jr., and Richard Zeckhauser, *An Economic Theory of Alliances,* Rand Corporation Paper 2992 (Santa Monica: 1964).

32. Rapoport, Anatol, *N-Person Game Theory* (Ann Arbor: University of Michigan Press, 1970), p. 303.

33. Riker, William H., *The Theory of Political Coalition* (New Haven: Yale University Press, 1962).

34. Rosenau, James N., "Intervention as a Scientific Concept," *Journal of Conflict Resolution,* 13 (June 1969), pp. 149–171.

35. Rothstein, Robert L., *Alliances and Small Powers* (New York: Columbia University Press, 1968).

36. Rubinstein, Alvin Z., *Yugoslavia and the Nonaligned World* (Princeton: Princeton University Press, 1970), p. 120.

37. Russett, Bruce M., *Community and Contention* (Cambridge, Mass.: MIT Press), 1963.

38. Schleicher, Charles P., *International Relations: Cooperation and Conflict* (Englewood Cliffs, N.J.: Prentice-Hall, 1962), p. 306.

39. Singer, J. David, and Melvin Small, "Alliance Aggregation and the Onset of War," in Singer, ed., *Quantitative International Politics* (New York: Free Press, 1968).

40. Steel, Ronald, *The End of Alliance: America and the Future of Europe* (New York: Viking, 1964), pp. 27–28.

41. Teune, Henry, and Sig Synnestvedt, "Measuring International Alignment," *Orbis*, 9 (Spring 1965), p. 189.

42. Thucydides, *The Peloponnesian War* (New York: Random House, 1951), book III, chap. IX, p. 151, paras. 10–11.

43. Torrance, E. Paul, "Some Consequences of Power Difference in Decision Making in Permanent and Temporary Three-Man Groups," in A. P. Hare, E. F. Borgatta, and R. F. Bales, eds., *Small Groups: Studies in Social Interaction* (New York: Knopf, 1955), pp. 491–492.

44. Waltz, Kenneth N., *Foreign Policy and Democratic Politics* (Boston: Little, Brown, 1967), pp. 67–68.

45. Wise, David, and Thomas B. Ross, *The Invisible Government* (New York: Bantam, 1965), pp. 116–121.

46. Wolfers, Arnold, "Stresses and Strains in 'Going it with Others,' " in Wolfers, ed., *Alliance Policy in the Cold War* (Baltimore: Johns Hopkins University Press, 1959), p. 8.

47. Wright, Quincy, *A Study of War*, abridged ed. (Chicago: University of Chicago Press, 1965), p. 122.

Suggested Reading

Axelrod, Robert, *Conflict of Interest* (Chicago: Markham, 1970).

Burgess, Philip M., and James A. Robinson, "The Alliance and the Theory of Collective Action: A Simulation of Coalition Processes," *Midwest Journal of Political Science*, 13 (May 1969), pp. 194–218.

Friedman, Julian R., Christopher Bladen, and Steven Rosen, eds., *Alliance in International Politics* (Boston: Allyn & Bacon, 1970).

Liska, George, *Nations in Alliance*, 2nd ed. (Baltimore: Johns Hopkins University Press, 1968).

Luce, Duncan R., and Howard Raiffa, *Games and Decisions* (New York: Wiley, 1957), especially chaps. 7, 10.

Neustadt, Richard E., *Alliance Politics* (New York: Columbia University Press, 1970).

Olson, Mancur, Jr., *The Logic of Collective Action* (Cambridge, Mass.: Harvard University Press, 1965).

Riker, William H., *The Theory of Political Coalitions* (New Haven: Yale University Press, 1962).

Russett, Bruce M., *Community and Contention* (Cambridge, Mass.: MIT Press, 1963).

Chapter 15
THE NORTH ATLANTIC TREATY ORGANIZATION

[N]o mystical, messianic movement—and particularly not that of the Kremlin—can face frustration indefinitely without eventually adjusting itself in one way or another to the logic of that state of affairs—George F. Kennan [4]

Relations between the Soviet Union and the West, and later between the Chinese People's Republic and the West, deteriorated after World War II. Mutually exclusive alignments began to alter the postwar environment radically. In February 1948 a Soviet-sponsored coup d'état in Czechoslovakia completed the division of Europe. The Korean War and the French colonial conflict in Indochina produced similar divisions in Asia. The world seemed split between the Soviet bloc and the Western allies. But as the years passed, events both within and between the blocs altered circumstances, and the carefully constructed military alliances of postwar years began to decline.

The period with which we are concerned here began when the former great powers of Europe found themselves in a confrontation with the greatest land-based military power in world history, poised on the frontiers of West Germany and behaving in what was considered an expansionist manner. Only the United States appeared capable of deterring Soviet aggression.

It was believed that a sufficiently clear postwar commitment by the United States would prevent the Soviet Union from aggression against western Europe. Twice in the twentieth century the United States had entered European wars to prevent domination of the continent by an adversary inimical to American interests, but both times the costs of the final military victory had been astronomical in terms of human suffering and economic devastation for victors as well as vanquished. The United States had remained neutral during World War I until 1917, and at the close of that war it had retreated into isolation. Two decades later American sympathy for Great Britain and France did not prevent the Nazis from conquering most of western Europe; again intervention was slow, coming only after the Japanese attack on Pearl Harbor, more than two years after the war had begun. Before American liberating armies arrived, continental Europe had suffered four bitter years of occupation.

Experiences during the two world wars made Europeans fear another, even one in which they would be assured of victory. The United States and the countries of western Europe shared the objective of *preventing* another war. It seemed desirable to deter a possible Soviet attack by committing the United States irrevocably to the defense of western Europe *before* a new war could begin. To make this commitment credible, the United States, Canada, and most nations of western Europe formed the North Atlantic Treaty Organization. The history of NATO illustrates many of the generalizations about integration, alliances, and formation of coalitions that we have already discussed.

THE OUTBREAK OF
THE COLD WAR

The wartime alliance among the United States, Great Britain, the Soviet Union, and their lesser partner France did not function smoothly. Collaboration was made possible only by the existence of a common threat and was carried out by means of agencies and high-level meetings. Before World War II Soviet leaders had long feared a Western coalition. The reluctance or inability of Great Britain and the United States to open a second front in Europe before 1944, despite repeated promises of an earlier invasion, caused Joseph Stalin to complain of Western deception [5].[1] In the meantime the Soviet Union bore the brunt of the strug-

[1] The "first front" had been opened when Germany invaded Russia in June 1941. The British withdrawal from Dunkirk in May–June and the surrender of France in June 1940 had brought an end to the land war in western Europe. Although a land war between Great Britain and Germany had continued in North Africa and a large-scale American and British invasion of North Africa had begun in November 1942, the Russians felt that it was a "side show" and that the main struggle was in Europe itself. The "second front," or invasion of France, repeatedly promised Stalin by Churchill and Roosevelt, did not take place until June 1944 at Normandy at least a year and a half after the decisive Soviet victory over the Germans at Stalingrad and the halting of the German

gle against Germany, suffering about 20 million deaths. Soviet mistrust of the West became so great that Soviet leaders apparently explored the possibility of a separate peace with Germany during the summer of 1943 [6]. Soviet antagonism toward noncommunist leaders of eastern Europe, particularly the Polish government in exile, on the other hand, fostered Western suspicions of ultimate Soviet objectives.

Anglo-American relations with France —also occasionally hostile—posed different problems. Unlike the Soviet Union, France had enjoyed cordial relations with its Western allies for a long time. Winston Churchill and Franklin D. Roosevelt, however, were disinclined to recognize Charles de Gaulle's Free French movement as the nation's sole representative. The necessity of dealing with the neutral Vichy commanders in North Africa, who were no friends of de Gaulle, would have rendered such recognition potentially damaging to the conduct of the war. De Gaulle's "invasion" of the tiny French islands of St. Pierre and Miquelon off the coast of Canada, in order to liberate them from Vichy control, was expressly opposed by the United States, Great Britain, and Canada.

President Roosevelt's attitude toward de Gaulle led him to propose a year-long occupation of liberated France so that a representative French government might emerge. In one message to Churchill he confided:

I am fed up with de Gaulle, and the secret personal and political machinations of that Committee [Free French Committee] in

advance into Russia. According to Alexander Werth, by the time the Normandy landing began,

The feeling widely expressed among ordinary Russian soldiers and civilians was that it would be "too easy," now that the Red Army had already pulled most of the chestnuts out of the fire, and that if the British and Americans were going to land in France now, it would be less out of any feeling of comradeship for the Russians than out of pure self-interest and even self-protection, since they feared that the Russians might now well smash Germany "single-handed" [11, p. 755].

the last few days indicates that there is no possibility of our working with de Gaulle. . . . I am absolutely convinced that he has been and is now injuring our war effort and that he is a very dangerous threat to us.[2]

Mutual distrust between the British and and Americans on one hand, and the French, on the other, which became obvious after de Gaulle's return to political power in 1958, was rooted in their wartime relations.

Even before the guns had been silenced fissures could be recognized within the alliance. Two main sources of discord were the future of defeated Germany and the distribution of benefits among the victors. Germany was divided first into three, then into four, occupation zones. Nevertheless, the allies initially agreed that it would be treated as a single economic unit, for the eastern sector was traditionally agricultural and the western sector predominantly industrial. They also agreed that Germany would pay reparations to the victors, particularly to the Soviet Union, which had suffered greater losses at the hands of the Nazis than had any other country. The Soviets were to receive all the industrial equipment in the Soviet zone, plus one-quarter of such equipment from the Western zones. The United States and Great Britain had agreed to this plan on condition that no reparations be required from current German production until the country had accumulated sufficient foreign-exchange reserves to purchase necessary imports. Otherwise, Great Britain, the United States, and France would have had to subsidize their former enemy economically, which would have entailed large-scale hardships for themselves, particularly for Great Britain.

The Soviet Union proceeded quickly to remove capital equipment from its own zone without informing the allies of what was being taken. Furthermore, it refused to permit shipment of agricultural goods to the Western zones. Soviet behavior in

Rumania and Hungary, former German allies, was equally ruthless. The American military commander in Germany, General Lucius Clay, responded by announcing suspension of reparations from the Western zones to the Soviet Union.

The United States and Great Britain were determined that their zones would become economically self-sufficient, so that they themselves would not have to underwrite the German economy and so that the country could remain free of Soviet control and contribute to the overall economic recovery of western Europe. To hasten the economic revival of the Western zones, American Secretary of State James Byrnes proposed in July 1946 that they be unified. France initially refused to support this plan because it feared a reunited Germany. Nevertheless, the British and American zones were unified in January 1947, and "Bizonia" came into existence.

Stalin's objectives in Germany were to obtain as much in reparations as possible to help finance the Soviet Union's economic reconstruction and to reduce the possibility of a German revival that might again threaten Soviet interests. The immediate result was to prolong the division of Germany and to eliminate Western influence from the Soviet zone. The differences in Soviet and Western objectives in Germany led to a rapid cooling of East-West relations. To this day Germany remains divided, and it has never signed a formal peace treaty with its former enemies.

A second major set of differences between the Soviet Union and the West involved the disposition of eastern Europe and the Balkan states. Great Britain and France had gone to war after the invasion of Poland, and especially among the British there was a great deal of popular sentiment for an independent and democratic Poland. Similar sentiments existed in the United States, which had a large Polish-American population. There was also much Western sympathy for Czechoslovakia, particularly because of the Munich betrayal and the traditional Western ori-

[2] This and other telegrams are quoted in David Schoenbrun, *The Three Lives of Charles de Gaulle* (New York: Atheneum, 1966), pp. 135–145.

entation of that country. The Soviet Union, however, had twice in the twentieth century been invaded by Germany through Poland, and, as President Roosevelt noted, it was understandably determined that this invasion corridor be closed from then on. Stalin insisted that Poland be strengthened enough to be able to close the corridor itself and alluded to a new *cordon sanitaire,* this time to protect, rather than to isolate, the Soviet Union.

During the final year of the war, the Soviet Union took steps to ensure that liberated eastern Europe would be governed by regimes friendly to its interests. With the Red Army rapidly overrunning this area, Winston Churchill reached an agreement with Stalin in October 1944 concerning the division of Eastern Europe and the Balkans into "spheres of interest." By the terms of their agreement, Rumania was to be 90 percent controlled by the Soviet Union and 10 percent controlled by others. Greece was to be 90 percent British and 10 percent Soviet; Yugoslavia and Hungary were to be 50 percent British and 50 percent Soviet; and Bulgaria 75 percent Soviet and 25 percent others.

The future of Poland, however, remained a source of contention and became a major test case of East-West relations. When Russian troops had entered the country the Soviet Union had established a "provisional government" of communist Poles in the city of Lublin. This government was substituted for the London government in exile, which had been recognized and assisted by the United States and Great Britain. In Stalin's view, the chief difficulty with the London government was that it was anti-Soviet and would, therefore, provide no guarantee against invasion from the West. In addition, the U.S.S.R. sought to eliminate the anticommunist elements within Poland. Noncommunist leaders of the Polish resistance were invited to Moscow, where they were arrested, tried, and sentenced to varying terms of imprisonment. Moreover, the advancing Red Army had halted its western drive at the gates of Warsaw, permitting the Germans to decimate the

Polish resistance movement, which had risen against the city's Nazi occupiers.

Despite these apparent provocations, the wartime allies sought, at the Yalta Conference of February 1945, to salvage an agreement about the future of Poland. It was agreed that a coalition government, the Provisional Government for National Unity, would be formed by merging the Lublin and London groups. It would then hold "free and unfettered elections," though it was understood that any Polish government would have to be "friendly" to the Soviet Union. Stalin, however, believed that no noncommunist government could fulfill this requirement. Given the Poles' traditional hatred of Russia, free elections would probably have returned a government hostile to the Soviet Union. Alexander Werth contends that Stalin "seems to have been impressed, soon after Yalta, by the great hostility that the Russians met in Poland, which led to his determination not to take any serious chances, either there or in any of the other east-European countries" [11, p. 877]. The subsequent postwar elections in Poland were rigged by the Soviet Union and its Polish supporters. Noncommunist leaders were driven out of the government, and many were arrested or exiled.

Elsewhere in Soviet-occupied eastern Europe the pattern was repeated. The Soviet Union insisted on the formation of coalition governments representing "antifascist and democratic" political parties. Many anti-Russian leaders in these countries were accused of having collaborated with the Nazis. Although large numbers of noncommunists had collaborated with the Nazi or Italian occupiers, many of the leaders accused of collaboration and excluded from the coalitions were in fact innocent of any wrongdoing. In certain countries, notably Hungary, free elections were held at the beginning, and pro-Soviet political parties received low percentages of the votes, to the discomfiture of Soviet observers. Subsequent elections were rigged and conducted amid suppression of political figures deemed "unfriendly" to Moscow. This process culminated in the arrest or elimination of opposition leaders and the merging of remaining political parties into a "front" dominated by the communists. This pattern recurred in Rumania, Bulgaria, Poland, Hungary, and Czechoslovakia.

Although these events in eastern Europe and the Balkans caused disappointment and concern in the West, Great Britain and the United States could do little to stop the trend, short of initiating another major war. Among the war-weary populations of Europe and North America such an undertaking, particularly directed against an ally whose cause had been publicly supported, would have been unthinkable. In fact, demand for repatriation and demobilization of wartime armies was rising, particularly in the United States. At Yalta, Roosevelt promised Stalin that American troops would be out of Europe within two years of the end of the war. The Red Army, as Hungarian communist leader Matyas Rakosi later pointed out, was the necessary instrument for transforming eastern Europe into "people's democracies" without proletarian revolutions [9]. Western anger at these events achieved little result except to irritate Soviet leaders and to convince them further that the United States and Great Britain sought "capitalist encirclement" of the Soviet Union.

Finally, in Czechoslovakia, the most Westernized and democratic of the Eastern European countries, a Soviet-inspired coup d'état occurred in February 1948 and resulted in the ouster of noncommunist parties from the government. The subsequent murder of Jan Masaryk, Czech foreign minister and son of the country's greatest national hero, created considerable outrage and chagrin in the West and added to what many Westerners saw as the tragedy of their postwar expectations. The Soviet Union had established "friendly" regimes in Eastern Europe, but at the cost of a permanent postwar settlement.

The key to European security was Germany. Its strategic position, highly trained population, and economic potential were the focus of both Western and Soviet attention. The five sessions of the Council of Foreign Ministers in 1946 and 1947 made little progress toward bridging the chasm between Western and Soviet perceptions of the problem of Germany. Inability to agree on whether economic or political unification of Germany should come first, coupled with Soviet rejection of the Marshall Plan, created a stalemate. By spring 1947 France was prepared to merge its zone with Bizonia. In the east the Soviet Union took steps to bind its zone of Germany more closely to the Soviet sphere of influence and to consolidate its control over key sectors of life in East Germany and elsewhere.

THE GENESIS OF NATO

These developments in eastern Europe and Germany were perceived by Western leaders as indications of Soviet expansionist aims. The interpretation was buttressed by Soviet behavior in areas outside Europe. Soviet interference in Iran continued until the end of 1946. Under United Nations pressure Soviet troops were finally withdrawn from that country in May, but a Soviet-supported separatist government persisted in Azerbaijan until December. Furthermore, the Soviets began to demand the cession of the Turkish provinces of Kars and Ardahan and a revision of the Montreux Convention governing use of the Dardanelles. Soviet activity in Manchuria, Soviet opposition to British and French colonialism in the Middle East, and the continuing success of Mao Tse-tung against the Chinese regime of Chiang Kai-shek intensified Western suspicions and animosity. On the other hand, certain Western behavior, like the sudden halt of American lend-lease, must have seemed precipitate and insensitive to the Soviet Union. The growing suspicion of the Soviet Union in the United States was indicated by President Truman's abrupt dismissal of Secretary of Commerce Henry Wallace, after the latter had argued publicly for a policy of conciliation toward the U.S.S.R.

In February 1947 the British government notified the United States that, owing to economic and financial difficulties, it could no longer assist Greece against growing communist subversion. The American response was prompt. Under the Truman Doctrine the United States offered assistance, not only to Greece and Turkey, which were immediately threatened, but also to all regimes threatened by communist expansion, regardless of their domestic orientations. The Truman Doctrine opened a new phase in American foreign policy, a phase during which American commitments assumed global proportions and American activities were focused on defeating communism wherever it appeared. The notion of "containment," altered and expanded in the Truman Doctrine, became the basis of American policy and was later institutionalized in NATO. Its original premise, as propounded by George F. Kennan, was that patient firmness on the part of the West would lead to "the breakup or the gradual mellowing of Soviet power" [4].

The next major American commitment in Europe was adoption of the Marshall Plan. Previous economic assistance to Europe had taken the form of limited contributions to the U.N. Relief and Rehabilitation Agency (UNRRA). The Marshall Plan involved massive American grants and loans to Europe and joint planning by European nations to ensure optimum use of American aid. As General George C. Marshall himself explained:

Aside from the demoralizing effect on the world at large and the possibilities of disturbances arising as a result of the desperation of the people concerned, the consequences to the economy of the United States should be apparent to all. It is logical that the United States should do whatever it is able to do to assist in the return of normal economic health in the world, without which there can be no political stability and no assured peace. [10]

The necessity for consolidating its new and shaky sphere of influence in eastern Europe and the growing hostility of its former wartime allies induced the Soviet Union to take a "hard line." Stalin insisted on the same ideological and political homogeneity within the eastern bloc that he expected within the Soviet Union itself. By the end of 1946 Soviet leaders had begun to emphasize the polarization of the world into two economic systems supported by two military blocs.

To bind other national communist parties still closer to the Communist Party of the Soviet Union (CPSU), the Communist Information Bureau (Cominform) was organized in September 1947. Represented in this group were the ruling communist parties of eastern Europe (except Albania), the CPSU, and the large Italian and French Communist parties. The Cominform provided an institutional framework for enforcing ideological and political uniformity within the bloc.

The most dangerous East-West split in the 1940s was centered on Berlin. Berlin was located in the Soviet zone of Germany, but it was also divided into four zones and governed by military commanders of the four powers. Western unification of their zones of Germany aroused vigorous protests from the Soviet Union. Increasing Soviet intransigence on "the German question" has been described by Clay:

I pointed out that I had no confirming intelligence of a positive nature, but that I did sense a change in the Soviet position which I was certain portended some Soviet action in Germany. I did not predict what course this action would take, though I did state that I was no longer adhering to my previous position that war was impossible. [2, p. 354]

After the initiation of a currency reform in the Western zones of Germany *and* Berlin the Soviet Union undertook to interrupt and then to blockade road, rail, and river traffic into the city. The Western allies had a choice of backing down or going to war. This unsatisfactory choice was evaded, however, thanks to technological ingenuity and sheer improvisation. By the spring of 1949 an Anglo-American airlift was ferrying up to 13,000 tons of supplies into Berlin each day. As neither side seemed prepared to start hostilities, a stalemate occurred. Although the blockade itself had been broken, there were now two governments in the city, though the fiction of four-power control continued. In the meantime two governments had come into existence in Germany as a whole. The growing American commitment to the defense of western Europe in general and to the preservation of an independent West Berlin as a symbol of this commitment was summed up by Clay: "When Berlin falls, western Germany will be next. . . . If we withdraw, our position in Europe is threatened. If America does not understand this now, does not know that the issue is cast, then it never will and communism will run rampant" [2, p. 361].[3] This commitment was affirmed symbolically when President Kennedy visited Berlin in 1961 and declared, "Ich bin ein Berliner!" ("I am a Berliner!").

The sharp division of Europe along ideological lines ensured a military "shield" behind which Western economic recovery could take place. In early recognition of this need, France and Great Britain concluded the Treaty of Dunkirk in March 1947; both countries agreed to mutual defense against a stipulated threat "by Germany." This phrase was understood to include Soviet aggression originating from the Soviet-occupied zone of Germany. In March 1948 the Netherlands, Belgium, and Luxembourg joined with France and Britain in signing the Brussels Pact, the military analogue of the Organization of European Economic Cooperation (OEEC), which had been established to coordinate administration of Marshall Plan aid from the United States. The formalization of alliance relationships was thus well under way.

Within a week after the signing of the Brussels Pact the Soviet blockade of Berlin began. In this climate the United States Senate adopted a bipartisan resolution,

[3] A possible break in the East-West stalemate over Berlin occurred in the summer of 1971, when a four-power agreement guaranteeing Western rights of access to the city was reached.

sponsored by Republican leader Arthur H. Vandenberg of Michigan, declaring American willingness to enter into joint military arrangements with the countries of western Europe. With this resolution as a basis, negotiations to create the North Atlantic Treaty Organization began. The treaty was signed on April 4, 1949, by representatives of Belgium, Canada, Denmark, France, Great Britain, Iceland, Italy, Luxembourg, the Netherlands, Portugal, and the United States. NATO was designed to make clear to any potential invader that the United States—with its powerful nuclear capacity—was firmly committed to the defense of western Europe.

The NATO concept was virtually unprecedented. It was a peacetime alliance intended to deter a potential adversary, rather than to defend against an actual attack or to seek revision of the status quo. Although other alliances, like the Grand Alliance of 1701, had incorporated the concept of deterrence, their scope had been far smaller and their aims far less ambitious. The core of the treaty was Article 5: "The Parties agree that an armed attack against one or more of them in Europe or North America shall be considered an attack against them all. . . ."

The treaty represented more than a vague agreement; in fact, a series of permanent organs was created to achieve its specific objectives. The Council of Ministers proceeded to establish financial, economic, and defense committees. The alliance thus took on aspects of a new international organization. In addition, the U.S. Congress quickly passed the Mutual Assistance Defense Act, which provided for arms and other kinds of military assistance to the member countries. In the first year alone $1 billion in military aid were channeled to the European allies.

NATO was initially based on four main assumptions. The first was that the Soviet Union entertained ambitions in western Europe; this assumption will probably never be conclusively proved or disproved. The second was that the countries of western Europe would be unable in the foreseeable future to defend themselves and that they were therefore vulnerable to Soviet blackmail. Third it was assumed that the Soviet Union was governed by rational men who could indeed be deterred by American nuclear weapons. Perhaps the most crucial assumption was that North America itself was safe from Soviet attack.

Under the terms of the treaty the United States would consider an attack on Europe an attack on itself and would respond accordingly. American strategy relied heavily on the ability of the Strategic Air Command to deliver a retaliatory nuclear strike against Soviet cities in the event of a Soviet invasion of Europe. NATO thus depended upon an American nuclear first-strike policy. This strategy was attractive for several reasons. First, the United States enjoyed a virtual monopoly of strategic nuclear power (even though the Soviet Union had exploded its first nuclear device in 1949). Second, it was relatively inexpensive for the United States because it did not require large land forces. It appealed to the Europeans because it seemed to require no large sacrifices for defense and would thus not divert scarce economic resources from their recovery programs. The threat of nuclear attack alone seemed sufficient to prevent a Soviet attack and to spare Europe the ravages of another war. As we shall see, many of these conditions changed in the ensuing decades, so that the original assumptions became less tenable.

NATO AND CHANGING CONDITIONS

The NATO allies held the Soviet Union accountable for the invasion of South Korea in June 1950, fearing that this event, which demonstrated that the American nuclear arsenal was not enough to prevent a major land war, promised increasing Soviet pressure in western Europe. Europe itself was still vulnerable to attack by the massive armies of the Soviet Union. NATO therefore adopted a new

"forward strategy" calling for the defense of Europe to begin at the Elbe river, which separates East Germany from West Germany, rather than at the Rhine river to the west as originally specified. Korea seemed to suggest that the American nuclear arsenal did not guarantee that a major land war could be avoided, and the European, particularly French, fear of fighting another such war made this strategy appealing.

But the forward strategy required sufficient conventional military resources, particularly ground troops, to withstand the Red Army. Only twelve understrength divisions were protecting Europe at that time. As long as American troops were needed on the frontiers of West Germany only to make the American nuclear threat credible, small forces made strategic sense. But these troops were scarcely enough to prevent a rapid Soviet advance westward. In the event of an attack any decision on the use of nuclear weapons would have to be made in haste. And, as the Soviets had meanwhile acquired nuclear weapons of their own —though of limited capability—such a rapid decision would be difficult to make. The new plan called for more allied troops to hold a Russian advance at the Elbe. They were to act as NATO's "shield" while strategic nuclear forces would serve as its "sword."

There were an estimated 175 Soviet divisions in eastern Europe in 1951; NATO set a goal of 96 divisions. The revised strategy called for the European countries to bear the major conventional burden and for the United States to continue to wield the nuclear sword. Massive European rearmament would, however, have entailed great sacrifices by the United States' allies and would have impaired their economic recovery. The defense of western Europe constituted a collective benefit for all members of the alliance, and each desired to reduce its own costs in providing such defense. A partial solution was to rearm West Germany, thus spreading costs and reducing them for each member of NATO. West Germany's industrial resources and geographical position made its defense imperative; it seemed logical to call on the Germans to contribute to achieving that objective.

What seemed logical in theory, however, was more difficult in practice. Rearming Germany under any conditions seemed disagreeable to many Europeans who remembered their experiences during World War II. The question was how could German participation in European defense be achieved without stirring the understandable anxieties of many Europeans.

The initial proposal was to form the European Defense Community (EDC) to pool western European military resources in a unified command structure. In effect, leaders envisioned a European army in which all German troops would remain under international control. The proposal seemed to complement the continental trend toward economic integration and to ensure against the resurgence of a national German army. A treaty setting up the EDC was signed on May 27, 1952.

It still had to be ratified by the member nations, however. The Benelux countries, though unenthusiastic about rearming Germany, did ratify it, because they saw it as a necessary step toward European unity. Italy also achieved a parliamentary majority in favor of ratification. In Germany itself, despite socialist opposition, Konrad Adenauer's Christian Democrats maintained their political control and endorsed the plan. The British government, though opposed to European integration at that time, supported EDC in order to bolster American enthusiasm for European defense. Only the French parliament remained. It was the French who had originally urged EDC on the other countries in NATO. Successive French governments, however, balked at the prospect of bringing the issue to a vote in the Chamber of Deputies because of intense parliamentary opposition.

The United States sought to bring pressure to bear on the French government. Secretary of State John Foster Dulles declared at a NATO meeting in December 1953, "[If] the European Defense Community should not become effective, that would compel an agonizing reappraisal of basic United States' policy."[4] Dulles' speech aroused great anger in the French government, which perceived the United States as insensitive to French national feelings.

In June 1954 a new French government was formed by Pierre Mendès-France, who sought unsuccessfully to convince the allies that there was not a majority in favor of EDC in the French Assembly; on August 30 the treaty was resoundingly defeated in the National Assembly. The vote may have been influenced by the acute problems that France was then experiencing in Indochina. It is possible that in return for a negative French decision on the EDC question, the Soviet Union was prepared to pressure Ho Chi Minh and the Viet Minh to accept a compromise solution to the Indochina conflict which would permit France an honorable disengagement; although widely believed, this hypothesis has never been proven.

A solution to the resulting impasse was finally achieved through a proposal by British Foreign Secretary Anthony Eden. French opposition to German rearmament was based largely on opposition to supranationalism and on fear of German resurgence. Eden proposed to admit Germany and Italy to the Brussels Pact Organization, to be renamed the Western European Union (WEU), and then to incorporate this organization into NATO. At a meeting in London allied representatives approved this scheme. To ease French fears of German rearmament, it was also agreed that Germany would not manufacture nuclear, biological, or chemical weapons. The Eden "package" was accepted by the French and thus solved a problem that had threatened to destroy the Western alliance.

The creation and consolidation of NATO illustrates the necessity for formalizing alliance structure as the number of

---

[4] *The New York Times*, December 15, 1953.

participants grows. It also shows that more formal structure and specification of obligations become necessary as allies come to share fewer interests. The German-rearmament question involved several divergent interests. The French feared German resurgence and sought retreat from Indochina. Great Britain, on the other hand, hoped for German rearmament to reduce economic costs but resisted participation in any supranational scheme.

CONFLICTS OF INTEREST: SUEZ AND HUNGARY, 1956

From its creation until the early 1950s NATO was regarded by its members as providing a "superior good," that is, a benefit valued so highly that they were willing to forgo other benefits to obtain it; other objectives were subordinated to the one common objective of deterring a possible Soviet invasion. In that period NATO was perceived by Europeans as vital, rather than as merely convenient. They were therefore prepared to surrender more of their respective autonomy than they otherwise would have done.

By the mid-1950s, however, deterring Soviet aggression had become a less salient objective. After the death of Stalin in 1953 East-West relations thawed somewhat. Cease-fires were arranged in Korea and Indochina, and in 1955 the Austrian State Treaty provided for the unification of Austria under a neutral regime. These events aroused new hope that the cold war was abating. As prosperity grew in Europe and the threat of Soviet aggression seemed to have eased, European leaders became preoccupied with more particularist interests.

The Hungarian and Suez crises in the autumn of 1956 cast the divergent interests of the NATO allies into sharp relief. As we suggested in Chapter 14, a reduction in the number and range of common interests tends to create instability in an alliance. Unlike the United States, which still considered containment of Soviet

communism its chief objective, Great Britain and France remained strongly interested in their colonial possessions and dependent upon foreign trade for economic prosperity. Indeed, Great Britain's reluctance to participate fully in the federation of Europe arose partly from its continuing involvement in the Commonwealth and the non-European focus of its foreign policy. France too was attempting to maintain its overseas empire in North Africa, where its resources were being drained in combating insurrection in Algeria. The United States refused to permit France to use NATO forces to put down the Algerian rebellion, even though the French argued that Algeria was a province of France. French interests in North Africa and British interests in the Middle East provided the bases for Anglo-French cooperation after President Gamal Abdel Nasser of Egypt nationalized the Suez canal on July 26, 1956.

Great Britain considered the canal essential to its security, for it functioned as the link between British possessions in Asia and on the Indian Ocean and the home islands. It was the route by which Great Britain imported its petroleum and was thus essential to the British economy. In 1954 Great Britain had agreed to a phased withdrawal of British troops from the canal zone, to be completed by mid-1956. In exchange Nasser had agreed to Anglo-French supervision of the canal's operation until 1969.

Within two weeks after the departure of British troops, however, Nasser had seized control of the canal and had nationalized it. The event which apparently precipitated the Egyptian action was an American withdrawal of an offer of funds for the construction of the Aswan High Dam, a vital scheme of Nasser's for the economic development of his country. His purposes were several. First, he was a nationalist leader with ambitions to lead a pan-Arab movement, and he believed that he could not afford to tolerate such an obvious vestige of colonial rule in Egypt. Second, Egypt had been receiving only 7 percent of the profits from the canal's operations, and sought to increase its share. Finally, Nasser wished to demonstrate his independence from the West as a bid for increased Soviet aid.

The British government was surprised and humiliated by the sudden seizure of the canal. The French also depended upon petroleum brought through the canal, and, furthermore, Premier Guy Mollet believed Nasser to be a key supporter of the Algerian rebel movement, which he was. Within a week after the nationalization the British government had decided to reestablish its control in the area by force if necessary [8]. The French agreed to join in overthrowing Nasser, in order to ease their difficulties in Algeria. The Anglo-French alignment was thus based on complementary, rather than common, interests. Both governments considered the overthrow of Nasser a way of achieving their separate objectives. Various forms of international consultation were attempted in the autumn of 1956, in order that a peaceful resolution to the crisis might be found, but the results were unsatisfactory to the British and French.

In the meantime a series of events in eastern Europe had caused the most serious upheaval within the Soviet bloc since the expulsion of Marshal Tito of Yugoslavia from the Cominform in 1948 for his insistence on following an independent line. Stirred by Nikita S. Khrushchev's condemnation of Stalin at the Twentieth Congress of the Soviet Communist Party in February 1956, intellectuals, students, and workers in Poland and Hungary had begun to press for liberalization of their communist regimes. In Poland a peaceful revolution brought the popular communist leader Wladislaw Gomulka to power in early October. Events in Hungary, however, went out of control, as a student-led revolution precipitated the overthrow of the existing regime. Imre Nagy, who had previously been expelled from the Hungarian Communist Party, was swept to power on a wave of popular sentiment, but even he was unable to control his supporters. Consequently, in the first days of November the Soviet Union intervened and crushed the Hungarian revolution by force.

The United States government assailed Soviet actions and attempted to rally world public opinion through the United Nations. At no time, however, did it contemplate military intervention in Hungary. American objectives in NATO centered around preserving the European status quo and deterring a Soviet attack on western Europe. Interfering in eastern Europe would have led to a dangerous collision with the Soviet Union, and, regardless of rhetoric, American leaders deemed such a collision unprofitable.

As the events in eastern Europe unfolded, the British and French completed their planning of Operation Musketeer. The two allies urged Israel to launch an attack on the Sinai peninsula, thus providing an excuse for their intervention. They could then argue that their action had been necessary to restore peace in the area and to prevent the canal from being closed. Logistics required Anglo-French mobilization a week before the Israeli attack, so that, when the Israelis began to move across Sinai on October 29, the British and French plan had already been put into operation secretly.

The United States, unaware of the plan, was embarrassed. Dwight D. Eisenhower was in the midst of an election campaign based on a platform of "peace and prosperity," and, furthermore, the administration considered its allies' behavior threatening to American influence in Asia and Africa. Furthermore, the Suez canal was considerably less important economically and politically to the United States than it was to its allies. Finally, the Anglo-French operation shifted world attention from eastern Europe to the Middle East, thus weakening American attempts to bring pressure upon the Soviet Union through the United Nations.

The Anglo-French operation was not the success that its sponsors had hoped for. The plan had depended largely upon speed of execution, but the British and French did not land troops in Egypt until after the Egyptians had blocked the canal by scuttling ships in it. In the meantime, the United States had joined the Soviet Union in condemning the invasion and supporting a General Assembly resolution calling for an immediate cease-fire in the Middle East. The Soviet Union threatened both Great Britain and France with nuclear attack, and the United States, far from coming firmly to the support of its allies, threatened them with economic sanctions. Against combined Soviet-American opposition Great Britain and France had little choice but to comply with the General Assembly's resolution. A United Nations force was sent to Egypt, and the British and French retired.

These events were a severe blow to NATO unity. The British and French felt betrayed by their American partner. It had been made clear to them that the United States would not permit the alliance to be used for objectives that were not common to all members; the United States, however, was unwilling to subordinate its objectives to those of its allies, no matter how salient the latter were. The United States government, annoyed at not having been kept informed, considered the Suez operation an example of colonial irresponsibility and parochial interests. Finally, it made clear that the dominant partner in the NATO alliance was the United States and that Great Britain and France had become "second-rate" powers, even "second-rate citizens." The overwhelming common interest that had led to creation of NATO in the first place was no longer sufficient to ensure cohesion.

DE GAULLE, GAULLISM, AND NATO

Since his participation in the Free French movement of World War II General de Gaulle's primary objective had been to restore the "grandeur" of France, that is, to regain for France the independence and pride that it had enjoyed before the disaster of 1940. Many other Europeans shared de Gaulle's aspirations for their own countries and had resented from the beginning their apparent dependence upon the United States. De Gaulle articulated not only French nationalism but European nationalism as well. He hoped to press for an alliance under French leadership, one that would put European interests first.

Until the 1960s Gaullist aspirations remained dormant. European economic and military weakness, the Soviet threat, and military technology combined to keep Europe in a secondary role in NATO. As these conditions changed, however, the inherent contradictions in the alliance began to emerge. NATO produced mainly collective benefits; under such circumstances there is little incentive for "junior" partners to contribute their shares to the costs of the alliance. That NATO is an asymmetrical alliance is reflected in the "overpayment" of costs by the United States and in American difficulties in maintaining cohesion in the alliance.

De Gaulle and his American allies agreed on one main point. For Europe to regain its influence, it was necessary to guarantee its security. But, whereas the Americans considered this security dependent upon an institutionalized alliance system in which the American commitment was beyond doubt, the French recognized that mutual interest in the independence of Europe alone was sufficient to guarantee American support in the event of war. The Gaullists viewed the American-dominated alliance system that had evolved since 1949 as a hindrance to French pursuit of vital interests. The Suez affair and subsequent events seemed to confirm their interpretation. Despite their belief in American willingness to maintain Europe free of Soviet control, the Gaullists argued that it was only natural, particularly in view of changes in military technology, that the interests of a superpower located thousands of miles from the Soviet border would often diverge from those of smaller nations located on the periphery of the Soviet bloc. The gradual détente between the United States and the Soviet Union after 1962, changes in American military strategy, and growing American concern about non-European issues like Cuba and Vietnam convinced de Gaulle and many other Europeans that the United States would sometimes sacrifice continental interests in pursuit of its own objectives.

A major opportunity for the French to pursue actively an independent policy occurred after changes in American strategy introduced by President John F. Kennedy and Secretary of Defense Robert S. McNamara after 1960. By that time both American and European cities had become Soviet "hostages." Soviet development of intercontinental ballistic missiles (ICBMs) laid the American heartland open to the threat of Soviet attack. Furthermore, the development of second-strike weapons systems made an American nuclear first strike against Soviet conventional attack unwise and unlikely. These weapons not only negated the previous assumptions of American policy but also made it realistic for American leaders to "pause" before retaliating against any Soviet move.

Although both the United States and western Europe continued to share the basic objective of deterring a Soviet attack on Europe, questions about the most effective ways to achieve it arose in the 1960s and 1970s. Was it still possible to threaten the Soviet Union with "massive retaliation" when it could respond in kind? Kennedy and McNamara concluded that it had become less possible for the United States to deter the Soviet Union from a conventional attack or a small-scale incursion in western Europe because a nuclear strike would bring corresponding reprisals on the United States.

The United States attempted to convince its allies of the desirability of substituting for the existing strategy of nuclear deterrence a more nearly traditional strategy of defense. "It is time," declared McNamara, "for the maps to change by which policy is charted and justified. The old ones, which assumed a U.S. nuclear monopoly . . . and a Communist monopoly of ground combat strength, are too far removed from reality to serve as even rough guides" [7]. Thenceforth the United States sought to develop an array of military resources, including increased conventional strength, to counter potential Soviet moves ranging from minor aggression to all-out nuclear war. By strengthening the conventional forces of NATO, particularly through the addition of more European divisions, the United States hoped to challenge Soviet conventional dominance of Europe. The earlier formula was reversed. NATO's land armies would become the "sword" and its nuclear strike force the "shield." To avoid nuclear warfare through miscalculation or rapid escalation and strengthen the credibility of its commitment to European security, the United States prepared to respond in kind to any Soviet thrust below the nuclear threshold. American planners foresaw a defense of Europe with ground forces in the event of a conventional Soviet attack. Only if it appeared that Europe was on the verge of being overrun would the United States consider resorting to a strategic nuclear response.

The strategy of "flexible response" was thus introduced in the early 1960s. It depended upon three conditions. First, NATO was to continue centralized command and control procedures. Obviously, if the allies were determined to pursue different strategies or if one of them was willing and able to use nuclear weapons early in a contest, McNamara's strategy of "slow escalation" would fail. The Americans believed it necessary that strategic nuclear weapons remain under the ultimate control of American officers, so that the escalation spiral could be coordinated and no "unauthorized" or "irresponsible" recourse to nuclear weapons could occur. Second, it was time for the Europeans to contribute more to their own defense, particularly in the form of ground troops. Finally, the strategy depended upon the dubious assumption that Soviet strategists would adopt a similar strategy, would "play the game."

McNamara's strategy played into de Gaulle's hands. Europeans feared that reliance on traditional defense would have no greater deterrent value than it had had in the past. Should it fail, the allies would find themselves engaged in a geographically "limited" war—limited, that is, to Europe. The United States might be cheered at the prospect of being able to defend Europe without incurring a Soviet attack on its homeland, but this did not hold the same appeal for many Europeans. Furthermore, NATO attempts to match Soviet firepower in Europe by resorting to "tactical" nuclear weapons seemed even less desirable to Europeans. Placing such weapons under the control of battlefield commanders seemed to negate the idea of centralized command and control. Furthermore, introduction of tactical nuclear weapons, far from compensating for NATO inferiority in ground troops, would give the Soviet Union additional advantages, for western Europe was geographically smaller and more densely populated than were eastern Europe and the Soviet Union, and thus more vulnerable to such weapons. As the Soviet Union had more troops than NATO, it would be able to replace the large numbers killed more easily. Also the ports in France and the Low Countries upon which NATO would have to depend for supplies were particularly vulnerable to such weapons.

Above all, however, such a limited war promised to be "unlimited" as far as Europe was concerned. De Gaulle asked whether or not the United States would always remain committed to Europe's defense. If escalation occurred, could Europe depend unconditionally upon American use of nuclear weapons that might invite retaliatory destruction of American cities? If Europe was uncertain of American intentions, was it wise to leave its destiny in American hands?

For France, de Gaulle answered, the only way to acquire political independence and military security was to develop its own nuclear arm, the *force de frappe*. American leaders argued that such a force would be militarily ineffective because it would be too small and too subject to rapid obsolescence to deter the Soviet Union. Americans considered it likely to be a *force de farce*. Furthermore, this

policy would be dangerous because it would undermine the effectiveness of the "flexible response" strategy, would provoke the Russians, and would encourage further proliferation of nuclear weapons among countries like India, Israel, Egypt, Japan, Germany, and even Indonesia. Not only would such a marginal force not deter the Russians; but as it would remain essentially a vulnerable weapons system for many years, it would also encourage a Soviet first strike against France and perhaps the United States in the event of conflict.

To fend off the French challenge to NATO, the Eisenhower administration in December 1960 and the Kennedy administration again in February 1963 proposed a scheme for sharing control of nuclear weapons known as the Multilateral Force (MLF). The scheme centered on the creation of a naval force manned by crews of mixed nationality. The idea was to permit the Europeans to have some voice in nuclear strategy by giving them a veto on the use of this fleet. It was a patchwork plan, however, and was greeted with noticeable lack of enthusiasm by many Europeans from the outset. First, even if the allies could agree on such a force, what would its strategic purpose be? If McNamara's strategy were adopted and the force became part of NATO's "shield," the Europeans would derive no benefit from it. On the contrary, they would have surrendered what nuclear weapons they possessed to no advantage. Second, even if the Europeans might have a veto in the MLF, they would have no greater influence over American nuclear strategy. The overwhelming majority of American strategic forces were to remain under American control anyway. The net result would be that Europe would surrender what little independence it had in these matters to no advantage. Eventually the proposal was quietly dropped by Lyndon B. Johnson.

Although American criticism of French efforts to create an independent nuclear striking force was largely justified in terms of coordinated alliance policy, such a force promised important political and psychological benefits to the French. An independent French deterrent would make it difficult for the United States to impose its strategic doctrine on NATO and would guarantee the French a voice in decisions on disarmament and arms control; the Americans and the Russians would no longer be able to conduct bilateral negotiations without consulting France.

Furthermore, the force could help to impose French strategic conceptions on NATO. A French threat to respond to Soviet provocation with nuclear weapons would increase the probability that the United States would have to come to France's aid. It would, in effect, force the Americans to make a decision that they might otherwise be reluctant to make. Even if such behavior did not galvanize American support, a sophisticated French striking force alone might deter a Soviet attack. The Russians would have to be convinced that the French were capable of destroying one or several Soviet cities; then France would possess a "minimum deterrent."

The nonmilitary benefits of an independent force would be even greater. De Gaulle considered the force a means to achieve influence over the United States and the Soviet Union in decisions affecting France—and Europe in general. France would no longer find itself helpless, as it had been in 1956. The pursuit of both European and French interests would be facilitated by French military independence, for de Gaulle thought that Europe required a renewed sense of solidarity, self-reliance, and independence. Nuclear weapons would permit European countries to pursue policies that were in their interests, even in the face of American or Soviet opposition.

FROM SUEZ TO SKYBOLT: THE UNRAVELING OF AN ALLIANCE

A series of events after the Suez episode seemed to confirm French fears about American-Soviet collaboration at the ex-

pense of Europe. The crisis over construction of the Berlin Wall in 1961 suggested American support for critical European objectives was only lukewarm. A major West German objective was reunification of the country, and American hesitation increased suspicion that the United States was less interested in German unification than in European stability and maintenance of the status quo. The continued division of Berlin showed that NATO could not help the Germans to attain their foremost national objective. Indeed, American proposals pertaining to Berlin after 1961 indicated readiness to concede certain rights in order to perpetuate stability in the region.

American behavior in this crisis gave the French yet another opportunity to proselytize the Gaullist philosophy. France saw the idea of an independent Europe as a means of assuaging German uneasiness. Through participation in the counsels of a revived and diplomatically active Europe, Germany was offered an alternative channel for its energies.

The Cuban missile crisis reinforced Gaullism in Europe because it illustrated that the United States was willing and able to drag Europeans into war over issues that did not directly concern them. Yet soon an even more divisive event occurred: the Kennedy administration's cancellation of the Skybolt research program. De Gaulle insisted that an independent Europe required British participation, yet such participation had been effectively blocked by a continuing British orientation toward the Commonwealth and by the Anglo-American "special relationship." This alliance of the "Anglo-Saxons" had been an irritant to de Gaulle since World War II, when he had been virtually excluded from major decisions. Furthermore, the Skybolt affair seemed to show that the British remained politically and psychologically dependent upon the Americans and that the United States would exploit the "special relationship" to spike de Gaulle's plans for an independent Europe.

The United States and Great Britain

shared close working relations in the field of nuclear energy, as in other fields. While opposing the French nuclear force, the United States had in effect underwritten an independent British deterrent. An amendment to the U.S. Atomic Energy Act of 1954 permitted American assistance to the British nuclear research program while barring such assistance to other allies, including France. By the end of the 1950s, however, the British nuclear strike force of V-bombers had become obsolete. The British had begun to develop a missile known as Blue Streak, but they abandoned it in 1960 in favor of cooperating with the United States on Skybolt. Skybolt was an air-to-surface missile that would, it was hoped, prolong the life of the obsolete British V-bomber force by permitting it to attack an enemy without having to fly to the target.

In December 1961 the United States government abruptly cancelled work on Skybolt, arguing that it had become more costly than it was worth. Although the decision was made on the basis of technical and financial considerations alone, the political repercussions were enormous. The British government of Harold Macmillan was immediately assailed by domestic critics for having wasted billions of dollars in developing an impotent deterrent. Furthermore, by canceling the project the United States seemed insensitive to British needs and national pride. It was as if the "special relationship" were taken for granted by the United States and that once again, as at Suez, when a choice had to be made between American and European interests the latter would suffer.

On December 18, 1962, President Kennedy met Macmillan on the island of Nassau in the Bahamas. They quickly reached a somewhat ambiguous agreement according to which the United States would supply Great Britain with Polaris missiles for which the British would provide submarines and nuclear warheads. The Americans made a similar offer to the French, but the latter did not yet have the capacity to manufacture either sub-

marines or warheads. In three days Macmillan had altered British strategy to suit American preferences without having consulted the French or any other of their NATO partners. It appeared to de Gaulle that the British valued a junior partnership with the United States more highly than equal participation in an independent Europe. As long as Great Britain preferred to orient its policies toward the United States and the Commonwealth, it could not, according to de Gaulle, adopt a "Europe-first" policy. Furthermore, the British had again shown how dependent they were upon the United States in matters of military security. Partly for these reasons de Gaulle announced his veto of the British application to join the European Common Market in January 1963.

American refusal to treat its NATO partners as political equals, along with its unilateral revisions of nuclear strategy and weapons development, further undermined NATO solidarity. All members still wanted to deter a Soviet attack, but developments in nuclear technology encouraged debate over how this objective could be achieved most efficiently. American interests and objectives were global; European interests and objectives were centered on the continent itself. By 1962 Great Britain and especially France had painfully divested themselves of most of their colonial empires in Africa and Asia and were reevaluating their foreign-policy priorities.

The United States seemed to become less and less responsive to Europe after 1960, and decisions on major matters like intervention in Vietnam were taken by the United States with little or no consultation with the NATO allies. The problem was exemplified by the Cuban crisis in 1962. When Kennedy's representative flew to Paris to speak with de Gaulle, the latter asked, "Are you consulting or informing me?" As de Gaulle expected, the answer was that the president's representative had come to *inform,* not to consult with, him [1]. The prospect of "annihilation without representation" is attractive to no actor in the contemporary system.

By 1972 reasons for the European

members of NATO to support actively an alliance that sharply circumscribed their alternatives yet involved real costs—without furnishing many benefits that could not also be achieved outside the alliance—were less compelling. If the American commitment to European security was genuine (and most Europeans believed that it was), American protection would be forthcoming even without the alliance. In addition, technological changes began to arouse fears in Europe that the American nuclear umbrella might actually not be available in the future. Finally, the probability of a Soviet attack on western Europe seemed much less by 1972. By 1970 the French were therefore prepared to withdraw from most alliance military activities; they forced NATO to move its headquarters and many of its installations out of France. The French hoped to transform the alliance from a primarily military association into an organization that would ensure political collaboration among allies. The regime of de Gaulle's successor, President Georges Pompidou, has largely continued de Gaulle's foreign policies. One study of European attitudes has confirmed that "nationality continues to be a far stronger determinant . . . of political attitudes" than does any other factor [3]. Apparent Soviet willingness to compromise on Berlin, Soviet calls for a European security conference, and continued Soviet preoccupation with China all contributed to further erosion of NATO unity in 1971–1972.

American attitudes toward Europe also appear to be changing. Burdened increasingly by global responsibilities, the United States has reduced its forces in Europe and has virtually ceased to publicize the concept of Atlantic community. Increasingly, Europeans and Americans are pursuing independent foreign policies. American actions in Cuba (1961, 1962), the Dominican Republic (1965), Indochina (1961–1972), and elsewhere have been undertaken with little attention to the views of NATO allies. Nor does NATO any longer provide such private benefits as economic prosperity to European members; in fact, it is increasingly an obstacle to independent behavior. For example, West Germany, under the socialist government of Willy Brandt, has on its own initiative adopted new policies, including negotiations with East Germany, the Soviet Union, and the nations of eastern Europe, to further the cause of German unification.

The survival of NATO, even in eclipse, attests to its adaptability over time and to the persistence of the forces promoting the alliance. Its members share common values and functional links. Although the common interest generated by the Soviet threat has declined, it has not disappeared. In its stead other, relatively minor interests in economic and military coordination are being served by NATO. The continuation of the alliance will depend upon the changing balance of integrative forces and perceived needs.

References

1. Abel, Elie, *The Missile Crisis* (New York: Bantam, 1966), p. 96.
2. Clay, Lucius, *Decision in Germany* (London: Heinemann, 1950).
3. Deutsch, Karl W., *et al., France, Germany, and the Western Alliance* (New York: Scribner's, 1967), p. 299.
4. Kennan, George F. [X], "The Sources of Soviet Conduct," *Foreign Affairs,* 25 (July 1947), p. 582.
5. Knapp, Wilfrid, *A History of War and Peace 1939–1965* (New York: Oxford University Press, 1967), p. 37.
6. Leonhard, Wolfgang, *Child of the Revolution,* trans. by C. M. Woodhouse (London: Collins, 1957), pp. 256–257.
7. McNamara, Robert S., "The Damage-Limiting Strategy," in Arthur L. Waskow, ed., *The Debate Over Thermonuclear Strategy* (Boston: Heath, 1965), p. 45.
8. Neustadt, Richard E., *Alliance Politics* (New York: Columbia University Press, 1970), p. 12.
9. Seton-Watson, Hugh, *The East European Revolution,* 3rd ed. (New York: Praeger, 1956), pp. 167–168.
10. U.S. Senate, Committee on Foreign Relations and State Department, *A De-*

cade of *American Foreign Policy: Basic Documents, 1941–1949* (Washington, D.C.: Government Printing Office, 1950), p. 1269.

11. Werth, Alexander, *Russia at War 1941–1945* (London: Pan Books, 1965).

Suggested Reading

Aron, Raymond, *The Great Debate* (Garden City, N.Y.: Doubleday, 1965).

Brzezinski, Zbigniew K., *Alternative to Partition* (New York: McGraw-Hill, 1965).

Deutsch, Karl W., *Arms Control and the Atlantic Alliance* (New York: Wiley, 1967).

Fox, W. T. R., and Annette Baker, *NATO and the Range of American Choice* (New York: Columbia University Press, 1967).

Furniss, Edgar, ed., *The Western Alliance, Its Status and Prospects* (Columbus: Ohio State University Press, 1965).

Hoffmann, Stanley, "De Gaulle, Europe, and the Atlantic Alliance," *International Organization*, 13 (1964), pp. 1–28.

Hoffmann, Stanley, *Gulliver's Troubles, Or the Setting of American Foreign Policy* (New York: McGraw-Hill, 1968).

Jackson, Henry A., ed., *The Atlantic Alliance: Jackson Subcommittee Hearings and Findings* (New York: Praeger, 1967).

Kissinger, Henry A., *The Troubled Partnership* (New York: McGraw-Hill, 1965).

Steel, Ronald, *Pax Americana* (New York: Viking, 1967).

Van der Beugel, Ernst, *From Marshall Plan to Atlantic Partnership* (New York: Elsevier, 1966).

Chapter 16

THE ROLE OF VIOLENCE IN INTERNATIONAL POLITICS

We see, therefore, that War is not merely a political act but also a real political instrument, a continuation of political commerce, a carrying out of the same by other means—Roger A. Leonard [25, p. 57]

Resorting to war involves both moral and empirical questions. In this and the following chapters we shall deal with such questions and the ways in which students of international politics have approached them. It is true, though perhaps unfortunate, that the most celebrated episodes in history have involved the sacrifice of men at war. The mass media, the schools, and national legends seem to conspire to fill our consciousness with tales of violence and battle. As Thomas Hardy declared, "War makes rattling good history but Peace is poor reading." Peaceful bargaining and diplomacy are actually more common but tend to be overlooked in comparison with more sanguinary events. We are more aware of failures in diplomacy that precipitate wars than of measures that prevent them. We count the wars that occur but not the wars that are avoided through skilled negotiation or statesmanlike leadership.

The recurrence of international violence throughout history and the nuclear sword of Damocles that hangs heavy over us now remind us that avoidance of large-scale violence is the sine qua non of continued civilization as we know it. Although advances in technology promote belief in human progress, this belief is undermined by the frequency of war, persecution of minorities, and civil strife. Of this contradiction George Bernard Shaw acidly exclaimed, "Nothing is ever done in this world until men are prepared to kill one another if it is not done."

A central question for historical analysis is whether violence is inherent in human behavior and society or a part of learned culture that can be eliminated. How we answer this question largely determines how we view the morality of violence. Those who consider violent behavior aberrant generally have sought to eliminate it or at least to bring it under control. They have proposed numerous solutions, ranging from selected child-rearing techniques to specific forms of government and social organization. On the other hand, those who have viewed violence as natural and inevitable have turned their attention to channeling it toward desired ends.

VIOLENCE IN THE MIDDLE AGES

The pre-Reformation Christian Church ascribed violence to the sinful nature of man—originating in the fall of Adam and Eve—and claimed that it should be eschewed by the true Christian, who, it was supposed, had been restored to the higher "law of God" by Christ. St. Augustine, one of the most prominent of the early Church philosophers, also blamed violence on the corrupting influence of original sin. According to Augustine, men are unable to achieve the harmony that God intended because of defective reason and will, owing to their progenitor's original violation of God's command.

The ideas of the medieval Church are still to be found in the work of contemporary philosophers. The late Reinhold Niebuhr, for example, argued that every human act has the potential for evil. Wars arise because of man's flawed nature, the "dark, unconscious sources in the human psyche" [33]. He therefore scoffed at "utopians" who believed it possible to eliminate violence and war entirely. Because of the existence of sin, which makes egoists of all men, he believed it is necessary to control domestic strife by threatening government coercion and to provide external protection against potential foes.

Like the Christian theologians Sigmund Freud and his followers have regarded violence as inherent in human nature. But unlike St. Augustine, who considered man's violence as representing the evil that conflicts with good, Freud interpreted it as instinctive behavior in conflict with the instinct for affection:

We assume that human instincts are of two kinds: those that conserve and unify, which we call "erotic" . . . and . . . the instincts to destroy and kill. . . . With the least of speculative efforts we are led to conclude that this latter instinct functions

in every living being, striving to work its ruin and reduce life to its primal state of inert matter. Indeed it might well be called the "death instinct. . . ." [14]

As did the theologians, Freud thought that violence must be regulated so that the positive side of man's nature can dominate.

The views of the Christian Church on the use of violence were important, especially in Europe during the Middle Ages. Taking advantage of class consciousness among knights, the medieval Church attempted to harness martial sentiments for its purposes and to circumscribe violence among Christians by surrounding it with rules, etiquette, and a code of chivalry. This code described an ideal warrior, who was to protect the orphan, the widow, and the poor; defend the Holy Church; spare the vanquished foe; refrain from giving a lady "evil counsel"; and help those in need or distress. "Thus," concludes Marc Bloch, "a modification of vital importance was introduced into the old ideal of war for war's sake, or for the sake of gain. With this sword, the dubbed knight will defend Holy Church, particularly against the infidel" [3, p. 318].

Various Church controls were also placed on the exercise of violence [3, pp. 412–420]; they included the right of sanctuary on consecrated land (usually a church). The Peace of God prohibited attacks on certain classes of people— men going to and from church, the poor, the clergy, and, as early as A.D. 990, merchants. Certain acts like killing peasants' livestock, plundering churches, destroying mills, and uprooting vines were also forbidden. People were encouraged and sometimes required by the Church to swear obedience to these controls, and often local princes enforced them.

As time went on, controls on the uses of violence proliferated and became more specific. The Truce of God was established in many parts of Europe; it forbade fighting on Sundays and the days just before that were necessary for preparing to worship God. In addition, peace was to be preserved on holy days and during the entire Christmas and Easter seasons. The Bishop of Cologne said in 1083 that the Truce of God was propounded

so that both those who travel and those who remain at home may enjoy security and the most entire peace, so that no one may commit murder, arson, robbery or assault, no one may injure another with a sword, club or any kind of weapon, and so that no one . . . may presume to carry arms, shield, sword or lance, or moreover any kind of armor [on the prohibited days]. [7]

Although these controls were aimed at individual violence, they also applied to "international" conflict, which in feudal times amounted to multiple individual conflicts.

The code of chivalry set the knight apart in a special class above all others except the clergy, which fitted closely with the military theory of the period, in which cavalry tactics were heavily emphasized. Warfare provided young nobles with the opportunity to engage in deeds of derring-do of which they could then boast to their friends and ladies. As armor became heavier—it often weighed more than 200 pounds—warfare became more conservative. Armies had to be carefully maneuvered into position as if they consisted of chess pieces, and battles took so long to plan and prepare that agreement between adversaries was often required before they could occur. Battles typically consisted of individual contests between knights, and casualty lists remained low because of the effectiveness of armor and the common practice of ransom, which turned knights into valuable prizes for capture; the death of a knight was a loss to both sides.

In the thirteenth and fourteenth centuries heavy plate armor developed to the point at which it became relatively safe to be a knight. The English, for instance, lost only thirteen men in the battle of Agincourt, one of the greatest clashes in the Hundred Years' War. By the fifteenth century death had been virtually elimi-

nated from warfare. For example, at the battle of Zagonara in Italy in 1423 two large armies struggled all day, and the outcome was described by Niccolò Machiavelli: "In this great defeat famous throughout all Italy no deaths occurred, except those of Ludovici degli Obizi, and two of his people, who having fallen from their horses were smothered in the morass" [30]. The battle of Castracaro in 1467 was decided without a drop of bloodshed, and Machiavelli recorded that "some horses were wounded and prisoners taken but no deaths occurred."

War in the Middle Ages was thus "limited." Both because of actors' limited capabilities and the fragile structure of feudal society, wars were regarded almost as social pastimes in which rules were to be strictly obeyed. In comparison, the restraints on combatants in modern warfare are much weaker. Truces, like those concluded in Vietnam from time to time, are often disregarded. The Japanese attack on Pearl Harbor was deliberately planned for a Sunday morning. Many medieval limitations on warfare have disappeared altogether.

IDEOLOGY AND VIOLENCE

Although men generally deplore violence, they tend to make exceptions when violence can be justified by ideals or sets of ideas. Although most people consider it immoral to resort to violence for personal advantage, they frequently regard some collective shibboleth like "defending free enterprise" and "forwarding the advance of communism" as legitimating *their* use of violence. Murder may be permissible, even encouraged, in the name of a transcendent cause, generally expressed in a complex of political and emotive symbols and myths. Thus, the murder of eleven Israeli athletes in September 1972 by Arab terrorists during the XXth Olympic games in Munich was hailed by many Palestinians as an act justified in the name of Palestinian liberation.

It is characteristic of normally peaceable men that they are willing to fight and die for "nation," "religion," "tribe," or "race." Studies have shown that human beings tend to view the groups of which they are members as possessing monopolies of virtue, whereas "outsiders" are considered untrustworthy or evil [43]. The concept of a superior in-group is fostered by schools, churches, parents, and politicians, and children are raised to respect the deeds and ideals of their group, whether it be the family, the nation, or some other.

The fundamental significance of the dichotomy between in-group and out-group is that men throughout history have willingly committed barbarous acts against other men in the name of their groups. National enemies have functioned as collective "scapegoats" against which men have been able to vent their prejudices. People who have experienced little economic or social success may find substitute gratification in the success of their groups and their ability to dominate other groups.[1]

Psychologists have suggested that the channeling of individual motives into collective action is an unconscious process. They argue that when an individual's desires are frustrated he tends to repress them, in order to avoid the social stigma that would result from antisocial behavior. Although all of us have at some time or another relieved our frustrations at the expense of others—by kicking the dog or yelling at the wife and children—a great deal of aggression is stored until it can be displaced on others in socially acceptable ways.[2] Furthermore, the guilt that may ensue from hurting friends or relatives does not ensue from hurting members of

an out-group, who, it may be alleged, are "inferior" or "wicked." Derogatory images of an enemy are created by those responsible for collective violence; the opponent is "dehumanized" so that he can be more willingly attacked. Terms like "krauts," "nips," "wogs," and "gooks" reflect this dehumanizing process. The process of dehumanization reached an extreme in the persecution of Jews in Germany during World War II.

People tend to project their own bad characteristics onto others. If a person is aggressive or frustrated, he commonly sees others this way, thus avoiding the painful admission that he himself may be at fault. When a nation increases its level of armaments, its citizens ordinarily interpret the increase as defensive and necessary to maintain international peace. When another nation does the same thing, however, the citizens of the first nation are likely to perceive the increase as evidence of aggressive designs.

The willingness of men to fight for ideals is not a recent development. At the same time that the medieval Church was attempting to minimize violence among Christians it encouraged violence against non-Christians or heretics. The Muslim rule of the Holy Land aroused the Church to mobilize against Islam. Although violence among the children of God, who had the means to rise above their natures, was considered evil and unnecessary, violence to save Christianity or to convert Muslims was applauded.

Islam, which had spread from Arabia across North Africa and into Europe, was regarded by its followers as the true faith; they too found it necessary to convert unbelievers by force. People who refused to be converted were sometimes enlightened through decapitation. The followers of Mohammad overthrew established regimes and set up Muslim governments. Mohammad's followers were mobilized by means of a guarantee that death in a holy war would be a certain path to heaven. The Church responded after 1100 by initiating the Crusades, an early example of ideologically justified violence;

---

[1] For a splendid fictional description of such substitute gratification, see Hans Helmut Kirst's novel about a small town in Germany during the Nazi era, *The Wolves* (New York: Coward-McCann, 1968).

[2] A study of the lynching of blacks in the American South has revealed that this behavior varied with the price of cotton! We may infer that those who committed these abominations were displacing frustration brought on by adverse economic conditions [20].

the idea was to convert infidels at sword's point.

Protestantism destroyed the ideological unity of Europe. The religious wars of the sixteenth and seventeenth centuries brought the violence and intensity of ideological warfare to the continent as a whole for the first time. For a century and a half after the Peace of Westphalia in 1648 European wars were conducted on the level of petty bickering. But the French Revolution, resulting in the overthrow of the French monarchy, represented the triumph of still another ideology—nationalism. It unified the French state, which had gradually evolved during the previous centuries, with the French nation: the community bound together through history and language. War was no longer merely the "trade of kings," and the explosive energy of mass violence became a factor in the politics of Europe.

The population of France was not notably larger than those of Austria, Prussia, Russia, and Great Britain, where the armies constituted less than 1 percent of the entire population. Yet in France mercenary soldiers were replaced by the *levée en masse,* and the French population as a whole recognized itself as guided by a common fate in the defense of collective values. The rate of military participation suddenly jumped to 5 percent, and the morale of the army improved as well. The *levée en masse* foreshadowed the mobilization of entire populations:

The young men shall go to battle; the
married men shall forge arms and transport
provisions; the women shall make tents and
clothes, and shall serve in the hospitals;
the children shall turn old linen into lint;
the old men shall repair to the public
places, to stimulate the courage of the
warriors and preach the utility of the
Republic and hatred of kings. [35]

Nationalism greatly increased the resources available to France and stimulated new goals, objectives, and policies that caused war in the interstate system for the next twenty years. The European consensus that had limited the scope and intensity of conflict since 1648 ended. French nationalism swept beyond the frontiers, and ideas of liberty, equality, and fraternity infected the whole continent. French "integration" thus diminished European prospects for peace.

The revolutionary armies of France were "the instrument, sharp and bloody as it might be, of civilization and progress" [46]. The French set out to undermine established European regimes and to bring to the other states of Europe the social, economic, and political reforms that they themselves had begun to enjoy. Inspired by lofty ideals, they thus sought to impose a new order, by force if necessary, on the peoples of Europe.

The rest of Europe recoiled in fear and horror from the excesses of the French Revolution. Edmund Burke, the English philosopher and formerly a defender of the American Revolution, commented indignantly of France that "In the groves of *their* academy, at the end of every vista, you see nothing but gallows" and predicted that "learning will be cast into the mire, and trodden down under the hoofs of a swinish multitude" [6].

French nationalism did indeed stimulate nationalism elsewhere in Europe, as in Spain and Germany, and brought in its train a new way of thinking and a new vocabulary. Diplomacy could no longer flourish, for revolutionaries and antirevolutionaries found it difficult to communicate with each other; the language of force thus became the common idiom.

The changes in tactics, strategy, and technology developed by the armies of Revolutionary France were exploited by Napoleon Bonaparte, whose Empire ultimately spanned Europe from the English Channel to the frontiers of Russia. The Napoleonic wars heralded the end of all wars in which noncombatants could be relatively safe.[3] Mass mobilization and participation were the keys to French military successes. The other states of Europe were quick to note that the French soldier, though conscripted into service

[3] For a description of the extent to which the Napoleonic wars engaged and affected whole nations, see Count Philippe-Paul de Ségur, *Napoleon's Russian Campaign* (Boston: Houghton Mifflin, 1958). Leo Tolstoy's epic *War and Peace* treats the same event in fiction.

for his country, fought better and more tenaciously than hired mercenaries did. Popular participation in war and politics necessitated inflammatory appeals to the populace, and these appeals ensured that war would become more violent and that governments would enjoy less flexibility in dealing with one another diplomatically, for, once popular support for a foreign policy had been aroused, it was very difficult for government to alter that policy.

The early nineteenth-century German philosopher Georg W. F. Hegel developed a theoretical model of the individual's relation to the nationalist state. The terrible effects of the Napoleonic wars on Prussia had created mistrust of democracy and parliamentarianism among elites in that country, and destruction by the French of feudal and traditional institutions had driven the Prussians to substitute for them a series of authoritarian states. Hegel himself eulogized the Prussian state.

Hegel believed that reason finds its expression in nature and the state, not in individual wisdom. He argued that the individual is meaningless outside the collectivity: "The march of God in the world, that is what the state is. . . . Man must therefore venerate the state as a secular deity" [18, pp. 618–619]. Hegel considered self-sacrifice in the service of the state as necessary and desirable and refused to recognize the legitimacy of individual claims against or resistance to the dictates of the state. War, he noted, "is not to be regarded as an absolute evil and as a purely external accident" [18, p. 622]. It was instead to be considered a healthy purgative for the body politic. It would allow men to appreciate the triviality of their daily existence and to share in deeds greater than themselves.

War has the higher significance that by its agency . . . the ethical health of peoples is preserved . . . just as the blowing of the winds preserves the sea from the foulness which would be the result of a prolonged calm, so also corruption in nations would be the product of prolonged . . . peace. [18, pp. 622–623]

When states are unable to agree, Hegel argued, war is the natural and only possible means for adjusting their claims and differences. Furthermore, war seemed to him the vehicle of human progress and the material expression of the dialectic in history. Heroes carried history forward on their swords and lances, and only victory could demonstrate national morality.

Hegel's belief in nationalism, war, and the authority of the state over the individual was the antithesis of the liberals' emphasis on the role of the individual and individual rights, the naturalness of peace, and the common interests of peoples everywhere. Hegel's belief in the genius of selected nations and the uniqueness of their achievements found a receptive climate in late nineteenth century Europe, and elements of Hegelian philosophy can be discerned in the doctrines of both Marxism and fascism.

Although certain nineteenth-century exponents of nationalism like Giuseppe Mazzini and Louis Kossuth emphasized its humane and liberal aspects, a more militant version gained support in Germany, as exemplified in the thought of Heinrich von Treitschke, a major historian of the Bismarckian era. Treitschke praised the virtues of military expansion and applauded Prussian military policies. He viewed nations purely as competitors in a totally anarchic system from which only the strong could emerge whole. Peace seemed to him a sign of weakness, even of effeminacy. "But God above will see to it that war will return again—a terrible medicine for mankind diseased" [4, p. 357]. Strong nations had an obligation to extirpate inferior races, as "the Redskins in America withered before the Basilisk eye of the Palefaces" [4, p. 359]. Treitschke considered most races inferior to the Germans, and he enjoined his nation to make its presence felt in Europe and in the world. The greatness of human history, he argued, "lies in the perpetual conflict of nations" [4, p. 353].

In the nineteenth century such theories of racial superiority, fostered by misunderstanding of Darwinian biology and genetics, increased the potential for international violence. At the turn of the twentieth century social Darwinism went hand in hand with the great surge of European and American imperialism in Africa, Asia, and Latin America and with an international climate saturated by notions of race and racial differences. Before World War I President Theodore Roosevelt and Kaiser Wilhelm spoke of the "yellow peril" and endorsed the idea of an alliance between Anglo-Saxons and Teutons. Industrialization would then permit men to fight one another on a scale previously unimagined.

Charles Darwin's theories in *The Origin of Species*—especially the idea that man had evolved from a lower order of animal—challenged the notion of man as a special creation of God. The idea of natural competition among men, comparable to competition among predatory beasts, took root in the political consciousness of Europe, already prepared by Marxist notions of class war and capitalism. Pseudoscientific theories of racial and ethnic superiority and of the necessity for ruthless competition in the social "jungle"—in which the weak must perish and only the strong might prosper—fell on receptive ears and flourished.

World War II witnessed unimagined excesses against both combatants and civilians. The war waged by Benito Mussolini and Adolf Hitler bore only slight similarity to a war initiated only for specific political ends. Fascism, the doctrine espoused by Mussolini, conceived of life as a struggle. It combined Hegel's and Treitschke's adoration of the state with selected tenets of Darwinism; war was viewed as the necessary medium through which men could prove their virility. "For Fascism," wrote Mussolini, "the tendency to Empire, that is to say, to the expansion of nations, is a manifestation of vitality; its opposite, staying at home, is a sign of decadence" [31]. The code of Mussolini's soldiers embodied the spirit of fascism:

1. Know that the Fascist . . . must not believe in perpetual peace. . . .

3. The nation serves even as a sentinel over a can of petrol. . . .

5. The rifle and the cartridge belt . . . are confided to you not to rust in leisure, but to be preserved in war. . . .

8. Mussolini is always right.

9. For a volunteer there are no extenuating circumstances when he is disobedient. [9, p. 392]

Hitler considered war an instrument for preserving racial purity and national survival. "We see before us," he declared, "the Aryan race which is manifestly the bearer of all culture. . . . Take away the Nordic Germans and nothing remains but the dance of apes" [9, p. 407]. The total war perpetrated by the Nazis evoked total war in reply, and the distinction between civilian and military virtually vanished.

The justification of wars in lofty moral terms—and thus in absolute terms—has become common in the twentieth century; this development has made it difficult for governments to wage limited war. They have become the prisoners of their own propaganda, surrender their flexibility, and lose their capacity to steer a course based on policies that will truly secure their objectives.

VIOLENCE AS ABERRATION

The liberal political philosophies of the eighteenth and nineteenth centuries generally considered violence among men abnormal and suggested various ways to eliminate its causes. The *philosophes* of prerevolutionary France, men like Voltaire, de Condorcet, Diderot, and the Marquis Helvétius—attacked intolerance, national aggrandizement, the balance-of-power system, and class or national differences. They stressed the value of the individual and the notion that common self-interest will lead mankind to choose peace over war. Progress was their fetish, and equal education and free trade were favored as means by which the natural harmony of men could be realized. Men could make use of their reason to the full and understand the laws of nature dictating the harmony of men only by shedding the "artificial" encumbrances that governments had placed upon them.

Liberals elsewhere embraced the creed of the *philosophes* and adapted it to the technical and industrial advances of the nineteenth century. Science was considered the vehicle that was to fulfill the promise of progress. John Stuart Mill considered education the means of realizing the liberal utopia. Adam Smith and other liberal economists stressed the necessity for removing obstacles to free enterprise and restrictions on international trade. Although Smith believed men to be naturally selfish, he argued that such individuals, competing with one another and acting in their self-interest, would cancel each other out, and economic well-being and prosperity for all would result.

Industrialization and the possibility of universal affluence for the first time in history raised hopes that peace could indeed be ensured. The promised end to scarcity of goods seemed to open new avenues into which man's energies could be directed. The American philosopher William James argued that war could no longer be profitable in the twentieth century: "Modern war is so expensive that we feel trade to be a better avenue to plunder" [22, p. 22].[4] James claimed that war is an outlet for human energies. Hardiness and discipline can indeed save people from the moral deterioration of pure pleasure, but their energies can be channeled instead into economically productive tasks:

To coal and iron mines, to freight trains, to fishing fleets in December, to dish-washing, clothes-washing, and window-washing, to road building and tunnel-making, to foundries and stokeholes, and to the frames of skyscrapers, would our gilded youth be drafted off . . . to get the childishness knocked out of them and to come back into society with healthier sympathies and soberer ideas. [22, p. 29]

These activities were to take the place of war and to inculcate the values of service without loss of life and treasure.

In contrast to James, Karl Marx and Auguste Comte saw in industrialization

itself the promise of permanent peace. Marx considered violence part of a historical process that might be harnessed to propel the "train of history" along its inevitable track more quickly. The capitalist state, "the engine of class despotism," was the means by which the bourgeoisie perpetuated its control of the economy and society. War, then, represented the international analogue of the class struggle, which would cease once the proletariat had seized power and socialism had eliminated classes. Wars would end when classless societies abolished state apparatuses.

Although agreeing with Marx that economics was the key to understanding history, Comte saw its specific historical role in a very different light. He argued that industrialization and technological progress will bring an end to war because material goods will be so plentiful that war will be less profitable than will investment in new industries. Comte claimed that militarism and commerce are incompatible and that individual success in industrial society will arise no longer from success in battle but rather from success in banking, industry, and commerce [2]. Comte was partly in error, for he did not foresee the rapidity with which the technology of war would develop or the degree of support that war would enjoy in the most technologically advanced societies.

Both Marx and Comte were optimists. They believed that an institution that had lost its principal function would cease to exist. War seemed to be losing its functions—the resolution of class antagonisms, the redistribution of scarce resources—and it would therefore have to disappear.[5] But revolution and the classless society did not come to the industrialized nations, nor did peace arise through industrialization. Instead wars became bloodier

---

[4] For an exposition of the thesis that war does not pay, see Norman Angell [1].

[5] A similar view of war was held by the economist Joseph A. Schumpeter, who declared: "It is an atavism in the social structure, in individual, psychological habits of emotional reaction. Since the vital needs that created it have passed away for good, it too must gradually disappear. . ." [39].

and more intense. Alexander Hamilton seems to have been partly justified in asking: "Has commerce hitherto done any thing more than change the objects of war? Is not the love of wealth as domineering and enterprising a passion as that of power and glory?" [17].

Some theorists tried to explain the failure of Marx's predictions by the resurgence of European imperialism and colonialism in the latter part of the nineteenth century. J. A. Hobson, an English economist, sought to prove that colonialism, though economically unprofitable for nations as a whole, is nevertheless quite profitable for certain economic elites. He argued that under the influence of these elites the industrialized nations fought among themselves for colonial concessions and economic privileges so that "their" capitalists might have opportunities to invest accumulated wealth [19].

Nikolai Lenin used a similar argument, in *Imperialism, the Highest Stage of Capitalism* (1916), to account for the failure of Marx's prediction of revolution. Lenin considered that capitalists need not only opportunities for investment of surplus capital but also raw materials and markets. The oppression and exploitation of the working class at home was thus exported to underdeveloped areas. The profits derived from exploiting these areas enabled the capitalist to "buy off" the proletariat with new economic benefits. Although imperialism has postponed revolution in the capitalist countries, according to Lenin, it has also increased the probability of violence among capitalist states as they vie with one another for new territories to delay the overproduction crisis. Imperialism is thus the final stage of capitalism; after it revolution will come.

INTERNATIONAL ORDER THROUGH INTERNATIONAL LAW

Over the centuries there has evolved a significant body of law designed to regulate and even to outlaw violence and war in the international system. International law is that body of principles which regulates intercourse among states. Law within states, whose governments have near-monopolies of the means of coercion, expresses the norms of society and functions to regulate and limit private use of force. International law differs from domestic state law in several ways, however. First, there is no binding arbiter to interpret and judge the law, except in relatively inconsequential matters. Second, international law has no agent capable of enforcing it, and victims of violations generally have no recourse other than self-help. International law recognizes such practices as retaliation precisely because of the absence of any superior enforcement agency. Finally, international law is based primarily on custom and precedent, rather than on legislation, and custom tends to evolve only slowly and then only in areas of activity in which international actors recognize common interests. There is little custom applicable to the areas of activity in which actors generally find themselves in conflict. The problem is not that conflict exists when there is an absence of law but rather that law cannot survive when conflict is too intense. That the second major source of international law is treaties suggests how much agreement is required among the strongest actors before law can be codified or have any impact on international behavior. Sometimes, however, international law has proved a great help in the daily intercourse of nations and has even been marginally effective in regulating warfare.

One of the earliest and most influential authors on the law of war was the seventeenth-century Dutch lawyer and theologian Hugo de Groot, better known as Hugo Grotius. In the introduction to his most famous treatise, *The Law of War and Peace (De Jure Belli et Pacis),* Grotius explains why he had been drawn to the subject:

Throughout the Christian world I observed a lack of restraint in relation to war, such as even barbarous races should be ashamed of; I observed that men rush to arms for slight causes, or no cause at all, and that when arms have once been taken up there is no longer any respect for law, divine or human; it is as if . . . frenzy had openly been let loose for the committing of all crimes. [15, p. 21]

Grotius set out to determine whether or not war is ever justified and, if it is, under what conditions. He answered the first question in the affirmative but added that "war ought not to be undertaken except for the enforcement of rights"; even then its conduct must be in accord with certain dictates of the law, derived from a combination of natural law and contract theory [15, p. 18]. We find here one of the earliest arguments for limited warfare. According to Grotius, war can justifiably be undertaken to defend oneself, to defend property, to enforce rights, or to punish violations of law. It is very much a remedy in an international system in which there is law but no way to enforce it. Agreements among nations are to be considered binding, as in contract law, and dealings among states are to be based on that law. Violation of an agreement may, according to Grotius, violate the rights of another party and lead to war. It is necessary to understand that such wars involve states, not populations, and that therefore civilians should not be mistreated in any way or held responsible for the actions of their rulers—a very reasonable notion in an age of absolute monarchy. Grotius' argument that under certain conditions states are justified in resorting to war suggests that he distinguished the needs of international society from those of domestic society, in which individual violence is almost totally outlawed [5].

Grotius believed that once a body of international law had been established and codified, states would acquire clear expectations of what their international agreements and obligations entailed. They would then be less apt to slip into war through mutual misunderstanding and might be able to curb the worst excesses of wartime conduct; Grotius was convinced that the rule of law should not cease to prevail once war has begun. International law also provides actors with a point of reference during disputes on various subjects without actual negotiation or communication among them.

Grotius' attempt to codify the law of warfare has been carried on with limited success. From time to time efforts have been made to outlaw war entirely, as in the Covenant of the League of Nations and the Kellogg-Briand Pact of 1928 (the Pact of Paris). Further efforts have also been made to limit the effects of war and outlaw certain practices that have seemed particularly abhorrent. Many of these attempts have taken the form of declaring certain weapons inadmissible in war; others have involved formal opening and cessation of hostilities, treatment of civilians and prisoners of war, and the rights of neutrals in wartime.

The signatories of the Declaration of St. Petersburg in 1868 agreed to the prohibition of certain types of explosives, and this agreement was extended during the international conferences at the Hague in 1899 and 1907 to include prohibition of the use of dumdum (expanding) bullets,[6] explosives dropped from aircraft and balloons, and certain gases. The Geneva Protocol of 1925 outlawed the use of poison gas and bacteriological weapons, and various regulations on the use of submarines have been adopted, particularly a ban on attacking unarmed merchant vessels. Such regulations have not been notably successful. Neither side used gas during World War II, though strategic considerations were a more important deterrent than were formal norms. Germany bombed civilian targets during the Spanish Civil War, and the bombing of industrial targets and civilian population centers was widely practiced by both sides during World War II.[7]

Technological advances like subma-

[6] In 1972 certain American domestic police forces, like that of Los Angeles, used dumdum bullets.

[7] Pablo Picasso's painting *Guernica* is a tribute to the Spaniards who perished in the first major aerial bombardment in history, directed at the Basque town of Guernica in northern Spain by the Germans in 1936. Of that incident Winston Churchill wrote, "Germany in particular used her air power to commit such experimental horrors as the bombing of the defenceless little township of Guernica" [8].

rines have posed difficult problems of adaptation for international law. Unrestricted submarine warfare by Germany during World War I seemed to violate freedom of the seas and the rights of neutral nations to transport goods without hindrance. Furthermore, submarines, unlike surface craft, cannot rescue survivors of a sinking ship—a customary practice in naval warfare. The United States had traditionally led the fight to ensure the rights of neutrals during wartime and was the leading neutral nation in the world in the first years of World War I. When the Germans sank the Lusitania, a British passenger vessel carrying munitions to England in May 1915, many American lives were lost, and American public opinion turned against Germany. Eventually the United States justified its entrance into the war as a response to Germany's continued sinking of neutral ships without warning. Restrictions on the use of submarines, however, would have particularly hampered Germany, which did not have a surface fleet comparable in size or strength to that of Great Britain. Furthermore, submarines that warn their prey before striking are rarely effective. The inconsistency of American "neutral" attitudes was apparent in its acceptance of the British blockade of German ports by a surface fleet as legitimate.

In January 1918 Woodrow Wilson reiterated in his Fourteen Points the American belief in freedom of the seas as a cardinal doctrine of international law, and after the war further efforts were made to restrict the use of submarines. Great Britain, France, Italy, Japan, and the United States agreed, as part of the London Naval Treaty of 1930, that submarines should be subject to the same restrictions as were surface vessels and that the indiscriminate sinking of merchant ships was illegal. The agreement was reaffirmed in 1936 and was signed by all the world's naval powers. After the outbreak of the Spanish Civil War in that year the United States, Great Britain, France, the Soviet Union, and others signed the Nyon Agreement condemning

unrestricted submarine warfare—but to little avail. During World War II German use of submarines against neutral shipping once again inflamed American public opinion.

Today submarines are among the most important weapons in the deterrent arsenals of the superpowers. American nuclear submarines, armed with Polaris and Poseidon missiles, cruise the seas, ready to launch nuclear attacks on Soviet cities in the event of war. The Soviet underseas fleet has a similar capability.

The doctrine of freedom of the seas is further limited by the use of blockades, the forcible prevention of entry or exit along an enemy coast. A blockade is "legal" when it is effective, and it was for the purpose of enforcing blockades that submarines were first used. A recent example of a blockade of dubious legality (because it was not aimed at a belligerent) was the United States' selective "quarantine" of Cuba in 1962; another was the American use of mines to blockade the harbors of North Vietnam in 1972.

Legal prohibitions on the use of weapons, then, have had only limited success. The United States, for example, has employed nontoxic gases against the North Vietnamese and the Viet Cong. Although the use of such gas seems to violate the moral taboo on such weapons, it has been argued that other weapons that would be even more destructive of life and property have not been outlawed. Paradoxically, there are no current prohibitions on the use of nuclear weapons, though all the nations that possess them, including the People's Republic of China, have declared unilaterally that they will not use them first. The bombings of the Japanese cities of Hiroshima and Nagasaki in August 1945 seem to have violated other rules of war, like requirements to exempt undefended civilian centers, hospitals, and religious and scientific enterprises from bombardment. Furthermore, it has been argued that nuclear weapons contain poisonous substances the release of which is illegal [12, 45]. The Nuclear

Test Ban Treaty, concluded in 1963 and signed by all nuclear powers except France and China, prohibits only the testing of nuclear devices in the atmosphere. The more recently concluded Nuclear Non-Proliferation Treaty is a further step toward moral condemnation of weapons of indiscriminate destruction. Surely, regardless of the law, the use of such weapons would violate the conscience of mankind and would invite the condemnation of most nations.

The treatment of prisoners of war and civilians has been the subject of many treaties and agreements, notably the Hague Regulations of 1907 and the Geneva Convention of 1949. Because of the unprecedented atrocities committed by Germany and Japan against civilian populations in occupied territories and against prisoners of war, German and Japanese leaders were made to stand trial after World War II. The only precedent for such trials was a provision in the Treaty of Versailles for the trial of Kaiser Wilhelm after World War I. The Kaiser, however, sought and was granted asylum in Holland and was never tried. The trials of other Germans for alleged war crimes in World War I were prosecuted with little energy or success in German courts.

The trials after World War II were unique in that they were conducted before international tribunals. A special war-crimes tribunal, composed of leading jurists from the United States, the Soviet Union, France, and Great Britain, was set up at Nürnberg to try German "war criminals." The defendants were accused of such offenses as crimes against peace, war crimes, and crimes against humanity; the traditional defenses of "superior orders" and *raison d'état* were not accepted. Crimes against peace entail conspiracy to wage or actual waging of aggressive war; this category is of dubious legality. Although certain defendants were charged with having violated the Kellogg-Briand Pact or other agreements, a problem in defining and identifying "aggression" arose. Grotius himself had failed to specify what constitutes aggression, and definition has become ever more difficult to agree on since the seventeenth century. Guerrilla and economic warfare, for example, have made the concept more ambiguous than ever before [40]. On one hand, the Soviet Union and Communist China define "wars of national liberation" as legitimate, whereas the United States considers some of them contrary to international law. There is not and has never been agreement on what constitutes aggression. Furthermore, international actors generally clothe their acts in the rhetoric of self-defense, and it is difficult to dispute their claims, especially as it is inevitable that "only the loser will pay." Because such acts had previously not been designated "crimes" the charges at Nürnberg had an ex post facto flavor. Few statesmen had ever seriously regarded war as other than a legitimate instrument of national policy.

Few of the accused at Nürnberg were charged with crimes against peace alone. Most were accused and found guilty of crimes against humanity and especially of war crimes. Crimes against humanity include genocide, murder, deportation, enslavement, and other barbarous acts against civilian populations for racial or political reasons, either before or during war; the attempt to pass judgment on acts committed in Germany and Japan *before* World War II involved creation of a new category of crimes. The main category of accusations, war crimes, included the wanton destruction of civilian centers, mistreatment of prisoners of war and of civilians in occupied territories, and so on.

The postwar trials were intended to establish the principle that men as individuals are responsible for their acts in time of war. The trials thus departed from the tradition of treating only states as responsible for the actions of their leaders. It has been argued that "individual responsibility for war crimes as well as crimes against peace and humanity will certainly serve as a serious warning to political and military leaders of various nations, especially those who are in a position to decide their national destinies"

[49]. This assertion appears, however, to express pious hope, rather than serious observation. Certainly evidence from the postwar world, ranging from Soviet behavior in eastern Europe to flagrant American disregard for the rules of war in Vietnam, as exemplified in the My Lai tragedy, points in a different direction. Furthermore, an actor rarely plans or conducts a war that he expects to lose. The precedent of individual responsibility has been established, but it is far from being rooted, for few political leaders *expect* that they will ever be held accountable for their decisions in this way.

VIOLENCE: ITS MANAGEMENT AND USES

Many political theorists have accepted violence as one of several possible means to achieve objectives and have sought to come to terms with it. Their analyses have occasionally been prescriptive, not in an ethical or moral sense, but in the sense of efficient achievement of objectives. To these thinkers violence and war have seemed "normal" international phenomena.

Unlike many of his predecessors Machiavelli was interested in the connection between violence and the "political" goals of men. Part of his interest arose from the changes in warfare brought about by the large-scale introduction of gunpowder and disciplined military organization during his lifetime. He was particularly perturbed by the disruption of the Italian city-state system caused by the French invasion of Italy in 1494.

Machiavelli argued that war and politics are intimately knit in a larger whole, in which they function as the indispensable means toward a greater end; he insisted that military power is the foundation on which a state is built. "A Prince should," he wrote, "have no other aim or thought . . . but war and its organization and discipline" [28, p. 53]. This Machiavellian imperative is well expressed in a chapter in *The Discourses* entitled "One's Country Must Be Defended, Whether With Glory or With Shame, It Must Be Defended Anyhow." "For where the very safety of the country depends upon the resolution to be taken, no considerations of justice or injustice, humanity or cruelty, nor of glory or of shame, should be allowed to prevail" [28, p. 528]. If one lost, everything that one sought to defend would also be lost; the successful defense of one's country and of its continued existence would be praiseworthy. Furthermore, although deceit is rarely desirable in personality, "in the conduct of a war it is laudable and honorable" [28, p. 526]. Machiavelli's argument, however, assumed that states fought only to defend their existences, rather than for marginal benefits.

At the heart of his view of international politics was the belief that "people cannot make themselves secure except by being powerful" [28, p. 108]. Men are neither particularly virtuous nor particularly evil by nature but, finding themselves in a state of competitive anarchy, must compete as best they can. One task that Machiavelli set himself was to advise leaders how best to survive and to prosper in the world in which they found themselves. Force, though not particularly desirable in itself, is, in Machiavelli's view, occasionally a necessary tool to achieve one's ends.

Machiavelli is often accused of having suggested that the end justifies the means, but, though there is some truth in this accusation, he did not favor the use of "immoral" over "moral" means. He considered "immoral" means justified only when no others were available. Although Machiavelli advised a prince who had come to power through villainy to kill all his enemies quickly, he also noted that such a prince is generally less secure than is one who has come to power lawfully. Under certain conditions cruelty is acceptable if it prevents greater harm and injustice later.

A prince . . . must not mind incurring the charge of cruelty for the purpose of keeping his subjects united and faithful; for . . . he will be more merciful than those who, from excess of tenderness, allow disorders to arise, from whence spring bloodshed and rapine; for these as a rule injure the whole community, while the executions carried out by the prince injure only individuals. [28, p. 60]

Machiavelli was concerned that force be employed *properly,* which meant using it to *minimize* violence. Again discussing cruelty, he wrote:

Well committed may be called these (if it is permissible to use the word well of evil) which are perpetrated once for the need of securing one's self, and which afterwards are not persisted in, but are exchanged for measures as useful to the subjects as possible. Cruelties ill committed are those which, although at first few, increase rather than diminish with time. [28, p. 34]

This argument is essentially the same one that American leaders have used to justify the use of nuclear weapons against Japan. Atomic bombs, it has been alleged, shortened the war and thus kept total casualties lower on both sides.

Machiavelli assumed the inevitable existence of violence in political life and tried to provide a guide for its most efficient and moral use. He devoted much of *The Discourses* to advice on military tactics and strategy, on such questions as when to fight and how to use the forces at one's command to greatest advantage. He was thus a "strategic thinker." In particular, he predicted some of the changes in warfare that actually occurred after the French Revolution and the rise of Napoleon. Shaken by the ease with which the French had defeated the mercenary armies of Italy, he called for the use of infantry and therefore conscription of citizens. The latter reform could come, however, only when wars were supported by the population. People had to be attracted to the political ideas for which wars were fought, and patriotism had to be encouraged so that Italy could be liberated.

It remained for a Prussian general, Carl Maria von Clausewitz, to work out a theory of violence suited to the new

age. The implications of violence fascinated him, and he had little use for earlier military theorists, except Machiavelli, whom he praised highly. As Machiavelli had been struck by the French invasion of Italy, Clausewitz was deeply impressed by the changes in warfare occasioned by the Napoleonic conquests. His theory of war began at the same point as did that of Machiavelli: War must be regarded as a whole and its parts subordinated to it. This whole included the reasons for which the war was being fought, and its parts included strategy and tactics by which it was fought.

For Clausewitz the main lesson of the Napoleonic period had been that war as a skirmish among hired armies seeking advantages while avoiding battle was obsolete. The rise of nationalism and the use of conscripted armies meant, according to him, that war would now involve and threaten whole nations. Sensing that the violence unleashed during the Napoleonic wars would permanently characterize modern warfare and could never again be banished, Clausewitz envisioned a form of "total warfare" that would involve entire peoples. The objectives of adversaries in such warfare would have to be the destruction of enemy forces, which could be achieved only by victory in battle. Clausewitz recognized, however, that when an enemy's weakness lay in its army's morale or in its relations with its allies, then it might be more efficient to exploit those weaknesses than to seek battle.

Clausewitz sought neither to glorify nor to ennoble war. For him it was a serious business, and he cautioned that it not be initiated frivolously. The concept of "total war" is merely an ideal type that rarely, if ever, occurs; but its possibility must be borne in mind as the theoretical totality toward which one's activities must be directed. Noting that accommodation becomes more difficult and political motives more obscure as "total war" approaches, Clausewitz recognized that his ideal type resembles what game theorists call a "zero-sum" encounter (see Chapter

17). Clausewitz understood that single events and battles affect later interactions and must therefore be undertaken with the final objective in mind. The end result is all important, and other considerations must be subordinated to it. Tactics are relevant only to the degree that they contribute to achieving the strategic outcome of the enterprise.

Clausewitz compared war to a "game" in which the interaction of chance and probability determine the outcome. The objective, in military terms the destruction of the enemy's forces and will to fight, is in fundamentals the achievement of specified political goals. "Theory demands," Clausewitz wrote, "that at the commencement of every War its character and main outline shall be defined according to what the political conditions and relations leads us to anticipate as probable" [25, p. 204; 34]. With a keen insight into the nature of violence as a form of coercive influence, he observed, "War . . . is an act of violence intended to compel our opponent to fulfill our will" [25, p. 41]. Wars are not just "fights" engendered by anger and animosity. They are "political acts," intended to do more than merely to hurt the adversary. Clausewitz argued that as wars always begin for political reasons, these reasons must be the constant preoccupation of the adversaries, for "if we reflect that War has its root in a political object, then naturally this original motive which called it into existence should also continue the first and highest consideration in its conduct" [25, p. 57].

Clausewitz distinguished among the uses of violence and determined which levels of violence and which tactics were most efficient in achieving different political ends. Despite his interest in the prospect of large-scale violence, he understood very well the role of limited warfare in attaining limited objectives. "If the aim of the military action," he wrote, "is an equivalent for the political object, that action will in general diminish as the political object diminishes, and in a greater degree the more the political object domi-

nates" [25, p. 49]. It is not appropriate to mobilize fully simply in order to achieve a border readjustment, and it is wise to accept defeat in a minor engagement when the anticipated gains from continuing the contest are smaller than are the anticipated costs. These ideas resemble the American strategic doctrine developed in the early 1960s and known as "flexible response," which calls for close matching of influence resources to objectives (see Chapter 18).

Having modified his original assumptions about absolute conflict, Clausewitz warned with some foresight that such war can be justified only in great national emergencies. He cautioned diplomats against becoming too dependent upon the advice of generals, for the latter tend to demand total victory, regardless of the costs or of the original reason for the contest. There is an echo of Clausewitz in Robert F. Kennedy's reflection about the Cuban missile crisis: "I thought, as I listened, of the many times that I had heard the military take positions which, if wrong, had the advantage that no one would be around at the end to know" [24].

Clausewitz considered violence an appropriate means for readjusting the international system without jeopardizing its existence and stability. His concern that minor objectives might lead to large-scale conflagrations compelled him constantly to admonish political leaders to keep their original objectives in mind. Previous wars had occasionally ballooned from small contests into virtually total wars, especially when they had come to involve ideological issues.

Both Clausewitz and Machiavelli assumed that violence is an integral part of politics and sought simply to counsel statesmen in its proper use. But changes in domestic and international systems had made calculated control of violence increasingly difficult for statesmen by the time that the nineteenth century drew to a close. World War I exemplified the "absolute war" that Clausewitz had feared.

ANTHROPOLOGICAL AND SOCIOLOGICAL FINDINGS ON THE CAUSES OF WAR

In the course of research to determine whether or not international war is in fact inevitable, anthropologists and sociologists have become divided along much the same lines that divide philosophers and statesmen. Some observers have sought to draw conclusions from the behavior of animals. Konrad Lorenz, for example, has declared, "There cannot be any doubt . . . that intraspecific aggression is, in Man, just as much of a spontaneous instinctive drive as in most other higher vertebrates" [27, 26]. But he and some others have admitted that the aggressive behavior of most other animals actually involves little physical harm to them.

Some students of animal behavior, however, dismiss the notion of instinctive aggression as presented by Lorenz:

The concept of a "drive" is at best a symbol of an unknown group of internal stimuli and physiological mechanisms affecting behavior. . . . There is no known physiological mechanism by which spontaneous internal stimulation for fighting arises. Rather, the physiological mechanisms for fighting are triggered by immediate external stimuli. There is much evidence that fighting can be suppressed by training. . . .[41]

From his long-term study of the behavior of dogs J. P. Scott has concluded that aggressive behavior can be learned and unlearned and that environmental factors are more important than are instinctive ones in triggering aggression. Scott and his colleagues are thus more optimistic than Lorenz is [42]. One difficulty in connection with such studies is their tendency to draw unverified analogies between animal behavior and human behavior. Indeed, as we have seen, there is considerable doubt whether or not the behavior of individuals is even analogous to that of such groups as national states.

Efforts have also been made, through the study of primitive tribes, to determine the role of war as a social institution. Investigation of the Hopi Indians, for instance, has revealed that intratribal conflict takes nonviolent forms [11]; investigation of the behavior of the Comanches has revealed that they became warlike only after their accustomed environment had been altered [23]. These efforts also suggest that war is the product of environmental, rather than of instinctive, factors. A large-scale cross-cultural study by Raoull Naroll has led him to doubt many of the major assumptions of deterrence theorists, who argue that military preparedness lessens the probability of war. Indeed, Naroll has found virtually no relationship between the incidence of war and military preparations for war among the forty-eight tribes that he has studied [32].

Social scientists have also sought to determine whether international conflict is related to or is the product of domestic strife. Again the results are inconclusive. On one hand, Pitirim Sorokin has argued that there is virtually no relationship between international and domestic conflict [47]; Samuel P. Huntington, on the other, has declared that there is a negative association [21]; still others have claimed a positive association [29]. Certain analysts have argued that national elites actually foster international conflict to promote domestic stability or at least that such conflict does serve such a purpose, whether intentionally or not [16, 10, 44]. Even large-scale statistical studies, based on factor and multiple-regression analysis, have failed to detect any convincing relationship between domestic and foreign conflict behavior [36, 37, 38, 13, 48].

The attempt to study international warfare by using animals, children, and so on as subjects poses many of the theoretical problems that we discussed in Chapter 2, notably a shift from one level of analysis to another. We must be skeptical of research reports that make claims about the sources of conflict at one level, like that of the international system, based on the study of behavior at a different level of analysis, like that of the family or a small group. It is, admittedly, difficult to conduct research on sources of conflict in the international system, and, for this reason, analogies with behavior in other arenas can have heuristic value. Nevertheless, the student should approach the conclusions drawn from such research with healthy skepticism.

SUMMARY

Since World War II the enormous potential for violence that men have created has stimulated many thinkers to reconsider the implications of force in the politics of the nuclear age. Contemporary strategic and game theorists have sought to analyze the uses that violence can serve and the limitations that must be imposed on its use as a mode of political influence. In the following chapters we shall turn our attention to the roles of threats and violence in international bargaining and diplomacy.

References

1. Angell, Norman, *The Great Illusion* (London: Heinemann, 1914).
2. Aron, Raymond, "War and Industrial Society," in Leon Bramson and George W. Goethals, eds., *War,* rev. ed. (New York: Basic Books, 1968), pp. 359–402.
3. Bloch, Marc, *Feudal Society,* trans. by L. A. Manyon, (Chicago: University of Chicago Press, 1964).
4. Bowle, John, *Politics and Opinion in the 19th Century* (New York: Oxford University Press, 1964).
5. Bull, Hedley, "The Grotian Conception of International Society," in Herbert Butterfield and Martin Wight, eds., *Diplomatic Investigations* (Cambridge, Mass.: Harvard University Press, 1968), pp. 51–73.
6. Burke, Edmund, *Reflections on the Revolution in France* (Garden City, N.Y.: Doubleday, 1961), pp. 91, 92.
7. Cantor, Norman, ed., *The Medieval World: 300–1300* (New York: Macmillan, 1963), p. 178.
8. Churchill, Winston S., *The Gathering Storm* (Boston: Houghton Mifflin, 1948), p. 214.
9. Cohen, Carl, ed., *Communism, Fascism and Democracy* (New York: Random House, 1962).
10. Coser, Lewis A., *The Functions of Social Conflict* (New York: Free Press, 1956).
11. Eggan, D., "The General Problem of Hopi Adjustment," *American Anthropologist,* 45 (1943), pp. 357–373.
12. Falk, Richard A., "The Shimoda Case: A Legal Appraisal of the Atomic Attacks upon Hiroshima and Nagasaki," *American Journal of International Law,* 59 (1965), pp. 759–793.
13. Feierabend, Rosalind L., "Aggressive Behaviors Within Polities, 1948–1962," *Journal of Conflict Resolution,* 10 (1966), pp. 247–271.
14. Freud, Sigmund, "Why War?" in Leon Bramson and George W. Goethals, eds., *War,* rev. ed. (New York: Basic Books, 1968), pp. 76, 77.
15. Grotius, Hugo, *Prolegomena to the Law of War and Peace* (New York: Bobbs-Merrill, 1957).
16. Haas, Ernst R., and A. S. Whiting, *Dynamics of International Relations* (New York: McGraw-Hill, 1956).
17. Hamilton, Alexander, John Jay, and James Madison, *The Federalist Papers,* (New York: Mentor, 1961), no. 6, p. 57.
18. Hegel, G. W. F., "Philosophy of Law," in William Ebenstein, ed., *Great Political Thinkers,* 4th ed. (New York: Holt, Rinehart and Winston, 1969).
19. Hobson, J. A., *Imperialism: A Study* (London: Allen & Unwin, 1902).
20. Hoveland, Carl I., and Robert R. Sears, "Correlations of Lynchings with Economic Indices," *Journal of Psychology,* 9 (1940), pp. 301–310.
21. Huntington, Samuel P., *Changing Patterns of Military Politics* (New York: Free Press, 1962).
22. James, William, "The Moral Equivalent of War," in Leon Bramson and George W. Goethals, eds., *War,* rev. ed. (New York: Basic Books, 1968).
23. Kardiner, A., *et al., The Psychological Frontiers of Society* (New York: Columbia University Press, 1945).
24. Kennedy, Robert F., *Thirteen Days* (New York: Norton, 1969), p. 48.
25. Leonard, Roger A., ed., *Clausewitz on War* (New York: Capricorn, 1967).
26. Lorenz, Konrad, *On Aggression* (New

York: Harcourt Brace Jovanovich, 1966).

27. Lorenz, Konrad, "Ritualized Fighting," in J. D. Carthy and F. J. Ebling, eds., *The Natural History of Aggression* (New York: Academic Press, 1964).

28. Machiavelli, Niccolò, *The Prince* and *The Discourses* (New York: Random House, 1950).

29. McKenna, J. C., *Diplomatic Protest in Foreign Policy* (Chicago: Loyola University Press, 1962).

30. Montross, Lynn, *War Through the Ages,* 3rd ed. (New York: Harper & Row, 1960), p. 199.

31. Mussolini, Benito, "The Doctrine of Fascism," in William Ebenstein, ed., *Great Political Thinkers,* 4th ed. (New York: Holt, Rinehart and Winston, 1969), p. 634.

32. Naroll, Raoull, "Does Military Deterrence Deter?" *Trans-Action,* 3 (January–February 1966), pp. 14–20.

33. Niebuhr, Reinhold, *Beyond Tragedy* (New York: Scribners, 1937), p. 158.

34. Parkinson, Roger, *Clausewitz* (New York: Stein & Day, 1971).

35. Ralston, David B., ed., *Soldiers and States: Civil-Military Relations in Modern Europe* (Boston: Heath, 1966), p. 66.

36. Rummell, R. J., "The Dimensions of Conflict Behavior Within and Between Nations," *General Systems,* 8 (1963), pp. 1–50.

37. Rummell, R. J., "Dimensions of Conflict Behavior Within Nations, 1946–1959," *Journal of Conflict Resolution,* 10 (1966), pp. 65–73.

38. Rummell, R. J., "Dimensions of Dyadic War, 1820–1952," *Journal of Conflict Resolution,* 11 (1967), pp. 176–183.

39. Schumpeter, Joseph A., "Imperialism as a Social Atavism," in Harrison M. Wright, ed., *The New Imperialism* (Boston: Heath, 1961), p. 53.

40. Scott, Andrew M., *The Revolution in Statecraft: Informal Penetration* (New York: Random House, 1965).

41. Scott, J. P., "On the Evolution of Fighting Behavior," *Science,* 148 (1965), p. 820.

42. Scott, J. P. and J. L. Fuller, *Genetics and the Social Behavior of the Dog* (Chicago: University of Chicago Press, 1965).

43. Sherif, Muzafer, *et al., Intergroup Conflict and Cooperation: The Robbers' Cave Experiment* (Norman: University of Oklahoma Press, 1961).

44. Simmel, George, *Conflict* (New York: Free Press, 1955).

45. Singh, N., *Nuclear Weapons and International Law* (New York: Praeger, 1959).

46. Sorel, Albert, "The Emergence of the Army as a Political Force," in David B. Ralston, ed., *Soldiers and States: Civil-Military Relations in Modern Europe* (Boston: Heath, 1966), p. 80.

47. Sorokin, Pitirim, *Social and Cultural Dynamics,* vol. 3 (New York: Bedminster, 1937).

48. Tanter, Raymond, "Dimensions of Conflict Behavior Within and Between Nations, 1958–60," *Journal of Conflict Resolution,* 10 (1966), pp. 48–64.

49. Tung, William L., *International Law in an Organizing World* (New York: Crowell, 1968), p. 457.

Suggested Reading

Banks, Arthur S., "Patterns of Domestic Conflict: 1919–39 and 1946–66," *Journal of Conflict Resolution,* 16 (March 1972), pp. 41–50.

Bramson, Leon, and George W. Goethals, eds., *War,* rev. ed. (New York: Basic Books, 1968).

Butterfield, Herbert, and Martin Wight, eds., *Diplomatic Investigations* (Cambridge, Mass.: Harvard University Press, 1968).

Earle, Edward M., ed., *Makers of Modern Strategy* (New York: Atheneum, 1967).

Leonard, Roger A., ed., *Clausewitz on War* (New York: Capricorn, 1967).

Meinecke, Friedrich, *Machiavellism* (New Haven: Yale University Press, 1957).

Morgenthau, Hans J., *In Defense of the National Interest* (New York: Knopf, 1951).

Morgenthau, Hans J., *Scientific Man vs. Power Politics* (Chicago: University of Chicago Press, 1946).

Ralston, David B., ed., *Soldiers and States: Civil-Military Relations in Modern Europe* (Boston: Heath, 1966).

Waltz, Kenneth N., *Man, the State, and War* (New York: Columbia University Press, 1959).

Chapter 17
GAMES AND ANALYSES OF CONFLICT

Diplomatic relations are not a game in the usual sense: The players are not there for their enjoyment. The slaughter on battlefields and the destruction caused by nuclear warfare are not subjects of amusement. . . . Certain abstractions, however, of part of a social or diplomatic process may be made—Martin Shubik [24]

Analyses of conflict based on some of the principles of game theory have informed numerous discussions of defense and arms control.[1] The use of the game analogy in analyzing conflict is part of a tradition that extends back much farther than the last two decades. War games have been used at least since the seventeenth century, when strategists cultivated a form of military chess. Military exercises have even had practical applications: both Japan and Germany played "games" in preparation for World War II. Before their attack on Pearl Harbor the Japanese staged a political-military game involving eleven other countries plus Japan [26, p. 219]. During the 1960s game analysis was used to clarify strategic policy options and to alert military officers to tactical considerations.

Direct application of formal game theory, an essentially deductive exercise, to the analysis and resolution of international conflict or to issues of national defense has so far been minimal, however. The most important contribution of game theory has been to provide a mode of thinking in which the systematic enumeration of alternative strategies and their related impacts on different players are emphasized. Calculations take into account the views and probable behavior of other players as conditions for decisions.

Diplomats involved in negotiations, generals engaged in warfare, and labor unions weighing strikes face conflicts in which they must take into account goals and objectives, other than their own, that will affect their ability to achieve their objectives. Such situations can be usefully studied as types of games. Raymond Aron has concluded:

The matrices of game theory render at least three services to the political scientists. They oblige them to accept a kind of discipline of thought, to analyze and enumerate all possible eventualities in a given situa-

---

[1] The pioneering work on this subject is John von Neumann and Oskar Morgenstern, *Theory of Games and Economic Behavior* (Princeton: Princeton University Press, 1944).

tion. They help them to construct ideal types of circumstances of conflict. . . . They permit the abstract formulation of the *dialectic of antagonism.* . . . [1, p. 772]

In this chapter we shall focus on decision making in situations in which an individual unit cannot control the actions of other units but in which the fates of all units are intertwined.

DEBATES AND FIGHTS

Anatol Rapoport has identified three types of conflict, each characterized by different conditions and consequences: debates, fights, and games [15].

Debates

Mutual efforts to persuade others to certain points of view constitute debate. Actors seek to alter one another's images of situations and of the interests at stake. The "great debate" between communism and capitalism has been cited by Rapoport as one of the fundamental processes in contemporary international society. Both sides wish to improve men's lives, yet each threatens the annihilation of the other in the process. As a debate it resembles those between Roman Catholicism and Protestantism 300 years ago and between Christianity and Islam 1,000 years ago. It too seems capable of resolution by mutual accommodation and conventions of tolerance—*provided that it remains a debate*, in which exchanges are verbal and ammunition consists only of new information and logical arguments. The debate aspect of this conflict is manifest in such international arenas as the United Nations, multinational conferences, and less formal but more frequent exchanges among diplomatic spokesmen.

Many aspects of negotiation take on the character of debates in which "the process of negotiation can be so gratifying to one's opponent or can entangle him so much in an obligation not to interrupt it that he will desist from some violent action he might have otherwise taken"

[10, p. 45]. Fred Iklé has distinguished five types of aims involved in negotiation: extension agreements, normalization agreements, redistribution agreements, innovation agreements, and effects unconnected with agreements [10, pp. 26–58]. Negotiation of extension agreements involves attempts to uphold existing arrangements and thus often to preserve gains already achieved. An example is the continuation of existing trade arrangements between two countries. A normalization agreement terminates an abnormal situation, as when an armed conflict is ended; negotiation usually involves securance objectives. Negotiation of redistribution agreements reflects efforts by one side to improve its position at the expense of the other; they too involve securance objectives, though conflict is likely to be greater than in the first two instances. An innovation agreement creates new relationships or new institutions among participants; again securance objectives predominate. The fifth type of negotiation is aimed at deterring an opponent, gaining information about its intentions, or achieving a propaganda victory at its expense.

Negotiations may involve all these types of objectives singly or in combination. Although debate may characterize all types of negotiations, those involving redistribution are most likely to exhibit characteristics of games. In practice, unless the two sides are prepared to be persuaded by the logic of each other's arguments, negotiations are unlikely to resemble debates.

The diffusion of ideas and culture across national boundaries represents a less formal but potentially more important mode of debate than that among ranking diplomats. In this sense debates on the social, economic, and cultural front tend to be long-term affairs in which the audience is an expanding proportion of the world's population over several generations. The resolution of such debates may be reflected more in intergenerational differences in attitudes within societies, rather than in differences among societies. As new generations come to power in different countries they bring with them their own images and understanding of national values and international issues, which will guide their implementation of new policies. Such policies reflect the "outcomes" of these long debates. The processes of debate and the resolution of conflict through debate constitute a slowly moving but pervasive force for change in international politics.

Fights

A "mechanical" quality pervades a fight. Once begun, the fight simply runs its course with little thinking by the adversaries. Calculations of gain and loss are forsaken. Arms races and other apparently deterministic processes seem to represent irresistible trends only marginally alterable by individual decisions and strategies. When men cannot avoid wars that they do not want or limit wars when they do occur, they find themselves unable to relate their initial objectives to the conflicts in which they find themselves. As we have seen in Chapter 16, Carl Maria von Clausewitz was particularly concerned lest "games" be transformed into "fights."

Uncontrolled escalation of war is one of these "fight" situations. Indeed, many social scientists believe that the use of nuclear or thermonuclear weapons would lead to a fight in which bargaining would be impossible and war could not be limited.

Military escalation produces the very conditions . . . which make it harder to stop and deescalate. Internally, if early escalations fail and produce counter-escalation, anger and frustration impel one upward; and if escalation succeeds, one is learning to use this means at the expense of others. . . . Externally, the early stages of escalation are more likely to produce hardening rather than softening of the opponent's resolve, thus forcing us to higher steps on the ladder than we had originally intended to reach. . . . The analogy with sexual arousal may be disturbing, but it is valid; as every practiced seducer knows, each threshold whose passage can be introduced makes it easier to induce passage of the next. [13]

Spiraling arms races and price wars resemble fights in which stimulus-response cycles are created and then become difficult to break [3]. As each actor raises his level of armaments, the second responds by raising his own. Lewis F. Richardson has used a mathematical model to examine the arms races before World Wars I and II, in order to illustrate "what people would do if they did not stop to think" [20]. Although it is clear that arms races do not invariably resemble the process described by Richardson, the consequences of large-scale war in the nuclear age promise to be so catastrophic that even small risks of loss of control cannot be tolerated calmly.[2]

The outcomes of wars and other "fights" can be studied as if they were determined by large-scale social and human processes. Rates of change that remain relatively fixed over decades thus serve as the prime targets of investigation. This type of conflict is structurally determined, and the variables, dimensions, and modes of analysis outlined in our discussion of structure in Chapters 5 and 6 provide the basis for such analysis. The focus in this chapter, however, is on neither debates nor fights; rather, it is on the calculations of men who find themselves in conflict, which may include decisions whether to fight or to debate.

GAMES AND GAME THEORY

Games frequently capture the dynamic interplay of competition and cooperation involving risky choices by international actors as they make "moves" in the real-life game of world politics. The gamelike qualities of international conflict have been formulated according to certain conventions partly based on mathematical procedures developed since World War II.

[2] For an attempt to refute Richardson, see Samuel P. Huntington, "Arms Races: Prerequisites and Results," in C. J. Friedrich and S. E. Harris, eds., *Public Policy: A Yearbook of the Graduate School of Public Administration* (Cambridge Mass.: Harvard University Press, 1958), pp. 41–86.

Elements of Game Analysis

In formal analysis of a game several elements can be distinguished: players, rules, strategies, and outcomes. Each player (or actor) is an autonomous decision-making unit, though not necessarily a single person. He has a unique set of objectives and operates according to his own decisions.

The rules of the game specify how resources like arms, income, and respect may be deployed. They can control occasions for choice and available alternatives, as in chess, in which it is stipulated that the king can move only one space at a time in any direction. Rules also specify the amount of information on past moves available to the players and the amount of communication permitted among them. In bridge, for example, partners can signal each other by means of certain bids, but they cannot show each other their cards or deliver kicks under the table. Finally, there are rules that specify the game's payoff structure. "Winner take all," for example, defines the distribution of payoffs in certain games.

A strategy specifies what each player *will* do at each juncture, or "play," of the game. Its logic is embodied in the phrase, "If he does X, I must do Y in order to win." A complete strategy specifies the moves of a player in all possible situations. A strategy that is "pure" accounts for all contingencies under a single instruction like "Damn the torpedos, full speed ahead." Usually, however, strategies are open-ended. President John F. Kennedy's warning in 1962 that missiles fired at the United States from Cuba would provoke a massive response against the Soviet Union clarified American strategy only for certain contingencies.

The outcome of the game includes the "payoff" that each player receives as a result of his joint strategies. Payoffs are usually defined as numerical values in a matrix of the possible strategies of the players. In each cell a number indicates the relative value for each player of the expected consequences. These numbers, or *utiles*, express in quantitative terms the levels of preference for each player. They represent a scale of values attached to outcomes in each intersection of players' choices. Such values are *not* comparable among players; ten utiles for player A are not necessarily greater than are five utiles for player B.

Game Theory

A formal branch of game analysis known as "game theory" emerged in the 1940s [12, 23]. By the 1950s it had made impressive strides toward establishing methods for solving problems of conflict that resemble games. Game theorists are able to "solve" games deductively using only a few axioms and assumptions. "Solutions" are arrived at through mathematical treatment of the specific context of the game; such solutions are essentially prescriptive outcomes: If a player wishes to maximize his utiles, he will follow the strategy prescribed by game theory. The game theorist asserts that to achieve a specific outcome, a specific strategy offers the best guarantee. Game theory is thus a theory of means, rather than of ends. It does not suggest to the player what his objectives *should* be. It seeks merely to afford a set of rules to facilitate the realization of the player's ends.

Game theory involves certain assumptions, for example, that all possible outcomes are known and that each player has a consistent pattern of preferences among them. It also assumes that each player seeks to maximize his utiles and can control his own behavior. Each player is assumed to have perfect knowledge of his opponent's preferences. Furthermore, according to the specific character of the game, other assumptions like "fairness" may be postulated.[3] Game-theoretical assumptions simplify reality. The theory is deductive because it is derived from a priori assumptions about human behavior that are then applied to specific cases. It

[3] "Fairness" is defined as rewarding each player according to his average contribution to determination of the outcome. See the differences among the Nash bargaining set, the Shapley value, and the Harsanyi solution discussed in Martin Shubik [23] and other sources.

is nonempirical because it is not anchored in observations of human behavior or other empirical referents. Although every game has an outcome, not all games have solutions. Furthermore, some assumptions by game theorists are not widely accepted; others yield solutions only in games that involve few, if any, real-world parallels.[4]

Before elaborating on the possible benefits of game-theoretical analyses of conflict, we must mention briefly some of the limitations and risks involved in direct application of game theory. In the early 1950s proponents of game theory were optimistic that it would provide a rigorous tool for analysis in decision making and that it would have an ever widening circle of applications to more complex situations as techniques for "solving" disparate games evolved. In the 1960s this expectation declined as it became apparent that large ranges of social action can be represented in game analyses only by severely simplifying or distorting reality. In addition, mathematicians have failed to develop more powerful techniques for "solving" complex games; indeed, the various "solution concepts" that have emerged in the literature often suggest different and sometimes incompatible solutions to the same games because they are based on different principles. Finally, various social analysts have questioned the basic thinking associated with game theory.[5] Although many of the questioners have been ill informed or have misrepresented the actual uses of game theory, some of their criticisms are valid. Conclusions reached through game-theoretical analysis have been challenged because they have been said to be based on a false assumption that moral and analytical concerns are separate. The association of analysis of military strategy based on games with mathematics, computers, and operations research has given it an air of scientific credibility, yet questions of ultimate justification have not been raised during such analysis. Deductions based on a priori assumptions have been justified only by the mode of analysis itself. Unfortunately, this approach not only ignores questions like Can war ever be justified? It also obscures questions of morality. As Aron has pointedly asked:

Can we give a cardinal or ordinal value to the stake of a strategic-diplomatic rivalry? . . . [I]s it not obvious that Laos, for the United States as for the Soviet Union, is worth less than Berlin? We do not disagree. But the mere notion of more and less does not suffice to permit a mathematically valid solution, hence a rational prescription. [1, p. 773]

We can distinguish among games by means of several criteria. A game may involve one person, two people, or n (three or more) people. When only one person plays, as in solitaire, he seeks to maximize his gains against "nature" or "chance." When two players are involved, each attempts to cooperate with or to best his opponent, depending upon the degree to which their interests are in conflict. Each player normally selects a strategy designed to maximize his payoff, despite the opponent's moves. In n-person games the players have the additional option of selecting partners, as well as strategies. In such contests alliances may be relevant to outcomes.

Games can also be differentiated according to the information available to players. Players may or may not possess perfect information about what has gone before. Information on what has gone before is important so that each player can know how his opponents play and whether or not they are trustworthy, yet in some games this knowledge may not be permitted. Furthermore, the rules of some games permit collusion among the players over division of the payoffs; others do

---

[4] Solutions are said to be *stable* when they are identical for each play. Often, however, a player can maximize his utiles by varying his choices (mixed strategies), thus varying outcomes. In addition, the outcomes of some games based on the solution principles of game theory are less desirable for players than are other possible outcomes; in still other games no general and defensible set of assumptions can be applied to reach solutions.

[5] See Albert Wohlstetter [26] for a discussion of these critiques and a defense of strategic thinking that does nevertheless acknowledge the severe limitations of game theory.

not. Collusion may increase the possibility of cooperative solutions.

Finally, the nature of the payoff structure is a critical variable. Some games, like poker and checkers, are totally competitive, whereas others permit, or even necessitate, cooperation. We can thus draw a major distinction between zero-sum and variable-sum games. The former involve pure competition among players; whatever one player gains is at the expense of another. When the losses of one player are subtracted from the gains of another, the result will equal zero. For instance, if two players have $10 between them, no matter how they divide it—$5 and $5, $7 and $3 and so on—the total sum will always be the same. Each additional dollar that one player gains is lost by his opponent. Although games of pure conflict are rare in international politics, they do occur, as, for example, over a disputed territory. When France lost Alsace-Lorraine to Prussia in 1870 its loss was equal to Prussia's gain. "Total war" can be a zero-sum game of ruin. When Rome fought Carthage in 149–146 B.C. the inevitable result was the destruction of one of them. At the urging of Cato the Elder and the Roman Senate, the Roman Republic initiated the Third Punic War so that Carthage might never again challenge Roman influence in the Mediterranean area. "Carthage must be destroyed," Cato reiterated until Rome at last launched its "final" campaign. When Carthage eventually capitulated, the survivors were "sold into slavery; the city was razed to the ground, and its site was doomed by exhaustive imprecations to utter desolation" [4].

The other major type of game, properly called the "variable-sum" game, though also often labeled the "mixed-motive" or "non-zero-sum" game, differs from the first in that the total payoff may vary, depending upon the joint strategies chosen by the players. Cooperation or strategic coordination usually increases the total sum of the payoffs. Such games also involve conflict of interests, as well as a cooperative aspect, though sometimes players

are independent of one another. The European Economic Community (EEC) has sought to increase the total payoff to participants by creating a free-trade area with common external tariffs, thus increasing the volume of trade among its members. Such economic cooperation has increased the total payoff that can be divided among members of the EEC.

Zero-Sum Games. A "solution" exists for every zero-sum game, regardless of the number of participants; this solution is based either on a fixed combination of choices or on some mixed strategy.[6] In a zero-sum game *that is to be played only once* there is no incentive for players to cooperate because only one outcome is at stake and any concession will be a permanent loss. Each player seeks to ensure the best outcome for himself, assuming that his opponent will do the same. This approach leads each player to adopt the strategy that guarantees him the best payoff under the worst possible conditions.

Figure 17.1 represents a zero-sum game between two players. Each box in the matrix represents a possible outcome. The first number in each box represents A's (row) payoff in that outcome; the second number represents B's (column) payoff. Each player must choose one of the two strategies open to him. If each player guarantees his best *payoff under the potentially worst conditions*, A will play his strategy 1 and B will play his strategy 2. The logic is clear. Player A sees that by

---

[6] A "solution" is the specified outcome of a game when each player adopts his most advantageous strategy. Solutions are reached through applying techniques and principles based on several important assumptions. To obtain a solution, the theorist must know the value to each player of the outcomes of all possible combinations of strategies. A variable-sum game may not have a solution, though additional assumptions about coalitions and "fairness" may help to achieve one. One technique for obtaining solutions is to reduce an *n*-person, variable-sum game to a set of two-person, zero-sum games. But the assumptions and techniques of formal game theory required to deduce solutions in such games strain the relation with reality. The direct relevance and applicability of mathematical game theory to interactions in complex international politics are thus severely circumscribed.

Player B
(column)

Player A (row)	Strategy 1		Strategy 2	
Strategy 1	+7	−7	−1	+1
Strategy 2	+5	−5	−3	+3

Figure 17.1. A Zero-Sum Game

choosing strategy 1 the least that he can win, regardless of what B does is −1; if he chooses strategy 2 he may lose 3. Player B reasons the same way. Strategy 2 guarantees a payoff of at least 1, regardless of what A does; strategy 1 could lose him as much as 7. B will decide to play strategy 2, regardless of what A does.

This type of reasoning is known as *maximin strategy*, for it guarantees the player a *maximum minimum*. It is a conservative strategy that entails the least possible risk for each player. From the matrix each player can see which strategy his opponent will probably choose and which strategy ensures his own lowest loss. There is no reason for either actor to choose another strategy in this game and no need for bargaining between them.

Maximin strategy is a basic element in game theory "rationality." It provides a rule for decision; that is, an actor should always expect the worst from his opponent (which in zero-sum games is the latter's best strategy) and be prepared to act accordingly. This reasoning assumes that the actor should always select the strategy that provides the best defense against the worst that an opponent can do. But this prescription assumes that each opponent will inevitably *intend* to maximize his payoffs at the other's expense; therefore each player is to attend to the opponent's capability, rather than to his probable behavior, for, as defined by maximin strategy, they are the same.

In the American debate over whether or not to construct an antiballistic-missile system, the government's decision to go ahead was based, it seems, on maximin strategy. Secretary of Defense Melvin Laird noted that the Soviet Union was building and had already begun to deploy a powerful missile, the SS-9, which *could* be employed in a first strike to neutralize American ability to retaliate. After five years of hesitation American leaders therefore ordered the construction and deployment of an antiballistic-missile system that they hoped would help to render "invulnerable" their own land-based strategic forces.

The question whether or not the Soviet Union *intended* to use its new weapons in a first strike was not raised. The intention was merely assumed, and the worst was expected. The Soviet Union may have developed the SS-9 to strengthen its retaliatory capability or to achieve added bargaining leverage. Such interpretations, however, do not allow for the most dangerous possible contingency as far as the United States is concerned. In such variable-sum games as an arms race, maximin strategies may not be the best.

In prescribing maximin strategy, game theory is no less moral than was Machiavelli. Neither specifically calls for unethical behavior, but both insist that men must be prepared for the depredations of others. As faulty or incomplete information makes it difficult to know the opponent's intentions, it is "safest" to base calculations on his capability of doing the worst. Capabilities are, after all, more easily estimated than are intentions.

The conservative bias of rigorous game analysis is more appropriate to acute conflicts of interest like war. As the zero-sum version resembles military conflict, it can be applied to questions of military doctrine.

A military commander . . . may select his course of action on the basis of his estimate of what his enemy *is able to do* to oppose him. Or, he may make his selection on the basis of his estimate of what the enemy *is going to do*. The former is a doctrine of decision based on enemy capabilities; the latter, on enemy intentions. . . . A commander is enjoined to select the course of action which offers the greatest promise of success in view of the enemy capabilities. [9, pp. 365–366]

In the battle of the Bismarck sea during World War II Major-General George C. Kenney, the American commander, and his staff used game analysis to determine their strategy. American intelligence had learned that the Japanese would attempt to reinforce and supply their troops on New Guinea by means of a convoy from the island of New Britain. The convoy would leave Rabaul on the eastern tip of New Britain and sail westward around New Britain to New Guinea. The Japanese convoy could sail either north or south of New Britain (Figure 17.2). Regardless of which route the Japanese chose, it would take them three days to arrive at New Guinea. The commander thus had two possible strategies: the northern route or the southern route.

General Kenney was determined to intercept and destroy the Japanese convoy and therefore had to decide where to concentrate his reconnaissance aircraft. The northern route usually had poor visibility, whereas the southern route was usually clear. Kenney's staff estimated the number of days that would be available for bombing the convoy, depending upon the strategies chosen by both Americans and Japanese. The matrix in Figure 17.3 illustrates the structure of the problem. The first number in each box represents the number of days available for bombing (the American payoff), and the second number represents the number of days during which no bombing could occur (the Japanese payoff).

American Strategies	Japanese Strategies	
	Northern route	Southern route
Observe northern route	2 1	2 1
Observe southern route	1 2	3 0

Figure 17.3. A Game Matrix of Strategies Available to the American and Japanese Commanders at the Battle of the Bismarck Sea

If both players observed a maximin strategy, the Americans would watch and the Japanese would take the northern route, which is precisely what occurred. The result was the battle of the Bismarck sea. Both players sought to guarantee their minimum security: For the Americans the number of days that would surely be available for bombing, for the Japanese the maximum number of days that would surely be free of bombing. The American strategy of observing the northern route guaranteed at least two days of bombing, no matter which route the Japanese chose. If the Americans had watched the southern route, they might have been able to bomb the Japanese for three full days, but only if the latter took the southern route. If the Japanese chose the northern route while the Americans conducted reconnaisance elsewhere, the Japanese convoy would have been vulnerable for only one day. When the Japanese commander chose the northern route, he guaranteed that the worst that could happen was two days of bombing. The alternative left him open to the possibility of three days of attack. Both commanders chose strategies yielding the highest minimum security level. The "worst" indeed did happen to the Japanese. Even though the Japanese commander lost most of his convoy in the ensuing battle, he could rest assured that he had chosen the safest strategy under the circumstances.[7]

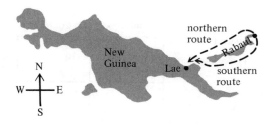

Figure 17.2. Two Possible Japanese Convoy Routes from Rabaul, New Britain, to Lae, New Guinea

[7] For a complete account of this episode, see O. G. Haywood, Jr. [9, pp. 365–385].

Purely mathematical game theory generally counsels decision makers against initiating tension-reducing policies that necessitate trusting the adversary. It emphasizes the most conservative strategy and thus discourages the use of rewards to test the adversary's intentions or to persuade him of one's own peaceful intentions. If we assume that the opponent is also aware of the tenets of game theory, then we must also assume that his decisions will be based on a similar calculus. Game-theoretical analysis may thus encourage mutual suspicion when reasons for it are otherwise lacking and may perpetuate hostility that already exists. Decision makers who follow game theory must take care lest their estimates become self-fulfilling prophecies. As Philip Green has declared, "Purely instrumental choice unhindered either by emotional or ideological blocks on the one hand, or by ignorance on the other, exists only in the abstract world of game theory" [7]. In international politics the distinction between zero-sum and variable-sum games is generally a perceptual one. Within limits, structure determines the degree of conflict among actors, but decision makers' perceptions and the resulting policies largely determine the degree to which a situation will resemble a zero-sum or a variable-sum game. Nearly all international interactions involve both overlapping and conflicting interests, and some mutual trust is required to enlarge the total payoff to be divided or at least to minimize losses. All too frequently game analogies among the mass public and occasionally among decision makers as well take the form of "sports" analogies. In sports there are usually winners and losers, and everyone wants to use all the resources that can be mustered to win, for "every game is important." In international politics this analogy is often dangerous.

Variable-Sum Games. Some characteristics of variable-sum game are well illustrated by the most popular example from game-theory literature, the "prisoners'

dilemma." It is a two-person game in which the payoffs are distributed so that, if the normal decision-making rules prescribed by zero-sum game theory are applied, the outcome is joint ruin! For players to avoid mutually undesirable consequences, they must cooperate. But the very structure of the situation suggests that they cannot cooperate without trusting each other and accepting the risk that their opponents will "defect" from the agreement. This game, attributed to A. W. Tucker, is illustrated in Figure 17.4 [24, pp. 37–38].

Two prisoners taken into custody by the police are interviewed separately by the district attorney. Each is told that if neither of them turns state's evidence the worst that he will receive is a light sentence. If both confess they will receive relatively heavy sentences. But, if one confesses and the other does not, the first will go free, and the second will receive the severest possible sentence. The numbers in Figure 17.4 represent the joint payoffs that each will receive from the alternative strategies. Each prisoner asks himself, regardless of what the other fellow does, in what situation will I be better off? Each observes that confessing will always place him in a better position than will not confessing. The paradox is that when both prisoners maximize their own perceived interests, the outcome (2:2) will be worse for each than if they had cooperated.

In the prisoners' dilemma each player calculates individually the expected value or payoff from his alternative strategies

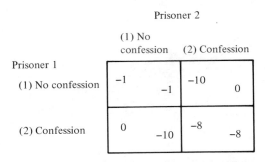

Figure 17.4. The Prisoners' Dilemma (a Variable-Sum Game)

so that the "natural" outcome is worse for both players than it might be if they cooperated. Regardless of which strategy the second prisoner selects, the first prisoner is *always* better off playing strategy 2, that is, defecting. The second prisoner is in the same position. It is for this reason that game theorists call 2:2 a "natural" or "equilibrium" solution. There is little incentive for either prisoner to seek an alternative outcome.[8] This mode of reasoning is an extension of the maximin principle developed in zero-sum games. The player examines the alternative strategies and corresponding payoff possibilities available, in order to find which strategy will guarantee the smallest possible loss, regardless of the opponent's choice.[9] In variable-sum games like the prisoners' dilemma such reasoning can prove disastrous. Instead of guaranteeing a player his best outcome, it may guarantee a payoff far lower than one that could be obtained through cooperation.

Actual situations corresponding to the prisoners' dilemma abound in international politics. Particularly relevant are those involving arms races, tariff policies, and alliances. Individual states may calcu-

[8] Various techniques for resolving this paradox have been proposed by game theorists, somewhat embarrassed by the unfortunate outcome prescribed by their normal approach. These techniques are based on additional assumptions of either "parallel reasoning" or "multiple plays." Morton Deutsch and his associates have concluded from extended laboratory research that the prisoners' dilemma can be resolved both competitively and cooperatively but that if one mode is used in early plays of the game, it tends to be self-perpetuating [5, 6]. Rapoport and Dale have found from experimental sessions with students that cooperation between players decreases in the course of the first few games but rises steadily after about fifty plays; it also increases as rewards for coordination and penalties for defection increase [16, 17, 19, 18, 14]. Many of these experimental findings have been summarized in Rapoport and A. Chammah, *Prisoner's Dilemma: A Study in Conflict and Cooperation* (Ann Arbor: University of Michigan Press, 1965).

[9] By calculating in similar fashion in a zero-sum game the players may frequently find one or more "saddlepoints," or solutions based on points of equilibrium. As such a game involves pure competition, neither player will then have an incentive to move from the saddlepoint.

late that more weapons or higher tariffs are in their interest, regardless of what other states do. But recognition that both sides forfeit comparative advantages in international trade or that a spiraling arms race frequently leads to greater national insecurity may make actors willing to enter into negotiations to reduce tariffs or armaments. Furthermore, international situations seldom resemble single games. Arms races and trade policy involve extended games with many individual opportunities for choice. Indeed, one of the major considerations in game analysis is not the outcome of a single "play" but whether or not this single instance is part of a series of plays in which the calculations and behavior in each are likely to affect outcomes in future plays. The images, preferences, and objectives of the players can change during a single play of the game or in the course of a series of plays (see Chapter 4, pp. 57–64). The definition of the game context depends upon the perceptions of the players. How they define the games in which they are involved has important policy consequences: They must decide whether or not the resolution of a single play in favor of one side will prove unfavorable to that side in the long run and whether or not the maximization of individual advantage at a single point in time will alter the opponent's values and preferences to make cooperation more difficult in the future.

In situations like an arms race, in which the prisoners' dilemma does not involve a single outcome, each actor may be tempted to arm to gain advantage over the other in subsequent plays. Furthermore, each is motivated by a desire to prevent the other from obtaining such an advantage. Although both actors may admit that they are better off not arming, they may continue to spend large sums on armaments, with mixed effects on their security and with real economic losses. Disarmament and arms control agreements pose a similar dilemma. Each actor has an incentive to "cheat" and to violate the agreement in order to gain an advantage over the other. Each actor, aware of these mutual incentives, also fears that the other will violate the agreement first and perhaps even gain a decisive advantage in the process. In these situations the "states are trapped in the double-defection box of a prisoners' dilemma" and cannot escape into the cooperative box without an agent to enforce cooperation and penalize cheating [25, p. 69].

As Thomas Schelling has pointed out, the race to mobilize at the outbreak of World War I has its counterpart in the "reciprocal fear of surprise attack" in the nuclear age [22, pp. 207–229]. Each of two nuclear powers, possessing a first-strike capability, is under strong pressure for preemptive attack in order to forestall a feared attack by the other. Even though equalizing capabilities provides few incentives for preemptive attack, the prisoners' dilemma has nevertheless operated in determining levels of preparedness for nuclear competition. Former Secretary of Defense Robert S. McNamara has succinctly outlined how:

In 1961, when I became Secretary of Defense, the Soviet Union possessed a very small operational arsenal of intercontinental missiles. However, they did possess the technological and industrial capacity to enlarge that arsenal very substantially over the succeeding several years.

Now, we had no evidence that the Soviets did in fact plan to fully use that capability. But as I have pointed out, a strategic planner must be "conservative" in his calculations; that is, he must prepare for the worst plausible case and not be content to hope and prepare merely for the most probable.

Since we could not be certain of Soviet intentions—since we could not be sure that they would not undertake a massive buildup—we had to insure against such an eventuality by undertaking ourselves a major buildup of the Minuteman and Polaris forces. . . .

Clearly, the Soviet buildup is in part a reaction to our own buildup since the beginning of this decade. Soviet strategic planners undoubtedly reasoned that if our buildup were to continue at its accelerated pace, we might conceivably reach, in time, a credible first-strike capability against the Soviet Union.

This was not in fact our intention. Our intention was to assure that they—with their theoretical capacity to reach such a first-strike capability—would not in fact outdistance us.

But they could not read our intentions with any greater accuracy than we could read theirs. And thus the result has been that we have both built up our forces to a point that far exceeds a credible second-strike capability against the forces we each started with. . . .

It is futile for each of us to spend $4 billion, $40 billion, or $400 billion—and at the end of all the spending, and at the end of all the deployment, and at the end of all the effort, to be relatively at the same point of balance on the security scale that we are now.[10]

There are two central elements in the structure of the prisoners' dilemma: the magnitude of the negative consequences in the double-defection strategy box (in the lower right-hand corner of Figure 17.4) and the assessment by each player of the likelihood that the other player can be trusted to cooperate. The importance of these two elements is illustrated by a comparison of two situations involving disarmament and preemptive attack.

Let us consider the two matrices in Figure 17.5. In the disarmament example player A may reason as follows (B's reasoning will be similar because he is confronted with an identical situation):

If both B and myself disarm, we would at least save the economic costs involved in developing and deploying weapons. Clearly, a 1:1 outcome is superior to a 2:2 outcome. But suppose that B does arm? I am clearly worse off, and he gains. Indeed, B has a real incentive to arm, at least when I am disarmed. Of the four possible outcomes, 1:2 is certainly the worst for me! Now, suppose that I arm; what happens? We may end up at 2:2, with both of us fully armed, and neither more secure than previously. Moreover, we will incur substantial economic costs. So, we are both somewhat worse off. But if I arm and he

[10] *The New York Times*, September 19, 1967.

Disarmament

Actor B

	(1) Disarm	(2) Arm
Actor A		
(1) Disarm	0 0	−30 +10
(2) Arm	+10 −30	−5 −5

First Strike

Actor B

	(1) No strike	(2) Strike
Actor A		
(1) No strike	0 0	−51 +5
(2) Strike	+5 −51	−50 −50

Figure 17.5. Possible Game Matrices for Disarmament and First-Strike Strategies

disarms, I am better off than in any of the other situations. Nevertheless, ignoring this possibility, let me examine whether or not it is worth taking a risk that B might disarm if I did. If I move to a disarmament strategy, I risk losing a great deal (25 utiles) to gain only a small amount (5 utiles). Why should I take this risk? If I remain armed, I can only lose a little, and, moreover, there is some chance that B might disarm, in which case I would gain a substantial advantage over him.

The negative payoff for double-defection is thus not great enough to induce player A to accept the risk involved in disarming. Indeed, the possible consequences for cooperating while the adversary defects are alarming. Furthermore, A finds it difficult to trust B, who is in an identical situation; it is unlikely that B will want to accept the risk of disarming either.

Determining whether or not to launch a first strike with nuclear weapons is somewhat different. The prisoners' dilemma still exists, but the values in the matrix have been altered to illustrate a more dangerous choice.[11] The assump-

tions that if neither actor strikes, the status quo will be maintained and that either will be devastated by an attack are similar to those of the second matrix in Figure 17.5 The small gain from a unilateral first strike is explained by the fact that the initiator undertakes this action largely as a defensive measure—not to gain an advantage but to prevent an opponent from gaining it. Let us again follow the reasoning of player A. Noting the 2:2 outcome, he recognizes that it is ruinous.

How can I escape the logic of this outcome? After all, my initiating a strike is clearly better for me, regardless of what my opponent does. But what are the stakes involved? If either of us strikes, he imposes great losses on the adversary but does not gain very much himself. On the other hand, if he decides not to strike I will be much better off (50 utiles). In this instance it is worthwhile for me to trust him, for he also gains relatively little from attacking. If we both attacked, we would both regret our behavior. If he declared that he would prefer a no-strike strategy, I would be inclined to believe him.

In this instance the structure of the situation places pressure on both players to cooperate to achieve the 1:1 outcome. Cooperation involves small risk to prevent unacceptable harm. In the disarmament example, on the other hand, cooperation involves large risk for relatively small gain. Although both situations are prisoners' dilemmas, the risks and incentives in the first-strike example make escape from the dilemma much more likely.

Another game situation frequently used by theorists of international relations is "chicken" (Figure 17.6). This game, once a popular way for teen-agers to prove their "courage," is like the prisoners' dilemma in that it has a ruinous outcome toward which each player is pulled; un-

---

[11] Although a simultaneous first-strike strategy cannot by definition occur, the game matrix in Figure 17.5 assumes nearly simultaneous action in the 2:2 outcome. One point of departure for analysis is the effect of second-strike capability, which will be discussed in Chapter 18.

Player B

	Swerve (Cooperate)	Not swerve (Defect)
Player A		
Swerve (Cooperate)	−5 −5	−5 +5
Not swerve (Defect)	+5 −5	−50

Figure 17.6. The Game of Chicken

like the prisoners' dilemma, however, this solution is not "natural." In the original version of this game, two cars speed toward each other, straddling the center lane of a drag strip; the object is to see which driver will lose his courage and swerve, thus "chickening out." The situations is defined by mixed motives, as is the prisoners' dilemma, but by contrast the strategy for winning is to create fear, rather than trust, in the opponent. In the prisoners' dilemma, when a player wants an opponent to cooperate, he seeks to communicate that he can himself be trusted, that both would thus be better off by cooperating, and that he intends to play cooperatively.[12] In chicken, the winning strategy is precisely the opposite. Each player tries to encourage his opponent's belief that he *will* "defect" from the mutual interest of avoiding a collision. Furthermore, the value of commitment in defecting, or mutually noncooperative strategy, is high for the rational adversary who recognizes the commitment *must* cooperate to avoid mutual disaster. The crucial difference between the two games is that penalties for double defection in chicken far exceed those in the prisoners' dilemma. Indeed, any player would prefer to swerve while the adversary wins than to collide.

In the prisoners' dilemma, the realization of the common interest may well be a primary desire of both parties, but neither can trust the other to collaborate in real-

---

[12] If this were a single-play game or an "end of the world" situation, each actor might communicate his intention to cooperate while actually planning to defect.

izing it; against the will of the parties, the situation degenerates into conflict. In chicken, one party willfully *creates* a conflict by challenging the other and threatens to *destroy* an already enjoyed common interest if it does not get its way in the conflict; the defending party may reciprocate with a similar threat. Typically, the common interest in chicken is something that is manipulated as a means of coercion, not something that is mutually sought. The spirit or leading theme of the prisoners' dilemma is that of the frustration of a mutual desire to cooperate. The spirit of a chicken game is that of a contest in which each party is trying to prevail over the other. [25, p. 84]

The juvenile hot-rodder swerves because he thinks that disaster is a probable outcome; he believes that his partner may not swerve. The more credible the determination of one's opponent, the more rational it becomes to swerve. Unlike the outcome of the prisoners' dilemma, the outcome in chicken varies widely according to the opponent's strategy.

For both games we have described only single plays, rather than successions of plays, which more closely represent real situations in international politics. We have also assumed simultaneous choices in each game, whereas in fact in an extended game we would have to specify whether or not each choice is succeeded by a response. In international politics actors tend to play sequentially, rather than simultaneously. For example, if one could develop a reputation for not swerving in several encounters of chicken, this reputation might be an important factor in subsequent games. Similarly, in more than 300 plays of one experimental game of prisoners' dilemma among students, Anatol Rapoport found that strategies of joint cooperation or defection tended to become "locked in" as players built reputations and sets of norms for trusting or distrusting each other.

Ironically, mutual perceptions of toughness promote cooperative responses by both players of chicken. When both parties find themselves facing the real possibility of all-out war, the desire to avoid such a disaster seems natural. Deterrence theory involves similar considerations, as each party emphasizes the possibility of mutual disaster to prevent the other from taking advantage of his own cooperative behavior.

The possibilities of a dynamic game in extended form are illustrated by "salami tactics." Salami tactics are an actor's deliberate provocation of a series of minor incidents or minor demands on an adversary. Each incident involves relatively low stakes unless the defender is prepared to go to war. From time to time, for example, the Soviet Union has employed salami tactics by harassing allied traffic heading toward the isolated city of West Berlin. According to Schelling:

"Salami tactics," we can be sure, were invented by a child; whoever first expounded the adult version had already understood the principle when he was small. Tell a child not to go in the water and he'll sit on the bank and submerge his bare feet; he is not yet "in" the water. Acquiesce, and he'll stand up; no more of him is in the water than before. Think it over, and he'll start wading, not going any deeper; take a moment to decide whether this is different and he'll go a little deeper, arguing that since he goes back and forth it all averages out. Pretty soon we are calling to him not to swim out of sight, wondering whatever happened to all our discipline. [21]

In each individual play of the game the adversary may consider resorting to war too destructive a response to a minor provocation. Over a long period the first actor may continue to incite minor crises and if the adversary fails to respond, may make still greater demands. If the game were to be played only one time, then resorting to war would clearly be an unrealistic strategy for the defender; the game would resemble chicken. But if the game is to be played over a long period of time, the prospective total losses of the defender may make the situation appear more like prisoners' dilemma. Assuming that the defender places some value on the specific shape of the future, he may view war as a "rational" strategy, even

though war will be disastrous for both players. We can envision a sequence of probes, counterprobes, and responses as actors seek to discover a rational pattern of behavior and to test each other's will. The defender ultimately may view "peace in our time" as less preferable than toleration of continued aggressions.

Martin Shubik has suggested such an extended game [24, pp. 62–65]. In Figure 17.7 the sequence of moves for two countries is outlined. Each part of the diagram portrays for each country a set of strategies that tend toward peaceful equilibrium. The flow charts are based on an extensive form of the game in which plays are sequential, rather than simultaneous. Finding the patterns of behavior and comparing them with possible real-world situations permit us to form an idea of how proposed strategies compare with actual ones. Extended repetitive games illustrate better than does simple deductive game theory the situations in which the available strategies, sequences of play, and payoffs resemble international behavior.

Simulation. Simulation is another approach to studying conflict in international politics that has gained currency during the last two decades. It involves an operating model in simplified form of the relations among units in a real world under laboratory conditions. Simulation resembles game theory in that it requires the analyst to specify precisely the variables and processes under investigation. In one sense simulation is simply an extension of games in a more complex form of modeling, allowing for change over time and for recycling of the decision-making context from period to period. In this way simulation permits the generation of data and the testing of hypotheses about reality.

Simulation offers a working model of the real world. It has been used in various fields, including research and teaching. As a research tool it enables the theorist to state hypotheses more clearly. Simulation models offer several advantages over verbal descriptions. They require that re-

Policy for country 1

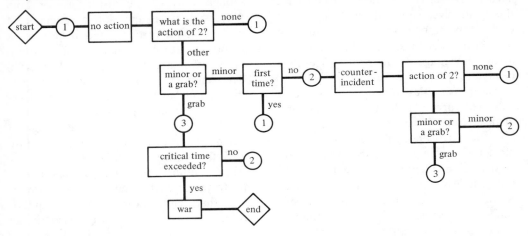

Policy for country 2

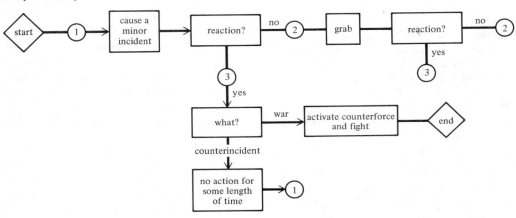

Figure 17.7. Flow Chart for a Two-Nation Interaction

Source: From M. Shubik, editor, *Game Theory and Related Approaches to Social Behavior*. Copyright © 1964 by John Wiley & Sons, Inc. Reprinted by permission.

Minor incident to start; if no counterincident takes place, grab; if a counterincident takes place, resume no action for some length of time, then try a minor incident again; if grabbing provokes nothing, keep grabbing; if it provokes war, fight.

No action as long as there is no action by the other. No action against the first minor incident; use counterincident on any subsequent incident. If any action is a grab, reply with a counterincident; if the grab continues beyond a certain time, then war; if minor incidents are resumed, employ counterincidents; if no action is resumed, then resume no action.

With the strategies as outlined . . . the second country will cause a minor incident which will go unanswered; it will then try for a grab which will provoke a reply. After this, there will be a series of testing and replies in the form of minor incidents. . . .

Danger of war will be less, the more both sides value the future, the more accurate the estimate of each other's strength, and the less random events clutter up communications encouraging incorrect inferences. For example, if nation 1 can communicate the existence of war as a policy to be taken if provoked or country 2 can make clear that counterincidents will deter it from "grabbing."

lationships be formally specified, thus reducing ambiguities; the parameters must be stated, so that the importance of each process is clearer. Theorists, by contrast, tend to use terms like "more" and "less." In simulation a great deal of information

about relationships among variables can be treated in more compact and manageable form, while at the same time the possibility that important relationships will be ignored is reduced.

Simulation as a teaching technique permits a more uncontrolled environment in which the personalities and even the fantasies of participants may affect outcomes. The results of such experiments may be useful either for the information that they provide on how individuals behave under stress and think about certain kinds of problems or for familiarizing participants with what it is like to face a difficult set of policy questions and arrive at consequential decisions under pressure of time.

In a study mentioned in Chapter 3 Charles and Margaret Hermann used simulation designed for teaching and research (Inter-Nation Simulation), to show how students, playing national-leadership roles based on those of the major powers before World War I, reenacted the steps leading to war. Two sets of students were used, one group whose personalities closely matched those of leading individuals in each state, and a second whose personalities were less closely matched. The situation was identical to World War I, except that names, dates, and other historical clues were not provided. The Hermanns found that the group with closely matched personalities presented demands and counterdemands parallel to those that had actually led to war. In the other group similar progress toward war occurred, except that efforts toward peace were greater, and individual behavior—like initiatives by the student playing the British foreign minister—were notably different from those that took place historically. Although this study neither validates the simulation method nor increases our certainty about the causes of World War I, it does provide insights into the possible uses of simulation.

The Inter-Nation Simulation (INS) employed by the Hermanns is a complex model involving both humans and computers. Humans serve as decision makers and are divided into nations which interact with one another as in the international system. The internal organization of each nation generally includes a central decision maker (head of state), an internal decision maker (economic adviser), an external decision maker (foreign policy adviser), and a decision maker with respect to force (defense adviser), as well as others. Decision makers in different nations are constrained by domestic and foreign variables that are provided by a set of computed programs. Some simulations involve only human participants without computers.

More formal models, usually involving complete computer simulations, offer a method that promises to allow researchers to handle the complexity that they find in international politics in a less simplified and more nearly realistic way. A study of multiply caused, interacting, and time-specific processes of change in the international political system may well be represented by simulation models portraying either portions (or subsystems) of the total process or even the entire system. Harold Guetzkow and Paul Smoker's work on various all-computer simulations and work by others at Northwestern University probably best represent this type [8].

THE VALUE OF GAME ANALYSIS

The Study of Structure

In the study of conflict in international politics, game analysis offers a valuable means both to clarify the structure of a situation and to specify the theoretical assumptions by which an actor may wish to formulate policies. Nevertheless, there are some disadvantages to its use. The most important contribution of this type of analysis is in the precision required to formulate a conflict situation and the deductive power that it permits. Obviously a bad "fit" between a game or simulation and a real conflict can lead to dangerously misleading conclusions. On the other hand, the task of specifying a game matrix, or the properties of a simulation, can help decision makers to clarify their information about a situation and reveal to them properties that are not immediately obvious.

What game theory allows is a kind of thumbnail sketch of the relevant structural features of a conflict. Let us see how it works. First, the distribution of relevant resources—that is, the resources of various kinds that each actor considers available to each player—is specified for each alternative strategy. Second, the distribution of attitudes within the situation is also represented in the game matrix by the values placed on various outcomes by the actors. In this way the matrix reveals the attitudes, values, and goals of leaders or, in traditional terms, the national interests of the actors. The magnitude and strength (positive or negative) of the utiles specified in the matrix represent crude approximations of how each player evaluates the likely outcome of each combination of strategies. Implicit theories about the causal relationships underlying a particular mix or sequence of decisions by actors help to stipulate the outcomes before they can be evaluated. In the simple chicken game, for instance, each player's choice of a strategy not to swerve supposedly yields the outcome of a serious collision. Previous experience, common sense, and physical laws all seem to justify this expectation about cause and effect. In this situation causal specification seems reasonably clear. But what about problems of disarmament? What is the relationship between disarmament (with and without inspection) and the probability of cheating on an arms-control agreement? How do we quantify cheating as an outcome? The issues here are far more complex, and consequently the specification of a matrix for the conflict situation demands not only subjective analysis but also more serious inquiry into the issues at stake. Specifying strategies, predicting the probable outcome from a particular mix of decisions, and evaluating individual payoffs to the actors are all steps that require investigation and specification of relevant aspects of international structure.

Analysis of structure can result in descriptions of various kinds of interdependence between two actors (for the sake of simplicity we need only use two). Different game structures represent different structural relations in the real world. In particular, the nature of interdependence can be clarified in this way.

Two actors are said to have interlocking fates when neither can achieve his preferred outcome without some action from the other. We suggested earlier that because of the respective geographical positions and resources of Brazil and India, military planning in the two countries is not interdependent. Let us assume that military planners in both these countries have surplus funds and must choose whether to build large or small navies. If we ignore alternative uses for the funds for a moment, we can construct a game matrix with plausible payoffs for India and Brazil (Figure 17.8). India will receive a payoff of four, rather than two, if it selects its second strategy, whereas Brazil will receive a payoff of three, rather than one, if it selects its second strategy. Planners in both countries would conclude that they would be better off with strategy 2, building a large navy. But *the choice of each is completely independent of the choice of the other.* In making their own decisions, the planners would not have to consider each other's decisions. Not only is there a solution (2:2) to this game, but also each actor can safely ignore the behavior of the other because they are not interdependent.

By contrast, three types of interdependence can be found in different game structures. Each of these games represents a "pure" type of interdependence, and for each there is a solution, though in one instance it presents a dilemma. We shall try to indicate the nature of each relationship by means of a concrete example that approximately parallels a real situation.

Mutual dependence is frequent in in-

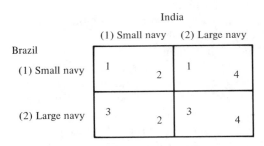

Figure 17.8. The Naval Game: An Example of Independence

ternational politics. If we look at major foreign-policy goals of Germany and Great Britain we may find (as in Figure 17.9) that each is relatively indifferent to its own choice of strategies but *unlike* the previous case, very concerned about the other's choice. Great Britain has been seeking admission to the European Common Market since the 1960s but requires the support of West Germany to succeed. West Germany, on the other hand, wants a British army to remain along the Rhine river and at other strategic points in Germany, in order to deter an attack from the east.

Weighing costs against benefits, Great Britain may be indifferent to whether it keeps troops in West Germany or withdraws them. Germany, on the other hand, cares a great deal about whether or not British troops remain. Conversely, West Germany may not care particularly whether or not Great Britain enters the Common Market, but Great Britain strongly desires such entrance. Here we have high interdependence—in the sense that *the outcome for each actor depends upon persuading the other to act in his favor.* Each actor is, however, indifferent as far as his own choice is concerned. The natural outcome of this situation would be 1:1, not because each player would choose the strategy best for himself, as in the earlier example, but because he would choose the strategy that would be best for his interdependent partner and thus indirectly for himself; in this way, both sides would realize desirable

outcomes. Such outcomes can be realized only through bargaining by parties aware of their mutual dependence.

The next example is of interdependence in which the players care about *both their own choices and those of their partners.* In autumn 1970, the United States proposed a cease-fire to the United Arab Republic and Israel, in order to end the fighting that had continued around the Suez canal intermittently since 1967.

In this instance difficult and delicate negotiations preceded formal announcement of acceptance of the cease-fire, first by the United Arab Republic and then by Israel. Let us suppose that the United States said to Egypt, "If you continue to fight, we will arm Israel, in which case Israel can maintain the status quo, but you will suffer a heavy drain on your economy, as you have in the fighting up to now, and you cannot count on the Russians to make it up" (see Figure 17.10). Either a cease-fire or continued mutual fighting (with United States support of Israel) would ensure general maintenance of the status quo, for Israel a positive value. On the other hand, should either country accept the cease-fire while the other continued to fight, the first would suffer tactical military losses, and the second would incur heavy losses of outside support. In this situation Israel would do whatever Egypt did, for Israel would be indifferent to the choice between mutual fighting and a cease-fire. Doubt whether or not it could trust Egypt might cause Israel to hesitate over an agreement.

Great Britain

Germany	(1) Maintain troop levels		(2) Withdraw troops from Germany	
(1) Support British application	3	6	−1	6
(2) Withhold support	3	−2	−1	−2

Figure 17.9. The German-British Tradeoff: An Example of Mutual Dependence

United Arab Republic (Egypt)

Israel	(1) Accept cease-fire		(2) Continue fighting	
(1) Accept cease-fire	4	4	−1	−1
(2) Continue fighting	−1	−1	4	−4

Figure 17.10. Egyptian-Israeli Cease-fire: A Dominant Solution

On the other hand, Egypt would clearly have one dominant strategy, to accept the cease-fire. In either instance Egypt would be better off accepting the cease-fire than it would be fighting, regardless of what Israel did. Egypt did in fact announce initial acceptance of the cease-fire; once this strategy of the Arab states had been revealed, Israel had little choice but to accept also. Although 1:1 is a natural solution in this interdependent situation, the actor with unambiguous preferences dominates determination of the joint outcome.

The final example takes the form of the prisoners' dilemma. Not only is there strategic interdependence, but each actor also has a clear preference among the available alternatives. Unfortunately, the choices are not mutually beneficial. We may imagine two military strategists, one in the United States and the other in the Soviet Union, both considering the use of nuclear weapons. Let us suppose that each country considers the other a threat and that each strategist considers that a successful first strike would yield a clear advantage to its initiator (see Figure 17.11). We assume that if both chose to attack first, the attacks would occur about simultaneously and would result in mutual massive destruction. But suppose that each strategist suspected that the adversary was prepared to launch such a first strike. Each could then reasonably conclude that regardless of what the adversary decided to do, it would be better off launching its own attack. Even though the best combined strategy for both actors would be for neither to attack, the absence of trust might lead them to select their second strategies and to invite mutual disaster.

Clarifying Tactics

Once the basic elements of the structural context of conflict have been specified, a further series of specifications is necessary to reveal how further manipulation of the situation may affect outcome. The first question is Who goes first? Let us consider the prisoners' dilemma, in which both players moving simultaneously produce a different situation from that in a serial game in which one completes his move (which has become known) before the other moves. If disarmament is the issue, the country that has the second move may announce, "I'll do whatever the first fellow does." If the first country believes the second, it can effectively choose a 1:1 or a 2:2 outcome. The sequence of action must therefore be specified.

A second question is How much conflict exists in the situation? The extent to which payoffs in each set tend to be zero-sum determines the intensity of the conflict. A high degree of conflict restricts an actor's bargaining opportunities and makes it difficult for the actor to undertake a cooperative move like compensating his opponent in some other sphere of activity [2].

A third structural feature that must be clarified is the amount of communication between actors. For instance, Rapoport found that when communication was possible in the prisoners' dilemma, cooperation occurred more readily. Communication was not the only factor affecting cooperation, however; initial instructions about the nature of the play and visual inspection of the game matrix itself also raised the percentage of cooperative choices (as opposed to defections) by players.

Still a fourth question is How much information is available to each player? In the simplest games we have assumed

United States

Soviet Union	(1) No first use		(2) First use	
(1) No first use	0	0	−50	10
(2) First use	10	−50	−45	−45

Figure 17.11. Surprise Attack: Interdependence and Cooperation

perfect information about the matrix, but in international politics negotiation is frequently based on informed guesses about the value preferences of other parties. Each party has defined a range of outcomes that it considers acceptable but that it may not wish to reveal to the other side, lest the latter then choose the least favorable portion of that range. If the two ranges do not overlap, it is unlikely that negotiations will succeed unless one or the other side alters its range during the course of negotiations. One never has perfect information, however, and negotiations often amount to series of guesses about what may induce the most concessions from the other and when the point of saturation has been reached [10, pp. 191–224].

A fifth area that must be specified is whether the game is to be a single or a repetitive one. The number of times that strategy choices are likely to be available within the given international structure is a basic factor affecting "rational" decision making. If we were certain in a prisoners' dilemma that the available choices were never to be repeated and that their consequences would have little or no impact on subsequent choices, we would expect a rational player always to "defect."

A final question about structure involves long-term versus short-term considerations for each actor. In repetitive play, similar to most international conflicts, the extent to which a player discounts future outcomes in favor of more immediate rewards has an important effect on the strategy that he chooses. For example, if war in the immediate future seems a real threat, then the player has a severely limited choice of strategies for deterring steady long-term aggression. If the long run were heavily discounted, the strategy for all-out war would *never* seem viable to the defensive player. As a result, it would be reasonable for the aggressive player to continue to "grab" because the mutually disastrous possibility of war would never be invoked by his opponent.

By determining these characteristics

while constructing the game matrix, we can clarify the constraints of the real world. Many of these features may be malleable, however. Tactics for modifying such elements of structure may be suggested to clarify or improve the strategic options available. For instance, if there is great uncertainty, a player may prefer to seek further information rather than opting for action. A decision to postpone a strategic decision in order to clarify an opponent's goals and intentions is, of course, opting for a strategy of inaction. An exhaustive consideration of policy alternatives would surely include this option.

When communication is possible, various tactics may be used to alter the structure of the situation in favorable ways. These tactics are intended to alter the opponents' image of its interests or probable actions.

Timing can affect tactics designed to reshape strategies. Determining who goes first in a situation and using initial actions to signal future intentions or commitment to future actions are important. An act that gives the opponent the "last clear chance" to avoid a mutually disastrous outcome (but only by responding favorably) illustrates such use of early initiatives. In chicken, when one driver throws aside his steering wheel, "locking himself" into a no-swerve strategy, he indicates his commitment (for his hands are tied) and gives his opponent the last chance to avoid mutual disaster. Schelling has speculated about the value of such bridge-burning activity to convince an advancing enemy of one's determination to fight and about the value of adopting strategies that place the burden of choosing to yield or to fight on the opponent [22, pp. 21–52]. Hardening one's "will" and surrendering control of the situation, however, ensure a loss of autonomy; hopes for a "good" outcome have been entrusted to an opponent in whom one seldom has much confidence. Furthermore, if strategies narrowing one's own options and giving the opponent the choice of saving the situation at the last moment are adopted by both sides, as they were to some extent by both Russia and Germany before World War I, the outcome may be rapid escalation toward war. Such strategies are thus often more risky than profitable.

Another element in timing is the lag between perception of an opponent's action and an effective response. Because of their fear of sneak attacks both the United States and the Soviet Union have established elaborate networks for monitoring each other's behavior. The Defense Early Warning line established by the United States and Canada is intended to reduce the lag between a Soviet attack and its detection by the North Atlantic defense system. The development of solid-fuel missiles and their maintenance under constant vigilance were undertaken partly in order to decrease the lag time in the United States' ability to respond to threatening situations. Because the fueling and firing of missiles now take only a few minutes, it has become possible to wait a little in a strategically dramatic situation, in order to clarify further the actions and intentions of a potential enemy and to be certain of what is happening.

The Continuum Between Conflict and Cooperation

Another value of game analysis is its power to clarify the integrative possibilities of various structural situations. Leon Lindberg has outlined a scale of bargaining styles associated with different types of games. The probabilities for cooperative interaction and the creation of integrated processes and organizations increase as the structural features of international situations shift from zero-sum to variable-sum forms and from single to multiple available values for division or exchange. In Table 17.1 each higher level represents greater expectation that actors may obtain objectives and satisfy values by engaging in cooperative behavior; it also represents a larger number of actors who can improve their positions by accommodation or alliance.

Various features or "subdimensions" of

this continuum of game types are also related to potential peaceful and integrative action. Some of those suggested by Lindberg are:

1. How many of the participants can improve their payoffs by "rational" strategies? The "efficiency" or "productivity" of the collective action—from low-level reordering of existing resources to creation of new ones.

2. The availability of side payments and hence the potential "logrolling" improves opportunities for mutual benefits in bargaining, not only because it increases chances for reaching settlement

but also because, by making it possible to compensate players, one can get decisions which benefit fewer than all the members of the winning coalition, thus further maximizing net productivity. If unlimited side payments are possible (complex logrolling), that is, if players are willing to make bargains involving a wide range of heterogeneous issues, the system's productivity is still further increased. It also reflects the range and distribution of preferences and intensities in the society (its cleavage structure).

3. The ranges of intensity of the communications among actors and their receptivity to one another's messages.

4. The possibility of learning or socialization resulting from participation in several bargaining games, so that companion norms may be internalized and trust promoted.

5. The congruence among actor's influence potential and the weight to be given to preferences of each in the collective ranking of preferences.

6. The extent to which players are responsive to environmental changes and external communications through changes in their images and goals. [11]

These factors, which can shape the bargaining possibilities in a conflict in international politics, also enhance the possibility of a peaceful integration. At the most favorable level in Table 17.1, level 5, these six helpful features are present, and new formal organizations and mechanisms (paths) for processing the composite demands of participants in the international arena may arise.

Table 17.1.
The Integrative Potential of Games

Social Level of Integration Potential	Game Structure (Context of Social Interaction)	Strategies Implied	Bargaining Style
1	competitive zero-sum (unit-veto model)	no possibility of increasing utiles through cooperation or collusion; individual rationality tends to maximize the gain of a single player, whose preference ordering must be accepted; loss for other players	little or no bargaining; involves making unacceptable demands, no changes in position; free use of threats (including threat to leave the system), ultimatums and *faits accomplis*; high hostility
2	competitive constant-sum (minimum-coalition model)	limited cooperation or collusion to maximize gain of winning coalition; increase only coalition benefits; loss to others; no side payments or important changes of position for members of winning coalition	as at level 1, except some cooperation or collusion among members of minimum winning coalition; some package deals on closely related matters
3	competitive variable-sum (simple logrolling model)	involves compromise of present interests, division of existing resources, or ratification of existing arrangements; side payments and exchanges of resources on limited range of closely related issues (some receiving more than others but all perhaps receiving something)	probable willingness to reach limited agreements of mutual interest; fewer threats and more exchanges though threats and bluffs still common; seek only to reorder existing resources without changing goals or preference orderings
4	mixed-motive variable-sum (complex logrolling model)	compromise, rearrangement of existing interests and resources, and establishment of new resources and institutions; basic goal to reorder resources within existing definitions of goals and interests or change "images" of players	unrestricted side payments and thus extensive logrolling and trades over wide ranges of issues seen not as unrelated but in context of a continuous decision process; more exchanges and fewer threats
5	cooperative variable-sum (progressive-taxation model)	cooperation to optimize interests of society itself; acceptance of overriding collective interest distinct from maximization of individual utiles	emergence of common interests perhaps transcending individual interests; basic transformation of images and goals; some acceptance of losses to increase benefits to others

Source: Adapted and simplified from Leon Lindberg, "Political Integration as a Multidimensional Phenomenon," *International Organization*, 24 (Autumn 1970), pp. 705-706.

CONCLUSION

The complexity, machinery, pomp, and apparent high scientific powers of game theory, computer techniques, simulation, and gaming are no substitute for substantive knowledge. Furthermore, there is a danger that a false sense of accuracy and precision will lead to a misemphasis in the study of political, sociological, or psychological problems. [24, p. 67]

It should be clear by now that most of the difficult choices in game analysis are made in setting up the framework of the game, not in analyzing it. Some of the difficulties of game theory thus arise from lack of "fit" with reality. Games tend to represent single events when in fact international politics is characterized by sequences of events. Images, preferences, and objectives are unchanging in a game matrix, but in reality there are critical changes in these factors. Another problem is the investigator's perception of the situation that he attempts to define as a game, for perceptions tend to be related to nationality. If one national actor believes that he understands what is at stake in a game, is there any guarantee that his opponent will see the situation similarly? For example, is the Vietnam War a struggle between the United States and North Vietnam, or is it part of some larger encounter among all the great powers, including Communist China and the Soviet Union? According to one view, in the 1950s the United States "succeeded" in deterring the Soviet Union from invading western Europe. But it is also possible that the Soviet Union never intended to invade, and then the deterrent force in Europe may have served as a needless provocation embittering Soviet-American relations. The analyst's institutional identifications may also affect his perceptions. Military strategists tend toward a zero-sum approach, seeing all conflict as win-or-lose struggle. Statesmen tend to include a broader spectrum of considerations, and they therefore rarely view conflict in zero-sum terms. Rather war seems to them merely an extension of diplomacy. To the extent that this latter view, posited by Clausewitz, is accurate, war may indeed be too serious a matter to be left to generals. Generals want to win, but in situations resembling the prisoners' dilemma a "winning" strategy may bring disaster.

References

1. Aron, Raymond, *Peace and War* (New York: Praeger, 1968).
2. Axelrod, Robert, *Conflict of Interest: A Theory of Divergent Goals with Applications to Politics* (Chicago: Markham, 1970).
3. Boulding, Kenneth E., *Conflict and Defense* (New York: Harper & Row, 1962), p. 25.
4. Carey, M., *A History of Rome,* 2nd ed. (New York: St. Martin's, 1957), p. 192.
5. Deutsch, Morton, "The Effect of Motivational Orientation upon Trust and Suspicion," *Human Relations,* 13 (1960), pp. 123–140.
6. Deutsch, Morton, and R. M. Krauss, "Studies of Interpersonal Bargaining," *Journal of Conflict Resolution,* 6 (1962), pp. 100–103.
7. Green, Philip, *Deadly Logic* (New York: Schocken, 1968), p. 98.
8. Guetzkow, Harold, "Some Correspondence between Simulations and 'Realities' in International Relations," in Morton Kaplan, ed., *New Approaches to International Relations* (New York: St. Martin's, 1968), pp. 202–269.
9. Haywood, O. G., Jr., "Military Decision and Game Theory," *Journal of the Operations Research Society of America,* 2 (1954), pp. 365–366.
10. Iklé, Fred C., *How Nations Negotiate* (New York: Praeger, 1967).
11. Lindberg, Leon, "Political Integration as a Multidimensional Phenomenon," *International Organization*, 24 (Autumn 1970), pp. 706–707.
12. Luce, R. Duncan, and Howard Raiffa, *Games and Decisions* (New York: Wiley, 1957).
13. Osgood, Charles E., "Escalation as a Strategy," *War/Peace Report* 5 (September 1965), p. 13.
14. Pilisuk, Mark, *et al.,* "War Hawks and Peace Doves: Alternate Resolutions of Experimental Conflicts," *Journal of*

Conflict Resolution, 9 (December 1965), pp. 491–508.

15. Rapoport, Anatol, *Fights, Games and Debates* (Ann Arbor: University of Michigan Press, 1960).

16. Rapoport, Anatol, "Formal Games as Probing Tools for Investigating Behavior Motivated by Trust and Suspicion," *Journal of Conflict Resolution,* 7 (September 1963), pp. 570–579.

17. Rapoport, Anatol, "A Note on the 'Index of Cooperation' for Prisoner's Dilemma," *Journal of Conflict Resolution,* 11 (March 1967), pp. 100–103.

18. Rapoport, Anatol, "Prospects for Experimental Games," *Journal of Conflict Resolution,* 8 (March 1964), pp. 36–49.

19. Rapoport, Anatol, and Phillip S. Dale, "The 'End' and 'Start' Effects in Iterated Prisoner's Dilemma," *Journal of Conflict Resolution,* 10 (September 1966), pp. 363–366.

20. Richardson, Lewis F., *Arms and Insecurity: A Mathematical Study of the Causes and Origins of War* (Chicago: Quadrangle, 1960), p. 12.

21. Schelling, Thomas C., *Arms and Influence* (New Haven: Yale University Press, 1966), pp. 66–67.

22. Schelling, Thomas C., *The Strategy of Conflict* (Cambridge, Mass.: Harvard University Press, 1960).

23. Shubik, Martin, ed., *Game Theory and Related Approaches* (New York: Wiley, 1964).

24. Shubik, Martin, "Game Theory and the Study of Social Behavior," in Martin Shubik, ed., *Game Theory and Related Approaches* (New York: Wiley, 1964).

25. Snyder, Glenn H., " 'Prisoner's Dilemma' and 'Chicken' Models in International Politics," *International Studies Quarterly,* 15 (March, 1971), pp. 66–103.

26. Wohlstetter, Albert, "Sin and Games in America," in Martin Shubik, ed., *Game Theory and Related Approaches* (New York: Wiley, 1964).

Suggested Reading

Axelrod, Robert, *Conflict of Interest: A Theory of Divergent Goals with Applications to Politics* (Chicago: Markham, 1970).

Iklé, Fred C., *How Nations Negotiate* (New York: Praeger, 1967).

Luce, R. Duncan, and Howard Raiffa, *Games and Decisions* (New York: Wiley, 1957).

Rapoport, Anatol, *Fights, Games and Debates* (Ann Arbor: University of Michigan Press, 1960).

Rapoport, Anatol, *Strategy and Conscience* (New York: Harper & Row, 1964).

Schelling, Thomas C., *Arms and Influence* (New Haven: Yale University Press, 1966).

Schelling, Thomas C., *The Strategy of Conflict* (Cambridge, Mass.: Harvard University Press, 1960).

Shubik, Martin, ed., *Game Theory and Related Approaches* (New York: Wiley, 1964).

Chapter 18
BARGAINING IN ANALYSES OF CONFLICT

A deterrence policy . . . constitutes a special kind of forecast, a forecast about the costs and risks that will be run by the party to be deterred, if certain actions are taken, and about the advantages that he will gain if these actions are avoided—W. W. Kaufmann [13]

Bargaining occurs both in high-risk international situations threatening war and in everyday contacts among actors. Actors continually communicate with one another, reshaping their images of one another's objectives, capabilities, and intentions. An actor may make a fundamental strategic choice to invest in nuclear weapons in order to build a deterrent or a large defense army, but the uses of these resources in influencing others involve considerations beyond those of basic investment decisions.

By now the general context of international conflict should be clear: Autonomous actors with both mutual and irreconcilable interests interact in order to attain outcomes designed at best to improve the situation for all and at worst to avert disaster for each.

DEFENSE, DETERRENCE, AND COERCIVE DIPLOMACY

Historically men have used strategies of defense and deterrence to secure objectives in international politics. Defense is a strategy for coping with an adversary's attack *after* it has occurred; by its very nature then, it is a passive strategy. An actor attempts to defend the status quo by accumulating resources to increase his capacity for warding off potential enemies. National states traditionally have used armies to defend territory and to protect such valuable resources as population, industrial capacity, and natural riches. International corporations retain phalanxes of attorneys whose task is to protect their interests against legal attacks, taxation, and nationalization by states in which production facilities and important markets are located. Defense is a passive strategy, then, because it aims at successful responses after a threatened action has been undertaken.

The capacity to defend oneself against adversaries may serve as a deterrent, but its rationale is self-protection not persuasion. Deterrence is a conscious strategy

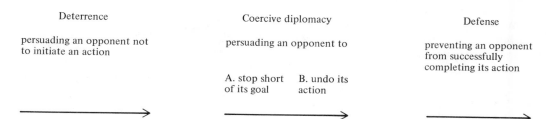

Figure 18.1. The Relations Among Coercive Diplomacy, Deterrence, and Defense
Source: Adapted from Alexander L. George, David K. Hall, and William R. Simons, *The Limits of Coercive Diplomacy* (Boston: Little, Brown, 1971), p. 24. Copyright © 1971 by Little, Brown and Company (Inc.). Reprinted by permission.

of mobilizing resources and applying threats and promises in order to influence others. It is an attempt to dissuade an opponent from an action *before* it is undertaken; in this sense, deterrence also serves a prevention objective.

Efforts to shape international norms and law in accordance with one's own values are ways in which actors quietly and undramatically pursue policies of deterrence.[1] As long as international law plays a relatively minor role in determining the behavior of international actors, however, policies aimed at persuading others through debate or moral consensus will have little deterrent effect. At the present level of development of the international system, actors' objectives are only marginally shaped by international norms. The more direct pressures of threats and rewards, coupled with capability to carry them out, remain the strongest pillar of a strategy of deterrence.

A deterrent strategy includes a set of policies for organization of weapons systems, their deployment and use, and communication to opponents of their effectiveness and one's own willingness to use them in specific contingencies. But threats to use weapons are not the only current form of deterrence. Statesmen have occasionally also sought to dissuade opponents through conciliation and appeasement. In

1938 British Prime Minister Neville Chamberlain attempted to satisfy Adolf Hitler's ambitions sufficiently to dissuade him from further aggressive behavior. The results suggest, not that Chamberlain was a fool, but too much "carrot" and too little "stick" may have the opposite effect from that intended.

Between the strategic extremes of deterrence and defense lies a range of policies called "coercive diplomacy." As defense of national territory after an attack becomes less possible and therefore less likely and because the utility of nuclear weapons in persuading adversaries not to initiate actions is more and more limited, the role of coercive diplomacy is increasing. It involves the threat or use of military force, coupled with promises designed to persuade an opponent *not to continue behavior already initiated* or *to reverse an action already completed.* President John F. Kennedy used coercive diplomacy in the Cuban missile crisis of 1962, when he sought to force the Soviet Union to withdraw missiles that had already been installed in Cuba. A strategy of deterrence would have been unsuccessful because the objective was one of securance rather than prevention. Figure 18.1 shows the relations between coercive diplomacy, on one hand, and deterrence and defense, on the other [8, pp. 1–35]. Persuading an opponent to cease an activity already underway is easier than persuading him to undo an action already completed. For example, the Arab states

---

[1] United Nations debates in which actors seek to gain acceptance for their views *before* other views can be articulated and gain acceptance illustrate this form of deterrent activity.

found it easier to persuade Israel to cease hostilities in 1967 than to withdraw from conquered territories.

In general, as we move from deterrence to defense, costs in committed resources necessary to achieve desired effects on an opponent increase. It may prove unnecessary actually to use military force as a deterrent; a credible threat is often sufficient.[2] In coercive diplomacy commitment may not be as sweeping as it is in defense, but some expenditure of resources is required. Coercive diplomacy constitutes the "murky sector" of international bargaining; it is used when deterrence has failed or when traditional defense is too costly. Limited military threats and tactics are aimed at raising costs and thus making it more difficult for an opponent to achieve his objective.

The central task of coercive diplomacy is "to create in the opponent the expectation of unacceptable cost of sufficient magnitude to erode his motivation to continue what he is doing" [8, pp. 26–27]. Alexander L. George has suggested two variants of coercive strategy, along with a number of intermediate mixes. First is the "try and see" approach (a weak variant), and second is the tacit ultimatum (a strong variant). The "try and see" approach involves a series of small incremental steps and waiting to see whether or not each has the desired effect. If the first step does not succeed, the second step follows, so that the contest slowly escalates. It is thus akin to salami tactics. By contrast, the tacit ultimatum involves a more severe formal purpose, a specific demand with an implicit or explicit time limit for compliance and a credible threat of punishment for noncompliance. The ultimatum need not be as unambiguous as that presented to Serbia by Austria-Hungary in 1914, but the intimidation must be clear and forcible.[3]

[2] If deterrence fails, however, and threats are carried out, the level of conflict may have no upper limit.
[3] For more comprehensive consideration of coercive diplomacy in specific situations, see Chapter 21.

THE EVOLUTION OF DETERRENT STRATEGY

The development of nuclear and thermonuclear weapons by the United States at the end of World War II propelled the world into a new era of international politics. Although many civilians were involved in the national mobilization efforts of World Wars I and II, populations as a whole were relatively immune from the threat of death. American national leaders still thought in terms of defense. Once war had begun, military forces were mobilized to defeat the enemy on the battlefield. There was little theoretical emphasis on avoiding war; most attention was devoted to winning it once it had begun.

Development of nuclear weapons is part of a technological revolution that has reduced the ability of nation-states to protect their civilian citizens. In the nuclear age it is no longer necessary to defeat an enemy's military forces in order to hurt his population. The bizarre but terrible prospect of two opposing armies battling one another after their homelands have been reduced to rubble now exists [25, pp. 25–26; 10]. Although the capacity to destroy the enemy totally has always theoretically existed, nuclear weapons and modern delivery systems make such destruction possible within hours instead of within months or years. Civilians have become hostages for the good behavior of their governments. One of the primary concerns of national leaders has thus been to avoid nuclear warfare while preserving their nations' essential interests and integrity.

In previous conflicts actors could afford to wait until the outbreak of war before developing strategies that would enable them to win. The United States managed to do so in both world wars. The prospect of nuclear warfare, however, requires many strategic choices to be made beforehand, for a surprise attack threatens to incapacitate the victim before his leaders can formulate a strategy. The emphasis has therefore shifted from defense to deterrence, from planning how to win a possible war to planning how to prevent an opponent from starting one. Although deterrent strategies did exist before, they have become primary in the nuclear age [19]. In contrast to coercive diplomacy, deterrence is *preventive diplomacy,* based on calculations about which combination of threats and promises will make an opponent refrain from certain behavior.

Deterrence theory lay at the heart of the cold war and has contributed to partial stability in international politics since World War II. The bipolar character of nuclear capabilities in the international system is a major source of this stability. The apparent initial success of deterrent strategy promoted competition between the United States and the Soviet Union for expanding alliances with other international actors. Later, as the two major protagonists came to recognize the increasing importance of their mutual interests, there was a partial détente in which they sought to contain local conflicts, especially those involving potential or even immediate conflict between them. In Southeast Asia and the Middle East the United States and the Soviet Union have sought either to limit the scope of the fighting or to control it (though favoring their own allies); in areas like the Congo and Cyprus, they have generally remained disengaged while intermittently supporting efforts to dampen conflict.

Two basic versions of deterrence theory have been developed: finite and minimum. Minimum-deterrence strategy is based on possession of "just enough" retaliatory capacity to do "unacceptable" damage to an enemy. Advocates of such a strategic posture argue that possession of a few relatively invulnerable weapons that can presumably destroy some of any potential enemy's cities serves as an adequate—and relatively inexpensive—deterrent, one that will not contribute to an arms race.

Those in favor of finite-deterrence strategy argue that a potential enemy may be able to improve his strategic position both quantitatively and qualitatively to the point at which he will be tempted to launch a first strike, thus destroying the defender's retaliatory capacity. They suggest that it is safer to insure against such a contingency by maintaining in readiness enough weapons to absorb an all-out first strike and still to retaliate. Neither position rests on the respected moral grounds of preventing harm to oneself by action against a guilty offender; as one critic has declared, "To be blunt, deterrence theory justifies the indiscriminate killing of innocent persons under certain circumstances" [9].

Among supporters of these two strategies there are variant positions. Finite deterrence, for example, may mean possession of enough strategic weapons not only to retaliate after an enemy counterforce attack (aimed at strategic-weapons installations, rather than at cities) but also to launch a first-strike counterforce attack, plus a reserve for destroying the opponent's cities in a later attack. Such a policy requires an enormous number of strategic weapons, as well as strategic "superiority" over the adversary. By contrast, proponents of a minimum-deterrence strategy may accept "inferiority" as still sufficient for a strategic balance. Richard M. Nixon's administration has developed a concept of strategic "sufficiency" that at first appeared to be less than "superiority" but more than "inferiority" or even "parity." The United States' decision in 1970 to go ahead with deployment of multiple-reentry nuclear warheads (MIRV), consisting of several warheads for each missile, reflected the effort to maintain "sufficient" retaliatory capability in the face of an increased number of Soviet missiles. The 1972 arms limitation agreement concluded by President Nixon and Party Secretary Leonid Brezhnev permitted the United States fewer missiles than the Soviet Union. With addition of MIRV they were deemed sufficient by American officials to deter any potential Soviet attack. It would appear that both sides have so many sophisticated strategic weapons that "superiority" and "inferiority" have become relatively meaningless terms in the arms race.

Since the mid-1950s, nuclear weapons have promoted mutual deterrence between the major blocs of actors. By tracing the development of this so-called "balance of terror" over time, we shall see how at different periods the balance has been characterized by varying degrees of stability and instability.

From 1945 to 1949 the United States had a monopoly of nuclear weapons. The Soviet Union, lacking such weapons, had only one possible strategy. The United States could have attacked or indulged in nuclear blackmail at that time, though there was no guarantee that it would then have secured its objectives. Deterrence created a severe problem for Soviet leaders. If they took Soviet nuclear inferiority very seriously, they should have been willing to sacrifice a great deal—perhaps even making large "side payments," if necessary—to persuade the United States not to attack. Soviet decision makers attempted to extricate themselves from this predicament in several ways. Foremost was their attempt to achieve a strategic choice by developing nuclear weapons themselves. In the meantime, however, other tactics were necessary. Joseph Stalin therefore refused to acknowledge the significance of nuclear weapons in modern warfare, denying that the United States had strategic advantages. In seeking to convince American leaders that he was not afraid of nuclear weapons, Stalin sought to communicate that he could not be deterred by them.

In spite of nuclear asymmetry, the Soviet Union enjoyed immense conventional military superiority, particularly in Europe. The United States could threaten to devastate Soviet cities in the event of a Russian attack on western Europe, thus deterring such an attack, but, with few long-range bombers, its ability to deliver many nuclear weapons in that period was uncertain. The Soviet Union, on the other hand, held Europe "hostage," threatening the allies with retaliation in the event of American misbehavior. The North Atlantic Treaty Organization was part of an American attempt to make its commitment to the defense of western Europe more credible to the Soviet Union, a step toward creation of a conventional deterrent.

By painting possible warfare as likely to be conventional and by claiming conventional superiority in the European theater, the Soviet Union gained a considerable measure of security. Its refusal to acknowledge the possible consequences of the American nuclear advantage rendered the Soviet Union relatively impervious to nuclear blackmail because the success of a threat is based on its communication to an adversary.

Once the Soviet Union had exploded an atomic bomb in 1949 (and a hydrogen bomb barely four years later) and the American buildup of conventional forces had been completed, a strategic balance began to emerge. The United States retained an advantage because, beside its enlarged conventional capability, it had a force of intercontinental bombers (under the Strategic Air Command) and base facilities along the Soviet periphery from which nuclear weapons could be delivered. Even as the strategic equation was being altered, however, Dwight D. Eisenhower's administration, impelled by a desire to cut military expenditures and to balance the budget, began in 1953–1954 to articulate a strategic posture largely predicated on assumptions of continued American superiority. This "new look" policy, which was to provide the United States with "more bang for the buck," stressed the role of air power and nuclear weapons at the expense of ground forces and conventional weapons. At the heart of the "new look" was the doctrine of "massive retaliation," which Secretary of State John Foster Dulles described as an effort to achieve "a maximum deterrent at a bearable cost." Dulles declared:

There is no local defense which alone will contain the mighty landpower of the Communist world. Local defense must be reinforced by the further deterrent of massive retaliatory power.

"The basic decision," said the Secretary, "was to depend primarily upon a great capacity to retaliate, instantly, by means and at places of our choosing" [30].

Increased Soviet strategic capability, the unlikelihood that the United States would rely on nuclear retaliation in small crises, and the increasing nervousness of the European allies rendered the administration's attempt to extend the range of the nuclear threat impractical. American unwillingness to assist France with direct military support during its struggle with Ho Chi Minh's guerrillas in Indochina in 1954 and the continued need for conventional forces in small crises like that in Lebanon in 1958 showed that the "new look" was obsolete and unusable virtually from the moment of its inception.

The strategy involved was based on a nuclear first strike. The United States reserved the right to launch a nuclear attack, including one against the Soviet Union, if the "communists" initiated a conventional war. In effect, this theory of "brinksmanship" had two main components. The first was a strong commitment to the principle of containing "communist" expansion; the second was a threat that the United States would unilaterally raise the stakes of a potential crisis to the point at which "things might get out of hand." It was an extremely dangerous and, as we shall see, unstable strategy, particularly as the Soviet Union also possessed nuclear weapons. As one writer has suggested, "The theory of deterrence . . . first proposes that we should frustrate our opponents by frightening them very badly and that we should then rely on their cool-headed rationality for our survival" [5]

Once the Soviets had acquired nuclear weapons, it was no longer possible or prudent for Soviet leaders to argue that nuclear technology had not altered the nature of warfare. It became increasingly clear that an actor's ability to eliminate his opponent's nuclear capability could have enormous payoffs. Paradoxically, this recognition increased the incentive for each to launch its attack first. The situation was unstable: Given circumstances in which each side could gain by

eliminating the opponent's nuclear retaliation force in a first strike, statesmen might envision a matrix like that in Figure 18.2, in which each state has only a brief time to choose between policies of restraint and attack.

"Peace" was obviously the mutually advantageous cooperative solution to this variable-sum game, but the rewards for "cheating" (launching a first strike) seemed high. In fact, the maximin solution was "mutual destruction," assuming that each country preferred that to being destroyed alone. The period from the early 1950s to the early 1960s was thus extremely unstable.

Because each side recognized the temptation of a possible first strike, both strove to increase the number of available strategies and thus the number of possible outcomes to the game. The United States attempted to retain nuclear superiority over the Soviet Union in order to be able to inflict "unacceptable damage" even after the latter had launched a surprise attack. In addition, elaborate warning systems were constructed to permit each actor to put its bombers quickly into the air in the event of attack. As long as manned bombers constituted most of the retaliatory force, these warning systems lent some stability to the international situation by making it difficult to destroy an opponent's retaliatory capability by surprise. The system remained basically unstable, however, because certainty of survival required actors to deploy their

| | Soviet Union | |
United States	Strike now	Wait to attack
Strike now	mutual destruction	Soviet Union destroyed, United States dominant in world affairs
Wait to attack	United States destroyed, Soviet Union dominant in world affairs	cold war (peace)

Figure 18.2. An Unstable Nuclear Balance

forces before they could be attacked. As failure to "retaliate" before being struck involved enormous risks, weapons were maintained on alert status and could be launched without delay or hesitation. This hair-trigger readiness was dangerous because of the perils of human or mechanical failure and "fatigue." Responsible leaders had little time to contemplate their moves. Unidentified "blips" on radar screens could bring both actors instantly to anxious alert. Soviet Foreign Minister Andrei Gromyko described in 1958 how it would be possible for "meteors and electronic interferences" to cause the Soviet Union to send its bombers aloft. Such a move would in turn cause the United States to send up its own aircraft, and each side might then conclude that the other was about to initiate an attack. In some respects the situation resembled the classical western gunfight: It put a high premium on "shooting first and asking questions afterward."

The strategic situation was altered once again by the Soviet Union's launching of the first sputnik and its testing of intercontinental ballistic missiles in 1957–1958. The ICBM permitted delivery of a nuclear weapon to its target within half an hour after its launching, thus reducing the available warning time in the United States to approximately fifteen minutes and sharply increasing strategic instability. The American response was to keep a certain percentage of its manned bombers in the air at all times and to accelerate its attempts to close the supposed "missile gap," for American leaders assumed that the Soviet Union would build as many nuclear missiles as it could.[4] Intermediate-range American missiles installed in Europe threatened the Soviet Union with devastating retaliation, though they were extremely vulnerable to an enemy first strike; as several hours were required to prepare these "first generation" missiles for launching, the incentive for preemptive or preventive attack against them was great.

[4] This assumption proved false, and the supposed missile gap "disappeared" in 1961.

In 1959 the United States began to deploy intercontinental missiles on "hardened" sites, sites relatively impervious to enemy attack (in underground silos, aboard railroad flatcars, geographically dispersed, and carried in submarines). A generation of missiles such as the Minuteman, using solid fuels that could be prepared for launching quickly, was developed shortly afterward. This advance was coupled with the dispersion of missiles and bombers to make them less vulnerable to enemy attack. As the United States began to develop a second-strike capability—the ability to absorb an enemy counterforce attack and to retaliate afterward—the strategic balance was temporarily destabilized even further. If one country could achieve a guaranteed second-strike capability before the other, it would be in an excellent position to engage in nuclear blackmail or even to launch its own first strike. The situation resembled the matrix in Figure 18.3.

This situation was disadvantageous to the Soviet Union, which then had only one acceptable strategy, whereas the United States had two possibilities open. Only the United States could "win." If the Soviet Union launched a preemptive attack, it would lose, whereas the United States could launch such an attack with some chance of victory. When the United States discovered that its adversary was also developing second-strike capability, it might have been tempted to launch a preventive first strike. Similar possibilities existed in relation to the development of antiballistic missiles and large-scale bomb-shelter programs. If only one country had an antiballistic-missile system, it would

	Soviet Union	
	Strike first	Wait
United States Strike first	mutual destruction	United States "wins"
Wait	mutual destruction	status quo (peace)

Figure 18.3. A Nuclear Balance with One Side Possessing Second-Strike Capability

	Soviet Union	
	Strike first	Wait
United States Strike first	mutual destruction	mutual destruction
Wait	mutual destruction	peace

Figure 18.4. A Strategic Balance with Mutual Possession of Second-Strike Capability

have a decisive second-strike advantage; the construction by only one side of a large-scale shelter system for its civilian population would have a slightly different destabilizing impact. The country that had taken the elaborate precaution of building such shelters would feel that it had less to fear from an enemy "counter-value" attack (attack on major population areas and industrial targets); its population would presumably no longer be "hostage," and it would therefore be immune to threats.

Both sides had developed some second-strike capability by 1963. Solid-fuel missiles at "hardened" sites reduced the incentive for either to attack first. The strategic calculus shifted to one of mutual "terror." Under these circumstances "peace" became a stable solution to the "game" because there were only negative payoffs for the actor who risked a first strike (see Figure 18.4).

In contrast to events in 1941, when Japan gained a substantial military advantage by its surprise attack on the United States' Pacific fleet at Pearl Harbor, today the global system offers few rewards for surprise attack, particularly to the superpowers.[5] The ability of each adversary to absorb an enemy attack and still to retaliate with deadly effectiveness

against enemy cities makes it unwise for either to contemplate a first strike; consequently, the fear of such an event declined in the United States and the Soviet Union during the 1960s.

In this atmosphere of reduced anxiety neither side requires weapons with hair-trigger mechanisms. Instead, sophisticated command and control procedures have been developed to reduce the probability of war arising from technical failure, human incompetence, or individual insanity. Invulnerable weapons systems reduce the need for rapid responses during crises, thus giving leaders time to consider alternatives and to negotiate.

Similarly, the development of such devices as space satellites, which enable adversaries to spy upon each other easily and to detect military preparations more accurately, makes surprise attack even less likely. When a state knows what a potential enemy is doing almost immediately, it is less likely to react rashly because of suspicions about the adversary's intentions. There is less need for instant alerts, during which human and technical errors are most likely. Mutual exchange of "secret" intelligence is in fact so useful a stabilizing force that it has even been suggested that the superpowers should voluntarily exchange spies who can report back to their governments.[6]

The international system of the 1970s is characterized by greater military stability than in any previous period since World War II. Paradoxically, this stability may be the result of improved weapons systems and the many nuclear devices that currently exist. If each side had only a few missiles, a quantitative lead would be significant, and the incentive for launching preemptive or preventive attacks would be greater.[7] Conversely, the

[5] In some arenas, however, comparable stability is lacking. In 1967, for example, the importance of air power in the Middle East gave Israel a strong incentive for a preemptive strike against Egyptian bases. After the June 1967 war the continuing importance of air power in the region led Israel to launch air strikes against Egypt to prevent the latter from acquiring parity or superiority in such power. Israel has thus followed a preventive strategy.

[6] In one instance, when United States radar picked up signals indicating possible enemy missiles, a check revealed that Nikita S. Khrushchev was attending a diplomatic party, and fears were dampened.
[7] A preemptive attack is a first strike initiated out of fear that the adversary is on the verge of doing the same. A preventive attack is an attempt to defeat or cripple an adversary before he acquires greater capability.

possession by each side of thousands of retaliatory weapons makes it virtually impossible for either to eliminate the other's ability to respond.

Not that strategic stability is guaranteed. The development of new weapons systems with greater accuracy and destructive potential could bring about new periods of dangerous instability. Technological developments of a qualitative nature may generate instability by threatening the second-strike capability of one side.[8] A case in point is the development by the Soviet Union of the capability to destroy American space satellites.

COMMUNICATIONS

Messages must be sent and received if threats and promises are to be conveyed and if capacity and will are to be confirmed. Communications are also important when mutual interests are perceived and negotiations likely. Communications may help to modify mutual expectations about the shared range of acceptable outcomes and to encourage the search for prominent solutions that "stand out." Signals from one actor to another are often verbal, but nonverbal signaling is also important; particularly in making one's intentions clear, "actions speak louder than words." Physical acts do not have any meaning as such, but in a given sequence of events, particular behavior may assume additional meaning from the "logic" of the situation or from a "fit" with shared images or memories of the past.

Perceptions of intentions are critical. When France engages in military maneuvers near the Swiss border, officials in Berne seldom lift an eyebrow, yet when British troops hold joint exercises in

Kenya, Somalia and Tanzania express alarm.[9] Behavior is susceptible to varying interpretations; its timing, the logic of the situation (interpretations emerging from the context of events in which an action occurs), and shared memories lend meaning to individual acts [15].

Most communication among international actors consists of both verbal and nonverbal behavior; often each reinforces the other. Sékou Touré, an African leftist leader, reportedly told President John F. Kennedy that the United States should pay attention to what Guinea *does* (for example, welcoming Peace Corps volunteers and expelling the Russian ambassador), rather than what it *says* (for example, denouncing American imperialism) [2]. In international politics mutual suspicion is common, and an actor's evaluation of verbal communications is based on both previous and current nonverbal behavior.

Communications can be used in bargaining to further an actor's objectives or to inhibit an adversary from achieving his own. For example, simple refusal to acknowledge receipt of some message or feigned ignorance of it can be a powerful bargaining tool. Urban pedestrians have long understood that one strategy in crossing a street crowded with slow-moving traffic is to avoid "seeing" or "hearing" approaching automobiles. By feigning ignorance they can usually cross, for drivers have few ways of threatening pedestrians, short of running them down. The analogous behavior in international politics is to feign ignorance of a deterrent threat, either by discounting the usefulness of nuclear weapons or by refusing to believe that the other state will dare to use them. If an actor is unaware of a threat or does not understand it, deterrence fails.

Another way to manipulate communication is to act irrationally or blindly, according to an inner impulse or a predetermined formula. This tactic prevents an opponent from improving his expecta-

---

[8] Qualitative changes lead to *substantial* differences: Just as nuclear weapons are qualitatively different from conventional ones, missiles are qualitatively different from manned bombers. The significance of quantitative changes was elaborated in the path-breaking article by Albert Wohlstetter, "The Delicate Balance of Terror," *Foreign Affairs*, 37 (January 1959), pp. 211–234.

[9] See *East African Standard*, January 24–27, 1971.

tions and is most frequently pursued by leaders willing to accept high risks. Adolf Hitler's unpredictability is legendary. "If France and England strike," he once declared, "let them do so. It is a matter of complete indifference to me" [4, p. 464]. His followers understood that his daring and unwillingness to bow to apparently adverse strategic calculations were responsible for Germany's bloodless victory in the Czechoslovak-Sudeten crisis of 1938. "The genius of the Führer," wrote General Alfred Jodl, "and his determination not to shun even a world war have again won victory without the use of force. The hope remains that the incredulous, the weak and the doubters have been converted . . ." [4, p. 469].

From time to time the leaders of the People's Republic of China, which suffers from strategic "inferiority," have dismissed the role of nuclear weapons as a determinant of the outcomes in future wars. China's own military weakness has been obscured by rhetoric about the American "paper tiger" in the Far East. Fears of Chinese "irrationality" have led American decision makers to pay more attention to China than its military capacity merits. Proposals to develop an "anti-Chinese" antiballistic-missile system around American cities are based on assessments of probable Chinese behavior; if the Chinese were "rational" they would be effectively deterred by American ability to destroy their country in a retaliatory strike, as the Russians have been.

By refusing to acknowledge or to "understand" their own strategic inferiority, Adolf Hitler, Joseph Stalin, and Mao Tse-tung have made themselves less vulnerable to the deterrent threats of their adversaries. The effect of this apparent irrationality has been described by one observer:

A high Chinese official was reported as saying that China could profitably fight a nuclear war, because even if the United States killed 300 million Chinese, there would still be . . . 300 million left. This statement . . . sent shivers through the western world, for it opened up the horrifying prospect of an enemy who could not be deterred. . . . Should the United States ever confront China armed with nuclear weapons and possessed of so grim a value scale, it will literally be faced with annihilation or surrender. [32]

The problem with "irrationality" is that the second actor may become convinced that bargaining is impossible and that both will engage in a zero-sum game, in which the first actor menaces life and limb. The former may then decide to cripple the enemy (or at least his offensive capability). The Soviet Union briefly but seriously considered a preventive attack to eliminate China's entire nuclear capability. Short of launching a first strike, however, the adversary of an apparently irrational actor faces difficult strategic choices because they are rationally calculable only when expectations are stable.

One of the most important uses of communications in bargaining is in manipulating the outcomes of competitive interaction. Commitments can be particularly effective in bargaining, as each side attempts to manipulate the other's perception of the interaction so that one's own determination makes continuation of the game seem less attractive. An army that "burns its bridges" behind it communicates unmistakably that it cannot retreat and that the enemy must fight if it is to advance farther. Similarly, a diplomat may suggest that he can make no further concessions because of the probable reaction of public opinion in his country or because the legislature that must approve any agreement will not go along. Such commitments effectively bind an actor to a limited range of possible outcomes and restrict the alternatives open to an adversary. They may thus increase the adversary's incentive to select the best alternative among those remaining.

Coercive and reward influence is the key to manipulation of outcomes. In bargaining, threats and promises are often used in tandem. The threat is a form of anticipated coercion; force need not be used but only signalled as a possibility if future behavior is not modified as desired. Successful threats are themselves inexpensive in terms of resource allocation, but, to make them believable, it is often necessary to have an enormous stockpile of military hardware. A promise, on the other hand, is an anticipated reward and does require investment of resources to fulfill it. Promises and threats communicate an actor's willingness to invest resources at some future time.

Threats and promises are effective only when their contents are clearly communicated to the opponent and only when the latter fully understands what he must do in order to avoid punishment or to gain rewards. Threats and promises must therefore be clearly linked to the initiating actor's objectives. His credibility can be maintained only if he carries out his threat in the event of the opponent's defiance. The American air strikes against North Vietnamese naval bases in August 1964 constituted such a clear and unmistakable signal, closely related to the alleged North Vietnamese naval attacks on American vessels in the Gulf of Tonkin. Similarly, promises must be carried out promptly and in good faith when the adversary complies.

Cooperative solutions are facilitated by communications. Communications take the simple form of common expectations between two actors. For instance, two people may be told that they will both receive prizes if, without speaking, they choose the same side of a coin ("heads" or "tails"), and that, if they actually select different sides of the coin, they will receive nothing. Cooperation is necessary to achieve the payoff, but neither person can coordinate his choice with that of the other. On the basis of shared memories and experiences they may nevertheless be able to achieve tacit cooperation and win the prizes. Each might pick "heads," expecting the other to do the same.

In crisis bargaining certain solutions seem to both parties to be "prominent" or obviously "fair" even without overt communications.[10] In sharing a reward, for example, two actors may find a fifty-fifty division, or "splitting the difference," reasonable and immediately attractive, without communicating. Even at the height of the cold war, the "iron curtain" served to limit the scope of the Soviet-American confrontation, despite rhetoric to the contrary. It was prominent because it marked the point to which Soviet troops had advanced westward and American and British troops eastward by the end of World War II. Similarly, the Berlin wall was a prominent solution to tension in Germany, one that the gaming division of the U.S. Defense Department had anticipated in scenarios.

The concept of a "prominent" solution seems particularly applicable to limiting war without negotiation. Geographical positions, the number of actors involved, and the types of weapons used, for instance, may tacitly limit the spread of conflict, thus permitting actors to communicate their intentions and their limits. Each participant can simply, by means of his actions, signal his intention to cooperate in some way. For example, American operations in the Korean War were limited to the Korean peninsula; American planes did not bomb north of the Yalu river (on the Chinese border), and in return American aircraft carriers were never attacked. Nevertheless, the two sides had never negotiated or formally agreed to such limitations. Conducting the war as a "police action" under United Nations auspices limited the war still further. Moreover, United Nations forces did not use nuclear, chemical, or bacteriological weapons—all available in the American arsenal.[11] Similarly, during World War II, which came as close as

---

[10] See Thomas C. Schelling, *The Strategy of Conflict* (Cambridge, Mass.: Harvard University Press, 1960), pp. 53–80, for an excellent analysis of the concepts of tacit bargaining and prominent solutions.

[11] The United States never formally declared war against either North Korea or China. Similarly, there was no formal declaration of war during the Vietnam conflict.

has any modern war to being "total," both sides observed certain tacit limitations; neither side employed poison gas, for example.[12]

COMMITMENT

Communication of intent is important in strategies of deterrence and coercive diplomacy. A strategic threat or promise requires assertion of commitment to one or another set of responses to initiatives by the other actor. Statesmen will insist, "We are *committed* to peace if you just behave thus and so." Commitment strengthens the certainty that promises or threats will be carried out should the specified circumstances arise. Statements of intent, like the Monroe Doctrine, and formal alliances are devices for strengthening an actor's resolve, beside conveying his determination to others. Commitments are thus important steps in a bargaining sequence and represent one way of manipulating both domestic calculations and analyses by others.

Commitment binds an actor to a certain strategy counter to one of an opponent's possible strategies. If a commitment is challenged, it may be necessary to carry out a threat, possibly to the detriment of both actors. If an actor has made threats or promises without carrying them out in the past, his credibility will be low. In a poker game, for example, a player whose bluff is successfully called on several occasions will find it difficult to bluff again. "Meeting one's commitments," even when they no longer seem wise, is valuable under certain circumstances in order to ensure the credibility of other commitments. When the general loss of

credibility is likely to be higher than the concrete loss from carrying out an otherwise unimportant threat, it may be rational to behave in a way that seems foolish when it is assessed in isolation from other considerations. There may at least be some benefit for the future, in the form of an enhanced bargaining reputation. In the first draft of a policy paper on American aims in Vietnam written for Secretary of Defense Robert S. McNamara in March 1965, Assistant Secretary of Defense John T. McNaughton concluded that "70 percent" of the American aim was "to avoid humiliating U.S. defeat (to our reputation as a guarantor)" [26]. American behavior, then, was partly motivated by the desire to enhance other commitments, despite higher costs in Vietnam.

Most threats are made in the expectation that they will not have to be fulfilled. If an actor is dealing with a rational opponent, commitment may be enough to ensure the desired outcome, no matter how dangerous carrying out the threat may seem. When an opponent is irrational, however, commitment is less useful and will not increase the probability of "winning."

The credibility of commitments is particularly important to an actor who threatens. Fooling or bluffing opponents involves convincing them that one is unalterably bound to a particular course of action; the simplest means is to *be* bound to that position. A bluff is most effective when it is not only a bluff, and a strong bargaining position results from public and irrevocable commitment to a course of action. In the game of chicken one driver can effectively communicate his commitment by throwing away the steering wheel; this action leaves no doubt in his opponent's mind about what he is going to do. His commitment becomes credible. The more credible a commitment, the higher is the probability that it will be honored by both sides. Such a commitment, however, limits an actor's future options, and creates a dilemma. Because information is at best imperfect,

[12] Several other such limitations were observed during World War II. Both sides respected the neutrality of Switzerland, Sweden, and Portugal because these countries served as convenient "listening posts," where adversaries could learn of one another's intentions and communicate with one another. Also, even while Great Britain and Germany were bombing each other, each spared the other's most famous university city—Oxford in England and Heidelberg in Germany.

an actor may be unwilling to wed himself to a course of action that may prove disastrous to himself, as well as to his opponent. Yet, if he does not commit himself forcibly enough, his resolution may be doubted.

Credibility can be achieved in various ways. An actor may establish "a point of no return" in time or in space: a point at which the commitment will surely be fulfilled. The "point of no return" may be a time limit, as in an ultimatum, or it may be a mutually recognized geographical boundary like a border or river. Two situations described in Chapter 19 ("The Chip on the Shoulder" and "The Bribe") include such points. When they are reached, the actor will carry out his threat or promise. An actor can also create a "trip wire" like token military forces, which must be overrun by an adversary seeking to alter the status quo. In effect, he is establishing a point of no return for the adversary.

Most of these methods do not bind an actor irrevocably to fulfill his threats or promises. To achieve complete credibility, an actor must render himself incapable of changing his mind and must communicate this intransigence to an opponent. In the film *Doctor Strangelove* the Soviet Union possesses a computer that will *automatically* initiate nuclear retaliation if the Soviet Union is attacked. The Soviet response is "out of human hands." The existence of this machine has not, however, been revealed to the people of the United States. The difficulties inherent in such irrevocable commitments are illustrated in the outcome of the film: The world is destroyed in an "accidental war."[13]

Complete credibility may be undesirable as it locks an actor into future positions from which he may wish to escape. The judgment whether or not an actor is bluffing must be subjective. France's decision to develop an independent nuclear deterrent arose partly from President Charles

de Gaulle's judgment that the American commitment to defend western Europe was not entirely firm or would not remain firm for the indefinite future. Indeed, most difficulties in preventing proliferation of nuclear weapons revolve around the question, Will one actor risk self-destruction in the defense of another?

The credibility of an actor's commitments depends largely upon his behavior. When his interests are obviously at stake, verbal commitment may be unnecessary, but when such interests are unclear, words may not suffice. The Communist Chinese threat to intervene in the Korean War was incredible to most American leaders in 1950, yet, largely because of the Korean intervention, the Chinese threat to defend North Vietnam in the 1970s has been believed. Chinese willingness to use troops in Korea convinced the United States more than any verbal communication could have done that China is prepared to intervene in Asia wherever its interests are threatened. In general the credibility of a commitment is proportional to the actor's certain losses should the opponent fail to modify his behavior.

It has been suggested that overall military superiority is essential to make commitments credible and that specific signals are helpful. But it is clear that in the example of deterrence, visible bonds between the actor and the area that he wishes to defend are vital. No one doubts, for example, that the United States would retaliate against an attack on its homeland, but the American will to deter attacks elsewhere has been questioned. When obvious interdependence has been generated by military cooperation or close political, economic, and cultural ties, the credibility of the American commitment to deterrence has remained high. The greater the interdependence and the longer its duration, the greater the credibility of a commitment will be [23, 24].

There are basically two kinds of commitment [31]. The first is "situational," commitment arising from the logic of a situation. Why does the United States not have to reiterate its determination to re-

[13] A similar situation has been described by Herman Kahn in his discussions of the "Doomsday Machine," the "Doomsday-in-a-Hurry Machine," and the "Homicide Pact Machine" [11].

taliate if attacked? Because any other course of action would clearly be against its interests. Certain areas of the world—like western Europe, Canada, and Japan—are important to the United States, regardless of treaties and other expressions of commitment. Any would-be aggressor understands that the United States will respond to threats in these areas, whether or not such a commitment is expressed. Similarly, the United States knows the importance of eastern Europe to the Soviet Union; even if the Warsaw Pact did not exist, the United States would be unlikely to interfere with Soviet interests in that area because of the high probability of Soviet response.

"Nonsituational" commitment, on the other hand, is defined more by the will and resolution of the actor than by any specific set of circumstances. The view is that the logic of a situation is never sufficient to guarantee credibility and that, therefore, commitments must be articulated and carried out. Commitment is viewed as a test of an actor's willingness to keep his word. Even if a specific commitment becomes a net liability, it is necessary to uphold it in order to preserve one's bargaining reputation. The nonsituational commitment, then, demonstrates an actor's resources and preferences for expenditures. If he reneges on one commitment, how can his allies and enemies trust his word in the future? Such a commitment is perceived as reflecting the actor's dedication and will. A commitment to punish aggression in all places, which is the assumption basic to the theory of collective security, can heavily burden a state. When this principle is at stake—and when one must take up the cudgels wherever peace is threatened—even when the specific engagement is not in one's short-run interest—"overcommitment" may tax both the resources and the credibility of the actor.

Threats and promises modify the strategic choices available to both adversary and initiator. In building coalitions, for example, one state frequently offers inducements in the form of "side payments," thus encouraging other states to accept a common strategy. This agreement may limit the range of strategies available to the alliance.

Making a commitment "public" can help to increase its force. President Kennedy announced publicly in 1961 that the United States would *not* supply air cover for an invasion of Cuba. During the Bay of Pigs invasion he was under considerable pressure to do so, but his earlier commitment made the cost incredibly prohibitive.

THE PROSPECT OF WAR AS A BARGAINING COUNTER

Commitment, threats, and communications all play a part in bargaining. The calculated use of violence is also important. In today's world, violence ranges from clandestine espionage to such brutal murders of civilians as have been committed by Germans in World War II and by Americans at My Lai and other Vietnamese villages. Uncontrolled brutality should be considered separately from violence as a bargaining counter. History is studded with examples of pure fights, activities that make sense only in true zero-sum games. But wanton destruction and "pure" revenge have been relatively infrequent. Arabs fighting the Jihad purportedly used to poison the wells of their enemies—until they were forced to retreat for the first time! Genghis Khan used to destroy completely the peoples that he conquered until he found that they were more valuable alive. For example, he could place captured women and children in front of his advancing hordes, which reduced his own losses and often paralyzed the will of his enemies. The European crusaders of the twelfth century also used violence wantonly. After suffering heavy losses at the siege of Jerusalem, they set the city afire and raped the women. Had they had time to consider the matter, they might well have only looted the town and married the women. Fortunately, such purposeless violence has been rare; it characterizes the acts of angry men or madmen who actually approve of extermination, and men wearing organizational blinders who can ignore the consequences of drawing zones on maps and labeling them "free fire."

The deliberate use of violence has frequently been a tool of diplomacy, however, designed to influence the opponent's behavior in conditions comparable to those of a variable-sum game. We have already noted how important threats of violence are when one wants an opponent to act peacefully or to refrain from certain behavior. Occasionally actual violence may be used to demonstrate one's will or capability as part of a strategy of deterrence. More often, violence may be incorporated into policies designed to force an opponent to surrender something that he values or to cease a particular undertaking. It is then part of coercive diplomacy. The most popular image of violence in international politics is of violence used to force an opponent to surrender, that is, to yield his decision-making capacity. The popular notions that war should somehow be decisive, yielding total victory, and that the military should direct it have obscured the basic fact that the use of violence to achieve such a broad objective as enemy surrender is rare.

One major trend in violent confrontations among international actors has been diffusion of the effects of conflict among all segments of the population. During most of the eighteenth century, wars were considered primarily engagements between two large military machines, preferably in thinly populated areas. When an army lost, the king's power to defend his state and his person was considerably diminished, and he generally acceded to the limited demands of his opponents. The outcome frequently mattered little to the average person, whose life was barely touched. In the French Revolution, however, the population exhibited a greater sense of participation, and war began to involve civilian soldiers. In the twentieth

century, wars have involved not only men drafted to defend their nation but also noncombatants. In World War II, for example, Hitler sent V-1 rockets ("buzz bombs") across the English channel, and allied planes fire-bombed cities like Tokyo and Dresden. In the Vietnam War killing civilians is commonplace; the Viet Cong plants bombs in crowded places and terrorizes whole villages, and American planes drop napalm on villages suspected of supporting the Viet Cong.

Violence against noncombatants may be an effective form of coercion; the resulting terror may induce the opponent to comply. The German bombing of refugees in the Spanish Civil War and in Belgium and France in 1940 had this effect. The "balance of terror" is the caution created by recognition of the damage that each side can do to the other. The only sane purpose of nuclear weapons is to deter. They cannot preserve values, lives, or property. Americans cannot save Washington, D.C., or Philadelphia with bombs and rockets; they can only hope to deter attack on these cities by threatening retaliation against Kiev and Moscow.

The prospect that the United States or the Soviet Union will be forced to submit, as Germany was after World Wars I and II, is remote. For that matter, such a fate is unlikely to befall any major national actor. Today a few men in an antiseptic room can initiate action that required multitudes to accomplish a few decades ago. In World War II, 50 million men and women were killed. In a nuclear World War III, that many Americans alone are likely to be killed in one day. It is not simply that future wars threaten more deaths; they threaten more deaths infinitely more quickly. To illustrate this point, Schelling has adopted a gruesome example:

Japan was defenseless by August 1945. With a combination of bombing and blockade, eventually invasion, and if necessary the deliberate spread of disease, the United States could probably have exterminated the population of the Japanese islands without nuclear weapons. . . .

Against defenseless people there is not much that nuclear weapons can do that cannot be done with an ice pick. And it would not have strained our Gross National Product to do it with ice picks. [25, p. 19]

Massive violence remains a threat, a deterrent that is, in the late President Eisenhower's word, "unthinkable." The "balance of terror" involves a contest of nerves and will; the use of violence is limited either to periodic crises or to debilitating bargaining for limited objectives.[14] In order to understand the significance of crises and limited warfare in the nuclear age, however, the salient features of "unthinkable" warfare must also be understood.

THINKING ABOUT UNTHINKABLE WARS

Technological factors partly account for the credibility of an actor's second-strike capability. But psychological factors are also important. Strategic capability does not ensure that an actor will be prepared to use nuclear weapons. It is generally assumed that both the United States and the Soviet Union would resort to nuclear retaliation in the event of attacks on their home territories, but this assumption is not as certain as it may appear at first. If an enemy first strike succeeded in destroying an actor's major cities but left his second-strike capability intact, what beside revenge would prompt the victim to retaliate? These weapons could be used only to wreak immense damage and the threat of their use, to extract indemnification. The credibility of an actor's deterrence policy is further reduced, when his own homeland is not the one threatened. Would the United States risk its own cities for London, Paris, or Berlin? Would a nuclear threat be a credible deterrent to guerrilla attacks in Asia or coups d'état in Latin America? Credibility clearly de-

pends upon two beliefs by a potential attacker: beliefs in the defender's capacity for destruction and in his willingness to use this capacity under certain circumstances.

There have been attempts to modify one implicit assumption in our analysis of the strategic balance between the United States and the Soviet Union: the assumption that total nuclear warfare is the only alternative to peace between the United States and the Soviet Union. It is *not* justified by current Soviet-American relations, however, nor is it justified by relations between the superpowers and lesser actors, though it informs the views of many Americans. This assumption is largely the product of a perceptual bias that has encouraged both sides to view the contest as a zero-sum game. Since World War II there have been many conflicts that have led to violence, yet none has resulted in nuclear exchange.

The importance of perceptual bias is illustrated by American images of the "communist" threat. This problem is particularly acute because the possibility of simplistic and ethnocentrically biased interpretation is high. An actor may "see" a gain for his adversary as a loss for himself, even though he has not really lost anything. This kind of bias was pronounced in the thinking of both the United States and the Soviet Union during the early years of the cold war, when slogans like "better dead than red" reflected zero-sum thinking. The high tension between the United States and the Soviet Union after World War II generated psychological blocks that made it difficult for either side to recognize changing international reality. Indeed, leaders on both sides consistently denied that changes were taking place. Stereotype thinking was common, and positive information about adversaries was ignored. One analyst discovered that when American school children were asked why Russians planted trees along roads, they answered that the trees "made work for the prisoners," whereas they believed that

[14] Not that such conflicts do not involve enormous loss of life. Recent civil wars in Nigeria, Pakistan, and Indonesia show that they do.

Americans planted trees for shade [3].[15] Stereotyping was accompanied by a kind of paranoia. Each side interpreted the proposals of the adversary as part of an effort to achieve gains at its own expense. The mere fact that the Soviet Union proposed general disarmament, for example, led American leaders to regard the move as a communist trap [29].

In the years immediately after World War II the spread of Soviet influence in eastern Europe and China was interpreted by many American officials as a gain for the Soviet Union and therefore as a loss for the United States. In the world "pie" a gain for the communists seemed to represent an automatic loss for the "free world." This climate of opinion distorted the policy of "containment" originally adopted by the United States (see Figure 18.5).

A more sober appraisal of postwar developments reveals that the "free world" did not exist as a coherent system and that the noncommunist sector of the globe actually included many independent countries divided by different systems of government and political interests. The United States could not "lose" China or eastern Europe, for it had never "had" them in the first place; but this notion of loss was widely accepted in the United States. As Figure 18.6 suggests, both the Soviet Union and the United States vastly expanded their influence and, as a result, found themselves in confrontation in a world without other "great" powers. Their differing ideologies fostered distrust, and escalating responses resulted in the cold war.[16] To a large extent, American and Soviet moves were *not* interdependent.

[15] For more information on the concept of the "mirror image," as well as on national images in general, see various articles in Herbert C. Kelman, ed., *International Behavior* (New York: Holt, Rinehart, and Winston, 1965), pp. 45–335. For changing American views of the Soviet Union, see Peter G. Filene, ed., *American Views of Soviet Russia, 1917–1965* (Homewood, Ill.: Dorsey, 1968).
[16] For a game-theory analogy to the cold war, see John C. Harsanyi, "Game Theory and the Analysis of International Conflict," *Australian Journal of Politics and History*, 11 (December 1965), pp. 292–304.

1944

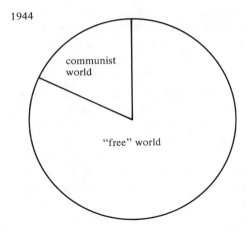

1950

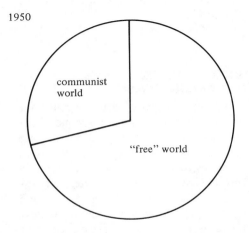

Figure 18.5. A Western Cold-War View of the Years 1944–1950

Secretary of Defense Robert S. McNamara's policy of building a diversified array of conventional weapons systems during the early years of the Kennedy administration was partly intended to provide the United States with the means to respond moderately to moderate provocations and to end American reliance on nuclear weapons that might compel unnecessarily large responses to minor incursions. This "damage-limiting" policy was intended to convey tacitly to Soviet leaders that the United States would not inevitably respond to an adversary's conventional military initiatives with nuclear weapons. It had the double effect of making American commitments more credible

1944

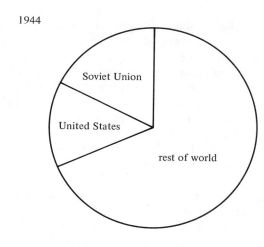

1950

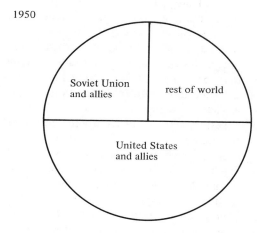

Figure 18.6. A Revised View of the Years 1944–1950

An Escalation Ladder: A Generalized Scenario[17]
Aftermaths

Civilian central wars
44. Spasms or insensate war
43. Some other kinds of controlled general war
42. Civilian-devastation attack
41. Augmented disarming attack
40. Countervalue salvo
39. Slow-motion countercity war
City-Targeting Threshold

Military central wars
38. Unmodified counterforce attack
37. Counterforce attack with avoidance
36. Constrained disarming attack
35. Constrained force-reduction salvo
34. Slow-motion counterforce war
33. Slow-motion counterproperty war
32. Formal declaration of general war
Central-War Threshold

Exemplary central attacks
31. Reciprocal reprisals
30. Complete evacuation (approximately 95 percent)
29. Exemplary attacks on population
28. Exemplary attacks against property
27. Exemplary attacks on military
26. Demonstration attack on zone of interior
Central-Sanctuary Threshold

Bizarre crises
25. Evacuation (approximately 70 percent)
24. Unusual, provocative, and significant countermeasures
23. Local nuclear war, military
22. Declaration of limited nuclear war
21. Local nuclear war, exemplary
"No Nuclear Use" Threshold

Intense crises
20. "Peaceful" worldwide embargo or blockade
19. "Justifiable" counterforce attack
18. Spectacular show or demonstration of force
17. Limited evacuation (approximately 20 percent)
16. Nuclear ultimatums
15. Barely nuclear war
14. Declaration of limited conventional war
13. Large compound escalation

[17] The source for this ladder is Herman Kahn, *On Escalation: Metaphor and Scenarios* (New York: Praeger, 1965), p. 39; published in the British Commonwealth by Phaidon Press Limited. Reprinted by permission.

and of lessening others' fear of rash American behavior. The new programs permitted the United States to abandon the Eisenhower-Dulles strategy of "massive retaliation" in favor of a strategy of "flexible response," in which American leaders could "maintain their options" during crises. "We . . . felt strongly," McNamara has written, "that the decision to employ such nuclear weapons should not be forced upon us simply because we had no other means to cope with conflict" [16].

Herman Kahn has suggested a forty-four-step "escalation ladder" culminating in full-fledged nuclear exchange.

12. Large conventional war (or actions)
11. Superready status
10. Provocative breaking off of diplomatic relations

  "Nuclear War Unthinkable" Threshold

Traditional crises
9. Dramatic military confrontations
8. Violent harassment
7. "Legal" harassment, retortions
6. Significant mobilization
5. Show of force
4. Hardening of positions, confrontations of wills

  "Don't Rock the Boat" Threshold

Subcrisis maneuvering
3. Solemn and formal declarations
2. Political, economic, and diplomatic gestures
1. Ostensible crisis

  Disagreement (cold war)

A rational actor would move up this ladder to the point at which he found continuing interaction no longer worth the costs of confrontation. In the extreme instance in which his homeland was threatened, he might move all the way to the top. Kahn has suggested several natural stopping points, or psychological "thresholds," that indicate quantum (qualitative) increases in the level of violence. But there is no logically compelling reason why conflict should be stopped before it reaches the highest levels if the push toward escalation—promoted by high stakes, domestic pressures, and high risks —is strong enough. Local conflicts can thus still be extremely dangerous [12, 22]. Mutual recognition of such thresholds can, however, facilitate tacit bargaining to halt escalation.

In particular, the "no nuclear use" threshold has been extremely important; leaders on both sides have been reluctant to proceed beyond this threshold for fear of total nuclear war. Although some strategists have favored the use of "tactical" nuclear weapons, as did Henry Kissinger from 1957 to 1961, the problems inherent in such use have generally led to reversals.[18] It would surely be difficult to

achieve mutual recognition of such limitations as "tactical nuclear weapons" or weapons of less than one megaton. One-megaton weapons are only slightly different from two- or even three-megaton weapons. The threshold between use and abstention from nuclear weapons, on the other hand, is clear.

Kahn has argued that other thresholds beside "no nuclear use" may be serviceable. Before 1963 such distinctions would have been virtually impossible to maintain because of the rapidity with which both sides would have lost control in a nuclear exchange. But recent development of mutual second-strike capabilities, by eliminating many previous time constraints, have increased the possibility that such thresholds as the central sanctuary, the central war, and city targeting may become tacit bargaining points. Escalation may result in destruction, first, of an actor's allies; second, of his military bases; third, of his outlying industrial plants; and, finally, of his population centers. At each stage there may be a pause for both sides to consider whether or not to halt hostilities. Such thinking is hypothetical at best, an extension of Carl Maria von Clausewitz's idea that different levels of violence can be used to achieve different objectives.

One trenchant criticism of such strategic thinking is that it treats nuclear warfare as "thinkable." Strategists influence the thinking of political leaders; in planning for contingencies like those suggested in the escalation ladder, an actor may tacitly accept the possibility of nuclear warfare and thus reduce popular revulsion toward it. Indeed, one critic has argued that nuclear war "could not occur if the strategists of both sides did not put forward convincing arguments about the necessity of possessing 'nuclear capabilities' and the will to use them" [20]. The actor, by treating nuclear warfare as feasible, may create a self-fulfilling prophecy; Kahn, on the other hand, believes that thinking about nuclear warfare makes it *less* likely.

---

[18] See Henry Kissinger, *Nuclear Weapons and Foreign Policy* (New York: Harper & Row,

1957), in which Kissinger states the position that he subsequently retracted.

STRATEGIC BARGAINING
OUT OF CONTROL

Fear and suspicion generated by conflict may impair actors' control. Escalation of violence may alter the participants' objectives, and stress may impair feedback mechanisms, thus preventing an actor from responding to a situation rationally. The resulting loss of control may generate unexpected and destabilizing behavior by one or both parties to a conflict. High stakes, uncertainty, and structurally unstable situations increase the possibility that controls will break down.

As the memories and psychological environment of an actor can distort his images of the world, threats and promises intended to influence him may not have that effect. The actor may fail to understand a threat or may interpret the promise of a reward as an attempt at coercion. American foreign aid, even when intended as rewards or as gestures of generosity, has often been interpreted by recipients—many of them only recently free from colonial domination—as an instrument of control.

Threats sometimes distort an adversary's ability to recognize signals and to respond rationally, for coercion can generate fear and hostility in the recipient; rewards often have the opposite effect. Continued application of either coercion or promises may condition the subject to react either favorably or hostilely to all further such stimuli [28]. Coercion disorients the subject. In human beings past experience conditions approaches to new stimuli. If coercion alone is used, "It becomes evident that future responses [to stimuli] will be made from this affective condition [fear and hostility] . . . with the probability of desperation behavior becoming greater and greater" [21]. Too often in coercive diplomacy the carrot is overlooked and the stick overemphasized. Exclusive reliance on coercion may produce an atmosphere of general fear and hostility. When journalists refer to periods of "high tension" they suggest that such an atmosphere dominates the psychological environment of the actors. Reliance by both Israel and the Arabs on coercion in their mutual relations since 1948 has created such a climate in the Middle East; a similar climate exists in Ulster between Protestants and Catholics. Social proximity and inequality between two groups promote such hostility; it then becomes difficult to bargain or behave rationally toward each other.

A mix of rewards and coercion seems to promise minimum distortion of communication between actors. The original concept of "containment" espoused by George F. Kennan in 1947 was aimed at preventing Soviet expansion without creating an undesirable psychological environment for the Soviet Union. As Kennan has written:

[T]he main element of any United States policy toward the Soviet Union must be that of a long-term, patient but firm and vigilant containment of Russian expansive tendencies. It is important to note, however, that such a policy has nothing to do with outward histrionics: with threats or blustering or superfluous gestures of outward "toughness." [14]

The Soviet Union was to be punished for undesirable behavior, yet a general environment of mutual suspicion was to be avoided; only Soviet attempts to expand would be opposed.

A psychological environment of mutual fear and hostility hampers bargaining, for conflicts come to resemble zero-sum games. Such mutual perceptions enhance the probability of rapid escalation, with accompanying risks of large-scale violence. Arab-Israeli relations after 1967, for example, were so completely dominated by hostility that nonviolent interaction, particularly face-to-face negotiation, was virtually impossible. To break the spiral of violence, it is necessary first to reduce the level of mutual distrust, so that a compromise settlement will become possible.

Various methods of reducing tensions among distrustful actors have been suggested. One is to increase communications and face-to-face contacts at all social levels [17]. Another is that such actors cooperate in achieving shared goals.

According to some psychologists and sociologists, as actors cooperate in matters of mutual concern, trust between them begins to grow, despite differing value systems [1]. Small controlled studies of intragroup conflict tend to support the conclusion that this method might effectively reduce tension.[19] In this spirit, it has been suggested that greater Soviet-American cooperation in the exploration of outer space, as agreed to in the Nixon-Brezhnev summit in the spring of 1972, might reduce tensions between the two countries and produce a "spillover" effect in their relations.

Another approach involves unilateral initiation of a series of steps that would be of advantage to the adversary. Because of the risks of distortion of information during periods of high tension, these steps must be designed in such a way as to communicate their conciliatory nature to the opponent. Otherwise, the opponent may interpret them as signs of weakness or treachery. Indeed, one adherent of this approach has suggested that unilateral renunciation of nuclear weapons may be the *only* initiative sufficiently impressive to overcome the adversary's fears [7]. For a while these conciliatory gestures must be continued regardless of the adversary's response. Eventually, however, the other side must show its receptivity to the initiator's overtures. If such unilateral approaches arouse positive responses, even more conciliatory activity can be undertaken: a "peace race" will have been launched. The most ambitious proposal along these lines, advanced by psychologist Charles Osgood, is "graduated reduction in tension" (GRIT). Osgood has argued that small unilateral gestures tied

to clear expectations of reciprocity may lead to deescalation of hostility and value conflict as each side "learns" to trust its opponent to act in mutually beneficial ways [18, 6].

Osgood's ideas received some confirmation between June and November 1963. In June President Kennedy gave a major address at The American University, in which he adopted a conciliatory tone toward the Soviet Union and announced unilateral cessation of nuclear testing in the atmosphere. Soviet leaders permitted Kennedy's speech to be published in full in the Soviet Union and withdrew their objections to a Western proposal in the United Nations. The United States then proceeded to withdraw its own objections to the restoration of full status to the Hungarian delegation to the United Nations. The Soviet Union next announced cessation of the production of strategic bombers. Several further steps were taken, including ratification of a treaty to ban nuclear testing in the atmosphere and conclusion of a sale of American wheat to the Soviet Union. Although the process ended with the assassination of President Kennedy and increasing American involvement in the Vietnam War, these events offer reason to believe that the GRIT approach has some validity.[20]

When an actor's commitment has been challenged or a destabilizing technological or diplomatic development has occurred, rapid increases in tension may ensue. Strategic thinking and analysis of bargaining may be useful tools for statesmen at such times. By trying to view a situation as others view it, by identifying and communicating with one another about potential prisoners' dilemmas, and by reminding powerful adversaries of the ranges of activity in which bargaining may make sense, actors can serve their paramount objectives. Precisely because

[19] One experiment involved two groups of young boys placed in a competitive situation. The two groups developed significant mutual mistrust and hostility, which carried over even outside the competitive environment. After a cooperative task was introduced, however, the two groups gradually lost their feelings of mutual hostility. As all the subjects had similar backgrounds, however, the problems of different value systems and different images of reality were not present to any great degree. Unfortunately, such differences may be significant in retarding international cooperation [27].

[20] For an analysis of this sequence of events, see Amitai Etzioni, "Disarmament and Arms Control Agencies," in P. F. Lazarsfeld, W. Sewell, and H. Wilensky, eds., *The Uses of Sociology* (New York: Basic Books, 1967), pp. 806–838.

such analyses do *not* serve to justify objectives but are, rather, examinations of the dynamics of pursuing them by undestructive means, they can be beneficial.

Conflicts among states may become clearer if we can separate elements of debate over values and goals from the nearly mindless hostility associated with fights; we must focus on frequently predominant elements that are more amenable to reasoned analysis. The challenge for statesmen, and for other responsible citizens as well, is to energize old mechanisms and to create new ones that may keep international conflict within tolerable bounds, balancing the objectives of their own nations against recognition that objectives may change and evolve in the continuing struggle for international survival.

In addition to the possible high risk of taking a small risk many times, current trends suggest other frightening possibilities. Although it seems unlikely, a technological breakthrough could make a first strike appear safe and attractive. A state that has achieved first-strike capacity against an opponent's second-strike capacity may be sorely tempted to use it. Another problem is the possible deterioration of values, so that mass deaths become acceptable. To calculate the uses of violence sanely, it may be necessary to discount the value of human life. Some would argue that the United States has already done so in Vietnam. For example, wide public support (between 70 and 80 percent of those questioned in opinion polls) for Lieutenant William Calley, who confessed having killed women and children, is evidence of this trend. A third problem involves political error; possibly one set of leaders will simply miscalculate the wills of their opponents—assuming their own wills to be of "steel" and those of others manipulable.

Threats and the use of violence in international politics remain important elements in game situations confronting international actors. Various such bargaining and game contexts resemble a stochastic or repetitive process in which the outcomes from one game shape the matrices and structure of the next. Over time reputations, credibility, and trustworthiness are established or undermined, and the value priorities of players are revealed in the choices that they make. When actors play several games simultaneously, they must control and rationalize their behavior in a variety of situations, not giving disproportionate attention to any one. Leaders must have sufficiently broad perspective to anticipate to some extent the next set of situations likely to confront them: The values assigned to outcomes by individual actors can be dangerous if the values of their opponents have been misread.

Finally, as Karl W. Deutsch has suggested, statesmen must remember that in nuclear warfare there is no learning. Our basic model of nuclear strategy must be one of "survival," not one of the "end of the world." The short-run perspective amplifies immediate fears and instincts, whether they encourage selling everything to buy "peace in our time" or risking everything to "end it now." These calculations are those of madmen and fools, but there is no guarantee that statesmen will never behave madly or foolishly.

References

1. Angell, Robert C., "Defense of What?" *Journal of Conflict Resolution,* 6 (June 1962), pp. 116–124.
2. Attwood, William, *The Reds and the Blacks* (New York: Harper & Row, 1967).
3. Bronfenbrenner, Urie, "The Mirror Image in Soviet-American Relations: A Social Psychologist's Report," *Journal of Social Issues,* 17 (1961), p. 46.
4. Bullock, Alan, *Hitler: A Study in Tyranny* (New York: Harper & Row, 1964).
5. Deutsch, Karl W., *The Nerves of Government* (New York: Free Press, 1963), p. 70.
6. Etzioni, Amitai, *The Hard Way to Peace* (New York: Collier, 1962).
7. Frank, Jerome D., "Breaking the Thought Barrier: Psychological Chal-

lenges of the Nuclear Age," *Psychiatry,* 23 (1960), pp. 263–265.

8. George, Alexander L., David K. Hall, and William R. Simons, *The Limits of Coercive Diplomacy* (Boston: Little, Brown, 1971).

9. Green, Philip, *Deadly Logic* (New York: Schocken, 1966), p. 225.

10. Herz, John H., *International Politics in the Atomic Age* (New York: Columbia University Press, 1959), pp. 167–223.

11. Kahn, Herman, "The Arms Race and Some of its Hazards," in Donald G. Brennan, ed., *Arms Control, Disarmament, and National Security* (New York: Braziller, 1961), pp. 89–129.

12. Kaplan, Morton A., "The Calculus of Nuclear Deterrence," *World Politics,* 11 (October 1958), pp. 20–43.

13. Kaufmann, W. W., ed., *Military Planning and National Security* (Princeton: Princeton University Press, 1956), p. 17.

14. Kennan, George F., *American Diplomacy 1900–1950* (New York: Mentor, 1952), p. 99.

15. McClelland, Charles A., "Action Structures and Communication in Two International Crises: Quemoy and Berlin," *Background,* 7 (1964), pp. 201–215.

16. McNamara, Robert S., *The Essence of Security* (New York: Harper & Row, 1968), p. 69.

17. Mills, C. Wright, *The Causes of World War III* (New York: Simon and Schuster, 1958), pp. 103 ff.

18. Osgood, Charles, *An Alternative to War or Surrender* (Urbana: University of Illinois Press, 1962).

19. Quester, George H., *Deterrence Before Hiroshima* (New York: Wiley, 1966).

20. Rapoport, Anatol, *Strategy and Conscience* (New York: Harper & Row, 1964), p. 191.

21. Raser, John, "Learning and Affect in International Politics," *Journal of Peace Research,* 2 (1965), p. 221.

22. Richardson, Lewis F., *Arms and Insecurity* (Chicago: Quadrangle, 1960), p. 12.

23. Russett, Bruce M., "The Calculus of Deterrence," *Journal of Conflict Resolution,* 7 (June 1963), pp. 97–109.

24. Russett, Bruce M., *Community and Contention: Britain and America in the Twentieth Century* (Cambridge, Mass.: MIT Press, 1963).

25. Schelling, Thomas C., *Arms and Influence* (New Haven: Yale University Press, 1966).

26. Sheehan, Neil, ed., *The Pentagon Papers* (New York: Bantam, 1971), p. 432.

27. Sherif, Muzafer, *et al., Intergroup Conflict and Cooperation: The Robbers' Cave Experiment* (Norman: University of Oklahoma Press, 1961).

28. Singer, J. David, "Inter-Nation Influence: A Formal Model," *American Political Science Review,* 57 (1963), pp. 420–430.

29. Spanier, J. W., and J. L. Nogee, *The Politics of Disarmament: A Study in Soviet-American Gamesmanship* (New York: Praeger, 1962).

30. U.S. Department of State, *Bulletin,* 30 (January 25, 1954), p. 108.

31. Weinstein, Franklin B., "The Concept of a Commitment in International Relations," *Journal of Conflict Resolution,* 13 (March 1969), pp. 39–56.

32. Wolff, Robert, "The Rhetoric of Deterrence," cited in Philip Green, *Deadly Logic* (New York: Schocken, 1966), p. 173.

Suggested Reading for Chapter 18 will be found at the end of Chapter 19.

Chapter 19
SOME APPLICATIONS OF STRATEGY IN INTERNATIONAL POLITICS

The thundering present becomes so soon the unchangeable past that seizing it at any moment of its acceleration is as dangerous as mounting a train gathering speed. To change the metaphor, every bird-shooter knows that you must lead your bird and swing with its flight
—Dean Acheson [2]

At the core of the foreign-policy process is the ability to look ahead systematically. The international actor must be aware of his own strengths and weaknesses and those of potential adversaries. A "winning strategy" maximizes the actor's values and minimizes opponents' bargaining advantages. If the actor is unsuccessful, he must discover what has been wrong with his strategy.

In practice strategies are often determined by bureaucratic struggle or conflict within the decision-making group.[1] Occasionally actors behave autistically, with little recognition of reality. In any event decision makers are often unwise and usually lack complete or even sufficient information.

Strategies may be more or less specific, depending upon the objectives that the actor seeks. "Grand strategies" like "world peace" and "world revolution" are difficult to translate into operational policies unless the actor is prepared to forgo advantages that might accrue from more specific, context-oriented strategies. "Grand strategy" is essentially a rule for decision making, one intended to have wide applicability to various situations over a long period of time. Nevertheless, "grand strategy" is often attractive to policy makers because it can be formulated apart from specific contexts, thus permitting evasion of many knotty problems inherent in decision making. Unfortunately, such strategy tends also to be dogmatic and undiscriminating, perhaps little more than a variant of ideology or a set of slogans with little utility in specific situations.

The evolution of the containment policy adopted by the United States in the immediate postwar years demonstrates how a specific strategy can be transformed into an all-encompassing strategy.[2] Origi-

[1] Neil Sheehan [16] has described an excellent example of the formulation of strategy in the Vietnam War.

[2] For a similar analysis of American policy in Korea, see Ernest R. May, "The Nature of Foreign Policy: The Calculated Versus the Axiomatic," *Daedalus*, 91 (Fall 1962), pp. 653–667.

nally accepted as a response to the spread of communist influence in Greece, it was converted through the Truman Doctrine into a broad and uncompromising statement of opposition to the general spread of communism and in favor of the status quo.[3] "I believe," said President Truman, "it must be the policy of the United States to support free peoples who are resisting subjugation by armed minorities or by outside pressures. I believe that we must assist free peoples to work out their own destinies in their own way." The doctrine was phrased in such a way that it could be applied to virtually any instance in which an established regime, of whatever political shade, was threatened by external attack or internal disruption. In criticizing the Truman Doctrine, George F. Kennan, author of the original containment policy, has noted, "I took exception to it primarily because of the sweeping nature of the commitments which it implied" [8]. Since its promulgation the decision rule contained in the Truman Doctrine has been applied with little discrimination not only in Europe but in Asia as well.[4]

In Chapter 17 we discussed maximin strategy, which can be applied to every decision. In practice, states often do not follow the course that a maximin strategy prescribes, however. The strategy tends to assume a zero-sum game and fails to allow for possible changes in the intentions of adversaries and irrationality on their part. The need for flexibility and the desire to meet new challenges and novel situations often compel decision makers to fashion strategies along lines more relevant to specific contexts. Their behavior is often based on a "nonstrategic calculus." President Dwight D. Eisenhower's decision to use a strategy of massive retaliation after 1953 was based more on financial considerations than on strategic ones. Similarly, when Secretary of De-

[3] For a detailed description of the formulation of the Truman Doctrine, see Joseph M. Jones [7].

[4] For evaluation of the contemporary implications of policies based on the Truman Doctrine, see J. William Fulbright, *The Arrogance of Power* (New York: Random House, 1966).

fense Robert S. McNamara finally accepted the proposal for constructing an antiballistic-missile system in 1968, he did so less for strategic reasons than to placate officials of the U.S. Air Force. As the history of the Truman Doctrine suggests, erroneous historical analogies often result from attempts to generalize a specific strategy to other contexts. George Santayana has cautioned that those who forget history are doomed to repeat it. We may paraphrase his warning: Those who remember history too well are doomed to misapply its lessons.

Even context-oriented strategies may require rapid revision by skilled political leaders. Most international situations are fluid, and problems shift constantly. Even within a single situation it may be imperative to alter strategy, for strategy is designed to serve an objective, and an objective depends in turn upon subjective assessment of the situation. It is also, then, frequently necessary to adapt objectives as new information permits reassessment of the situation. For this reason, a determination not to adopt any rigid decision rule may be profitable. A rigid decision rule, especially one favored by representatives of the military services, can be dangerous in a nuclear era, for it can bias strategic thinking about options controlled by the military. For example, after 1965 a dispute about the utility of continued bombing in North Vietnam arose in the United States government. McNamara argued that bombing was at best marginally useful. The Joint Chiefs of Staff insisted that it was vital to the war effort. President Lyndon B. Johnson could obviously not obtain unbiased information from his military advisers. Of the advice that he received during the Cuban missile crisis President John F. Kennedy remarked: "One thing this experience shows is the value of sea power and air power; an invasion would have been a mistake—a wrong use of our power. But the military are mad. They wanted to do this" [15].

In an era characterized by rapidly evolving crises and swift change, pragmatism and incrementalism are often most appropriate. Failure to readjust strategy in the midst of a bargaining sequence can have various undesirable consequences, including an escalation spiral that may lead to thermonuclear warfare. The greater an actor's reliance on axiomatic decision rules, the less is his ability to revise his behavior when the situation warrants. Sometimes also nonsituational commitments of the sort that have been held by the American government in the Vietnam War may prove unproductive and incompatible with the requirements of bargaining.

THE QUESTION OF PLANNING

The accumulation of information and the analysis of its implications for future strategy are crucial to successful foreign policy making. In a sense all members of a foreign-policy establishment are engaged in planning, for they must all consider how today's news will affect tomorrow's events. In addition, however, tailoring good policy requires large inputs of current data, a theoretical framework in which to view them, and the time and wisdom to understand their relevance for the future.

In order to think ahead and to plan strategy, decision makers require accurate information about the world in which they operate. This information originates in a host of governmental and nongovernmental institutions and agencies, from secret intelligence agencies to the academic community. Good intelligence operations, however, involve more than simply amassing information and passing it on. Selection and interpretation of information are required as well. Raw data have little use until their relevance to policy problems has been established and they have been communicated in comprehensible form. It is crucial that such information be presented clearly and concisely because decision makers are often required to move quickly and must cope with competing demands on their time and atten-

tion. Former Secretary of State James F. Byrnes, for instance, was forced to attend international meetings on 350 of the 562 days that he spent in office. He simply did not have time to cope with large amounts of unrefined information.

Officials must attempt, with the aid of intelligence evaluations, to define situations and to develop appropriate strategies for dealing with them. They must establish priorities among competing objectives and weigh short- and long-range consequences against each other—all under the pressure of time and on the basis of "incomplete" information. This pressure helps to explain why decision makers are reluctant to relinquish future alternatives by committing themselves irrevocably to untested courses of action now. Rapidly unfolding events give persuasive reasons for retaining maximum flexibility and altering established patterns of behavior only very slowly. Unfortunately, too much flexibility may generate a purely "reactive" strategy lacking decisiveness, imagination, and initiative.

Planning suggests a *systematic* attempt to anticipate the future and to prepare for it. The pressures of the present, however, preclude much planning beyond the immediate tomorrow. As Dean Acheson has succinctly put it: "One can think under pressure, but not contemplate. Ruminants lie down to ruminate" [3].[5] The military establishment has found planning particularly useful. Even the most limited military operations require complex schedules for logistics and coordination. The more comprehensive the advance planning for possible military eventualities, the more efficient and effective the actor's response will be when they arise. But, as the events of 1914 remind us, an actor can become the prisoner of his plans. In their haste to implement a strategy worked out some time before, leaders can lose sight of their primary objectives. Today this danger may be even greater, for the military services plan weapons systems many years

[5] The authors have it on good authority, however, that ruminants do not lie down to ruminate.

ahead. Yet political predictions are not projected into the distant future. Political attitudes may therefore be shaped by possession of weapons planned long before, when political *conditions* were different. The broader and more detailed the attempt to plan for military contingencies, the greater are the uncertainties involved. No actor can plan for all contingencies, nor can plans take into account more than a few elements of the situations that will actually arise.

An actor's future military capability rests in large measure on his present decisions. Weapons development, procurement, and deployment take time, including time for budgetary and scientific planning. The incorporation of a certain type and level of capability into strategy also reveals basic assumptions about the future. Nevertheless, political planning is even more elusive. It is necessary to take into account not only one's own preferences but also those of other actors with different backgrounds and frames of reference. For this reason the politician who relies on maximin strategy in effect abdicates his responsibility to plan for political eventualities.

Questions about what is going to happen and what the United States should do in the event of the death of a foreign leader, the overthrow of a friendly or an unfriendly regime, or the outbreak of civil war in a neutral country are likely to preoccupy American government planners. But it is even more difficult to anticipate all the political contingencies than it is to anticipate the military ones, not to mention anticipating them in such detail that appropriate strategies are ensured. Under President Eisenhower and later under President Richard M. Nixon many planning papers were prepared and submitted to the National Security Council, but rarely, if ever, did they prove applicable. The main value of such planning has been the intellectual stimulation involved and the heuristic use of the "scenarios." Such plans may also alert decision makers to areas of particular interest and to possible alternative courses of action. But they rarely, if ever, provide decision makers with accurate "maps" of the future.

Before the outbreak of the Korean War in 1950 Secretary of State Acheson announced that the American Pacific defense perimeter was considered to run through Japan and the Philippines and to include neither South Korea nor Taiwan. Nevertheless, this theoretical boundary did not prevent American officials from reevaluating the probable consequences of inaction after the unexpected North Korean attack in June. Ultimately they recommended to President Harry S. Truman that the United States disregard its previous plans and intervene. Acheson has recalled the events:

"Thought" would suggest too orderly and purposeful a process. It was rather to let various possibilities, like glass fragments in a kaleidoscope, form a series of patterns of action and then draw conclusions from them. Our recommendations for the President dealt with the next twenty-four hours or so, which was as far as we could see at the time. [1, p. 405]

Another type of planning involves projection of significant trends in international politics and economics so that long-term political and economic programs can be designed. If foreign-assistance programs, for example, were planned only one year in advance it would be impossible to ensure the most efficient use of current and future resources; many long-term programs are financed year to year, but they are planned farther ahead.

Finally, some planning occurs even at the level of "grand strategy" and is intended to provide a framework for more context-oriented programs. This kind of planning generally involves questions of "national purpose," or goals. It is, however, never sufficiently detailed to provide operational direction. For example, "grand strategy" was useless to President Johnson when he found it necessary to approve tactical bombing of North Vietnam on a day-to-day basis.

THE TACTICAL ELEMENTS OF STRATEGY

Elements of strategy are related to the types of objectives and influence that we discussed in Chapter 4. Strategy is the specific application of types of influence to attainment of selected objectives, with attention to possible unanticipated effects.

An actor's choice of objective is the first step in interaction. The objective must be at once important enough to the actor to convince any adversary that it will be seriously pursued yet sufficiently limited so that the adversary is not forced into intransigence in response. This objective must also be clear to the adversary, so that response can be at the appropriate level. It is difficult even to surrender when one does not know what specific conditions the opponent is after.

As we suggested in Chapter 18, effective communication of an objective to an adversary requires credibility. To convince the opponent that an objective is important, it is necessary also to convince him that one is prepared to take certain critical steps to achieve it. This necessity is fundamental to a strong bargaining position, for bargaining leverage is based on "the ability to set the best price for yourself and fool the other man into thinking this was your maximum offer" [11].

Four kinds of strategic situation are common in contemporary international politics: avoidance-coercion, avoidance-reward, securance-coercion, and securance-reward.

Chip on the Shoulder: Avoidance-Coercion

A strategy of deterrence falls clearly into the avoidance-coercion category. The United States and the Soviet Union have both built large second-strike nuclear forces to persuade each other not to initiate certain courses of action. The threat of coercion has been central: Partial or total destruction of the adversary's homeland will ensue if he behaves in certain undesirable ways. The objective of deter-

ring an attack on one's homeland is clear, and compliance is therefore easier. In addition, there can be a very clear line, crossing which will bring the threatened response. Once the line has been crossed, however, deterrence has failed.

Credible commitment is a central feature of deterrence. Although it may be mutually undesirable for a threat to be carried out, actors may consider themselves as involved in a stochastic (random) sequence of events. Present coercion may be necessary temporarily, in order to prevent future violations of certain prohibitions. It is believed that present "pain" will serve as a lesson. American interventions in Korea and South Vietnam have been justified partly by such arguments. The communists have been supposed to learn that aggression will be followed by retaliation so that they will refrain from future aggression.

The credibility of a deterrent threat is, however, reduced in situations that do not involve an actor's homeland or core values. As we have suggested, it is doubtful that an actor will risk self-destruction in order to protect an ally or will carry out large-scale threats in response to minor provocations. Nuclear weapons are not an effective deterrent against guerrilla attacks, wars of national liberation, and international monetary speculation. Deterrent threats must be tailored to the events that the actor wishes to prevent. The United States could credibly threaten to defend Europe with conventional weapons if it were attacked or it could threaten to send military and economic assistance to a country in danger of communist subversion. Paradoxically, the very limitations of such threats enhance their credibility. While threats must promise punishment sufficient to deter the potential aggressor, if too much is threatened they will be "incredible."

Protection Money: Avoidance-Reward

The avoidance-reward relation between objective and influence has been scornfully dubbed "appeasement," especially when it has failed. It is essentially an attempt to "pay" another actor to refrain from a specified course. At Munich British Prime Minister Neville Chamberlain agreed to reward Adolf Hitler with the Sudetenland in return for promises to temper future demands and to refrain from initiating hostilities.

Rewards, like coercion, generate expectations of further behavior of the same kind. It has been argued that Hitler believed that Great Britain would stand aside when Germany annexed Poland, as it had done when the Nazis occupied Czechoslovakia. Unlike a deterrent threat, which has failed as soon as it must be fulfilled, the promise of a reward must be fulfilled eventually. After the reward, however there may be no incentive for the recipient to abstain any longer unless further rewards are promised or unless a threat has been combined with the original promise.

Rewards may have to be given frequently to further an avoidance objective. But an actor may then become so dependent upon the rewards that stopping them will be interpreted as coercion, as the United States has discovered after having provided economic and military aid to certain countries for several years in order to ensure their continued allegiance to the West. Rather than manifesting "gratitude" for past rewards, these countries are quick to take offense at any suggestion that the accustomed rewards may stop. Alexander Hamilton once argued that no nation should base its policy on expectations of gratitude: "It is necessary then to reflect, however painful the reflection, that gratitude is a duty, or sentiment, which between nations can rarely have any solid foundation" [12].

The continual use of rewards to achieve an avoidance objective is also expensive. The late Senator Everett M. Dirksen of Illinois had a favorite story about a constituent for whom he had done many favors. When the Senator stopped by during a campaign to elicit this particular voter's support and reminded him of all the favors that he had received, the con-

stituent replied, "Yes, but what have you done for me lately?" The implications of the remark were not lost on the Senator: The constituent was suggesting that he might vote for Dirksen's opponent if the Senator did not provide him with further rewards. In attempting to rally support for itself on various issues, the United States has often reminded other countries of past American aid and has frequently received replies similar to that of Senator Dirksen's constituent. Coercion may be added to rewards in order to reduce the overall cost of attempts at influence.

Arm Twisting: Securance-Coercion
Unlike an avoidance objective, the prevention of a specific action, a securance objective involves alteration of another actor's current behavior, perhaps to new types of behavior. In bombing North Vietnam between 1965 and 1968, for example, the United States was seeking to persuade Hanoi both to stop assisting the Viet Cong in the south and to join in negotiating an end to the conflict. The use of coercion under those circumstances was intended to remind the adversary that he would have to endure still greater losses if he did not modify his behavior in a desirable direction. Securance-coercion is simply a more academic term for what is commonly known as "arm twisting" or "putting the heat on." When a man twists his opponent's arm, it is not the adversary's pain that convinces him to alter his behavior; it is the belief that still further pain is in store unless he submits.

As our discussion of coercive bargaining suggested, a threat unaccompanied by actual coercion is not as useful in securance as in avoidance, for in the former there is no threshold at which the threat will automatically be carried out. An adversary can use delaying tactics more easily, and it is therefore more difficult to persuade him to do something than it is to prevent him from doing something. During the Cuban missile crisis, for instance, the United States used several threats to force the Soviet Union to remove its missiles from Cuba. If, however, instead of capitulating, the Soviet Union had decided merely to halt construction of the missile sites before they became operational, the United States would have faced a dilemma. Soviet action other than that specified would have forced the United States to decide whether to back down or to carry out its threats and thus incur the responsibility for starting a nuclear war.

Moderate coercion, with the threat of more to come, is sometimes a useful response to delaying tactics. The initial coercion signals that the initiator is serious and will not wait long; it can be effectively combined with a threat that includes an arbitrary time limit by which the adversary must comply. The threat then becomes an ultimatum. The carrying out of an ultimatum, like the carrying out of a deterrent threat, can have mutually disastrous consequences.

Bribe: Securance-Reward
The combination of a securance objective and the use of rewards to achieve it—in effect, a bribe—is relatively common in international politics. Like avoidance-coercion, this combination incorporates a clear point at which promised action must be undertaken. When the desired modification of behavior occurs—*and only then*—the promise must be translated into a reward. Furthermore, the reward need be given only once because the objective will have been achieved.

In June 1947 Secretary of State George C. Marshall announced a program of large-scale American economic assistance to the war-torn countries of Europe. The Marshall Plan was an example of the use of rewards to achieve a securance objective. It was intended "to bring about conditions in Europe and in our relations with the U.S.S.R. which would cause Soviet leaders to decide that their interests were better served by negotiating a political and economic settlement and collaborating with the United States on European

matters..." [7, p. 243]. Beside this "bribe" to the Soviet Union, the Plan offered economic recovery, stability, and reorganization to several countries in both western and eastern Europe, in return for economic and political "friendship" with the United States. The Soviet Union, fearful that the Plan would lead to extension of American influence in eastern Europe and the undermining of its own influence there, rejected the "bribe" and pressured the eastern European countries, notably Czechoslovakia, to do the same. The Soviet leaders were wary lest American assistance lead to eastern European economic and political dependence upon the United States, and they were in a position to prevent it: Pressure on the Czechoslovak government to reject the American offer was followed shortly by a communist coup d'état in Czechoslovakia. The Marshall Plan was accepted in western Europe, and the improved economic conditions that it fostered made governments better able to resist both internal and external communist pressures.

The bribe aspect of this combination was perhaps most blatant in the United States' exchange of approximately $53 million worth of drugs, chemicals, medical equipment, and baby food for the 1,179 Cubans who had been captured by Fidel Castro's army after the ill-fated Bay of Pigs invasion. The exchange, technically undertaken through private agencies, had the support of the Kennedy administration which, in the words of Senator Barry Goldwater of Arizona, lent "the prestige of the government to this surrender by blackmail" [6].

Comparison of Tactical Combinations
The discussion so far enables us to compare these four combinations with three main variables: the presence or absence of a "point of no return," the costs of success, and the costs of failure.

As Table 19.1 suggests, a "chip on the shoulder" strategy is inexpensive because the threat does not have to be fulfilled. If deterrence fails, however, the costs of

Table 19.1.
*Comparison of Four Combinations of Influence and Objectives**

	Point of No Return	*Cost of Success*	*Cost of Failure*
Chip on the shoulder	present	minimal	very large
Protection money	absent	large	variable
Arm twisting	variable	variable	variable
Bribe	present	variable	minimal

*This table includes not all possible combinations but only those that are likely to occur.

carrying out the threat may be exorbitant. "Protection money" has relatively high initial costs in resource allocation, for, as we have suggested, the promise must often be carried out repeatedly if the objective is to be achieved. If the opponent indulges in the forbidden behavior despite the rewards received, the costs will be determined largely by the resources already allocated and the losses suffered in failing to attain the objective. The costs of "arm twisting" equal the investment of resources necessary to obtain modification of an adversary's behavior. On the other hand, it is a high-risk strategy. Finally, the failure of a "bribe" entails minimal costs because the reward need never be given, while its success, when rationally offered, entails benefits in excess of costs.

STRATEGIC COSTS

As we have suggested, an international interaction may involve several types of costs. In selecting from alternative strategies an actor must assess these costs systematically and comparatively. In particular, he must avoid two common errors: defining costs too narrowly and omitting consideration of the costs of failure.

Various kinds of costs must be considered in choosing strategies. We shall outline only a few, in order to illustrate the complexity of the problem. Some of these costs obviously defy quantification, but they should not be overlooked for that reason.

Resource Costs

Resource costs are obvious and can often be expressed in quantitative terms: money spent, troops lost, material assistance granted, and so on. When resource costs are emphasized to the detriment of nonmaterial costs, however, evaluations may be distorted. During the Vietnam War the Pentagon's preference for releasing casualty figures obscured the additional costs in loss of American prestige and the adverse effects of an unpopular war on American morale. Similarly, although the American invasion of Cambodia in spring 1970 resulted in capture of large amounts of enemy supplies and weapons, the psychological cost of invasion of a small neutralist country was domestic unrest. As Erich Fromm has suggested, "It is a psychological fact that acts of brutality have a brutalizing effect on the participants and lead to more brutality" [4].

Psychological Costs

Psychological costs are very difficult to estimate but nevertheless real. They include intellectual and emotional anguish entailed by various courses of action. Such anguish can be intense, for example, when action has resulted in many deaths. When Chamberlain was finally forced to admit that his policy of appeasing Hitler had failed and that Great Britain would have to go to war, he reminded the House of Commons "how he prayed that it would never fall upon him to ask the country to accept the 'awful arbitrament of war'" [13]. An individual forced to witness what he strongly believes to be unjust, even if that injustice is committed by his own government, can also undergo intense suffering. If an individual firmly believes in a certain policy or strategy, it may pain him to change his mind. A decision maker firmly wedded to a certain course of behavior will have difficulty in evaluating its success objectively or in accepting new information that invalidates his deeply held beliefs. Men who cannot admit to mistakes that they have made are more dangerous as leaders today than ever before.

Decision and Information Costs
It takes time and energy to arrive at decisions. Obtaining information is expensive and evaluating it is even more expensive in terms of time. Too much information and its insufficient organization cause overloading, but inadequate and inaccurate information may result in bad decisions. Time is often essential, particularly during crises, and alternatives may be foreclosed if decisions take too long.

Inertia Costs
Failure to make decisions may also entail costs. Such failure is, of course, actually a type of decision that precludes other alternatives. When decision makers attempt to reduce costs of information and decisions, they often incur inertia costs. Unproductive but inexpensive strategies may thus be continued even though top leaders recognize that change would be desirable.

Opportunity Costs
Because resources are scarce, when an actor adopts one course of action he may have to forgo others. Sending troops to one country may prevent military intervention in another country. Soviet efforts to achieve a détente in Europe in the late 1960s seem partly stimulated by the increasing hostility of communist China. The Soviet Union wished to be free to redeploy troops stationed in the German Democratic Republic to the Soviet fron-

tier with China. In attempting to achieve one objective, an actor may thus have to give up other highly prized objectives.

Intergame Costs
Closely related to opportunity costs are intergame costs, the contingent effects of one policy or strategy on another interaction in which the actor is engaged. In 1970 Soviet efforts to achieve a relaxation of tension in Europe and to conclude a European-security treaty were impaired by Soviet assistance to the United Arab Republic against Israel and by attempts to increase Soviet influence throughout the Mediterranean area. Similarly, American efforts to reach agreement with the Soviet Union on various questions of mutual interest, including arms limitations, were undermined by continuing American involvement in Indochina.

Responsibility Costs
An actor may be criticized by others for his responsibility for a particular course of action. The Arab countries hold the United States responsible for continuing hostilities in the Middle East because of its assistance to Israel. The United States severely criticized the irresponsibility of the British and French invasion of Suez in 1956.

Bargaining Costs
The greater the conflict between the objectives of actors and the more nearly exclusive they are, the greater are the compromises usually necessary to achieve negotiated settlement or even a beginning to negotiations. In both the Korean and Vietnam wars the adversaries were so far apart at the beginning of negotiations that considerable time and effort was required to reach agreement even on the most superficial issues. When two sides are initially far apart and influence is not too asymmetrical, it is generally necessary that both make considerable concessions. If they are too far apart, however, they

may prefer simply to accuse each other of not negotiating seriously: a reasonable psychological defense but poor strategy if agreement is the objective.

The Costs of Failure

International actors do not attempt to bring influence to bear in a situation unless they see some prospect for success. If the objective is sufficiently important, actors may overestimate the chances of success and underestimate the possibilities of failure.[6] They then may fail to weigh carefully the potential gains and costs of failure. Unexpected failure may have great negative consequences like loss of domestic support, a decline in international prestige, or a weakened strategic position. Failure at deterrence may mean not only loss of the objective but also outbreak of large-scale violence with devastating consequences for both actors.

CONFLICT IN OBJECTIVES AND STRATEGIES: THREE EXAMPLES

North Vietnam

In February 1965 the Johnson administration decided to begin bombing in North Vietnam. This decision convinced some members of the administration that the American effort was expanding well beyond what American objectives required and might have undesirable unanticipated effects. Their argument was "for a political approach to guerrilla warfare and for the use of American power not to escalate but to deter the Communist side from escalating" [5, pp. 536–537].

In recalling the decision to initiate

[6] A good example of such self-delusion has been provided by Special Assistant to President Johnson, Robert W. Komer's assessment of the American position in Vietnam in February 1967: "[W]e are winning the war in the South. ... [W]e are grinding the enemy down. ... And the cumulative impact ... is beginning to tell. ... Indeed my broad feeling, with due allowance for over-simplification, is that our side now has ... all the men, money and other resources needed to achieve success ..." [16, p. 555].

bombing, former Assistant Secretary of State for Far Eastern Affairs Roger Hilsman has pointed out that officials favored the decision for different reasons. Some thought that bombing would punish North Vietnam and thus compel it to end hostilities. Others doubted this possibility but favored bombing because they thought that it would stop, or at least reduce, the flow of supplies and men to the south. A third group argued that even if the bombing did not halt the flow of supplies and men, it would so increase the costs to the North Vietnamese as to improve the morale of the beleaguered South Vietnamese [5, p. 531; 16, pp. 307–381].

There was thus no essential agreement on the basic rationale of escalation. These three arguments refer to objectives of different domains and scopes. The fundamental discrepancies, perhaps not immediately discernible even to those who made the decision, made it difficult for the United States to convey clearly to North Vietnam what the American objective was. Furthermore, there was no clearly indicated "point of no return" beyond which the adversary could expect coercion to be increased; it was not even clear that coercion would be increased under *any* circumstances.

The ambiguities inherent in this policy caused further difficulties, for they resulted in inability to decide when to halt the bombing. Those who had thought that the bombing would end the war were proved wrong and then had to vote either for intensifying bombing or for stopping it altogether. Those who had argued that bombing would interrupt North Vietnamese assistance to the Viet Cong could be expected to support the policy even after the illusions of the first group had been shattered. When it became apparent that the bombing was having only marginal effects on the flow of supplies, there was still the third group, which could insist that bombing was beneficial to South Vietnamese morale. It was not clear to anyone in the government or outside it under what conditions the United States would stop the bombing and thus how the adversary could comply with American demands short of abject surrender. There were no criteria by which to judge the success or failure of the policy; the bombing continued until 1968 almost on its own momentum. This "bombing strategy" was not a true strategy at all because it lacked essential elements of a decision rule. American failure to match objectives to resources and to provide such a decision rule were succinctly summarized in a report by the Institute for Defense Analyses in August 1966:

In general, current official thought about U.S. objectives in bombing NVN implicitly assumes two sets of causal relationships:
1. That by increasing the damage and destruction of resources in NVN, the U.S. is exerting pressure to cause the DRV to stop their support of the military operations in SVN and Laos; and
2. That the combined effect of the total military effort against NVN—including the U.S. air strikes in NVN and Laos, and the land, sea, and air operations in SVN—will ultimately cause the DRV to perceive that its probable losses accruing from the war have become greater than its possible gains and, on the basis of this net evaluation, the regime will stop its support of the war in the South.

These two sets of interrelationships are assumed in military planning, but it is not clear that they are systematically addressed in current intelligence estimates and assessments. Instead, the tendency is to encapsulate the bombing of NVN as one set of operations and the war in the South as another set of operations, and to evaluate each separately; and to tabulate and describe data on the physical, economic, and military effects of the bombing, but not to address specifically the relationship between such effects and the data relating to the ability and will of the DRV to continue its support of the war in the South.

The fragmented nature of current analyses and the lack of adequate methodology for assessing the net effects of a given set of military operations leaves a major gap between the quantifiable data on bomb damage effects, on the one hand, and policy judgments about the feasibility of achieving a given set of objectives, on the other. Bridging this gap still requires the exercise

of broad political-military judgments that cannot be supported or rejected on the basis of systematic intelligence indicators. It must be concluded, therefore, that there is currently no adequate basis for predicting the levels of U.S. military effort that would be required to achieve the stated objectives—indeed, there is no firm basis for determining if there is *any* feasible level of effort that would achieve these objectives. [16, pp. 506–507]

Korea

The Korean War illustrates not only the effects of contradictions among a set of objectives but also the consequences of shifting objectives. After the beginning of the war in 1950 the United States sought to design a set of policies that would achieve at least three different objectives. It wanted to liberate South Korea and to contain North Korean aggression; to "teach" the North Koreans and other potential adversaries that "aggression does not pay"; and to prevent expansion of the conflict. The first was a securance objective, the second an avoidance objective, and the third a prevention objective. The initial policy was to fight a limited war under United Nations auspices in order to force the communists back to the 38th parallel dividing North and South Korea. This limited effort would perhaps have enabled the United States to repel the North Koreans and to contain the conflict, but it was not sufficient to avoid the Chinese People's Republic's alteration of its security goals when it felt endangered.

The relatively moderate early American response seemed to demonstrate American caution. Then, on September 13, 1950, American units under the command of General Douglas MacArthur achieved one of the most stunning tactical successes in modern military history. In an amphibious landing at Inchon American troops outflanked the North Korean armies and began a successful campaign to drive the invaders out of South Korea. The very success of the operation encouraged expansion of the securance objective, however. It suddenly seemed possible not only to drive the aggressor out of South Korea but also to reunite the entire Korean peninsula under a regime friendly to the West. The tremendous success of the Inchon operation in the teeth of great risks seems to have caused MacArthur to lose his sense of prudence and to become overconfident. "The golden moment to transmute our victory at Inchon into a political peace had arrived," he wrote [9].

United Nations forces pushed north of the 38th parallel until they had almost reached the Yalu river, which forms the border with China. The move north, however, conveyed a clear threat to China, which was not at all convinced that the United States intended to stop at the Manchurian frontier. The objective of preventing expansion of the war was temporarily subordinated to the objective of "liberating" all Korea. The Chinese perceived that the race north would bring at worst an immediate threat to their autonomy and at best an unfriendly regime and a permanent military threat on their borders. Although partly aware of the contradictions among its objectives, the United States military command decided to reunite Korea without foreseeing the effects that this course might have on the Chinese. The problem was complicated by lack of communication between the American and Chinese governments. Chinese intentions and perceptions were thus overlooked in efforts to achieve a quick military victory and "get the boys home by Christmas." The attitude of American leaders, influenced by MacArthur's optimism, is described in President Truman's memoirs: "[Acheson] pointed out that it was agreed that General MacArthur's directive should not now be changed and that he should be free to do what he could in a military way . . . one problem was that we lacked any direct contacts with the Peiping regime . . ." [17, 18].

At the end of November the Chinese struck back at MacArthur's forces and opened "one of the major decisive battles of the present century, followed by the longest retreat in American history" [10]. The consequences of the attempt to reunite Korea were far-reaching. Although the border was ultimately stabilized near the 38th parallel, the effect of Chinese victory was to increase communist morale and to convince the Chinese that they could fight the United States on equal terms. Not only did the Americans fail in their objective of preventing expansion of the war; the Korean campaign also failed to convince the United States' adversaries that "aggression does not pay." On the contrary, it stimulated the Chinese belief that the United States was vulnerable if proper tactics were adopted. Less ambitious objectives—like those originally sought by American leaders—might have met with greater success at less cost.

French Indochina

The first war in Indochina illustrates the possible effects of conflicting objectives. As the war moved into its critical phase in early 1954, the French took an enormous risk in hopes of reversing their rapidly deteriorating position. In placing their best troops at Dien Bien Phu, deep inside Viet Minh territory, the French gambled on luring their adversary into a decisive battle. The move was foolish and resulted in disaster, for the communists were able to mass superior firepower around the beleaguered garrison and to place it under siege. By late April the fall of Dien Bien Phu was imminent, and observers thought that defeat might so demoralize the French army that it would mutiny. At the very least the French would be unable to continue fighting, for all reserves were already committed at Dien Bien Phu, and their loss would irreparably weaken the army.

At that time the United States was underwriting approximately 75 percent of the costs of the war, for Secretary of State John Foster Dulles was determined to hold the line against further communist successes. Dulles' "grand strategy" was based on a decision rule requiring resistance to communist encroachment at every point. In a speech delivered only a month before the fall of Dien Bien Phu, President Eisenhower set forth the assumption on which the decision rule was based: "You have a row of dominoes set up, you knock over the first one, and what will happen to the last one is that it will go over very quickly. So you have a beginning of a disintegration that would have the most profound consequences." The "domino theory" shaped the ways in which American decision makers evaluated the impending loss of Dien Bien Phu and much of Indochina to the communist forces of Ho Chi Minh and General Vo Nguyen Giap.

By mid-March the Pentagon had begun to plan an air strike against communist positions around Dien Bien Phu. Operation Vulture, as the plan was called, was strongly backed by Chairman of the Joint Chiefs of Staff Admiral Arthur Radford and warmly received by the French, who saw in it a possibility for obtaining better peace terms. Dulles then briefed a selected group of congressional leaders in order to solicit support for Operation Vulture. They raised two main questions: Would an air strike be sufficient, and, if not, would American troops be committed after that? Second, did the United States have the support of its allies, particularly the British?

The second question reflected doubts that the United States should undertake unilateral action at the risk of alienating a close ally. Because the United States valued its close working relations with the British and regarded maintenance of the Western alliance as its primary objective, congressional leaders refused to support the plan until they could be assured that the British would also support it. On April 23 Dulles contacted British Prime Minister Anthony Eden and informed him that Dien Bien Phu would fall within seventy-two hours unless there was an air strike. He asked Eden for support.

Although the British, too, did not wish to see Indochina fall under communist rule, they believed that the risks entailed in the proposed operation outweighed any possible gains. Eden, convinced that only

a conflict on the scale of the Korean War could effectively stop the communists in Indochina and wishing to avoid such a war, refused his consent. As a result, the operation was canceled, Dien Bien Phu fell, and major Asian land war for the United States was temporarily averted. Two actors can share an objective but can attach strikingly different values to it; the British scale of preferences differed from that of Dulles. Furthermore, American preference for not endangering its relations with Great Britain prompted it to forgo exerting influence in Indochina. Joint strategy proved impossible becaue the images of the situation held by allied leaders were poles apart [14].

CONCLUSIONS

As these brief accounts have illustrated, the formulation and execution of a successful strategy constitute no mean feat. Contradictions between long- and short-range demands, conflicts among differing objectives, and difficulties in implementing strategy all suggest that the rational use of violence is easier to contemplate than to implement. In recalling the period in which he entered the State Department Acheson has stated the problem for men who make decisions: "Not only was the future clouded . . . but the present was equally clouded. . . . The significance of events was shrouded in ambiguity. We groped after interpretations of them . . ." [1, p. 3]. As long as men are forced to plan strategy in the complex world of international politics, there will be many chances for error and miscalculation.

References

1. Acheson, Dean, *Present at the Creation* (New York: Norton, 1969).
2. Acheson, Dean, "The President and the Secretary of State," in Don K. Price, ed., *The Secretary of State* (Englewood Cliffs, N.J.: Prentice-Hall, 1960), p. 47.
3. Acheson, Dean, "Thoughts About Thought in High Places," in Andrew M. Scott and Raymond H. Dawson, eds., *Readings in the Making of Amer-*

ican Foreign Policy (New York: Macmillan, 1965), p. 295.

4. Fromm, Erich, "The Case for Unilateral Disarmament," in Donald G. Brennan, ed., *Arms Control, Disarmament, and National Security* (New York: Braziller, 1961), p. 190.

5. Hilsman, Roger, *To Move a Nation* (Garden City, N.Y.: Doubleday, 1967).

6. Johnson, Haynes, *The Bay of Pigs* (New York: Norton, 1964), p. 238.

7. Jones, Joseph M., *The Fifteen Weeks* (New York: Harcourt Brace Jovanovich, 1955), p. 243.

8. Kennan, George F., *Memoirs 1925–1950* (Boston: Little, Brown, 1967), pp. 319–320.

9. MacArthur, Douglas, *Reminiscences* (New York: McGraw-Hill, 1964), p. 357.

10. Marshall, S. L. A., *The River and the Gauntlet* (New York: Morrow, 1952), p. 1.

11. Morgan, J. N., "Bilateral Monopoly and the Competitive Output," *Quarterly Journal of Economics,* 63 (August 1949), p. 376.

12. Morris, Richard B., ed., *The Basic Ideas of Alexander Hamilton* (New York: Pocket Books, 1957), p. 288.

13. Nicolson, Harold, *Diaries and Letters 1930–1939* (New York: Atheneum, 1966), p. 417.

14. Roberts, Chalmers M., "The Day We Didn't Go to War," *The Reporter,* September 14, 1954. See also *The Pentagon Papers, op. cit.,* pp. 1–13.

15. Schlesinger, Arthur M., Jr., *A Thousand Days* (Boston: Houghton Mifflin, 1965), p. 831.

16. Sheehan, Neil, ed., *The Pentagon Papers* (New York: Bantam, 1971).

17. Truman, Harry S., *Memoirs,* vol. 2 (Garden City, N.Y.: Doubleday, 1956), p. 380.

18. Whiting, Allen S., *China Crosses the Yalu* (New York: Macmillan, 1960).

Suggested Reading

Bloomfield, Lincoln P., and Amelia C. Leiss, *Controlling Small Wars* (New York: Knopf, 1970).

Edwards, David V., *Arms Control in International Politics* (New York: Holt, Rinehart and Winston, 1969).

Green, Philip, *Deadly Logic* (New York: Schocken, 1966).

Halperin, Morton H., *Defense Strategies for the Seventies* (Boston: Little, Brown, 1971).

Iklé, Fred C., *How Nations Negotiate* (New York: Praeger, 1967).

Jervis, Robert, *The Logic of Images in International Politics* (Princeton: Princeton University Press, 1970).

Kahn, Herman, *On Escalation: Metaphors and Scenarios* (New York: Praeger, 1965).

Kahn, Herman, *On Thermonuclear War* (Princeton: Princeton University Press, 1960).

Kissinger, Henry A., *Necessity for Choice* (New York: Harper & Row, 1961).

Knorr, Klaus, *On the Uses of Military Power in the Nuclear Age* (Princeton: N.J.: Princeton University Press, 1966).

Parkinson, Roger, *Peace for our Time: Munich to Dunkirk—The Inside Story* (New York: McKay, 1971).

Quade, Edward S., ed., *Analysis for Military Decisions* (Chicago: Rand McNally, 1965).

Quester, George, *Deterrence Before Hiroshima* (New York: Wiley, 1966).

Rathjens, George W., *The Future of the Strategic Arms Race* (New York: Carnegie Endowment for International Peace, 1969).

Schelling, Thomas C., *Arms and Influence* (New Haven: Yale University Press, 1966).

Young, Oran R., *The Poltics of Force* (Princeton: Princeton University Press, 1968).

Chapter 20
INTERNATIONAL CRISES

*In a Nuclear Age, nations must make
war as porcupines make love—carefully.*[1]

Although many international events are dangerous, an international crisis represents an immediate and heightened danger to the values and goals of international actors. In 1962, for example, American leaders considered the introduction of Soviet missiles into Cuba not simply a further step in the continuing degeneration of American-Cuban relations but also a grave threat to the United States' strategic position in the world. Something of the unpredictable and dangerous nature of that confrontation has been captured by Arthur M. Schlesinger, Jr.: "The Soviet Union had never before placed nuclear missiles in any other country. . . . Why should it now send nuclear missiles to a country thousands of miles away, lying within the zone of vital interest of their main adversary, a land, morover, headed by a willful leader?" [14, p. 795].

Although the term is ofen used loosely, "crisis" denotes a systemic phenomenon with specific characteristics. Crises arise suddenly, raise the probability of violence, and thus threaten the existing system. They are contests for high stakes, which reach their peaks rapidly and permit decision makers only short times in which to respond.

Crisis situations seem to have temporal limits during which an actor feels pressured to respond before the situation can change radically. The lag between perception of the challenge and response to it is necessarily short. In the Cuban missile crisis, for instance, American leaders believed that they had to act before the recently introduced Soviet missiles could be made operational. Otherwise, they feared an immediate and unfavorable alteration in the distribution of power.

Finally, although a long chain of events may have led up to a crisis, the rapid spiral of crisis itself is generally unanticipated by important decision makers [5] (see Chapter 8, pp. 160–165). The Cuban confrontation had been preceded by several years of growing animosity between the United States and Cuba. Economic and diplomatic relations had been

---

[1] From a sign in a briefing room of the U.S. State Department in October 1962 [6, p. 215].

severed, and hostilities had culminated in the abortive American-sponsored Bay of Pigs invasion in April 1961. The introduction of Soviet offensive weapons in the summer and autumn of 1962 created a very different issue, only tenuously connected with general American hostility toward Fidel Castro's regime. Roger Hilsman, a member of John F. Kennedy's administration at the time, has described this feeling:

The United States, of course, would also have liked to see the end of the Soviet military presence in Cuba and the end of Castro's totalitarian Communist regime. But here is where the importance of means began to be felt. The full panoply of American military power was appropriate to getting the missiles out of Cuba. . . . The first step was the missiles. [6, p. 202]

In the same way the sequence of events immediately prior to the outbreak of war in Europe in 1914, including the assassination of the Archduke Francis Ferdinand at Sarajevo, had not been predicted despite the conflicts that had taxed the European system during the previous two decades and had sustained the atmosphere of suspicion and tension among the major European powers.

Crises tend to escalate dangerously as the participants attempt to raise the stakes higher in order to gain an advantage. The Cuban missile and the 1914 crises demonstrate that such spirals quickly reach the threshold of either recovery or disaster. Secretary of State Dean Rusk commented during the Cuban affair that the Americans and Russians were "eyeball to eyeball" and that the Russians "blinked first" [6, p. 219].

It has been argued that the "nearly constant presence of pressure and the recurrence of crises" are actually stabilizing elements in international politics and that, as major actors became more skilled in crisis bargaining and more practiced in making decisions under stress, recurring crises will substitute for war [16]. But when the major actors possess thermonuclear weapons the cost of miscalculations

that might cause one or both sides actually to carry out their threats can be high. Although wars among great powers may be less frequent than they have been in previous eras, *any* war threatens catastrophe.

SYSTEM ANALYSIS AND INTERNATIONAL CRISIS

The system approach to crisis assumes that international actors interact in patterned ways through established structures. To avoid a major breakdown of the system, instability and rapid changes in the pattern of relations among actors or in the structures of the system must be limited and controlled by at least ad hoc procedures. Crisis can be defined as rapid change in systemic variables such that parameters are on the verge of change, disrupting the system. The systemic approach implies that an observer can determine the existence of a crisis "objectively," according to certain criteria and without reference to the perceptions of decision makers. Crises, it is said, can be "mapped" according to events in a stochastic chain. As each event succeeds another, the choices available to decision makers are increasingly restricted [13, 12].

This approach involves a difficult analytical problem. Decision makers do not always recognize the existence of crises and may evaluate sequences differently from the ways in which other observers evaluate them. We must ask whether or not there is a crisis unless at least two sets of decision makers define it as such. The answer is apparently no. In 1969, for instance, the North Koreans shot down an American reconnaisance aircraft. The incident was fraught with danger and uncertainty. Had the United States responded sharply to the provocation, a threat of war would have arisen. Instead, the Nixon administration chose to treat the incident without urgency, and it soon faded from public consciousness. In this instance the outcome was largely determined by American perceptions and unwillingness to escalate the situation.

When international systems lack elasticity and appropriate regulatory mechanisms, crises tend to bring war and systemic breakdown. In 1914 factors like rigid alliances, widespread nationalism, slow and easily clogged channels of communication among national leaders, and the exigencies of military technology made it difficult for the European state system to adapt to rapid changes. Studies of this crisis, we may recall, have generated some very disquieting hypotheses, focusing on the problem of adequate communications. For example, one study has concluded, "If a state's perception of injury to itself is 'sufficiently' great, this perception will offset perceptions of insufficient capability, making the perception of capability much less important a factor in a decision to go to war" [17]. In 1914, at least, the "common sense" idea that actors will not go to war if they think that they will lose was not valid. Instead Kaiser Wilhelm declared, "If we are to bleed to death, England shall at least lose India" [8]. Changes were too great and too rapid for the system to cope with them. On the other hand, certain factors in the contempory system seem to permit more effective adjustment to crises than was possible in 1914.

The United Nations and certain regional organizations like the Organization of American States (OAS) can act as intermediaries between powerful actors and can contain localized conflicts so that they do not spread through the system.[2] When Israel, Great Britain, and France attacked Egypt in 1956 and again when riots and disorder broke out in the Congo (Zaïre) in 1960, the United Nations helped to supervise withdrawal of foreign troops and replaced them with international military forces. It thus provided a mechanism for

preventing these conflicts from spreading and allowed the major powers to avoid primary responsibility and the dangers that it might entail.

Furthermore, certain technological changes like the emergency teletype connection between Moscow and Washington, D.C.; invulnerable missile bases that ensure nuclear second-strike capability; and observational ("spy in the sky") satellites have enhanced the stability of the contemporary system. The "hot line," for instance, reduces the probability of war from miscalculation, technical error, or neglect.

Technological change today, however, occurs with such rapidity that there is a problem of lag. Weapons systems are planned ten years before they can be deployed. They are planned, therefore, on the basis of assumptions about the international system that may well be invalid by the time that the weapons have become operational. The Maginot Line in France, for example, was constructed between World Wars I and II in order to prevent German invasion. It was simply outflanked so that during most of World War II these expensive fortresses were used to house homeless refugees.

Crises often involve amplifying, rather than corrective, feedback. Panics, arms races, and esclation spirals reflect amplifying feedback. In arms races or situations involving mutually exclusive commitments, an increase in arms or commitment by one side tends to evoke a matching response from the other, thus generating a dangerous and costly spiral that may reach no point of equilibrium short of war. During the rush to war in 1914 mobilization by one state stimulated mobilization by others. When one side committed itself more deeply to a violent course of action, the others responded in kind. As one party perceived himself threatened, he responded with hostility. The other side, perceiving the hostility, intensified his own hostility.

The outcome of the crisis might have been different had the actors' responses to

---

[2] For an evaluation of the crisis circumstances in which third parties can act as intermediaries, see Oran R. Young, *The Intermediaries* (Princeton: Princeton University Press, 1967).

others' initiatives been less hostile than the initiatives themselves. "Underresponse" can initiate a "dampening" process in which a modus vivendi is attained.[3]

Such a "dampening" process seems to have occurred during the Quemoy-Matsu crisis of 1958. The roots of this crisis went back to the period immediately after the overthrow of the Chinese nationalist regime of Chiang Kai-shek by the communists under Mao Tse-tung in 1949. Chiang, driven from the Chinese mainland, established a rival government on the island of Taiwan and retained control over several small islands off the Chinese coast, including Quemoy, Matsu, and the Pescadores. These islands became a major object of contention between the communist government on the mainland and the Taiwan regime.

In late August 1958 the communists began an intensive bombardment of Quemoy and Matsu. It appeared for a time that this bombardment was a prelude to invasion of the islands and perhaps even of Taiwan itself. The United States had been allied with Chiang Kai-shek's regime since 1950, but the American attitude toward defense of the islands, located in Amoy and Foochow harbors, was ambiguous. Initially the United States mobilized massive naval strength in the western Pacific, but in the meantime the bombardment severed nationalist supply lines to the islands. In September American vessels began to convoy supplies to these nationalist garrisons, which had been rapidly reinforced by the Taiwan regime, but the United States still refrained from launching attacks against the mainland, and American vessels were instructed to fire only in self-defense.

Instead of increasing the level of violence, the Chinese communists proposed a resumption of ambassadorial talks in Warsaw, which had been suspended be-

[3] Similarly, when two people begin to argue and one raises his voice, the other often responds in a still louder tone. If one of the participants lowers his voice during the argument, it is likely that the other will do so as well.

fore the crisis, and tacitly indicated their readiness to end the escalation by bombarding the islands only on even-numbered days of the month. Although the issue of control over the islands remained unsettled, the crisis itself gradually faded. The political issues underlying a crisis are often not resolved but are either temporarily shelved or carefully evaded. The attitude of adversaries under such circumstances is similar to that expressed by Henry Cabot Lodge, Jr., a former American ambassador to the United Nations:

I see some things that you cannot solve, now. Maybe in 10 years you can, but you can't do it now, and the best thing you can do is to sort of spin it out and drag it along and temporize and pettifog, and that way they don't shoot each other, and that is that much clear gain. [4]

Certain factors affect the probability that escalation will pass some critical threshold beyond which neither side can reverse the process without "losing." First, there are considerations of the future and of other potential enemies. If an adversary seems to have long-range aggressive designs, overresponse to his initial moves is likely, for the stakes are greater than the immediate issue alone would suggest. An actor worried about future encounters may wish to prove that "aggression does not pay." His response will be more moderate if he perceives that the initial move is limited, justified, or brought on by pressures of public opinion and the like beyond the adversary's control.

British and French reactions to Adolf Hitler's demands on Czechoslovakia in 1938 were moderate, partly because the leaders hoped (and some even believed) that the Nazi desire for annexation of the Sudetenland was legitimate and represented the last territorial claim that Hitler would make in Europe. To foster this illusion, Hitler declared on September 26, 1938, that when the Sudeten question had been resolved, "there is for Germany no further territorial problem in Europe."

An actor's response will also be more moderate if other potential enemies seem to require attention. The initial American response to the invasion of South Korea in June 1950, for example, was limited because Harry S. Truman's administration feared that the Soviet Union would take advantage of American preoccupation in the Far East to threaten western Europe. The United States did not want to endanger other, more important objectives by acting precipitately in Korea.

Other important factors include efforts and pressures by third parties to induce peaceful settlement. The nineteenth century Concert of Europe and the contemporary United Nations have played such a role. Sometimes a single country will offer its "good offices" to settle a dispute, thus moderating the behavior of the involved parties. A third party may have the advantage of being able to offer a solution or to make suggestions that the principals can not suggest for fear of losing international prestige or inviting domestic opposition. President Theodore Roosevelt successfully mediated the Russo-Japanese War in 1905, earning for himself one of the few Nobel Peace prizes ever awarded to an advocate of imperialism. In negotiations at Tashkent, Soviet Premier Alexei Kosygin assisted India and Pakistan to resolve their conflict over the borders of Kashmir in 1965.

A third group of factors includes the resources available during a crisis. The fewer the actor's resources, the more likely he is to "underrespond" to an adversary's initiative. A crisis or a conflict may end if the participants simply run out of resources. The Chaco War, fought between Paraguay and Bolivia in 1932–1935 over an uninhabited wilderness rumored to contain oil deposits, ended when the reservoirs of men of combat age in the two countries were exhausted. The India-Pakistan cease-fire agreement in 1965 occurred after both armies had depleted their petroleum and ammunition reserves.

Technology may also shape the course of a crisis. As we have suggested, certain weapons systems act as incentives to over-

reaction; others encourage actors to respond with caution. Finally, there are many psychological variables that can affect decision makers' responses. Memories of the adversary's past behavior, expectations of his future behavior, and the decision makers' own goals can influence choices. During the Cuban missile crisis Robert F. Kennedy argued successfully against an air strike because he believed that the basic values of the United States made secret attack indefensible. He passed to his brother a note that read, "I now know how Tojo felt when he was planning Pearl Harbor" [9].

Corrective feedback may encourage an actor to alter the direction of his behavior and may therefore serve as a crucial steering mechanism for improving policy. Whether or not a corrective signal is properly sent and received can critically affect the outcome of a crisis. When two drivers, though aware of imminent collision, step on their accelerators instead of their brakes and aim their automobiles at each other, deadly consequences ensue. In international politics such "steering pathologies" may occur when an actor's information is inadequate or incorrect or cannot be used effectively. For example, if one state fails to receive, to understand, or to believe a deterrent threat, the danger increases. When time is short sudden changes occur, and the outcome is unpredictable; actors may fail to make normal corrective adjustments.

Premier Nikita S. Khrushchev's misunderstanding of President Kennedy's repeated warnings against the introduction of offensive Soviet weapons into Cuba reflected failure to recognize corrective information. Khrushchev apparently believed that the President lacked the will to carry out his threats. This illusion may have been fostered by the summit meeting between the two leaders in Vienna in 1961, at which Khrushchev was able to "bully" Kennedy, and by Kennedy's failure to respond vigorously to the erection of the Berlin wall. The image of the President that Khrushchev formed during these events may have distorted his interpretations of Kennedy's warnings in the spring and summer of 1962.

The American government also overlooked corrective information because the bureaucracies either disbelieved or sifted out intelligence reports indicating the introduction of offensive missiles into Cuba. Nevertheless, because it was believed that the Soviet Union desired a détente with the United States (a belief that it did not wish to relinquish), and because Khrushchev was expected to behave differently, the situation was not perceived until more evidence was available [10].

The failure to make corrective policy adjustments also may result in systemic overload. When too many demands are placed on a single system in too short a time, its capacity to process inputs and the actor's ability to make satisfactory decisions are severely tested; the system may break down. Even an individual decision maker may break down under demands that he is unable to cope with. A political system subject to strong conflicting claims is vulnerable to such crises as took place in the Weimar Republic in 1933, the French Fourth Republic in 1958, and the Congo in 1960. Demand overload is most dangerous when communications become clogged, as during crises when there is a failure to relay messages quickly and accurately. The communications systems existing in 1914 were unable to handle the increased volume of messages. Consequently misunderstandings and miscalculations about the demands of the actors contributed to the outbreak of war.

The overload problem can be eased either by reducing the demands on the system or by improving mechanisms for handling them. The creation of additional communication and information-processing facilities for periods during which input is great is one way to increase the capacity of a system. Supplementary channels can be opened to handle larger volumes of messages and can substitute for regular channels that become dysfunctional.

THE SYSTEMIC APPROACH AND THE RESOLUTION OF INTERNATIONAL CRISES

Crises may encompass elements of cooperation, as well as of competition [11]. In some outcomes, like nuclear warfare, where *both* adversaries can lose, actors may at least wish to cooperate to avoid the costs of major conflict, even while they continue to compete for the stakes in the contest.

Crises are rarely perceived as having no further consequences, and each actor must consider the possible effects of a lasting crisis or its resolution on future interactions with the same adversary or others. An actor may thus seek to prove that he cannot be "pushed around" by taking greater risks to attain a short-term objective than ordinarily seem worthwhile.

The combination of competitive and cooperative interests characteristically leads to bargaining in which actors in pursuit of goals seek to alter the preferences of opponents, in order to maximize their own benefits at minimum cost. The degree to which an interaction is competitive or cooperative is determined by participants' perceptions of each other's intentions and capabilities and of the structure of the international situation when the crisis begins.

Point 1 in Figure 20.1 represents this beginning point, and the curved line suggests the range of possible outcomes from bargaining. Any change to a point above 1 is a gain for actor A, and any change to a point to the right of it is a gain for actor B. The shaded area represents bargaining outcomes of mutual, though not necessarily identical, advantage. Any point on the curve of this area, such as 4, represents an efficient solution, because neither party can receive more without the other's receiving less. This is known as a "Pareto optimal solution." The smaller the shaded area, the fewer opportunities for mutually profitable outcomes there are, and the more competitive the situation is [2]. If there were *no* shaded area, it would be a zero-sum contest in which point 1, which would also represent the

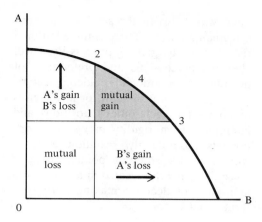

Figure 20.1. Schematic for Mixed-Motive Interaction

solution "*no* agreement," would be on the curve, and any other solution would represent a loss for one of the contestants. Crises may thus result in no change, in mutual gain, in mutual loss, or in gains for some actors and losses for others.[4]

A crisis tends to have a "life cycle," consisting of a series of "moves" by which adversaries initiate and respond. Each actor attempts to avoid sudden disasters, war, or capitulation as he searches for a mutually "acceptable" solution. To make continuation of the crisis appear less attractive, each actor attempts to manipulate incentives and costs for the adversary.

As long as the crisis continues, actors may also try various policy alternatives. A "high level" move, with high risk of war, would be Soviet seizure of Berlin or invasion of western Europe—or American intervention in eastern Europe. Soviet curtailment of American transit rights to Berlin, on the other hand, is a lower-level move, designed to maintain a crisis and likely to evoke American responses short of major retaliation. The Soviet blockade

[4] The upper left-hand quadrant of Figure 20.1 represents a gain for actor A and a loss for actor B, whereas the lower right-hand quadrant represents the reverse. The lower left-hand quadrant represents mutual loss. Clearly, the location of point 1, at which the crisis begins, helps to determine the extent of possible cooperation and conflict, as well as the symmetry or asymmetry of the bargaining situation.

of Berlin in 1948 was a low-level move to which the Western powers responded by successfully supplying the city by means of an airlift. A series of low-level moves, sometimes called "salami tactics," is less likely to provoke major retaliation because no one such move is likely to alter the situation substantially. If a low-level move meets no resistance and earns high rewards, it may encourage still more daring moves.

There is real difficulty in communicating the intention behind a move to the other player. There is no assurance that what is intended by one actor as a non-threatening move will be perceived as such by the other. The greater the competition and mistrust in an interaction, the more likely misunderstandings are. Tacit signaling of concessions and mutual adjustments can ease this problem to some extent, especially if both actors share a common cultural background. In international politics, however, players often have different backgrounds, which may result in different perceptions of the same event or signal.

When one actor possesses a significant strategic advantage, he can raise the stakes in a crisis without fear of major warfare. Even if this actor suffers from localized military inferiority in a particular confrontation, he may still be able to "win" by convincing his adversary of his own willingness to escalate.

International structure, particularly the distribution of resources and attitudes, affects the behavior of actors during crises. Once both sides possess invulnerable nuclear retaliation forces, there is a strong incentive *not* to indulge in uncontrolled escalation or major provocation. The existence of relative second-strike parity since about 1963 and the common recognition of the effects of nuclear warfare partly explain Soviet and American reluctance to confront each other. Localized military superiority has usually dictated how a crisis will be resolved, which helps to explain why the Soviet Union did not meet effective American opposition to its intervention in Hungary in 1956 or to the erection of the Berlin wall in 1961. Similarly, local military superiority permitted the United States to intervene unilaterally in the Dominican Republic in 1965 and strengthened the American bargaining position during the Cuban missile crisis.

Sometimes the values that adversaries attach to their objectives outweighs military considerations. During crises both sides telescope and intensify manipulative bargaining of the sort that we examined in Chapter 18. Bluffs, threats, and promises, all of which affect the credibility of commitments, become critical in determining outcomes. Commitments are expressed in messages to an adversary indicating the high value of an objective and willingness to take risks to ensure its attainment, regardless of possible consequences. As in a poker game, the player with the more convincing commitment may "win," despite strategic or tactical inferiority. Nazi Germany was militarily inferior to its potential opponents between 1933 and 1939. Nevertheless, Adolf Hitler rearmed the nation and reoccupied the Rhineland, thus overthrowing the restrictions of the Versailles Treaty, then succeeded in gaining control of Austria and Czechoslovakia without resorting to war. His success arose mainly from his ability to manifest greater resolve in his undertakings than his British and French adversaries did. Time after time Hitler acted against the advice of his generals, who feared the consequences of military inferiority. "The whole contrast becomes once more acute," wrote General Alfred Jodl at the time of the Munich crisis, "between the Führer's intuition that we *must* do it this year, and the opinion of the Army that we cannot do it yet, as most certainly the Western Powers will interfere, and we are not as yet equal to them" [3]. Hitler's attitudes weighed more than did the beliefs of his generals or the capabilities of the adversaries.

Several possible difficulties in strategic bargaining during crises merit our special attention. First, actors may attach different values to the stakes of interaction. As we have suggested, there is no assurance that adversaries will distinguish in the

same way between threatening and nonthreatening moves. There is the additional risk that the bargaining process itself will alter the perceptions and preferences of the players. Emotional or ideological rigidity can make it difficult for adversaries to appreciate each other's positions and intentions; such rigidity may "lock" opponents into a deadly escalation sequence with no stable stopping points. Some of these dangers are revealed in a critical examination of decision making during international crises.

CRISIS DECISION MAKING: THE CUBAN EXAMPLE

The perception of crisis hinges on interaction between the structure of the situation and the views of decision makers. Sometimes leaders fail to recognize the existence of crisis situations; at other times they invest events with greater significance than will be accorded to them in retrospect. President Kennedy, speculating on why he acted as he did in the Cuban missile crisis in 1962, claimed that he had no choice. "I think," he said, "there are certain compulsions on any major power" [14, p. 830]. Such a view rests on a belief in an objective or systemic basis for crises.

The Cuban example appears to fulfill all our criteria for a crisis. First, it was almost totally unanticipated; despite the suspicions of a few individuals like Senator Kenneth Keating of New York and Central Intelligence Agency Director John McCone, no serious consideration was given to the possibility that the Soviet Union would install offensive missiles outside its own territory. Indeed, the administration had taken care to play down the danger of Soviet action in Cuba as a counter to Republican efforts to make the "Cuban threat" a major issue in the November 1962 congressional elections.

Second, the focus of the conflict was well defined: The issue was the presence of missiles in Cuba. The Kennedy administration perceived both domestic political consequences and global strategic consequences of the Soviet action. Finally, the possibility that the Soviet missiles would be made operational or that a security leak would shift initiative to the Russians compelled a swift decision.

On October 14, 1962, an American U-2 reconnaissance aircraft made the first aerial survey of western Cuba since early September. It took photographs that clearly revealed missile-construction sites in the area of San Cristóbal. There had been several earlier clues to what was happening in Cuba, but national intelligence estimates had discounted the possibility that offensive missiles—that is, medium- and long-range surface-to-surface missiles—were being secretly introduced into Cuba.

The photographs were shown to several high-ranking officials in the Defense and State departments and in the White House, and the reaction of Deputy Secretary of Defense Roswell Gilpatric, "that the United States and the Soviet Union stood at the beginning of a decisive confrontation," was general [1, p. 18]. Gilpatric made certain that the interpreters of the photographs rechecked their findings before finally accepting the evidence that Khrushchev had violated his previous assurances to President Kennedy.

The formation of an Executive Committee (Ex Comm) to shape policy for the Cuban crisis was swift and orderly; Ex Comm was carefully selected and limited in size. As in most crises, decision making was centralized at high levels of government, and bureaucratic channels were bypassed. In crises the structure of decision groups and the distribution of influence among large bureaucracies are less influential (though not uninfluential) in the decisions that are reached. At such times members of a small decision group like Ex Comm are less constrained by bureaucratic affiliations and parochial departmental roles than they are in situations involving incremental change and budgetary distribution or redistribution. Recall that social variables are also less important in crises than in other situations, but

idiosyncratic variables may be *more* critical.

The first meeting of Ex Comm was "dominated by somber reflections concerning the nature of the challenge from Moscow" [1, pp. 34–35]. The participants' reflections constituted an initial attempt to articulate and integrate their individual perceptions in a cogent explanation by which to guide later action. The group speculated about Soviet motives, considered the implications of the missiles for national security, and anticipated the decisions that would have to be made. The discussion appears to have resembled a restrained form of "brainstorming"; opinions and interpretations were welcomed in hopes that they might present a "handle" on the situation. The major importance of this meeting was in permitting determination of both the "objective" characteristics of the situation (what had happened and why) and its "subjective" characteristics (its importance to the men in the room and to the United States). The situation was being defined, and interpretations of reality were being offered; these interpretations could be tested as new information was received, but the suddenness of the Cuban crisis and the need for secrecy and haste meant that argument, logic, and expertise were the only available tests for the group's speculations. Furthermore, the nature and timing of the Soviet move threatened not only the interests of the United States but also the political interests of President Kennedy. His personal reputation and that of the United States government were both at stake. He was already subject to domestic pressures to "do something" about Cuba, and the successful introduction of Soviet offensive weapons into Cuba would severely damage the reputation for effectiveness of his administration. Soviet action challenged Kennedy's public pledges not to tolerate a Soviet presence and violated Soviet promises not to deploy such weapons. To this degree social and role variables *did* intrude, and an understanding of them is necessary to explain certain aspects of American and Soviet behavior.

The formulation of alternative policies is an integral part of the process of defining a situation and clarifying objectives. Once the Soviet challenge had been perceived, possible responses were discussed; the process of decision making had begun. Rusk has described Ex Comm's method of presenting alternatives as "boxing the compass"; and several possible courses of action, ranging from informal diplomatic contacts to unilateral military action, were considered. The group tried to project the probable results of each proposed course and to anticipate possible complications. "We discussed what the Soviet reaction would be to any possible move by the United States, what our reaction with them would have to be to that Soviet reaction and so on, trying to follow each of these roads to their ultimate conclusion."[5] Former Ambassadors to the Soviet Union Charles Bohlen and Llewellyn Thompson were called upon for their opinions of probable Soviet reactions; military leaders described requirements for both an air strike and an invasion of Cuba; the group as a whole assessed the likely political consequences at home and abroad of various courses of action. As the meetings continued, papers and memoranda were written and submitted, and "war games" were conducted. But the unexpectedness of the event and the necessity for continuing secrecy limited the available knowledge. Uncertainty was manifest throughout the crisis. Although it behaved in an orderly and rational way, the group had to choose among only a limited portion of "all the alternatives." The exigencies of the crisis seem to have generated many new ideas, and this freedom of thinking was encouraged by President Kennedy's decision not to attend some of the sessions so that his presence would not inhibit discussion. At this stage systemic variables were paramount, and American leaders seemed mainly concerned about minimizing threats to the United States from Soviet missiles.

The next stage in the process was in-

ternal consensus building, the welding of individual opinions and ideas into group decisions. Consensus building in the missile crisis centered on resolving the differences between those who preferred to blockade Cuba and those who favored an air strike. Although other alternatives were considered, the members of Ex Comm soon gravitated toward one or the other of these two positions, and "nearly every man in the room changed his position at least once—and some more than once—during that anxious week of brainstorming" [1, p. 57]. Discussion was largely unstructured, and ideas were freely exchanged. Each position was tested and retested. As opinion began to coalesce about the two alternatives and the final choice was narrowed, the deliberations became more structured.

President Kennedy finally chose a "selective quarantine." In making this decision he seems to have been particularly persuaded by two lines of argument. The first was Robert F. Kennedy's insistence that a sneak attack on Cuba by the United States would violate American norms and traditions and would alienate world public opinion. This argument illustrates the effect of individual values and collective memory. Secretary of Defense Robert S. McNamara's insistence that the blockade would permit the United States greater flexibility during the later stages of the crisis was also persuasive. He believed that an air strike would be irreversible and might result in the deaths of innocent civilians, as well as of Russian advisers and technicians in Cuba, whereas the blockade would allow the United States to test Soviet reactions while keeping control of the situation. McNamara's evaluation was based mainly on strategic considerations, whereas Robert Kennedy's was determined by an awareness of social characteristics, but both men seemed acutely aware that Soviet perceptions were a significant, though relatively unknown, variable in the crisis. On this point the contrast with European leaders in 1914 is striking!

According to one presidential adviser,

"President Kennedy, aware of the enormous hazards in the confrontation with the Soviets . . . made certain that his first move did not close out either all his options or all of theirs" [15]. A distinction was made between the use of coercive threats and the perpetration of violence, and, partly for this reason, the United States initiated a "selective quarantine" around Cuba, rather than taking the bolder step of attacking Soviet missile bases. The President's announcement of the quarantine on October 23 emphasized that "force shall not be used except in case of failure or refusal to comply with directions . . . after reasonable efforts have been made to communicate them to the vessel or craft, or in case of self-defense." He was well aware of what constituted a "rational" bargaining process.

Once the decision group had achieved consensus, the new policy had to be communicated to others in a manner that would minimize opposition and facilitate implementation. There are two central questions about building an external consensus in a crisis: How does the need for external support affect the decision-making process, and how is this support obtained once policy has been decided? Questions about the needs of the bureaucracies and about social factors like public opinion intrude once again at this point.

Although deliberations during the Cuban crisis proceeded in secret, the world outside was by no means forgotten. Several participants argued with an eye to tradition and the need for legal rationalization. They recognized that American behavior would ultimately have to be justified before others. The Pearl Harbor analogy was mentioned against the alternative of surprise attack, whereas concern for "freedom of the seas" was a point against the blockade. Eventually the blockade was justified by the right of the Organization of American States to take collective action to preserve hemispheric security. Normative questions could not be excluded from these deliberations. An elaborate scenario was drawn up to ensure that the American action and "legitimat-

ing" reasons for it would be communicated and publicized accurately and effectively.

Congressional leaders and allies were informed; they accepted the decision and promised whatever support was necessary. The role of the allies was, however, minimal. American efforts in the United Nations were not expected to yield major results, but they did embarrass the Soviet Union and prevented it from mobilizing world opinion against the blockade. The Organization of American States was important, and the United States did secure its full support for the quarantine. To avert potential domestic opposition, President Kennedy released the U-2 photographs of Soviet installations in Cuba; his television speech of October 22 had an electric impact on American public opinion, galvanizing support for the administration despite the partisan atmosphere aroused by the impending congressional elections.

Kennedy began by explaining what had occurred and what the implications of Soviet bases in Cuba were: "Several of them include medium-range ballistic missiles, capable of carrying a nuclear warhead for a distance of more than 1,000 nautical miles. Each of these missiles in short is capable of striking Washington, D.C., the Panama Canal, Cape Canaveral. . . . " He proceeded to hold the Soviet Union responsible for the crisis and accountable for what might ensue. Carefully he showed how closely Cuba and the Soviet Union were linked in the enterprise, in order to prevent the latter from fobbing off its responsibility on Castro. He summed up:

[T]his secret, swift and extraordinary build-up of Communist missiles—in an area well known to have a special and historical relationship to the United States . . . in violation of Soviet assurances, and in defiance of American and hemispheric policy . . . is a deliberately provocative and unjustified change in the *status quo* which cannot be accepted by this country, if our courage and our commitments are ever to be trusted again by either friend or foe.

The effect of the quarantine was to leave it to the Soviet Union to seize the "last clear chance" to avoid escalation. The United States had drawn a line around Cuba, and it was now up to Khrushchev to halt the shipment of offensive weapons to the island. To assure the Soviet leaders of his resolve, Kennedy ordered mobilization and a state of military readiness. Military aircraft were dispersed to civilian airfields; troops were massed in the southeastern United States, and the Navy began to tighten the ring around Cuba. The message was clear and unmistakable: The United States was committed to this course of action and was prepared to suffer whatever consequences might ensue. American moves contained the implicit threat of intensifying the crisis unless the Soviet Union backed down. The threat was clearly understood by Khrushchev, and the Soviet Union, suffering from an approximate inferiority of 10 to 1 in the number of strategic missiles at its disposal, as well as from a marked local disadvantage in the Caribbean, ultimately agreed to withdraw the missiles.

In exchange for Soviet compliance with American demands, President Kennedy issued a unilateral promise that the United States would not invade Cuba and praised the Soviet Premier for his prudence, which provided the Soviet Union an opportunity for graceful exit; too great a "loss of face" or prestige might have tempted it to escalate the crisis instead. Putting the opponent "up against a wall" may simply force him to fight, even though the conflict may result in mutually devastating consequences.

References

1. Abel, Elie, *The Missile Crisis* (Philadelphia: Lippincott, 1966).
2. Axelrod, Robert, *Conflict of Interest* (Chicago: Markham, 1970), chap. 2.
3. Bullock, Alan, *Hitler: A Study in Tyranny* (New York: Harper & Row, 1964), p. 450.
4. Claude, Inis L., Jr., *Swords into Plowshares,* 3rd ed. (New York: Random House, 1964), p. 217.
5. Hermann, Charles F., "Some Consequences of Crisis Which Limit the Viability of Organizations," *Administrative Science Quarterly,* 8 (1963), pp. 61–82.
6. Hilsman, Roger, *To Move a Nation* (Garden City, N.Y.: Doubleday, 1967).
7. Holsti, Ole, Richard Brody, and Robert North, "Measuring Affect and Action in International Reaction Models: Empirical Materials from the 1962 Cuban Crisis," in James N. Rosenau, ed., *International Politics and Foreign Policy,* rev. ed. (New York: Free Press, 1969), p. 694.
8. Holsti, Ole R., Robert C. North, and Richard A. Brody, "Perception and Action in the 1914 Crisis," in J. David Singer, ed., *Quantitative International Politics* (New York: Free Press, 1968), p. 137.
9. Kennedy, Robert F., *Thirteen Days* (New York: Norton, 1969), p. 31.
10. Knorr, Klaus, "Failures in National Intelligence Estimates: The Case of the Cuban Missiles," *World Politics,* 16 (April 1964), pp. 455–467.
11. Luce, R. Duncan, and Howard Raiffa, *Games and Decisions* (New York: Wiley, 1957).
12. McClelland, Charles A., "Action Structures and Communication in Two International Crises: Quemoy and Berlin," *Background,* 7 (1964), pp. 201–215.
13. McClelland, Charles A., "The Acute International Crisis," *World Politics,* 14 (October 1961), pp. 182–204.
14. Schlesinger, Arthur M., Jr., *A Thousand Days* (Boston: Houghton Mifflin, 1965).
15. Sorenson, Theodore, *Decision-Making in the White House* (New York: Columbia University Press, 1963), pp. 20–21.
16. Waltz, Kenneth N., "The Stability of the Bipolar World," *Daedalus,* 93 (Summer 1964), pp. 892–907.
17. Zinnes, Dina A., Robert C. North, and Howard E. Koch, Jr., "Capability, Threat, and the Outbreak of War," in James N. Rosenau, ed., *International Politics and Foreign Policy* (New York: Free Press), 1961, p. 470.

Suggested reading for Chapter 20 will be found at the end of Chapter 21.

Chapter 21
CUBA AND VIETNAM: A COMPARATIVE ANALYSIS

In all civilizations, the long-run trend of war has been toward increasing destructiveness of life and property in spite of its declining frequency. Each period of battle concentration has tended to be more serious than the previous one
—Quincy Wright [11]

There are few more dangerous practices in international politics than drawing unwarranted conclusions from a previous event. The tendency of statesmen to assume that successes or failures in the past provide suitable guides for the present and future leads to "decision by analogy." The use of analogies is no substitute for systematic investigation, for rarely, if ever, do all the conditions of one historical event reappear in another. The statesmen of 1914 mistakenly acted on assumptions left over from the Franco-Prussian War of 1870, and catastrophe ensued. Western politicians in the 1930s tried to avoid the mistakes of 1914 and encouraged the aggressive designs of Adolf Hitler and Benito Mussolini. It is imperative that decision makers be aware not only of what the present has in common with the past but also of how they differ.

OBJECTIVES AND INFLUENCE IN THE CUBAN MISSILE CRISIS

The Cuban crisis was not simply dangerous; it was also very complex. Ex Comm adopted a set of securance and prevention objectives and devised a combination of rewards and threats to attain them. The United States sought not only to secure termination of the Soviet buildup in Cuba but also to obtain removal of existing Soviet missiles from the Caribbean. This second objective required persuading the Soviet Union to undo something it had already done, whereas the first required the Soviet Union only to cease a specific activity. Clearly, the former kind of objective is more difficult to achieve than the latter, for most actors are less inclined to retreat than simply to desist. Furthermore, it is possible to persuade an actor to desist from an activity by making a threat contingent on future behavior and leaving it up to the adversary whether or not that threat will be carried out. To undo a *fait accompli*, however, an actor must initiate coercive behavior against the adversary—which presumably threatens greater harm to the adversary than he will endure from acquiescence.

Aside from these securance objectives, the United States was also determined to deter Soviet provocation elsewhere, as in Berlin, where the Soviet Union enjoyed an overwhelming tactical advantage, and to prevent uncontrolled escalation and the concomitant risk of large-scale violence.

This combination of American objectives created a dilemma for Ex Comm. To bring an end to Soviet shipments of offensive weapons to Cuba and to achieve the dismantling of existing weapons, President John F. Kennedy had to convince Nikita S. Khrushchev of his willingness to accept risks. And to ensure the removal of Soviet missiles it was also necessary to invoke a threat that would convey urgency to the Soviet Union. If uncontrolled escalation was to be prevented, on the other hand, it was necessary to maintain strict control over American military activities and to proceed prudently in order to avoid either provoking the adversary unduly or making American threats seem "incredible" bluffs. Prudent bargaining also requires lengthening decision time and pausing between steps in the ladder of escalation so as to ascertain the intentions of the adversary and avoid misunderstandings. The blockade of Cuba was actually only the first step, after which Kennedy could stop and review the results. The blockade itself consisted of a set of discrete moves. First, the actual interdiction of shipping to Cuba was delayed for many hours after Kennedy's televised announcement of October 22. Second, the line of quarantine, originally intended to stretch about 800 miles around Cuba, was tightened to within 500 miles to permit the Soviet Union more time to consider its response.[1] Third, American vessels were ordered to fire only at the rudders of blockade runners and to intercept only non-Soviet ships at first. These precautions were intended to

[1] The Navy preferred the 800-mile distance so that its vessels would be out of range of planes based on Cuba.

minimize the danger of rapid Soviet-American confrontation.

The more slowly an actor escalates, the smaller is the impact of each step. Such incrementalism permits the opponent time to deal with each step individually and to prepare for what may come. Lyndon B. Johnson's policy of slow and deliberate increases in the bombing of North Vietnam during 1965, though an excellent illustration of presidential control, permitted North Vietnam to absorb the impact of each increment more easily, to reply with escalating steps of its own, and to prepare its citizens for what was to come. The Joint Chiefs of Staff complained in October 1966 that two years before they had

recommended a "sharp knock" on NVN military assets and war-supporting facilities rather than the campaign of slowly increasing pressure which was adopted. Whatever the political merits of the latter course, we deprived ourselves of the military effects of early weight of effort and shock, and gave to the enemy time to adjust to our slow quantitative and qualitative increase of pressure. [9, p. 552]

When the sequence of coercion unfolds slowly, the risk that it will get out of hand is minimized, but its impact on the opponent is also diminished.

Recalling the options that Ex Comm favored—quarantine or air strike—it is clear that the former promised minimum risk of uncontrollable escalation and the latter the dramatic impact necessary to achieve both securance objectives. The quarantine was also appropriate to demonstrate Kennedy's determination, to provide dramatic impact and to signal to the Soviet Union that the United States was unwilling to acquiesce in the continuing buildup in the Caribbean. The quarantine did, however, lack an obvious connection with the objective of having weapons already in place removed from Cuba.

Preference for the blockade was based on Kennedy's assumption that Khrushchev had miscalculated American resolve and willingness to take risks; Khrushchev apparently did not think the young American President particularly "tough-minded." The President himself was acutely aware of the difficulty of communicating his own resolve to Khrushchev without resorting to force; he was deeply concerned lest his desire for détente be misinterpreted as a manifestation of weakness. The depth of his concern was reflected in a comment during the Berlin crisis of 1961: "If Khrushchev wants to rub my nose in the dirt, it's all over. That son of a bitch won't pay any attention to words. He has to see you move" [8, p. 391].

Khrushchev was like a poker player who sees that his opponent is unable to call his bluff. Against this background, the value of the blockade option becomes clearer. Any less daring move—for example, a diplomatic offensive in the United Nations—would have been ineffective by itself and would have signaled acquiescence to the Soviet *fait accompli*. A stronger signal, like bombing or invasion of Cuba, would have severely threatened Soviet prestige, killed Cubans and Russians, and probably initiated hostilities before bargaining could begin. The blockade, on the other hand, registered Kennedy's determination without threatening Khrushchev's prestige so heavily and left open to the Soviet Premier several "face-saving" options that would permit genuine bartering of concessions.

When the administration first learned of the introduction of Soviet missiles into Cuba, there was disagreement about the strategic meaning of the move. Secretary of Defense Robert S. McNamara, for example, argued that "a missile is a missile" and "It makes no great difference whether you are killed by a missile fired from the Soviet Union or from Cuba" [3, p. 195]. Others disagreed, arguing that the intermediate- and medium-range ballistic missiles in Cuba would expose American strategic bombers in the Southeast to attack with virtually no warning time. Furthermore, such missiles would also subject large areas of Latin America to Soviet nuclear blackmail. Regardless

of the actual strategic meaning of the move, it is clear that the political consequences of permitting the Soviet provocation to go unchallenged would have been serious, for it would have appeared to have shifted the strategic balance. It was therefore necessary that the missiles be removed, and obtaining this removal would be even more difficult once they had been made operational. The Soviet Union would then have achieved a substantial psychological victory without deploying expensive intercontinental ballistic missiles and could have silenced increasing Chinese criticism of Soviet caution.

Khrushchev later argued that the Soviet Union was merely attempting to deter a possible American attack on Fidel Castro's regime. The truth of this claim is in doubt, for the number and range of Soviet missiles and bombers in Cuba were greater than would have been necessary to deter such a move [4]. "Minimal deterrence" would have been sufficient. There was the further possibility that the Soviet Union intended to use the missiles as a counter in bargaining with the United States for the removal of American missiles from Greece and Turkey. This hypothesis was partly borne out during the crisis by Soviet demands for such a quid pro quo. But as an explanation this hypothesis seems inadequate because of the magnitude of the Soviet investment and the likelihood that Soviet leaders knew that the United States was planning to remove the obsolete weapons from Greece and Turkey in the near future anyway. It is also possible that the Soviet Union hoped that the missiles in Cuba would increase its bargaining leverage on a whole range of issues, including that of Berlin.

The blockade strategy permitted the President to control the escalation process and to signal his determination without resorting to force; it also proved sufficient to bring about cessation of further shipments of offensive weapons to Cuba. Although the blockade did not achieve all its objectives, the President retained an arsenal of alternatives that would have been progressively more onerous for Cuba and the Soviet Union. Force was reserved for an ultimate showdown, rather than used as the point at which bargaining would begin. Force could be used later, and the President took care to make this possibility very clear. The Soviet Union was aware that the selective quarantine was merely an initial step on the ladder of escalation and was guided in its response by the knowledge that the President would otherwise take further steps on that ladder. Ex Comm had not yet decided whether or not to escalate when the Soviet Union agreed not to challenge the American blockade and began to cut its losses.

The blockade served to structure the bargaining sequence in Kennedy's favor. Some observers have overlooked the fact that the crisis was a variable-sum game involving bids and communication, as well as coercion and opposing interests. From the beginning the President was aware that Khrushchev could not simply be coaxed into dismantling and removing the missiles; he had to receive something in return. Ultimately the United States pledged not to invade Cuba. A positive incentive was thus an integral part of the final bargain.

One major problem was timing: when to offer concessions and when to apply coercive pressures. Certain members of Ex Comm favored making concessions to the Soviet Union at an early stage of the crisis, but Kennedy demurred. His brother Robert remarked to presidential adviser Arthur M. Schlesinger, Jr., on October 22: "We will have to make a deal at the end, but we must stand absolutely firm now. Concessions must come at the end of negotiation, not at the beginning" [8, p. 811]. Until the President was satisfied that Khrushchev had been convinced of his determination and had initiated steps to remove the Soviet provocation, he wanted to retain his freedom of maneuver and make no commitments that would impair his control of the situation. Robert Kennedy recalled that the President had mulled over the idea of a summit meeting with Khrushchev and had rejected it as "useless until Khrushchev first ac-

cepted, as a result of our deeds as well as our statements, the U.S. determination in this matter. . . . The President wanted to have some cards in his own hands" [6, pp. 66–67].

The final outcome was that Soviet ships on their way to Cuba stopped dead and did not challenge the quarantine. The Soviet decision to halt shipments to Cuba may also have been a response to the American Navy's action in forcing Soviet submarines in the Caribbean to the surface to identify themselves. The tension was further eased when both sides accepted a proposal by U Thant that Soviet ships temporarily stay away from the area of the blockade and that the United States try to avoid confrontation with them. An earlier proposal by the Secretary-General that both arms shipments to Cuba and the quarantine be voluntarily suspended had been rejected by Kennedy because he thought that it would lessen the pressure on Soviet leaders without assuring the United States that missiles already in Cuba would be removed. U Thant's second proposal resulted partly from American advice. Undersecretary of State George Ball is reported to have instructed United Nations representative Adlai Stevenson:

The Secretary General ought to be doing everything possible to avert an encounter between ships at sea in the next twenty-four hours. We need time for the Soviet Union to think things over and for diplomacy to have a chance to work. Why don't you get him to issue an appeal to the Russians to stop their ships for a time? We could have a shooting war by tomorrow afternoon. [1]

U Thant's role in the crisis illustrates the use of ancillary channels of communication by both sides. Third parties can make proposals that neither of the principals can put forward directly. Furthermore, normal channels of communication tend to become overloaded during crises. Khrushchev took advantage of a visit to Moscow by Westinghouse Corporation executive William Knox to transmit his views to the American President, and messages were also passed through other unorthodox channels. The availability of alternative channels of communication proved particularly important after the quarantine had succeeded in halting the weapons shipments but before agreement on removal of Russian weapons already on the island had been reached. On Friday, October 26, an American journalist, John Scali, was approached by Alexander S. Fomin of the Soviet embassy in Washington, D.C. Fomin suggested a possible resolution of the impasse: the dismantling of Soviet missiles, to be verified by the United Nations, in return for an American pledge not to invade Cuba. These terms were incorporated in the bargain that was finally struck some days later. Scali reported his conversation with Fomin to the State Department and was taken to see Secretary of State Dean Rusk. The Secretary gave Scali a message to pass on to Fomin: "I have reason to believe that the USG [United States government] sees real possibilities and supposes that the representatives of the two governments in New York could work this matter out with U Thant and with each other. My impression is, however, that time is very urgent" [3, p. 218]. Rusk then emphasized to Scali "that time was very, very short—no more than two days" [3, p. 218].

Later that same day a letter, probably written by Khrushchev personally, arrived; it incorporated the terms of the deal that Fomin had suggested. The next day another letter arrived specifying a further condition: that American missiles be removed from Turkey. It is possible that other members of the Soviet Politburo had put pressure on Khrushchev to raise the price or even that the second letter had been written first but delivered later because of a more elaborate clearance procedure. At any rate, it created a new dilemma for Kennedy because there was a strong feeling in the United States that such a swap would be "fair" and that American missiles in Turkey were obsolete anyway.[2] Had the President accepted such a trade the United States

---

[2] For example, influential columnist Walter Lippmann had suggested such a trade in a newspaper article on October 25.

would have seemed ready to surrender the interests of its allies when its own interests were threatened. Such an impression would have had a very unfavorable impact on the North Atlantic Treaty Organization, already troubled by the suspicions of Charles de Gaulle (see Chapter 15). Instead of responding to the new demand, the President accepted his brother's suggestion that he simply ignore the second letter and negotiate with the Russians only on the basis of the first one. Robert Kennedy met with Soviet Ambassador Anatoly Dobrynin and presented him with a virtual ultimatum: an unambiguous threat that the United States would escalate the crisis if the Soviet Union did not agree to dismantle and withdraw its missiles from Cuba very soon. Kennedy reported his encounter with Dobrynin:

> We had to have a commitment by tomorrow that these bases would be removed. I was not giving them an ultimatum but a statement of fact. He should understand that if they did not remove these bases, we would remove them. . . . We had only a few more hours—we needed an answer immediately from the Soviet Union. I said we must have it the next day. [6, pp. 108–109]

Kennedy also made it clear that American missiles in Turkey and Italy would be removed in the near future but not in such a way that Soviet pressure would appear to be the cause. An additional reward for Soviet compliance with American demands was thus added to the package. On Sunday, October 28, Khrushchev agreed to withdraw the Soviet missiles from Cuba.

SOBERING CONTRASTS BETWEEN THE CUBAN CRISIS AND THE VIETNAM WAR

The Cuban crisis of 1962 was something of a watershed in the cold war; the first crisis of the nuclear age that had pitted the two superpowers directly against each other, with Armageddon threatening. It revealed that the two nations not only had competing interests but also shared certain objectives, like the desire to avoid nuclear warfare. The crisis in many ways offers a textbook example of the uses of manipulative coercion in diplomacy and of the techniques of crisis diplomacy. But overgeneralization from the Cuban crisis would be unwise. A combination of good fortune, skill, and chance conditions enabled the United States to test successfully the will of the Soviet Union without resorting to large-scale violence. Some observers have argued that the crisis proved that the threat of force is rational in a nuclear age, though force itself is not. Others have suggested that American determination in any crisis will guarantee attainment of American objectives. Both these conclusions are ill founded and dangerous, for they reflect ignorance of the special circumstances that favored Kennedy's use of threats and facilitated bargaining between the Soviet Union and the United States.

Several structural characteristics of the crisis especially merit our attention. In October 1962 the United States enjoyed both strategic and tactical military superiority. American long-range bombers and missiles assured Kennedy of a strategic military advantage that an American president no longer enjoys. Indeed, one explanation of Soviet behavior in the autumn of 1962 is as an effort to right the strategic imbalance quickly and inexpensively. The geographical position of Cuba and its vulnerability to American naval, air, and amphibious forces assured the United States of a conventional military superiority that it does not enjoy in areas like Berlin and Cambodia. Cuba's vulnerability was a factor because the United States had military forces that could have exploited it. Kennedy also had command of sufficient rewards to offer to Khrushchev, and he could offer them in a way calculated to permit his adversary a dignified retreat.

The Soviet leader was rapidly made aware of American determination to achieve objectives, regardless of the costs. The Soviet Union could recognize also the United States' special interest and his-

toric responsibility in Latin America[3]— public articles of faith since promulgation of the Monroe Doctrine of 1823. Economic, cultural, and military ties between the United States and the nations of Latin America—in the Rio Pact, the Organization of American States, and the Alliance for Progress, among others—are the tangible expressions of this special interest. Such concern lent American determination in the Cuban crisis greater credibility than is possible in Southeast Asia or Africa. The President's determination was further enhanced by domestic political support for a "hard line" toward Cuba.

The bargaining process itself was facilitated by several factors. First, only two actors were involved, thus simplifying calculations for both. The only possible intruder, Castro, was studiously ignored by both, in order to avoid complications. Second, both actors were superpowers with global responsibilities and overlapping mutual interests. Consequently, both sought to avoid undermining other objectives, and both had much to lose in the event of war. Finally, the central American objective in Cuba was limited and clear: Kennedy wanted the Soviet missiles out.

If this discussion has helped to explain Kennedy's success in the Cuban crisis, it should also clarify why both Lyndon B. Johnson and Richard Nixon have fared so poorly in Indochina. Since 1965 it has no longer been certain that the United States enjoys substantial strategic superiority over the Soviet Union. Furthermore, as the Soviet Union was basically a bystander in the Vietnam War, limiting itself to supplying arms to North Vietnam and the Viet Cong, the issue did not directly involve the two superpowers. Instead, the United States and its South Vietnamese ally were confronting two minor international actors, North Vietnam and the Viet Cong; China stood

[3] The United States, on its part, recognizes the Soviet Union's special interest in eastern Europe, which helps to explain why it did not intervene in the East Berlin uprising of 1953, the Hungarian revolution of 1956, or the occupation of Czechoslovakia in 1968.

aside but had a major stake in the outcome. Under these circumstances strategic asymmetry would be basically irrelevant to the conflict anyway, and threats to raise the conventional threshold would have been either incredible or provocative to the United States' adversaries and shocking to its friends.

The United States enjoyed the dubious tactical advantages of air and naval superiority in a conflict conducted largely along guerrilla lines. The adversary was on home terrain, with widespread support from the people. Its proximity to the Soviet Union and China and limited requirements meant few unsurmountable logistical problems. Guerrilla warfare puts a premium on political agitation and selective terrorism. Local recruitment and relatively minor outside support were all that was required to sustain what became essentially a war of attrition. The North Vietnamese and Viet Cong also were able to take advantage of sanctuaries in neighboring Cambodia and Laos, despite American and South Vietnamese intervention in those countries in 1970.

As the United States' adversaries were not major powers and were conducting political or military operations under conditions for which they were well prepared, air and naval superiority had little meaning. First of all, at the beginning of large-scale American intervention North Vietnam and the Viet Cong were on the verge of overthrowing the regime in Saigon and replacing it with a communist government. This objective was central to the North Vietnamese and the Viet Cong, who had fought for almost three decades against the Japanese, the French, and the United States to achieve an independent and united Vietnam. Unlike Soviet objectives in Cuba, the unification of Vietnam was the focal point of North Vietnamese foreign policy. But North Vietnam was not a superpower and did not need to weigh its objective against global obligations and conflicting requirements. The unification of Vietnam was the very cornerstone of Ho Chi Minh's foreign policy and that of succeeding leaders.

There was thus extreme asymmetry between the two sides' objectives. The United States had to weigh its behavior in Vietnam against the requirements of its policies elsewhere. In Europe discontent with the United States' Asian policy was growing and American obsession with Southeast Asia was considered to have weakened its commitment to the defense of Europe. Vietnam was essentially of secondary interest to the United States; imprudent escalation by the United States could have led to one or more of the following undesirable consequences:

1. Ending the growing détente between the United States and the Soviet Union and halting progress toward mutual understanding on matters of European security, the Middle East, and strategic arms control.
2. Putting an end to the Sino-Soviet split.
3. Bringing about massive Chinese intervention.
4. Permitting the Soviet Union to make advances in other areas, notably the Mediterranean basin and the Middle East.
5. Creating unprecedented revulsion against American foreign policy among the small nonaligned nations of Africa and Asia, which perceived the unequal conflict as having racial overtones.
6. Dislocating the American economy and perpetuating neglect of major domestic needs while causing large-scale domestic dissatisfaction.

These restraints on American freedom to use threats or coercion were buttressed by the obvious limitation on how far North Vietnam and the Viet Cong could be coerced. As rapid large-scale escalation might have been counterproductive to American interests elsewhere, the United States at first announced that the bombing of the north would be limited. The Johnson administration made it clear that the city of Hanoi, the port of Haiphong, and the Red river dikes protecting North Vietnam's main rice-growing area would not be touched. Indeed, the accidental American bombing of the dikes in the summer of 1972 touched off widespread protests against American policy throughout the world. Once these targets were off limits, however, there was little else of value in underdeveloped North Vietnam that the administration could threaten to destroy. Indeed, at the beginning of the bombing, the Pentagon was able to identify only eight industrial targets worth destroying. All the thatched huts, sampans, and pontoon bridges in Vietnam were scarcely worth a fraction of a united Vietnam to Hanoi's leaders. The United States could surely have bombed North Vietnam "back into the Stone Age," as was suggested by General Curtis LeMay, but the journey would not have been very long. The threat could have profoundly disturbed a major industrialized and urbanized nation like the United States or the Soviet Union, but could have only limited impact on an agrarian country with much less to lose. Furthermore, it is unclear to what extent North Vietnam could be held accountable for the behavior of the Viet Cong in South Vietnam anyway.

Bargaining was complicated by the involvement of several parties and potential adversaries, each with different objectives and interests.[4] The United States was hampered by having to negotiate an accord that would also be acceptable to the government of South Vietnam, whose interests did not invariably coincide with American objectives. The military regime in South Vietnam was simultaneously weak and truculent. Its bargaining strength vis-à-vis its American ally rested on that very weakness. The likelihood of its rapid collapse without American support—combined with little prospect of a new regime favorable to the United States—meant that its leaders could pursue dictatorial policies while resisting American demands for social and economic reform. Its foreign policies were uniformly more belligerent than those of the United States, and its leaders behaved in ways that embarrassed Washington. Involvement of weaker allies with somewhat divergent objectives had complicated previous situ-

ations for the United States. In 1958 the Chinese nationalist Chiang Kai-shek involved the United States in the defense of Quemoy and Matsu by placing the best men in his army on those offshore islands; the army thus became a hostage to American behavior, for Taiwan warned that the troops might have to surrender to the communists if no assistance were received from Dwight D. Eisenhower's administration. In 1951 President Syngman Rhee of South Korea succeeded in delaying an American agreement with China on the disposition of prisoners of war by ordering the release of all North Korean and Chinese prisoners in South Korean camps. The risks to a major power of relying on weak allies were graphically illustrated by the way in which Austria-Hungary drew Germany into war in 1914.

Compared with Kennedy's objectives in the Cuban crisis, Johnson's and Nixon's objectives in Vietnam remained cloudy. The United States has no traditional interests in Southeast Asia, and its interference in that area, only recently free of French colonialism, smacked of imperialism. Furthermore, there were no rewards that could sufficiently compensate Vietnamese communists for renunciation of their objective.[5]

Finally, Vietnamese doubts of American willingness to continue an expensive and frustrating war of attrition were fostered by deep divisions in American public opinion. Indeed, public revulsion against the war put an end to the career of President Johnson. One study has found that in the mid-1960s the American public was suprisingly well informed about Vietnam and that 86 percent of the public knew that Congress had not declared war; 68 percent knew that North Vietnam was being bombed. According to the investigators, "It is our impression that [these figures] represent fairly high levels of information on an issue of for-

[4] For an excellent discussion of this complex situation, see Donald A. Zagoria, *The Vietnam Triangle* (New York: Pegasus, 1967).

[5] At one stage President Johnson spoke vaguely of American assistance in the economic development of the Mekong delta after the war, but the offer evoked little response from the other side.

eign policy" [10]. The sharpness of the divisions in public opinion were suggested in the 1968 election survey conducted by the Survey Research Center of the University of Michigan; it was found that 20 percent were in favor of withdrawal, 38 percent in favor of continuing the same course of action, 35 percent in favor of escalation, and 7 percent not answering. Despite substantial American commitment of troops and material, American resolve could be questioned by the Vietnamese Communists as larger segments of the public became disenchanted with the war.

SOME DIFFICULTIES IN THE MANAGEMENT OF CRISES

Each crisis, then, is to some extent unique. Its characteristics ultimately determine the nature and intensity of the interaction and the specific moves of the adversaries. As these characteristics are rarely known or understood before the crisis erupts, it is difficult to plan behavior in advance. Information on an opponent's attitudes, intentions, and resolution is difficult to obtain, and evaluations are usually based on guesswork. Nevertheless, both the Cuban and Vietnam examples serve to highlight several general problem areas in the management of crises: risk, will, promises and threats, and timing.

In attempting to manipulate an adversary during a crisis the question of risk is central. It is imperative that an actor base his demands on knowledge of the adversary's ability to comply—and thus of his perceptions. American efforts to persuade Japan to cease its expansion in Asia in 1940–1941 by denying to it the resources with which to wage war ultimately drove the Japanese to initiate war against the United States itself. Recalling the period of increasing American economic restrictions on the Japanese just before Pearl Harbor, Dean Acheson, then assistant secretary of state, insisted: "The Japanese military leaders were not rational regarding their interests and purposes, which an oil embargo would

threaten. Furthermore, our discussions were not analytical or quantitatively precise, but rambling and argumentative" [2].

As demands increase, resistance to them will probably also increase. Coercion tends to breed resistance, suspicion, and hatred, and to make bargaining more difficult. The German blitz of Great Britain during World War II and the American bombing of North Vietnam strengthened the morale of the victims and hardened their attitudes toward their tormentors. A study conducted by the Institute for Defense Analyses has concluded:

The indirect effects of the bombing on the will of the North Vietnamese to continue fighting and on their leaders' appraisal of the prospective gains and costs of maintaining the present policy have not shown themselves in any tangible way. Furthermore, we have not discovered any basis for concluding that the indirect punitive effects of bombing will prove decisive in these respects. [9, p. 504]

In selecting a course of action an actor must seek to avoid endangering other salient objectives. It is not only a question of whether or not coercion will ensure the objectives but also of whether or not it may broaden the conflict, as it did when the Chinese intervened in Korea in 1950. This problem raises the particularly thorny balance between controlling a crisis to prevent large-scale conflict and making a dramatic impact to convince the adversary of one's determination and deter his behavior by the prospect of further costs. An actor must often choose between prudence and effectiveness.

Related to the question of risk is that of will. Is the opponent sufficiently impressed with one's resolve? How impressed is the initiator with the opponent's will to resist? The answers to these questions determine the credibility of threats. We emphasize again that a threat has little value unless it is understood and believed by the adversary. Although Great Britain and France guaranteed the independence of Poland in 1939, their previous vacillation toward Adolf Hitler and Benito

Mussolini, which reached a climax in the appeasement at Munich, led Germany to believe that they were bluffing. This belief was confirmed by the knowledge that Poland was far less defensible than, for example, Czechoslovakia had been. Czechoslovakia had had a large and well-equipped army. Czech terrain, unlike the Polish plains, was suitable for defense against Hitler's mobile panzers. There had long been an Anglo-French commitment to the defense of Czechoslovakia, and it had been buttressed by Western sympathy for Czechoslovak democracy. Parallel commitment to Poland after German absorption of Czechoslovakia seemed only a sop aimed primarily at satisfying Western public opinion. The Czechs had also been promised support by Soviet Russia. Hitler may have reasoned that as the British and French had been unwilling to go to war to save Czechoslovakia, even under such compelling circumstances, they would certainly not fight for Poland.

A third problem confronting decision makers during crises is to devise the appropriate mix of threats and promises as an incentive to persuade an opponent to alter his behavior. If the threat is too great, it may stiffen the adversary's resistance and force him to fight; the Austro-Hungarian ultimatum to Serbia in 1914 was so extreme in its demands that it left the Serbs no other choice but war or capitulation. The offer of compensation without threats, on the other hand, may simply encourage an aggressive adversary to raise his demands. Appalled by continued British appeasement of Hitler, Winston Churchill remarked that his country was "nosing from door to door like a cow that has lost its calf, mooing dolefully now in Berlin and now in Rome—when all the time the tiger and the alligator wait for its undoing" [7]. The Anglo-French attempt to appease Hitler in the 1930s was partly the result of trying to avoid the mistakes of 1914. Leaders believed the error to have been unwillingness to compromise and to compensate the opposition. Although that explanation may clarify the outbreak of World War I,

its lesson was inapplicable to the conditions of the 1930s.

A fourth related problem is that of timing. At what point in the crisis should an actor offer rewards? At what point should he make threats? When should he open negotiations? In the Cuban crisis direct negotiations too early might have robbed Kennedy of the initiative and would surely have given the Soviet Union time to complete the installation of missiles in Cuba. In Vietnam the problem has presented itself differently. Each side has been prepared to negotiate seriously only when it has seemed to be winning. Both of these situations were determined by key decisions, and not by systemic characteristics as was the allied victory.

The problems of timing and devising an appropriate mix of threat and promise were central to the resolution of the American-Japanese conflict in 1945. Japan was being gradually defeated in a war of attrition. By the spring of 1945 it was no longer a question of which side would ultimately win the war but upon what terms Japan would surrender. The United States refused to offer terms and demanded "unconditional surrender." Nevertheless, the "island hopping" campaign in the Pacific—including the battles for Saipan, Iwo Jima, and Okinawa—suggested that Japan still retained a capacity for fierce and tenacious resistance. American intelligence revealed that the Japanese armies in China and the home islands were still intact and might extract a heavy price for an American invasion of Japan. Although the bargaining situation was asymmetrical, Japan did have the capacity to raise the costs of American total victory very high.

The United States' problem was how to obtain Japanese surrender most economically. It was decided to increase military pressure and eventually to drop atomic bombs on Hiroshima and Nagasaki on August 6 and August 9, 1945, respectively. On August 10 Japan surrendered on the condition that the emperor would not be ousted. This condition was expected by most American policy makers and was accepted as an important face-saving gesture for the Japanese. The United States thus made a concession of psychological importance to the Japanese in order to obtain their surrender and to facilitate the subsequent occupation and administration of their country.

It has been assumed by many observers that the Japanese decision to surrender was *caused* by the dropping of the bombs, the sudden intensification of coercion, but this interpretation remains unproved and even dubious. It is based on the fallacy that because one event precedes another in time, it also *causes* the second event [5]. In the first place, Japan was already suffering equivalent losses in life and property from large-scale strategic bombing. A fire-bomb raid on Tokyo, for instance, had cost more lives than the bombing of Hiroshima did. The Japanese had asked the Soviet Union to mediate the conflict and were prepared to surrender on any "reasonable" terms, but the Russians had temporized and had not reported Japanese peace feelers; in fact, the Soviet Union soon entered the war on the allied side. This declaration of war erased Japan's last hope that the Soviet Union might be persuaded to mediate and strongly influenced the Japanese to accept peace terms that would safeguard the position of the emperor.[6]

It is possible that had the United States offered in the early summer of 1945 the concession that it finally made anyway, hostilities could have been terminated earlier. As it was, the dropping of atomic bombs ensured for the United States the moral stigma of having been the first (and so far the only) nation to use nuclear weapons.

References

1. Abel, Elie, *The Missile Crisis* (Philadelphia: Lippincott, 1966), p. 138.

[6] By the terms of Yalta agreements with the United States, the Soviet Union was obliged to declare war on Japan within three months after the conclusion of the war in Europe.

2. Acheson, Dean, *Present at the Creation* (New York: Norton, 1969), pp. 19–20.
3. Hilsman, Roger, *To Move a Nation* (Garden City, N.Y.: Doubleday, 1967).
4. Horelick, Arnold, "The Cuban Missile Crisis: An Analysis of Soviet Calculations and Behavior," *World Politics,* 16 (April 1964), pp. 363–390.
5. Kecskemeti, Paul, *Strategic Surrender* (Stanford: Stanford University Press, 1958), pp. 155–211.
6. Kennedy, Robert F., *Thirteen Days* (New York: Norton, 1969).
7. Nicolson, Nigel, ed., *Harold Nicolson: Diaries and Letters 1930–1939* (New York: Atheneum, 1966), p. 328.
8. Schlesinger, Arthur M., Jr., *A Thousand Days* (Boston: Houghton Mifflin, 1965).
9. Sheehan, Neil, ed., *The Pentagon Papers* (New York: Bantam, 1971).
10. Verba, Sidney, *et al.*, "Public Opinion and the War in Vietnam," *American Political Science Review,* 61 (June 1967), p. 320.
11. Wright, Quincy, *A Study of War,* abridged ed. (Chicago: University of Chicago Press, 1964), p. 404.

Suggested Reading

Abel, Elie, *The Missile Crisis* (Philadelphia: Lippincott, 1966).
Allison, Graham T., "Conceptual Models and the Cuban Missile Crisis," *American Political Science Review,* 63 (September 1969), pp. 689–718.
George, Alexander L., David K. Hall, and William R. Simons, *The Limits of Coercive Diplomacy* (Boston: Little, Brown, 1971).
Hermann, Charles F., *Crises in Foreign Policy* (Indianapolis: Bobbs-Merrill, 1969).
Hilsman, Roger, *To Move a Nation* (Garden City, N.Y.: Doubleday, 1967).
Hoopes, Townsend, *The Limits of Intervention* (New York: McKay, 1969).
Kecskemeti, Paul, *Strategic Surrender* (New York: Atheneum, 1964).
Kennedy, Robert F., *Thirteen Days* (New York: Norton, 1969).
Pool, Ithiel de Sola, and Allen Kessler, "The Kaiser, The Tsar, and the Computer: Information in a Crisis," *American Behavioral Scientist,* 8 (May 1965), pp. 31–38.

Pruitt, Dean G., "Stability and Sudden Change in Interpersonal and International Affairs," *Journal of Conflict Resolution,* 13 (March 1969), pp. 18–38.

Pruitt, Dean G., and Richard C. Snyder, eds., *Theory and Research on the Causes of War* (Englewood Cliffs, N.J.: Prentice-Hall, 1969).

Sheehan, Neil, ed., *The Pentagon Papers* (New York: Bantam, 1971).

Sigal, Leon V., "The 'Rational Policy' Model and the Formosa Straits Crisis," *International Studies Quarterly,* 14 (June 1970), pp. 121–156.

Wohlstetter, Roberta, "Cuba and Pearl Harbor," *Foreign Affairs,* (July 1965), pp. 691–707.

Wohlstetter, Roberta, *Pearl Harbor: Warning and Decision* (Stanford: Stanford University Press, 1962).

Part IV
SECURITY AND SURVIVAL

So far we have sought to illuminate the conceptual, structural, and process features of international politics. We turn now to the exploration of some other implications of this analysis. Too frequently those who construct an intellectual framework do not actually act and think within the framework that they have devised.

> In relation to their systems, most systematizers are like a man who builds an enormous castle and lives in a shack beside it; they do not live in their own enormous buildings. But spiritually this is a decisive objection. Spiritually speaking a man's thought must be the building in which he lives—otherwise everything is topsy-turvy.[1]

If modern man is to survive, his intellectual devices must be honest and effective. To reorder his world, he must first understand it. Creating richer and more accurate maps of human activity that can be widely shared is critical to resolving problems satisfactorily. But until recently the study of international politics had been undertaken mainly with an eye toward securing and enhancing the values of particular units within the international system. Simplistic, rather than simplifying, assumptions were made, and mere catalogues of international activities were prepared.[2] Policy prescriptions derived from nearly all normative *and* empirical writings have been "ethnocentric," guided by the intention of instructing actors how to maximize their international status in relation to others. Competitive criteria, however, are suitable only for an international system in which there is a generous margin for error, a system that can tolerate national advantages. His-

[1] Sören Kierkegaard, quoted in Henry Beck, "The Rationality of Redundancy," *Comparative Political Studies*, 3 (January 1971), p. 476.
[2] See, for instance, Hans Morgenthau's assumptions about power in *Politics Among Nations* (New York: Knopf, 1967); see also the escape into a systemwide viewpoint in J. W. Burton, *Systems, States, Diplomacy and Rules* (Cambridge: Cambridge University Press, 1968).

torically, conflict has been a major instrument for implementing decisions and forcing adjustments in international politics. With the advent of the nuclear age the continued acceptance of violent conflict as a systemic norm has become perilous not only for individual actors but for the entire system as well. Consequently, it is necessary to seek cooperative solutions to global problems and to construct overall strategies for change, rather than simply piecemeal efforts.

As the structural features of our global political system are altered, new institutions and mechanisms are required to permit new allocations to be implemented effectively. Imagination and creativity, prerequisites for social innovation, are furthered by clarification of the present and forecasts of the future. In this last, brief part of the book, we shall turn to intellectual tasks that the previous analysis has only implied. We shall seek to clarify revolutionary transformations now challenging the system. Overpopulation, racism, nuclear warfare, nationalism, and the international economy are global problems with momentous implications for political relations among states and even for their survival as sovereign units. Failure to acknowledge these problems and to attempt to resolve them equitably will ensure more decades of "crisis" and unstable change. We must become conscious of our own roles, small as they may be, in shaping the power processes of the world and act deliberately and rationally to help construct a better future. We cannot afford to indulge ourselves in the naïve assumption that responsibility for more fundamental human problems lies elsewhere.

In these last two chapters we explicitly acknowledge values and purposive choice as essential components in any complete political analysis. Although scientific investigation necessitates suspension of value judgments as much as possible, value preferences must at some point be reintroduced into social analysis, in order to ensure that we ask important questions and use productivity and "corrective" capacities to respond to trends that threaten not merely one life style or another but also basic biophysical survival itself.

Chapter 22
PROJECTIONS AND THE WORLD REVOLUTION

No-one is wise enough alone—Titus
Plautus [17]

In October 1962 the two most powerful
actors in the world confronted each other
anxiously, and the world awaited the outcome of a crisis in which it had no part
but in which it had an enormous stake. In
a sense the fate of much of mankind was
in the hands of only two men, John F.
Kennedy and Nikita S. Khrushchev.
Either of them could have ordered a nuclear attack that would have triggered
massive destruction throughout the world.
Although the crisis has subsided, the supreme power of a few key leaders remains essentially the same. Never have
the lives of so many been subject to the
decisions of so few.[1]

Is it reasonable to entrust to a very few
men such responsibility? Most of us who
remain outside the highest councils of
government profess an often naïve faith
that leaders will cope wisely with such
massive responsibility. We trust them to
do what is right. *We have very little
choice.*

There remains something in all of us of the
childish belief that there is a world of
grownups *who know*. There *must* be—
because we, evidently, *don't know*. It is
very shocking then to suspect that the
knowers do not exist at all. Everyone is
groping around in the dark, just as we
are. [4]

Awareness of the precarious nature of
human comprehension, the enormous responsibility placed on a few men, and the
growing need to anticipate potentially
overwhelming problems encourages us,
the authors, to reveal some of our hopes
and fears as political scientists. Our values are shaped by what we perceive as
the disorderly state of international politics and by the persistence of problems
that have defied all efforts to resolve
them. It may be that the existing structures of national states are "cognitive
traps" for their citizens, who are like
passengers in a defective airplane—they
cannot bail out, even though a safe land-

[1] Anatol Rapoport makes this point in *The
Big Two* (New York: Pegasus, 1971).

443

ing seems increasingly improbable. To cope with the problems of increased interdependence, crowded populations, and rapid technological change that have been unleashed in modern international society, we need intellectual resources that will ensure the functioning of critical faculties under stress, as well as individual participants who have inclusive "maps" of social processes and understand their own roles in those processes.

In an age of unprecedented change and technical sophistication it has become feasible and even vital to look into the future and to choose boldly the kind of world that we want to live in. Like the Greek oracle at Delphi we must interpret current international trends and speculate about their probable consequences. Some trends are ominous, and we must prepare ourselves to cope with them or to alter them.

Planning, by its very nature, is not a mechanical process. Central to it is the problem of choice—both for the ends desired and for the allocation of resources. Thus planning and rationality are one. All this puts us on the threshold of an ancient and persistent human quest: to choose our futures. And what is central, therefore, to the present future studies is not an effort to "predict" the future, as if this were some far-flung rug of time unrolled to some distant point, but the effort to sketch "alternative futures"—in other words, the likely results of different choices, so that the polity can understand the costs and consequences of different desires. [2, p. xxvi]

Until today it has been possible, indeed even ethically justifiable, to ignore the future, rather than to become the slaves of future generations or to impose our preferences on them. The progress of Western civilization has been largely based on the assumption that the future will tend to its own problems and that we must work out limited solutions to those immediately confronting us.

We have arrived, however, at a point at which change is so rapid that its consequences are thrust upon us, rather than

on posterity. In one sense we already live in the future; the impact of our actions is likely to be felt during our lifetimes. The distinction between the "long" and the "short" run is breaking down. John Maynard Keynes' observation that "in the long run we are all dead" is no longer true—or perhaps it has an ominous sort of truth. The aim of the social scientist to predict and to develop strategies for the future, then, is not the result of simple altruism but rather the product of hard-headed recognition that certain trends threaten catastrophe for those alive now.

ON LOOKING AHEAD

A prediction is a stated expectation about future events that will subsequently be verified or disproved. Its purpose in the social sciences is to permit some control over such circumstances as election results and over larger patterns affecting entire groups. It must allow for unforeseen, even uncontrollable, events. Although certain events remain difficult to predict, others are less so, and some trends can even be manipulated when political will is sufficient. Just as the natural scientist has sought to tame the natural environment, so the political scientist must seek to control the political environment. In attempting to attach probabilities to an event or trend before it unfolds, we endeavor to gain time to plan for it intelligently and creatively.[2] The farther into the future we wish to see, the less accurate our predictions are likely to be. Studies of the success of past predictions, notably of population projections, suggest that fifteen years are about as far ahead as accuracy can be trusted.

In predicting we usually seek to describe a spectrum of future alternatives and to assign probabilities to the occurrence of each. In assessing trends we must also distinguish between those that

---

[2] Only predictions for specific points in time can be called "forecasts."

seem controllable and those that do not.[3] Finally, it is necessary to assign priorities among future alternatives. The political scientist as a specialist in policy construction seems particularly suited to this last task. He should attempt to prescribe policies that will enable national actors and the international system as a whole to adapt to change in an orderly manner [14].

Several prediction techniques have already been developed; they range from individual intuition and systematic group forecasting to complex computer-based techniques. Indeed, institutions for dealing with questions about the future have been established in various parts of the world. As we suggested in Chapter 5, extrapolation of current trends into the future on the assumption that rates of change will continue is a frequent first approximation for forecasting.[4]

When we try to penetrate the future and to analyze it, we cannot escape dealing with normative, as well as with empirical, concerns. The latter provide us with an outline of probable change; whether or not such trends as population growth and ecological decay can be altered by human design, we do not know. If we assume that they cannot, however, we shall fall into despair.

The normative element in analyzing trends is based on a fundamental belief that future alternatives do exist and that, through human ingenuity, we can alter probable outcomes to accord more fully with our desires. We can predict widespread starvation in the year 2000, but we must also be convinced that it is within our powers to avoid this calamity. To believe such a situation probable without seeking to avert it is morally unacceptable.

The process of looking into the future thus involves setting goals related to perceived needs and wants, establishing priorities among values, and devising strategies by which we may attain a better future than that foreseen. As one team of observers has suggested: "The determinative acts as a 'push' from the past. . . . Its most probable path is implicit in what already exists just as the essential nature of the oak is implicit in the acorn. . . . [The] normative or goal-directed acts as a pull toward the future" [20, pp. 8–10]. To reduce the gap between probable and preferred futures, we must seek to foster corrective behavior and to devise policies based on the "enlightened self-interest" of goal clarification.

When statesmen attempt to exercise influence through analysis of trends and matching expected with preferred futures, the probability that they will secure their goals is greater. Analysis can yield more valid theories, so that the consequences and contingent effects of various alternative policies can be more reliably predicted. Second, analysis can clarify the relations among values, goals, and objectives, so that normative assumptions and empirical components can be scrutinized for possible erroneous assumptions. Finally, the orientation to the future required for analysis of trends expands a decision maker's time horizon and makes him more willing to adjust to long-term problems and to discount ill-advised short-term policies.

TRENDS

Trend analysis stipulates the rate, magnitude, and range of change that occurs in a given feature of the international system (or some smaller arena) over a given period. Two major types of such trends can be distinguished: technological and social trends. Many that seem to have similar and important consequences—increasing the interdependence and vulnerability of human social systems at

[3] One criterion for satisfactory theory, as discussed in Chapter 2, is how much control of future events it allows for.
[4] A description of the Delphi technique can be found in Yehezkel Dror, *The Prediction of Political Feasibility*, Rand Corporation Paper No. 4044 (Santa Monica: April 1969). For discussion of scenario writing, see Herman Kahn and Anthony Weiner [2].

practically all levels—have been widely perceived, though not forecast with accuracy. These trends tend to reinforce one another, which means that they have little autonomy.

Types of Trends

For example, industrialization and the development of new energy sources altered the structure of the state system in the nineteenth century. As industrialization expanded military capacity, the European system spread beyond the Western Hemisphere and became global in scope. Actors who had formerly found themselves in only episodic contact with one another began to pursue continuous relationships. They simultaneously had more to share and more to quarrel about. Internal developments in transportation and communications permitted governments to mobilize national resources and populations more quickly and efficiently. New social classes and elites arose with urbanization. Finally, both totalitarian and democratic regimes emerged during the course of these changes.

Technological change has also had consequences for actors' objectives. The acquisition of territory, for example, has become less important as the desire to share in new technologies and to impose grandiose ideologies upon others has become more salient. Indeed, technological changes have rendered relatively unimportant geographical areas once deemed strategically vital, whereas other areas have become important. The advent of airplanes and "supertankers" to transport oil, for example, as well as the breakup of colonial empires, have reduced the strategic significance of the Suez canal, whereas nuclear-powered submarines have made the Arctic and Antarctic regions more important.

Technological trends include changes in economic interdependence, communications capacity, and destructiveness of weapons. Economies of conglomeration— as reflected in international marketing facilities and management—and economies

of scale have operated, through the spread of industrialization, to increase the interdependence of production facilities and to expand the population that services or works in these facilities. One result is increasingly linked fates of those in connected industries: American automobile workers in Detroit, Volkswagen workers in Germany, and assembly-line workers in Latin America and Africa, for example. Suppliers of oil, thanks to a steady rise in demand and decentralization of facilities, have also entered into interdependencies that cut across ideological divisions.[5] A second technological trend has been growth in communications capacity, marked at all points by improved reception facilities (greater literacy, more radios, and so forth) and greater channel capacity (including decentralization through proliferation of special language broadcasts on radio and television, as well as direct cable facilities in which thirty or more channels can operate simultaneously). A rise in media "participation" is also likely as special interest groups achieve the resources required to produce low-budget films and other programs [9].

The speed of communication has also increased. Within a few hours of the death of President John F. Kennedy, the news had circled the world and had penetrated rural areas of Latin America, Asia, and Africa. Terms like "world village" and "spaceship earth" reflect the disappearance of time and space barriers, described in Chapter 5.

Rapid communications have made it possible for statesmen to contact one another almost immediately. No longer do ambassadors enjoy plenipotentiary powers to negotiate on behalf of national leaders. The impact of changes in communications on the nature of diplomacy can be noted in the continuous control that President Kennedy exercised over his subordinates

---

[5] See, for instance, *Atlas* (March 1971), "The Mystery of Israel's Disappearing Tankers," pp. 26–28, for a report that in 1970 Israeli oil pipelines carried oil bound for Soviet-bloc countries.

throughout the world during the Cuban crisis of 1962 and in President Lyndon B. Johnson's ability to direct his field commanders in Vietnam. The increased capacity and speed of communications, however, have in turn created new stresses for national leaders. The new communications systems that have ensured greater informational inputs to decision-making systems, advances in weapons-delivery systems, and so forth have reduced the time available for decisions during acute crises. Despite technological advances, therefore, the possibilities of systems overload may actually have increased.

A third major technological trend is the growth of weapons capacity and sophistication. Aside from biological and chemical weapons, the scope, volatility, and utility of which are uncertain, nuclear weapons have enormously increased man's destructive potential. Countries with advanced industrial plants and political will already have this potential and can acquire more. The difference between current weapons systems and what may be achieved with new breakthroughs seems less important than do the effects that spreading nuclear capabilities can produce. Technological change has increased the interrelation of activities and the diffusion of physical and economic capacities. Possibilities for the next half century include advances in chemistry, biology, and engineering that will permit us to shape human learning, personality, and heredity. We may see evolve data-storage facilities with public access that will have enormous impact on the legal and medical professions, thermonuclear electric power, limited weather control, inexpensive nonnarcotic drugs that will produce personality changes like improved learning ability, inexpensive contraceptives that can be administered through drinking water, and even chemical control of the aging process [5].

But such technological innovations, designed to cope with existing problems, may generate new problems, as improvements in weapons technology in the twentieth century may have contributed to

greater demands to avoid large-scale warfare, but also to a reduction of limitations on conflict, particularly in relation to noncombatants.

Social trends must also be examined. We may note the potential both for integration resulting from interdependencies and for intensified nationalism and decentralization of political units. Trends in many social indicators are relevant to international outcomes. They include defense expenditures, per capita gross national product, the gap between rich and poor countries, crime rates, international travel, and population mobility. Social and technological trends are intimately related in practice, as in the case of global population growth. Our discussion of this topic is designed to demonstrate the purpose and value of trend analysis. The "population problem" is, in fact, a group of problems involving values and norms, as well as questions of technology. Furthermore, its effects spill over onto a variety of other interdependent trends affecting international politics, including decentralization of communications and rising nationalism in an increasingly interdependent world.

Projecting a trend like population growth requires analysis, first, of the forces affecting change and growth; second, of the consequences that make growth a problem; and, finally, of the possible outcomes of different responses.

Population Trends

Figure 22.1 illustrates the acceleration in the growth of world population since 1650. The populations of Europe and North America grew faster than did that of the rest of the world during the nineteenth century, thanks to a decline in death rates (especially in Europe) and to migration (especially to North America). In the first half of the twentieth century, although growth continued high in these more "developed" regions, the growth rates in the rest of the world jumped ahead, so that they are now highest in the poorer, less industrialized countries of

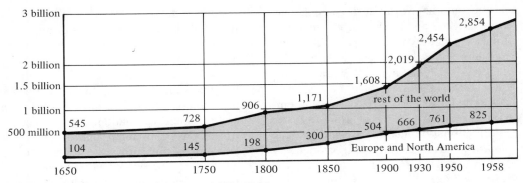

Figure 22.1. Estimated Population, 1650–1958

Source: Dennis H. Wrong, *Population and Society,* 2nd ed. (New York: Random House, 1961), p. 13. "Europe" includes all the present Soviet Union.

Asia, Africa, and Latin America, some of which are already densely populated. This set of changes can be seen in Figure 22.2.

These growth trends are the products of several social changes, occurring at different times in different regions and including both technological innovations and the alteration of customs and mores.

Medical efforts to prolong life and to lower infant mortality, and more efficient food production and housing have contributed heavily to rapid growth. Unless family norms change so that women marry later and have fewer children, high birth rates will continue to fuel it. Furthermore, this growth will be unevenly distributed both by political unit and by the already existing population densities

of different countries, as Table 22.1 makes clear. Without social change material constraints of various kinds will operate. More than double the food needed in 1958, for instance, will be required by 2000 [12]. Even if new land and techniques are found to provide it, shelter and material goods, especially those related to energy consumption, are likely to become scarcer per capita.

At current rates of growth we can predict that, even if human ingenuity could sustain life for everyone (an unlikely prospect), in 900 years the earth's population would be 60 million billion. The British physicist J. H. Fremlin has described the possibility of housing such masses in a continuous 2,000-story building covering the planet. The upper 1,000

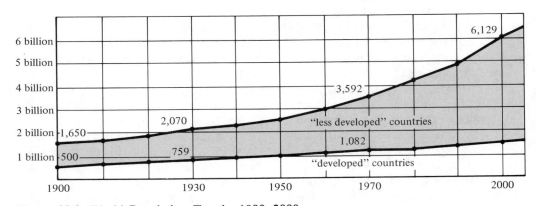

Figure 22.2. World Population Trends, 1900–2000

Source: Data and definitions are taken from J. D. Durand, "World Population Estimates, 1750–2000," *Proceedings at the World Population Conference, 1965,* vol. 2 (New York: United Nations, 1967), p. 21.

Table 22.1.

Selected Countries with High and Low Rates of Population Increase

Country	Population (in millions)	Rate of Annual Increase (in percentages)	Population Density (per square kilometer)
Countries with High Rates			
Africa			
Kenya	10.2	2.9	17
Libya	1.8	3.0	1
United Arab Republic	31.8	3.0	30
Zambia	4.1	3.0	5
Asia			
Ceylon	12.2	2.8	175
China (Taiwan)	13.5	2.7	356
India	523.0	2.5	163
Iran	26.5	3.0	15
Lebanon	2.6	2.5	237
Malaysia	8.7	3.2	7
Mongolia	1.2	3.0	1
Philippines	35.9	3.5	112
Thailand	33.7	3.1	61
Turkey	33.8	2.9	41
South America			
Brazil	88.3	3.2	10
Colombia	19.7	3.2	16
Costa Rica	1.6	3.5	29
Dominican Republic	4.0	3.6	77
Ecuador	5.7	3.4	19
El Salvador	3.3	3.7	141
Guatemala	4.9	3.1	42
Honduras	2.5	3.5	21
Mexico	47.3	3.5	22
Paraguay	2.2	3.2	5
Peru	12.8	3.1	9
Venezuela	9.7	3.6	10
Countries with Low Rates			
Europe			
Austria	7.4	0.4	87
Belgium	9.7	0.6	312
Czechoslovakia	14.4	0.5	111
Denmark	4.8	0.8	111
Finland	4.7	0.7	14
France	50.4	1.0	90
East Germany	17.1	0.2	148
West Germany	60.3	0.6	232
Hungary	10.2	0.3	109
Ireland	2.9	0.4	41
Luxembourg	0.3	0.5	130
Poland	32.3	0.8	101
Rumania	19.4	0.6	81
Sweden	7.9	0.8	17

Source: Demographic Yearbook, 1967 (New York: United Nations, 1968).

stories would contain only the apparatus for running this gigantic warren. Ducts, elevator shafts, and other equipment would occupy about half the space in the bottom 1,000 stories. This arrangement would leave four square yards of floor space for each person but would permit him to choose his friends from among 10 million people in his section of the building [13]. Although this prospect is somewhat fanciful, it does suggest that we must deal not only with simple statistics but also with the problem of what life styles we wish to have. According to recent United Nations estimates, world population by 2000 will be almost 6.5 billion, compared with 3.5 billion in 1969. India and China alone are expected to have populations in excess of 1 billion people each by then.

In the underdeveloped areas of the world, food production falls farther behind population growth each year. Fertility rates are correlated negatively with per capita income and standard of living. It is currently estimated that at least half the people in the world are undernourished at best. In 1966, because of serious agricultural failures in several areas, the global population increase of 70 million was accompanied by a reduction in net food production averaging 2 percent per person.

The distribution of food resources is, of course, uneven. In 1952 only ten countries produced more food than they consumed. Science and technology, by making greater yields per acre possible and developing new sources of nutrition, may delay the time when population far outdistances food production, but at current growth rates massive famine is likely by the end of this century. Urbanization and technology have already reduced the fertile areas of many countries. Moreover, as populations increase further, countries will be less able to transfer food surpluses. Certain developed countries like Great Britain and certain less developed countries like India are already dependent upon imports of raw materials and agricultural products to support their populations.

The gap between rich and poor promises to widen as time goes on. Countries like Ceylon, Taiwan, Pakistan, and India, where married couples usually want three or more children each, already had some of the highest birth rates in the world in 1969. Agrarian couples generally want larger families to assist in tilling the land, and their attitudes complicate the problem of modernizing their societies. Governments are only beginning to involve themselves in "family planning." The impact of population trends on international politics is manifold, affecting both structural features, like distribution of resources, and actors' systemic objectives (through effects on values). The most likely general effect will be to increase world conflict. The highest growth rates tend to be in the poorest countries. Although the current rates of 3.0 percent or higher may decline (a 3-percent rate means that the population doubles about every twenty-three years), burgeoning populations in poor countries for the next thirty to fifty years seem certain. This growth will retard other development in several ways. First, it will encourage adoption of labor-intensive techniques that ensure lower productivity per capita. Second, it will create a large "dependent" population. Sometimes half a country's population will be fifteen years old or younger and therefore mainly consumers, rather than producers.

If population growth retards development and simultaneously lowers per capita income, the frustrations of this relative deprivation in the poorer states will be intense. These states' ability to create disturbances in international politics will increase owing to systemic interdependence and to at least some absolute gains in resources, including population.

Although economic deterioration will be felt most severely in less developed states, population growth also has negative consequences in store for industrialized states. High social and political costs seem likely as built-in inflation of expectations (of ever-higher living standards) provokes increased frustration. Urban growth will place increasing pressure on welfare, transportation, sewage, and other facilities, which may become overloaded and break down.

Other costs of crowding can also be enumerated. Already we are aware of the aesthetic impact of pollution in the seas, the air, and the land. The effects on our chances for future survival are only beginning to be understood, however. For instance, men use chemicals to control insect damage to crops, yet certain insect strains have become immune to existing pesticides; the pesticides themselves may have deleterious effects on the organic compounds required for soil productivity. And it is difficult to estimate the total impact of continued use of DDT and similar compounds that have been in use for only about twenty-five years.

At least 70 percent of our total oxygen is the product of photosynthesis in planktonic diatoms in the oceans. Nevertheless, throughout the world countries continue to dump large quantities of pollutants into the sea with little regard for the consequences. It is possible that continued dumping may seriously impair oceanic photosynthesis. No single actor is capable of reversing the trend, and the problem will grow worse. As actors begin to exploit the resources of the seas in the quest for new sources of energy and food, pollution will increase. Exploitation of the oceans clearly requires interstate cooperation, rather than international competition. It exemplifies the type of problem that calls for system-level regulation instead of national self-help.[6]

Many of us have recently become more aware of air pollution. The aesthetic problem is already obvious to residents of Tokyo, Shanghai, Los Angeles, and New York. Scientists are currently attempting to determine its cumulative impact on health, especially its relation to diseases like tuberculosis and cancer. In addition, air pollution destroys plant life, thus reducing sources of both oxygen and food. It affects the way in which the sun's

rays reach the surface of the earth and how they are radiated back into space. If these rays are unable to penetrate the pollution layer, unexpected weather changes may result. It has been suggested that should shifting pockets of polluted air trap heat on earth and prevent its radiation back into space, the resulting temperatures may melt the polar ice caps and cause mammoth flooding.

Another heavy cost of population growth seems to be a decline in respect for individuals and the increase of "antisocial" behavior and conflict. Although the relationship between these two changes is surely complex, crowded urban areas and poverty (both by-products of "overpopulation") are closely associated with high crime rates. Crowded courts, hospitals, and welfare rolls reduce the attention that individuals receive, whereas impersonal and slow bureaucratic procedures increase the sense of distance between individuals and collective social goods. These systemic changes are likely to conflict with the current value placed on individual human dignity. Crowded metropolises like Calcutta, Hong Kong, and Tokyo already suggest the probable features of population growth in many other areas of the globe: Declines in living standards, health, transportation, and privacy are likely as various limits in the environment are reached.

Greater overpopulation and ecological catastrophes are probably unavoidable unless new controls are created at the level of the international system. In recent years some international "ecological law" has been established: the Geneva Convention on the High Seas (1958) and the Convention for the Prevention of Pollution of the Sea by Oil (1954, amended in 1962), for example. Efforts have also been made to establish legal norms for radioactive pollution of the seas, pollution of Antarctic waters, rocket-exhaust pollution of the upper atmosphere, pollution of international rivers, and radioactive pollution from the testing of nuclear weapons [15]. Most of these problems, however, are peripheral and have only minor political significance. There are no

[6] For a discussion of the political problems involved in competition for oceanic resources, see Wolfgang Friedmann, *The Future of the Oceans* (New York: Braziller, 1971).

international regulatory agencies with authority to prevent such disasters in international waters as spills of oil tankers.

To determine optimum world population and distribution, it would be necessary to begin with value judgments about standards of living and international distribution of resources. We would have to inquire about the ideal size of a community for various activities and which individual rights and freedoms are really compatible with collective values (can everybody own and drive cars, dispose of all the waste that he wishes, and have as many children as he fancies?). Then alternative policies for altering current trends would have to be considered. Solutions might involve complex legal and cultural changes. Controlling the sizes of families would be one possible solution, though, as we have already suggested, it would require more than simple technological and administrative advances. Fundamental revision of the cultural norms of great numbers of individuals—norms that are propagated and supported by institutions like the Roman Catholic Church—would also be required. As with other questions of social engineering, this one would involve questions of democratic control and collective versus individual rights. Emphasizing the "rights" of parents to bear as many children as they wish or can support is socially immoral, for it evades the fundamental question of how many children are compatible with the collective good. So far, there have been few successes in international "family planning," and many national programs are minimal, aimed mainly at helping middle-class populations to *plan,* rather than to limit, their families.[7] In the United States little is being done to formulate a coherent population policy. In 1968 the Department of Health, Education and Welfare (HEW) assigned less than one-quarter of 1 percent of its budget to population control. This figure is equivalent, as Paul R. Ehrlich has pointed out, to the amount appropriated for rat control [10]!

The human population *will* stop growing. This halt must come through either a decrease in the birth rate, or an increase in the death rate, or both. A corollary of this is that anyone or any organization opposing reduction in the birth rate is automatically an agent for eventually increasing the death rate. [11]

One deceptively simple solution to the population problem that has been proposed is to produce more food. Yet little new land is available for agricultural production, and most of the land farmed today is relatively poor. There have been attempts to exploit less fertile areas, but the costs are enormous and the results often disappointing, as shown by the low yields of the "virgin lands" program of the 1950s and 1960s that aimed at expanding cultivatable land in the Soviet Union.

It has been believed that man's success in adapting to his changing environment is illustrated by the way in which the human population has expanded into all parts of the globe. But mere numbers may not represent successful adaptation, and unchecked population growth must inevitably lead to ecological decline. A given environment is able to support only a limited population. Although the limit can be increased through technological innovation, it still remains a limit. Indeed, there is a "law of the minimum," which predicts that "whichever requisite of life is in shortest supply in a particular environment determines, like the weakest link of a chain, the maximum population which can be supported in that environment" [7]. Furthermore, the "maximum" population is probably not the "optimum" population, the population that can be "best" supported qualitatively by the environment. Occasional suggestions about what would constitute the political and economical optimum number of citizens

[7] Some countries with high growth rates, like Nigeria, Brazil and Burma, have no programs at all, whereas others like Mexico and the Philippines, where the Roman Catholic Church is strong, have made only minor efforts. See Bernard Berelson, *Studies in Family Planning,* No. 39 (New York: Population Council, 1969).

in a community have been made.[8] Clearly, an optimum number must be based on a reconciliation of diverse human demands and needs, as well as on profound ethical considerations. Political stability, economic productivity, and social and cultural welfare must all be considered from a global point of view. The determination of what population would be optimal and the policies to achieve it are beyond the capabilities of any single actor in the international system.

The examination of trends to clarify future alternatives and to compare them with preferred outcomes reveals that many current trends—and some very disturbing ones—are unfolding at exponential rates, rather than in steady absolute increments.[9] But prediction from existing trends is often dangerous. The National Resources Planning Board predicted in the 1930s that the United States' population would peak at 165 million in the 1960s and decline to 130 million by the year 2000. The error resulted from extrapolation from trends current during the Great Depression, without predicting the impact of postwar prosperity on population growth in the United States [3, p. 123]. We must be alert to the possibility that existing trends will not continue unimpeded at current rates, and we must consider both the *range* of likely future characteristics and the *factors* that will affect rates of change.

Some trends may end when they have produced what we call "step-level change." Development of military technology and growth in productive capacity have already produced such change. Weapons

[8] Jean Jacques Rousseau, for instance, argued that a small, relatively isolated community on the model of Sparta is culturally and politically preferable to any alternative. For a more recent effort of this kind, see Robert A. Dahl, "The City in the Future of Democracy," *American Political Science Review*, 61 (December 1967), pp. 953–970.

[9] When marked on a graph each trend rises ever more steeply, rather than in a straight line. Some of the trends described in Chapter 5— population growth, the destructive radius of weapons, speed over intercontinental distances, the growth of technical knowledge, and so on— follow exponential patterns.

developments were partly responsible for bipolarity after World War II; only two "great powers" existed, and they were antagonistic. With the reduction in costs of nuclear weapons, miniaturization of the components of such weapons, diffusion of technical knowledge, and expansion of governmental capacity, more actors will possess some military autonomy, and some will even have nuclear weapons. We foresee the continuing decline of bipolarity as the political blocs and stability of the past twenty-five years erode.

We can also foresee the termination of some growth rates in some countries because of an end to the demand for them. It is unlikely, for instance, that the very high rate of increase in the explosive power of weapons will continue, for little use can be found for larger weapons. Furthermore, debate on the supersonic transport plane in the United States has suggested that there are limits to the demand for increasing speed in transportation. These rates of growth will slow down, not because of conscious governmental regulation, but because of waning social demand. Some growth rates will slow down because of the depletion or exhaustion of the resources necessary to maintain them; for instance, existing energy sources may be used up. Until new technological breakthroughs occur, we can place finite limits on the amounts of energy consumption possible for any country.

Of most importance to the social scientist, however, are those rates of change that although alterable by social regulation, could nevertheless end in disaster if permitted to continue unchecked. The population problem and its potential effects on the quality of life illustrate this type of trend.

SURVIVAL AS A COLLECTIVE ENTERPRISE

In efforts to control existing trends several barriers must be overcome. Some problems are not easily resolved because of technological limitations. For example, the international system currently has only finite amounts of energy resources, partly because of the existing level of technology. On the other hand, some undesirable trends continue merely because of human ignorance. Man could not exploit the resources of the Western Hemisphere until he realized that the earth is not flat. Finally, certain problems persist because of existing values. Pollution of the seas and the air has not been effectively countered partly because we have previously favored free enterprise and relatively unrestricted economic competition and have left "free" such public resources as air and water.

This last point deserves special attention. Some of our oldest and most deeply felt values have contributed to a climate that prevents resolution of major current problems. One historian has pointed out that man's insensitivity to nature arises partly from the Judeo-Christian notion that man can make use of the fruits of the earth as he sees fit because they have been created for his pleasure [18]. Our existing values are largely based on competitive criteria. Countries evaluate their success in comparison with that of other countries. Such "other-oriented" criteria are, however, unrewarding in the long run. They contribute to trends like the stockpiling of military armaments. An actor may find himself superior to his neighbors but, nevertheless, worse off absolutely than he might have been had he not adopted competitive criteria to determine policy. The positive "kill ratios" achieved by the United States in Vietnam may reflect comparative success over the adversary, but they have provided no absolute criterion by which to evaluate American foreign-policy performance.

Survival of the species must be the fundamental goal of men. Such survival involves the continuous satisfaction of basic psychological and biological needs. As a minimum we require air and water, nutrition, and shelter. Most of the species that have ever existed are already extinct; there is no guarantee that man will evade the same fate. It is through evolution that creatures earn survival. Adaptive physical structure and behavior maximize chances of survival, but, as the environment changes, behavior that was once adaptive may become less so. Until now it has seemed that technological advances have facilitated human adaptation, but many current trends suggest that we must now rapidly find methods to cope with and regulate these very technological innovations and their consequences. Although man has unique abilities to learn and to create and is thus better able to adapt to changing circumstances than is any other animal, we have no reason to believe that he will in fact use this potential.[10]

It is through learning that men are able to adapt to their changing environment, for learning is the means by which men can evaluate the success or failure of their behavior and correct it. Man's institutions, innovations, and patterns of behavior are presumably the fruit of his learned responses to external challenges. His invention of political institutions like the state has served his needs in particular circumstances. His customs also reflect attempts to satisfy fundamental needs. The human infant, for example, remains helpless longer than do the young of any other species. Consequently, methods of child rearing based on the family unit and division of labor within it have been encouraged. Furthermore, man's aggressiveness has apparently helped him to overcome various threats from both natural forces and other men. Political theorists have long observed that governments and other instruments of political control can limit and channel such behavior. Competition is itself a means of regulating aggressive behavior. Institutions and forms of behavior that have proved adaptive at specific stages of development may, however, become obsolete or even maladaptive when their utility is limited to specific situations and specific needs. One of the greatest of our problems is to determine when institutions and norms are no longer suitable for current use and

[10] For a provocative essay arguing for an evolutionary model in political science, see Peter A. Corning [6].

must be abandoned regardless of their former utility.

While the condition of the individual is certainly an important ingredient in the condition of the society, it is an insufficient measure of the whole. This is because in any aggregate (such as human society) in which the whole is greater than the sum of the parts, statistics based on the state of the parts frequently fail to show the state of the relations *between the parts*. [20, p. 14]

The survival of the individual is inextricably bound up with the survival of the collectivity. Only through the collectivity is division of labor in the tasks necessary to ensure life possible. Increasingly, the nature of the problems that beset men defy individual or even national solutions.

Some current changes in the international system seem to promise a brighter future, however. For the first time in history most adults are literate. Advances in communication through speech, writing, printing, and electronic transmission have "opened" national frontiers and have speeded the exchange of new ideas and habits. Since the introduction of a new generation of communications satellites to encircle the globe, "the printed word . . . will be capable of being transmitted as easily and as widely as the voice, so that facsimile mail can be transmitted from point to point in a fraction of a second" [1]. The exponential growth rate in the speed of communications has been complemented by similarly explosive rates in the diffusion of new ideas. These changes may permit leaders to keep abreast of the growing demands of populations and to respond more quickly to them. Furthermore, our interest in the future has been stimulated by the development of such approaches as cybernetics, information theory, simulation, linear programming, and game theory, all of which help us to look ahead with greater precision.[11]

That the world has become "smaller"

[11] For a stimulating discussion of the impact of technological innovations like computers on international politics, see Zbigniew K. Brzezinski, *Between Two Ages* (New York: Viking, 1970), pp. 3–62.

does not mean that institutions have kept pace. A fundamental problem for future adaptation revolves around the relationship between structure and process in international politics. If they become "out of phase," process may spill over into new paths that lack institutional solidarity. Moribund structures can prevent new institutional solutions to problems generated by change in social and technological processes. Although structures can adapt to changed conditions, too great a lag may be destructive. The basic federal arrangements in the United States reflect this type of problem. The federal system was worked out 200 years ago when the population of the United States was mainly rural and spread thinly in historically distinct areas. Yet long-term forces of change and modernization in the United States have been accompanied by enormous growth at the national level, and earlier conditions no longer exist. As the eruption of problems confronting American cities indicates, individual states are ill prepared to promote corrective policies. Although the federal system is commendable in some ways, it is difficult to believe that most American political scientists today would fully recommend it. The scale of problems for one thing has grown vastly.

The same type of difficulty exists within the international system as a whole. Technological and attitudinal changes call for wider systemic or regional regulation, as opposed to local or national regulation. Whether or not more formal international structures are available to regulate these processes, their consequences will be international in scope. Although many trends contribute to the interdependence of actors and to the links between domestic and international politics, they may not also contribute to political integration. Indeed, national attempts to resolve what are essentially global problems may actually prove dysfunctional. In an international economic crisis each state may be tempted to raise tariffs or to compete more vigorously for scarce resources. The total impact of such national behavior will, however, undoubtedly exacerbate the crisis still further. Without a more integrated system, actors' responses to social processes and incompatible goals may increase the difficulties facing the international system.

This analysis suggests the need for new mechanisms to *adjust political pressures nonviolently by acting as safety valves,* to *redistribute scarce resources more equitably* (perhaps through some form of international progressive tax), and to *provide greater redundancy* in the system so that normal activity can continue even when one element of the structure fails.[12] Most international actors, however, are not prepared to assign prerogatives to a central decision-making unit like the United Nations. Nevertheless, they will be less and less able to gain satisfactory outcomes from purely self-interested policies, and many of them may eventually conclude that it is better to settle for partial "sovereignty" than to defend total autonomy. Under these conditions we may see an increase in "transitional" politics, in which states and other actors more frequently collaborate in joint enterprises and organizations to defend themselves and to achieve equitable distribution of rewards. A period of "collaborationist" politics may then follow; actors would form defensive alliances within the system to defend compatible interests against systemic environmental threats. Weak states already behave in this fashion, and in the next stage of international politics powerful states may follow suit.

SHAPING FUTURE CHANGE
It is likely that by the year 2000 men will no longer be engaged in agriculture, and many will be involved in science and technology. Urbanization has already gone farther than had previously been considered possible, and the process is unlikely to end in the foreseeable future. By the

---

[12] Various redundancies are built into spaceships, for example, so that if one system fails, a ship will not necessarily be doomed.

end of the century "It will be a mankind that is literate, a mankind that works in nonagricultural employment . . . a mankind that lives in towns, a mankind with unprecedented amounts of capital goods and mechanical energy at its disposal for production or destruction" [8]. In many countries peasant man has become modern man and has moved from a parochial life style, in which the level of efficiency and productivity depend upon his personal skill and natural environment, to a new setting in which his temporal and spatial horizons are expanded and he is predisposed toward planning, rationality, and scientific interpretation of natural phenomena. "The simple sociological fact is," Daniel Bell has observed, "that in a complex interconnected society *the conditions* of happiness for the mass of the people . . . involve a high degree of collective action . . ." [3, p. 120].

In a world populated by "modern" men the meaning of "security" and "insecurity" and the nature of politics have changed. This second major type of change parallels that of the growth of resources and the increase in technical efficiency as we move from peasant to modern society, from self-help to systemic control. In peasant societies the individual is forced back upon his own resources and those of his family. Fulfillment of his needs rarely involves insuperable political questions. Although feudal kingdoms and even the infant national states of the seventeenth century offered higher levels of recourse and enforcement of law and order than in previous centuries, the fundamental problems of survival—from securing food and shelter to ensuring the safety of person and family—were still left to the individual. In modern society, on the other hand, increasing diversification and specialization in occupational skills and functions have stimulated growth of political and social institutions designed to deal with problems that were formerly solved by the individual on his own or as a member of a small group. Choices of what news is transmitted; how wealth is redistributed; what protection is afforded to the young, the needy, the infirm, and the aged; and what military and police strategies are adopted may then be determined at the system level, even if formal institutions are unprepared and most people do not like it.

The satisfaction of peasant needs involves relatively minor political questions. By contrast, the satisfaction of the needs of the modern city dweller involves major political questions and interests. Public services are required and demanded. Each individual is dependent upon others, and the fabric of urban society, though it has become more complex, has also become in many ways more fragile—as strikes by public workers in many countries have illustrated. Government budgets have increased rapidly to provide public services in areas in which private self-help is no longer sufficient. The modern, urbanized individual is capable of providing for only a limited portion of his needs.

Given the means at his disposal . . . and given the configuration (and hazards) of his specific social environment, he must attend to a number of personal and family needs. Yet, whether he is aware of it or not, that individual is also dependent upon many others in his community, as well as public services, city and state governments, major subsystems of the American economy, the Federal government, and international politics—to the extent that events and activities at each of these other levels (or among them) affect his personal chances of survival and reproductive success. [6]

Most individuals have greater technical skills than their predecessors had and manifest keener awareness of the behavior and attitudes of others near and far. Politics has thus become more important, and fewer individuals are prepared to accept meekly and unquestioningly the governmental policies that affect them. The growth of nongovernmental organizations, ranging from mobs and political parties to multinational corporations, attests that a greater proportion of individuals is caught up in interdependent political networks than ever before.

There is a paradox for modern man. He has more advantages (like housing and education) than his predecessors had, yet he has come to expect them. As he is more able to compare and contrast his lot with those of others, he perceives his level of satisfaction in more *relative* terms than he previously did and evaluates his needs less in relation to his own previous position than in relation to the positions of his fellows. Whereas the peasant may have been satisfied with subsistence, modern man "needs" his television and his automobile. As his horizons have expanded, so has his level of aspirations. The more the individual possesses, the greater seems to be his determination to acquire more. Increased productivity, greater efficiency, and the rapid march of technology have brought man to a point at which the fruits of his interdependence are bitter indeed. The problems of rising pollution, the "overkill" capacity of nuclear weapons, and decreasing natural resources per capita were not foreseen by individuals in their quests for increasing affluence. Man is therefore probably *less secure* in his collective existence now than when he had not advanced so far.

But man has no reason to assume that the global political system will yield better and better adaptations to his situation. Changes in international politics generated by such exogenous factors as technological growth are not guaranteed to produce satisfying consequences. Trends that may individually have predictable consequences may in combination produce unexpected, and sometimes unfortunate step-level changes or systemic transformation. For instance, as individuals in developed countries improve their standards of living, consume more, and dispose of more, their very "progress" may cause a decline in the quality of their lives and the breakdown of traditional mediating institutions without substitution of viable alternatives. For example, because modern man consumes so much more than his predecessor did, he creates much more waste as well. Ironically, in modern societies the population problem may be far greater than it is in under-developed societies because of the far greater economic and social infrastructure required to support a modernized population. It has been estimated that one affluent American is likely to consume and dispose of forty-seven times more than does his counterpart in a less-developed area of the world. Furthermore, satisfying individual needs creates a tremendous aesthetic problem for society as open lands disappear and air and water are misused:[13] "We must expect, therefore, that the future will disclose dangers. It is the business of the future to be dangerous. . ." [19].

Change appears to be a process that occurs at several levels simultaneously. The first level lies deep, and change is slow; such change affects underlying cultural patterns and includes "diffusion of Western culture," "urbanization," "modernization," and so on. It tends to be fairly stable and slow, but it has enormous long-term consequences. These consequences are not easily detectable in particular events, however. A second level of change encompasses short-term adjustments like business cycles and economic fluctuations. Other changes of this order include advances in weapons technology taking several years. The actual consequences wrought by these changes tend to be relatively immediate, usually occurring within five to ten years, though they may affect memories longer.

A third level of change includes developments known as "accidents." Social scientists frequently treat these kinds of changes as random, or error, variables when they design formal models. As Aristotle pointed out, however, accidents are *not* random. An accident is an unusual or unexpected juxtaposition of circumstances that cannot normally be predicted by underlying or even fluctuating models of change. It turns out that we need fairly specific hypotheses and the-

ories to explain accidents. Such events may be matters of grave concern in making immediate policy. For example, the assassinations of Archduke Francis Ferdinand and President Kennedy had important psychological and catalytic effects, even though they may not have had abiding structural consequences.

The salient time horizon for most policy makers is from three months to a year. They focus most attention on individual arguments of other leaders and day-to-day events, which may offer important signals but seldom yield clues to fundamental international change. Social scientists, on the other hand, tend to concentrate on middle-range and long-range trends and their effects. Such trends usually have little relation to questions of day-to-day policy, though they promise to shape the contexts in which future policy will be made. It is in studying and helping to shape these more basic trends that political scientists can contribute most.

In seeking to foster adaptive policies, the political scientist must be active, rather than passive. He must seek to bring about positive change in orderly fashion. He must make fundamental normative judgments based on his knowledge of political life and on the probable social consequences of predicted change. The problem of population growth and its negative consequences of pollution and decline in individuality suggest the role that a political scientist can play in social change. First, by identifying and describing a problem and its probable consequences he can alert people to the potential seriousness of current trends before disaster occurs. Second, he can analyze the causes of the problem. His third task is to propose corrective policies based on theories about causal factors.

Toward the end of *The Prince,* Niccolò Machiavelli exclaims that "fortune is the ruler of half our actions," like an "impetuous river that, when turbulent, inundates the plains, casts down trees and buildings, removes earth from this side and places it on the other; everyone flees before it, and everything yields to its fury

[13] For a particularly frightening vision of life in 1999, see the science-fiction novel by Harry Harrison, *Make Room! Make Room!* (Garden City, N.Y.: Doubleday, 1966).

without being able to oppose it." The task of the political scientist is, as Machiavelli has suggested, to "make provision against it by dikes and banks, so that when it rises it will either go into a canal or its rush will not be so wild and dangerous" [16].

References

1. Asimov, Isaac, "The Fourth Revolution," *Saturday Review,* 53 (October 24, 1970), p. 19.
2. Bell, Daniel, "Introduction," in Herman Kahn and Anthony J. Weiner, eds., *The Year 2000* (New York: Macmillan, 1967).
3. Bell, Daniel, "The Study of the Future," *The Public Interest,* 1 (Fall 1965).
4. Berger, Peter, *The Precarious Vision* (Garden City, N.Y.: Doubleday, 1961), pp. 83–84.
5. Brigard, Raul de, and Olaf Helmer, *Some Potential Societal Development— 1970–2000,* Institute for the Future, Report R-7 (Middletown, Conn.: April 1970), pp. 81–104.
6. Corning, Peter A., "The Biological Bases of Behavior and Some Implications for Political Science," *World Politics,* 23 (April 1971), p. 363.
7. Corning, Peter A., "Toward an Evolutionary-Adaptive Theory of Politics" (unpublished manuscript, Fordham University, 1971), p. 29.
8. Deutsch, Karl W., "The Future of World Politics," *Political Quarterly,* 37 (January–March 1966), 15.
9. Deutsch, Karl W., and Manfred Kochen, "Toward a Rational Theory of Decentralization," *American Political Science Review,* 63 (September 1969), pp. 734–749.
10. Ehrlich, Paul R., *The Population Bomb* (New York: Ballantine, 1968), p. 89.
11. Ehrlich, Paul R., "World Population: A Battle Lost?" in Walt Anderson, ed., *Politics and Environment* (Pacific Palisades, Calif.: Goodyear, 1970).
12. Farmer, Richard N., *et al., World Population—The View Ahead* (Bloomington: Indiana University Bureau of Business Research, 1968), p. 87.
13. Fremlin, J. H., "How Many People Can the World Support?" *New Scientist,* 24 (October 29, 1964), p. 287.
14. Jouvenel, Bertrand de, "Political Science and Prevision," *American Political Science Review,* 59 (March 1965), pp. 29–38.
15. Livingston, Dennis, "Pollution Control: An International Perspective," in Walt Anderson, ed., *Politics and Environment* (Pacific Palisades, Calif.: Goodyear, 1970), pp. 319–335.
16. Machiavelli, Niccolò, *The Prince* and *The Discourses* (New York: Modern Library, 1950), p. 91.
17. Plautus, Titus Maccius, *Miles gloriosus,* III, 3, ed. by Mason Hammond (Cambridge, Mass.: Harvard University Press, 1963).
18. White, Lynn, Jr., "The Historical Roots of Our Ecological Crisis," *Science,* 155 (March 10, 1967), pp. 1203–1207.
19. Whitehead, Alfred North, *Science and the Modern World* (New York: Macmillan, 1929), p. 298.
20. Wilson, Albert, and Donna Wilson, "Toward the Institutionalization of Change," Institute for the Future, Report R-11 (Middletown, Conn.: August 1970).

Suggested reading for Chapter 22 will be found at the end of Chapter 23.

Chapter 23
A FUTURE
FOR MANKIND?

Efforts to produce theory that is more policy-relevant need to be supplemented with analytical studies of the role of judgment and the nature of different kinds of judgment. By careful observation, we may be able to "decompose" complex judgments and diagnose their ingredients and perhaps begin to say something useful by identifying the conditions, procedures, and analytical devices that favor better performance in this respect—Alexander L. George [6]

If we think of international politics as a system of organized complexity, we may be able to grasp more fully the nature of the human process in this environment and perhaps to equip ourselves better for planning individual, national, and global strategies to replace the haphazard approach of contemporary policy makers [2]. Organized complexity cannot be understood only in relation to a few variables. Nor can we understand the unique outcomes of such complexity by conceiving of it as disorganized. Insurance companies and demographers regularly use statistical techniques to describe disorganized complexities that they must account for and control in their own interests. For example, the probable life span of a class of insurance-policy holders, defined by health, age, and other characteristics, can be dependably predicted. But statistical probabilities are of limited use in international politics, for the class of outcomes is of a different order. As an alternative we must develop mental maps and perhaps quantitative models of the principal components of international politics. We attempt to do so by using theory, as described in Chapter 2, to improve our own mental maps, to attempt policy formulations, and to correct and recast our ideas in the light of new evidence or more careful examinations of history. We should attempt to examine all levels or types of relevant change, relating outcomes to the effects of broad shifts in process, cyclical fluctuations, and "accidents." This general activity constitutes the most important work of political scientists in policy formulation, a necessary prerequisite to policy prescription.

SYSTEMIC PROCESS ANALYSIS: GAMBLER'S RUIN AND UNCERTAINTY

If one looks over the major decisions about initiating war . . . the probability of a major decision being realistic may well have been less than one-half, on the average. That is to say, if in the last half-century states-men made major decisions on matters of war and peace, the chances were better than even that the particular decision would be wrong. [4, p. 13]

As we have suggested, there is an increasing need for new forms of system-level control in international politics. As demands increase and more individuals and groups throughout the world become "politicized," existing mechanisms will surely be taxed, for the "reality" that they are designed to control will change. New crises are inevitable.[1] The stakes involved will also increase, and the margin of permissible error will shrink. When we turn to simple policy problems confronting national and international leaders but with ramifications affecting international activity, it is clear that for each decision of the same magnitude less and less time is available. The changes that generate the need for decisions are beginning to outpace our capacity to anticipate them and their consequences. Paradoxically, such advances in technology as the spread of nuclear weapons and delivery systems have increased the potential consequences of leaders' mistakes, yet decision making in the international system still proceeds as it did two decades ago.[2] In addition, the rapidity of change has given us less time to prepare for demands and needs that will arise in the future. New types of industry, new drugs, and new social activities are appearing more rapidly than are codes and regulations to deal with them and to separate their malevolent from their benevolent aspects.

Individual risks become greater as they accumulate. The gambler knows that although he has a 90 percent chance of

[1] The proliferation of "microsovereignties" like the Maldive Islands, Fiji, and Lesotho has produced a class of actors who may be unable to cope by themselves with either internal or external stresses.
[2] In the past we have been rather inept at foreseeing accurately the impacts of technological developments. In 1910, for instance, Marshal Ferdinand Foch of France commented after an aerial show: "All very fine for sport, you know. But the airplane's no use to the army."

success at any given moment in time, risking all his holdings seven times will reduce his chances of success to less than 50 percent. But the parallel between politics and gambling is misleading, for it assumes a universe of fixed probabilities. If we spin a roulette wheel often enough, every number will come up an equal number of times. But the universe of political choice involves constantly changing probabilities and few "spins of the wheel." The gambler's risks are based on determined features, whereas the politician's risks are based on changing odds and circumstances. International politics involves processes in which risks may increase or decrease as learning and social invention change the mood and structure of the situation.

As social scientists we try to chart changes and assess the ways in which various processes are interrelated. We have rejected the notion that an underlying purpose shapes change; needs do not necessarily lead to solutions. Functionalism assumes too much in this respect. We must focus instead on a changing environment and purposive actors. Goal attainment requires active pursuit of objectives, and patterned activity of this kind constitutes what we call "coping mechanisms." Changes in the environment alter the contributions of such mechanisms to goal fulfillment. Actors can analyze trends to detect when goals are not being fulfilled and can adjust their behavior accordingly: the basic notion of corrective feedback. Single actors in international politics have, however, been able to effect only marginal direct or indirect changes in the shifting environment of politics, whereas exogenous cultural and technological forces have had great effects on changing the environment, as illustrated in Figure 23.1.

The role of decision makers, nevertheless, is important. It is the malleable element, the point of choice toward which analysis must be aimed. We might look at the "hits and misses" of decision makers, the times they were successful and unsuccessful in securing desired out-

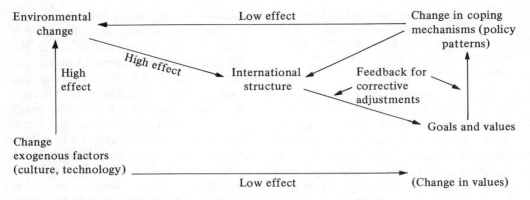

Figure 23.1. Macro Process in International Politics: A Crude Chart

comes. In the nineteenth century, with relatively decentralized decision making aimed at "balance of power," only a few minor wars occurred. The serenity of the system survived until 1914; even afterwards old outlooks prevailed and Europe remained the focus of world politics until World War II. These two wars are indicative of the type of political errors that statesmen make. It might be difficult to recover, however, from future mistakes of this magnitude [9].

Responses to a poll conducted by the Rand Corporation in 1964 indicate that defense experts thought there was a 10 percent probability of major war within ten years and a 25 percent probability of such war in twenty-five years [1]. Since 1945 war has been common throughout the world, and the hopes initially raised by the United Nations have not been remotely fulfilled. Quincy Wright, a pioneer in contemporary approaches to international relations, has argued that the probability of war increases as technological and intellectual distances between states decrease more rapidly than do psychological and social distances.[3] His conclusion is that there is a danger-

[3] Psychological distance refers to the degree of hostile sentiment of the government and people of one member of the pair to the other; social distance to the degree in which they differ in culture, institutions and ideologies; technological distance to the absence of communication and other contacts between them; intellectual distance to the disparity of their scientific and technological skills [12, p. 12].

ous probability of general war before the year 2000, though we do not know how much "out of phase" these rates of change must be before the probabilities of war become great. "Technological and intellectual distances have shrunk rapidly in the modern world under the influence of new inventions facilitating communication and education in the world as a whole. At the same time national sentiments, revolutionary ideologies and unsettled political disputes have shrunk less rapidly or have been increased" [12, p. 13].

Governmental budgetary processes reflect the increasing lag behind demands characteristic of modern politics. Although some efforts have been made in recent years to extend the period between an executive's initial formulation of a proposed budget and the point at which the money is actually spent, the problem of identifying what will be the salient problems in two or three years has really not been incorporated in planning. Many local and national governments find themselves in budget-making "crises," authorizing sums to deal with problems that have caught legislators by surprise. The speed of change thus threatens the effectiveness of decision-making apparatuses. In earlier centuries, when environmental change was slower and more predictable, the margin for error permitted "muddling through." Unplanned responses to short-term demands, a symptom of decision overload, is rapidly becoming a luxury that most nations can ill afford. We can foresee that trends like population growth will certainly slow down—if not because of new cultural norms like those that have already slowed them in industrial states, then because famine deaths will rise as land and resources become insufficient. But this latter type of "solution" is irresponsible and unacceptable. "We have," as one observer has declared, "a limited amount of time to break loose from habit, inertia, and administrative routine, to decide which trends we most need to control, and to devise ways of doing it" [11].

A second feature of decision overload is the increasing number of participants in the process. It is not simply that "too many cooks spoil the broth" but also that, as problems become more diverse and require greater specialization for full comprehension, more specialists and specialized processing are needed. We can thus expect at practically all organizational levels the crisis that students of development call the "participation explosion." Let us consider the problem of the American National Security Council, with its special secretariat appointed by the White House. It has grown from a single man to a small office to a complex establishment—and has finally outgrown even the White House staff. The result is that less thought and less interaction are now possible in governmental decision making. More participants but no more available time means that each individual has less opportunity to speak with others about a problem or to understand fully the views of other participants. One consequence has been the increasing demand for information summaries and the presentation of policy options as simple alternatives; such demands increase the possibility of information distortion, as layers for screening, interpreting, reviewing, reinterpreting, and writing position papers proliferate between the policy makers and the immediate arena of action. Given the burgeoning amounts of incoming information and the multiplying layers of bureaucracy required simply to keep abreast of it, it is virtually impossible for high-

level policy makers to escape isolation from reality. If human capacity to process information and to make decisions remains relatively constant while the information fed into the process expands geometrically and the number of links increases, the probability of correct assessments shrinks.

The problems of distortion and overload can arise both in the policy process of an individual country and in the self-contained communications networks of many smaller communities. As groups and classes once remote from one another become interdependent and find themselves in mutual communication, variations in their resources and life styles become more salient. In earlier centuries peasants and noblemen, for instance, had little to say to one another; their relations were sporadic, and they thought of each other only in stereotypes. In the modern world we no longer do so as easily. As the political process becomes more precarious because of structural changes in the last decade, cultural, economic, and other processes become more interdependent. A civil war like that in Nigeria in 1967–1970 has global consequences; 100 years ago it might not even have been reported outside Africa. Indeed, most Africans would not have learned of it. Political exchanges are also becoming more tightly intertwined over a broader domain. These changes place greater burdens on the flow of communications and greater demands on policy makers for political solutions to new problems, removal of dissatisfactions, and elimination of relative privation. Failures in this regard spawn separatist movements and radical ideologies, which result from withdrawals of trust combined with the increase in interdependence. But failures become more probable. Current elites find that more is demanded of them, while at the same time fewer and fewer resources, especially of reliable information and time, are available for coping with these demands. As decisions affect more and more individuals, more of the world's people are becoming informed about them and more determined to be heard. Social unrest and civil wars in countries like Pakistan, the Congo, Uganda, and the Sudan have made many of them simply more difficult to govern. Leaders must pay greater attention than ever before to the demands of lower-class groups. Foreign policy receives less attention, and decisions in this realm must take greater cognizance of the needs and demands of the citizens. The primacy of external events in shaping foreign policy may no longer be possible. To an ever greater extent foreign-policy decisions are interlocked with domestic considerations, and leaders, whose principal aim is to retain or increase domestic support, tend to ignore international pressures or structural propensities and consequences.[4] In the past it was confidently predicted that technological advances would break down national barriers. In fact, government innovations like passports, control of mass media, and economic regulations have actually increased obstacles to free interstate movement.

Furthermore, as the Franco-Algerian and American-Vietnamese conflicts illustrated, it is becoming more difficult and more costly for one actor to intervene effectively in the territory of another. Penetration is easier, but not control. In the eighteenth and nineteenth centuries strong countries could control and govern weaker ones at low cost, often simply by "showing the flag" or "gunboat diplomacy." Today it is not uncommon for entire populations to resist successfully even the most dedicated foreign attempts to control them. Threats and violence are less effective means of achieving objectives than they formerly were, and, as nuclear weapons spread and the means of conducting biological warfare become known,

such tactics become increasingly dangerous.

We thus find ourselves facing a truly frightening paradox. At a time when difficult problems like pollution, population, and economic development require greater international attention, coordination, and planning, and increased system-level regulation, actors are under more and more pressure to respond according to domestic needs. Indeed, frequently they continue to respond in ways that were successful in earlier centuries but are less relevant to contemporary problems. As we suggested in Chapter 8, incrementalism is the dominant mode of formulating public policy, particularly in developed and highly bureaucratic states. Policy making thus "tends to follow the line of least resistance," with few goals other than regime or personal maintenance [5].

We have argued that as demands on the international system increase, the need for appropriate coping mechanisms at the system level also grows. With few exceptions, however, effective decisions continue to be made at the national level, and only the most naïve optimist would predict that this pattern will change in the near future. Under these circumstances the least that a political scientist can seek is to ensure that the increasing interdependence among both small human systems like the family and community and larger units within the international system will bring about a new approach by political leaders. Such leaders should abandon Thomas Hobbes' assumptions about human nature and game theorists' assumptions about strategy. In the cause of human survival we must reject the maximin approach and begin to expect, perhaps to demand, that players in the game do their "best," rather than their "worst," by their opponents.

Political scientists are accustomed to dealing with concepts of survival and adaptation in terms of separate national entities.[5] They have concerned themselves

---

[4] Pierre Salinger in his novel, *On Instructions of My Government* (Garden City, N.Y.: Doubleday, 1971), has argued that a president can lead the United States to the brink of disaster by weighing domestic considerations too heavily and ignoring the causal nexus of international politics on which the policy will bear. Karl W. Deutsch has argued that since 1913 the ratio of foreign trade to gross national product has fallen in most countries, indicating an increasing tendency by actors to look inward [5, pp. 20–21].

[5] See, for example, James N. Rosenau, *The Adaptation of National Societies: A Theory of Political System Behavior and Transformation* (New York: McCaleb-Seiler, 1970).

with insuring the basic values of national actors against internal and external depredations. In this sense foreign policy is considered the means by which nation-states adapt to systemic stresses. Their main goals have been to ensure the security and integrity of their national units against external threats, but national integrity and autonomy may, in fact, run counter to the political development of the international system as a whole.[6] As the geographical dispersion of nuclear weapons suggests, there is tension between the requirements of national autonomy and the demands of systemic survival. As long as the state is treated as the only instrument through which populations can satisfy their most vital needs, adaptation of the larger system will be anchored to parochialism expressed through mechanisms, organizations, and leaders whose purposes are increasingly unrelated to coping with threats to basic values. If and when such institutions fail, we can regard their continuation as simply anachronistic.

Scholars of international politics must shift their focus from prescriptions for individual nation-states to prescriptions for the global community as a whole. The justification for such a radical intellectual reorientation is the need to seek new forms when old ones prove inadequate. The inability of many national units and other international actors either to provide the range of public services demanded of them or to regulate their own behavior equitably is increasingly apparent. This conclusion is not a universal condemnation of national leaders; instead it embodies recognition that we must restructure the outlooks of national leaders, a very difficult task.

Survival through corrective adjustment to a changing environment, then, is the fundamental task facing the international system, but it is by no means clear that the system is capable of such adaptation.

The goal of survival is not necessarily its only goal, but it is surely the one that must be achieved if any others are to be attained. In the long run the survival of individuals depends upon survival of the global collectivity. The survival of the international system, however, depends on the survival of neither specific national units nor individuals. The task of preserving the greater collectivity must take precedence over perpetuation of any of its parts.

In prescribing specific modes of behavior for actors, the political scientist has the opportunity to make a profound contribution. Such prescriptions inevitably raise normative questions and dilemmas. He must identify those norms and patterns of behavior that inhibit the satisfaction of human needs and must put forward policies to foster their satisfaction. Once again the level of analysis problem is relevant. Clearly, practices that satisfy individual demands contribute in some way to overcoming systemic stresses. As we have seen, however, the survival of the collectivity is not necessarily identical with the survival of its parts or of any specific individuals. Indeed, as we suggested in Chapter 12, "development" means more than simply the modernization of individual societies. It means increased probability that the system as a whole will survive for the foreseeable future. Despite liberal doctrines of "progress," development is not a one-way process [8]. If we can identify processes and institutions that contribute to individual and collective needs, then we must insist on adopting them, even if we must violate traditional norms and even if they require changes beyond the "incremental" innovations that are more readily accepted. If we fail to do so, we may be remembered as Captain E. J. Smith of the *Titanic* is remembered; he claimed that the art of shipbuilding had reached the point at which disaster to a modern ocean-going vessel was unimaginable. "I will say," he remarked, "that I cannot imagine any condition which could cause [this] ship to founder. I cannot conceive of any vital

[6] Indeed, integration, cooperation, and even conquest contributing to the formation of larger and more comprehensive actors can be considered mechanisms by which small states can compensate for narrow resource bases [3].

disaster happening to this vessel. Modern ship-building has gone beyond that."[7]

As analysts of international politics we must be conscious of our role in the social process, serving as active, rather than passive, agents in political transactions. As Harold D. Lasswell has reminded us:

We may be without conscious interest in our "power" position in society, but we cannot escape from the "power" implications themselves. We may be so devoted to a compulsive neurotic ritual of collecting, ordering, condensing, and expelling data that the political implications, aside from modest incomes and great deference from other compulsive personality types, are ignored. We may be oral, impressionistic, agile, and facile, welcoming mainly the approbation of other oral erotics; but the "power" consequences remain none the less. Those who declare that they want truth and are indifferent to control may, indeed, get truth; they are bound to have some control. The mere fact of persisting in a network of interpersonal relations means that one finds a place in, and partly modifies the shape and composition of the current value pyramid, whether one keeps this in mind or not. If one has no clear understanding of the consequences of his acts, he is unable to defend his acts rationally; what he does takes on the color of capricious indulgences, naïvely functioning to relieve the recurring stresses of the living organism, extracting tributes of esteem and purchasing power from some, and receiving sympathetic comprehension from the few whose autobiographies include enough parallelisms to his own biopsychic characteristics and cultural techniques. [10]

The political scientist, as a participant in and an observer of social processes, has an obligation to call for such minimal reform. Seeking means to animate this reform is our principal task, both as teachers and as scholars. Political scientists must view themselves as "helmsmen" in an uncharted world, rather than simply as advisers to competitive princes. They must begin to consider themselves as "traitriots," as Morton Grodzins has so colorfully expressed it, that is, as patriots

to the greater needs of human survival rather than to narrowly defined national interests [7]. With Thomas Jefferson we "like the dreams of the future better than the history of the past."

References

1. Bloomfield, Lincoln, *Disarmament and Arms Control* (New York: Foreign Policy Association, 1968), p. 22.
2. Brunner, Ronald D., and Gary D. Brewer, *Organized Complexity: Empirical Theories of Political Development* (New York: Free Press, 1971).
3. Corning, Peter A., "Toward An Evolutionary-Adaptive Theory of Politics" (unpublished paper, Fordham University, 1971), pp. 14–22.
4. Deutsch, Karl W., "The Future of World Politics," *Political Quarterly,* 37 (January–March 1966), pp. 9–32.
5. Dror, Yehezkel, *Public Policymaking Reexamined* (San Francisco: Chandler, 1968), p. 87.
6. George, Alexander L., *et al., The Limits of Coercive Diplomacy* (Boston: Little, Brown, 1971), p. xvii.
7. Grodzins, Morton, *The Loyal and the Disloyal* (Chicago: University of Chicago Press, 1965), pp. 208–216.
8. Huntington, Samuel P., "Political Development and Political Decay," *World Politics,* 17 (April 1965), pp. 386–430.
9. Kahn, Herman, *Thinking About the Unthinkable* (New York: Avon, 1962), p. 22.
10. Lasswell, Harold D., *World Politics and Personal Insecurity,* rev. ed. (New York: Free Press, 1965), p. 16.
11. Russett, Bruce M., "Ecology of Future International Politics," *International Studies Quarterly,* 11 (March 1967), p. 30.
12. Wright, Quincy, "On Predicting International Relations: The Year 2000," University of Denver Graduate School of International Studies, Monograph No. 1 (Denver: 1969–1970).

Suggested Reading

Bell, Daniel, and Mancur Olsen, Jr., "Toward a Social Report," *Public Interest,* 15 (Spring 1969), pp. 72–84.

---

[7] *The New York Times*, April 16, 1912.

Brzezinski, Zbigniew K., *Between Two Ages* (New York: Viking, 1970).

Choucri, Nazli, "Population Dynamics and International Violence: Propositions, Insights, Evidence," paper delivered at the American Political Science Association meetings, Washington, D.C., September 5–9, 1972.

Corning, Peter A., "The Biological Bases of Behavior and Some Implications for Political Science," *World Politics,* 23 (April 1971), pp. 321–370.

Deutsch, Karl W., "The Future of World Politics," *Political Quarterly,* 37 (January–March 1966), pp. 9–32.

Drucker, Peter, *The Age of Discontent: Guidelines to Our Changing Society* (New York: Harper & Row, 1969).

Duncan, Otis Dudley, "Social Forecasting: The State of the Art," *Public Interest,* 17 (Fall 1969).

Erlich, Paul R., and Anne H. Erlich, *Population, Resources, Environment: Issues in Human Ecology* (San Francisco: Freeman, 1970).

Haas, Ernest B., "Toward Controlling International Change—A Personal Plea," *World Politics,* 17 (October 1964), pp. 1–12.

Kahn, Herman, and A. J. Weiner, *The Year 2000* (New York: Macmillan, 1967).

Wright, Quincy, "On Predicting International Relations: The Year 2000," University of Denver Graduate School of International Studies, Monograph No. 1 (Denver: 1969–1970).

Indexes

AUTHOR INDEX

SUBJECT AND NAME INDEX

Franz Joseph, emperor of Austria, 36, 39
FRELIMO, 193
Fremlin, J. H., 448
French East India Company, 239
French Revolution, 26, 342, 351, 394
Friendship, trade and, 25
Functional linkage, 292–293, 299
Functionalism, 207, 283–286, 461
Future change, 456–459

G

Gambetta, Léon, 34
Gambling, politics and, 461
Game analysis
  elements of, 359
  value of, 371–376
Game theory, 12, 313 *n.*, 356–379
  assumptions in, 359–360, 361 *n.*, 365 *n.*, 464
  chicken game, 367–368, 372, 391
  difficulties, 378
  fairness and, 359, 361 *n.*
  mathematical, 361 *n.*, 364
  outcomes, 359–361, 364–365, 372
  payoff strategy, 361–368, 372, 374
  prisoners' dilemma, 364–368, 374, 375, 378
  saddlepoints, 365 *n.*
  salami tactics, 369
  simulation, 369–371
  solutions, 359–361
    equilibrium, 365
  variable-sum games, 361, 364–369, 385, 394, 432
  war and, 351–352, 354, 356, 363, 369, 378, 385, 395
  zero-sum games, 361–364, 389, 393, 395, 404
Gandhi, Mahatma, 271
Garrison state hypothesis, 95–96, 271 *n.*
Gasperi, Alcide de, 297
Gaullism, 331–334
General Agreement on Tariffs and Trade (GATT), 6, 209, 235
General Motors Corporation, 83, 128, 135, 141, 239, 243
Geneva Convention (1949), 349
Geneva Convention on the High Seas, 451
Geneva Protocol (1925), 347
Genghis Khan, 393

Genocide Convention, 224
Geographical distance, 28, 95
Geographical resources, 99–100, 148
Germany
  as aggressor, 40–41, 49
  and Alsace-Lorraine, 34, 40, 41
  Austria-Hungary and, 35–38, 41, 74, 314
  and Balkans, 34, 36–38, 74
  and Belgium, 33, 37, 38, 40, 41, 74, 75
  colonial expansion, 34, 40, 50
  consolidation of (1870), 33, 40
  and Czechoslovakia, 420, 424
  East, 262, 327, 336
  France and, 16–17, 27, 33–38, 40, 41, 49–51, 74, 75, 328–329, 437–438
  and Great Britain, 34–37, 41, 49–51, 66, 68, 75, 321 *n.*, 408, 437–438
  and Italy, 41, 95
  mobilization for World War I, 38, 40, 68, 74
  naval armament, 34–36, 41
  Nazi. *See* Hitler, Adolf
  occupation zones, 322
  persecution of Jews, 341
  and Poland, 51, 408
  railroad network, 68
  reparations payments, 51, 322
  and Russia, 34–38, 41, 68, 74
  Soviet Union and, 114, 147, 155, 178, 262, 321–324, 326
  and Spanish Civil War, 347, 394
  and Sudetenland, 266, 420
  United States and, 51
  West. *See* West Germany
Ghana, 193, 296
Gilpatric, Roswell, 425
Gini index, 92 *n.*
Global system, 16
  decision making in, 264
  interdependence in, 263, 264, 304
  origins, 263
  regional subsystems and, 264 *n.*
  rise of dominance, 130
  values of, 258
Goals. *See also* Objectives
  compatibility of, 112–118
  compromise among, 60
  conflicting, 17, 60, 112–118, 124, 125
  contradictory, 59–60